THE TIMES
THE SUNDAY TIMES

KT-439-178

Good University Guide

2020

John O'Leary

WITHDRAWN

REFERENCE ONLY
Not to be taken away from the Learning Centre

S085177

HAM REF
HAM CARLEARK
REF 378.41 OUE

Published in 2019 by Times Books

An imprint of HarperCollins Publishers
Westerhill Road
Bishopbriggs
Glasgow G64 2QT
www.harpercollins.co.uk
times.books@harpercollins.co.uk

First published in 1993. Twenty-fifth edition 2019

© Times Newspapers Ltd 2019

The Times is a registered trademark of Times Newspapers Ltd

ISBN 978-0-00-832548-0

Patrick Kennedy was the lead consultant with Andrew Farquhar for UoE Consulting Limited, which has compiled the main university league table and the individual subject tables for this *Guide* on behalf of *The Times*, *The Sunday Times* and HarperCollins Publishers.

Please see chapters 1 and 13 for a full explanation of the sources of data used in the ranking tables. The data providers do not necessarily agree with the data aggregations or manipulations appearing in this book and are also not responsible for any inference or conclusions thereby derived.

Project editor: Alan Copps
Design and layout: Davidson Publishing Solutions

All rights reserved. No part of this publication may be reproduced, stored in a retrieval system or transmitted, in any form or by any means electronic, mechanical, photographing, recording or otherwise without the prior written permission of the publisher and copyright owners.

The contents of this publication are believed correct at the time of printing. Nevertheless the publisher can accept no responsibility for errors or omissions, changes in the detail given or for any expense or loss thereby caused.

HarperCollins does not warrant that any website mentioned in this title will be provided uninterrupted, that any website will be error free, that defects will be corrected, or that the website or the server that makes it available are free of viruses or bugs. For full terms and conditions please refer to the site terms provided on the website.

A catalogue record for this book is available from the British Library.

Printed and bound by CPI Group (UK) Ltd, Croydon, CR0 4YY.

MIX
Paper from
responsible sources
FSC™ C007454
FSC
www.fsc.org

This book is produced from independently certified FSC™ paper to ensure responsible forest management.

For more information visit: www.harpercollins.co.uk/green

SOUTHALL AND WEST
LONDON COLLEGE
LEARNING CENTRE

Contents

THE LEARNING CENTRE
EALING, HAMMERSMITH AND WEST LONDON COLLEGE
GLIDDON ROAD
LONDON W14 9BL

About the Author

John O'Leary is a freelance journalist and education consultant. He was the Editor of *The Times Higher Education Supplement* from 2002 to 2007 and was previously Education Editor of *The Times*, having joined the paper in 1990 as Higher Education Correspondent. He has been writing on higher education for more than 30 years and is a member of the executive board of the QS World University Rankings. He is a member of the Higher Education Commission and the author of *Higher Education in England*, published in 2009 by the Higher Education Funding Council for England. He has a degree in politics from the University of Sheffield.

Acknowledgements

We would like to thank the many individuals who have helped with this edition of *The Times and Sunday Times Good University Guide*, particularly Rosemary Bennett, Education Editor of *The Times*, Alastair McCall, Editor of *The Sunday Times Good University Guide*, and Patrick Kennedy, the lead consultant with Andrew Farquhar, for UoE Consulting Limited, which has compiled the main university league table and the individual subject tables for this *Guide* on behalf of *The Times*, *The Sunday Times* and HarperCollins Publishers.

To the members of *The Times and Sunday Times Good University Guide* Advisory Group for their time and expertise: Patrick Kennedy, Consultant, Collective Intelligence Limited; Christine Couper, Head of Planning and Statistics, University of Greenwich; James Galbraith, Senior Strategic Planner, University of Edinburgh; Alison Hartrey, Head of Planning, SOAS, London; Mark Langer-Crame, Senior Planning Officer, Cardiff University; Daniel Monnery, Head of Corporate Strategy, Northumbria University; Aaron Morrison, Principal Planning Officer, De Montfort University; Jackie Njoroge, Head of Strategic Planning, Manchester Metropolitan University; Komal Patel, Strategic Planning Officer, Imperial College, London; Dr Sarah Taylor, Head of Strategy Development, Aberystwyth University; David Totten, Head of Planning, Queen's University, Belfast; Jenny Walker, Planning Officer, Loughborough University; to James McLaren, Denise Jones and Pip Day of HESA for their technical advice; to Kathryn Carlson, Biba Kang, Martin Ince and Sue O'Leary for their contributions to the book.

We also wish to thank all the university staff who assisted in providing information for this edition.

Timeline to a University Place

This book is designed to help you find a university place in September 2020. That may seem a long time away, but a decision that can change your life needs a lot of consideration. Add to that the fact that the application process is somewhat long-winded and there is less time than you might think – for example, if you want to study medicine starting in September 2020 you will have to have had some practical experience of helping to care for people, have taken an aptitude test during the summer and completed your application by 15 October 2019, almost a year before your studies will start. Planning well ahead of application and decision deadlines will always give you greater flexibility and choice. The less time you give yourself, the more limited will become your choices.

So where to start? The dates below indicate the key staging points along the way to a university place.

Key dates
February to July 2019
This is the time to develop your thoughts on the subject you would like to study and on where you would like to be at university. See overleaf for where to find advice in this book on choosing a subject and a university.

March 2019 onwards
Attend university open days. Open Days are a good way to gain a personal impression of what a university feels like, where it is located, and what studying in a particular department or faculty would be like. You will only have the time and resources to attend a small number of Open Days, so careful planning is necessary, not least because Open Days at different universities can often clash. The calendar for Open Days for 2019 (as announced by the beginning of the year) appears alongside each university's profile in Chapter 15.

July 2019
Registration starts for UCAS Apply, the online application system through which you will make your application. You will have a maximum of five choices when you come to complete your application form.

September 2019
UCAS will begin to accept completed applications.

15 October 2019
Deadline for applications to Oxford or Cambridge (you can only apply to one of them), and for applications to any university to study medicine, dentistry or veterinary science. Note that for some courses you will need to have completed a pre-application assessment test by this date.

15 January 2020
Deadline for applications for all other universities and subjects (excluding a few art and design courses with a deadline of 24 March 2020). It is advisable to get your application in ahead of this deadline; aim for the end of November 2019.

End of March 2020

Universities should have given you decisions on your applications by now if you submitted them by 15 January 2020.

April onwards

Apply for student loans to cover tuition fees and living costs.

Early May 2020

You will need to have responded to all university decisions. You have to select first choice, if your first offer is conditional, a second choice, and reject all other offers. Once you have accepted an offer, apply for university accommodation if you are going to require it.

4 August 2020

Scottish examination results. If your results meet the offer from your first choice (or, failing that, your second choice), your place at university will be confirmed. If not, you can enter Clearing for Scottish universities in order to find a place on another course.

13 August 2020

A-level results announced. If your results meet the offer from your first choice (or, failing that, your second choice), your place at university will be confirmed. If not, you can enter Clearing to find a place on another course offered by any university.

Mid to late September 2020

Arrive at university for Freshers' Week.

How This Book Can Help You

The process of making a successful application to university has many stages. Fundamental to the whole process are your decisions on which subject to pick and where to study it.

How do I choose a course?

As you will be taking a course that will last three or sometimes four years, you will need enthusiasm for, and some aptitude in, the subject. The options of studying full-time or part-time also need to be considered.

» The first half of chapter 2 provides advice on choosing a subject area and selecting relevant courses within that subject.

» Chapter 13 provides details for 67 different subject areas (as listed on page 36). For each subject there is specific advice and a league table that provides our assessment of the quality of universities offering courses.

How will my choice of subject affect my employment prospects?

As the course you choose will also influence your job prospects at its conclusion, your initial subject decision will have an impact on your life long after you complete your degree.

» The employment prospects and average starting salaries for the main subject groups are given in chapter 3.

» The subject tables in chapter 13 give the employment prospects for each university offering a course.

» Universities are now doing more to increase the employability of their graduates. Some examples are given in chapter 3.

How do I choose a university?

While choosing your subject comes first, the place where you study will also play a major role. You will need to decide upon what type of university you wish to go to: campus, city or smaller town? How well does the university perform? How far is the university from home? Is it large or small? Is it specialist or general? Do you want to study abroad?

» Central to our *Guide* is the main *Times and Sunday Times* league table in chapter 1. This ranks the universities by assessing their performance not just according to teaching quality and the student experience but also through seven other factors, including research quality, the spending on services and facilities, and graduate employment prospects.

» The second half of chapter 2 provides advice on the factors to consider when choosing a university.

» Chapter 15, the largest chapter in the book, contains two pages on each university, giving a general overview of the institution as well as data on student numbers, contact details, accommodation provision, and the fees for 2019–20. Note that fees and student support for 2020–21 will not be confirmed until August 2019, and you must check these before applying.

» For those considering Oxford or Cambridge, details of admission processes and of all the undergraduate colleges can be found in chapter 14.

» If you are considering studying abroad, chapter 11 provides guidance and practical information.

» Specific advice for international students coming to study in the UK is given in chapter 12.

How do I apply?

» Chapter 5 outlines the application procedure for university entry. It starts by advising you on how to complete the UCAS application, and then takes you through the process that we hope will lead to your university place for autumn 2020.

Can I afford it?

Note that most figures in chapters 4 and 7 refer to 2019 and there will be changes for 2020, which you will need to check.

» Chapter 4 describes how the system of tuition fees works and what you are likely to be charged, depending upon where in the UK you plan to study.

» Chapter 7 provides advice on the tuition fee loans and maintenance loans that are available, depending upon where you live in the UK, other forms of financial support (including university scholarships and bursaries), and how to plan your budget.

» Chapter 8 provides advice on where to live while you are at university. Sample accommodation charges for each university are given in chapter 15.

How do I find out more?

The Times and Sunday Times Good University Guide website at **https://www.thetimes.co.uk/gooduniversityguide** will keep you up to date with developments throughout the year and contains further information and online tables (subscription required).

You can also find much practical advice on the UCAS website (**www.ucas.com**), and on individual university websites. There is a wealth of official statistical information on the Unistats website (**www.unistats.ac.uk**).

Introduction

There are times when it makes sense to delay an application to university – if there may be imminent change in fee levels, for example. But 2020 will not be one of them because it will see the end of a decade-long decline in the number of 18-year-olds in the population. Indeed, the competition for higher education places may never be as low again. The size of age group that takes much the biggest share of undergraduate places is about to take off, growing by almost a quarter in the following decade.

Universities show no sign of reducing the number of places on offer. Why would they when fees are their main source of income, and they have been warned that there will be no bailouts for those in financial trouble? While the number of applicants dropped by 44,000 in 2017, the eventual intake was within 525 of the previous year. Many universities are now struggling to fill their places, and are responding with a growing number of unconditional offers and increased marketing of their courses. More than 7% of offers were unconditional in 2018, and 23% of applicants received one.

By 2020, there may also be fewer applicants from other EU countries if the current fee arrangements do not survive Brexit, although the decline in the value of the £ has made the UK a more affordable study destination for those from other countries who already have to pay (higher) international fees. At the time of writing, this was shrouded in uncertainty, but universities were concerned about the consequences for their research budgets and staffing, as well as student recruitment.

Those thinking of starting a degree in 2020, therefore, should be in a buyer's market. But is a degree still worth the price you will have to pay? Not if you listen to many of today's politicians and commentators. Graduates are left with unmanageable debts after sub-standard teaching on courses that lead nowhere, they say. Partly as a result of the negative publicity universities have received over the past 18 months in particular, as many as three-quarters of people think higher education represents poor value for money.

In fact, Government statistics show graduates earning over £100,000 more on average than non-graduates over a working lifetime, as well as being much less likely to be unemployed and more likely to remain healthy. But, as this *Guide* has demonstrated over a quarter of a century, there are wide variations between universities and courses

Taking all graduates together, apprentices earn more at the age of 21 and those whose highest qualifications are good-grade GCSEs earn a similar amount. By the age of 24, however, graduates are ahead and by the age of 30, the gap is £5,000 – or £10,000 compared with the GCSE cohort. But the Institute for Fiscal Studies has reported that the male graduates of 23 institutions continued to earn less than non-graduates and the same was true for female graduates at nine institutions. At the other end of the scale, there were 36 institutions for men and ten for women where graduates were earning more than £60,000 after ten years – far more than those with lower qualifications.

The fine detail that is becoming available on employment rates and salary levels well into graduates' careers makes it more important than ever – and easier – to carry out thorough research before completing an application, or deciding not to do so. There are more options for 18-year-olds to go straight into work, perhaps through the halfway house of a degree apprenticeship, with the attractive combination of a qualification without fees, for those who are sure of their early career aspirations.

As yet, however, school and college leavers are as likely as before to opt for traditional higher education. Last year's decline was driven by the lower number of 18-year-olds, not a loss of faith in universities. In international terms, the salary premium enjoyed by UK graduates is still higher than in most other parts of the world, even if it has declined somewhat with the sharp rise in the proportion of the working-age population with a degree – 42% now, compared with 24% in 2002.

New statistics will continue to come thick and fast, however, to test that proposition. The Government planning to use graduate salary averages in the next round of its Teaching Excellence Framework, for example. With so many more graduates competing for jobs, a degree will never again be an automatic passport to a fast-track career. But it is a fair assumption that most of the better-paid jobs in the future will require post-school education, whether it is a traditional degree, a higher-level apprenticeship, or in-company training.

Even for those who cannot or do not wish to afford the costs associated with three or more years of full-time education when they leave school, university remains a possibility. As well as degree apprenticeships, the modular courses adopted by most universities enable students to work through even a traditional degree at their own pace, dropping out for a time if necessary, or switching to part-time attendance. Distance learning is another option, and advances in information technology now mean that some nominally full-time courses are delivered mainly online.

Most graduates do not regret their decision to go to university. Students from all over the world flock to British universities, and they offer a valuable resource for those on their doorstep. No league table can determine which is the right university for any candidate, but this *Guide* should provide some of the information necessary to draw up a shortlist for further investigation and make the right choice in the end.

The methodology for the new edition remains stable. The *Guide* has always put a premium on consistency in the way that it uses the statistics published by universities and presents the results. The overriding aim is to inform potential students and their parents and advisors, not to make judgments on the performance of universities. As such, it differs from the Government's Teaching Excellence Framework (TEF), which uses some of the same statistics but makes allowance for the prior qualifications of students and uses an expert panel to place the results in context. Our tables use the raw data produced by universities to reflect the undergraduate experience, whatever advantages or disadvantages those institutions might face. We also rank all

132 universities, while the TEF uses only three bands, leaving almost half of the institutions in our table on the same middle tier.

The TEF represents the first official intervention in this area since the Quality Assurance Agency's assessments of teaching quality were abolished more than a decade ago. Scores in those reports correlated closely with research grades, and the first discussions on the framework in the Coalition Government envisaged one comparison taking account of both teaching and research. This remains our approach, to look at a broad range of factors (including the presence of excellent researchers on the academic staff) that will impact on undergraduates

An era of change

Higher education has undergone numerous changes in the 25 years that this book has been published, and more are likely in England, with another review taking place as this book went to press. In England, the Office for Students has taken on the responsibilities for regulating universities that were the province of the Higher Education Funding Council. Research will be overseen by a different body, making universities less able to juggle their finances between different budgets.

In the short term, fees of £9,250 are here to stay in England and Wales, following the announcement of a three-year freeze and the adoption of a new system in the Principality. In Scotland, too, the current regime of free higher education for Scottish residents and those from other EU countries is unlikely to change. However, it is impossible to be sure how long the Conservatives' minority government will last and Jeremy Corbyn's Labour Party is committed to abolishing fees if it wins power.

The pattern of applications and enrolments has already changed since the introduction of higher fees. Students are opting in larger numbers for subjects that they think will lead to well-paid jobs. While there has been a recovery in some arts and social science subjects, the trend towards the sciences and some vocational degrees is unmistakeable. Languages have suffered particularly – perhaps partly because they tend to be four-year degrees – and so have courses associated with parts of the economy that were hardest hit in the recession. Building is one example, where numbers are only now beginning to recover even though the subject is in the top ten for employment prospects, with four out of five graduates going straight into a professional job.

The vast majority of students take a degree primarily to improve their career prospects, so some second-guessing of the employment market is inevitable. But most graduate jobs are not subject-specific and the best brains in the country are hard-pressed to predict employment hotspots four or five years ahead, when today's applicants will be looking for jobs. Computer science is a good example of the pitfalls. Demand for the subject plummeted when the "dotcom bubble" burst and courses closed. Now much of the IT industry is booming again and there is a skills shortage. Applications for the subject have shot up, but no one can be certain of market conditions in such a fast-moving industry so far ahead.

Just as it may be unwise to second-guess employment prospects, the same goes for the competition for places in different subjects. Universities may close or reduce the intake to courses that have low numbers of applicants while some of the more selective institutions may make more places available, especially to candidates who achieve good grades at A-level. Bristol, Birmingham, Exeter and University College London have all taken hundreds more students than usual since the restrictions were relaxed for high-grade candidates. Now others plan to follow suit – as long as they can attract enough students.

Even before the increase to £9,250 fees in 2017, it seems that universities of all types saw the expansion of undergraduate provision as a sensible strategy. But even those that are expanding may do so only in areas where they are strong and extra students can be taught at reasonable cost. Applicants are still best advised to go for the courses and universities that meet their requirements, rather than trying to second-guess the system.

Using this *Guide*

The merger of *The Times and The Sunday Times* university guides five years ago began a new chapter in the ranking of higher education institutions in the UK. The two guides had 35 editions between them and, in their new form, provide the most comprehensive and authoritative assessments of undergraduate education at UK universities.

This year we have added a new table – and chapter – on social inclusion. They look at universities' success (or otherwise) in recruiting students from those sectors of the population that are traditionally underrepresented in higher education. These include ethnic minorities, working-class students, those who live in deprived areas and the disabled. We also compare universities' performance in admitting students from non-selective state schools. The figures in chapter 6 are not used in our main table because they are not, in themselves, measures of quality, but they will be of interest to many applicants.

There are two new names in the main table this year: Leeds Arts University and Ravensbourne University London, both specialist arts institutions with long pedigrees which received university status since the last edition of the *Guide*. They have experienced contrasting fortunes on their debuts in the table, with Leeds Arts on the verge of the top 50 and Ravensbourne in last place, as many debutants have been in the past. Specialist institutions in particular often find that their positions change substantially in their early years in the table.

Wolverhampton has rejoined after several years in which it boycotted league tables. Only one public university with a focus on full-time undergraduate education – University College Birmingham – is now absent. UCB believes that its high proportion of students taking further education students would make for misleading results, so it continues to instruct the Higher Education Statistics Agency not to release data on its performance and is missing from the institutional and subject tables. Private universities such as the University of Law, Regent's University and UPP University, do not currently have the necessary data to be included.

Some famous names in UK higher education have never been ranked because they do not fit the parameters of a system that is intended mainly to guide full-time undergraduates. The Open University, for example, operates entirely through distance learning, while the London and Manchester Business Schools have no undergraduates. Other specialist institutions, including a number of university colleges, appear in relevant subject tables only.

There are now 67 subject tables, and others will be added in due course. Successive surveys have found that international students are more influenced by subject rankings than those for whole institutions, and there is no reason to believe that domestic applicants think differently.

Since the separation of NSS scores, outlined above, there has been no change in the basic methodology behind the tables, however. The nine elements of the main table are the same, with the approach to scores in the 2014 Research Excellence Framework mirroring as closely as possible those for previous assessments. In order to reflect the likelihood of undergraduates coming into contact with outstanding researchers, the proportion of eligible academics entered for assessment is part of the calculation, as well as the average grades achieved.

This year's tables

This year's results again show considerable movement, perhaps reflecting the high level of competition for undergraduates. The division of NSS scores continues to have an effect, with the four sections of the survey categorised as 'Teaching Quality' given more weight than the remaining five. The survey itself was extended and toughened up in 2017, causing a general decline in scores and making the results less comparable with the previous year.

There were changes, too, in the graduate employment market, with slightly lower unemployment in 2017 – the year in which the latest available employment survey took place.

As in last year's *Guide*, there was considerable variation in the amounts spent on student facilities and some universities (but by no means all) saw further increases in the proportion of students awarded good honours.

It seems, however, that nothing can shake the dominance of Cambridge and Oxford at the head of the main table – and the majority of the subject tables. Cambridge has maintained a clear lead over its ancient rival, although the gap has narrowed slightly. St Andrews remains the nearest challenger, with Imperial College London hot on its heels in fourth place. Cambridge also tops 29 of the subject tables, compared with six at Oxford. Throughout all the years of the *Guide*, Oxford and Cambridge have seldom been challenged, especially in terms of the undergraduate education they offer.

Guide Award Winners

University of the year	**Loughborough**
Runner up	**Swansea**
Shortlisted	**Aberdeen**
	Nottingham
	St Andrews
Scottish University of the year	**Aberdeen**
Welsh University of the year	**Swansea**
Modern University of the year	**Creative Arts**
Sports University of the year	**Nottingham**
International University of the year	**Nottingham**
University of the year for	
Teaching quality	**Aberystwyth**
Student experience	**Coventry**
Graduate employment	**London South Bank**
Social Inclusion	**De Montfort**
Student retention	**Leeds Arts**

St Andrews remains easily Scotland's top university in the table and Queen's, Belfast the same in Northern Ireland, while in Wales, Swansea has won back the top spot from Cardiff for the second time in three years. Other changes in the upper reaches of the table have seen Loughborough and the London School of Economics each move up two places. Finishing fifth, Loughborough is in its highest-ever position and has been rewarded with the title of *Sunday Times* University of the Year. A little further down, Aberdeen is up 14 places and back in the top 30 as Scottish University of the Year.

The biggest rise of all is 25 places by the University of the Creative Arts, in 33rd place, matching the highest position ever achieved by a post-1992 university and helping it to the title of Modern University of the Year. Others celebrating impressive rises include St Mary's, Twickenham (up 22 places to 77th) and Oxford Brookes and the University of the Arts London, which both rose 21 places. Those going in the other direction include the Royal Agricultural University (down 29 places to 115th) and Hull (down 28 places to 103rd).

More modern universities than ever feature above some older foundations. The first edition of *The Times Good University Guide* predicted the development of a new pecking order in an era of growing competition between universities, many of which had just acquired that title. It has taken longer than many expected and the top 30 places in the table are still monopolised by old universities, but the previous binary division is breaking down.

Making the right choices

Anyone hoping to embark on a degree in 2020 (or any other time) will be well advised to tread carefully and muster as much comparative information as possible before making their choices. This *Guide* is intended as a starting point, a tool to help navigate the statistical minefield that will face applicants, as universities present their performance in the best possible light. There is advice on fees and financial questions, as well as all-important employment issues, along with the usual ranking of universities and 67 subject tables.

While some of the leading universities have expanded considerably in recent years, most will remain selective, particularly in popular subjects. Overall, 76.7% of applicants found places in 2018, but that does not mean that they secured the university or course of their dreams. The demand for places is far from uniform, and even within the same university the level of competition will vary between subjects. The entry scores quoted in the subject tables in Chapter 13 offer a reliable guide to the relative levels of selectivity, but the figures are for entrants' actual qualifications. The standard offers made by departments will invariably be lower.

Making the right choice requires a mixture of realism and ambition. Most sixth-formers and college students have a fair idea of the grades they are capable of attaining, within a certain margin for error. Even with five choices of course to make, there is no point in applying for a degree where the standard offer is so far from your predicted grades that rejection is virtually certain. If your results do turn out to be much better than predicted, there will be an opportunity through the Adjustment system, or simply through Clearing, to trade up to an alternative university.

Since the relaxation of recruitment restrictions, universities that once took pride in their absence from Clearing have continued to recruit after A-level results day. As a result, the use of insurance choices – the inclusion of at least one university with lower entrance standards than your main targets – has been declining. It is still a dangerous strategy, but there is now more chance of picking up a place at a leading university if you aimed too high with all your first-round choices. Oxford and Cambridge will not be appearing in the Clearing lists, but there is a wider range of universities to choose from than ever before. Some may even come to you if you sign up for the new arrangements introduced by UCAS two years ago, which allow universities to approach unplaced candidates on Results Day if their grades are similar to other entrants'.

The Adjustment Period that runs for five days after results have been published is reserved for those with better grades than the offer they have accepted to approach other universities. Although only 880 students found places this way in 2018, the system offers a valuable safety net for those in this happy position. Universities at the very top of the table may be full, but there should be more opportunities elsewhere.

The long view

School-leavers who enter higher education in 2020 were not born when our first league table was published and most will never have heard of polytechnics, even if they attend a university that once carried that title. But it was the award of university status to the 34 polytechnics, a quarter of a century ago, that was the inspiration for the first edition of *The Times Good University Guide*. The original poly, the Polytechnic of Central London, had become the University of Westminster, Bristol Polytechnic was now the University of the West of England

and – most mysteriously of all – Leicester Polytechnic had morphed into De Montfort University. The new *Guide* charted the lineage of the new universities and offered the first-ever comparison of institutional performance in UK higher education.

The university establishment did not welcome the initiative. The vice-chancellors described the table as "wrong in principle, flawed in execution and constructed upon data which are not uniform, are ill-defined and in places demonstrably false." The league table has changed considerably since then, and its results are taken rather more seriously. While consistency has been a priority for the *Guide* throughout its 25 years, only six of the original 14 measures have survived. Some of the current components – notably the National Student Survey – did not exist in 1992, while others have been modified or dropped at the behest of the expert group of planning officers from different types of universities that meets annually to review the methodology and make recommendations for the future.

While ranking is hardly popular with academics, the relationship with universities has changed radically, and this *Guide* is quoted on numerous university websites. As Sir David Eastwood, now vice-chancellor of the University of Birmingham, said in launching an official report on university league tables that he commissioned as Chief Executive of the Higher Education Funding Council for England: "We deplore league tables one day and deploy them the next."

Most universities have had their ups and downs over the years, although Oxford and Cambridge have tended to pull away from the rest. Both benefited from the introduction of student satisfaction ratings and from the extra credit given to the top research grades – the two measures that carry an extra weighting in our table. They also have famously high entry standards, much the largest proportions of first and upper-second class degrees and consistently good scores on every other measure. Several other famous names have been among the chasing pack throughout. Imperial College and University College London have seldom been out of the top five, while the London School of Economics, Durham, Warwick and, in recent years, St Andrews have all been fixtures in the top ten.

There have been spectacular rises, however. Coventry, for example, was only 12 places off the bottom a dozen years ago and is now well inside the top 50, having reached the highest position ever for a modern university three years ago. The University of the Creative Arts, which now enjoys that distinction, was not even a university until 2008.

Since this book was first published, the number of universities has increased by a third and the full-time student population has rocketed. Individual institutions are almost unrecognisable from their 1993 forms. Nottingham, for example, had fewer than 10,000 students then, compared with more than 30,000 now. Manchester Metropolitan, the largest of the former polys, has experienced similar growth. Yet there are universities now which would have been too small and too specialist to qualify for the title in 1992. The diversity of UK higher education is celebrated as one of its greatest strengths, and the modern universities are neither encouraged nor anxious to compete with the older foundations on some of the measures in our table.

The coming years, let alone the next 20, may see another transformation in the higher education landscape, with the private sector competing strongly with established universities in some fields and distance learning becoming more popular as there is greater investment in Massive Open Online Courses (MOOCs) and the cost of full-time degrees rises. There may, indeed, be university closures and mergers, although they have been predicted before and seldom come about. Universities are among the most enduring of the UK's institutions, and will take some shifting.

1 The University League Table

What Makes a Top University?

Some changes have been forced upon us. Universities stopped assessing teaching quality by subject, when this was the most heavily weighted measure in the table, for example. However, the subsequent development of the National Student Survey (NSS) has enabled the student experience to be reflected in the table. More than two thirds of final year undergraduates give their views on the quality of their courses, a remarkable response rate that makes the results impossible to dismiss.

Three years ago, we split the student satisfaction measure in two while keeping the overall contribution of the NSS to the table unchanged, and we have retained this approach. The "teaching quality" indicator reflects the average scores of the survey's sections on teaching, assessment and feedback, learning opportunities and academic support, while the "student experience" indicator is drawn from the average of the sections on organisation and management, learning resources, the student voice and the learning community, as well as the final question on overall satisfaction. Teaching quality is favoured over student experience and accounts for 67% of the overall student satisfaction score, with student experience making up the remaining 33%.

The basic information that applicants need in order to judge universities and their courses does not change, however. A university's entry standards, staffing levels, completion rates, degree classifications and graduate employment rates are all vital pieces of intelligence for anyone deciding where to study.

Research grades, while not directly involving undergraduates, bring with them considerable funds and enable a university to attract top academics.

Any of these measures can be discounted by an individual, but the package has struck a chord with readers. The ranking is the most-quoted of its type both in Britain and overseas, and has built a reputation as the most authoritative arbiter of changing fortunes in higher education.

The measures used are kept under review by a group of university administrators and statisticians, which meets annually. The raw data that go into the table in this chapter and the

67 subject tables in chapter 13 are all in the public domain and are sent to universities for checking before any scores are calculated.

The various official bodies concerned with higher education do not publish league tables, and the Higher Education Statistics Agency (HESA), which supplies most of the figures used in our tables, does not endorse the way in which they are aggregated. But there are now numerous exercises, from the Teaching Excellence Framework to the annual "performance indicators" published by HESA on everything from completion rates to research output at each university, that invite comparisons.

Any scrutiny of league table positions is best carried out in conjunction with an examination of the relevant subject table – it is the course, after all, that will dominate your undergraduate years and influence your subsequent career.

How *The Times and Sunday Times* league table works

The table is presented in a format that displays the raw data, wherever possible. In building the table, scores for student satisfaction (combining the teaching quality, student experience scores) and research quality were weighted by 1.5; all other measures were weighted by 1.

For entry standards, student/staff ratio, good honours and graduate prospects, the score was adjusted for subject mix. For example, it is accepted that engineering, law and medicine graduates will tend to have better graduate prospects than their peers from English, psychology and sociology courses. Comparing results in the main subject groupings helps to iron out differences attributable simply to the range of degrees on offer. This subject-mix adjustment means that it is not possible to replicate the scores in the table from the published indicators because the calculation requires access to the entire dataset.

The indicators were combined using a common statistical technique known as z-scores, to ensure that no indicator has a disproportionate effect on the overall total for each university, and the totals were transformed to a scale with 1,000 for the top score. The z-score technique makes it impossible to compare universities' total scores from one year to the next, although their relative positions in the table are comparable. Individual scores are dependent on the top performer: a university might drop from 60% of the top score to 58% but still have improved, depending on the relative performance of other universities.

Only where data are not available from HESA are figures sourced directly from universities. Where this is not possible scores are generated according to a university's average performance on other indicators, apart from the measures for research quality, student–staff ratio and services and facilities spend, where no score is created.

The organisations providing the raw data for the tables are not involved in the process of aggregation, so are not responsible for any inferences or conclusions we have made. Every care has been taken to ensure the accuracy of the tables and accompanying information, but no responsibility can be taken for errors or omissions.

The Times and The Sunday Times league table uses nine important indicators of university activity, based on the most recent data available at the time of compilation:

» Teaching quality
» Student experience
» Research quality
» Entry standards
» Student–staff ratio

» Services and facilities spend
» Completion
» Good honours
» Graduate prospects

Teaching quality and student experience

The student satisfaction measure has been divided into two components which give final-year undergraduates' views of the quality of their courses. The National Student Survey (NSS) published in 2018 was the source of the data.

Where no data was available in the 2018 survey the score from the 2017 survey was used. Where neither 2018 nor 2017 NSS data was available, the 2016 scores for Teaching Quality and Student Experience were adjusted by the overall percentage point change between 2016 and 2018. The adjusted scores were used for z-scoring only, and do not appear in the final table.

» The National Student Survey covers eight aspects of a course, with an additional question gauging overall satisfaction. Students answer on a scale from 1 (bottom) to 5 (top) and the score in the table is the percentage of positive responses (4 and 5) in each section

» The teaching quality indicator reflects the average scores of the first four sections, which contain 14 questions

» The student experience indicator is drawn from the average scores of the remaining four sections, containing 12 questions, and the additional question on overall satisfaction.

» Teaching quality accounts for 67% of the overall score covering student satisfaction, with student experience making up the remaining 33%.

» The survey is based on the opinion of final-year undergraduates rather than directly assessing teaching quality. Most undergraduates have no experience of other universities, or different courses, to inform their judgements. Although all the questions relate to courses, rather than other aspects of the student experience, some types of university – notably medium-sized campus universities – tend to do better than others.

Research quality

This is a measure of the quality of the research undertaken in each university. The information was sourced from the 2014 Research Excellence Framework (REF), a peer-review exercise used to evaluate the quality of research in UK higher education institutions undertaken by the UK Higher Education funding bodies. Additionally, academic staffing data for 2013–14 from the Higher Education Statistics Agency have been used.

» A research quality profile was given to every university department that took part. This profile used the following categories: 4* world-leading; 3* internationally excellent; 2* internationally recognised; 1* nationally recognised; and unclassified. The Funding Bodies have directed more funds to the very best research by applying weightings, and for the 2015 *Guide* we used the weightings adopted by HEFCE (the funding council for England) for funding in 2013–14: 4* was weighted by a factor of 3 and 3* was weighted by a factor of 1. Outputs of 2* and 1* carried zero weight. This meant a maximum score of 3. In the interests of consistency, the above weightings continue to be applied this year.

» The scores in the table are presented as a percentage of the maximum score. To achieve the maximum score all staff would need to be at 4* world-leading level.

» Universities could choose which staff to include in the REF, so, to factor in the depth of the research quality, each quality profile score has been multiplied by the number of staff returned in the REF as a proportion of all eligible staff.

Entry standards

This is the average score, using the new UCAS tariff (see page 32), of new students under the age of 21 who took A and AS Levels, Scottish Highers and Advanced Highers and other equivalent qualifications (eg, International Baccalaureate). It measures what new students actually achieved rather than the entry requirements suggested by the universities. The data comes from HESA for 2016–17 and has been converted into points from the new tariff because this is the system used by current applicants. The original sources of data for this measure are data returns made by the universities themselves to HESA.

» Using the UCAS tariff, each student's examination results were converted to a numerical score. HESA then calculated an average for all students at the university. The results have then been adjusted to take account of the subject mix at the university.

» A score of 144 represents three As at A-level. Although all but five of the top 40 universities in the table have average entry standards of at least 144, it does not mean that everyone achieved such results – let alone that this was the standard offer. Courses will not demand more than three subjects at A-level and offers are pitched accordingly. You will need to reach the entry requirements set by the university, rather than these scores.

Graduate prospects

This measure is the percentage of the total number of graduates undertaking further study or in a professional job six months after graduation. The professional employment marker is derived from the latest Standard Occupational Classification (SOC2010) codes. The data came from the HESA Destination of Leavers from HE (DLHE) Record for 2017 graduates.
The results have been adjusted for subject mix.

» HESA's survey of graduates six months after graduation is the only research to show what at least 80% of them do immediately after leaving university.

Good honours

This measure is the percentage of graduates achieving a first or upper second class degree. The results have been adjusted to take account of the subject mix at the university. The data comes from HESA for 2016–17. The original sources of data for this measure are data returns made by the universities themselves to HESA.

» Four-year first degrees, such as an MChem, are treated as equivalent to a first or upper second.

» Scottish Ordinary degrees (awarded after three years of study) are excluded.

» Universities control degree classification, with some oversight from external examiners. There have been suggestions that since universities have increased the numbers of good honours degrees they award, this measure may not be as objective as it should be. However, it remains the key measure of a student's success and employability.

Completion

This measure gives the percentage of students expected to complete their studies (or transfer to another institution) for each university. The data comes from the HESA performance indicators published in March 2018 and based on students entering in 2015–16.

» This measure is a projection, liable to statistical fluctuations.

Student-staff ratio

This is a measure of the average number of students to each member of the academic staff, apart from those purely engaged in research. In this measure a low value is better than a high value. The data comes from HESA for 2016–17. The original sources of data for this measure are data returns made by the universities themselves to HESA.

» The figures, as calculated by HESA, allow for variation in employment patterns at different universities. A low value means that there are a small number of students for each academic member of staff, but this does not, of course, ensure good teaching quality or contact time with academics.

» Student/staff ratios vary by subject; for example the ratio is usually low for medicine. In building the table, the score is adjusted for the subject mix taught by each university.

» Adjustments are also made for students who are on industrial placements, either for a full year or for part of a year.

Services and facilities spend

The expenditure per student on staff and student facilities, including library and computing facilities. The data comes from HESA for 2015–16 and 2016–17. The original data sources for this measure are data returns made by the universities to HESA.

» This is a measure calculated by taking the expenditure on student facilities (including sports, grants to student societies, careers services, health services, counselling, etc.) and library and computing facilities (books, journals, staff, central computers and computer networks, but not buildings) and dividing this by the number of full-time-equivalent students. Expenditure is averaged over two years to even out the figures (for example, a computer upgrade undertaken in a single year).

2019 rank	2018 rank		Teaching quality (%)	Student experience (%)	Research quality (%)	Entry standards (UCAS pts)	Graduate prospects (%)	Good honours (%)	Completion rate (%)	Student–staff ratio	Service & facilities spend per student (£)	Total	Page
1	1	Cambridge	n/a	n/a	57.3	225	86.8	92.6	98.6	11.0	3,708	1,000	
2	2	Oxford	n/a	n/a	53.1	217	83.5	93.7	98.5	10.5	3,455	971	
3	3	St Andrews	86.2	85.2	40.4	206	79.6	90.1	96.0	11.6	2,721	898	
4	4	Imperial College London	75.1	78.8	56.2	219	90.4	90.2	96.6	11.4	3,656	871	
5	=7	Loughborough	82.5	84.5	36.3	162	86.9	84.3	92.3	13.8	3,047	818	
6	6	Lancaster	81.4	81.8	39.1	158	89.1	76.5	92.6	12.7	3,244	817	
7	5	Durham	78.8	75.9	39.0	198	84.9	90.8	96.1	14.9	2,888	813	
8	=7	University College London	72.8	73.2	51.0	191	83.8	90.8	94.1	10.3	2,733	788	
9	11	London School of Economics	66.1	64.5	52.8	204	86.2	88.8	96.0	11.9	3,023	786	
10	9	Warwick	77.8	78.4	44.6	182	83.2	84.4	96.1	12.8	2,563	785	
11	10	Leeds	81.3	81.6	36.8	168	81.2	86.6	92.5	13.2	3,110	778	
12	14	Exeter	80.6	80.9	38.0	176	85.5	86.3	95.4	16.1	2,745	777	
13	12	Bath	79.0	80.7	37.3	186	87.5	86.2	95.1	15.8	2,486	766	
14	15	Birmingham	79.2	78.2	37.1	166	85.8	85.8	94.5	14.8	2,840	731	
15	13	East Anglia	79.0	78.5	35.8	153	77.1	87.8	90.6	13.4	3,005	719	
16	18	Nottingham	78.9	77.9	37.8	164	86.0	84.9	93.3	13.9	2,508	716	
17	20	Glasgow	79.1	79.6	39.9	201	85.3	84.1	88.6	14.9	2,316	714	
18	30	Southampton	78.7	78.1	44.9	159	82.1	82.4	92.4	12.9	2,220	708	
=19	25	Manchester	77.1	76.6	39.8	168	80.7	81.7	93.0	13.4	2,898	702	
=19	=16	Bristol	75.7	74.1	47.3	184	80.6	89.3	95.6	13.6	2,139	702	
21	26	Newcastle	78.8	79.1	37.7	161	85.8	81.3	94.7	13.8	2,200	697	
22	=16	York	81.3	79.3	38.3	160	82.0	80.6	92.5	14.6	1,909	692	
23	19	Surrey	78.6	79.2	29.7	164	81.0	85.3	90.6	15.7	2,714	684	
24	=28	Royal Holloway, London	80.3	78.3	36.3	142	73.5	80.0	93.0	15.2	2,530	679	
25	21	Sheffield	78.4	80.3	37.6	156	84.4	80.6	93.0	14.7	2,334	676	

2019 rank	2018 rank	Teaching quality (%)	Student experience (%)	Research quality (%)	Entry standards (UCAS pts)	Graduate prospects (%)	Good honours (%)	Completion rate (%)	Student-staff ratio	Services & facilities spend per student (£) Total	Page
26	40 Aberdeen	79.6	79.9	29.9	182	80.9	85.4	89.5	15.4	2,369	672
27	23 Dundee	83.0	82.0	31.2	174	81.7	81.2	87.1	14.5	2,203	668
28	24 Edinburgh	72.8	72.4	43.8	182	77.5	86.5	92.0	12.6	2,195	667
29	22 Essex	80.4	79.7	37.2	117	74.3	78.8	86.2	16.3	3,408	664
30	=36 Swansea	80.7	81.5	33.7	138	85.6	77.8	90.2	15.4	2,375	662
31	42 Liverpool	79.5	80.0	31.5	146	85.4	79.3	90.5	13.5	2,302	659
32	35 Cardiff	78.5	77.3	35.0	155	81.7	78.9	92.4	13.5	2,267	646
=33	33 Harper Adams	83.1	81.6	5.7	128	72.9	66.2	90.3	15.7	3,459	643
=33	58 University for the Creative Arts	84.4	80.7	3.4	142	72.7	74.1	83.6	13.2	2,657	643
=35	=28 King's College London	73.1	71.2	44.0	170	84.5	86.4	87.4	12.5	2,570	636
=35	39 Heriot-Watt	75.8	75.6	36.7	167	79.3	76.8	84.6	16.7	3,219	636
37	=47 Nottingham Trent	83.8	82.5	6.5	144	81.7	71.9	85.8	14.8	2,320	631
=38	38 Queen's, Belfast	77.9	77.5	39.7	152	82.4	80.0	91.2	15.8	2,288	629
=38	34 Leicester	76.7	76.9	31.8	136	75.4	79.0	92.7	13.7	2,664	629
40	32 Reading	76.7	72.2	36.5	138	76.0	79.1	92.1	15.0	2,560	624
41	27 Sussex	75.2	74.3	31.8	144	80.4	75.9	91.6	16.4	2,709	622
42	54 Lincoln	83.1	82.4	10.3	129	81.4	73.5	88.7	14.9	2,054	614
43	=47 Buckingham	84.9	83.2	n/a	128	81.5	68.7	84.0	11.3	2,344	613
=44	41 Strathclyde	76.3	76.3	37.7	202	79.6	82.0	86.5	19.8	1,819	608
=44	45 Stirling	79.1	76.3	30.5	161	78.7	79.5	85.5	15.5	1,823	608
=46	44 Coventry	83.4	83.6	3.8	127	80.9	73.5	86.0	14.6	2,305	595
=46	43 Queen Mary, London	73.2	73.9	37.9	148	78.7	79.8	91.9	13.1	2,524	595
=48	50 Keele	83.3	83.4	22.1	128	82.1	71.4	89.6	14.2	1,962	592
=48	=47 Aberystwyth	86.5	84.1	28.1	119	78.2	67.3	83.2	16.6	1,838	592
50	52 Liverpool Hope	85.1	83.3	9.2	116	83.8	65.9	81.0	14.5	2,094	590

2019 rank	2018 rank		Teaching quality (%)	Student experience (%)	Research quality (%)	Entry standards (UCAS pts)	Graduate prospects (%)	Good honours (%)	Completion rate (%)	Student-staff ratio	Services & facilities spend per student (£)	Total	Page
=51	53	Portsmouth	81.6	81.0	8.6	119	85.4	75.2	85.1	15.4	2,169		584
=51	51	Arts University, Bournemouth	80.7	78.5	2.4	161	80.5	67.5	89.3	15.7	1,786		584
53	=36	Soas, University of London	75.0	71.8	27.9	148	70.9	80.5	82.6	12.3	2,376		583
54	—	Leeds Arts	85.4	82.7	n/a	167	57.1	73.8	90.5	12.5	1,238		574
55	31	Kent	77.2	77.0	35.2	138	78.3	78.5	88.3	18.4	1,762		570
56	46	Aston	79.0	78.3	25.8	137	79.1	81.3	90.7	20.1	1,937		565
57	=63	Staffordshire	84.6	80.6	16.5	116	80.8	68.4	76.4	14.5	2,180		562
58	57	West of England	84.2	84.0	8.8	128	76.3	75.3	84.3	18.4	2,440		560
59	=61	Edge Hill	82.9	81.1	4.9	131	77.2	71.9	85.4	15.2	2,191		558
60	73	Ulster	82.4	81.5	31.8	126	71.9	73.5	82.9	17.1	1,910		550
61	66	Northumbria	79.9	79.4	9.0	145	75.4	77.0	86.2	16.7	2,257		549
62	65	Huddersfield	81.4	78.6	9.4	129	80.0	74.4	82.5	17.0	2,234		541
=63	84	Oxford Brookes	79.7	78.4	11.4	130	77.4	74.6	87.8	16.1	2,069		540
=63	55	Bangor	83.3	81.5	27.2	134	67.8	69.3	88.2	16.7	1,747		540
65	=67	De Montfort	82.1	81.7	8.9	113	83.8	71.3	83.6	19.4	2,181		530
66	60	Norwich Arts	82.0	77.0	5.6	144	60.6	72.8	87.2	15.8	2,176		528
67	=70	Sheffield Hallam	82.4	80.8	5.4	124	73.8	75.3	86.3	16.9	2,128		527
68	=75	City	77.8	78.8	22.6	142	73.4	71.8	87.2	17.9	2,352		523
69	80	Manchester Metropolitan	79.2	77.2	7.5	133	70.7	70.4	82.9	15.3	2,599		520
70	74	Roehampton	77.7	77.4	24.5	109	72.2	68.9	81.2	14.7	2,216		519
71	=63	Goldsmiths, London	74.8	70.1	33.4	132	58.3	83.9	79.2	14.7	2,539		518
72	=86	Plymouth	82.5	80.1	15.9	128	73.6	73.0	85.1	15.9	1,763		517
73	=61	Chester	83.2	79.9	4.1	115	70.1	65.8	82.6	15.3	2,838		515
74	=70	Liverpool John Moores	80.4	79.2	8.9	141	74.9	76.0	86.0	17.3	1,730		514
75	81	Derby	83.8	80.0	2.5	119	76.2	66.5	82.2	15.1	2,015		511

2019 rank	2018 rank		Teaching quality (%)	Student experience (%)	Research quality (%)	Entry standards (UCAS pts)	Graduate prospects (%)	Good honours (%)	Completion rate (%)	Student-staff ratio	Services & facilities spend per student (£)	Total	Page
76	59	Brunel	73.8	74.4	25.4	132	70.9	75.1	87.1	16.4	2,370		505
77	99	St Mary's, Twickenham	83.4	81.0	4.0	120	72.6	72.2	80.0	15.7	1,749		504
78	79	Bournemouth	78.6	77.2	9.0	123	68.7	78.9	84.1	17.0	2,278		499
79	85	Winchester	81.7	80.2	5.8	113	63.7	77.6	87.7	16.3	1,605		496
80	=75	St George's, London	72.7	71.7	22.2	166	93.8	75.7	92.6	12.4	2,505		495
=81	88	Salford	81.8	79.1	8.3	128	73.6	69.6	81.5	15.0	2,014		494
=81	83	Gloucestershire	81.9	79.7	3.8	124	72.9	71.8	83.4	19.0	2,007		494
83	56	West London	79.2	77.3	1.6	120	74.0	72.4	76.5	15.6	2,893		492
84	69	Falmouth	80.5	74.6	4.6	121	77.0	72.6	88.4	18.4	1,456		491
=85	92	Teesside	82.5	78.9	3.6	120	81.3	66.0	81.6	17.2	2,399		489
=85	=100	Solent	82.0	78.8	0.5	117	70.4	71.3	78.7	15.7	2,166		489
=87	105	Birmingham City	82.3	80.3	4.3	128	76.8	68.6	83.6	18.1	2,026		488
=87	=67	Leeds Trinity	83.9	82.3	2.0	101	68.1	78.6	83.4	19.5	1,895		488
89	104	Wales Trinity St David	85.4	80.8	2.6	106	66.0	69.0	78.2	15.0	1,961		480
89	89	Hertfordshire	80.1	79.0	5.6	119	80.6	65.9	81.7	17.9	2,439		476
91	=102	Worcester	83.6	81.6	4.3	119	75.0	65.6	84.9	16.7	1,519		474
92	=100	West of Scotland	82.6	79.2	4.3	142	80.7	70.3	80.9	22.1	2,166		473
93	96	Sunderland	82.1	79.0	5.8	120	67.1	66.7	78.1	15.6	2,303		472
=94	115	Arts London	76.3	70.9	8.0	139	72.2	65.8	84.1	14.4	1,805		471
=94	72	Chichester	80.2	79.1	6.4	125	64.6	69.4	88.2	15.1	1,531		471
96	82	Robert Gordon	80.3	77.5	4.0	159	81.1	71.0	85.8	20.6	1,448		469
97	=102	Queen Margaret, Edinburgh	78.4	74.7	6.6	149	72.9	78.7	80.1	18.5	1,728		467
98	=75	Bradford	74.7	75.6	9.2	130	82.8	77.3	82.1	16.8	2,021		462
99	97	Northampton	80.8	76.6	3.2	108	68.2	68.8	82.9	18.7	2,946		460
100	=109	Greenwich	78.8	76.9	4.9	135	70.3	74.1	80.9	17.9	2,203		458

SOUTHALL AND WEST
LONDON COLLEGE

2019 rank	2018 rank		Teaching quality (%)	Student experience (%)	Research quality (%)	Entry standards (UCAS pts)	Graduate prospects (%)	Good honours (%)	Completion rate (%)	Student–staff ratio	Services & facilities spend (per student £)	Total	page
101	=109	Glasgow Caledonian	78.5	76.1	7.0	165	73.7	72.8	84.9	19.2	1,588		455
102	118	York St John	81.1	79.2	4.1	115	73.6	64.7	84.6	17.4	1,831		453
=103	=75	Hull	78.5	75.8	16.7	123	76.0	67.3	82.2	18.3	2,153		450
=103	94	Bath Spa	79.1	74.8	7.9	122	66.9	74.6	85.3	19.9	1,851		450
=105	93	Central Lancashire	78.6	76.5	5.6	130	76.9	70.4	78.9	16.4	1,875		446
=105	98	Abertay	79.2	77.0	5.1	157	73.4	70.4	74.9	18.5	1,905		446
107	=106	London South Bank	77.1	75.2	9.0	107	87.7	68.9	77.0	16.5	2,084		442
108	90	Cardiff Metropolitan	77.7	77.9	3.9	126	65.9	65.2	79.5	16.5	2,599		440
109	=119	Plymouth Marjon	36.3	82.6	0.0	129	63.7	65.5	84.1	22.7	1,884		436
=110	91	Middlesex	75.0	73.9	9.7	118	73.5	67.4	72.8	16.6	3,170		432
=110	117	Kingston	78.3	77.2	5.1	127	64.5	70.1	81.2	16.0	2,362		432
=110	=119	South Wales	81.7	78.1	4.0	130	63.4	67.4	79.2	15.1	1,721		432
113	95	Bishop Grosseteste	80.8	74.8	2.1	112	72.9	66.4	91.5	22.0	1,833		430
=114	=106	Westminster	73.4	74.0	9.8	124	70.4	71.9	82.9	17.0	2,022		428
=115	114	East London	81.4	80.1	7.2	114	65.3	63.9	73.3	17.0	2,449		424
=115	=86	Royal Agricultural University	75.4	75.3	1.1	123	63.5	65.8	95.2	21.6	2,529		424
117	126	Buckinghamshire New	83.5	81.0	1.5	112	68.8	56.6	76.2	16.0	2,327		417
118	111	Canterbury Christ Church	80.0	75.4	4.5	111	64.7	70.7	79.5	15.2	1,913		413
119	121	Newman	81.2	78.5	2.8	120	64.7	65.3	77.8	16.0	1,623		408
120	116	Edinburgh Napier	72.8	72.3	4.6	150	73.8	74.7	81.5	18.8	1,796		401
121	108	Bedfordshire	81.6	79.7	7.0	97	70.6	63.5	72.8	17.6	2,157		400
122	113	Anglia Ruskin	82.4	79.1	5.4	106	68.3	71.3	79.2	18.2	1,520		396
123	112	Brighton	77.3	73.4	7.9	118	67.2	69.3	85.5	18.2	1,497		375
124	123	Leeds Beckett	80.8	80.5	4.1	114	63.2	65.9	76.0	19.4	1,633		367
125	125	Cumbria	77.2	71.5	1.2	120	73.6	61.1	83.5	16.7	1,550		355

2019 rank	2018 rank		Teaching quality (%)	Student experience (%)	Research quality (%)	Entry standards (UCAS pts)	Graduate prospects (%)	Good honours (%)	Completion rate (%)	Student-staff ratio	Services & facilities spend per student (£)	Total	page
126	124	Bolton	85.6	82.0	2.9	114	57.4	59.4	68.9	14.7	1,352	349	
127	–	Wolverhampton	79.8	78.3	5.9	110	68.9	64.0	70.3	20.0	1,859	345	
128	122	Birkbeck	77.3	73.9	34.6	102	69.0	57.2	64.3	15.8	1,189	329	
129	127	Glyndŵr	80.3	73.2	2.3	112	63.5	66.6	71.1	19.2	1,570	317	
130	129	Suffolk	75.8	70.9	n/a	123	65.0	66.2	69.5	17.6	2,290	313	
131	128	London Metropolitan	78.5	74.6	3.5	102	70.7	52.3	68.8	21.6	1,970	280	
132	–	Ravensbourne, London	71.9	67.9	n/a	109	68.7	65.6	77.9	28.8	1,731	257	

Notes on the Table

Leeds Arts University and Ravensbourne University, London are included this year for the first time. The University of Wolverhampton has returned after a nine-year boycott of league tables.

University College Birmingham continues to block the release of its performance data and does not appear in this year's table.

2 Choosing What and Where to Study

Choosing a degree is one of the biggest decisions any student will ever take – both in terms of the likely costs and the influence it may have on the direction of his or her life. That is not just a matter of future earning power, although the current political and media debates might suggest that it is. Many graduates end up living and working near their university; they often make their closest friends in their student days and may even meet their future partner there. And that is without considering the three or four years you will spend as an undergraduate, which should develop your intellect and shape you as a person.

Of course, with fees now exceeding £9,000, no one is suggesting that you should ignore career prospects – although it is dangerous to read too much into employment statistics that are collected only six months after graduation. Indeed, any assumptions about the link between particular courses and future salaries are no more than that; the world is changing too rapidly to pick winners several years ahead of joining the graduate labour market, although some subjects and universities have a record that inspires more confidence than others. This chapter will suggest some of the signs to take into account in selecting the course that is right for you, if indeed you are certain that your immediate future should be in higher education at all.

Most young people with the necessary qualifications to go to university decide that it is right for them – half the working age population of London now consists of graduates. But applications and enrolments since the introduction of much higher fees are beginning to show clear patterns that favour particular subjects and universities – and may make life increasingly difficult for others. It is not surprising that growing numbers should decide to play it safe, as they see it, in choosing what and where to study. Although most graduate jobs continue to be open to students of any discipline, some arts subjects may now seem more of a gamble, and there may be pressure at home to go for a science or business subject if you have the right qualifications.

Your choices must be realistic, however. The course must not only be within your capabilities, but will have to maintain your interest for at least three years – possibly much longer than that if it is then going to determine your field of employment. Ideally, higher education should broaden your options in later life, not narrow them. Most of today's graduates will work in several different fields during their careers. In any case, no one can be sure which skills will be required in four or more years' time, when today's applicants enter the graduate labour market.

Some subjects and universities will be more marketable than others, but which ones? This *Guide* may give some pointers – medicine is unlikely to go into decline, for example – but times do change. Computer science, for instance, went through years of falling numbers after the dotcom bubble burst, before recovering strongly in recent years. Applications for the group of subjects that includes architecture and building are only now returning to the totals reached before the recession.

Why applicants have reached some of the conclusions they have remains a mystery. Languages, for example, have been hardest hit in terms of applications and enrolments. Yet business leaders are constantly stressing the need for linguists. In this case, decisions made on entry to the sixth-form may be the biggest factor behind falling applications – the numbers taking languages at A-level have been dropping for a number of years, perhaps because they are seen as more difficult than other arts subjects.

There will be a number of different factors influencing your choice of university and course, ranging from the limitations imposed by your qualifications to favoured geographical locations. You may want to stay within reach of home – or to get as far away as possible. You may have heard good things about a particular course from friends, or a teacher. This *Guide* – and the tables it contains – offers a reality check to supplement such opinions, and the opportunity to narrow down your options.

What influences a choice?

Most important factors in choosing a university (median marks out of 10)

1	The course: curriculum, assessment type and structure	8.4
2	Reputation of the University	7.7
3	University's perceived ability to boost career	7.1
4	Accessibility by major transport	6.7
5	Facilities: gym, library, IT and labs	6.3
6	Distance from family home	6.1
7	Affordability of town/city	6.1
8	Availability of accommodation	5.9
9	Support services: enrichment, counselling and diversity	5.8
10	Culture: arts, food and attractions	5.7
11	Size of town or city	5.6
12	Nightlife	4.6
13	Sports available	3.9
14	Family or friends' links with university	3.9
15	Regional weather	3.6

Source: SPCE Labs 2018 (sample of 2,000 current and past UK students)

Is higher education for you?

Before you start, there is one important question to ask yourself: what do you want out of higher education? The answer will make it easier to choose where (and if) to be a student. With nearly three in ten school-leavers going on to university, it is easy to drift that way without much thought, opting for the subject in which you expect the best A-level grades, and looking for a university with a reasonable reputation and a good social life. Your career will look after itself – you hope.

With graduate debt soaring, however, and job prospects varying widely between subjects and universities, now is the time to look at your own motivation. Fewer young people than predicted have opted out of higher education since higher fees were introduced, but apprenticeships and big firms' training schemes are now offering attractive alternatives. Many of those who do choose higher education appear to be rethinking their choice of course to give themselves the best possible chance of a satisfying and lucrative career.

Love of a subject is an excellent reason for taking a degree, and one that allows you to focus almost exclusively on the search for a course that corresponds with your passions. If, however, higher education is a means to an end, you need to think about career ambitions and look carefully at employment rates for any courses you might consider. These are examined in more detail in chapter 3.

Many graduates look back on their student days as the best years of their lives, and there is nothing wrong with wanting to have a good time. Remember, though, that you will be paying for it later (literally) and there will be more studying than partying. If you have not enjoyed sixth-form or college courses, you may be better off in a job and possibly becoming one of the hundreds of thousands each year who return to education later in life.

Setting your priorities

Even in the world of £9,250 fees, there are good reasons to believe that the right degree will still be a good investment. Most research suggests that, on average, a degree would add more than £100,000 to lifetime earnings. A recent Labour Force Survey showed working-age graduates earning almost 50% more on average than non-graduates – a bigger premium than graduates enjoy in most countries.

The majority of graduate jobs are not subject-specific; employers value the transferable skills that higher education confers. Rightly or wrongly, however, most employers are influenced by which university a graduate attended, so the choice of institution remains as important as ever. The Institute for Fiscal Studies (IFS) found that the male graduates of 23 universities and the female graduates of nine were earning less than those without degrees after ten years. Although most of the IFS report focused mainly on 2012-13, there is little reason to think that this has changed.

Those who want to add value to their degree in the jobs market will find that growing numbers of universities are offering employment-related schemes that are considered in more detail in chapter 3. In many cases, this will involve work experience or extra activities organised by the careers service. A growing number of universities now run certificated employability programmes, while others, such as Liverpool John Moores, have built such skills into degree courses. Such programmes are also highlighted in chapter 3 and in the university profiles in chapter 15.

Narrowing down the field

Once you have decided that higher education is for you, the good news is that, as long as you start early enough, finding the right university can be relatively straightforward. Media attention focuses on the scramble for places on a relatively small proportion of courses where competition is intense, but there are plenty of places at good universities for candidates with the basic qualifications – it's just a matter of finding the one that suits you best. For older applicants, relevant work experience and demonstrable interest in a subject may be enough to win a place.

If anything, the problem is that of too much choice, although universities have reduced the number of degree combinations in anticipation of tougher financial conditions. Students prepared to move away from home will still have more than 100 universities and numerous specialist colleges to consider, most with hundreds – even thousands – of course combinations on offer. Institutions come in all shapes and sizes, so there is work to do at the outset narrowing down your options.

Most applicants start by choosing a subject, rather than a university, and this may reduce the field considerably – there are only eight institutions offering veterinary medicine for example, although the total is around 100 in subjects such as psychology, law and English. By the time you have factored in personal preferences about the type or location of your ideal university, the list of possibilities may already be reduced to manageable proportions.

After that, you can take a closer look at what the courses contain and what life is really like for students. Prospectuses and university websites will give you an accurate account of course combinations, and important facts like the accommodation available to new students, but it is their job to sell the university. To get a true picture, you need more – preferably a visit not just to the university, but to the department where you would be studying. If that is not possible, there are plenty of other sources of objective information, such as the National Student Survey (which is available online, with a range of additional data about the main courses at each institution, at **www.unistats.com**).

A few students' unions publish alternative prospectuses, giving a "warts and all" view of the university, and those that do not provide this service may be able to arrange a brief discussion with a current student, either by phone or email. Your school or college may put you in contact with someone who went to a university that you are considering. Guides and collections of statistics may give you valuable information about a course or a university, but there is no substitute for personal experience.

What to study?

Most people seeking a place in higher education start by choosing a subject and a course, rather than a university. If you take a degree, you are going to spend at least three years immersed in your subject. It has to be one you will enjoy and can master – not to mention one that you are qualified to study. Many economics degrees require maths A-level, for example, while most medical schools demand chemistry or biology. The UCAS website (**www.ucas.com**) contains course profiles, including entrance requirements, which is a good starting point, while universities' own sites contain more detailed information. In chapter 13, we describe 67 subject areas and provide league tables for each of them.

Your school subjects and the UCAS tariff

The official yardstick by which your results will be judged is the UCAS tariff, which gives a score for each grade of most UK qualifications considered relevant for university entrance, as well as for the International Baccalaureate (IB). The tariff changed in 2017. The new points system is shown on page 32, but most applicants are not affected – two thirds of offers are made in grades, rather than tariff points. This allows universities to stipulate the grades that they require in particular subjects, if they wish, and to determine which vocational qualifications are relevant to different degrees. In certain universities, some departments, but not others, will use the tariff to set offers. Course profiles on the UCAS website and/or universities' own sites should show whether offers are framed in terms of grades or tariff points. It is important to find out which, especially if you are relying on points from qualifications other than A-level or Scottish Highers, more of which are included in the new tariff.

Entry qualifications listed in the *Guide* relate not to the offers made by universities, but to the actual grades achieved by successful candidates who are under 21 on entry. For ease of comparison, a tariff score is included even where universities make their offers in grades.

"Soft" subjects

There is a related issue for many of the most selective universities about the subjects studied in the sixth-form or at college. Not only have growing numbers of students been applying with vocational (usually BTEC) qualifications, but the variety of A-level courses now available includes many subjects that top universities usually will not consider on a par with traditional academic subjects.

UCAS tariff scores for main qualifications:

A-levels		AS levels	
Grade	**Points**	**Grade**	**Points**
A*	56	A	20
A	48	B	16
B	40	C	12
C	32	D	10
D	24	E	6
E	16		

Scottish Advanced higher		Scottish higher	
Grade	**Points**	**Grade**	**Points**
A	56	A	33
B	48	B	27
C	40	C	21
D	32	D	15

International Baccalaureate			
Higher level		Standard level	
H7	56	S7	28
H6	48	S6	24
H5	32	S5	16
H4	24	S4	12
H3	12	S3	6

The Extended Essay and Theory of Knowledge course are awarded A 12, B 10, C 8, D 6, E 4

For other qualifications see: ucas.com/ucas/ucas-tariff-points

For many years, a minority of universities have refused to accept General Studies as a full A-level for entrance purposes (although even some leading universities do). The growth of supposedly "soft" subjects, such as media studies and photography, has prompted a few universities to produce lists of subjects that will only be accepted alongside at least two traditional academic subjects.

The Russell Group of 24 leading universities publishes an extremely useful report, called *Informed Choices*, on the post-16 qualifications preferred by its members for a wide range of degrees. Although it names media studies, art and design, photography and business studies among the vocational subjects that would normally be given this label, it does not subscribe to the notion of a single list of "soft" subjects. The report suggests you choose at most a single vocational course and primarily select from a list of "facilitating subjects", which are required for many degrees and welcomed generally at Russell Group universities. The list comprises: maths and further maths, English, physics, biology, chemistry, geography, languages (classical and modern) and history. In addition, their guide indicates the "essential" and "useful" A-level subjects for 60 different subject areas studied at Russell Group universities.

For most courses at most universities, there are no such restrictions, as long as your main subjects or qualifications are relevant to the degree you hope to take. Nevertheless, when choosing A-levels it would be wise to bear the Russell Group lists in mind if you are likely to apply to one or more of the leading universities. At the very least, it is an indication of the subjects that admissions tutors may take less seriously than the rest. Although only the London School of Economics has published a list of "non-preferred" subjects (see page 33), others may adopt less formal weightings.

Vocational qualifications

The Education Department downgraded many vocational qualifications in school league tables from 2014. This has added to the confusion surrounding the value placed on diplomas and other qualifications by universities. The engineering diploma has won near-universal approval from universities (for admission to engineering courses and possibly some science degrees), but some of the other diplomas are in fields that are not on the curriculum of the most selective universities. Regardless of the points awarded under the tariff, it is essential to contact universities direct to ensure that a diploma or another vocational qualification will be an acceptable qualification for your chosen degree.

Admission tests

The growing number of applicants with high grades at A-level has encouraged the introduction of separate admission tests for some of the most oversubscribed courses. There are national tests in medicine and law that are used by some of the leading universities, while Oxford and Cambridge have their own tests in a growing number of subjects. The details are listed on page 34. In all cases, the tests are used as an extra selection tool, not as a replacement for A-level or other general qualifications.

Making a choice

Your A-levels or Scottish Highers may have chosen themselves, but the range of subjects across the whole university system is vast. Even subjects that you have studied at school may be quite different at degree level – some academic economists actually prefer their undergraduates. not to have taken A-level economics because they approach the subject so differently. Other students are disappointed because they appear to be going over old ground when they continue with a subject that they enjoyed at school. Universities now publish quite detailed syllabuses, and it is a matter of going through the fine print.

"Traditional academic" and "non-preferred" subjects

The London School of Economics expects applicants to offer at least two of the traditional subjects listed below, while any of the non-preferred subjects listed should only be offered with two traditional subjects.

Traditional subjects

- Ancient history
- Biology
- Classical civilisation
- Chemistry
- Computing
- Economics
- Electronics
- English
- Further mathematics
- Geography
- Government and politics
- History
- Law
- Mathematics
- Modern or classical languages
- Music
- Philosophy
- Physics
- Psychology
- Religious studies
- Sociology

Non-preferred subjects

- Any Applied A-level
- Accounting
- Art and design
- Business studies
- Citizenship studies
- Communication and culture
- Creative writing
- Design and technology
- Drama/theatre studies
- Film studies
- Health and social care
- Home economics
- Information and communication technology
- Leisure studies
- Media studies
- Music technology
- Physical education/ Sports studies
- Travel and tourism

General studies, critical thinking, thinking skills, knowledge and enquiry and project work A-levels will only be considered as fourth A-level subjects and will not therefore be accepted as part of a conditional offer.

Admissions tests

Some of the most competitive courses now have additional entrance tests. The most significant tests are listed below. Note that registration for many of the tests is before 15 October and you will need to register for them as early as possible. All the tests have their own websites. Institutions requiring specific tests vary from year to year and you must check course website details carefully for test requirements. In addition over 50 universities also administer their own tests for certain courses. Details are given at: **www.ucas.com/ucas/undergraduate/getting-started/entry-requirements/admissions-tests**

Law
Law National Admissions Test (LNAT): for entry to law courses at Bristol, Durham, Glasgow, King's College London, Nottingham, Oxford, SOAS, University College, London. Register from August; tests held from September to January.

Mathematics
Mathematics Admissions Test (MAT): for entry to mathematics at Imperial College, London and mathematics and computer science at Oxford. Test held in early November.

Sixth Term Examination Papers (STEP): for entry to mathematics at Cambridge and Warwick (also encouraged by Bath, Bristol, Imperial College London, King's College London, Loughborough, Nottingham, Southampton and University College London). Register by end April; tests held in June.

Medical subjects
BioMedical Admissions Test (BMAT): for entry to medicine at Brighton and Sussex Medical School, Cambridge (also for veterinary medicine), Imperial College London, Keele (international applicants only), Lancaster, Leeds (also for dentistry), Oxford and University College London. Register by 1 October; test held early November.

Graduate Medical School Admissions Test (GAMSAT): for graduate entry to medicine and dentistry at Cardiff, Exeter, Liverpool, Nottingham, Plymouth, St. George's, University of London, Swansea, Keele and St Andrews and Dundee in partnership with University of the Highlands & Islands (Scotgem). Register by early August; test held mid-September

Health Professions Admissions Test (HPAT–Ulster): for certain health profession courses at Ulster.Register by start January; test held late January.

UK Clinical Aptitude Test (UKCAT): for entry to medical and dental schools at Aberdeen, Aston, Birmingham, Bristol, Cardiff, Dundee, East Anglia, Edinburgh, Exeter, Glasgow, Hull York Medical School, Keele, King's College London, Leicester, Liverpool, Manchester, Newcastle, Nottingham, Plymouth, Queen Mary, University of London, Queen's University Belfast, Sheffield, Southampton, St Andrews, St George's, University of London, Warwick. Register between May and mid-September; tests held between July and early October.

Cambridge University
Pre-interview or at-interview assessments take place for all subjects. Full details given on the Cambridge admissions website. See also STEP and BMAT above.

Oxford University
Pre-interview tests take place in many subjects that candidates are required to register for specifically by early October. Full details given on the Oxford admissions website. Tests held in early November, usually at candidate's educational institution. See also LNAT, MAT and BMAT above.

The greater difficulty comes in judging your suitability for the many subjects that are not on the school or college curriculum. Philosophy and psychology sound fascinating (and are), but you may have no idea what degrees in either subject entail – for example, the level of statistics that may be required. Forensic science may look exciting on television – more glamorous than plain chemistry – but it opens fewer doors, as the type of work portrayed in *Silent Witness* is very hard to find.

Academic or vocational?

There is frequent and often misleading debate about the differences between academic and vocational higher education. It is usually about the relative value of taking a degree, as opposed to a directly work-related qualification. But it also extends to higher education itself, with jibes about so-called "Mickey Mouse" degrees in areas that were not part of the higher education curriculum when most of the critics were students.

Such attitudes ignore the fact that medicine and law are both vocational subjects, as are architecture, engineering and education. They are not seen as any less academic than geography or sociology, but for some reason social work or nursing, let alone media studies and sports science, are often looked down upon. The test of a degree should be whether it is challenging and a good preparation for working life. Both general academic and vocational degrees can do this.

Nevertheless, it is clear that the prospect of much higher graduate debt is encouraging more students into job-related subjects. This is understandable and, if you are sure of your future career path, possibly also sensible. But much depends on what that career is – and whether you are ready to make such a long-term commitment. Some of the programmes that have attracted public ridicule, such as surf science or golf course management, may narrow graduates' options to a worrying extent, but often boast strong employment records.

As you would expect, many vocational courses are tailored to particular professions. If you choose one of these, make sure that the degree is recognised by the relevant professional body (such as the Engineering Council or one of the institutes) or you may not be able to use the skills that you acquire. Most universities are only too keen to make such recognition clear in their prospectus; if no such guarantee is published, contact the university department running the course and seek assurances.

Even where a course has professional recognition, bear in mind that a further qualification may be required to practise. Both law and medicine, for example, demand additional training to become a fully qualified solicitor, barrister or doctor. Nor is either degree an automatic passport to a job: only about half of all law graduates go into the profession. Both law and medicine

Most popular subject areas by applications 2017		Most popular subjects by acceptances 2017	
1 Nursing	188,110	1 Nursing	28,620
2 Law	118,565	2 Psychology	21,680
3 Psychology	115,850	3 Law	21,455
4 Design	93,765	4 Design	18,815
5 Computer Science	92,955	5 Computer Science	18,475
6 Management Studies	82,530	6 Sport & Exercise Science	15,110
7 Business Studies	69,170	7 Business Studies	14,475
8 Medicine	68,655	8 Management Studies	14,415
9 Sport & Exercise Science	67,710	9 Social Work	13,265
10 Subjects Allied to Medicine	60,175	10 Subjects Allied to Medicine	11,410
Source: UCAS applications 2017		Source: UCAS acceptances 2017	

Subject areas covered in this *Guide*

The list below gives each of the 67 subject areas that are covered in detail later in the book (in chapter 13). For each subject area in that chapter, there is specific advice, a summary of employment prospects and a league table of universities that offered courses in 2016–17, ranked on the basis of an overall score calculated from research quality, entry standards, teaching quality, student experience and graduate employment prospects.

Accounting and Finance
Aeronautical and Manufacturing
  Engineering
Agriculture and Forestry
American Studies
Anatomy and Physiology
Animal Science
Anthropology
Archaeology and Forensic Science
Architecture
Art and Design
Biological Sciences
Building
Business Studies
Celtic Studies
Chemical Engineering
Chemistry
Civil Engineering
Classics and Ancient History
Communication and Media Studies
Computer Science
Creative Writing
Criminology
Dentistry
Drama, Dance and Cinematics
East and South Asian Studies
Economics
Education
Electrical and Electronic Engineering
English
Food Science
French
General Engineering
Geography and Environmental Sciences

Geology
German
History
History of Art, Architecture and Design
Hospitality, Leisure, Recreation and Tourism
Iberian Languages
Italian
Land and Property Management
Law
Librarianship and Information Management
Linguistics
Materials Technology
Mathematics
Mechanical Engineering
Medicine
Middle Eastern and African Studies
Music
Nursing
Other Subjects Allied to Medicine
Pharmacology and Pharmacy
Philosophy
Physics and Astronomy
Physiotherapy
Politics
Psychology
Radiography
Russian
Social Policy
Social Work
Sociology
Sports Science
Theology and Religious Studies
Town and Country Planning and Landscape
Veterinary Medicine

also provide a route into the profession for graduates who have taken other subjects. Law conversion courses, though not cheap, are increasingly popular, and there are a growing number of graduate-entry medical degrees.

One way to ensure that a degree is job-related is to take a "sandwich" course, which involves up to a year in business or industry. Students often end up working for the organisation which provided the placement, while others gain valuable insights into a field of employment – even if only to discount it. The drawback with such courses is that, like the year abroad that is part of most language degrees, the period away from university inevitably disrupts living arrangements and friendship groups. But most of those who take this route find that the career benefits make this a worthwhile sacrifice.

Employers' organisations calculate that more than half of all graduate jobs are open to applicants from any subject, and recruiters for the most competitive graduate training schemes often prefer traditional academic subjects to apparently relevant vocational degrees. Newspapers, for example, often prefer a history graduate to one with a media studies degree; computing firms are said to take a disproportionate number of classicists. A good degree classification and the right work experience are more important than the subject for most non-technical jobs. But it is hard to achieve a good result on a course that you do not enjoy, so scour prospectuses, and email or phone university departments to ensure that you know what you are letting yourself in for. Their reaction to your approach will also give you an idea of how responsive they are to their students.

Studying more than one subject

You may find that more than one subject appeals, in which case you could consider Joint Honours – degrees that combine two subjects – or even Combined Honours, which will cover several related subjects. Such courses obviously allow you to extend the scope of your studies, but they should be approached with caution. Even if the number of credits suggests a similar workload to Single Honours, covering more than one subject inevitably involves extra reading and often more essays or project work..

The number taking such degrees is falling, but there are advantages to them. Many students choose a "dual" to add a vocational element to make themselves more employable – business studies with languages or engineering, for example, or media studies with English. Others want to take their studies in a particular direction, perhaps by combining history with politics, or statistics with maths. Some simply want to add a completely unrelated interest to their main subject, such as environmental science and music, or archaeology and event management – both combinations that are available at UK universities.

At most universities, however, it is not necessary to take a degree in more than one subject in order to broaden your studies. The spread of modular programmes ensures that you can take courses in related subjects without changing the basic structure of your degree. You may not be able to take an event management module in a single-honours archaeology degree, but it should be possible to study some history or a language. The number and scope of the combinations offered at many of the larger universities is extraordinary. Indeed, it has been criticised by academics who believe that "mix-and-match" degrees can leave a graduate without a rounded view of a subject. But for those who seek breadth and variety, close scrutiny of university prospectuses is a vital part of the selection process.

What type of course?

Once you have a subject, you must decide on the level and type of course. Most readers of this *Guide* will be looking for full-time degree courses, but higher education is much broader than that. You may not be able to afford the time or the money needed for a full-time commitment of three or four years at this point in your life.

Part-time courses

Tens of thousands of people each year opt for a part-time course – usually while holding down a job – to continue learning and to improve their career prospects. The numbers studying this way have dropped considerably, but loans are available for students whose courses occupy between a quarter and three-quarters of the time expected on a full-time course. Repayments are on the same conditions as those for full-time courses, except that repayments will begin after three years of study even if the course has not been completed by then. The downside is that many universities have increased their fees in the knowledge that part-time students will be able to take out student loans to cover fees and employers are now less inclined to fund their employees on such courses. At Birkbeck, University of London, for example, a compromise has been found with full-time courses taught in the evening. For courses classified as part-time, students pay fees in proportion to the number of credits they take.

Part-time study can be exhausting unless your employer gives you time off, but if you have the stamina for a course that will usually take twice as long as the full-time equivalent, this route should still make a degree more affordable. Part-time students tend to be highly committed to their subject, and many claim that the quality of the social life associated with their course makes up for the quantity of leisure time enjoyed by full-timers.

Distance learning

If you are confident that you can manage without regular face-to-face contact with teachers and fellow students, distance learning is an option. Courses are delivered mainly or entirely online or through correspondence, although some programmes offer a certain amount of local tuition. The process might sound daunting and impersonal, but students of the Open University (OU), all of whom are educated in this way, are frequently among the most satisfied in the country, according to the results of the annual National Student Survey. Attending lectures or oversized seminars at a conventional university can be less personal than regular contact with your tutor at a distance.

Of course, not all universities are as good at communicating with their distance-learning students as the OU, or offer such high-quality course materials, but this mode of study does give students ultimate flexibility to determine when and where they study. Distance learning is becoming increasingly popular for the delivery of professional courses, which are often needed to supplement degrees. The OU now takes students of all ages, including a growing number of school-leavers, not just mature students.

In addition, there is now the option of Massive Open Online Courses (MOOCs) provided by many of the leading UK and American universities, usually free of charge. As yet, such courses are the equivalent of a module in a degree course, rather than the entire qualification. Some are assessed formally but none is likely to be seen by employers as the equal of a conventional degree, no matter how prestigious the university offering the course. That may change – some commentators see in MOOCs the beginning of the end of the traditional, residential university – but their main value at the moment is as a means of dipping a toe in the water of higher education. For those who are uncertain about committing to a degree, or who simply want to learn more about a subject without needing a high-status qualification, they are ideal.

A growing number of UK universities are offering MOOCs through the Futurelearn platform, run by the Open University (**www.futurelearn.com**). But the beauty of MOOCs is that they can come from all over the world. Perhaps the best-known providers are Coursera (**www.coursera.org**), which originated at Stanford University, in California, and now involves a large number of American and international universities including Edinburgh, and edX (**www.edx.org**), which numbers Harvard among its members. MOOCs are also being used increasingly by sixth-formers to extend their subject knowledge and demonstrate their enthusiasm and capability to admissions tutors. They are certainly worth considering for inclusion in a personal statement and/or to spark discussion at an interview.

Foundation degrees

Even if you are set on a full-time course, you might not want to commit yourself for three or more years. Two-year vocational Foundation degrees have become a popular route into higher education in recent years. Many other students take longer-established two-year courses, such as Higher National Diplomas or other diplomas tailored to the needs of industry or parts of the health service. Those who do well on such courses usually have the option of converting their qualification into a full degree with further study, although many are satisfied without immediately staying on for the further two or more years that completing a BA or BSc will require.

Other short courses

A number of universities are experimenting with two-year degrees, encouraged by the Government, squeezing more work into an extended academic year. The so-called "third semester" makes use of the summer vacation for extra teaching, so that mature students, in particular, can reduce the length of their career break. Several universities are offering accelerated degrees as part of a pilot project initiated under the last government. But only at the University of Buckingham, the UK's longest-established private university, is this the dominant pattern for degree courses. Other private institutions – notably BPP University – are following suit.

Other short courses, usually lasting a year, are designed for students who do not have the necessary qualifications to start a degree in their chosen subject. Foundation courses in art and design have been common for many years and are the chosen preparation for a degree at leading departments, even for many students whose A-levels would win them a degree place elsewhere. Access courses perform the same function in a wider range of subjects for students without A-levels, or for those whose grades are either too low or in the wrong subjects to gain admission to a particular course. Entry requirements are modest, but students have to reach the same standard as regular entrants to progress to a degree.

Higher and Degree Apprenticeships

Apprenticeships have been a serious alternative to university for more than a decade. But now students can have the best of both worlds at a growing number of universities, with higher or degree apprenticeships, which combine study at degree level with extended work experience with a named industrial or business partner. The programmes are already popular, but are only available in a limited range of subjects, such as accountancy, healthcare sciences, management and some branches of engineering. A survey by *The Sunday Times* found only about 8,500 people taking degree apprenticeships in 2018, but universities were planning for 14,000 this September, with more expected subsequently.

Such apprenticeships take up to five years to complete and leave the graduate with a Bachelor's or even a Master's degree. Employers including Deloitte, BMW and the BBC are offering higher-level apprenticeships, although naturally not all are with household names such as these. Students are a paid employee of the sponsoring company, with a contract of employment and holiday entitlement, as well as wages of up to £300 a week. Some are available through UCAS, but most require a direct application. The best starting point to weigh up the options is the gov.uk website, which has a 'Find an Apprenticeship' section. Once you register you can set up email and text alerts to inform you about new apprenticeship roles. You can also find a range of vacancies at ratemyapprenticeship.co.uk, which carries thousands of reviews.

Further details of the structure of courses and the areas in which apprenticeships are available can be found at **www.gov.uk/government/publications/higher-and-degree-apprenticeships**. In addition, Which? University and the National Apprenticeship Service have produced a more detailed publication, *The Complete Guide to Higher and Degree Apprenticeships*, which is available online and in print.

Yet more choice

No single guide can allow for personal preferences in choosing a course. You may want one of the many degrees that incorporate a year at a partner university abroad, or to try a six-month exchange on the Continent through the European Union's Erasmus Programme. Either might prove a valuable experience and add to your employability. Or you might prefer a January or February start to the traditional autumn start – there are plenty of opportunities for this, mainly at post-1992 universities.

In some subjects – particularly engineering and the sciences – the leading degrees may be Masters courses, taking four years rather than three (in England). In Scotland, most degree courses take four years and some at the older universities will confer a Masters qualification. Those who come with A-levels may apply to go straight into the second year. Relatively few students take this option, but it is easy to imagine more doing so in future at universities that charge students from other parts of the UK the full £9,250 for all years of the course.

Where to study

Once you have decided what to study, there are still several factors that might influence your choice of university or college. Obviously, you need to have a reasonable chance of getting in, you may want reassurance about the university's reputation, and its location will probably also be important to you. On top of that, most applicants have views about the type of institution they are looking for – big or small, old or new, urban or rural, specialist or comprehensive. Campus universities tend to produce the highest levels of student satisfaction, but big city

---

Universities with highest and lowest offer rates

Highest		Lowest	
1 Aberystwyth	98.5%	1 Oxford	23.0%
2 Portsmouth	93.9%	2 University of the Arts London	30.2%
3 Bangor	93.8%	3 Cambridge	31.2%
4 Roehampton	93.7%	4 Leeds Arts	38.3%
5 Wolverhampton	93.1%	5 London School of Economics	38.4%
6 Sussex	92.6%	6 Imperial College London	43.6%
7 Winchester	92.4%	7 Edinburgh	50.4%
8 Lincoln	91.7%	8 St Andrews	50.2%
9 Swansea	91.7%	9= Queen Margaret	52.9%
10 Newman	91.5%	9= St George's, London	52.9%

UCAS 2017 applications

UCAS 2017 applications

universities continue to attract sixth-formers in the largest numbers. You may surprise yourself by choosing somewhere that does not conform to your initial criteria, but working through your preferences is another way of narrowing down your options.

Best paid graduates

(Median salary six months after graduating)

1	Imperial College London	£30,000
2	London School of Economics	£29,000
3	Oxford	£27,040
4	Cambridge	£27,000
5	St George's, London	£26,600
6	Warwick	£26,500
=7	Bath	£26,000
=7	King's College London	£26,000
=7	London South Bank	£26,000
=7	University College London	£26,000

HESA 2017 graduates

Entry standards

Unless you are a mature student or have taken a gap year, your passport to your chosen university will probably be a conditional offer based on your predicted grades, previous exam performance, personal statement, and school or college reference. A growing number of universities have followed Birmingham's lead in making unconditional offers to candidates in selected subjects who have a strong academic record and are predicted high grades. With ministers making critical comments about the practice, it remains to be seen whether the trend will continue for courses beginning in 2020.

Supply and demand dictate whether you will receive an offer, conditional or otherwise. Beyond the national picture, your chances will be affected both by the university and the subject you choose. A few universities (but not many) at the top of the league tables are heavily oversubscribed in every subject; others will have areas in which they excel, but may make relatively modest demands for entry to other courses. Even in many of the leading universities, the number of applicants for each place in languages or engineering is still not high. Conversely, three As at A-level will not guarantee a place on one of the top English or law degrees, but there are enough universities running courses to ensure that three Cs will put you in with a chance somewhere.

University prospectuses and the UCAS website will give you the "standard offer" for each course, but in some cases, this is pitched deliberately low in order to leave admissions staff extra flexibility. The standard A-level offer for medicine, for example, may not demand A*s, but nearly all successful applicants will have one or more.

Most popular universities by applications 2017

1	Manchester	63,590
2	Edinburgh	62,480
3	Leeds	58,560
4	Birmingham	55,340
5	Manchester Met	53,335
6	Nottingham	47,485
7	University College London	43,930
8	King's College London	43,820
9	Bristol	43,355
10	Exeter	41,000

UCAS applications 2017

As already noted, the average entry scores in our tables give the actual points obtained by successful applicants – many of which are far above the offer made by the university, but which give an indication of the pecking order at entry. The subject tables (in chapter 13) are, naturally, a better guide than the main table (in chapter 1), where average entry scores are influenced by the range of subjects available at each university.

Location

The most obvious starting point is the country you study in. Most degrees in Scotland take four years, rather than the UK norm of three. It goes without saying that four years cost more than three, especially given the loss of the year's salary you might have been earning after graduation. A later chapter will go into the details of the system, but suffice to say that students from Scotland pay no fees, while those from the rest of the UK do. Nevertheless, Edinburgh and St Andrews remain particularly popular with English students, despite charging them £9,250 a year for the full four years of a degree starting in 2018. The number of English students going to Scottish universities has increased almost every year since the fees went up, despite the fact that there would be no savings, perhaps because the institutions have tried harder to attract them. Fees – or the lack of them – are by no means the only influence on cross-border mobility: the number of Scots going to English universities rose sharply, in spite of the cost, probably because the number of places is capped in Scotland, but not any longer in England.

Close to home

Far from crossing national boundaries, however, growing numbers of students choose to study near home, whether or not they continue to live with their family. This is understandable for Scots, who will save themselves tens of thousands of pounds by studying at their own fees-free universities. But there is also a gradual increase in the number choosing to study close to home either to cut living costs or for personal reasons, such as family circumstances, a girlfriend or boyfriend, continuing employment or religion. Some simply want to stick with what they know.

The trend for full-time students who do go away to study, is to choose a university within about two hours' travelling time. The assumption is that this is far enough to discourage parents from making unannounced visits, but close enough to allow for occasional trips home to get the washing done, have a decent meal and see friends. The leading universities recruit from all over the world, but most still have a regional core.

University or college?

This *Guide* is primarily concerned with universities, the destination of choice for the vast majority of higher education students. But there are other options – and not just for those searching for lower fees. A number of specialist higher education colleges offer a similar, or sometimes superior, quality of course in their particular fields. The subject tables in chapter 13 chart the successes of various colleges in art, agriculture, music and teacher training in particular. Some colleges of higher education are not so different from the newer universities and may acquire that status themselves in future years, as two did last year and one more in the current academic year.

Further education colleges

The second group of colleges offering degrees are further education (FE) colleges. These are often large institutions with a wide range of courses, from A-levels to vocational subjects at different levels, up to degrees in some cases. Although their numbers of higher education students have been falling in recent years, the new fee structure presents them with a fresh opportunity because they tend not to bear all the costs of a university campus. For that reason, too, they may not offer a broad student experience of the type that universities pride themselves on, but the best colleges respond well to the local labour market and offer small teaching groups and effective personal support.

FE colleges are a local resource and tend to attract mature students who cannot or do not want to travel to university. Many of their higher education students apply nowhere else. But, as competition for university places has increased, they also have become more of an option for school-leavers to continue their studies, as they always have done in Scotland.

Their predominantly local, mature student populations do FE colleges no favours in statistical comparisons with universities. But it should be noted that the proportion of college graduates unemployed six months after graduation is often lower than at universities, as are average graduate salaries. Indeed, 14 further education colleges secured 'gold' ratings in the first year of the Government's Teaching Excellence Framework (TEF) – although more than twice as many found themselves in the 'bronze' category.

Both further and higher education colleges are audited by the Quality Assurance Agency and appear in the National Student Survey, as well as the TEF. In all three, their results usually show wide variation. Some demonstrate higher levels of satisfaction among their students than most universities, for example, while others are at the bottom of the scale.

Private universities and colleges

The final group of colleges that present an alternative to university was insignificant in terms of size until recently, but may also prosper under the current fee regime, as well as the most recent legislation. This is the private sector, seen mainly in business and law, but also in some other specialist fields.

By far the longest established – and the only one to meet the criteria for inclusion in our main table – is the University of Buckingham, which is profiled on pages 358–359. The best-known "newcomer" currently is BPP University, which became a full university in 2013 and offers degrees, as well as shorter courses, in both law and business subjects. Like Buckingham, BPP offers two-year degrees with short vacations to maximise teaching time – a model that other private providers are likely to follow. Fees were £9,000 a year for UK students taking BPP's three-year degrees in 2018 and £13,500 a year for the accelerated version. International students paid £12,500 and £18,750 respectively.

The New College of the Humanities, which graduated its first students in 2015, started out with fees of nearly £18,000 a year for all undergraduates, guaranteeing small-group teaching and some big-name visiting lecturers in economics, English, history, law and philosophy. The college is now matching the 'public sector' at £9,250 a year and is being bought by the Boston-based Northeastern University. At present, the college offers University of London external degree courses and Combined Honours degrees validated by Solent University.

Two other private institutions have been awarded university status. Regent's University, attractively positioned in London's Regent's Park, caters particularly for the international market with courses in business, arts and social science subjects priced at £16,400 a year for 2017–18. However, about half of the students at the not-for-profit university, which offers British and American degrees, are from the UK or other parts of Europe. The University of Law, as its name suggests, is more specialised. It has been operating as a college in London for more than 100 years and claims to be the world's leading professional law school. Law degrees, as well as professional courses, with fees for three-year degrees set at £9,250 in 2019–20 for UK and EU students and £11,100 for the two-year version. For non-EU students, the equivalent fees are £13,500 and £16,100 respectively. The university is about to open its eleventh campus, in Nottingham, to add to those in London, Birmingham, Bristol, Chester, Guildford, Manchester and Leeds, as well as at Exeter, Reading, and Liverpool universities.

There are also growing numbers of specialist colleges offering degrees, especially in the business sector. GSM London (formerly the Greenwich School of Management), with more than 3,500 students on two London campuses, is probably the largest in terms of full-time students, but there are others that have forged partnerships with universities or are going it alone. The ifs School of Finance, for example, also dates back more than 100 years and now has university college status (as ifs University College) for its courses in finance and banking.

Some others that rely on international students have been hit by tougher visa regulations, but the Government is keen to encourage the development of a private sector to compete with the established universities. Two newcomers will focus on engineering, for example. The Dyson Institute of Engineering and Technology, based at Malmesbury, in Wiltshire, welcomed its first 33 undergraduates in 2017. Funded entirely by Sir James Dyson, there are no fees, and students will work at the nearby Dyson headquarters for 47 weeks a year. The New Model in Technology and Engineering, in Hereford, has received more than £20m in Government funding and promises to "totally reimagine and redesign the higher education experience". It will take its first students in 2020. For details of these institutions see pages 585–587.

City universities

The most popular universities, in terms of total applications, are nearly all in big cities with other major centres of population within the two-hour travelling window. For those looking for the best nightclubs, top sporting events, high-quality shopping or a varied cultural life – in other words, most young people, and especially those who live in cities already – city universities are a magnet. The big universities also, by definition, offer the widest range of subjects, although that does not mean that they necessarily have the particular course that is right for you. Nor does it mean that you will actually use the array of nightlife and shopping that looks so alluring in the prospectus, either because you cannot afford to, because student life is focused on the university, or even because you are too busy working.

Top 10 Universities for Quality of Teaching, feedback and support 2018 % satisfied with teaching quality		Top 10 Universities for Overall Student Experience 2018	
1 Aberystwyth	86.5%	1 St Andrews	85.2%
2 Plymouth Marjon	86.3%	2 Loughborough	84.5%
3 St Andrews	86.2%	3 Aberystwyth	84.1%
4 Bolton	85.6%	4 West of England	84.0%
=5 Leeds Arts	85.4%	5 Coventry	83.6%
=5 Wales Trinity St David	85.4%	6 Keele	83.4%
7 Liverpool Hope	85.1%	7 Liverpool Hope	83.3%
8 Buckingham	84.9%	8 Buckingham	83.2%
9 Staffordshire	84.6%	9 Leeds Arts	82.7%
10 University for the Creative Arts	84.4%	10 Plymouth Marjon	82.6%

Source: National Student Survey 2018   **Source:** National Student Survey 2018

Campus universities

City universities are the right choice for many young people, but it is worth bearing in mind that the National Student Survey shows that the highest satisfaction levels tend to be at smaller universities, often those with their own self-contained campuses. It seems that students identify more closely with institutions where there is a close-knit community and the social life is based around the students' union rather than the local nightclubs. There may also be a better prospect of regular contact with tutors and lecturers, who may also live on or near the campus. Few UK universities are in genuinely rural locations, but some – particularly among the more recently promoted – are in relatively small towns. Several longer-established institutions in Scotland and Wales also share this type of setting, where the university dominates the town.

Importance of Open Days

The only way to be certain if this, or any other type of university, is for you is to visit. Schools often restrict the number of open days that sixth-formers can attend in term-time, but some universities offer a weekend alternative. The full calendar of events is available at www.opendays.com and on universities' own websites. Bear in mind, if you only attend one or two, that the event has to be badly mismanaged for a university not to seem an exciting place to someone who spends his or her days at school, or even college. Try to get a flavour of several institutions before you make your choice.

How many universities to pick?

When that time comes, of course, you will not be making one choice but five; four if you are applying for medicine, dentistry or veterinary science. (Full details of the application process are given in chapter 5.) Tens of thousands of students each year eventually go to a university that did not start out as their first choice, either because they did not get the right offer or because they changed their mind along the way. UCAS rules are such that applicants do not list universities in order of preference anyway – indeed, universities are not allowed to know where else you have applied. So do not pin all your hopes on one course; take just as much care choosing the other universities on your list.

The value of an "Insurance Choice"

Until recently, nearly all applicants included at least one "Insurance Choice" on that list – a university or college where entry grades were significantly lower than at their preferred institutions. This practice has been in decline, presumably because candidates expecting high grades think they can pick up a lower offer either in Clearing or through UCAS Extra, the service that allows applicants rejected by their original choices to apply to courses that still have vacancies after the first round of offers. However, it is easy to miscalculate and leave yourself without a place that you want. You may not like the look of the options in Clearing, leaving yourself with an unwelcome and potentially expensive year off, at a time when jobs are thin on the ground.

The lifting of recruitment restrictions in 2015 has increased competition between universities and seen more of the leading institutions taking part in Clearing. For those with good grades, this makes it less of a risk to apply only to highly selective universities. However, if you are at all uncertain about your grades, including an Insurance Choice remains a sensible course of action – especially since entry requirements have risen in recent years in response to increased demand for places. Even if you are sure that you will match the standard offers of your chosen universities, there is no guarantee that they will make you an offer. Particularly for degrees demanding three As or more at A-level, there may simply be too many highly qualified applicants to offer places to all of them. The main proviso for Insurance Choices, as with all others, is that you must be prepared to take up that place. If not, you might as well go for broke with courses with higher standard offers and take your chances in Clearing, or even retake exams if you drop grades. Thousands of applicants each year end up rejecting their only offer when they could have had a second, Insurance Choice.

Reputation

The reputation of a university is something intangible, usually built up over a long period and sometimes outlasting reality. Before universities were subject to external assessment and the publication of copious statistics, reputation was rooted in the past. League tables are partly responsible for changing that, although employers are often still influenced by what they remember as the university pecking order when they were students.

The fragmentation of the British university system into groups of institutions is another factor: the Russell Group (**www.russellgroup.ac.uk**) represents 24 research-intensive universities, nearly all with medical schools; the million+ group (**www.millionplus.ac.uk**) contains many of the former polytechnics and newer universities; the University Alliance (**www.unialliance.ac.uk**) provides a home for 18 universities, both old and new, that did not fit into the other categories; while GuildHE (**www.guildhe.ac.uk**) represents specialist colleges and the newest universities. The Cathedrals Group (**www.cathedralsgroup.ac.uk**) is an affiliation of 16 church-based universities and colleges, some of which are also members of other groups.

Many of today's applicants will barely have heard of a polytechnic, let alone be able to identify which of today's universities had that heritage, but most will know which of two universities in the same city has the higher status. While that should matter far less than the quality of a course, it would be naïve to ignore institutional reputation entirely if that is going to carry weight with a future employer. Some big firms restrict their recruitment efforts to a small group of universities (see chapter 3), and, however short sighted that might be, it is something to bear in mind if a career in the City or a big law firm is your ambition.

Facilities

A 2015 survey commissioned by university directors of estates found that the quality of campus facilities was an important factor in choosing a university for two thirds of applicants. Only the course and the university's location had a higher priority. Accommodation is the main selling point for those living away from home, but sports facilities, libraries and computing equipment also play an important part. Even campus nightclubs have become part of the facilities race that has followed the introduction of top-up fees.

Many universities guarantee first-year students accommodation in halls of residence or university-owned flats. But it is as well to know what happens after that. Are there enough places for second or third-year students who want them, and if not, what is the private market like? Rents for student houses vary quite widely across the country and there have been tensions with local residents in some cities. All universities offer specialist accommodation for disabled students – and are better at providing other facilities than most public institutions. Their websites give basic information on what is provided, as well as contact points for more detailed inquiries.

Checklist

Choosing a subject and a place to study is a major decision. Make sure you can answer these questions:

Choosing a course

» What do I want out of higher education?
» Which subjects do I enjoy studying at school?
» Which subject or subjects do I want to study?
» Do I have the right qualifications?
» What are my career plans and does the subject and course fit these?
» Do I want to study full-time or part-time?
» Do I want to study at a university or a college?

Choosing a university

» What type of university do I wish to go to: campus, city or smaller town?
» How far is the university from home?
» Is it large or small?
» Is it specialist or general?
» Does it offer the right course?
» How much will it cost?
» Have I arranged to visit the university?

Special-interest clubs and recreational facilities, as well as political activity, tend to be based in the students' union – sometimes knows as the guild of students. In some universities, the union is the focal point of social activity, while in others the attractions of the city seem to overshadow the union to the point where facilities are underused. Students' union websites are included with the information found in the university profiles (chapter 15).

Sources of information

With more than 130 universities to choose from, the Unistats and UCAS websites, as well as guides such as this one, are the obvious places to start your search for the right course. Unistats now includes figures for average salaries at course level, as well as student satisfaction ratings and some information on contact hours, although this does not distinguish between lectures and seminars. The site does not make multiple comparisons easy to carry out, but it does contain a wealth of information for those who persevere. Once you have narrowed down the list of candidates, you will want to go through undergraduate prospectuses. Most are available online, where you can select the relevant sections rather than waiting for an account of every course to arrive in the post. Beware of generalised claims about the standing of the university, the quality of courses, friendly atmosphere and legendary social life. Stick, if you can, to the factual information.

If the material that the universities publish about their own qualities is less than objective, much of what you will find on the internet may be completely unreliable, for different reasons. A simple search on the name of a university will turn up spurious comparisons of everything from the standard of lecturing to the attractiveness of the students. These can be seriously misleading and are usually based on anecdotal evidence, at best. Make sure that any information you may take into account comes from a reputable source and, if it conflicts with your impression, try to cross-check it with this *Guide* and the institution's own material.

Useful websites

The best starting point is the UCAS website (**www.ucas.com**). On the site there is extensive information on courses, universities and the whole process of applying to university. UCAS has an official presence on Facebook (**www.facebook.com/ucasonline**) and Twitter (**@UCAS_online**) and now also has a series of video guides (**www.ucas.tv**) on the process of applying, UCAS resources and comments from other students.

For statistical information which allows limited comparison between universities (and for full details of the National Student Survey), visit: **www.unistats.com**.

On appropriate A-level subject choice, visit: **www.russellgroup.ac.uk/for-students/school-and-college-in-the-uk/subject-choices-at-school-and-college/**

Narrowing down course choices: **www.ukcoursefinder.com**.

For a full calendar of university and college open days: **www.opendays.com**.

Students with disabilities:
Disability Rights UK: **www.disabilityrightsuk.org/how-can-we-help**

3 Assessing Graduate Job Prospects

Most students go to university primarily in order to improve their chances of a lucrative and/or fulfilling career. They may love their subject and expect to have a good time as an undergraduate but, with fees at £9,250 a year in England, graduate employment prospects are bound to influence course choices. They will not be the only factor for most applicants, but it is clear from admissions statistics that they are playing an important role.

But how can you be sure, four or five years before joining the employment market, whether a degree is a worthwhile investment and, if so, which course to choose? The answer, of course, is that you cannot be sure, and there are plenty in the media, Parliament and elsewhere who doubt the value of higher education. But the evidence thus far is that the right degree will pay off in financial terms, as well as giving you the widest choice of future employment.

That, of course, begs another set of questions about which courses at which universities are likely to be 'right' for the employment market. Analysts are constantly claiming that many of the jobs available to the graduates of the future do not exist yet, while a growing proportion of the current options will disappear through automation and the impact of technology on current occupations. No doubt they are right, but employers will still need the analytical skills that come with a well-rounded degree, particularly if accompanied by work-related experience outside the classroom or laboratory.

For now, the UK Labour Force Survey, run by the Office for National statistics, finds that while 75% of the overall workforce is employed, the figure rises to 82% for graduates. Between the ages of 22 and 29, the employment rate for graduates is 90%, compared with 78% for non-graduates. They remain at an advantage even though the percentage of graduates in the workforce rose from 24% to 40% between 2002 and 2017. (Although the headline rate of registered unemployment may be only around 4%, the Labour Force Survey also includes those classed as "economically inactive", i.e. not employed and not seeking employment.)

In salary terms, 21-year-old graduates earned less than people of the same age with an apprenticeship, but by the age of 24 – and for all subsequent age groups – graduates were ahead. By the age of 39, graduates were earning an average of £35,000, while those who left education with A-levels or their equivalent averaged £22,000 and those with GCSEs at A* to C £19,000.

Averages conceal a huge variety of outcomes, but these certainly point to continuing advantages conferred by a degree.

Even these figures understate the advantages of a degree for your employment potential. The 2018 Labour Force survey also makes it clear that a degree is a growing expectation in certain lines of work: 40% of graduates work in the public sector, health, or education, and a further 21% in banking and finance. Energy, water, fisheries, agriculture and forestry attract only 2% of all graduates, less than their share of the workforce as a whole.

Of course, what matters to readers of this book is how the market will look in a post-Brexit world, struggling to cope with the fourth industrial revolution, not the picture today. For all the uncertainties, there would have to be seismic changes in the economy for graduates not to be in a much better position than those without a degree. That has been the case for several decades, and all projections suggest that a growing proportion of the jobs created in the coming years will require a degree.

This does not mean, however, that every degree will be a passport to a well-paid job, nor that it will be worth the debts that graduates are going to accrue in the current era of high fees. Recent salary figures for graduates five and ten years into their careers show startling differences between universities and subjects in the earning power of their graduates.

Graduate employment and underemployment

An average graduate earns at least £100,000 more than a non-graduate over a working lifetime. However, competition for graduate jobs remains stiff. There are 14 million graduates in the UK, and in Inner London they make up 56% of the adult population. Even in the North East, Britain's least graduate region, 34% of those over 20 have a degree. As a result, today's graduates may take longer than their predecessors to find the right opening, and may experiment with internships before committing themselves.

This change in employment patterns explains why underemployment has become a hot topic in the public debate about higher education. It is an important subject, but is also one with little precision and where the practice of collecting employment data only six months after graduation can be extremely misleading. This *Guide* uses the definition of a graduate job from

Median earnings by degree subject five years after graduation (2010 graduates)

Medicine and Dentistry	£47,300	Historical & Philosophical Studies	£25,400
Economics	£37,900	Law	£25,200
Veterinary Science	£34,900	Biological Sciences	£24,500
Mathematical Sciences	£33,100	Social Studies	£24,500
Engineering and Technology	£32,600	Combined Subjects	£24,200
Architecture, Building and Planning	£30,900	English Studies	£24,000
Nursing	£28,500	Education	£23,700
Computer Science	£27,800	Mass Communications & Documentation	£22,800
Languages	£27,400	Psychology	£22,600
Physical Sciences	£27,100	Agriculture & Related Subjects	£20,500
Business & Administrative Studies	£26,800	Creative Arts & Design	£20,200
Subjects Allied to Medicine	£26,400		

Source: Department for Education, Graduate Outcomes March 2018

the Higher Education Statistics Agency (HESA). But employers' ideas of which jobs require a degree, and of the jobs for which they prefer graduates, change over time. Nurses now require a degree, partly because the job has changed and requires skills that were not needed 20 years ago. The same is true of many occupations. In others it may be possible to do the job without a degree, but having one makes it much easier to get hired in the first place.

Nevertheless, a survey by consultants Accenture found that 60% of 2013 and 2014 graduates considered themselves underemployed or working in a job that did not require a degree. Eight out of ten said they had considered the availability of jobs in their intended field before selecting their degree course, but only 55% were working in their chosen field. Almost 60% said they would take a lower salary for a more fulfilling job.

The graduate labour market

Government reports take a longer-term view of the whole labour market. The findings continue to support the case for taking a degree if you have the opportunity. The first "experimental statistics" from its Longitudinal Education Outcomes (LEO) data were published at the end of 2016, showing average salaries and employment status three, five and ten years after graduation. You may be encouraged by the long-term effects of higher education that they revealed. Looking at 2003/04 graduates, it showed that 55% of graduates a year out of college had steady employment, but that a decade after graduation, the figure had hit 69%. In addition, the data shows that graduates are on a steadily ascending salary ladder, with median earnings rising from £16,500 a year after graduation to £31,000 a decade after. The figures also show predictable differences between subjects in employment and salary rates, some of which are shown in the tables in this chapter. While the institutional comparisons would require more work to be consistent with other measures in the *Guide*, they did illustrate the lasting impact of university choice. Among law graduates, for example, the top earners from Oxford and Cambridge average more than £75,000 (and the lowest some £35,000) after five years, compared with under £10,000 for low earners from the University of East London.

Overall, however, graduates continued to earn £10,000 a year more than non-graduates in 2017, according to the Department for Education. This may be a smaller premium than they enjoyed before the financial crash – it was over 50% in 2006 – but it remains one of the biggest differentials in the Western world. The material in this *Guide* – particularly in the subject tables – should help to create a more nuanced picture. A close examination of individual universities' employment rates in your subject – possibly supplemented by the salary figures on the Unistats website (**www.unistats.com**) – will tell you whether national trends apply to your chosen course.

There is now much more information available on graduate salaries, much of it broken down by subject and university. But caution should be applied when using the long-term data, persuasive though it may look. The most recent reports relate to those who graduated in 2008, at the height of the global economic downturn and recession in the UK – hopefully not the most typical conditions on which to base decisions. Some reports also use quite large groups of subjects, within which there may be significant differences. Veterinary science was listed among the least well-paid groups for female students at the age of 29, for example. That is because it straddles animal science, one of the bottom four subjects for graduate starting salaries in 2017, and veterinary medicine, one of the top three.

Inevitably, future graduate expectations are clouded by the uncertainty caused by Brexit. But even without this big unknown, there would be swings in employment trends before anyone starting a degree course in 2020 manages to graduate. The latest analysis of the graduate

What graduates are doing six months after graduation by subject studied

Subject	Professional job %	Professional job and studying %	Studying %	Non-professional job and studying %	Non-professional job %	Unemployed %	Professional job and/or studying %
=1 Dentistry	96	2	1	0	0	1	**99.3**
=1 Medicine	95	1	3	0	0	1	**99.3**
3 Nursing	94	1	1	0	1	2	**96.9**
4 Veterinary medicine	94	0	2	0	1	3	**96.5**
5 Physiotherapy	94	2	1	0	2	2	**95.9**
6 Radiography	94	1	1	0	2	3	**95.5**
7 Pharmacology & pharmacy	72	10	10	1	4	3	**92.8**
8 Land and property management	79	3	5	0	5	9	**86.6**
9 Civil engineering	67	3	14	1	6	9	**84.8**
10 Building	75	4	5	0	7	9	**84.1**
11 Subjects allied to medicine	62	3	16	2	10	6	**83.4**
12 Town and country planning and landscape	58	6	16	2	11	8	**81.2**
13 Architecture	68	4	9	0	10	9	**81.1**
14 Electrical and electronic engineering	64	2	14	1	10	9	**80.2**
15 Mechanical engineering	62	2	15	1	10	10	**80.0**
16 Physics & astronomy	38	3	38	1	10	11	**79.8**
17 Chemical engineering	52	2	24	1	7	13	**79.4**
18 General engineering	59	2	18	0	9	12	**79.0**
19 Anatomy & physiology	42	4	31	2	14	8	**78.8**
20 Law	33	6	34	5	14	8	**78.2**
21 Economics	56	5	16	1	11	11	**77.8**
22 Materials technology	49	2	24	2	11	11	**77.7**
23 Chemistry	39	2	34	2	12	10	**77.5**
24 Computer science	64	2	11	1	11	12	**77.4**
25 Russian	50	0	23	4	13	10	**77.1**
26 Mathematics	45	4	26	1	13	11	**76.6**
27 Food science	54	3	16	3	16	8	**75.8**
28 Education	56	2	16	2	19	5	**75.5**
29 German	50	4	20	2	17	8	**75.4**
30 Social work	59	3	10	2	18	8	**74.5**
=31 Aeronautical and manufacturing engineering	57	2	15	1	14	12	**74.2**
=31 Geology	31	2	38	3	15	10	**74.2**
33 Theology & religious studies	32	3	33	5	18	8	**73.7**
34 Politics	41	3	26	4	17	10	**73.1**
=35 Accounting & finance	53	8	9	2	18	10	**72.3**
=35 French	48	3	19	2	18	10	**72.3**
37 Middle Eastern and African studies	43	3	24	2	14	14	**71.9**
38 Celtic studies	23	6	41	2	25	3	**71.5**
39 Biological sciences	30	2	35	3	18	10	**71.3**

Subject	Professional job %	Professional job and studying %	Studying %	Non-professional job and studying %	Non-professional job %	Unemployed %	Professional job and/or studying %
40 Sport science	39	5	23	4	23	6	**70.6**
41 Geography & environmental sciences	39	3	26	3	19	11	**70.3**
42 Business studies	55	3	10	2	20	10	**69.5**
43 Classics & ancient history	33	3	31	3	20	11	**69.4**
44 Librarianship & information management	55	4	9	1	19	12	**69.1**
45 Iberian languages	47	3	18	2	21	10	**69.0**
46 English	34	3	26	5	23	8	**68.7**
47 Music	41	5	19	3	25	7	**68.2**
48 History of art, architecture and design	37	2	26	3	23	9	**67.9**
49 Philosophy	35	3	26	4	19	13	**67.8**
50 History	31	3	29	4	22	10	**67.7**
51 Linguistics	39	3	22	3	26	7	**66.9**
52 Archaeology and forensic science	35	3	25	5	23	11	**66.5**
53 Italian	44	3	16	2	22	12	**66.3**
54 Art & design	54	1	8	2	25	10	**65.3**
55 Psychology	30	5	24	6	26	9	**65.0**
56 Anthropology	36	3	24	2	21	15	**64.7**
57 East and south Asian studies	45	1	16	2	21	15	**64.0**
58 Communication and media studies	49	2	10	2	27	10	**63.0**
=59 Social policy	35	4	21	3	26	11	**62.7**
=59 Drama, dance and cinematics	49	2	9	2	29	9	**62.7**
61 American studies	32	1	24	5	27	11	**62.2**
62 Criminology	34	3	20	5	31	8	**61.2**
63 Hospitality, leisure, recreation & tourism	48	1	7	2	31	10	**58.7**
=64 Agriculture and forestry	43	5	8	2	28	14	**57.8**
=64 Sociology	30	2	21	5	32	10	**57.8**
66 Creative writing	27	3	21	5	30	13	**56.8**
67 Animal science	25	2	18	4	44	6	**49.1**
AVERAGE	**52**	**3**	**17**	**2**	**17**	**8**	**74.3**

Note: Thhe table is ranked on the proportion of graduates in professional jobs and/or further study six months after leaving university. This total is shown in the final column in bold. **Source:** Higher Education Statistics Agency, 2016–17

employment market by recruitment specialist High Fliers found employers expecting to take 3.8% more graduates in 2018. However, the High Fliers survey covers only the upper end of the market. For the boom years of graduate employment to return, there will have to be stronger recruitment by small and medium-sized companies as well. Increasingly, there will also be a greater proportion of self-employed graduates – and not simply because they cannot find the jobs they want. Many universities report growing demand for the services they provide for students who want to set up their own companies.

What graduates earn six months after graduation by subject studied

Subject	Professional employment (£)	Non-professional employment (£)
=1 Dentistry	31,000	—
=1 Medicine	31,000	—
3 Veterinary Medicine	30,000	—
=4 Chemical Engineering	27,500	18,000
=4 General Engineering	27,500	16,380
=6 Economics	27,000	18,000
=6 Mechanical Engineering	27,000	17,500
8 Electrical and Electronic Engineering	26,500	16,497
=9 Aeronautical and Manufacturing Engineering	26,000	17,000
=9 Building	26,000	17,316
=9 Civil Engineering	26,000	15,808
=9 Physics & Astronomy	26,000	16,500
=9 Social Work	26,000	16,000
=14 Computer Science	25,000	16,500
=14 Land and Property Management	25,000	—
=14 Librarianship & Information Management	25,000	16,881
=14 Materials Technology	25,000	18,000
=14 Mathematics	25,000	17,472
19 Middle Eastern and African Studies	24,000	15,000
=20 Politics	23,000	17,000
=20 Town and Country Planning and Landscape	23,000	17,000
=22 Chemistry	22,500	16,653
=22 Education	22,500	15,933
24 Radiography	22,125	—
25 Physiotherapy	22,100	16,575
=26 Accounting & Finance	22,000	18,000
=26 Agriculture and Forestry	22,000	18,000
=26 Anatomy & Physiology	22,000	15,600
=26 Business Studies	22,000	17,971
=26 East and South Asian Studies	22,000	16,500
=26 Food Science	22,000	17,000
=26 French	22,000	17,500
=26 Iberian Languages	22,000	17,000
=26 Nursing	22,000	18,000
=26 Other Subjects Allied to Medicine	22,000	16,000
=26 Philosophy	22,000	17,000
37 Classics & Ancient History	21,600	16,000
38 Geography & Environmental Sciences	21,505	16,643
39 Theology & Religious Studies	21,500	15,912
=40 Biological Sciences	21,000	16,000
=40 Geology	21,000	16,575

Subject	Professional employment	Non-professional employment
=40 German	21,000	18,000
=40 History	21,000	16,497
=40 Italian	21,000	17,400
=40 Russian	21,000	16,000
46 History of Art, Architecture and Design	20,280	16,000
=47 American Studies	20,000	17,000
=47 Anthropology	20,000	17,063
=47 Architecture	20,000	16,640
=47 Hospitality, Leisure, Recreation & Tourism	20,000	17,000
=47 Linguistics	20,000	16,354
=47 Social Policy	20,000	16,224
=47 Sociology	20,000	16,400
=47 Criminology	20,000	17,000
55 Law	19,998	17,000
=56 English	19,500	16,224
=56 Psychology	19,500	16,500
58 Archaeology and Forensic Science	19,185	16,536
=59 Art & Design	19,000	15,808
=59 Celtic Studies	19,000	—
=59 Communication and Media Studies	19,000	16,185
=59 Pharmacology & Pharmacy	19,000	16,640
=59 Sport Science	19,000	16,000
=59 Animal Science	19,000	17,056
65 Drama, Dance and Cinematics	18,720	16,000
66 Music	18,500	16,380
67 Creative Writing	18,000	16,068
TOTAL	**22,128**	**16,640**

Note: The salaries table is ranked by the median salary of those in professional employment in each subject area.

Source: Higher Education Statistics Agency, Destination of Leavers from Higher Education, 2016–17

Subject choice and career opportunities

For those thinking of embarking on higher education in 2020, the signs are still positive. But in any year, some universities and some subjects produce better returns than others. The tables here give a more detailed picture of the differences between subjects, while the rankings in chapters 1 and 13 include figures for each university and subject area. There are a few striking changes, but mainly among subjects with relatively small and fluctuating numbers of graduates.

This is the fifth year of a classification developed by HESA to distinguish between "graduate-level" work and jobs that do not normally require a degree. In the employment table, subjects are ranked on "positive destinations", which include professional jobs and further study, whether or not combined with a job. Some similar tables do not make a distinction between different types of job. These tend to give the misleading impression that all universities and subjects offer uniformly rosy employment prospects.

The definition of a graduate job is a controversial one. The statistics include internships and temporary jobs, which may or may not lead to permanent employment. New universities in particular often claim that the whole concept of a graduate job immediately after graduation fails to reflect reality for their alumni, especially in subjects such as media studies or art. In any case, a degree is about enhancing your whole career, your way of working and your view of the world, not just your first job out of college.

That said, these tables will help you assess whether your course will pay off in career terms, at least to start with. They show both the amount you might expect to earn with a degree in a specific subject, and the odds of being in work. They reflect the experience six months after graduation of those who competed their degrees in 2017, and the picture may have improved by the time you leave university. But there is no reason to believe that the pattern of success rates for specific subjects and institutions will have changed radically.

The table of employment statistics does reveal some unexpected results. For example, only 68% of business studies graduates are working in graduate jobs or doing further study. Accounting and finance graduates are only two percentage points better off. The social workers and town and country planners fare a lot better. The figures also explode a few popular myths, such as the suggestion that young people avoid engineering because salaries are low. All six branches of engineering are in the top dozen subjects for graduate earnings, and five of them are in the top 20 for successful graduate destinations.

The employment table also shows that graduates in some subjects, especially sciences such as physics, chemistry and geology, are more likely to undertake further study than in others, such as those in art and design or hospitality. In Celtic studies, almost half of graduates continued to study, and the figure is above 30% for several branches of science. A range of professions now regard a Master's degree as a basic entry-level qualification.

Those going into subjects such as art and design appreciate that it, too, has its own career peculiarities. Periods of freelance or casual work may be an occupational hazard at the start of a career, and perhaps later on as well. Less surprisingly, doctors and dentists are virtually guaranteed a job if they complete a degree, as are nurses. HESA found that only one graduate in 100 in medicine or dentistry was unemployed six months after graduating. The picture is pretty similar for vets and physiotherapists.

The second table, on pages 54–55, gives average earnings of those who graduated in 2017, recorded six months after leaving university. It contains interesting, and in some cases surprising, information about early career pay levels. Few would have placed social work in the top ten for graduate pay. However, nursing is now one of a large group of subjects sharing 26th place, having been in the top 20 a few years ago. The cause may be a general ban on big pay rises in the National Health Service, abandoned by the government in late 2017.

It is important, of course, to consider the differences between starting salaries and the long-term prospects of different jobs. After all, those years at university should teach you about the benefits of long-term strategic thinking. Over time, the accountants may well end up with bigger rewards, despite being only £91 a year better off than the nurses in our early-career snapshot.

In any case, it is important to realise that once you ignore the stellar incomes available to medics and other elite professionals, there does seem to be a general level of early graduate incomes that varies less than you might think from subject to subject. Eleven subjects ranging from accountancy to food science and Iberian languages tie for 26th spot in our salary ranking.

A further six tie for 40th. But the difference between these two groups is less than £1,000 a year, with the first set on £22,000 and the second on £21,100. That's why you should consider the lifetime earnings you might derive from these subjects, and your own interests and inclinations, at least as much as this snapshot.

There are reasons for longer-term optimism in HESA surveys on the occupations and views of graduates three and a half years into their careers. The last one, published in 2017, painted a more positive picture than surveys conducted six months after graduation. Of the UK graduates surveyed, 88% were in employment, 6% were studying full-time and 2.2% were unemployed. The majority of those who had been unemployed six months after graduation were in work by this stage. The median salary of these 2013 graduates was £27,000 for those in full-time work and £25,500 overall. And 87.5% were fairly or very satisfied with their careers to date.

Enhancing your employability

Universities are well aware of the difficulties of graduate employment, and have been introducing all manner of schemes to try to give their graduates an advantage in the labour market. Many have incorporated specially designed employability modules into degree courses; some are certificating extra-curricular activities to improve their graduates' CVs; and yet others are stepping up their efforts to provide work experience to complement degrees.

Opinion is divided on the value of such schemes. Some of the biggest employers restrict their recruitment activities to a small number of universities, believing that these institutions attract the brightest minds and that trawling more widely is not cost-effective. In 2017–18, High Fliers reported that the universities most targeted were Manchester, Birmingham, Warwick, Bristol and University College London. These companies, often big payers from the City of London and including some of the top law firms, are not likely to change their ways at a time when they are more anxious than ever to control costs. Widening the pool of universities from which they set out to recruit is costly, and can seem unnecessary if employers are getting the people they think they need. They will expect outstanding candidates who went to other universities to come to them, either on graduation or later in their careers.

The best advice for those looking to maximise their employment opportunities (and who isn't?) must be to go for the best university you can. But most graduates do not work in the City and most students do not go to universities at the top of the league tables.

University schemes

If a university offers extra help towards employment, it is worth considering whether its scheme is likely to work for you. Some are too new to have shown results in the labour market yet, but they may have been endorsed by big employers or introduced at an institution whose graduates already have a record of success in the jobs market. They might involve classes in CV writing, interview skills, personal finance, entrepreneurship and negotiation skills, among many other topics. There can be guest lectures and demonstrations, or mock interviews, by real employers, to assess students' strengths and weaknesses. In time, these extras may turn into mandatory parts of a degree, complete with course credits.

Hertfordshire is one institution which has demonstrated a sustained focus on its students' job prospects. Employer groups are consulted on the curriculum and often supply guest lecturers on degree courses. Like some other universities, such as Derby, it offers career development support to graduates throughout their working lives and has an outstanding record for graduate employment. The University of Exeter is helping students to build their employability skills and certificating them. It believes that the Exeter Award will encourage employers to take more notice of graduate attainment beyond exam results. It says "Student Employability is a key resource for students, graduates and graduate recruiters. We have over 40 staff working to help improve student chances of getting a great job after they graduate."

The value of work experience

The majority of graduate jobs are open to applicants from any discipline. For these general positions, employers tend to be more impressed by a good degree from what they consider a prestigious university than by an apparently relevant qualification. Here numeracy, literacy and communications – the arts needed to function effectively in any organisation – are of vital importance. Specialist jobs, for example in engineering or design, are a different matter. Employers may be much more knowledgeable about the quality of individual courses, and less influenced by a university's overall position in league tables, when the job relies directly on knowledge and skills acquired as a student. That goes for medicine and architecture as well as computer games design or environmental management.

In either case, however, work experience has become increasingly important. It is common for major and less major employers to hire graduates who had already worked for them, whether in holiday jobs, internships or placements. Sandwich degrees, extended programmes that include up to a year at work, have always boosted employment prospects. Graduates – often engineers – frequently end up working where they undertook their placement. And while a sandwich year will make your course longer, it will not be subject to a full year's fees.

Many conventional degrees now include shorter work placements that should offer some advantages in the labour market. Not all are arranged by the university. Most big graduate employers offer some provision of this nature, although access to it can be competitive.

A growing (but, as yet, relatively small) number are also offering degree apprenticeships, in partnership with a wide range of universities. Even Cambridge has some at postgraduate level, and is developing more. They generally take longer than a traditional degree, but there are no fees and apprentices are paid a salary. Although there is no guarantee of employment at the end of the course, employment rates from sandwich degrees suggest that companies are likely to want to retain those in whom they have invested considerable time and money.

If you opt for a traditional degree without a work placement, you may want to consider arranging your own part-time or temporary employment. The majority of supposedly full-time students now take jobs during term time, as well as in vacations, to make ends meet. But such jobs can boost your CV as well as your wallet. Even working in a bar or a shop shows some experience of dealing with the public and coping with the discipline of the workplace. Inevitably, the more prosperous cities are likely to offer more employment opportunities than rural areas or conurbations that have been hard hit in the recession.

Consider part-time degrees

Another option, also favoured by ministers in successive governments, is part-time study. Although enrolments have fallen sharply both before and since the big 2012 increases in fees, there are now loans available for most part-time courses. Employers may be willing to share the cost of taking a degree or another relevant qualification, and the chance to earn a wage while studying has obvious attractions. Bear in mind that most part-time courses take twice as long to complete as the full-time equivalent. If your earning power is linked to the qualification, it will take that much longer for you to enjoy the benefits.

Plan early for your career

Whatever type of course you choose, it is sensible to start thinking about your future career early in your time at university. There has been a growing tendency in recent years for students to convince themselves that there would be plenty of time to apply for jobs after graduation, and that they were better off focusing entirely on their degree while at university. In the current employment market, all but the most obviously brilliant graduates need to offer more than just a degree, whether it be work experience, leadership qualities demonstrated through clubs and societies, or commitment to voluntary activities. Many students finish a degree without knowing what they want to do, but a blank CV will not impress a prospective employer.

Half of the leading employers in the High Fliers surveys mentioned above say that they are not interested in graduates without previous work experience and that any such applicants would have "little or no chance" of a place on their graduate programmes. Nearly half of all final year students in the survey had done course placements, internships, or vacation work with graduate employers whilst at university, completing an average of more than six months work experience. He may be overstating the case, but Martin Burchall, High Fliers' managing director, claimed that work placements and internships were now "just as important as getting a 2:1 or first-class degree".

However, nobody knows what the future holds, especially in today's turbulent times. You may not walk straight into your dream job upon graduation. But if you don't, the effects will not be fatal. A survey by graduate careers web site magnet.me in 2017 found that 33% of 2016 graduates left their first job after university in the first 12 months, up from 28% a year earlier. Most said that the roles didn't match what they were told when applying.

It seems from the survey that the graduate recruitment market is an unsophisticated one, with too many generic applications for underspecified jobs. The rise of online job-hunting may be part of the problem. Physical attendance at recruitment fairs, where the student and recruiter at least meet in the flesh, is on the wane. But despite these pressures most graduates – as we saw in the three-and-a-half-year survey mentioned above – do find their way through this baffling maze, and end up with satisfying and rewarding working lives.

Useful websites

Prospects, the UK's official graduate careers website: **www.prospects.ac.uk**
For career advice, internships and student and graduate jobs: **www.milkround.com**
High Fliers: **www.highfliers.co.uk**

SOUTHALL AND WEST LONDON COLLEGE LEARNING CENTRE

4 Understanding Tuition Fees

Giving advice on tuition fees for courses beginning in 2020 is an extremely risky business. At the time of writing, the latest review of higher education funding in England was still taking place, with leaks suggesting that fees in some or all subjects could be reduced from £9,250 to £6,500. A general election was not beyond the bounds of possibility, with Labour set to promise to abolish fees altogether. Both prospective students and the universities they might want to attend were left in a state of unprecedented uncertainty.

This chapter is, necessarily, written on the premise of no change, which is at least likely in Scotland, Wales and Northern Ireland. The Scottish government has been adamant that it will not abandon its no fees policy for Scots, the Welsh Assembly has only recently reformed its student finance system, and Northern Ireland has no government of its own to consider potential change.

In England, for 2019–20 anyway, all universities are planning on the assumption that fees for full-time honours degrees will remain at £9,250. Even the small discount previously applied by University College, Birmingham has now vanished. However, bursaries and fee waivers will bring the actual cost down for those from low-income families.

Those bursaries, scholarships and fee waivers mean that the actual amounts students pay in fees in England, let alone other parts of the UK, will vary much more widely than media reporting might suggest. But this only matters to those who qualify for an award, usually by virtue of family income or their academic performance; most students will pay the maximum. Some universities are charging an average fee after bursaries that is quite a lot lower than the headline £9,250. Last year the lowest for a mainstream university was £8,065 at Bournemouth. These discounts may or may not be enough to persuade you to apply there, but should obviously be viewed alongside the course offering from each institution and the lifetime earnings it might lead to. Some further education colleges – where nearly 200,000 students are studying on higher education courses – offer average fees of less than £6,000 after accounting for financial support, or £6,000-8,000 if you are paying the full price. However, FE colleges may not all be in the business of affordable higher education. Bradford College is charging £7,950 for bachelor-level courses in 2018–19 and £8,750 in 2019–20, only a whisker short of the full fee at the city's nearby university.

This *Guide* quotes the higher headline fees, but even these will vary according to whether you are from inside or outside the EU, studying full-time or part-time, and whether you are taking a Foundation degree or an Honours programme. Non-European medical students at Imperial College, London, will pay £41,000 a year for their clinical years, a figure that will rise with inflation. Meanwhile, UK and EU students taking some Foundation degrees at nearby Kingston University will pay £5,300, although some Foundation years there will cost up to £7,800 for 2019 entry. Here we focus on full-time Honours degrees for British and other EU undergraduates: these students make up the biggest group on any UK campus, and are the group for whom maximum fees shot up to £9,000 in 2012.

One twist to bear in mind is that some universities guarantee that your fee will be fixed at the first year level for the whole of your course. Reading is an example. Manchester, on the other hand, warns that fees may go up, even for existing students, as and when the government raises the maximum it can charge.

Fees and loans

Student numbers dropped in the first year of higher fees, in 2012, but prospective students now appear to have resigned themselves to the new regime. In 2017, admissions body UCAS reported that applications from 18-year-olds had held firm even as the number of people in this age group fell a little. However, there were falls in applications from older people and in some subjects, as well as for part-time courses, which have been particularly badly hit.

There is little sign that applicants are basing their choices on the marginal differences in fee levels and bursaries at different universities, and numbers from the poorest socio-economic groups are at record levels, although they remain severely under-represented compared with more affluent groups. Concern remains, however, over the impact on part-time courses and, in years to come, on the numbers prepared to continue to postgraduate study.

Most readers of *The Times and The Sunday Times Good University Guide* will be choosing full-time undergraduate or Foundation degree courses. The fees for 2019 entry are listed alongside each university's profile in chapter 15, and the last access agreements for universities in England, including details of bursaries and scholarships, are on the website of the former Office for Fair Access (**www.offa.org.uk**). In future, this information will be published by the new Office for Students (OfS) in access and participation plans, the first of which will relate to the 2019–20 academic year.

Institutions in Scotland, Wales and Northern Ireland will continue to have lower charges for their own residents, but will charge varying amounts to students from other parts of the UK. Only those living in Scotland and studying at Scottish universities will escape all fees, although there will be reduced fees for those living in Wales and Northern Ireland.

The number of bursaries and scholarships offered to reduce the burden on new students has been falling since OFFA suggested that such initiatives do little to attract students from low-income households. As a result, the government has turned the grants paid to the poorest students into loans. While this decision may not affect many of those qualifying for the new loans, because repayment will only begin if and when they have paid off the loans for their tuition fees, there are signs that the fear of yet more debt may be the final straw that puts some off higher education.

Variations among universities

The lowest full-time fee at an English university in 2018/19 will probably be the £4,000 a year cost of a Foundation degree in education or theology at York St John University. In Northern

Ireland you can start a Foundation Degree for £2,600 a year. But even there, UK Honours degree students from outside the Province will pay £9,250 and local and EU students, up to £4,160.

At most university-level institutions, every course will cost £9,250 and at several others the only exceptions will be during work placements or years abroad, when fees cannot exceed £1,850 (20% of the full-year fee) for work placements and £1,385 for a year abroad, and are often less.

Many universities will continue to devote a substantial proportion of the income they receive from higher fees to access initiatives, whether in the form of bursaries or outreach activities. In the case of the London School of Economics, a third of its additional fee income above £6,000 is spent in this way and yields some bursaries of up to £4,000 a year. A more usual figure is in the 15-30% range. Generosity is at its minimum in the West Midlands, at 10.1% of higher fee income for access expenditure at Newman University and 10.6% for Wolverhampton. Their neighbour University College Birmingham manages 71.9%. Nationally, over £800 million of this cash was available in 2018–19.

These measures appear to be having some success in attracting students from disadvantaged backgrounds. OFFA, the body set up to close this gap (and now replaced by the Office for Students), says: "Currently, young people from the most advantaged neighbourhoods are nearly two-and-a-half times more likely to go to higher education than young people from the most disadvantaged neighbourhoods." The government has set a challenging target of getting 28% of young people from the least privileged backgrounds in university by 2020.

Fees for students from other EU countries are the same as for those from the UK, but charges will be higher, sometimes massively higher, for those from other countries.

The new fees regime has had less effect on the demand for higher education than many universities dared hope in the run-up to the fees hike, but financial considerations will still be important to the decision-making process for many students. In the current economic circumstances, students will want to keep their debts to a minimum and are bound to take the cost of living into account. They will also want the best possible career prospects, and may choose their subject accordingly.

Alternative options

Some further education colleges will offer substantial savings on the cost of a degree, or Foundation degree, but they tend to have very local appeal, and generally offer a limited range of vocational subjects. Similarly, the private sector may be expected to compete more vigorously in future, following the success of two-year degrees at the University of Buckingham and BPP University in particular. Most will continue to undercut traditional universities, although Regent's University, one of the latest to be awarded that title, is charging £17,500 in the current year for all students, irrespective of their place of origin, although less for some foundation years. The New College of the Humanities, also in London, surprisingly reduced its charges to the standard £9,250 for 2018–19 and is maintaining them at that level for 2019–20, having originally come in at twice the price charged by mainstream institutions.

Impact on subject and university choice

Fee levels have had little impact on students' choices of university, but that is not the case for choices of subject. Predictions that old universities and/or vocational subjects would prosper at the expense of the rest have been shown to be too simplistic. Some, but not all, arts subjects have suffered, while in general science courses have prospered. For many young people, the options have not changed. If you want to be a doctor, a teacher or a social worker, there is no alternative to higher education. And, while there are now more options for studying post A-level, it remains to be seen whether they offer the same promotion prospects as a degree.

Even among full-time degrees, the pattern of applications and enrolments has varied considerably since the introduction of higher fees. In 2018, the big losers among disciplines included technology subjects and languages and literature, European and global. Winners included medicine and, perhaps unexpectedly, the social sciences. Notably less popular are melange degrees such as combinations of the arts, sciences and social sciences, or combined arts and sciences. Perhaps these choices seem too indecisive for the modern age. There was a small decline in applicant numbers, and less prestigious institutions felt the pinch the most.

In general terms, over the six years since higher fees were introduced, science and business subjects have done better than the arts, as students have made their own assumptions about future career prospects. Acceptances for computer science were up by almost 50% in the first five years of higher fees, for example, while in French the decline was close to 40%. But there are plenty of exceptions – the numbers taking anthropology degrees have doubled since the last year before £9,000 fees came in – and a decline in applications can be good news for the applicant if entry requirements are reduced as a result.

Anyone hoping to start a course in 2020 would be unwise to jump to conclusions about levels of competition in different subjects. Universities vary the courses they offer, in response to the perceived demand from students, much more frequently than they used to. A drop in applications may mean less competition for places, or it may lead universities to close courses and possibly even intensify the race for entry. The only reliable forecast is that competition for places on the most popular courses will remain stiff, just as it has been since before students paid any fees.

There is considerable enthusiasm in the current UK government for the radical idea of delivering degrees in two years. At the moment, support for this concept comes mainly from private institutions. The University of Law, for example, already does degrees in this way. It charges £11,100 per year, a saving of £5,550 on a three-year course, which the same institution also offers, alongside less expensive online options. A two-year course also gets you into the workforce faster and reduces spending on living costs. However, this approach also cuts out much chance of holiday earnings and of sandwich courses or placements, where students can often get paid and gain work experience. It remains to be seen whether the idea will catch on with traditional universities and if so, whether it will be applicable to the full range of academic subjects.

Finally, there is the option of studying for a degree with no fees at all, by taking a degree apprenticeship sponsored by an employer. So far, the range of subjects in which these are available is relatively narrow – they have to go through a cumbersome accreditation procedure – but a growing number of universities are beginning to offer them. The numbers taking degree apprenticeships are still small, but a big increase is planned for 2019 and it is safe to assume that this will continue in 2020.

Naturally enough, many degree apprenticeships are in professional areas, such as policing and social work, but there are others in the sciences, business subjects and some social sciences. Students spend the majority of their time at work with their sponsoring employer – and receiving a wage, rather than having to access loans – with varying periods at university.

Degree apprenticeships – known as graduate apprenticeships in Scotland – are too new to be certain of the long-term prospects for those who take them. For those who last the course of up to five years, the immediate employment levels are guaranteed to be excellent, and many employers expect to pay those who complete the qualification more than traditional graduates because they will have been with them for longer and be more valuable in the short term. But it is impossible to say whether the qualification will have the same currency and be as portable as a traditional degree in mid-career.

Getting the best deal

There will still be a certain amount of variation in student support packages in 2019/20, so it will be possible to shop around, particularly if your family income is low. But remember that the best deal, even in purely financial terms, is one that leads to a rewarding career. By all means compare the full packages offered by individual universities, but consider whether marginal differences in headline fees really matter as much as the quality of the course and the likely advantages it will confer in the employment market. For an English student, annual earnings of £40,000 mean student finance repayments of £1,350 per year, while Scottish students can save themselves £27,750 by opting to study north of the border. That is a very different matter to the much smaller saving that is available to students in England, particularly if the Scottish university is of comparable quality to the alternatives elsewhere. So it is all a matter of judgement.

Those who are eligible for means-tested bursaries may not be able to ignore the financial assistance they offer. No one has to pay tuition fees while they are a student, but you still have to find thousands of pounds in living costs to take a full-time degree. In some cases, bursaries may make the difference between being able to afford higher education and having to pass up a potentially life-changing opportunity. Some are worth up to £3,000 a year, although most are less generous than this, often because large numbers of students qualify for an award.

Some scholarships are even more valuable, and are awarded for sporting and musical prowess, as well as academic achievement. Most scholarships are not means-tested, but a few are open only to students who are both high performers academically and from low-income families.

How the £9,250 fee system works

What follows is a summary of the position for British students at the start of 2019. While there are substantial differences between the four countries of the UK, there is one important piece of common ground. Up-front payment of fees is not compulsory, as students can take out a fee loan from the Student Loans Company to cover them (see chapter 7). This is repayable in

---

Tuition fees

The figures below show the maximum fees that students can be charged in 2019–20.

Domicile of student	Location of institution			
	England	Scotland	Wales	Northern Ireland
England	£9,250	£9,250[1]	£9,000	£9,250
Scotland	£9,250	No fee	£9,000	£9,250
Wales[2]	£9,250	£9,250	£9,000	£9,250
Northern Ireland	£9,250	£9,250[1]	£9,000	£9,250
European Union	£9,250	No fee	£9,000	£4,160
Other international	Variable	Variable	Variable	Variable

[1] Note that Honours degrees in Scotland take four years and some universities charge £9250 for each year.

[2] Students whose home is in Wales will be entitled to tuition fee loans and means-tested maintenance grants. Correct at time of going to press.

instalments after graduation when earnings reach £25,000 for English students, a threshold set by the Government.

Undergraduate fees are remaining unchanged at £9,250, and this is the most you can borrow to pay fees, with lower sums for private colleges (up to £6,165) and part-time study, where the cap is £6,935 at public institutions and £4,625 at private ones. There are different levels of fees and support for UK students who are not from England. Students from other EU countries will pay the same rate as home students in the UK nation in which they study. Those from outside the EU will usually pay quite a lot more than home and European students. The latest information on individual universities' fees at the time of going to press is listed alongside their profiles in chapter 15.

With changes, large or small, becoming almost an annual occurrence, it is essential to consult the websites of the relevant Government agencies.

Fees in England

In England, the maximum tuition fee for full-time undergraduates from the UK or anywhere in the European Union will be £9,250 a year in 2019/20. As we have seen, most courses will demand fees of £9,250 or close to it.

In many public universities, the lowest fees will be for Foundation degrees and Higher National Diplomas. Although some universities have chosen to charge the same for all courses, in many universities and further education colleges, these two-year courses will remain a cost-effective stepping stone to a full degree or a qualification in their own right. Those universities that offer extended work placements or a year abroad, as part of a degree course, will charge much less than the normal fee for the "year out". The maximum cost for a placement year is 20% of the tuition fee (£1,850), and for a full year abroad, 15%. If you spend only part of the year abroad, you will probably have to pay the whole £9,250.

Fees in Scotland

At Scottish universities and colleges, students from Scotland and those from other EU countries outside the UK pay no fees directly. The universities' vice-chancellors and principals have appealed for charges to be introduced at some level to save their institutions from falling behind their English rivals in financial terms, but Alex Salmond, when he was Scotland's First Minister, famously declared that the "rocks will melt with the sun" before this happens.

Students whose home is in Scotland and who are studying at a Scottish university apply to the Student Awards Agency for Scotland (SAAS) to have their fees paid for them. Note, too, that three-year degrees are rare in Scotland, so most students can expect to pay four years of living costs.

Students from England, Wales and Northern Ireland studying in Scotland will pay fees at something like the level that applies in England and will have access to finance at similar levels to those available for study in England. It is worth noting, however, that some courses offer considerable savings. Robert Gordon University in Aberdeen, for example, has a fee of £5,000 per year for some four-year courses, including a BA in Accounting and Finance.

The majority of Scottish universities offer a "free" fourth year to bring their total fees into line with English universities, but Edinburgh and St Andrews are charging £9,250 in all four years of their degree courses.

Fees in Wales

In previous years, Welsh universities have applied a range of fees up to £9,000, but all have now opted for £9,000. Students who live in Wales will be able to apply for a Tuition Fee Loan as well as a Tuition Fee Grant, wherever they study. You can get a combined loan and grant for up to £9,000 if you study in Wales, or £9,250 for Scotland, England or Northern Ireland, but only a loan, of up to £6,165, for study in a private institution.

Fees in Northern Ireland

The two universities of Northern Ireland are charging local students £4,160 a year. Students can receive a fee loan to postpone paying this until their earnings are above £18,330 for 2018/19. For students from elsewhere in the UK, the fee is £9,250 for Queen's, Belfast and for the University of Ulster. It is £4,160 for EU students from outside the UK.

Useful websites

With changes, large or small, becoming more frequent, it is essential to consult the latest information provided by Government agencies. It is worth checking the following websites for the latest information:

England: **www.gov.uk/student-finance**
Wales: **www.studentfinancewales.co.uk**
Scotland: **www.saas.gov.uk**
Northern Ireland: **www.studentfinanceni.co.uk**
Office for Students (OfS): **www.officeforstudents.org.uk**

5 Making Your Application

Applying to university is deceptively simple. It all takes place online and there is abundant help available. But too many people take their eye off the ball at this crucial stage in the process. Surprising numbers of applicants each year spell their own name wrongly, or enter an inaccurate date of birth, or the wrong course code. And that is to say nothing of the damage that can be done in the personal statement and teachers' references.

While UCAS will decode misspelt names, other errors in grammar or spelling present admissions officers with an easy starting point in cutting applications down to a more manageable number. Of course, your grades will be the most important factor in winning a degree place, but what goes on the application form is more important than many students realise. The art of conveying knowledge of, and enthusiasm for, your chosen subject – preferably with supporting evidence from your school or college – can make all the difference.

In years to come, applications may be made after students have their results, but for the moment decisions have to be made well before that point. You will be able to make up to five choices, although you do not have to use all five if you do not want to. Some people make only a single application, perhaps because they do not want to leave home or they have very particular requirements – but you will give yourself the best chance of success if you go for the maximum.

At the time of writing, no major changes were planned for 2019. There has been a trial of names-blind applications at 16 universities to test whether this would counter unconscious bias among admissions officers, but the results were inconclusive. Perhaps the most important recent change allowed candidates to submit a new personal statement if their initial applications are unsuccessful and they use the UCAS Extra process. This and other changes are outlined below.

The application process

Most applications for full-time higher education courses go through UCAS, although there is still a different process for the music conservatoires. The trend is towards the UCAS model even among specialist providers, however: recruitment to nursing and midwifery diploma and degree courses in Scotland switched to the UCAS system in 2010, and the art and design courses that used to recruit using the separate "Route B" scheme have also moved to the main system.

Some universities that have not filled all their places, even during Clearing, will accept direct applications up to and sometimes after the start of the academic year, but UCAS is both the official route and the only way into the most popular courses.

All UCAS applications are made online. The Apply electronic system is accessed via the UCAS website and is straightforward to use. For those who do not have the internet at home and prefer not to use school or college computers, the UCAS website lists libraries all over the UK where you can make your application. Apply is available 24 hours a day, and, when the time comes, information on the progress of your application may arrive at any time.

Registering with Apply

The first step in the process is to register. If you are at a school or college, you will need to obtain a "buzzword" from your tutor or careers adviser – it is used when you log on to register. It links your application to the school or college so that the application can be sent electronically to your referee (usually one of your teachers) for your reference to be attached. If you are no longer at a school or college, you do not need a "buzzword", but you will need details of your referee. More information is given on the UCAS website.

To register, go to the UCAS website and click on "Apply". The system will guide you through the business of providing your personal details and generating a username and password, as well as reminding you of basic points, such as amending your details in case of a change of address. You can register separate term-time and holiday addresses – a useful option for boarders, who could find offers and, particularly, the confirmation of a place, going to their school when they are miles away at home. Remember to keep a note of your username and password in a safe place.

Throughout the process, you will be in sole control of communications with UCAS and your chosen universities. Only if you nominate a representative and give them your unique nine-digit application number (sent automatically by UCAS when your application is submitted), can a parent or anyone else give or receive information on your behalf, perhaps because you are ill or out of the country.

Video guides on the application process are available on the UCAS website. Once you are registered, you can start to complete the Apply screens. The sections that follow cover the main screens.

Personal details

This information is taken from your initial registration, and you will be asked for additional information, for example, on ethnic origin and national identity, to monitor equal opportunities

---

The main screens to be completed in UCAS Apply

» Personal and contact details and some additional non-educational details for UK applicants.
» Student finance, a section for UK-resident applicants.
» Your course choices.
» Details of your education so far, including examination results and examinations still to be taken.
» Details of any jobs you have done.
» Your personal statement.
» A declaration that you confirm that the information is correct and that you will be bound by the UCAS rules.
» Pay for the application (applications for 2019 cost £24, or £18 to apply to just one course).
» A reference from one of your teachers.

in the application process. UK students will also be asked to complete a student finance section designed to speed up any loan application you might make.

Choices

In most subjects, you will be able to apply to a maximum of five universities and/or colleges. The exceptions are medicine, dentistry and veterinary science, where the maximum is four, but you can use your fifth choice as a back-up to apply for a different subject.

The other important restriction concerns Oxford or Cambridge, because you can only apply to one or the other; you cannot apply to both universities in the same year, nor can you apply for more than one course there. For both universities you may need to take a written test (see page 34) and submit examples of your work, depending on the course selected. In addition, for Cambridge, many subjects will demand a pre-interview assessment once the university has received your application from UCAS, while the rest will set written tests to be taken at interview.

The deadline for Oxbridge applications – and for all medicine, dentistry and veterinary science courses – is 15 October. For all other applications the deadline is 15 January (or 24 March for some specified art and design courses). The other exceptions to this rule are the relatively small but growing number of courses that start in January or February. If you are considering one of these, contact the university concerned for application deadlines.

Most applicants use all five choices. But if you do choose fewer than five courses, you can still add another to your form up to 30 June, as long as you have not accepted or declined any offers. Nor do you have to choose five different universities if more than one course at the same institution attracts you – perhaps because the institution itself is the real draw and one course has lower entrance requirements than the other. Universities are not allowed to see where else you have applied, or whether you have chosen the same subject elsewhere. But they will be aware of multiple applications within their own institution. Remember that it is more difficult to write a convincing personal statement if it has to cover two subjects.

For each course you select, you will need to put the UCAS code on the form – and you should check carefully that you have the correct code and understand any special requirements that may be detailed on the UCAS description of the course. It does not matter what order you enter in your choices as all your choices are treated equally. You will also need to indicate whether you are applying for a deferred entry (for example, if you are taking a gap year – see page 78).

Education

In this section you will need to give details of the schools and colleges you have attended, and the qualifications you have obtained or are preparing for. The UCAS website gives plenty of advice on the ways in which you should enter this information, to ensure that all your relevant qualifications are included with their grades. While UCAS does not need to see qualification certificates, it can double-check results with the examination boards to ensure that no one is tempted to modify their results.

In the Employment section that follows, add details of any paid jobs you have had (unpaid or voluntary work should be mentioned in your personal statement).

Personal statement

As the competition for places on popular courses has become more intense, so the value attached to the personal statement has increased. Admissions officers look for a sign of potential beyond the high grades that growing numbers of applicants offer. Many academics responsible for admissions value success in extracurricular activities such as drama, sport or the Duke of Edinburgh's Award scheme. But your first priority should be to demonstrate an enthusiasm for and understanding of your subject beyond the confines of the exam syllabus.

This is not easy in a relatively short statement that can readily sound trite or pretentious. You should resist any temptation to exaggerate, let alone lie, particularly if there is any chance of an interview. A claim to have been inspired by a book that you have not read will backfire instantly under questioning and, even without an interview, academics are likely to see through grandiose statements that appear at odds with a teacher's reference.

Genuine experiences of after-hours clubs, lectures or visits, work experience or actual reading around the syllabus are much more likely to strike the right note. If you are applying for medicine, for example, any practical work experience or volunteering in medical or caring settings should be included. Take advice from teachers and, if there is still time before you make your application, look for some subject-related activities that will help fill out your statement.

UCAS top ten personal statement tips

1 Express interest in the subject and show real passion.
2 Go for a strong opening line to grab the reader's attention.
3 Relate outside interests to the course.
4 Think beyond university.
5 Get the basics right.
6 Don't try to sound too clever.
7 Take time and make it your best work.
8 Don't leave it until the last minute – remember the 15 January deadline!
9 Get a second opinion.
10 Honesty is the best policy

Admissions officers are also looking for evidence of character that will make you a productive member of their university and, eventually, a successful graduate. Taking responsibility in any area of school or college life suggests this – leading activities outside your place of learning even more so. Evidence of initiative and self-discipline is also valuable, since higher education involves much more independent study than sixth-formers are used to.

Your overall aim in writing your personal statement is to persuade the admissions officer to pick yours out from the piles of applications. That means trying to stand out among an often rather dull and uniform set of statements based around the curriculum and the more predictable sixth-form activities. Everyone is going to say they love reading, for example; narrow your interest down to an area of (real) interest. Don't be afraid to include the unusual, but bear in mind that an academic's sense of humour may not be the same as yours.

Give particular thought to why you want to study your chosen subject – especially if it is not one you have taken at school or college. You need to show that your interests and skills are well suited to the course and, if it is a vocational degree, that you know how you envisage using the qualification. Admissions officers want to feel that you will be committed to their subject for the length of the course, which could be three, four or even five years, and capable of achieving good results. If your five choices cover more than one subject, be careful not to focus too much on one; try to make more general comments on your academic strengths and enthusiasms. And, since the same statement goes to all your chosen departments, avoid expressing any preference for an individual institution.

Your school or college should be the best source of advice, since they see personal statements every year, but there are others. The UCAS website has a useful checklist of themes that you may wish to address, while sites such as www.studential.com also provide tips. But do not fall into the trap of cutting and pasting from the model statements included on such sites –

both UCAS and individual universities have software that will spot plagiarism immediately. In one year, no fewer than one in 20 applicants came to grief in this way. Plagiarists of this type are unlikely to be disqualified, but they destroy the credibility of their application.

Try not to cram in more than the limited space will allow – admissions officers will have many statements to go through, and judicious editing may be rewarded. As long as you write clearly – preferably in paragraphs and possibly with sub-headings – it will be up to you what to include. It is a personal statement. But consider the points listed below and make sure that you can answer all the questions raised. Once you have completed your statement show it to others you trust. It is really important to have others read your statement before submitting it – sometimes things that are clear to you may not be to fresh eyes.

The Apply system allows 4,000 characters (including spaces) or 47 lines for your statement. While there is no requirement to fill all the space, it should not look embarrassingly short. Indeed, your statement now has to be at least 1,000 characters long. UCAS recommends using a word-processing package to compile the statement before pasting it into the application system. This is because Apply will time-out after 35 minutes of inactivity, so there is a danger of losing valuable material. Working offline also has the advantage of leaving you with a copy and making it easier to show it to others.

References

Hand in hand with your personal statement goes the reference from your school, college or, in the case of mature students, someone who knows you well, but is not a friend or family member. Since 2014, even referees who are not your teachers have been encouraged to predict your grades, although they are allowed to opt out of this process. Whatever the source, the reference has to be independent – you are specifically forbidden to change any part of it if you send off your own application – but that does not mean you should not try to influence what it contains.

Most schools and colleges conduct informal interviews before compiling a reference, but it does no harm to draw up a list of the achievements that you would like to see included, and ensure your referee knows what subject you are applying for. Referees cannot know every detail of a candidate's interests and most welcome an aide-memoire.

The UCAS guidelines skirt around the candidate's right to see his or her reference, but it does exist. Schools' practices vary, but most now show the applicant the completed reference. Where this is not the case, the candidate can pay UCAS £10 for a copy, although at this stage it

---

Key points to consider in writing your personal statement

» What attracts you to this subject (or subjects, in the case of dual or combined honours)?

» Have you undertaken relevant work experience or voluntary activities, either through school or elsewhere?

» Have you taken part in other extra-curricular activities that demonstrate character – perhaps as a prefect, on the sports field or in the arts?

» Have you been involved in other academic pursuits, such as Gifted and Talented programmes, widening participation schemes, or courses in other subjects?

» Which aspects of your current courses have you found particularly stimulating?

» Are you planning a gap year? If so, explain what you intend to do and how it will affect your studies. Some subjects – notably maths – actively discourage a break in studies.

» What other outside interests might you include that show that you are well-rounded?

Timetable for applications for university admission in 2020
At the time of writing UCAS had not confirmed the exact dates for the application schedule. Please check the UCAS website for the most recent information.

2019

January onwards	Find out about courses and universities. Check schedule of open days.
February onwards	Attend open days.
early July	Registration starts for UCAS Apply.
mid September	UCAS starts receiving applications.
15 October	Final day for applications to Oxford and Cambridge, and for most courses in medicine, dentistry and veterinary science.

2020

15 January	Final day for all other applications from UK and EU students including all art and design courses except t hose which have a 24 March deadline (specified in UCAS Course Search).
16 January–end June	New applications continue to be accepted by UCAS, but only considered by universities if the relevant courses h ave vacancies.
late February	Start of applications through UCAS Extra.
24 March	Final day for applications to art and design courses that specify this date.
end March	Universities should have sent decisions on all applications received by 15 January.
early May	Final time by which applicants have to decide on their choices if all decisions received by end March (exact date for each applicant will be confirmed by UCAS). **If you do not reply to UCAS, they will decline your offers.** UCAS must have received all decisions from universities if you applied by 15 January.
early June	Final time by which applicants have to decide on their choices if all decisions received by early May.
start of July	Any new application received from this time held until Clearing starts. End of applications through UCAS Extra.
5 July	International Baccalaureate results published.
4 August	SQA results published. Scottish Clearing starts.
13 August	A-level results published. Full Clearing and Adjustment starts.
end August	Adjustment closes. Last time for you to meet any offer conditions, after which university might not accept you.
late October	End of period for adding Clearing choices and last point at which a university can accept you through Clearing.

is obviously too late to influence the contents. Better, if you can, to see it before it goes off, in case there are factual inaccuracies that can be corrected.

Timing

The general deadline for applications through UCAS is 15 January, but even those received up to 30 June will be considered if the relevant courses still have vacancies. After that, you will be limited to Clearing, or an application for the following year. In theory – and usually in practice – all applications submitted by the January deadline are given equal consideration. But the best advice is to get your application in early: before Christmas, or earlier if possible. Applications are accepted from mid-September onwards, so the autumn half-term is a sensible target date for completing the process. Although no formal offers are made before the deadline, many admissions officers look through applications as they come in and may make a mental note of promising candidates. If your form arrives with the deadline looming, you may appear less organised than those who submitted in good time; and your application may be one of a large batch that receives a more cursory first reading than the early arrivals. Under UCAS rules, last-minute applicants should not be at a disadvantage, but why take the risk?

Next steps

Once your application has been processed by UCAS, you will receive an email confirming that your application has been sent to your university choices and summarising what will happen next. The email will also confirm your Personal ID, which you can use to access "Track", the online system that allows you to follow the progress of your application. Check all the details carefully: you have 14 days to contact UCAS to correct any errors. Universities can make direct contact with you through Track, including arranging interviews.

After that, it is just a matter of waiting for universities to make their decisions, which can take days, weeks or even months, depending on the university and the course. Some obviously see an advantage in being the first to make an offer – it is a memorable moment to be reassured that at least one of your chosen institutions wants you – and may send their response almost immediately. Others take much longer, perhaps because they have so many good applications to consider, or maybe because they are waiting to see which of their applicants withdraw when Oxford and Cambridge make their offers. Universities are asked to make all their decisions by the end of March, and most have done so long before that.

Interviews

Unless you are applying for a course in health or education that brings you into direct contact with the public, the chances are you will not have a selection interview. For prospective medics, vets, dentists or teachers, a face-to-face assessment of your suitability will be crucial to your chances of success. Likewise in the performing arts, the interview may be as important as your exam grades. Oxford and Cambridge still interview most applicants in all subjects, and a few of the top universities see a significant proportion. But the expansion of higher education has made it impractical to interview everyone, and many admissions experts are sceptical about interviews.

What has become more common, however, is the "sales" interview, where the university is really selling itself to the candidate. There may still be testing questions, but the admissions staff have already made their minds up and are actually trying to persuade you to accept an offer. Indeed, you will probably be given a clear indication at the end of the interview that an offer is on its way. The technique seems to work, perhaps because you have invested time and nervous energy in a sometimes lengthy trip, as well as acquiring a more detailed impression of both the department and the university.

The difficulty can come in spotting which type of interview is which. The "real" ones require lengthy preparation, revisiting your personal statement and reading beyond the exam syllabus. Impressions count for a lot, so dress smartly and make sure that you are on time. Have a question of your own ready, as well as being prepared to give answers.

While you would not want to appear ignorant at a "sales" interview, lengthy preparation might be a waste of valuable time during a period of revision. Naturally, you should err on the side of caution, but if your predicted grades are well above the standard offer and the subject is not one that normally requires an interview, it is likely that the invitation is a sales pitch. It is still worth going, unless you have changed your mind about the application.

Offers

When your chosen universities respond to your application, there will be one of three answers:

» Unconditional Offer (U): This used to be a possibility only if you applied after satisfying the entrance requirements – usually if you are applying as a mature student, while on a gap year, after resitting exams or, in Scotland, after completing Highers. However, a growing number of universities competing for bright students now make unconditional offers to those who are predicted high grades – just how high will depend on the university. If you are fortunate (and able) enough to receive one, do not assume that grades are no longer important because they may be taken into consideration when you apply for jobs as a graduate.

» Conditional Offer (C): The vast majority of students will still receive conditional offers, where each university offers a place subject to you achieving set grades or points on the UCAS tariff.

» Rejection (R): You do not have the right qualifications, or have lost out to stronger competition.

Unconditional offers have been the subject of considerable controversy over the past year, following evidence from UCAS that applicants who received them were much more likely than others to miss their predicted grades. Far from targeting only the very brightest students, almost a quarter of all applicants received one in 2018. In the previous year, students with BBB at A-level were the most likely to receive an unconditional offer. And, while one university – St Mary's, Twickenham – has announced that it is ending the practice, many more are expected to carry on in 2019.

One danger, from the student's point of view, is that an unconditional offer might tempt a candidate to lower his or her sights and accept a place that would not have been their first choice otherwise. As long as this is not the case, however, there is no reason to spurn such an offer if it comes, as long as you do not take your foot off the pedal in the run-up to examinations.

If you have chosen wisely, you should have more than one offer to choose from, so you will be required to pick your favourite as your firm acceptance – known as UF if it was an unconditional offer and CF if it was conditional. Candidates with conditional offers can also accept a second offer, with lower grades, as an Insurance Choice (CI). You must then decline any other offers that you have.

You do not have to make an Insurance choice – indeed, you may decline all your offers if you have changed your mind about your career path or regret your course decisions. But most people prefer the security of a back-up route into higher education if their grades fall short.

Some 37,500 took up their Insurance Choice in 2017. You must be sure that your firm acceptance is definitely your first choice because you will be allocated a place automatically if you meet the university's conditions. It is no good at this stage deciding that you prefer your Insurance Choice because UCAS rules will not allow a switch.

The only way round those rules, unless your results are better than your highest offer (see Adjustment, below), is through direct contact with the universities concerned. Your firm acceptance institution has to be prepared to release you so that your new choice can award you a place in Clearing. Neither is under any obligation to do so but, in practice, it is rare for a university to insist that a student joins against his or her wishes. Admissions staff will do all they can to persuade you that your original choice was the right one – as it may well have been, if your research was thorough – but it will almost certainly be your decision in the end.

UCAS Extra

If things do go wrong and you receive five rejections, that need not be the end of your higher education ambitions. From the end of February until the end of June, you have another chance through UCAS Extra, a listing of courses that still have vacancies after the initial round of offers. Extra is sometimes dismissed (wrongly) as a repository of second-rate courses. In fact, even in the boom years for applications, most Russell Group universities still have courses listed in a wide variety of subjects.

You will be notified if you are eligible for Extra and can then select courses marked as available on the UCAS website. In order to assist students who choose different subjects after a full set of rejections in their original application, you will be able to submit a new personal statement for Extra. Applications are made, one at a time, through UCAS Track. If you do not receive an offer, or you choose to decline one, you can continue applying for other courses until you are successful. About half of those applying through Extra normally find a place. Increases in the success rate from the initial round of applications prompted a fall of more than 20% in the numbers using Extra in 2018, but it remains a valuable route for those who need it.

Results Day

Rule Number One on results day is to be at home, or at least in easy communication – you cannot afford to be on some remote beach if there are complications. The day is bound to be stressful, unless you are absolutely confident that you achieved the required grades – more of a possibility in an era of modular courses with marks along the way. But for thousands of students, Track has removed the agony of opening the envelope or scanning a results noticeboard. On the morning of A-level results day, the system informs those who have already won a place on their chosen course. You will not learn your grades until later, but at least your immediate future is clear.

If you get the grades stipulated in your conditional offer, the process should work smoothly and you can begin celebrating. Track will let you know as soon as your place is confirmed and the paperwork will arrive in a day or two. You can phone the university to make quite sure, but it should not be necessary and you will be joining a long queue of people doing the same thing.

If the results are not what you hoped – and particularly if you just miss your grades – you need to be on the phone and taking advice from your school or college. In a year when results are better than expected, some universities will stick to the letter of their offers, perhaps refusing to accept your AAC grades when they had demanded ABB. Others will forgive a dropped grade to take a candidate who is regarded as promising, rather than go into Clearing to recruit an unknown quantity. Admissions staff may be persuadable – particularly if there are extenuating personal circumstances, or the dropped grade is in a subject that is not relevant to your chosen course. Try to get a teacher to support your case, and be persistent if there is any prospect of flexibility.

If your results are lower than predicted, one option is to ask for papers to be re-marked, as growing numbers do each year. The school may ask for a whole batch to be re-marked, and you should ensure that your chosen universities know this if it may make the difference to whether or not you satisfy your offer. If your grades improve as a result, the university will review its decision, but if by then it has filled all its places, you may have to wait until next year to start.

If you took Scottish Highers, you will have had your results for more than a week by the time the A-level grades are published. If you missed your grades, there is no need to wait for A-levels before you begin approaching universities. Admissions staff at English universities may not wish to commit themselves before they see results from south of the border, but Scottish universities will be filling places immediately and all should be prepared to give you an idea of your prospects.

Adjustment

Adjustment

If your grades are better than those demanded by your first-choice university, there is now an opportunity to "trade up". The Adjustment Period runs from when you receive your results until 31 August, and you can only use it for five 24-hour periods during that period, so there is no time to waste. First, go into the Track system and click on "Register for Adjustment" and then contact your preferred institutions to find another place. If none is available, or you decide not to move, your initial offer will remain open. The number of students switching universities in this way has not increased as much as many observers expected, perhaps because Clearing has become much more flexible, but there were still approaching 900 successful candidates in 2018. The process has become as established part of the system and, without the previous restrictions on the number of students they could recruit, many leading universities see it as a good source of talented undergraduates. UCAS does not publish a breakdown of which universities take part – some, such as Oxford and Cambridge, simply do not have places available – but it is known that many students successfully go back to institutions that had rejected them at the initial application stage. Even if you are eligible for Adjustment, you may decide to stick with the offer you have, but it is worth at least exploring your options.

Clearing

If you do not have a place on Results Day, there will still be plenty of options through the UCAS Clearing scheme. More than 66,000 people – one successful applicant in eight – found a place through this route in 2018, despite another drop in the number of applicants. With recruitment restrictions lifted, universities that used to regard their absence from Clearing as a point of pride are appearing in the vacancy lists. It is likely that this trend will continue in 2020, as more universities seek to expand, particularly in arts, social science and business subjects.

Although the most popular courses may still fill up quickly, many remain open up to and beyond the start of the academic year. And, at least at the start of the process, the range of courses with vacancies is much wider than in Extra. Most universities will list some courses, and most subjects will be available somewhere.

Clearing runs from A-level Results Day until the end of September, matching students without places to full-time courses with vacancies. As long as you are not holding any offers and you have not withdrawn your application, you are eligible automatically. You will be sent a Clearing number via Track to quote to universities.

There are now two ways of entering Clearing: the traditional method of ringing universities that still have vacancies, or by using the system introduced in 2017 which allows universities to approach candidates with suitable grades for one of their courses. You will be given the option of signing up for this service in an email from UCAS and issued with a code word to be used by universities contacting you on Results Day or subsequently. You will be approached by a maximum of five universities or colleges. UCAS advises students to approach universities themselves in any case, but the new system does add an extra string to their bow and may take some of the anxiety out of Clearing.

Assuming you are making your own approaches, the first step is to trawl through the lists on the UCAS website, and elsewhere, before ringing the university offering the course that appeals most, and where you have a realistic chance of a place – do not waste time on courses where the standard offer is far above your grades. Universities run Clearing hotlines and have become adept at dealing with a large number of calls in a short period, but you can still spend a long time on the phone at a time when the most desirable places are beginning to disappear. If you can't get through send an email setting out your grades and the course that interests you.

The best advice is to plan ahead and not to wait for Results Day to draw up a list of possible Clearing targets. Many universities publish lists of courses that are likely to be in Clearing on their websites from the start of August. Think again about some of the courses that you considered when making your original application, or others at your chosen universities that had lower entrance requirements. But beware of switching to another subject simply because you have the right grades – you still have to sustain your interest and be capable of succeeding over three or more years. Many of the students who drop out of degrees are those who chose the wrong course in a rush during Clearing.

In short, you should start your search straight away if you do find yourself in Clearing, and act decisively, but do not panic. You can make as many approaches as you like, until you are accepted on the course of your choice. Remember that if you changed your personal statement for applications in Extra, this will be the one that goes to any universities that you approach in Clearing, so it may be difficult to return to the subjects in your original application.

Most of the available vacancies will appear in Clearing lists, but some of the universities towards the top of the league tables may have a limited number of openings that they choose not to advertise – either for reasons of status or because they do not want the administrative burden of fielding large numbers of calls to fill a handful of places. If there is a course that you find particularly attractive – especially if you have good grades and are applying late – it may be worth making a speculative call. Sometimes a number of candidates holding offers drop grades and you may be on the spot at the right moment.

What are the alternatives?

If your results are lower than expected and there is nothing you want in Clearing, there are several things you can do. The first is to resit one or more subjects. The modular nature of most courses means that you will have a clear idea of what you need to do to get better grades. You can go back to school or college or try a "crammer". Although some colleges have a good success rate with retakes, you have to be highly focused and realistic about the likely improvements. Some of the most competitive courses, such as medicine, may demand higher grades for a second application, so be sure you know the details before you commit yourself.

Other options are to get a job and study part-time, or to take a break from studying and return later in your career. You may have considered an apprenticeship before applying to university, but the number and variety are growing all the time, so it may be worth another look. The UCAS Progress service provides information on apprenticeship opportunities post-16 and a new search tool has been established for higher and degree apprenticeship vacancies.

The part-time route can be arduous – many young people find a job enough to handle without the extra burden of academic work. But others find it just the combination they need for a fulfilling life. It all depends on your job, your social life and your commitment to the subject you will study. It may be that a relatively short break is all that you need to rekindle your enthusiasm for studying. Many universities now have a majority of mature students, so you need not be out of place if this is your chosen route.

Taking a gap year

The other popular option is to take a gap year. In most years, about 7% of applicants defer their entry until the following year while they travel, or do voluntary or paid work. A whole industry has grown up around tailor-made activities, many of them in Asia, Africa or Latin America. Some have been criticised for doing more for the organisers than the underprivileged communities that they purport to assist, but there are programmes that are useful and character-building, as well as safe. Most of the overseas programmes are not cheap, but raising the money can be part of the experience.

Various organisations can help you find voluntary work. Some examples include vInspired (**www.vinspired.com**), Lattitude Global Volunteering (**www.lattitude.org.uk**) and Plan my Gap Year (**www.planmygapyear.co.uk**). Voluntary Service Overseas (**www.vsointernational.org**) works mainly with older volunteers but has an offshoot, run with five other volunteering organisations, International Citizen Service (**www.volunteerics.org**), that places 18–25-year-olds around the world.

The alternative is to stay closer to home and make your contribution through organisations like Volunteering Matters (**http://volunteeringmatters.org.uk**) or to take a job that will make higher education more affordable when the time comes. Work placements can be casual or structured, such as the Year in Industry Scheme (**www.etrust.org.uk**). Sponsorship is also available, mainly to those wishing to study science, engineering or business. Buyer beware: we cannot vouch for any of these and you need to be clear whether the aim is to make money or to plump up your CV. If it is the second, you may end up spending money, not saving it.

Many admissions staff are happy to facilitate gap years because they think it makes for more mature, rounded students than those who come straight from school. The longer-term benefits may also be an advantage in the graduate employment market. Both university admissions officers and employers look for evidence that candidates have more about them than academic ability. The experience you gain on a gap year can help you develop many of the attributes they are looking for, such as interpersonal, organisational and teamwork skills, leadership, creativity, experience of new cultures or work environments, and enterprise.

There are subjects – maths in particular – that discourage a break because it takes too long to pick up study skills where you left off. From the student's point of view, you should also bear in mind that a gap year postpones the moment at which you embark on a career. This may be important if your course is a long one, such as medicine or architecture.

If you are considering a gap year, it makes sense to apply for a deferred place, rather than waiting for your results before applying. The application form has a section for deferments. That allows you to sort out your immediate future before you start travelling or working, and leaves you the option of changing your mind if circumstances change.

Useful websites

The essential website for making an application is, of course, that of UCAS:
www.ucas.com/ucas/undergraduate/apply-and-track

For applications to music conservatoires: **www.ucas.com/ucas/conservatoires**

For advice on your personal statement:
www.ucas.com/ucas/16-18-choices/search-and-apply/writing-ucas-progress-personal-statement

Gap years

To help you consider options and start planning: **www.independentgapadvice.org**
For links to volunteering opportunities in the UK: **www.do-it.org**
For links to many gap year organisations: **www.yearoutgroup.org**

6 Where Students Come From

Who goes where?

Why does it matter who goes to our universities? Should universities be agents of social change or should they choose their students regardless of their social, economic or educational background? This is a controversial issue and one that is moving steadily up the political agenda with universities on notice that – for some of them, at least – there will need to be a tangible shift in their recruitment patterns in the immediate future.

Nicola Dandridge, chief executive of the newly-created Office for Students, was explicit when she said recently: "There is general agreement about the need to improve access to higher education. But some continue to argue that the buck stops with schools, and that universities have neither a role nor a responsibility to bring about change. I don't accept this.

"Many universities need to make the way they recruit students fairer and more transparent. Many institutions have made significant progress to open up…opportunities to the widest possible cross-section of society. They have a genuine commitment to ensuring that an applicant's background does not act as a barrier to success. But we need more urgency and to see swifter progress. And if we do not see this, the Office for Students has the powers and commitment to take swift and tough action."

A Sutton Trust report published in December 2018 highlighted the lack of progress to which Dandridge refers. Eight schools – Eton College, St Paul's School, London and Westminster School among them – had as many Oxbridge acceptances over a three-year period as another 2,894 schools or colleges put together, about three-quarters of all schools and colleges. Sixty per cent of those educated at independent schools attend a Russell Group university, compared to just under 25% of those educated in comprehensive schools or sixth form colleges, the report shows.

The desire to see accelerated change on social inclusion is driven by a number of factors. The first is financial. Widening participation initiatives cost £887.7m in 2016–17 – a record sum – and up by nearly 30% on the £690.7m spent in 2010-11. Spending that sort of money demands tangible results. Widening participation covers everything from outreach work in schools or with young people more generally – an area which has seen one of the biggest growths in spending – through to academic and pastoral support of current students and support for progression from higher education into work and further study. Even when set against the overall expenditure on higher education of £34.5bn, the spend on widening participation is still significant. And it prompts questions when, for some universities, the proportion of students admitted from under-represented groups remains stubbornly low.

The second driver for change arises from the relaxing of the rules relating to student recruitment. The Government abolished the cap on student numbers in 2015, allowing universities for the first time to recruit as many students as they felt capable of educating. This change offers universities an unprecedented opportunity to expand the reach of higher education into groups within society which have been largely bystanders as higher education participation grew more generally. While it is true that most universities can point to record *numbers* of students from under-represented groups, too little progress has been made on increasing the *proportion* of those groupings in the wider student body. It is no longer a zero-sum game for universities: they can recruit more from under-represented groups while still offering the same number of places as before to those from their traditional recruiting grounds.

The dividend from widening participation can be uncovering students of great potential who would not have been admitted otherwise. Research has shown that students from disadvantaged backgrounds and/or schools with poor higher education progression rates often go on to outperform others at university who were admitted holding higher grades.

A third factor is the heightened awareness among applicants themselves of the composition of the student body within the universities they are applying to and whether or not it is reflective of the wider society they come from or the working world they will progress into once they graduate. That awareness is driven by the plethora of data now available on universities, more than at any point in their history. The data covers everything – the financial health of universities and student opinion on their courses (via the National Student Survey); performance measures on graduate employability and student retention; and data on the socio-economic background of the students who enroll.

The table

This impetus led to the creation of our first social inclusion ranking for British universities. We resisted any temptation to include some or all the measures contained within it as part of our wider academic ranking, published on pages 22–27. There is good reason for this: a university with a poor record for social inclusion may still have an excellent record for teaching and research. It might be a very good university with an outstanding global and national reputation, but with a socially-narrow recruitment profile. This table identifies the universities with socially broad and narrow intakes. We intend to publish it annually and to amend the indicators used as more sophisticated measures become available while others are discontinued. By using the two multi-indicator, multi-institution tables that we publish together (alongside the relevant subject table) prospective students can identify the universities which are the best fit for them academically and where they might feel most at home socially. The importance of that last factor, in particular, will vary from applicant to applicant.

Based on the most recent data available at the time of compilation, *The Times and The Sunday Times* social inclusion ranking uses seven equally-weighted indicators covering student recruitment proportions from:

> » non-selective state schools
> » black ethnic minority applicants
> » the most deprived neighbourhoods
> » disabled students

> » all ethnic minorities
> » working class backgrounds
> » mature students older than 21

With the exception of the admissions data for non-selective state schools, all the other indicators are in the public domain. The uniqueness of this social inclusion ranking is in combining these several strands of data together for the first time to build an overall picture of the social mix at each institution.

The table is presented in a format that displays the raw data in all instances (the percentage proportions of entrants or the wider student body drawn from each of the seven categories). No adjustment is made for university location, so a university with a strong, local recruitment pattern in an area of low ethnic minority population will not do well on the two measures covering the ethnicity of the intake. This was most notably the case with Glyndŵr, the most socially inclusive university in the UK according to our ranking, but which had just 2.5% of its 2017 entrants drawn from ethnic minorities with just 1.3% black.

However, by combining the seven indicators using a common statistical technique known as z-scoring, we have ensured no single indicator has a disproportionate effect on the overall total for each university. The totals for each university were transformed to a scale with 1,000 for the top score and the performance of all universities measured relative to that of the university ranked No. 1.

Just as with our academic ranking, the organisations providing the raw data for the table are not involved in the process of aggregation, and are not responsible for any conclusion or inferences we have made. Every care has been taken to ensure the accuracy of the table and accompanying analysis, but no responsibility can be taken for errors or omissions.

The indicators used and what can be learned from them are outlined in turn below.

Non-selective state school admissions

For many years, the Higher Education Statistics Agency has published as part of its annual Performance Indicators, the proportion of students admitted to universities from all state schools. Among the entrants included in this proportion are those attending the 164 state grammars in England and the voluntary grammars in Northern Ireland. However, state school admissions to all universities stripped of the academically-selective grammar school sector have not been published before. Removing the grammar school sector from the equation reveals the proportion of students admitted to each university in 2016–17 from the largely non-selective state secondary schools attended by around 80% of university applicants.

At six universities, fewer than half the students admitted came from comprehensives and academies – Oxford (39.4%), Imperial College London (39.9%), Cambridge (40.1%), the London School of Economics (44.7%), Durham (46.4%) and the Royal Agricultural University (48.4%). (We have discounted the proportion of admissions from non-selective schools at Queen's Belfast from this analysis as Northern Ireland's two universities recruit predominantly from within the province and the proportions of selective and non-selective schools are broadly balanced.) Oxford is the only university in the country where privately-educated students are the biggest school grouping (42.3% independent/39.4% non-selective/18.3% grammar schools), while at LSE, St George's London, Imperial and Cambridge, more than one in five students are recruited from selective grammars.

The majority of universities (91 in all) admit more than 80% of their students from non-selective state schools, and just 25 take less than 70% of their intake from this demographic, 17 of these universities being members of the Russell Group of highly-selective, research-led universities.

All ethnic minority admissions

Data gathered from the 2017 admissions cycle by UCAS shows the proportion of entrants to each university drawn from black, Asian, mixed and other ethnic minorities.

Five London universities – all with more than two-thirds of their students drawn from ethnic minorities – rank immediately behind Aston which recruited 72.4% of its students from ethnic minorities in 2017, and Bradford (72.2%). The most ethnically diverse London universities are City, University of London (71.6%), Middlesex (69.6%), Brunel, London (69.5%), East London (67.2%) and London Metropolitan (67.1%). Just outside this group – and the eighth most ethnically-diverse university in the UK – is Queen Mary, London where a shade under 66% of students are BAME, by some distance the most diverse of the Russell Group student communities.

The least ethnically diverse university is Harper Adams, in rural Shropshire and specialising in predominantly land-based courses, where 0.8% of the intake was drawn from ethnic minorities in 2017. Harper Adams is followed by Bishop Grosseteste, in Lincoln (1.4%), Ulster (2.2%), Wrexham Glyndŵr (2.5%) and Queen's Belfast (3%).

Black ethnic minority admissions

The decision to isolate – and effectively double count – black ethnic minority admissions was a deliberate one. While as a group, black students are actually over-represented across higher education as a whole – making up 8% of the university population, roughly double their proportion among 18-24-year-olds more generally – their numbers in the most selective universities are small. Recent figures showed that ten out of 32 Oxford colleges did not admit a single black British A-level student in 2015, while at Cambridge one college did not admit any black students from 2012-16 and six colleges admitted fewer than ten black British students in the same five-year period.

Our data, drawn again from 2017 UCAS admissions data shows a wide variation from 0% to 38% for admission of black students across 130 institutions. Harper Adams is once again bottom with no black students recorded by UCAS among 2017 admissions and London Metropolitan is top with 37.6% of admissions being black students. The top two universities overall for ethnic diversity Aston (72.4%) and Bradford (72.2%) admit many fewer black students, 15.2% and 9% respectively, reflecting the strong local recruitment profile of both universities, located in two of England's biggest Asian population centres.

Bedfordshire, London South Bank, East London, Northampton and West London universities all saw more than one third of admissions drawn from black ethnic minorities in 2017. The UCAS data shows that black admissions at Cambridge and Oxford totaled 2.1% and 2% respectively.

Working class backgrounds

This indicator is most likely making its only appearance in the social inclusion ranking because HESA stopped publishing it two years ago. The data covers entrants to UK universities in 2014–15 who were deemed to come from socio-economic classification 4, 5, 6 or 7, in effect working class backgrounds. The classification given to university entrants was based on information students provided on the occupation of their parent or guardian who earned the most. The indicator used to be part of the HESA dataset on widening participation, but was discontinued on the basis that it was of poor quality and a judgment on socio-economic classification could not be made accurately based on the information students provided.

The Times and The Sunday Times Good University Guide editorial team felt this aspect of student opinion on their social background to be worth including, even if only once, in the new ranking. It had been employed by HESA for 13 years, beginning in 2002-03.

The data showed more than half the students were from working class backgrounds at ten universities, headed by Bradford (58.3%), Wolverhampton (56.9%) and Middlesex (56.3%). At the opposite end of the social scale were the universities with the fewest number of working class students as a proportion of their young entrants – in other words, the most middle class universities – which were Oxford (10%), Cambridge (10.2%), and Durham and St Andrews (both 14.2%). Twenty of the 25 universities with the smallest proportion of working class students were from the highly-selective Russell Group.

The most deprived neighbourhoods

This data is drawn again from the 2017 UCAS admissions cycle and looks at the home postcode of all university recruits, putting them into one of five pots, according to the level of participation in higher education. This indicator records the proportion of students who fall into Quintile 1 – the 20% of areas that have the lowest participation rates in higher education.

Like all indicators, this one has limitations, chief among which is that London has relatively high participation rates in higher education, so very few London-based university entrants fall into Quintile 1, meaning that London universities score relatively poorly across the board on this measure, even if they have a socially diverse intake of students.

Unsurprisingly, therefore, the universities of Sunderland (34.8%) and Teesside (33.2%) record the highest proportions of students recruited from Quintile 1. Both institutions recruit heavily within northeast England, which has the lowest participation rates in higher education in England. Imperial College London and St Andrews have the lowest rates of recruitment from Quintile 1, standing at just 3.5% in both instances.

Mature students

The proportion of entrants to university aged over 21 on admission is calculated from the overall number of entrants recorded by HESA in 2016–17 with all young entrants discounted. Mature students are returners to education and often win places with "life" qualifications, rather than A-levels. This immediately makes the group more diverse than the young entrants would be, who come mostly straight from school or via a gap year.

The age of the student population can have a major impact on the social scene on campus. Older students, particularly those with partners (and even children) are less likely to be found clubbing or propping up the bar late into the evening. Universities with a very small proportion of mature undergraduates – the LSE (1.5%), St Andrews (2.1%), Oxford (2.8%) and Bath (3%) – are likely to have a livelier campus social life than Birkbeck, London (69% mature admissions), London Metropolitan (68%), Wrexham Glyndŵr (63.8%) and Suffolk (59.1%).

Disabled students

This indicator measures the proportion of all students in higher education in receipt of Disability Support Allowance (DSA). It is part of the bigger HESA dataset on widening participation, published in February 2018 and is based on data from the 2016–17 academic year.

As with the other indicators, there is a significant difference between the universities at the top – Glyndŵr where HESA records 26.7% of students in receipt of DSA and Trinity St David (18.2%) – and those at the bottom – Glasgow Caledonian (1.3%) and West of Scotland (2.2%).

The overall picture

It is not possible to appear near the top of the social inclusion ranking if an institution is only achieving well on one or two of the measures of social inclusion that *The Times and The Sunday Times* have chosen. Success in the table comes from broadly-based achievement in recruiting from areas of society least represented in higher education. Equally, a university that appears near the bottom is not just falling short in one or two regards; it reflects a pattern of recruitment – or non-recruitment – from swathes of society.

A different set of metrics looking at the same subject matter might produce a very different looking table, which is why it is necessary to be clear about what is being measured here. Based on the measures we have chosen the top three in the academic rankings – Cambridge, Oxford and St Andrews – appear in the bottom three (in a different order) for social inclusion. London Metropolitan, next to bottom in the academic ranking, is next to top for social inclusion. Sixteen of the bottom 20 universities for social inclusion are Russell Group universities.

Some of the universities near the foot of our table point to their excellent record on progression and degree outcomes for those students they admit from some of the categories of students we have included in our ranking. They are right to do this, which is why De Montfort University is our University of the Year for Social Inclusion. De Montfort ranks 16th overall for social inclusion, but also sits in the top 20 in the UK for graduate prospects and student experience in our main academic ranking. Having a socially diverse student body should not legitimise failure in the graduate jobs market or a ruinous degree completion rate. That benefits no-one, wastes money, and ultimately does not help the majority of students given a shot at higher education that has been denied them elsewhere.

Used in conjunction, our academic and social inclusion rankings seek to provide an intriguing insight to likely academic and professional success, the quality of the student experience, and the mix of students likely to be found in the university lecture theatres and the after-hours clubs and bars. They also indicate the likelihood of an application being successful in the first place.

Social Inclusion Rankings

Institution	State educated (non-grammar) (%)	Ethnic (all, %)	Ethnic (Black, %)	Working class (%)	Deprived areas (%)	Disabled (%)	Mature (%)	Total
1 Wrexham Glyndŵr	99.3	2.5	1.3	46.2	30.8	26.7	63.8	1000
2 London Metropolitan	96.5	67.1	37.6	51.4	7.6	6.1	68.0	958
3 London South Bank	97.2	64.6	34.0	50.7	7.3	11.9	51.1	956
4 Wolverhampton	97.1	50.9	22.6	56.9	23.8	7.4	45.2	929
5 Bolton	98.7	38.2	15.8	52.5	25.6	11.5	48.3	926
6 Bedfordshire	97.6	60.9	34.0	50.1	10.9	5.0	56.4	909
7 East London	96.3	67.2	33.7	54.7	9.0	6.4	44.5	908
8 West London	95.5	63.0	33.3	49.9	6.3	6.0	56.5	892
9 Newman	98.5	49.1	11.7	56.2	20.5	10.1	30.3	859
10 Birkbeck, London	87.8	n/a	n/a	42.8	n/a	6.6	69.0	852
11 Bradford	93.7	72.2	9.0	58.3	15.6	9.2	22.0	831
12 Northampton	96.2	46.6	33.6	40.2	15.2	6.5	32.3	828
13 Suffolk	98.5	13.2	6.9	44.8	30.6	7.2	59.1	827
14 Middlesex	96.7	69.6	27.1	56.3	5.3	4.5	27.6	816
15 Teesside	98.4	12.2	3.1	45.7	33.2	9.7	39.3	805
16 De Montfort	94.9	52.8	21.8	43.1	14.9	10.6	15.4	799
17 Sunderland	97.9	13.9	3.9	44.9	34.8	4.4	53.0	794
18 Kingston	93.5	59.6	23.8	47.3	6.9	7.2	31.8	793
19 Greenwich	92.5	51.4	20.4	54.0	9.1	4.7	40.5	791
20 Wales Trinity St David	98.5	7.8	1.9	42.4	14.9	18.2	42.5	784
21 Roehampton	94.2	56.9	23.2	43.0	5.5	5.7	45.6	783
22 Staffordshire	98.5	18.6	7.0	47.6	27.3	7.1	35.8	775
23 Plymouth Marjon	94.7	4.8	0.7	37.0	23.8	16.8	38.7	769
24 Anglia Ruskin	92.4	31.3	15.7	38.9	16.6	5.7	53.1	763
25 Birmingham City	97.2	52.5	16.3	46.9	14.1	5.3	26.5	762
26 Bishop Grosseteste	96.1	1.4	0.7	44.0	22.9	13.1	36.3	742
27 Canterbury Christ Church	93.2	26.0	17.6	39.8	17.3	6.4	34.5	735
28 Hertfordshire	94.9	56.4	22.1	42.5	7.9	5.3	23.2	734
29 Buckinghamshire New	93.9	43.0	19.8	46.2	9.0	4.3	33.7	731
30 Derby	95.2	22.8	8.7	38.6	23.3	7.8	30.2	727
31 Huddersfield	96.0	36.2	5.2	46.2	17.2	8.7	21.4	721
32 Central Lancashire	96.8	23.1	5.0	45.1	21.6	5.3	35.7	717
33 Coventry	92.3	52.9	20.6	41.7	11.7	4.0	18.3	708
=34 Salford	96.5	30.8	7.4	42.2	21.0	5.0	28.3	706
=34 Arts London	91.6	29.8	8.6	33.1	7.1	17.4	20.1	706
36 Brunel, London	89.9	69.5	18.4	43.3	4.1	7.1	11.0	705
37 Westminster	94.2	62.8	13.8	49.3	5.6	4.3	20.1	704
38 Cumbria	95.5	8.9	2.1	41.9	22.9	7.2	35.8	693
=39 Creative Arts	92.3	24.6	8.3	39.0	11.7	13.4	15.7	689

Institution	State educated (non-grammar) (%)	Ethnic (all, %)	Ethnic (black, %)	Working class (%)	Deprived areas (%)	Disabled (%)	Mature (%)	Total
=39 South Wales	95.9	10.6	2.9	42.0	22.7	8.0	28.0	689
41 Essex	90.8	44.4	22.3	38.3	12.8	4.3	14.5	685
42 Worcester	94.6	13.2	5.2	36.9	17.3	9.1	34.3	682
43 City, London	86.4	71.6	15.0	46.0	4.5	3.8	16.8	678
44 Sheffield Hallam	93.1	17.9	4.3	40.8	21.5	7.6	16.9	662
=45 Solent	96.4	17.3	6.6	43.8	16.7	6.6	19.7	659
=45 Aston	87.2	72.4	15.2	42.1	9.8	3.0	4.5	659
47 Cardiff Metropolitan	93.5	13.9	4.3	38.4	20.3	8.0	22.3	658
48 Hull	89.5	14.3	4.9	33.2	26.5	6.0	25.7	654
=49 Leeds Trinity	95.0	20.1	3.0	42.3	20.7	6.2	17.2	652
=49 Edge Hill	96.7	7.2	2.2	39.1	21.7	6.8	26.2	652
51 Liverpool Hope	90.2	9.3	2.4	43.2	21.1	8.8	17.0	651
52 Manchester Metropolitan	93.8	30.0	5.6	41.5	16.9	5.7	15.0	646
53 Portsmouth	91.8	29.2	9.6	32.9	14.6	8.6	14.7	645
=54 St George's, London	60.3	64.7	17.3	30.4	5.8	7.2	32.6	643
=54 Norwich Arts	93.9	10.8	2.0	37.6	17.6	12.3	9.7	643
56 St Mary's, Twickenham	91.5	28.8	11.4	38.8	6.4	7.9	22.8	641
57 Kent	91.0	35.1	15.8	32.5	10.5	8.1	9.5	640
=58 Brighton	89.8	21.8	5.9	34.2	12.5	9.6	24.6	639
=58 Goldsmiths, London	87.6	47.2	12.9	30.8	4.7	7.9	24.3	639
=58 West of England	90.3	16.3	4.5	30.2	16.6	9.8	26.5	639
61 Ravensbourne, London	93.1	37.5	13.1	39.5	6.3	7.0	13.0	637
62 Soas, London	74.0	60.2	12.0	35.7	4.6	8.6	16.5	633
63 Chester	93.8	9.8	3.1	33.9	20.7	7.4	23.5	631
64 Queen Mary, London	78.4	65.9	10.0	37.0	4.5	8.1	11.0	630
65 Gloucestershire	92.4	10.3	4.0	36.4	15.7	9.1	19.9	625
66 Winchester	92.1	10.4	2.6	30.4	15.2	12.9	14.1	621
67 Keele	83.0	32.4	8.0	32.1	17.5	7.4	13.0	620
68 Plymouth	87.3	10.0	2.2	31.9	16.7	8.6	28.6	611
69 West of Scotland	98.2	9.2	2.6	40.6	8.9	2.2	49.6	609
70 Chichester	95.4	6.9	2.2	31.9	18.4	9.0	16.5	608
71 Highlands and Islands	96.1	3.3	0.7	46.2	6.8	4.4	45.4	607
=72 Lincoln	93.2	9.3	2.1	37.1	19.1	8.2	10.8	606
=72 Northumbria	90.7	10.4	2.0	37.2	20.2	5.8	20.5	606
74 Bangor	89.3	7.7	1.6	34.9	15.3	9.3	22.7	605
75 Arts Bournemouth	95.1	11.9	2.6	30.4	10.6	12.7	10.4	597
=76 Liverpool John Moores	90.7	11.2	2.9	39.6	20.6	4.2	16.8	596
=76 Nottingham Trent	90.4	22.9	8.1	33.1	14.9	6.0	12.5	596
=78 Leeds Beckett	92.8	20.6	4.3	35.4	18.3	4.9	12.1	594

Social Inclusion Rankings cont

Institution	State educated (non-grammar) (%)	Ethnic (all, %)	Ethnic (Black, %)	Working class (%)	Deprived areas (%)	Disabled (%)	Mature (%)	Total
=78 Falmouth	90.6	6.4	0.8	27.5	10.9	15.3	12.6	594
80 Leicester	80.3	49.2	17.7	26.9	9.8	5.2	7.6	593
=81 Abertay	95.4	6.2	0.9	33.8	8.8	7.8	35.7	592
=81 Bath Spa	89.2	9.1	2.1	33.1	13.1	10.9	15.7	592
=83 Leeds Arts	95.0	9.4	1.7	38.2	10.3	11.3	7.2	591
=83 Bournemouth	90.0	15.7	4.6	31.4	12.0	8.7	19.1	591
85 Harper Adams	71.8	0.8	0.0	44.4	7.0	16.2	14.8	589
86 York St John	93.5	5.6	0.9	34.9	17.3	8.0	10.0	576
87 Queen Margaret, Edinburgh	93.2	10.7	2.0	34.4	8.1	7.4	26.7	574
88 Aberystwyth	90.8	6.1	0.6	33.8	12.5	9.7	11.9	563
89 Robert Gordon	93.8	10.1	2.4	32.0	4.4	8.7	26.4	562
90 Edinburgh Napier	92.5	7.7	1.9	31.1	9.2	4.7	33.5	549
91 Glasgow Caledonian	96.4	11.3	2.4	34.7	8.8	1.3	35.5	547
92 Stirling	87.9	6.5	1.8	32.1	8.3	6.4	29.3	543
93 East Anglia	78.6	19.6	5.4	25.0	13.0	8.1	12.9	540
94 King's College London	61.4	50.7	10.6	26.2	4.5	5.4	22.4	532
95 Surrey	78.6	33.9	6.7	28.6	7.6	4.7	14.4	524
96 Oxford Brookes	66.9	16.4	4.5	27.9	8.7	8.9	22.7	523
97 Buckingham	69.4	n/a	n/a	25.0	n/a	4.1	40.9	521
98 Dundee	86.1	9.1	1.7	29.1	6.9	5.0	22.2	496
99 Royal Holloway, London	74.1	36.3	5.6	28.4	5.1	6.1	6.1	495
100 Swansea	85.5	13.9	2.4	27.9	10.4	4.5	13.3	494
101 Ulster	62.8	2.2	0.3	44.6	9.0	4.7	24.9	491
102 Manchester	70.0	29.7	4.3	21.5	9.3	7.5	9.0	489
103 Sussex	79.0	19.7	4.0	22.5	8.2	6.8	9.1	481
104 Reading	73.3	24.1	5.4	27.3	6.0	6.3	6.8	476
105 Loughborough	69.7	23.3	6.9	21.9	7.3	8.4	3.5	475
106 Cardiff	76.5	15.3	2.7	23.8	10.8	5.7	11.2	473
107 Sheffield	74.0	18.4	3.4	21.2	11.0	6.9	7.4	472
108 Liverpool	76.7	15.2	2.4	25.9	10.8	5.3	9.7	471
109 Heriot-Watt	78.8	14.9	3.1	26.1	6.3	5.1	15.6	469
110 Lancaster	79.9	15.5	3.0	23.9	10.7	5.4	4.7	464
111 Royal Agricultural	48.4	n/a	n/a	29.9	n/a	10.4	11.7	461
112 Nottingham	64.0	27.8	7.6	20.3	8.6	5.5	9.3	458
113 Southampton	71.7	21.6	4.6	23.1	8.7	4.6	10.3	455
=114 Strathclyde	89.5	8.7	1.2	25.9	5.6	3.0	14.1	445
=114 Aberdeen	76.1	10.1	2.6	25.0	3.7	5.7	16.8	445
116 Birmingham	67.3	27.2	4.7	22.8	7.1	5.4	4.9	442
=117 Leeds	68.4	18.7	2.9	22.5	8.5	5.5	7.9	437

Institution	State educated (non-grammar) (%)	Ethnic (all %)	Ethnic (black %)	Working class (%)	Deprived areas (%)	Disabled (%)	Mature (%)	Total
=117 Warwick	58.4	33.1	7.0	19.3	6.6	5.1	9.8	437
119 York	68.9	13.0	3.0	19.6	9.0	5.5	7.2	420
120 London School of Economics	44.7	48.8	4.7	21.1	7.1	4.3	1.5	405
=121 Newcastle	65.0	13.2	2.3	20.3	9.3	4.9	5.8	403
=121 Glasgow	78.8	8.1	0.8	21.4	4.2	3.3	15.1	403
123 University College London	50.4	49.6	5.1	19.0	3.9	2.7	10.1	402
124 Queen's Belfast	34.3	3.0	0.4	31.9	7.6	6.4	19.6	386
125 Imperial College, London	39.9	47.8	5.1	16.2	3.5	4.1	11.5	382
126 Exeter	56.2	11.1	2.0	15.5	7.7	6.9	6.5	377
=127 Bath	55.5	15.1	1.8	18.2	5.5	5.5	3.0	357
=127 Edinburgh	60.2	10.2	0.6	18.7	4.1	5.4	6.7	357
129 Bristol	50.5	16.0	2.2	14.7	5.2	5.1	5.6	339
130 Durham	46.4	12.5	1.3	14.2	6.4	5.3	5.7	326
131 Cambridge	40.1	21.3	2.1	10.2	4.4	4.6	4.3	298
132 St Andrews	54.0	10.5	1.3	14.2	3.5	3.2	2.1	296
133 Oxford	39.4	17.6	2.0	10.0	4.1	5.6	2.8	293

7 Financing Your Studies

The simmering political debate about student finance tends to concentrate on fee levels and repayments. The huge figures for total debt accumulated by successful graduates may make good headlines, but for those who have decided to aim for a degree the most immediate concern is how to make ends meet for three or four years (if not more) at university. How much money will they need and where it will come from?

Students are notoriously bad at estimating how much they will spend in the course of a term, as well as assessing how much they will earn after graduation, when the time may come to repay their loans. More than a quarter do not budget at all, according to research for the NatWest Student Living Index, but half admit that money worries are causing them stress.

So, if you can see your way past those scary totals, this chapter looks at the funding available to students in different parts of the UK, how to plan for a possibly precarious existence and then pay back what is required as a graduate. Of course, by September 2020, or at some point during your degree, everything may change. Fees may be reduced – or even abolished – but you can only plan on the basis of the current system. At the time of writing, that means fees of £9,250 in England (nothing in Scotland) with student loans both for fees and maintenance.

What will not change is the need to find enough money to live on at university and the likelihood that, for most, some debt will be involved. Under the current system, those debts are likely to be considerable but, assuming they come mainly from student loans, should always be manageable and may well not be repaid in full. You will not repay anything until you are earning £25,000 a year and then only 9% of anything above that amount, however much you earn.

When you do get a student loan, however, your first surprise is that the interest clock starts ticking on it from the day the first payment hits your bank account, usually the first day of your first term. It keeps ticking until the April after you finish the course, which is when you might or might not start repaying. If you are a part-time student, and earning over £25,000, you'll have to start repaying four years after you started getting the loan, even if you are still studying.

During your course, the interest rate on your loan will be RPI plus 3%. RPI, the Retail Price Index, is a standard measure of UK inflation and at the time of writing, RPI plus 3% adds up to a total of 6.3%. That would mean interest of £393 a year on a single year's tuition fee of £9,250. The interest you are racking up will, paradoxically, go down to RPI alone if you leave college and get a job paying less than £25,000 a year. Then it goes onto a sliding scale of RPI plus up to 3%

until you reach a salary of £45,000, after which it remains at RPI plus 3%, however much you earn. Note that as with much else in this chapter, these threshold numbers are likely to change over time, usually upwards. Note too that the rate of RPI plus 3% will be applied to your debt automatically if you don't keep in touch with the Student Loans Company and inform them of your circumstances.

One constant, however, is that after 30 years in England (the figure varies elsewhere in the UK), the debt is written off. Because the repayments seem modest for anyone with a qualifying income, and because of the 30-year rule, student debt is a lot more forgiving than a mortgage or a credit card, where the bills keep on coming even if you are out of work. The Student Loans Company is, after all, probably the only lender in Britain who will hand you tens of thousands of pounds without a credit check.

The last significant change in this system, in 2016/2017, was the abolition of grants for students from low-income families in England, and their replacement by loans. As with the introduction of fees, there is no immediate impact on students. Repayments still begin only after graduation, and when the borrower's salary reaches £25,000. But the prospect of yet more debt does appear to be deterring some applicants from this already under-represented section of society. That did not happen when fees went up in 2012, but no one can be sure what will happen over time.

There are different arrangements in other parts of the UK, which are addressed later in this chapter. But wherever you study, there are two quite different timescales to consider: in the short term you need to ensure you have enough money to live on and maybe have some fun, while the long term calculation is whether your degree is value for money. Most commentary on the subject conflates the two, focusing on the total debt that the average student will have at graduation. That is likely to be an intimidating figure, and one that should not be ignored by those contemplating a degree, but it has little to do with whether you can afford three or more years as an undergraduate.

Affordability

The introduction of £9,000 fees, now fixed at a maximum of £9,250 for three or four-year courses, added enormously to graduates' debts. But tuition fee loans are paid straight to the university, so the student's calculation is about bridging the gap between a maintenance loan and the real cost of living. In England, a maintenance loan was worth up to £8,700 (or £11,354 in London) in 2018/19. The maximum figure was reduced to £7,234 for those living with parents. With hall fees topping £5,000 a year at some universities, that might seem an attractive option. (For a year when you were studying abroad for at least one term, the maximum award was £9,963.)

There will be a financial gap for most students. But don't panic. Students have always had a challenge to make ends meet, typically through a combination of parental help, part-time employment and institutional bursaries.

Analysis by the National Union of Students suggests that it is not possible to get by on student loans alone. Savings, earnings, and help from family and friends have to be added to the pot. The information provided here will help you understand how big your pot needs to be, and what you can expect to be added and taken away from it. But it takes careful budgeting to avoid adding credit card debt to the income-contingent variety offered by the Government and repaid (or not) over 30 years.

Value for money

Only when you are sure you can cope with the costs of student life should you move on to the longer-term question of whether your chosen degree will make it worth repaying £40,000 or more in student loans. Even in purely financial terms, there are too many uncertainties to be sure of the answer. You may never earn the £25,000 a year which triggers repayments, although few students go to university with that expectation and in practice, very few will be in that position. At the other extreme, your degree may help you land such a well-paid job that university was cheap at the price. Most graduates will be somewhere in the middle, and the system is too new for any to have experienced the impact of loan repayments of 9% of salary above the threshold for more than a few years.

Contrary to some alarmist media coverage of graduate employment prospects, most surveys suggest that on average, a degree is still a worthwhile investment in terms of future salary expectations, even after adding in the amount you might have earned while you were a student.

In 2018 the Department for Education published figures showing, in a somewhat broad-brush way, that graduates with a bachelor-level degree earn about £10,000 a year more than non-graduates, with an extra £5,000 a year mark-up for a higher degree, and that this premium had held steady for a decade. However, the *Financial Times* pointed out that over that decade, the median non-graduate income had risen from about £19,000 to about £23,000 while the graduate premium had stayed unchanged, in effect falling as a percentage of total income.

The Government's decision to raise the threshold for starting repayments from £21,000 to £25,000 is expected to mean that, on average, graduates pay back £15,700 less over a full career. The biggest advantage, obviously, will be for those on relatively low incomes.

This *Guide* should help to fill in some of the detail on employment rates for different courses at different universities, while salary data by course is available on the Unistats website. But no one can be certain of salary prospects over an entire career, which is increasingly likely to span several forms of employment. Many satisfying jobs are open only to graduates, while in others the majority of new entrants have degrees.

Planning your finances

Like maximum fees, national student support schemes are the responsibility of the devolved UK administrations. There are separate sections for Northern Ireland, Wales and Scotland that follow the advice given for English students below.

At the time of writing, the government had decided to keep the basic rate of fees at £9,250 per year for England, partly as a political response to its unpopularity with young people. This standstill is bad news for university finance managers, who might have expected an inflation-linked increase, but is excellent for you. Despite this stasis, it is essential to consult the information provided by Government agencies. It is worth checking the following websites for the latest information:

» England: **www.gov.uk/student-finance**
» Wales: **www.studentfinancewales.co.uk**
» Scotland: **www.saas.gov.uk**
» Northern Ireland: **www.studentfinanceni.co.uk**

Student loans for English students

More than 80% of students take out a student loan, and it is not difficult to see why. The National Union of Students estimates that undergraduates spend £12,000 a year outside London and £13,500 in the capital. While some other estimates are marginally lower, most students find it impossible to cover all their living costs without a loan or significant family support. NUS research suggests that money worries are among students' biggest concerns and are one of the

Scottish maintenance bursaries and loans 2018–19[1]

Young student (under 25 at start of course)				Independent student			
Income	Bursary	Loan	Total	Income	Bursary	Loan	Total
£0–£18,999	£1,875	£5,750	£7,625	£0–£18,999	£875	£6,750	£7,625
£19,000–£23,999	£1,125	£5,570	£6,875	£19,000–£23,999	0	£6,750	£6,750
£24,000–£33,999	£500	£5,750	£6,250	£24,000–£33,999	0	£6,250	£6,250
£34,000 and over	0	£4,750	£4,750	£34,000 and over	0	£4,750	£4,750

Repayments start at a salary above £17,775. Any outstanding amount will be written off after 35 years.

[1] The Scottish Government had not announced all maintenance loan details for 2019/20 at the time of going to press. But it had pledged bursaries of £8,100 for nursing and midwifery students, rising to £10,000 in 2020/21. It had also pledged that EU students in 2019/20 (in common with Scottish students) would not have to pay tuition fees.

main reasons why they might drop out of a course or consider doing so. Incidentally, anyone who drops out of university still has to repay the loan they ran up while there. The only ways out of paying are to wait 30 years, become permanently unable to work or die. Unpaid student debt does not become a charge against an estate.

Most experts such as Martin Lewis of moneysavingexpert.com, who writes regularly on student finance, agree that student loans are a good deal compared with other forms of borrowing. In particular, he counsels against using family savings to pay fees upfront, especially since the Government's own estimates suggest that most graduates will not repay the whole amount that they borrow.

Tuition fees loan
You can borrow up to the full amount needed to cover your tuition fees wherever you study in the UK, and this loan is not dependent upon your household income.

Maintenance loan for a first-year English student 2018–19

Household income	Living at home	Living away from home but not in London	Living away from home in London
£25,000 and below	£7,324	£8,700	£11,354
£30,000	£6,707	£8,076	£10,719
£35,000	£6,090	£7,452	£10,084
£40,000	£5,473	£6,828	£9,449
£42,875	£5,118	£6,469	£9,083
£45,000	£4,855	£6,204	£8,813
£50,000	£4,238	£5,579	£8,178
£55,000	£3,621	£4,955	£7,543
£58,215 and above	£3,224	–	–
£60,000	–	£4,331	£6,907
£62,215 and above	–	£4,054	–
£65,000	–	–	£6,272
£69,860 and above	–	–	£5,654

Tuition fees loans for part-time students

The most that universities or colleges could charge for part-time courses in 2018–19 was 75% of the full-time fee, a maximum of £4,625 per year at private institutions and £6,935 per year at public ones. New part-time students were able to apply for a tuition fee loan that was not dependent on household income or on age, a factor that led to some courses having a surprising number of pensioner students. Eligibility depended on the "intensity" of the course being at least 25% of a full-time course. So, if a course takes six years to complete and the full-time equivalent takes three, the intensity will be 50%. In practice, most courses achieve more than 25% intensity.

Maintenance loan

Maintenance loans are means-tested. The amount you can borrow depends on several factors, including your family income, where you intend to study, and whether you expect to be living at home.

Although you are legally an adult, your student finance options depend heavily on your family income, frequently termed "household income", which in practice usually means your parents' earnings. If your parents are separated, divorced or widowed, only the income of the parent with whom you normally live will be assessed. However, if that parent has married again, entered into a civil partnership, or has a partner of the opposite sex, then both their incomes will be taken into account. If you are over 25, married, or in some other way visibly independent of your parents, you can avoid having their income taken into account. If you have not been in contact with them for a year or more, you can apply as "estranged." This is a complex field

---

Funding timetable

It is vital that you sort out your funding arrangements before you start university. Each funding agency has its own arrangements, and it is very important that you find out the exact details from them. The dates below give general indications of key dates.

March/April

» Online and paper application forms become available from funding agencies.
» You must contact the appropriate funding agency to make an application. This will be the funding agency for the region of the UK that you live in, even if you are planning to study elsewhere in the UK.
» Complete application form as soon as possible. At this stage select the university offer that will be your first choice.
» Check details of bursaries and scholarships available from your selected universities.

May/June

» Funding agencies will give you details of the financial support they can offer.
» Last date for making an application to ensure funding is ready for you at the start of term (exact date varies significantly between agencies).

August

» Tell your funding agency if the university or course you have been accepted for is different from that originally given them.

September

» Take letter confirming funding to your university for registration.
» After registration, the first part of funds will be released to you.

touching on issues such as forced marriage orders. It requires genuine evidence, not just a statement from you that you have fallen out with your parents.

For courses starting in or after autumn 2018, the maximum loan for those living at home is £7,324, but only if the combined household income is £25,000 or less. The size of the loan is then reduced on a sliding scale to £3,224 for incomes over £60,000. For students living away from home outside London, the maximum loan is £8,700, and for those living away from home in London, £11,354, but again these are rates for a household income of £25,000 or less. For students outside London, the loan is reduced on a sliding scale to £4,054 for those whose parents earn £65,000 and above, while for students in London the loan reduces to £5,654 for incomes of £69,860 and above. You can get up to £9,963 for a year studying abroad as part of a UK course. Final-year students receive less than those in earlier years.

Sixty-five per cent of the maintenance loan is available to you regardless of your family circumstances, while the remaining 35% is means-tested. Note, too, that there is extra cash available for future teachers, social workers and healthcare workers, including doctors and dentists.

This means that students who would have qualified for maintenance grants under the old system and are studying away from home will be able to borrow up to £17,950. In London the maximum will be £20,604; and for those living in the parental home £16,574. These sums exclude interest.

Scams

One new hazard for students seeking loans emerged last year in the form of an email scam that appears to offer tax refunds in an attempt to steal personal data and money. The scammers are using fake university addresses or even aping the branding of the GOV.UK website or credit card companies and the emails guide students through links to websites where they are instructed to enter personal and bank details.

HMRC said this was the first time it had seen such an attack directly targeting university students in high volumes. It said it would never inform anyone about tax refunds by email, text or voicemail and that any such communication should be regarded as a scam. If you get such a message, don't click on it and forward it to HMRC's phishing email address that can be found on its website.

Repaying loans

As we have seen, full-time students begin accumulating interest from day one of their course and will start repaying in the April after graduation if they earn over £25,000. They will then pay 9% of their income above £25,000, but repayments will stop during any period in which annual income falls below the threshold. Repayments are normally taken automatically through income tax and National Insurance. If the loan has not been paid off after 30 years, no further repayments will be required. During the repayment period, the amount of interest will vary according to how much you earn. If you earn less than £25,000, interest will be at the rate of inflation as measured by the Retail Price Index; between £25,000 and £41,000 you will be charged inflation plus up to 3%; and if you earn over £41,000, interest will be at inflation plus the full 3%.

The Student Loan Company website (**www.studentloanrepayment.co.uk**) has information to guide prospective students through these arrangements and gives examples of levels of repayment.

Student loans and grants for Northern Ireland students

Maintenance loans for 2018–19 vary from a maximum of £3,750 for students living at home, £4,840 for those studying away from home, up to £5,770 for those living overseas and £6,780 for those studying in London (only 25% of the loan is means-tested). There are also extra sums for people taking courses longer than 30 weeks a year, worth up to £108 a week if you are in London.

Maintenance grants range from £3,475 for students with household incomes of £19,203 or below, to zero if the figure is £41,540 or above. Your maximum loan is reduced by the size of any grant you receive. Loan repayments of 9% of salary start once your income reaches £18,330 for 2017–18, less than in England, and interest is calculated on the retail price index or 1% above base rate, whichever is lowest, again less than for England. The loan will be cancelled after 25 years, also quicker than in England.

As in England, there are also special funds for people with disabilities and other special needs, and for those with children or adult dependants. Students studying in the Republic of Ireland can also borrow up to €3,000 a year to pay their Irish student fees and may be able to get a bursary to study there. Tuition fee loans are available for the full amount of tuition fees, regardless of where you study in the UK.

Fees for local students at the province's two universities are a lot lower than for England, Scotland or Wales, at £4,160 for 2018/19.

Student loans and grants for Welsh students

For 2018/19, the maximum maintenance award is £7,650 for students living at home, £9,000 for those living away from home and outside London, and £11,250 for those living in London. The cunning part is that these sums are mainly an outright grant to those from less prosperous households. So if total household income is £18,370 or less, £8,100 of the £9,000 is a grant and only £900 a loan, but if income is over £59,200, then £8,000 is repayable and only £1,000 is a grant. The same logic applies to other levels of support, while part-time students can get a loan or grant up to the precise figure of £4,987.50.

Tuition fee loans are available to cover the first £9,000 of tuition fees in Wales, or £9,250 for Welsh students in Scotland, England or Northern Ireland (£6,165 for a private provider). If you are studying part-time in Wales you can apply for a loan of up to £2,625, elsewhere in the UK you can apply for up to £6,935 or if your course is offered by a private provider, £4,625.

Repayment of loans starts once a graduate's income reaches £25,000. Interest repayments and the length of loan are as for England (see above). In addition, students in Wales are also able to apply for Welsh Government support for parents of young children, for adult learners, for those with adult dependants and for those with disabilities. This support can cover carer costs as well as equipment and general expenditure.

Student loans and grants for Scottish students

Scottish students pay no tuition fees at their own universities and the Scottish Government has a commitment to a minimum income of £7,625 a year for students from poorer backgrounds. So, in 2018/19, students from a family with an income below £19,000 could get a £1,875 Young Students' Bursary (YSB) as well as a loan of £5,750. The bursary component does not have to be repaid, but the loan does. It tapers off to zero for family incomes of £34,000, at which point the maximum loan also falls from £5,750 to £4,750. The loan does not vary in size depending on whether you live at home or where you are studying in the UK. Higher loans but more limited bursaries are available for "independent" students – those who are married, mature (25 or over) or without family support.

Note that you must be under 60 on the first day of your course. Repayment of the loan starts when your income reaches £18,330 and is set at 9% of your income above that threshold. The

Scottish government, whose Student Awards Agency Scotland runs this system, plans to raise the repayment threshold to £25,000 in 2021, to match England. Interest is linked to the Retail Price Index. Repayments will continue until the loan is paid off, with any outstanding amount being cancelled after 35 years, five years later than for the English.

As elsewhere in the UK, there are special funds for people with disabilities and other special needs, and for those with children or adult dependants. No tuition fee loans are required by Scottish students studying in Scotland, but such loans are available for Scottish students studying elsewhere in the UK.

A review of the student support system was announced in October 2016, led by Jayne-Anne Gadhia, former CEO of Virgin Money. She recommended a minimum student income of £8,100 a year.

Living in one country, studying in another

As each of the countries of the UK develops its own distinctive system of student finance, the effects on students leaving home in one UK nation to go and study in another have become knottier. UK students who cross borders to study pay the tuition fees of their chosen university and are eligible for a fee loan, and maybe a partial grant, to cover them. They are also entitled to apply for the scholarships or bursaries on offer from that institution. Any maintenance loan or grant will still come from the awarding body of their home country. If you are in this position, you must check with the authorities in your home country about the funding you are eligible for.

While the UK remains in the European Union, EU students from outside the UK must be charged the same tuition fees as those paid by nationals of the country where they are studying, rather than the higher – often much higher – fees paid by students from outside the EU. They can also apply for a fee loan and may be considered for some of the scholarships and bursaries offered by individual institutions. Only students who have been living and studying in the UK for at least three years can apply for a maintenance loan or grant. Those who haven't, will need to apply for assistance from the authorities in their own country. Tuition fee rules for non-UK European Union students are the same in Scotland as for Scottish students – that is, they do not have to pay tuition fees. There are also no fees to pay for exchange students coming to the UK, including those on the Socrates Programme.

Applying for support

English students should apply for grants and loans through Student Finance England, Welsh students through Student Finance Wales, Scottish students through the Student Awards Agency for Scotland, and those in Northern Ireland through Student Finance NI or their Education and Library Board. You should make your application as soon as you have received an offer of a place at university. Maintenance loans are usually paid in three instalments a year into your bank or building society account. European Union students from outside the UK will usually be sent an application form for tuition fee loans by the university that has offered them a place. Don't expect things to happen automatically. For instance, you will have to tell the finance system to pay your fees to the college. You'll never see this money yourself, only the repayments you end up making.

University scholarships and bursaries

As well as taking out student loans for both tuition and living costs, you can shop around for university bursaries, scholarships and other sponsorship packages, and seek out supplementary support to which you may be entitled. There may be reductions for a range of other groups, including local students, which vary widely from university to university and which are usually detailed on university websites. The details of the financial support offered by all universities in England are listed in the access agreements published on the website of the Office for Students, **www.officeforstudents.org.uk**.

Nevertheless, UK students are said to be missing out on over £150 million in scholarships, according to research by The Scholarship Hub, a free online database of over 3,000 scholarships and bursaries. Leading organisations offering scholarships, grants or bursaries to UK students said they often struggle to get enough suitable applicants.

A bewildering variety of awards are on offer at UK universities. Most bursaries are dependent on your financial circumstances, while scholarships are available through open competition. In general, bursaries that provide students with the money to make ends meet at university have (rightly) proved more popular than fee waivers giving relief from repayments that may stretch over 30 years. Some universities offer eligible students the choice of accommodation discounts, fee waivers or cash. Most also have hardship funds for those who find themselves in financial difficulties. Many charities for specific industries or professions have a remit to support education, and many have bursaries for anyone studying a related subject. It might be worth seeking out some options online. The Directory of Grant-Making Trusts **https://www.dsc.org.uk/publication/the-directory-of-grant-making-trusts-201819/** lists a wealth of bodies that make one-off or regular awards to all kinds of causes, often including deserving students.

Do take note of the application procedures for scholarships and bursaries. They vary from institution to institution, and even from course to course within individual institutions. There may be a deadline you have to meet to apply for an award. In some cases, the university will work out for you whether you are entitled to an award by referring to your funding agency's financial assessment. If your personal circumstances change part-way through a course, your entitlement to a scholarship or bursary may be reviewed.

If you feel you still need more help or advice on scholarships or bursaries, you can usually find it on a university's website or in its prospectus. Most institutions also maintain a helpline. Some questions you will need answered include whether the bursary or scholarship is automatic or conditional and, if the latter, when you will find out whether your application has been successful. For some awards, you won't know whether you have qualified until you get your exam results. Another obvious question is how the scholarship or bursary on offer compares with awards made by another university you might consider applying to. Watch out for institutions that list entitlements that others don't mention, but which you would get anyway.

Students with disabilities

Extra financial help is available to disabled students, whether studying full-time or part-time, through Disabled Students' Allowances, which are paid in addition to the standard student finance package. They are available for help with education-related conditions such as dyslexia, and for other physical and mental disabilities. They do not depend on income and do not have to be repaid. The cash is available for extra travel costs, equipment and to pay helpers. For 2018–19 the maximum for students in England for a non-medical helper is £21,987 a year, or £16,489 a year for a part-time student. In addition, there is a maximum equipment allowance of £5,529 for the duration of the course and £1,847 for general expenses a year, although the government warns that most students get less than these amounts. There is also needs-based funding for travel costs. For postgraduates, the maximum award is a flat payment of £10,993 for full-time students and less for those studying part-time.

The National Health Service has its own Disabled Students Allowance system, worth a look if you are in the health field. On that theme, the NHS Business Services Authority has a Student Services Arm which runs the NHS Learning Support Grants and the NHS Education Support Grant, again worth investigating if you are planning to study health or social work.

Further sources of income

If you are feeling daunted by the potential costs of study, take comfort from this section, which outlines just some of the ways you can raise additional funds.

Taking a gap year

Gap years (see chapter 5) have become increasingly popular both for travelling and to earn some money to help pay for higher education. Many students will simply want to travel, but others will be more focused on boosting the bank balance in preparation for life as a student. Work opportunities can be structured or casual. An example of the structured variety in the science and engineering field is EDT (**www.etrust.org.uk**).

Further support

There are various types of support available for students in particular circumstances, other than the main loans, grants and bursaries.

» Undergraduates in financial difficulties can apply for help to their university's student hardship fund. These are allocated to provide support for anything from day-to-day study and living costs to unexpected or exceptional expenses. Many universities have committed to increasing the size of their hardship funds. The university decides which students need help and how much money to award them. These funds are often targeted at older or disadvantaged students, and at finalists who are in danger of dropping out. The sums range up to a few thousand pounds, are not repayable and do not count against other income.

» Students with children can apply for a Childcare Grant, worth up to £164.70 a week if you have one child and up to £282.36 a week if you have two or more children under 15, or under 17 with special needs; and a Parents' Learning Allowance, for help with course-related costs, of between £50 and £1,669 a year.

» Any students with a partner, or another adult family member who is financially dependent on them, can apply for an Adult Dependants' Grant of up to £2,925 a year for 2018/19.

Part-time work

The need to hold down a part-time job during term time is now a fact of life for almost half of students. Students from a working-class background are more likely to need to earn while they learn.

If you need to earn during term time, it is important to ensure that you do not work so many hours that it affects your studies. A survey by the NUS found that 59% of students who worked felt it had an impact on their studies, with 38% missing lectures and over a fifth failing to submit coursework because of their part-time jobs. You may find that new universities are better geared-up to cope with working students than more traditional institutions.

Student employment agencies, which can now be found on many university campuses, can help you get the balance right. These introduce employers with work to students seeking work, sometimes offering jobs within the university itself. But they also abide by codes of practice that regulate both minimum wages and the maximum number of hours worked in term time (typically 15 hours a week). Some firms, such as the big supermarkets, offer continuing part-time employment to their school part-time employees when they go to university. Some students make use of their expertise in areas like web design to earn some extra money, but most take on casual work in shops, restaurants, bars and call centres.

Most students, including those who don't work during term time, get a job during vacations. A Government survey found that 86% of students in their second year of study or above worked during their summer vacation. Most of this kind of work is casual, but some is formalised in a scheme like STEP (**www.step.org.uk**) or may be part of a sponsorship programme. Many vacation jobs are mundane, but it is possible to find more interesting work. Some students broaden their experience by working abroad, others work as film extras, take on tutoring, or do a variety of jobs at big events such as festivals. It is also a good idea to try to use the summer holidays to get some work experience in a field that has some relevance to your career aspirations. Even if you don't get paid, this can significantly enhance your chances of finding employment after graduation. Many new graduates end up being hired by businesses where they have previously worked.

What you will need to spend money on
Living costs

Certain costs are unavoidable. You have to have a roof over your head, eat enough, clothe yourself, and probably do a certain amount of travelling. But the cost of even these essential items can be cut significantly through a mixture of shopping around and careful budgeting. If you set aside a certain amount of money a week for food, you will find it goes much further if you keep takeaways and ready-meals to a minimum and stick to a shopping list when you go to a supermarket. Some catering outlets at your university or in the students' union may well offer good value meals, but probably the most economical way to eat is to cook and share meals with fellow students with whom you may be living in a shared house. Make sure you make full use of student travel cards and other offers and facilities available locally to help you cut the cost of travel. In certain locations, a bicycle is a worthwhile investment (as is buying a lock for it).

If you can keep your essential costs down, you will have more for what you would probably prefer to spend your money on – going out and personal items. Most students spend a proportion of their budget on socialising, and this is certainly an important part of the university experience. You can have plenty of fun and keep your leisure costs down by making the most of your student union's facilities and events.

It is easy to let "other costs" get out of hand to the extent that they start to eat into your budget for day-to-day living. Mobile phone bills are a case in point: the latest edition of an annual survey of student life by NatWest put average spending at £15 per month, but extras like downloading games or music, or sending pictures, can add significantly to your bill. Most of all, try to avoid getting tied up with an expensive and inflexible contract.

The same survey shows that students spend £121 a month on groceries and household items, £41 on alcohol, but under £15 on books and other course-related material. An earlier survey by Sodexo suggested that half of all students have altered their eating and socialising habits for lack of money.

SOUTHALL AND WEST LONDON COLLEGE LEARNING CENTRE

Studying costs

A NUS survey estimated that the average student spent about £1,000 a year on costs associated with course work and studying, mainly books and equipment. The amount you spend will be determined largely by the nature of your course. Additional financial support may be available for certain expenditure, but this is unlikely to cover you fully for spending on books, stationery, equipment, fieldwork or electives. A long reading list could prove very expensive if you tried to buy all the required books brand new. Find out as soon as possible which books are available either in your university library or local libraries. Another approach is to buy books second-hand from students who no longer need them. Your students' union or your university may run second-hand book sales or offer a service helping students to buy and sell books.

Overdrafts and credit cards

Other costs it is best to avoid are the more expensive forms of debt. Many banks offer free overdraft facilities for students, but if you go over the limit without prior arrangement, you can end up paying way over the odds for your borrowing. Credit cards can be useful if managed properly. The best way to manage a credit card is to set up a direct debit to pay off your balance in full every month, which means you will avoid paying any interest. One of the worst ways is to pay only the minimum charge each month, which can cost you a small fortune over a long period. If you are the kind of person who spends impulsively and doesn't keep track of your spending, you are probably better off without a credit card. Have a debit card instead. That way, you can't spend money you don't have.

Insurance

One kind of additional spending that can save you money is getting insurance cover for your possessions. Most students arrive at university with laptops and other goodies such as games consoles, sports equipment or musical instruments, mobile phones and bikes that are tempting to thieves. It is estimated that around a third of students fall victim to crime at some point during university. If you shop around, you should be able to get a reasonable amount of cover for these items without it costing you an arm and a leg. It may also be possible to add this cover cheaply to your parents' domestic contents policy.

Planning your budget

One in four freshers spend their first student loan instalment within a month, according to Endsleigh Insurance. But university websites, the National Union of Students (**https://www.nus.org.uk/en/advice/money-and-funding/money-management-tips**) and many others offer guidance on preparing a budget, usually with the basic headings provided for you to complete. First, list all your likely income (bursaries, loans, part-time work, savings, parental support) and then see how this compares with what you will spend. Try to be realistic, and not too optimistic, about both sides of the equation. With care, you will end up either only slightly in the red, or preferably far enough in the black for you to be able to afford things you would really like.

Above all, keep track of your finances so that your university experience isn't ruined by money worries, or finding you can't go to the ball because the cash machine has eaten your card. Spreadsheets make doing this simpler, and it is one skill you can learn at college that you are going to need for the rest of your life.

If all else fails, your campus almost certainly has a student money adviser who is a member of NASMA, the National Association of Student Money Advisers. You can find them via **www.nasma.org.uk**. NASMA reports that some students, especially those with children, are struggling financially. However, there are often bargains available in student shops well below high street prices.

More than two-thirds of young people aged 18–24 say they received no financial education at school. This chimes with the experience of NASMA, which finds that many students have low levels of basic financial awareness and planning ability. In addition, advisers have noticed that students are increasingly likely to spend money they cannot afford on TV and online gambling, so try to avoid this temptation.

Useful websites

For the basics of fees, loans, grants and other allowances:
www.gov.uk/student-finance
www.gov.uk/browse/education/student-finance

UCAS provides helpful advice: **www.ucas.com/ucas/undergraduate/undergraduate-finance-and-support**

For England, visit Student Finance England: **www.sfengland.slc.co.uk**
Office for Fair Access: **www.offa.org.uk**
Ofice for Students: **www.officeforstudents.org.uk**
For Wales, visit Student Finance Wales: **www.studentfinancewales.co.uk**
For Scotland, visit the Student Awards Agency for Scotland: **www.saas.gov.uk**
For Northern Ireland, visit Student Finance Northern Ireland: **www.studentfinanceni.co.uk**

All UK student loans are administered by the Student Loans Company: **www.slc.co.uk**

For guidance on the tax position of students, visit HM Revenue and Customs:
www.gov.uk/student-jobs-paying-tax

For finding out about availability of scholarships: **www.scholarship-search.org.uk**

8 Finding Somewhere to Live

Students spend an average of £130 a week on rent, according to the 2018 National Student Accommodation Survey, and the average maintenance loan provides only £139 a week. So it is no exaggeration to say that choosing where to live is the most important decision a student has to make, after the choice of course. Getting it right will have an impact on your entire university experience. It will determine how much money you have left for other activities, but more importantly, will influence your work and your whole state of mind. Particularly in your first year – and especially if it is your first time away from home – you are likely to be happier and more successful academically in accommodation of reasonable quality, preferably in a setting that helps you meet other students.

Fortunately, there is more choice than ever, with a range of private providers supplementing what universities and individual landlords provide. Many universities guarantee to provide accommodation for first-year undergraduates, and even those which cannot do this will offer help in finding somewhere of reasonable quality.

Of course, whatever you choose has to be affordable, but if your budget will stand it, you may well start off in a hall of residence or university flat. Three-quarters of applicants hope to live in halls, but only 60% actually do so, according to a 2016 report by Unite Students. The company's most recent UK survey showed halls gaining in popularity among second and third-year undergraduates, with the proportion opting for shared houses in their second year falling to little more than half.

With tastes apparently changing and the numbers going to university remaining high, student housing has become the biggest growth area in the property market. Rents have been rising at more than 3% a year and billions of pounds have been committed to student residences.

Particularly in the big student cities, but increasingly in other university towns as well, student accommodation now comes in all shapes and sizes – and prices. Despite considerable investment in housing by universities themselves, property consultant JLL estimates that more than a third of residential places for students are now in private hands. Most of the developments are in big complexes, but there are also niche providers such as Student Cribs, which convert properties to a rather higher spec than the traditional landlord and rent them to students.

Of the big providers, Unite Students has 50,000 beds in 22 towns and cities, some provided in partnership with universities and others in developments that serve more than one institution. UPP manages 35,000 residential places in complexes it has built for universities and where rents are negotiated with the university, often in consultation with the students' union. The National Student Accommodation Survey found that 10% of students were living in private halls in 2018, up from 8% two years ago.

There is now an award for the best private halls of residence – won in 2018 by Host, which has accommodation in 19 UK cities. A 2017 survey by StudentCrowd found that traditional campus universities such as St Andrews and Lancaster tend to have well-liked halls, although some inner-city institutions such as Northumbria also appear in the top 50.

For most students, it will not matter whether the owner of their accommodation is the university, a private landlord or larger organisation if the quality and the price are right. But successive reports by the National Union of Students (NUS) have told a story of increasingly unaffordable rents, often poor facilities and rushed decisions by inexperienced students. While those who can afford it – or think they can – are living in luxury, NUS has found others coping with mice, slugs, mould, cold, or all of these. So it is worth putting some effort into basic decisions on this subject.

Living at home

Although student loan repayments start only after graduation, many undergraduates are understandably cautious about the debts they run up. So the option of avoiding big accommodation charges is a tempting one for those who are attracted by a local university. The pattern of recent applications shows that the trend towards studying at home is accelerating, albeit only gradually, and there is no reason to think that this will change in the near future. Indeed, it may be a permanent shift, given the rising costs of student housing and the willingness of many young people to live with their parents well into their twenties.

Term-time type of accommodation of full-time and sandwich students

University maintained property	19.4%
Private-sector halls	7.8%
Parental/guardian home	18.8%
Own residence	16.7%
Other rented accommodation	29.8%
Other	3.4%
Not known	3.9%
HESA 2016 (adapted)	

The proportion of students living at home was already rising before undergraduate fees went up. For 2016/17 it was estimated that 338,000 students were living with their parents. Including mature students, many of whom live at home because of their own family commitments, the proportion is now close to 20%. Among younger students, women are more likely than men to stay at home, and Asian women are particularly likely to take this option. Home study is also four times more common at post-1992 universities than older institutions, again reflecting the larger numbers of mature students at the newer universities and a generally younger and more affluent student population at the older ones. Research has shown that these students spend less time on campus than others and are less involved in campus sports and activities. In London, University College has published advice for students on coping with long commuting. The National Student Accommodation Survey puts students' average journey time to lectures at 20 minutes, but 30 minutes in London.

For those considering studying from home, there are important considerations, of which the relationship with your parents and the availability of quiet space are the most obvious. You will still be entitled to a maintenance loan, although for 2018–19 it is a maximum of £7,324 in England, rather than £8,700 if you were living away from home outside London. There may be advantages in terms of academic work if the alternative involves shopping, cooking and cleaning as well as the other distractions of a student flat. The downside is that you may miss out on a lot of the student experience, especially the social scene and the opportunity to make new friends.

A 2018 report by the Higher Education Policy Institute found that students who live at home are less likely than others to say they are learning a lot at university, and a survey by the Student Engagement Partnership suggests that they find life unexpectedly "tiring, expensive and stressful". Issues affecting their quality of life include travel, security and the lack of their own space. But remember that you can always move on later if you think you are missing out – many initially home-based students do so in their second year.

Top Ten Problems for Student Tenants

1	Noisy housemates	52%
2	Damp	38%
3	Housemates stealing food	37%
4	Lack of water/heating	34%
5	Disruptive building work	22%
6	Rodents and pests	18%
7	Inappropriate landlord visits	14%
8	Dangerous living conditions	8%
9	Break-in or burglary	6%
10	Bedbugs	4%

Source: National Student Accommodation Survey 2018

Based on 2,246 responses **www.savethestudent.org**

Living away from home

Most of those who can afford it, still see moving away to study as integral to the rite of passage that student life represents. Some have little option, for instance if the course they want is not available locally in spite of the expansion of higher education. Others are happy to travel to secure their ideal place and widen their experience. If you insist on a degree from a household-name global university, the odds are that you'll have to travel to get there.

For the lucky majority, the search for accommodation will be over quickly because the university can offer a place in one of its halls of residence or self-catering flats. The choice may come down to the type of accommodation and whether or not to do your own cooking. But for others, there will be an anxious search for a room in a strange city. Most universities will help with this if they cannot offer accommodation of their own.

Going to university will oblige those who take the 'away' route to think for the first time about the practicalities of living independently. This can make the decision about where to live – in terms of location and the type of accommodation – doubly difficult. It may even influence your choice of university, since there are big differences across the sector and the country in the cost and standard of accommodation, and in its availability.

How much will it cost?

Rents vary so much across the UK that national averages are almost meaningless. The 2018 NatWest Student Living Index found a range from £339 a month in Belfast and £373 in Glasgow to £668 in London and £604 in Cambridge, the next-dearest. All but five of the 35 student cities in the survey averaged more than £400 a month. However accurate such figures may be, they conceal a wide range of actual rents, particularly in London. This was always the case, but has become even more obvious with the rapid growth of a luxury market at the same time as many students are willing to accept sub-standard accommodation to keep costs down.

A series of recent reports suggest that the need for good Wi-Fi has overtaken reasonable rents as students' top priority in choosing accommodation. A big bedroom with a double bed was the other top priority for British students, according to a Europe-wide survey for the Uniplaces website. But obviously you have to be able to afford the rent in the first place. The last annual NUS/Unipol survey found a dwindling amount of "affordable" housing, judged against the loans available to students, adding that "The challenge of affordability is a long-standing one, and seems to grow more severe with each cycle of this survey." Another issue raised in this survey is the need for cash up front for deposits, and/or a guarantee, probably from your parents, that the rent will be paid.

Most universities with a range of accommodation find that their most expensive rooms fill up first, and that students appear to have higher expectations than they used to. More than half of all the rooms in the NUS survey had ensuite facilities.

It is important to remember that both your living costs and your potential earnings should be factored into your calculations when deciding where to live. While living costs in London are by far the highest, potential part-time earnings are, too. Taking account of both income and outgoings, the NatWest index made Hull the most affordable student city, followed by Cardiff and Leicester. Liverpool was the dearest on this measure, ahead of London. Students were found to earn the most in London, followed by Canterbury – £1388 and £1368 per term-time month respectively.

The choices you have

The NUS puts accommodation into 16 categories, ranging from luxurious university halls to a bedsit in a shared house. The choices include:

» University hall of residence, with individual study bedrooms and a full catering service. Many will have ensuite accommodation.
» University halls, flats or houses where you have to provide your own food.
» Private, purpose-built student accommodation.
» Rented houses or flats, shared with fellow students.
» Living at home.
» Living as a lodger in a private house.

This chapter will help you decide where you would like to live and whether you can afford it.

Making your choice

Finance is not the only factor you should consider when deciding where to live. It is worth investing time to find the right place, and to avoid the false economy of choosing somewhere cheap, where you may end up feeling depressed and isolated. Most students who drop out of university do so in the first few months, when homesickness and loneliness can be felt most acutely.

Being warm and well fed is likely to have a positive effect on your studies. Perhaps for these reasons, most undergraduates in their first year plump for living in university halls, which offer a convenient, safe and reliable standard of accommodation, along with a supportive community environment. The sheer number of students – especially first years – in halls also makes this form of accommodation an easy way of meeting people from a wide range of courses and making friends.

If meals are included, this extra adds further peace of mind both for students and their parents. The last NUS survey, which covered students in 2015–16, found that the difference in cost between full board and self-catering was less than £40 a week on average, not unreasonable for two hot meals a day. But only 7.6% of places are now catered, compared with 27% in 1994. Most are self-catering, with groups of students sharing a kitchen.

Wherever you choose to live, there are some general points you will need to consider, such as how safe the neighbourhood seems to be, and how long it might take you to travel to and from the university, especially during rush hour. A survey of travel time between term-time accommodation and the university found that most students in London can expect a commute of at least 30 minutes and often over an hour, while students living in Wales are usually much less than 30 minutes away from their university.

In chapter 15, we provide details of what accommodation each university offers, covering the number of places, the costs, and their policy towards first-year students.

What universities offer

You might think that opting to live in university accommodation is the most straightforward choice, especially since first-year students are invariably given priority in the allocation of places in halls of residence, and it is possible to arrange university accommodation in advance and at a distance. Searching for private housing can often be a matter of having to be in the right place at the right time. However, you may still need to select from a range of options, because most universities will have a variety of accommodation on offer. You will need to consider which best suits your pocket and your preferred lifestyle.

New student accommodation

At the top end of the market, private firms usually lead the way, at least in the bigger student cities. Companies such as UPP, Unite Students and Liberty Living offer some of the most luxurious student accommodation the UK has seen, either in partnerships with universities or in their own right. Rooms in these complexes are nearly always ensuite and with internet access, and may include other facilities such as your own phone line and satellite TV. Shared kitchens are top-quality and fitted out with the latest equipment.

This kind of accommodation naturally comes at a higher price, but offers the advantages of flexibility both in living arrangements and through a range of payment options. An earlier NUS survey found little difference between the rents charged by higher education institutions for their own accommodation and those for rooms managed by private companies under contract, but private providers operating outside institutional links charged over £20 a week more.

Halls of residence

Many new or recently refurbished university-owned halls offer a standard of accommodation that is not far short of the privately-built residences. This is partly because rooms in these halls can be offered to conference delegates during vacations. Even though these halls are also at the pricier end of the spectrum, you will probably find that they are in great demand, and you may have to get your name down quickly to secure one of the fancier rooms. That said, you can often get a guarantee of some kind of university accommodation if you give a firm acceptance of an offered place by a certain date in the summer. If you have gained your place through Clearing, this option may not apply, although rooms in private halls might still be on offer at this stage.

While a few halls are single-sex, most are mixed, and often house over 500 students. In student villages the numbers are now counted in thousands. They are therefore great places for making friends and becoming part of the social scene. Most of the university applicants surveyed for the 2017 Reality Check report by the Higher Education Policy Institute, in association with

Unite, regarded the course and their accommodation as the two key places to meet new friends. Many also agreed that the ability to make friends was more important than the specification of the accommodation. Two-thirds put a priority on the availability of social events where they lived, particularly in their first term.

One possible downside is that big student housing developments can also be noisy places where it can be difficult at times to get down to some work. In another Unite survey, 44% of those responding identified noise as the biggest challenge in student accommodation. For those who had experienced it, peace and quiet was a higher priority than access to public transport or good nightlife. The more successful students learn, before too many essay deadlines and exams start to loom, to get the balance right between all-night partying and escaping to the library for some undisturbed study time. Remember that some libraries, especially new ones, are now open 24 hours a day.

University self-catering accommodation

An alternative to halls, now offered by most universities, are smaller, self-catering properties fitted out with a shared kitchen and other living areas. The Reality Check report found that 83% of female university applicants, and 79% of the men, felt confident of their cooking abilities. The women were also more likely to say they could clean the house and cope with laundry. But students looking for a more independent and flexible lifestyle often prefer this option, which is now the norm at many universities. As well as having to feed yourself, you may also have heating and lighting bills to pay. University properties are often on campus or nearby, so travel costs should not be a problem.

Catering in university accommodation

Many universities have responded to a general increase in demand from students for a more independent lifestyle by providing more flexible catering facilities. A range of eateries, from fast food outlets to more traditional refectories, can usually be found on campus or in student villages. Students in university accommodation may be offered pay-as-you-eat deals as an alternative to full-board packages.

What after the first year?

After your first year of living in university residences you may well wish, and will probably be expected, to move out to other accommodation. The main exceptions are the collegiate universities – particularly Oxford and Cambridge – which may allow you to stay on in college for another year or two, and particularly for your final year. Students from outside the EU are also often guaranteed accommodation. At a growing number of universities, where there is a sufficiently large stock of residential accommodation, it is not uncommon for students to move back in to halls for their final year.

Practical details

Whether or not you have decided to start out in university accommodation, you will probably be expected to sign an agreement to cover your rent. Contract lengths vary. They can be for around 40 weeks, which includes the Christmas and Easter holiday periods, or for just the length of the three university terms. These term-time contracts are common when a university uses its rooms for conferences during vacations, and you will be required to leave your room empty during these weeks. It is therefore advisable to check whether the university has secure storage space for you to leave your belongings. Otherwise you will have to make arrangements to take all your belongings home or to store them privately between terms. International students may be offered special arrangements by which they can stay in halls during the short vacation periods. Organisations like **www.hostuk.org** can arrange for international students to stay in a UK family home at holiday times such as Christmas.

Parental purchases

One option for affluent families is to buy a house or flat and take in student lodgers. This might not be the safe financial bet it once appeared, but it is still tempting for many parents. Agents Knight Frank have had a student division since 2007, mostly working with new developers to sell specially adapted homes. Those who are considering this route tend to do so from their first year of study to maximise the return on the investment.

Being a lodger or staying in a hostel

A small number of students live as a lodger in a family home, an option most frequently taken up by international students. The usual arrangement is for a study bedroom and some meals to be provided, while other facilities such as the washing machine are shared. Students with particular religious affiliations or those from certain countries may wish to consider living in a hostel run by a charity catering for a specific group. Most of these are in London.

Renting from the private sector

Around a third of students live in privately rented flats or houses. Every university city or town is awash with such accommodation, available via agencies or direct from landlords. Indeed, this type of accommodation has grown to the point where so-called "student ghettoes", in which local residents feel outnumbered, have become hot political issues in some cities. Into this traditional market in rented flats and houses have come the new private-sector complexes and residences, adding to the options. Some are on university campuses, but others are in city centres and usually open to students of more than one university. Examples can be seen online; some sites are listed at the end of this chapter.

While there are always exceptions, a much more professional attitude and approach to managing rented accommodation has emerged among smaller providers, thanks to a combination of greater regulation and increasing competition. Nevertheless, it is wise to take certain precautions when seeking out private residences.

How to start looking for rented property

Contact your university's accommodation service and ask for its list of approved rented properties. Some have a Student Accommodation Accreditation Scheme, run in collaboration with the local council. To get onto an approved list under such schemes, landlords must show they are adhering to basic standards of safety and security, such as having an up-to-date gas and electric safety certificate. University accommodation officers should also be able to advise you on any hidden charges. For instance, you may be asked to pay a booking or reservation fee to secure a place in a particular property, and fees for references or drawing up a tenancy agreement are sometimes charged. The practice of charging a "joining fee", however, has been outlawed.

It would be wise to speak to older students with first-hand experience of renting in the area. Certain companies in the area may be notorious among second and third years and you can try to avoid them. In addition to websites and accommodation services designed for students, you can also use sites such as Gumtree that cater for the population at large.

Making a choice

Once you have made an initial choice of the area you would like to live in and the size of property you are looking for, the next stage is to look at possible places. If you plan to share, it is important that you all have a look at the property. If you will be living by yourself, take a friend with you when you go to view a property, since he or she can help you assess what you see objectively, and avoid any irrational or rushed on-the-spot decisions. Don't let yourself be pushed into signing on the dotted line there and then. Take time to visit and consider a number of options, as well as checking out the local facilities, transport and the general environment at various times of the day and different days of the week.

If you are living in private rented accommodation, it is likely that at least some of your neighbours will not be students. Local people often welcome students, but resentment can build up, particularly in areas of towns and cities that are dominated by student housing. It is important to respect your neighbours' rights, and not to behave in an anti-social manner.

Preparing for sharing

The people you are planning to share a house with may have some habits that you find at least mildly irritating. How well you cope with some of the downsides of sharing will be partly down to the kind of person you are – where you are on the spectrum between laid back and highly strung – but it will help a lot if you are co-habiting with people whose outlook on day-to-day living is not too far out of line with your own. According to Unite Students, 31% of female students find sharing more difficult than they had expected, compared with 22% of men.

Some students sign for their second year houses as early as November. While it is good to be ahead of the rush, you may not yet have met your best friends at this stage. If you have not selected your own group of friends, universities and landlords can help by taking personal preferences and lifestyle into account when grouping tenants together.

Potential issues to consider when deciding whether to move into a shared house include whether any of the housemates smoke, or own a loud musical instrument. It will also be important to sort out broadband arrangements that will work for everyone in the house, and that you will be able to arrange access to the university system. It is a good idea to agree a rota for everyone to share in the household cleaning chores from the start. Otherwise, it is almost certain that you will live in a state of unhygienic squalor or that one or two individuals will be left to clear up everyone else's mess.

The practical details about renting

It is a good idea to ask whether your house is covered by an accreditation scheme or code of standards. Such codes provide a clear outline of what constitutes good practice as well as the responsibilities of both landlords and tenants. Adhering to schemes like the National Code of Standards for Larger Student Developments compiled by Accreditation Network UK (**www.anuk.org.uk**) may well become a requirement for larger properties, including those managed by universities, now that the Housing Act is in force.

At the very least, make sure that if you are renting from a private landlord, you have his or her telephone number and home address. Some can be remarkably difficult to contact when repairs are needed or deposits are due to be returned.

Multiple occupation

If you are renting a private house it may be subject to the 2004 Housing Act in England and Wales (similar legislation applies in Scotland and Northern Ireland). Licenses are compulsory for all private Houses in Multiple Occupation (HMOs) with three or more storeys and that house five or more unrelated residents. The provisions of the Act also allow local authorities to designate whole areas in which HMOs of all sizes must be licensed. The regulations may be applied in sections of university towns and cities where most students live. This means that a house must be licensed, well-managed and must meet various health and safety standards, and its owner subject to various financial regulations.

Tenancy agreements

Whatever kind of accommodation you go for, you must be sure to have all the paperwork in order and be clear about what you are signing up to before you move in. If you are taking up residence in a shared house, flat or bedsit, the first document you will have to grapple with is a tenancy agreement or lease offering you an 'assured shorthold tenancy'. Since this is a binding legal document, you should be prepared to go through every clause with a fine-tooth comb. Remember that it is much more difficult to make changes or overcome problems arising from unfair agreements once you are a tenant than before you become one.

You would be well advised to seek help in the likely event of your not fully understanding some of the clauses. Your university accommodation office or students' union is a good place to start – they should know all the ins and outs and have model tenancy agreements to refer to. A Citizens Advice Bureau or Law Advice Centre should also be able to offer you free advice. In particular, watch out for clauses that may make you jointly responsible for the actions of others with whom you are sharing. If you name a parent as a guarantor to cover any costs not paid by you, they may also be liable for charges levied on all tenants for damage that was not your fault. A rent review clause could allow your landlord to increase the rent at will, whereas without such a clause, they are restricted to one rent rise a year. Make sure you keep a copy of all documents, and get a receipt (and keep it somewhere safe) for anything you have had to pay for that is the landlord's responsibility.

Security in rented accommodation

Students in private housing are twice as likely to be burgled as those in university halls. When looking at accommodation, use this NUS security checklist:

» Check that the front and back doors are fitted with five-lever mortise locks in addition to standard catch locks.
» Make sure the door to your room has a lock, and always lock up when you leave it, especially for long periods such as during vacations.
» Check the locks and catches on accessible windows, especially those at ground-floor level.
» Before you move in, try to talk to neighbours about how safe the area is and whether there have been many instances of burglary.
» Ask your landlord to ensure that all previous tenants and holders of keys no longer have copies.
» If you find a property that you like but have some security concerns, discuss these with the letting agency or landlord.

Contracts with private landlords tend to be longer than for university accommodation. They will frequently commit you to paying rent for 52 weeks of the year. Leaving aside the cost, there are probably more advantages than disadvantages to this kind of arrangement. It means you don't have to move out during vacation periods, which you will have to in most university halls. You can store your belongings in your room when you go away (but don't leave anything really valuable behind if you can help it). You may be able to negotiate a rent discount for those periods when you are not staying in the property. The other advantage, particularly important for cash-strapped students, is that you have a base from which to find work and hold down a job during the vacations. Term dates are also not as dictatorial as they might be in halls; if you rent your own house then you can come back when you wish.

Deposits

On top of the agreed rent, you will need to provide a deposit or bond to cover any breakages or damage. This will probably set you back the equivalent of another month's rent. The deposit should be returned, less any deductions, at the end of the contract. However, be warned that disputes over the return of deposits are common, with the question of what constitutes reasonable wear and tear often the subject of disagreements between landlord and tenant. To protect students from unscrupulous landlords who withheld deposits without good reason, the 2004 Housing Act introduced a National Tenancy Deposit Scheme under which deposits are held by an independent body. This is designed to ensure that deposits are fairly returned, and that any disputes are resolved swiftly and cheaply. You may also be asked to find guarantors for your rent payments – in practice, usually your parents.

Inventories and other paperwork

You should get an inventory and schedule of condition of everything in the property. This is another document that you should check very carefully – and make sure that everything listed is as described. Write on the document anything that is different. The NUS even suggests taking photographs of rooms and equipment when you first move in (setting the correct date on your camera), to provide you with additional proof should any dispute arise when your contract ends and you want to get your deposit back. If you are not offered an inventory, then make one of your own. You should have someone else witness and sign this, send it to your landlord, and keep your own copy. Keeping in contact with your landlord throughout the year and developing a good relationship with him or her will also do you no harm, and may be to your advantage in the long run.

You should ask your landlord for a recent gas safety certificate issued by a qualified CORGI engineer, a fire safety certificate covering the furnishings, and a record of current gas and electricity meter readings. Take your own readings of meters when you move in to make sure these match up with what you have been given, or make your own records if the landlord doesn't supply this information. This also applies to water meters if you are expected to pay water rates (although this isn't usually the case). The NUS issues its own advice on how to keep down energy bills, at http://studentswitchoff.org/save-energy-rented-accommodation.

Finally, students are not liable for Council Tax. If you are sharing a house only with other full-time students, then you will not have to pay it. However, you may be liable to pay a proportion of the Council Tax bill if you are sharing with anyone who is not a full-time student. You may need to get a Council Tax exemption certificate from your university as evidence that you do not need to pay Council Tax.

Safety and security

Once you have arrived and settled in, remember to take care of your own safety and the security of your possessions. You are particularly vulnerable as a fresher, when you are still getting used to your new-found independence. This may help explain why so many students are burgled or robbed in the first six weeks of the academic year. Take care with valuable portable items such as mobile phones, tablet computers and laptops, all of which are tempting for criminals. Ensure you don't have them obviously on display when you are out and about and that you have insurance cover. If your mobile phone is stolen, call your network or 08701 123123 to immobilise it. Students' unions, universities and the police will provide plenty of practical guidance when you arrive. Following their advice will reduce the chance of you becoming a victim of crime, and help you to enjoy living in the new surroundings of your chosen university town.

Useful websites

For advice on a range of housing issues, visit: **www.nus.org.uk/en/advice/housing-advice**

The Shelter website has separate sections covering different housing regulations in England, Wales, Scotland and Northern Ireland: **www.shelter.org.uk**

As examples of providers of private hall accommodation, visit:
www.upp-ltd.com
http://www.unitestudents.com/
www.libertyliving.co.uk
http://thestudenthousingcompany.com
www.student-cribs.com

A number of sites will help you find accommodation and/or potential housemates, including:
www.accommodationforstudents.com
www.uniplaces.com
www.sturents.com,
 www.studentpad.co.uk
www.studentcrowd.com
www.let4students.com
http://student.spareroom.co.uk
http://uk.easyroommate.com

Accreditation Network UK is at **anuk.org.uk**

www.hostuk.org helps international students meet British people and families in their homes

9 Enjoying University Sport

There may never be a better opportunity to pursue your favourite sport, take up a new one, or simply to keep fit than during your undergraduate years. Practically every university now has excellent sports facilities and even the most demanding course timetable will leave room to take advantage of them. More than half of all students exercise regularly, according to research published in 2018, and another 40% do so for at least half an hour a week.

The quality of the sports facilities will not be the clinching factor in most applicants' choice of university – and nor should it be – but nearly a third say it played some part in their decision-making. Universities are well aware of this and have upgraded their provision accordingly. Some of the best and most extensive sports facilities in the UK are on campuses. Such has been the scale of investment in recent years that nationally, they are said to be worth an astonishing £20 billion. Birmingham is planning a £55m sports centre, including the only 50m pool in the region, to add to its already impressive facilities. Nottingham opened a £40m sports complex in 2016, which was one of the factors behind its selection as our latest Sports University of the Year. Solent is opening a £28m sports development in the next few months. Such facilities attract elite performers and are often used for high-level teaching, but they are also available for day-to-day use by undergraduates.

Especially at the big universities – but also at many of the smaller ones – sporting provision is now both diverse and high quality. Half of all universities were chosen as training bases for Great Britain squads in the run-up to the 2012 Olympic Games and 30 hosted other nations' teams. Comparing such facilities is not easy, but most universities display them prominently on their websites. There are brief descriptions of the bigger developments in the university profiles in Chapter 14.

At the elite level, university sport has never been stronger. At the Rio Olympics in 2016, over half Team GB's medals were won by university students or alumni. Five of the gold medal-winning ladies hockey team (and the coach) were Loughborough graduates, for example. Indeed, Loughborough would have been 17th in the overall medal table in Rio, and it was not the only successful university – St Mary's, Twickenham, would have been 25th. Such successes are the result of considerable investment in sports scholarships and training programmes, as well as campus facilities.

Naturally, most students will never aspire to such heights, but may still welcome the chance to use top-grade facilities. Research for British Universities and Colleges Sport (BUCS) suggests that at least 1.7 million students take part in regular physical activity, from gym sessions to competitive individual or team sports. There are good reasons, beyond fitness, for doing so, according to BUCS reports. Those who were physically active expect higher grades and are more confident of securing a graduate job than less active students. And in 2013, graduates who had played and/or volunteered in sport were found to be earning at least £4,000 more than those who had not, and were 25% less likely to have been unemployed. Nine out of ten employers thought that participation in university sport helped to develop valuable skills in potential employees.

Sporting opportunities

Some specialist facilities may be reserved at times for elite performers, but all universities are conscious of the need for wider access. Surveys show that two-thirds of sessions at university sports facilities are taken by students, roughly a quarter by the local community and the rest by staff. Many institutions still encourage departments not to schedule lectures and seminars on Wednesday afternoons, to give students free time for sport. There are student-run clubs for all the major sports and – particularly at the larger universities – a host of minor ones. In addition, there are high-quality gyms, with staff on hand to devise personalised training regimes and to run popular activities such as Zumba and Pilates. The cost varies widely between universities, and membership fees can represent a large amount to lay out at the start of the year, but most provide good value if you are going to be a regular user.

Sport for all

For most universities, it is in the area of "sport for all" that most attention has been focused. Beginners are welcomed and coaching provided in a range of sports, from Ultimate Frisbee to tai-chi, that would be difficult to match outside the higher education system. Check on university websites to see whether your usual sport is available, but do not be surprised if you come across a new favourite when you have the opportunity to try out something different as a student. Many universities have programmes designed to encourage students to take up a new sport, with expert coaching provided.

All universities are conscious of the need to provide for a spread of ability – and disability. Sports scholarships for elite performers are now commonplace, but there will be plenty of opportunities, too, for beginners. University teams demand a hefty commitment in terms of training and practice sessions – often several times a week – and in many sports standards are high. University teams often compete in local and national leagues.

For those who are looking for competition at a lower level, or whose interests are primarily social, there are thriving internal, or intramural, leagues. These provide opportunities for groups from halls of residence or faculties, or even a group of friends, to form a team and participate on a regular basis. A BUCS survey found 41,000 participants in the intramural programmes of 41 institutions. The largest programme was at the University of Brighton, where more than 6,000 students were playing sports ranging from football, rugby and badminton to softball, orienteering and fencing. Nor is university sport a male preserve – student teams were among the pioneers in mixed sport and are still strong in areas such as women's cricket, football and rugby.

Some universities have cut back sports budgets, but representative sport continues to grow. There are home nations competitions at international level in some sports and in London, 35 institutions take part in the London Universities Sport League. This now involves almost 450 teams – male, female and mixed – competing at a variety of levels in 14 different sports, not all of which are in the main national competitions.

First-year sport

Halls of residence and university-owned flats will often have their own sports teams. At some universities, these are part of the intramural network of leagues, while others have separate arrangements for first years. In such cases, a Sports Captain, elected the year previously as part of the Junior Common Room, takes responsibility for organising trials and picking the teams, as well as arranging fixtures for the year. Hall sport is a great way of meeting like-minded people from your accommodation and over the course of the years, friendly rivalries often develop with other halls or flats. Generally there will be teams for football (both five and 11-a-side), hockey, netball, cricket, tennis, squash, badminton and even golf. If your lodgings are smaller then don't worry, they are often twinned with similar flats to enable as many first-year students as possible to get involved in freshers' sport.

Other opportunities

You may even end up wanting to coach, umpire or referee – and this is another area in which higher education has much to offer. Many university clubs and sports unions provide subsidised courses for students to gain qualifications that may be of use to the individual in later life, as well as benefiting university teams in the short term. Or you might want to try your hand at some sports administration, with an eye to your career. In most universities there is a sports (or athletic) union, with autonomy from the main students' union, which organises matches and looks after the wider interests of those who play. There are plenty of opportunities for those seeking an apprenticeship in the art of running a club, or larger organisation. Solent University, for example, deploys students on volunteer coaching placements in local schools and community groups, working with Southampton FC's Saints Foundation. The placements increase a university's community engagement as well as enhancing student employability.

Universities that excel

A few universities are known particularly for sport. Exeter and Loughborough men's teams have played national Premier League hockey, for example, while Bath, Loughborough and Northumbria have teams in the Netball Super League. The University of London women's volleyball team has won the English Volleyball Championships, and "Team Bath" have tasted success in the FA Cup. Several of this elite group had a head start as former physical education colleges. Loughborough is undoubtedly the best-known of them, but Leeds Beckett and Brunel are others with a similar pedigree. Other universities with different traditions, such as Bath and East Anglia, also have a variety of outstanding facilities, while the likes of Stirling and Cardiff Metropolitan have the same in a narrower range of sports.

As in so much else, Oxford and Cambridge are in a category of their own. The Boat Race and the Varsity Match (in rugby union) are the only UK university sporting events with a big popular following – although there are varsity matches in many university cities that have become big occasions for students – and there is a good standard of competition in other sports. But you should not assume that success in school sport will be a passport to an Oxbridge place, for the days of special consideration for sporty undergraduates are long since over.

Representative sport

Competitive standards have been rising in university sport, as have the numbers taking part in it. More than 6,000 students competed in ten sports at the 2018 BUCS Nationals in Sheffield. BUCS (**www.bucs.org.uk**) runs competitions in 47 sports, and ranks participating institutions based on the points earned in the competitive programme. Over 4,700 teams compete in BUCS leagues, making the organisation the largest provider of league sport across Europe. More than a third of those teams are female and many others mixed. There is also international competition in a number of sports, and the World Student Games have become one of the biggest occasions in the international sporting calendar.

BUCS is the national organisation for higher education sport in the UK, providing a comprehensive, multi-sport competition structure and managing the development of services and facilities for participative, grass-roots sport and healthy campuses, through to high-performance elite athletes. Its mission is to raise the profile of student sport and drive the university sport agenda by influencing government and key stakeholders in the sector.

British Universities and Colleges Sports (BUCS) league table positions

University	2017–18	2016–17	2015–16	University	2017–18	2016–17	2015–16
Loughborough	1	1	1	Cambridge	31	18	16
Nottingham	2	4	4	Sheffield Hallam	32	20	23
Durham	3	2	2	Strathclyde	33	26	34
Exeter	4	5	5	Manchester Metropolitan (MMU)	34	36	38
Bath	5	6	7	Essex	35	34	32
Edinburgh	6	3	3	West of England (UWE)	36	28	35
Bristol	7	9	13	Leicester	37	39	46
Birmingham	8	7	6	Oxford Brookes	38	35	31
Newcastle	9	10	9	Reading	39	44	39
Cardiff	10	11	11	East Anglia	40	43	55
Stirling	11	12	17	Aberdeen	41	50	42
Nottingham Trent	12	15	19	York	42	46	40
Leeds Beckett	13	14	12	Brunel	43	38	36
Northumbria	14	8	8	Lancaster	44	49	45
Oxford	15	13	10	Hertfordshire	45	45	44
Manchester	16	17	18	Queen Mary, University of London	46	=64	58
Swansea	17	33	33	Portsmouth	47	55	41
St Andrews	18	25	29	Kent	48	48	51
Sheffield	19	19	21	Dundee	49	54	54
Cardiff Metropolitan	20	21	15	Sussex	50	41	43
Glasgow	21	22	26	Plymouth	51	51	53
Imperial College	22	24	24	East London	52	42	48
University College London	23	27	27	LSE	53	53	62
Leeds	24	16	14	St Mary's, Twickenham	54	47	59
King's College London	25	37	37	Brighton	55	61	52
Warwick	26	23	20	Gloucestershire	56	40	49
Liverpool	27	30	25	Chichester	=57	56	57
Bournemouth	28	31	30	Royal Holloway	=57	62	56
Surrey	29	29	28	Derby	59	57	64
Southampton	30	32	22	South Wales	60	59	50

University	2017–18	2016–17	2015–16	University	2017–18	2016–17	2015–16
Liverpool John Moores	61	66	69	Teesside	=105	103	101
Heriot-Watt	62	=64	60	Universities at Medway	=105	=122	
Coventry	63	52	47	UCFB (Football Business)	107	116	
Worcester	64	60	61	Leeds Trinity	108	107	116
Hartpury University centre	65	=68	76	Highlands and Islands	109	112	110
De Montfort	66	75	84	Bedfordshire	110	=95	82
Bangor	67	63	66	University of London	111	71	77
Chester (Chester)	68	72	72	St George's, London	112	108	107
Aberystwyth	69	=68	70	Royal Agricultural University	113	115	118
Robert Gordon	70	74	68	Bolton	114	=136	143
Lincoln	71	73	67	Cranfield University	115	117	
Central Lancashire	72	67	63	London Metropolitan	116	124	131
Hull	73	76	79	Royal Veterinary College	=117	126	—
Solent	74	58	71	Bishop Burton College, Yorks	=117	111	—
Canterbury Christ Church	75	78	73	Greenwich	119	113	111
Keele	76	77	73	Bath Spa	120	119	119
City, London	77	86	87	FXU (Falmouth and Exeter Union)	121	104	104
Plymouth, Marjon	78	82	75	Suffolk	122	=154	141
Anglia Ruskin	79	70	65	University of the Arts London	123	=128	130
Edinburgh Napier	80	79	83	Newman	124	118	126
Edge Hill	81	80	85	Chester (Warrington)	=125	130	124
Abertay	82	85	93	Wrexham Glyndŵr	=125	=138	125
Winchester	83	100	100	Queen's, Belfast	=127	106	102
Middlesex	84	81	78	SOAS	=127	132	142
Kingston	85	84	80	Doncaster College & Uni centre	=127	135	
Glasgow Caledonian	86	88	90	Goldsmiths	130	121	138
West of Scotland	87	=95	109	West London	=131	=122	135
Staffordshire	88	90	99	Writtle University College	=131	=146	—
York St John	89	94	86	Scotland's Rural College	133	—	—
Sunderland	90	99	92	Edinburgh College	134	=136	—
Aston	91	89	97	Cumbria	135	145	121
London South Bank	92	92	96	South Glos & Stroud College	=136	=128	—
Salford	93	=101	88	Brooksby Melton College	=136		
Harper Adams	94	98	103	Tottenham Hotspur Foundation	=136	=138	—
Bradford	95	87	89	University for Creative Arts	139	152	144
Roehampton	96	91	91	Trinity Saint David (Swansea)	=140	127	127
Wolverhampton	97	93	98	Bishop Grosseteste	=140	=138	135
Queen Margaret Edinburgh	98	110	115	New College Lanarkshire	=140	=148	—
Liverpool Hope	99	105	105	AECC University College	=140		
Northampton	100	83	81	Moulton College	=140		
Huddersfield	101	=101	95	Trinity Saint David (Carmarthen)	145	125	108
Birmingham City	102	109	117	City of Glasgow College	146	=154	—
Westminster	103	114	112	Leeds City College	=147		
Buckinghamshire New	104	97	94	Richmond, American University	=147	=138	—

University	2017–18	2016–17	2015–16	University	2017–18	2016–17	2015–16
University College Birmingham	=147	=138	128	West College Scotland	=151	=138	
UCEN Manchester	=147			Glasgow Clyde College	=151	153	
West Lothian College	=151	=154		Glasgow Kelvin College	=151	=148	–
Regent's University, London	=151			Ravensbourne	=151		
Dundee & Angus College	=151	134					

University sports facilities

Even the smallest university should provide reasonable indoor and outdoor sports facilities – a sports hall, modern gym equipment and outdoor pitches (usually including an all-weather surface and floodlights). Many will also have a swimming pool and extras such as climbing walls, but some smaller universities make arrangements for students to use local sports centres and clubs when it is not feasible to provide for minority sports. The same goes for the really expensive sports, like golf, which is usually the subject of an arrangement with one or more local clubs that give students a discount. Specialist facilities, like boat houses and climbing huts, obviously depend on location, but the most landlocked university is likely to have a sailing club that organises regular activities away from campus, and a skiing club that runs at least annual trips to the mountains.

Developments at many universities have come in partnership with local authorities or national sporting bodies. University campuses are ideal locations for national coaching centres, and many have been established in recent years. Although elite coaching generally takes place in closed sessions, students may occasionally find themselves rubbing shoulders with star players.

Universities now boast a significant proportion of the UK's 50-metre pools, for example, the latest of which, at the University of Surrey, has some of the most advanced facilities in the country. Innovative schemes include Leeds Beckett's development of the Headingley cricket and rugby league grounds, providing teaching space for students during the week and improved facilities for players and spectators on match days.

Beyond scrutinising the website and prospectus for the extent of university facilities, there are two important questions to ask: how much do they cost and where are they? Neither is easy to track down on the average university website.

How much?

University prospectuses tend to major on the quality of the sports facilities without being as forthcoming about the prices. Students who are used to free (if inferior) facilities at school often get a nasty surprise when they find that they are expected to pay to join the Athletic Union and then pay again to use the gym or play football. Because most university sport is subsidised, the charges are reasonable compared to commercial facilities, but the best deal may require a considerable outlay at the start. Some campus gyms and swimming pools now charge more than £300 a year, for example, which is still considerably cheaper than paying per visit if you intend to use the facilities regularly (and provides an incentive to carry on doing so). Some universities are offering sports facility membership as part of the £9,250 fee, but most offer a variety of peak and off-peak membership packages – some for the entire length of your course.

Outdoor sports are usually charged by the hour, although clubs will also charge a membership fee. You may be required to pay up to £60 for membership of the Athletic Union (although not all universities require this). Fees for intramural sport are seldom substantial; teams will usually pay a fee for the season, while courts for racket sports tend to be marginally cheaper per session than in other clubs.

How far away?

The other common complaint by students is that the playing fields are too far from the campus – understandable in the case of city-centre universities, but still aggravating if you have to arrange your own transport. This is where campus universities have a clear advantage. For the rest, there has to be some trade-off between the quality of outdoor facilities and the distance you have to travel to use them. But universities are beginning to realise that long journeys depress usage of important (and expensive) facilities, and some have tried to find suitable land closer to lectures and halls of residence. Indoor sports centres should all be within easy reach.

Sport as a degree subject

Sports science and other courses associated with sport had seen consistent increases in applications until the imposition of higher fees, and their popularity has now returned. Over 15,000 students started courses in 2017, making it one of the ten most popular degree choices. A separate ranking for the subject is on page 274. If you are hoping to be rewarded with an academic qualification for three years on the sports field, you will be disappointed because there is serious science involved.

However, sport is a growing employment field and one that demands qualifications like any other. It is even spawning whole new higher education institutions. The University College of Football Business (UCFB) is already offering undergraduate degrees at Wembley Stadium, its original home at Burnley's Turf Moor ground, and at the Etihad Stadium, in Manchester. And now Gary Neville, the former Manchester United captain and television pundit, is planning to open University Academy '92, in Manchester, in partnership with Lancaster University, offering sport, business and media degrees, from September 2019.

Many existing degrees in the sports area focus on management, with careers in the leisure industry in mind – golf course management, for example, has proved popular with students despite being a target of those who see anything beyond the traditional academic portfolio as "dumbing down". The question is not whether the courses are up to standard, but whether a less specialised one will offer more career flexibility if a decline in popularity for the particular sport limits future opportunities.

Sports scholarships

The number and range of sports scholarships have expanded just as rapidly as courses in the subject, but the two are usually not connected. Sports scholarships are for elite performers, regardless of what they are studying – indeed, they exist at universities with barely any degrees in the field. Imported from the USA, scholarships now exist in an array of sports. At Birmingham University, for example, there are specialist golf awards (as there are at a number of other universities) and a scholarship for triathletes, as well as others open to any sport.

The value of scholarships varies considerably – sometimes according to individual prowess. The Royal and Ancient scholarships for golfers, for example, range from £500 for promising handicap golfers to £10,000 for full internationals, and are available at 17 universities. All of them demand that you meet the normal entrance requirements for your course and maintain the necessary academic standards, as well as progressing in your sport. In practice, most departments will be flexible about attendance and deadlines, as long as you make your requests well in advance.

Many sports scholarships offer benefits in kind, in the form of coaching, equipment or access to facilities. The Government-funded Talented Athlete Scholarship Scheme (TASS), which is restricted to students at English universities who have achieved national recognition at under-18 level and are eligible to represent England in one of 32 different sports, is one such example. No fewer than 165 current or former TASS athletes took part in the Rio Olympics and Paralympics, winning 78 medals, 35 of them gold. The scholarships are worth £3,500 a year and can be put towards costs such as competition and training, equipment or mentoring. In 2018–19, more than 600 student athletes were supported across a wide range of sports. The Scottish equivalent, Winning Students Scotland awards scholarships worth up to £6,000 a year for training, competition fees and other expenses such as student accommodation. Further details of the two schemes are available at **www.tass.gov.uk** and **www.winningstudents-scotland.ac.uk**.

Leading performers in many sports still look first to US universities – often unfamiliar ones – for sports scholarships. In some sports, such as American football or basketball, this is the main route into professional sport, while in others it may provide bigger awards – and in some cases better coaching – than are available in the UK. Half of the UK's six-strong tennis team at the 2017 World Student Games were from US universities, including Clemson University, in South Carolina, and the University of North Florida – neither of them household names on this side of the Atlantic. For the most promising athletes, US scholarships can cover the full cost of university; for others they may be worth only a few thousand dollars, but may make the difference in gaining admission. Further details are available at **www.fulbright.org.uk/study-in-the-usa/undergraduate-study/funding/sports-scholarships**.

Part-time work

University sports centres are an excellent source of term-time (and out-of-term) employment. You may also be trained in first aid, fire safety, customer care and risk assessment – all useful skills for future employment. The experience will help you secure employment in commercial or local authority facilities – and even for jobs such as stewarding at football grounds and music venues. Most universities also have a sabbatical post in the Athletic Union or similar body, a paid position with responsibility for organising university sport and representing the sporting community within the university.

10 How Parents Can Help

Parents play a delicate role both as their children go through the admissions process for higher education and when they are at university. Many take an active role in selecting courses, may have their say subsequently on the quality of the student experience – and, of course, contribute large sums towards funding their children's time at university. Under such circumstances, there is a thin line between helping and meddling. But it is a balance that every parent wants to get right – and naturally the same applies to step-parents and guardians.

Opinion has shifted recently about how active parents should be – indeed, whether they have a role at all – if and when a student has left home. Any more than occasional encouragement used to be described dismissively as 'helicopter parenting', but greater awareness of particular mental health issues facing students is beginning to change attitudes. Most students are adults, capable of making their own decisions, but some still require help and advice, especially if it is their first foray beyond the family home.

The introduction of £9,000 fees was meant to make the student responsible for his or her higher education – including paying for it – but parents' involvement has, if anything, increased under the current system. That is because most parents are paying towards students' living costs, not their tuition. Maintenance loans may be larger than they were, but very few students will get by on them alone. For undergraduates outside London, they range from £8,700 for students with a family income below £25,000 to £4,054 if the family income is above £65,000 for 2018–19. Those parents who can, are often anxious to spare their children yet more debt on top of the cost of tuition. Surprising numbers of students from affluent families are not taking out loans at all and are relying instead on support from parents or sometimes grandparents. Up to half the students at some leading universities are doing without Government maintenance loans, although throughout England, well over 80% are taking them up.

Nearly half of all parents in the UK think university is now poor value for money, according to a survey by HSBC. But a larger proportion also believe that higher education is essential to their children's career prospects and are willing to help them through it. Nine out of ten expect to make a financial contribution to their children's time at university – and to spend up to eight years paying off the debts they incur in the process.

Operating the "bank of mum and dad" may be the most indispensable role played by parents, but there are plenty of others, from chauffeur on open days to cookery coach in anticipation of their first experience of living away from home. The scale of parental involvement naturally depends on individual relationships, but the right advice and encouragement before, during and after the selection process can be invaluable. Many parents have been to university themselves and will be more adept than a teenager at reading between the lines of a self-congratulatory prospectus or website. But it is important to remember who is going to be the student and not to allow your own (inevitably dated) preconceptions to muddy the waters. Those who are not graduates are just as capable of doing the necessary research to offer a second opinion on universities and courses.

Laying the ground

The first thing any parent can do to smooth the path to university is to be encouraging about the value of higher education. Ideally, this should have started long before the application process, but it is especially important at this point. Now that student debt and variable graduate employment prospects have become frequent media topics, it is only natural for sixth-formers and others to have second thoughts about higher education.

The lure of a regular wage packet will be tempting, should one be available, and there are plenty of young people who are not suited to full-time higher education. More big companies are choosing to employ promising 18-year-olds, rather than rely entirely on graduate recruitment, and there has been a rapid development of higher-level apprenticeships. Even after the years of enormous university expansion, most people still do not go to university. Nevertheless, those who are capable of going generally do not regret the decision. Many people look back on their student days as the best period of their life, as well as the one that shaped their personality and their career. Time as a student should still pay off for the individual in terms of lifetime earnings, as well as personal development. A little reassurance at this stage may make all the difference.

There are important decisions to be made before the sixth-form even begins because the choice of A-levels or vocational qualifications – and even GCSEs – can close off avenues at degree level. A core of traditional academic subjects will help to keep options open, but there are specific requirements for some degrees that can easily be overlooked until it is too late. Maths A-level will be needed for many economics courses, for example, as well as for most sciences.

Making the choice

Any parent wants to help a son or daughter through the difficult business of choosing where and what to study. How big a role you play will depend on a number of factors, not the least of which is the extent to which your advice is wanted. If the quality of advice available at school or college is good, parental involvement may be marginal. But often that is not the case, and you may have to call on other resources, including your own research. Avoid second-hand opinions gleaned through the media or dinner party gossip. You may think that some subjects are a sure-fire route to lucrative employment, while others are shunned by employers, but are you right? And do you really know the strengths and weaknesses of more than 100 universities? Above all, do not try to rewind your own career decisions through your children. The fact that you enjoyed – or hated – a subject or a university does not mean that they will. You may have always regretted missing out on the chance to go to Oxbridge or to become a brain surgeon, but they have their own lives to lead. Students who switch courses or drop out frequently complain that they were pressured into their original choice by their parents. The tables in chapters 1 and 3 offer a reality check, but even they cannot take account of the differences within institutions. The subject tables in chapter 13 show that the best graduate employment rates are often not at the obvious universities.

Parents are encouraged by many schools and colleges to play an active role in the process of choosing a course. At the most basic (but vital) level, this means keeping an eye on deadlines, but it is also about acting as a sounding board and trying to guide your child towards the right university and course. Check that choices are being made for sensible reasons, not on the basis of questionable gossip or trivial criteria. But beyond that, you should stay in the background unless there is a very good reason to play a more substantive role. Make a point of looking for important aspects of university life that the applicant might miss. Security, for example, does not usually feature near the top of a teenager's list of priorities, nor do other practical issues, such as the proximity of student accommodation to lectures, the library and the students' union.

Many universities now publish guides specifically for parents and put on programmes for them at open days. The latter may be a way of separating prospective applicants from their more demanding "minders", but the programmes themselves can be interesting and informative. Do not worry that you will be an embarrassment by attending open days – many thousands of parents do so, and you may add a critical edge to the proceedings. Like prospectuses, open days are part of the sales process, and it is easy for a sixth-former to be carried away by the excitement surrounding a lively university campus. You are much more likely to spot the defects – even if they are ignored in the final decision. The open days in 2019 that had been announced at the time of going to press are included alongside each university's profile, in Chapter 15. As open days at popular institutions are often on the same day, providing assistance in planning open day visits is important. Where there is a clash, universities and individual departments are always happy for prospective applicants to visit on another occasion. Ring ahead or email the department to see if an academic will be available to answer questions.

Most of today's sixth-formers and college students seem happy to have their parents' help and advice – even if they do not take it in the end. Research by the Knowledge Partnership consultancy found that more than half of the parents of first-year undergraduates felt they had exerted some influence on their children's choices of university and course, although only about 7% characterised this as "a lot".

UCAS also publishes its own guide for parents, offering useful tips and outlining the deadlines that applicants will have to meet. The school should be on top of the timing and offering the necessary advice, but there is no harm in providing a little back-up, especially on parts of the process that take time and thought, such as writing the personal statement. There is little a parent can do as the offers and/or rejections come rolling in, other than to be supportive. If the worst happens and there is a full set of rejections, you may have to start the advice process all over again for a new round of applications through UCAS Extra. If so, a cool head is even more necessary, but the same principles apply.

Results Day

Then, before you know it, results day is upon you. Make sure you are at home, rather than in some isolated holiday retreat. Your son or daughter needs to have access to instant advice at school or college, and to be able to contact universities straight away if Clearing or Adjustment is required. And your moral support will be much more effective face to face, rather than down a telephone line. Whatever happens, try not to transmit the anxiety that you will inevitably be feeling to your son or daughter, especially if the results are not what was wanted. It is easy to make rash decisions about re-sitting exams or rejecting an insurance offer in the heat of the moment. Try to slow the process down and encourage clear and realistic thinking. Make sure you know in advance what might be required, such as where to access Clearing lists, and if

Clearing or Adjustment is being used, you will need to be on hand to offer advice and help with visits to possible universities. For most applicants, Clearing or Adjustment is all but over in a week, so the agony should be short-lived.

Before they go

Little more than a month after the tension of results day, everything should be ready for the start of term. Unless your son or daughter chooses to stay at home to study – as one in five now does, either in their own or their parents' home – there will be forms to fill in to secure university accommodation, as well as student loans to sort out and registration to complete. You can perform useful services, like supplying recipe books if the first year is to be spent in self-catering accommodation, but now is the time for independence to become reality. Make sure that important details like insurance are not forgotten, but otherwise stand clear.

Then it is just a matter of agreeing a budget, assuming you are in a position to make a financial contribution. How large that contribution is will depend on family circumstances and your attitude to independent living. Some parents want to ensure that their children leave university debt-free; others could never afford to do that. The important thing is that students and parents know where they stand.

Student finance and parental involvement

After a mortgage, a university degree can be the most significant debt families have to repay, according to HSBC. The debt usually combines student loans for tuition fees and maintenance and is repayable only when a graduate is paid £25,000 a year and can never amount to more than 9% of his or her salary above that threshold. The immediate priority, however, is budgeting for the cost of living, which the National Student Money Survey puts at £770 a month – more in London and less in some other university towns and cities.

Hundreds of thousands of undergraduates – particularly mature students – pay their own way through university. Many undergraduates of all ages supplement their income with term-time and vacation jobs. But every survey shows that families play an important (and growing) role where students move straight from school to higher education. More than half of all students consider the family contribution crucial to their ability to afford a university education. This proportion may rise following the withdrawal of grants for students from the poorest families, although there is actually be more cash available through the replacement loan system.

Costs are likely to be higher if the choice is an overseas university, although most American institutions have generous scholarships and employment opportunities. Even so, HSBC found that most parents were prepared to pay more for the experience, although they would prefer that their children stayed closer to home.

A frank discussion on what the family can afford is essential before the student leaves home. It is all too easy for a young person who has never had to budget for themselves to get into financial difficulties in the social whirl that is the first term of a degree course. In the worst cases, this can lead to excessive term-time employment to keep up with spiralling debts and pressures that contribute towards a student dropping out.

After they've left

Any new student is going to be nervous if he or she is leaving home for the first time and having to settle into a strange environment. But in most cases it is not going to last long because everyone is in the same boat and freshers' weeks hardly leave time for homesickness. In any case, they will not want to let their apprehension show. The people who are most likely to be emotional are the parents – especially if they are left with an empty nest for the first time. It can take a while to get used to an orderly, quiet house after all those years of mayhem.

Resist any temptation to decorate a newly-departed student's bedroom and turn it into an office – it is more common than you might think, and psychologists say it can do lasting damage to family relationships. Keep in touch by phone, text or email, but try not to pry. You're not going to be told everything anyway – which is probably just as well. They will be back soon enough and, just as you were getting used to having the place to yourself, a weekend visit or the Christmas vacation will remind you of how things used to be. If things are not going smoothly at university, this may be the time for more reassurance – more students drop out at Christmas of their first year than at any other time.

Keeping in contact

Growing numbers of parents now want to play their part in ensuring that their children get value for money at university, but there is a fine line between constructive involvement and unwelcome interference. Universities report that anxious mothers and fathers are more inclined than ever to question what their children are getting for their now substantial fees. There have been stories of parents challenging not just the amount and quality of tuition, but even the marking of essays and exams. The phenomenon, first reported in the USA, has given rise to the phrase "helicopter parents" – so called because they hover over their children's education when they should be letting go. No one wants to think of themselves in that category, but it is not surprising – or reprehensible – that parents are taking more of an interest.

One of the reasons that some overstep the mark is that they are shocked that the amount of teaching and size of seminar groups are not what they recall from their own "free" higher education. The new fees were meant to herald improvements in the student experience, including more contact hours, but these have been marginal in most universities so far. It may be that fewer and larger seminars are here to stay in the arts and social sciences, where almost all state support for teaching was withdrawn, and more learning opportunities will be provided online.

An associated reason for greater parental involvement is that family relationships have changed. Many teenage applicants are glad to accept a lift to an open day to get a second opinion on a university and their prospective course. They are also more likely than previous generations of students to come home at the weekend – or to live there in the first place – and to air any grievances. It is up to each family to decide when parental intervention is justified – and would be welcomed. Universities are in a difficult position when such intervention takes place; traditionally, they have only been prepared to deal with students, not parents. But recent tragic cases have encouraged greater flexibility.

The majority of students will go through their time at university without major mishaps, but parents are often the first to spot signs of unhappiness. They should not be afraid to discuss it and, if necessary, take things further with the university. Most students' unions, as well as universities themselves, have professional counselling services that are a good starting point.

Useful websites

Many universities have sections on their websites for parents of prospective students.
UCAS has a Parents section and a guide on its website:
www.ucas.com/ucas/undergraduate/getting-started/ucas-undergraduate-parents-and-guardians
To find out more about open days, visit: **www.opendays.com**

11 Going Abroad to Study

Millions of students across the world now go abroad to take a degree, but relatively few of them are from the UK. Although the numbers have been growing, British students remain reluctant to study in another country – sometimes because of poor linguistic skills, more often because they are satisfied with what they have at home. UK universities are second only to those in the US in all the international rankings and, at present at least, there are plenty of places available.

There is evidence, however, that going abroad, even for part of a degree, may be good for future career prospects. Surveys can exaggerate the impact because the minority who choose to go abroad – and can afford to do so – may be more outgoing and have other advantages in any case. Nevertheless, one recent report found that UK students who study abroad are 9% more likely to gain a 1st or 2:1 degree and 24% less likely to be unemployed after they graduate.

There has been speculation ever since £9,000 fees were introduced that more students would apply to universities on the Continent, where the equivalent charges are low or even non-existent. Schools say that many more sixth-formers are considering it and the numbers going abroad as part of a UK degree have grown by 50% in recent years, topping 30,000. But France still has three times as many studying abroad and Germany more than four times as many, according to UNESCO. Nepal, with half the UK's population, has roughly the same number of students overseas.

The Government and universities themselves have been encouraging students to take advantage of overseas opportunities, but the predicted surge in applications to European universities has yet to materialise. There has been an increase in the numbers going to universities in the USA, where the fees gap has narrowed, at least with state universities, but it is still very much a minority pursuit. There were over 10,000 UK students at US universities last year, but many were postgraduates and/or the children of Britons working on that side of the Atlantic.

Research by the British Council has shown that one student in three is interested in some form of overseas study. And there is now a wide range of opportunities for them to consider. Some universities have international summer schools and many degrees include the opportunity of a semester or a year abroad, either studying or with an employer.

Some of the obstacles that have held British students back are now being removed. The maximum fee for a year abroad while studying at a UK university is £1,385, for example, and many universities are charging less than that. But there is still one important disincentive to taking a full degree overseas: although support from the Student Loans Company continues for a year abroad during a UK degree course, it is not available for degrees from non-UK institutions.

Universities in some countries – notably the Netherlands and the USA – now mount frequent recruitment campaigns in the UK. Numbers of British students have been rising sharply at Dutch universities, where fees in 2019/20 will be little more than €2,000 for most courses, but they still account for only about 1,000 of the 2.5-million UK student population. How Brexit will affect fees for UK students at EU universities in the long term is impossible to tell. Leading independent schools report serious interest in American universities and attendance at the Fulbright Commission's recruitment fairs continues to rise, but the numbers enrolling remain modest, despite attractive incentives in the form of scholarships, bursaries and campus employment opportunities.

Nevertheless, it would be surprising if high fees at home and an increasingly international graduate labour market did not encourage continuing growth in overseas study. Most students who go abroad are motivated by a desire to study at a "world-class" institution, according to a study commissioned by the Government. Often the trigger is failure to win a place at a leading UK university and being unwilling to settle for second best. Other motivations include a desire for adventure and a belief that overseas study might lead to an international career. The question is how to judge a university that may be thousands of miles from home against more familiar names in the UK. This chapter will make some suggestions, including the use of the growing number of global rankings that are available online.

It is possible to have your academic cake and eat it by going on an international exchange or work placement organised by a UK university, or even to attend a British university in another country. Nottingham University has campuses in China and Malaysia; Middlesex can offer Dubai or Mauritius, where students registered in the UK can take part or all of their degree. Other universities, such as Liverpool, also have joint ventures with overseas institutions which offer an international experience (in China, in Liverpool's case) and degrees from both universities.

In most cases, however, an overseas study experience means a foreign university – through a partnership with a UK institution. Until recently, this was usually for a postgraduate degree – and there are still strong arguments for spending your undergraduate years in the UK before going abroad for more advanced study. Older students taking more specialised programmes may get more out of an extended period overseas than those who go at 18 and, since first degrees in the UK are shorter than elsewhere, it may also be the more cost-effective option.

If cost is the main consideration, however, even the generally longer courses at Continental universities can work out cheaper than a degree in the UK. The main obstacle, apart from British students' traditional reluctance to take degrees anywhere else, concerns the language barrier. Although there are now thousands of postgraduate courses taught in English at Continental universities, first-degree programmes are still much thinner on the ground. A few universities, like Maastricht and others in the Netherlands, are offering a wide range of subjects in English. But most European universities teach undergraduates in the host language – and, up to now, that has always deterred UK students.

The obvious alternative lies in American, Australian and Canadian universities, all of which are keen to attract more international students. Here, cost and distance are the main obstacles. Four-year courses add considerably to the cost of affordable-looking fees, while the state of the £ has been another serious disadvantage. Add in the natural reluctance of most 18-year-olds to commit to life on the other side of the world (or even just the Atlantic), and the prospect of a dramatic increase in student emigration is considerably reduced.

Where do students go to?

There is remarkably little official monitoring of how many students leave the UK, let alone where they go. But it seems that for all the economic advantages of studying in Continental Europe, the USA remains by far the most popular student destination. Most surveys put Canada, France and Germany, Ireland and Australia as the biggest attractions outside the USA.

A few British students find their way to unexpected locations, like South Korea or Slovakia, but usually for family reasons or to study the language. The figures suggest that British students are more attracted to countries that are familiar or close at hand, and where they can speak English. Many are doubtless planning to stay in their adopted country after they graduate, although visa regulations may make this difficult.

Studying in Europe

More than 10,000 UK students now attend Continental European universities and colleges, according to UNESCO. But international statistics pick up those whose parents emigrated or are working abroad, as well as those who actually leave the UK to take a degree. A minority are undergraduates, if only because the availability of courses taught in English is so much greater at postgraduate level.

The increased interest in Continental universities arises both from the generally low fees they charge and from the growth in the number of courses offered in English. Some countries charge no fees at all, even to international students, and public universities in the European Union are obliged to charge other member countries' students the same as local residents, as well as allowing them to get a job while studying. Of course, at some point after the UK ceases to be a member, students will not enjoy these advantages, but fee levels will remain lower than at home across most of Europe.

At present, undergraduates can study at a French university for €170 a year but, not surprisingly, nearly all first degrees are taught in French. Only 108 of the 1,386 programmes taught in English and listed on the Campus France website (**www. campusfrance.org/en**) are at the Licence (Bachelors equivalent) level – and 26 of them have some teaching in French. Germany is much the same, despite attracting large numbers of international students. The DAAD website (**www.daad.de/en**) lists 226 undergraduate programmes taught wholly or mainly in English, but many are at private universities like Jacobs University in Bremen, which charges up to €20,000 a year. There are cheaper alternatives in the public sector, where tuition fees have been abolished, but they remain relatively scarce.

Any potential saving has to be considered with care. In spite of the Bologna process – an intergovernmental agreement which means that degrees across Europe are becoming more similar in content and duration – most Continental courses are longer than their UK equivalents, adding to the cost and to your lost earnings from attending university. And, of course, you will have higher travel costs. It is harder to generalise about the cost of living. It can be lower than the UK in southern Europe, but frighteningly high in Scandinavia.

Obviously, the cost of an international experience and the commitment involved is much reduced if you opt for an exchange scheme or other scheme arranged by a UK university, many of which have partners all over the world. There are opportunities for everything from a summer school of less than a month to a full year abroad, and a number of universities now have targets to increase the numbers taking advantage of such schemes.

The most common offering is the EU's Erasmus scheme, which funds exchanges of between three months and a year, the work counting towards your degree. More than 2 million students throughout Europe have used the scheme, and there are 2,000 universities to choose from in 30 countries. It is uncertain whether UK students will have access to the scheme after Brexit but, for the moment at least, applications are made through universities' international offices, and must be approved by the UK university as well as by the Erasmus administrators. Erasmus students do not pay any extra fees and they are eligible for grants to cover the extra expense of travelling and living in another country.

Studying in America

American universities remain the first choice of British students going abroad to take a degree, just as the UK is the first choice for Americans. Regardless of any special relationship, this is not surprising since international rankings consistently show US and UK universities to be the best in the world (as well as teaching in English). Around half of the British students taking courses in the USA are undergraduates.

Already by far the most popular student destination, the attractions of an American degree have multiplied since fees trebled in England. The Fulbright Commission, which promotes American higher education, has seen a 30% increase in the number of Britons taking US university entrance exams. Even before the latest rise in UK fees, the top American universities had seen demand rise sharply, and this is spreading to universities further down the rankings.

The sheer depth of the US university system means that if you are thinking of studying abroad, the USA is almost bound to be on the list of possibilities. Tuitión fees at Ivy League institutions are notoriously high – Harvard's are $46,340 in 2018–19 and the university put the full cost of attendance at $67,580 a year plus health insurance of $3,364 – but generous student aid programmes ensure that most pay far less than the "sticker price". Outside the Ivy League, the fee gap for UK students was narrowing, but fees at many state universities have shot up in the last few years as politicians have tried to balance the books. Texas A&M University, for example, ranked in the top 200 in the world, puts undergraduates' total costs at $55,000. Fees are up to $28,000 at the State University of New York, although the university puts the total cost for those living on campus at up to $42,000. Only at much lower-ranked state universities do the costs compare with those in the UK. At South Dakota State University, for example, the annual cost is put at around $24,000 for a four-year degree.

Top Ten destinations for UK undergraduates studying abroad

1	United States	10,279
2	Netherlands	2,060*
3	Australia	2,019
4	France	1,999
5	Germany	1,798*
6	Ireland	1,791
7	Canada	1,632
8	Denmark	898
9	Bulgaria	890
10	United Arab Emirates	869

Source: 2017 Unesco figures *2016 figure

Best Student Cities ranking

1	London	United Kingdom
2	Tokyo	Japan
3	Melbourne	Australia
4	Montreal	Canada
5	Paris	France
6	Munich	Germany
7	Berlin	Germany
8	Zurich	Switzerland
9	Sydney	Australia
10	Seoul	South Korea

QS ranking 2018

The individual systems of state universities and private universities mean that there is a great variation in the financial support given to international students. Fulbright advises students considering a US degree to assess and negotiate a funding package at the same time as pursuing their application. Otherwise, they may end up with a place they cannot afford, losing valuable time in the quest for a more suitable one.

Which countries are best?

Anyone going abroad to study will be in search of a memorable and valuable all-round experience, not just a good course. Most international students are motivated by location – both the country and the city in which a university is based – as well as by the reputation of the institution. QS publishes an annual ranking of student cities, based on quality of life indicators as well as the number of places at world-ranked universities. London topped the ranking in 2018, with Tokyo second, Melbourne third and Montreal fourth.

Many Asian countries are looking to recruit more foreign students, both as part of a broader internationalisation agenda and to compensate for falling numbers of potential students at home. Japan is a case in point. The high cost of living may put off many potential students, as may the unfamiliarity of its language, but more support is being offered to attract foreign students and more courses are being taught in English. However, as with any non-English speaking country, the language of instruction is only part of the story. You will need to know enough of the local language to manage the shops and the transport system, and, of course, to make friends and get the most out of being there.

Another option of growing interest is China, although Western students are often put off by the dormitory accommodation that is the norm at most universities. The country has already grown massively in importance. Its university system is growing in quality, with the leading institutions climbing the world rankings and improving their facilities. Familiarity with China is unlikely to be a career disadvantage for anyone in the 21st century. Some see Hong Kong, which has several world-ranked universities and a familiar feel for Britons, as the perfect alternative to mainland Chinese universities.

Will my degree be recognised?

Even in the era of globalisation, you need to bear in mind that not all degrees are equal. At one extreme is the MBA, which has an international system for accrediting courses, and a global admissions standard. But with many professional courses, study abroad is a potential hazard. To work as a doctor, engineer or lawyer in the UK, you need a qualification which the relevant professional body will recognise. It is understandable that to practise law in England, you need to have studied the English legal system. For other subjects, the issues are more to do with the quality and content of courses outside UK control.

There are ways of researching this issue in advance. One is to contact NARIC, the National Recognition Centre for the UK (**www.naric.org.uk**). NARIC exists to examine the compatibility and acceptability of qualifications from around the world. The other approach is to ask the UK professional body in question – maybe an engineering institution, the relevant law society or the general teaching, medical or dental councils – about the qualification you propose to study for.

Which are the best universities?

Going abroad to study is a big and expensive decision, and you want to get it right. Whether your ultimate aim is to become an internationally mobile high-flyer, or simply to broaden your experience, you will want to know that the university you are going to is taken seriously around the world.

At the moment, there are three main systems for ranking universities internationally. One is run by QS (Quacquarelli Symonds), an educational research company based in London (**www.topuniversities.com**). Another is by Shanghai Ranking Consultancy, a company set up by Shanghai Jiao Tong University, in China, and is called the Academic Ranking of World Universities (ARWU) (**www.shanghairanking.com**). The third is produced by *Times Higher Education* (**www.timeshighereducation.com/world-university-rankings**), a weekly magazine with no connection to *The Times*, which published the QS version until 2010.

There are several more international ranking systems that an online search might throw up, but most are either specialist – like the Webometrics ranking of universities' web activity – or limited in their readership and influence. Some are still developing: the European Commission's U-Multirank (**www.umultirank.org**), for example, remains limited in the subjects it covers, but may become a more widely-used source of information in time.

The QS system uses a number of measures including academic opinion, employer opinion, international orientation, research impact and staff/student ratio to create its listing, while the ARWU uses measures such as Nobel Prizes and highly-cited papers, which are more related to excellence in scientific research. *Times Higher Education* added a number of measures to the QS model, including research income and a controversial global survey of teaching quality.

Naturally, the different methodologies produce some contrasting results – the three main rankings each have a different university at the top, for example. The table on these pages is a composite of the three main rankings, which places Stanford at the top and includes four UK universities in the top 20. In practice, however, if you go to a university that features strongly in any of the tables, you will be at a place that is well-regarded around the world. After all, even the 200th university on any of these rankings is an elite institution in a world with more than 4,000 universities.

These systems tend to favour universities which are good at science and medicine. Places that specialise in the humanities and the social sciences, such as the London School of Economics, can appear in deceptively modest positions. In addition, the rankings tend to look at universities in the round, and contain only limited information on specific subjects. QS published the first 26 global subject rankings in 2011 and has since increased this to 42. One advantage of the QS ranking system is that 10% of a university's possible score comes from a global survey of recruiters. So you can look at this column of the table for an idea about where the major employers like to hire. Note that the author of this *Guide* has a role in developing the QS rankings.

Other options for overseas studies

For the growing numbers who want to study abroad without committing themselves to a complete degree, a number of options are available. A language degree will typically involve a year abroad, and a look at the UCAS website will show many options for studying another subject alongside your language of choice. UK universities offer degrees in information technology, science, business and even journalism with a major language such as Chinese.

Many universities offer a year abroad, either studying or in a work placement, even to those who are not taking a language. At Aston University, for example, 70% of students do a year's work placement and a growing number do so abroad. China and Chile have been among recent destinations. Other universities offer the opportunity to take shorter credit-bearing courses with partner institutions overseas. American universities are again the most popular choice. The best

Top Universities in the World

Rank	Institution	Country
1	Stanford University	USA
2	Massachusetts institute of Technology (MIT)	USA
3	Harvard University	USA
4	Cambridge University	UK
5	Oxford University	UK
6	California Institute of Technology	USA
7	Princeton University	USA
8	University of Chicago	USA
9	Yale University	USA
10	Federal Institute of Technology, Zurich	Switzerland
11	Columbia University	USA
=12	University College, London	UK
=12	Imperial College, London	UK
14	Cornell University	USA
=15	University of California, Berkeley	USA
=15	University of Pennsylvania	USA
17	Johns Hopkins University	USA
18	University of California, Los Angeles	USA
19	University of Michigan, Ann Arbor	USA
20	Duke University	USA
21	University of Toronto	Canada
22	University of Edinburgh	UK
=23	Northwestern University	USA
=23	Tsinghua University	China
25	University of California, San Diego	USA
26	University of Tokyo	Japan
27	New York University	USA
28	University of Washington	USA
29	University of Melbourne	Australia
=30	University of Manchester	UK
=30	Peking University	China
32	National University of Singapore	Singapore
33	University of Wisconsin, Madison	USA
34	King's College, London	UK
35	University of British Columbia	Canada
36	Kyoto university	Japan
37	Federal Institute of Technology, Lausanne	Switzerland
38	Australian National University	Australia
39	University of Texas at Austin	USA
=40	University of Munich	Germany
=40	McGill University	Canada
42	Technical University Munich	Germany

Rank	Institution	Country
43	Ecole Normale Superieur, Paris	France
44	Heidelberg University	Germany
45	Nanyang Technological University	Singapore
=46	University of Illinois at Urbana-Champaign	USA
=46	Carnegie Mellon University	USA
48	Hong Kong University	Hong Kong
49	London School of Economics	UK
=50	University of North Carolina at Chapel Hill	USA
=50	University of Sydney	Australia
52	University of Queensland	Australia
53	Washington University in St Louis	USA
54	Hong Kong University of Science and Technology	Hong Kong
55	Georgia Institute of Technology	USA
56	Sorbonne University	France
57	Karolinska Institute	Sweden
58	University of California, Santa Barbara	USA
59	Seoul National University	South Korea
60	University of Bristol	UK
61	Chinese University of Hong Kong	Hong Kong
62	University of Minnesota, Twin Cities	USA
=63	University of Copenhagen	Denmark
=63	Brown University	USA
65	Delft University of Technology	Netherlands
66	KU Leuven	Belgium
67	University of Amsterdam	Netherlands
68	University of Zurich	Switzerland
69	University of California, San Francisco	USA
70	University of Southern California	USA
71	Utrecht University	Netherlands
72	Rockefeller University	USA
=73	University of Maryland, College Park	USA
=73	Purdue University, West Lafayette	USA
=73	Monash University	Australia
76	University of Warwick	UK
=77	Zhejiang University	China
=77	Boston University	USA
79	University of Colorado at Boulder	USA
=80	Rice University	USA
=80	Leiden University	Netherlands
=80	KAIST (Korea Advanced Institute of Technology)	South Korea
83	University of Paris-Sud	France
84	University of Groningen	Netherlands
=85	Pennsylvania State University – University park	USA
=85	Erasmus University, Rotterdam	Netherlands

=87	University of Texas Southwestern Medical Center at Dallas	USA
=87	Uppsala University	Sweden
89	Vanderbilt University	USA
90	Ohio State University – Columbus	USA
91	University of California, Davis	USA
92	University of Helsinki	Finland
93	City University of Hong Kong	Hong Kong
=94	Tokyo Institute of Technology	Japan
=94	Wageningen University	Netherlands
=96	University of Geneva	Switzerland
=96	Shanghai Jiao Tong University	China
98	University of Glasgow	UK
=99	Ghent University	Belgium
=99	McMaster University	Canada

Averaged from positions in the QS World University Ranking (QS), the Academic Ranking of World Universities (ARWU) and *Times Higher Education* (THE) for 2018

approach is to decide what you want to study and then see if there is a UK university that offers it as a joint degree or with a placement abroad. Make sure that all the universities involved are well-regarded, for example by looking at their rankings on one or other of the websites of global rankings.

Useful websites

Prospects: studying abroad: **www.prospects.ac.uk/postgraduate-study/study-abroad**
Association of Commonwealth Universities: **www.acu.ac.uk**
Campus France: **www.campusfrance.org/en**
College Board (USA): **www.collegeboard.org**
DAAD (for Germany): **www.daad.de/en**
Study in Holland: **www.studyinholland.co.uk**
Education Ireland: **www.educationinireland.com/en**
Erasmus Programme (EU): **www.erasmusplus.org.uk**
Finaid (USA): **www.finaid.org**
Fulbright Commission: **www.fulbright.org.uk**
Study in Australia: **www.studyinaustralia.gov.au**
Study in Canada: **www.studyincanada.com**

SOUTHALL AND WEST
LONDON COLLEGE
LEARNING CENTRE

12 Coming to the UK to Study

Universities are understandably anxious about the long-term consequences of tougher visa controls and leaving the European Union but, for the moment at least, the referendum vote and its subsequent uncertainties have indirectly helped to boost international recruitment. The fall in the value of the £ has made a degree at a UK university better value for money than it has been for some years. And, now that the Government has reassured European students that they will pay the same fees and remain eligible for loans if they come in 2019–20, applications from the continent have remained steady, while those from the rest of the world are continuing to rise. EU students will still pay no fees in Scotland.

This could mean slightly tougher competition for places in 2019, but with the number of British school-leavers continuing to decline, universities will be keen to attract international students. As yet, no decisions have been announced for 2020-21, other than to assure EU students already on courses that their fees will not rise. It would not be surprising if this encouraged an unusually high number of applications from European students this year, as those contemplating entry in 2020 bring forward their applications, if they have the flexibility to do so.

Universities in the UK have been a magnet for international students for many years – only the huge higher education system in the USA attracts more. Global surveys have shown that UK universities are seen as offering high quality in a relatively safe environment, with the added advantage of allowing students to learn and immerse themselves in English. Even after the fall in the value of the £, the UK remains an expensive destination by international standards, but shorter than average courses both at undergraduate and Master's level redress the balance to some extent. The UK's 11% share of the world's young people who choose to study outside their own country is important to its universities and welcomed by British students.

More than 4 million people now travel abroad to study, and universities in many parts of the world compete aggressively to attract them. The students concerned may see other countries' universities as better than their own, or they may want to master another language and/or experience another culture, but most also see international study as a boost to their career prospects. Surveys in a number of countries have shown that employers – particularly those engaged in global markets – favour applicants with an international education.

While international students have continued to favour UK universities, the numbers of undergraduates coming from individual countries have varied considerably over recent years and the UK's overall 'market share' has declined. The source of most stability has been China, which sends four times as many students as any other country and increased the number of undergraduate entrants by another 10% in 2017. Elsewhere, there has been more fluctuation, often due to economic or political factors. Most significant has been the decline in students coming from the Indian sub-continent, where tougher visa policies have hit hardest. But even here there was a significant upturn in 2017, with 12% more Indian students accepting places.

Universities in the UK continue to be extremely proactive in the recruitment of international students, participating in international fairs and sometimes opening their own offices in target countries. The fees such students pay is the obvious motivation, but universities also value the cultural richness that a diverse international intake contributes to student life.

Why study in the UK?

Aside from the strong reputation of UK degree courses and the opportunity to be taught and surrounded by English, research shows that most graduates are handsomely rewarded when they return home. A Government-commissioned report showed that UK graduates earn much

The top countries for sending international students to the UK

EU countries (top 20)		%	Non-EU countries (top 20)		%
France	8,348	9.8	China	38,567	26.5
Italy	7,141	8.4	Hong Kong (Special Administrative Region of China)	13,688	9.4
Cyprus (European Union)	6,989	8.2			
Romania	6,670	7.8	Malaysia	12,870	8.8
Germany	5,981	7.0	United States	5,802	4.0
Bulgaria	5,425	6.4	Singapore	5,723	3.9
Spain	5,391	6.3	India	5,649	3.9
Poland	5,149	6.1	Nigeria	5,390	3.7
Ireland	5,096	6.0	Norway	3,524	2.4
Greece	4,811	5.7	Korea (South)	3,038	2.1
Lithuania	3,507	4.1	Canada	2,980	2.0
Portugal	2,460	2.9	Saudi Arabia	2,736	1.9
Sweden	2,080	2.4	Russia	2,649	1.8
Belgium	2,010	2.4	United Arab Emirates	2,554	1.8
Hungary	1,665	2.0	Kuwait	2,317	1.6
Finland	1,594	1.9	Pakistan	2,236	1.5
Czech Republic	1,512	1.8	Qatar	2,194	1.5
Netherlands	1,509	1.8	Switzerland	2,194	1.5
Slovakia	1,278	1.5	Thailand	1,863	1.3
Latvia	1,102	1.3	Vietnam	1,712	1.2
			Oman	1,467	1.0
Total (all non-UK EU)	**85,103**		**Total (all non-EU)**	**145,805**	

Note: First degree non-UK students

higher salaries than those who studied in their own country. The starting salaries of UK graduates in China and India were more than twice as high as those for graduates educated at home, while even those returning to the USA enjoyed a salary premium of more than 10%.

Some premium is to be expected – you are likely to be bright and highly motivated if you are prepared to uproot yourself to take a degree. And, unless they have government scholarships, most students have to be from a relatively wealthy background to afford the fees and other expenses of international study. A higher salary will probably be a necessity to compensate for the cost of the course. But the scale of increase demonstrated in the report suggests that a UK degree remains a good investment. Three years after graduation, 95% of the international graduates surveyed were in work or further study. More than 90% had been satisfied with their learning experience and almost as many would recommend their university to others.

A popular choice

Nearly all UK universities are cosmopolitan places that welcome international students in large numbers. Almost one student in five is from outside the UK – 6% from the EU and 14% from the rest of the world. Recent surveys by i-graduate, the student polling organisation, put the country close behind the USA among the world's most attractive study destinations. More full-time postgraduates – the fastest-growing group – come from outside the UK than within it. In many UK universities you can expect to have fellow students from over 100 countries.

More than 90% of international students declare themselves satisfied with their experience of UK universities in i-graduate surveys, although they are less enthusiastic in the Government's National Student Survey and more likely than UK students to make official complaints. Nevertheless, satisfaction increased by eight percentage points in four years, according to i-graduate, reflecting greater efforts to keep ahead of the global competition. International students are particularly complimentary about students' unions, multiculturalism, teaching standards and places of worship. Their main concerns tend to be financial, partly because of a lack of employment opportunities. In one survey, only 56% were satisfied with the ability to earn money while studying, and ministerial statements suggest that controls on this, and particularly on the opportunity to work after completing a degree, are unlikely to be eased.

One way round this in a growing number of countries is to take a UK degree through a local institution, distance learning or a full branch campus of a UK university. Indeed, there are now more international students taking UK first degrees in their own country than there are in Britain. The numbers grew by 70% in a decade and are likely to rise further if UK Government policies obstruct universities' efforts to increase the number of students coming to Britain. Most branch campuses are in Asia or the Middle East, but some universities, such as King's College London, are now planning campuses in other parts of the EU.

Where to study in the UK

The vast majority of the UK's universities and other higher education institutions are in England. Of the 132 universities profiled in this *Guide*, 107 are in England, 15 in Scotland, eight in Wales and two in Northern Ireland. Fee limits in higher education for UK and EU students are determined separately in each administrative area, which in some cases has brought benefits for EU students. All undergraduates from other EU countries are currently charged the same fees as those from the part of the UK where their chosen university is located, which is why EU students currently pay no tuition fees in Scotland, for example. With the UK set to leave the EU in March 2019, it is unclear whether these arrangements will continue for students starting in 2020, or what system might replace it.

Within the UK, the cost of living varies by geographical area. Although London is the most expensive, accommodation costs in particular can also be high in many other major cities. You should certainly find out as much as you can about what living in Britain will be like. Further advice and information is available through the British Council at its offices worldwide, at more than 60 university exhibitions that it holds around the world every year, or at its Education UK website (**www.educationuk.org**). Another useful website for international students is provided by the UK Council for International Student Affairs (UKCISA) at **www.ukcisa.org.uk**.

Universities in all parts of the UK have a worldwide reputation for high quality teaching and research, as evidenced in global rankings such as those shown on pages 133–135. They maintain this standing by investing heavily in the best academic staff, buildings and equipment, and by taking part in rigorous quality assurance monitoring. The new Office for Students will be the chief regulatory body for higher education in England, overseeing organisations such as the Quality Assurance Agency for Higher Education (QAA), which remains the arbiter of standards. Professional bodies also play an important role in relevant subjects.

Although many people from outside the UK associate British universities with Oxford and Cambridge, in reality most higher education institutions are nothing like this. Some universities do still maintain ancient traditions, but most are modern institutions that place at least as much emphasis on teaching as on research and offer many vocational programmes, often with close links to business, industry and the professions. The table below shows the universities that are

The universities most favoured by EU and non-EU students

Institution (top 20)	EU students	Institution (top 20)	Non-EU students
Coventry University	2,412	The University of Manchester	5,565
University College London	2,401	Coventry University	4,980
The University of Aberdeen	2,366	The University of Liverpool	4,739
King's College London	2,313	University College London	4,662
The University of Glasgow	2,284	University of the Arts, London	4,364
The University of Edinburgh	2,007	The University of Edinburgh	3,800
University of the Arts, London	1,820	The University of Sheffield	3,226
The University of Manchester	1,780	University of Nottingham	2,952
The University of Westminster	1,602	Imperial College of Science, Technology and Medicine	2,929
The University of Warwick	1,553	King's College London	2,885
The University of Essex	1,407	The University of Warwick	2,656
Middlesex University	1,380	The University of Birmingham	2,508
Imperial College of Science, Technology and Medicine	1,321	The University of St Andrews	2,275
The University of Bath	1,275	The University of Sussex	2,184
The University of Kent	1,250	The University of Leeds	2,180
The University of Southampton	1,242	The University of Exeter	2,173
Queen Mary University of London	1,225	City, University of London	2,139
The University of Exeter	1,158	Newcastle University	2,089
The University of Greenwich	1,103	The University of Bristol	1,998
The University of Cambridge	1,061	The University of Portsmouth	1,965

Note: First degree non-UK students

most popular with international students at undergraduate level. Although some of those at the top of the lists are among the most famous names in higher education, others achieved university status only in the last 25 years.

What subjects to study?

One of the reasons for such diversity is that strongly vocational courses are favoured by international students. Many of these in professional areas such as architecture, dentistry or medicine take one or two years longer to complete than most other degree courses. Traditional first degrees are mostly awarded at Bachelor level (BA, BEng, BSc, etc.) and last three to four years. There are also some "enhanced" first degrees (MEng, MChem, etc.) that take four years to complete. The relatively new Foundation degree programmes are almost all vocational and take two years to complete as a full-time course, with an option to study for a further year to gain a full degree. The table below shows the most popular subjects studied by international students. Remember, though, that you need to consider the details of any university course that you wish to study and to look at the ranking of that university in our main league table in chapter 1 and in the subject tables in chapter 13.

The most popular subjects for international students (excluding 'Other')

Subject Group	EU students	Non-EU students	Total students	% of all international students
Business Studies	12,525	26,078	38,604	16.7
Accounting & Finance	2,440	14,541	16,982	7.4
Law	3,932	10,277	14,209	6.2
Computer Science	6,120	5,132	11,252	4.9
Art & Design	4,024	6,969	10,993	4.8
Economics	2,906	7,267	10,173	4.4
Mechanical Engineering	2,030	6,084	8,114	3.5
Politics	3,698	3,769	7,467	3.2
Biological Sciences	3,823	3,421	7,243	3.1
Psychology	3,835	3,065	6,899	3.0
Electrical & Electronic Engineering	1,297	5,116	6,414	2.8
Communication & Media Studies	3,028	3,143	6,171	2.7
Mathematics	1,625	4,363	5,987	2.6
Drama, Dance & Cinematics	2,955	2,088	5,043	2.2
Medicine	1,104	3,651	4,755	2.1
Architecture	1,644	2,911	4,554	2.0
Civil Engineering	836	3,633	4,469	1.9
Hospitality, Leisure, Recreation & Tourism	2,260	1,923	4,183	1.8
Chemical Engineering	576	2,901	3,477	1.5
Other Subjects Allied to Medicine	1,467	1,890	3,357	1.5
Total	**85,103**	**145,805**	**230,908**	

English language proficiency

The universities maintain high standards partly by setting demanding entry requirements, including proficiency in English. For international students, this usually includes a score of at least 5.5 in the International English Language Testing System (IELTS), which assesses English language ability through listening, speaking, reading and writing tests. Under visa regulations introduced in 2011, universities are able to vouch for a student's ability in English. This proficiency will need to be equivalent to an "upper intermediate" level (level B2) of the CEFR (Common European Framework of Reference for Languages) for studying at an undergraduate level (roughly equivalent to an overall score of 5.5 in IELTS).

There are many private and publicly funded colleges throughout the UK that run courses designed to bring the English language skills of prospective higher education students up to the required standard. However, not all of these are Government approved. Some private organisations such as INTO (**www.intohigher.com**) have joined with universities to create centres running programmes preparing international students for degree-level study. The British Council also runs English language courses at its centres around the world.

Tougher student visa regulations were introduced in 2012 and have since been refined. Although under the current system, universities' international students should not be denied entry to the UK, as long as they are proficient in English and are found to have followed other immigration rules, some lower-level preparatory courses taken by international students have been affected. It is, therefore, doubly important to consult the official UK government list of approved institutions (web address given at the end of this chapter) before lodging an application.

How to apply

You should read the information below in conjunction with that provided in chapter 5, which deals with the application process in some detail.

Some international students apply directly to a UK university for a place on a course, and others make their applications via an agent in their home country. But most applying for a full-time first degree course do so through the Universities and Colleges Admissions Service (UCAS). If you take this route, you will need to fill in an online UCAS application form at home, at school or perhaps at your nearest British Council office. There is plenty of advice on the UCAS website about the process of finding a course and the details of the application system (**www.ucas.com/ucas/undergraduate/getting-started/ucas-undergraduate-international-and-eu-students**).

Whichever way you apply, the deadlines for getting your application in are the same. For those applying from within an EU country, application forms for most courses starting in 2020 must be received at UCAS by 15 January 2020. Note that applications for Oxford and Cambridge and for all courses in medicine, dentistry and veterinary science have to be received at UCAS by 15 October 2019, while some art and design courses have a later deadline of 24 March 2020.

If you are applying from a non-EU country to study in 2020, you can submit your application to UCAS at any time between 1 September 2019 and 30 June 2020. Most people will apply well before the 30 June deadline to make sure that places are still available and to allow plenty of time for immigration regulations, and to make arrangements for travel and accommodation.

Entry and employment regulations

Visa regulations have been the subject of continuing controversy in the UK and many new rules and regulations have been introduced, often hotly contested by universities. Recent governments have been criticised for increasing visa fees, doubling the cost of visa extensions, and ending the right to appeal against a refusal of a visa.

The current points system for entry – known as Tier 4 – came into effect in 2009. Under this scheme, prospective students can check whether they are eligible for entry against published criteria, and so assess their points score. Universities are also required to provide a Confirmation of Acceptance for Studies (CAS) to their international student entrants, who must have secured an unconditional offer, and the institution must appear as a "Tier 4 Sponsor" on the Home Office's Register of Sponsors. Prospective students have to demonstrate that, as well as the necessary qualifications, they have English language proficiency and enough money for the first year of their specified course. This includes the full fees for the first year and, currently, living costs of £1,265 a month, up to a maximum of nine months, if studying in London (£1,015 a month in the rest of the UK). Under the new visa requirements, details of financial support are checked in more detail than before.

All students wishing to enter the UK to study are required to obtain entry clearance before arrival. The only exceptions are British nationals living overseas, British overseas territories citizens, British Protected persons, British subjects, and non-visa national short-term students who may enter under a new Student Visitor route. Visa fees have been increased again (to £348 for a Tier 4 visa, plus £150 a year healthcare surcharge). As part of the application process, biometric data will be requested and this will be used to issue you with a Biometric Residence Permit (BRP) once you have arrived in the UK. You will need a BRP to open a bank account, rent accommodation or establish your eligibility for benefits and services or to work part-time, for example. The details of the regulations are continually reviewed by the Home Office. You can find more about all the latest rules and regulations for entry and visa requirements at **www.gov.uk/tier-4-general-visa**.

The rules and regulations governing permission to work vary according to your country of origin and the level of course you undertake. If you are from a European Economic Area (EEA) country (the EU plus Iceland, Liechtenstein and Norway) or Switzerland, you do not need permission to work in the UK, although you will need to be ready to show an employer your passport or identity card to prove you are a national of an EEA country. However, the regulations that will apply after the UK leaves the EU are unknown at the time of writing and you will need to check for the latest information before making an application.

Students from outside the EEA who are here as Tier 4 students are allowed to work part-time for up to 20 hours a week during term time and full-time during vacations. These arrangements apply to students on degree courses; stricter limits were introduced in 2010 for lower-level courses. If you wish to stay on after you have graduated, you can apply for permission under Tier 2 of the points-based immigration system, but you will need a sponsor and the work must be considered "graduate level", commanding a salary of at least £20,800. The reforms abolished the Tier 1 two-year, post-study period for graduates who do not have such a sponsor. They will be required to apply for a new visa from scratch. Full details are on the Home Office study visas website above.

The Tier 1 Graduate Entrepreneur Scheme enables up to 2,000 graduates to remain in the UK if they have "genuine and credible business ideas and entrepreneurial skills". Successful applicants, who will be selected by their university, will be allowed to stay in the UK for 12 months, with the possibility of a further 12-month extension.

Bringing your family

Since 2010, international students on courses of six months or less have been forbidden to bring a partner or children into the UK, and the latest reforms extend this prohibition to all undergraduates except those who are government sponsored. Postgraduates studying for 12 months or longer will still be able to bring dependants to the UK, and most universities can help to arrange facilities and accommodation for families as well as for single students. The family members you are allowed to bring with you are your husband or wife, civil partner (a same-sex relationship that has been formally registered in the UK or your home country) or long-term partner and dependent children. You can find out more about getting entry clearance for your family at **www.ukcisa.org.uk**.

Support from British universities

Support for international students is more comprehensive than in many countries, and begins long before you arrive in the UK. Many universities have advisers in other countries. Some will arrange to put you in touch with current students or graduates who can give you a first-hand account of what life is like at a particular university. Pre-departure receptions for students and their families, as well as meet-and-greet arrangements for newly-arrived students, are common. You can also expect an orientation and induction programme in your first week, and many universities now have "buddying" systems where current students are assigned to new arrivals to help them find their way around, adjust to their new surroundings and make new friends. Each university also has a students' union that organises social, cultural and sporting events and clubs, including many specifically for international students. Both the university and the students' union are likely to have full-time staff whose job it is to look after the welfare of students from overseas.

International students also benefit from free medical and subsidised dental and optical care and treatment under the UK National Health Service (non-EU students will have had to pay a healthcare surcharge when paying for their visa to benefit from this), plus access to a professional counselling service and a university careers service.

At university, you will naturally encounter people from a wide range of cultures and walks of life. Getting involved in student societies, sport, voluntary work, and any of the wide range of social activities on offer will help you gain first-hand experience of British culture, and, if you need it, will help improve your command of the English language.

Useful websites

The British Council, with its dedicated Study UK site designed for those wishing to find out more about studying in the UK:
https://study-uk.britishcouncil.org/

The UK Council for International Student Affairs (UKCISA) provides a wide range of information on all aspects of studying in the UK:
www.ukcisa.org.uk

UCAS, for full details of undergraduate courses available and an explanation of the application process:
www.ucas.com/ucas/undergraduate/getting-started/ucas-undergraduate-international-and-eu-students

For the latest information on entry and visa requirements:
www.gov.uk/tier-4-general-visa

Register of sponsors for Tier 4 educational establishments:
www.gov.uk/government/publications/register-of-licensed-sponsors-students

For a general guide to Britain, available in many languages:
www.visitbritain.com

13 Subject by Subject Guide

The rankings of whole institutions capture all the headlines when university guides appear, but recent surveys suggest that students take more notice of the subject tables. Knowing where a university stands in the pecking order of higher education is a vital piece of information for any applicant, but the quality of the course is what matters most – particularly in the short term. Your chosen course, rather than the character of the whole university, will determine what you get out of taking a degree and may have a big bearing on your employment prospects. As the 2014 Research Excellence Framework confirmed, the most modest institution may have a centre of specialist excellence, and even famous universities have mediocre departments. This chapter offers some pointers to the leading universities in a wide range of subjects. With a number of universities reviewing the courses they will offer in the future, it is possible that not all institutions listed in a particular subject area will be running courses in 2020.

The subject tables in this *Guide* include scores from the National Student Survey (NSS). These distil the views of final-year undergraduates on various aspects of their course, with the results presented in two columns. The teaching quality indicator reflects the average scores of the sections of the survey focusing on teaching, assessment and feedback, learning opportunities and academic support. The student experience indicator is drawn from the average of the organisation and management, learning resources, student voice and learning community sections, as well as the overall satisfaction question. The three other measures used are research quality, students' entry qualifications and graduate employment prospects. None of the measures is weighted. A full explanation of the measures is given on the next page.

Many subjects, such as dentistry or sociology, have their own table, but others are grouped together in broader categories, such as "other subjects allied to medicine". Scores are not published where the number of students is too small for the outcome to be statistically reliable. Cambridge is again the most successful university. It tops 29 of the 67 tables, while Oxford leads in six subjects and Glasgow in four. Imperial College London, Lancaster, Loughborough and St Andrews are all top in three subjects, Bath, Birmingham, Durham, Edinburgh and Leeds in two each. Ten other universities are top in one subject.

Research quality

This is a measure of the quality of the research undertaken in the subject area. The information was sourced from the 2014 Research Excellence Framework (REF), a peer-review exercise used to evaluate the quality of research in UK higher education institutions, undertaken by the UK Higher Education Funding Bodies. The approach mirrors that in the main table, with the REF results weighted and then multiplied by the percentage of eligible staff entered for assessment.

For each subject, a research quality profile was given to those university departments that took part, showing how much of their research was in various quality categories. These categories were: 4* world-leading; 3* internationally excellent; 2* internationally recognised; 1* nationally recognised; and unclassified. The funding bodies decided to direct more funds to the very best research by applying weightings. The English, Scottish and Welsh funding councils have slightly different weightings. Those adopted by HEFCE (the funding council for England) for funding in 2012–13 are used in the tables: 4* is weighted by a factor of 3 and 3* is weighted by a factor of 1. Outputs of 2* and 1* carry zero weight. This results in a maximum score of 3. In the interest of consistency, the above weightings continue to be applied this year.

The scores in the table are presented as a percentage of the maximum score. To achieve the maximum score, all staff would need to be at 4* world-leading level.

Universities could choose which staff to include in the REF, so, to factor in the depth of the research quality, each quality profile score has been multiplied by the number of staff returned in the REF as a proportion of all eligible staff.

Entry standards

This is the average new UCAS tariff score for new students under the age of 21, based on A and AS-Levels and Scottish Highers and Advanced Highers and other equivalent qualifications (including the International Baccalaureate), taken from HESA data for 2016–17. Each student's examination grades were converted to a numerical score using the new UCAS tariff to make the figures more accessible to those applying in 2020, who will be using the new system. The points used in the revised tariff appear on page 32.

Teaching quality and student experience

The student satisfaction measure is divided into two components. These measures are taken from the National Student Survey (NSS) results published in 2018 and 2017. A single year's figures are used when that is all that is available, but an average of the two years' results is used in all other cases. Students at some universities boycotted the 2018 NSS, leaving individual departments below the 50% threshold for publication. Where 2018 NSS data was not available, the last available scores for Teaching Quality and Student Experience were adjusted to reflect changes in satisfaction rates nationally, and are not shown in the final table.

The NSS covers eight aspects of a course, with an additional question gauging overall satisfaction. Students answer on a scale from 1 (bottom) to 5 (top) and the score in the table is calculated from the percentage of positive responses (4 and 5) in each section. The teaching quality indicator reflects the average scores for the first four sections of the survey. The student experience indicator is drawn from the average scores of the remaining sections and the additional question on overall satisfaction. Teaching quality is favoured over student experience and accounts for 67% of the overall student satisfaction score, with student experience making up the remaining 33%.

Graduate prospects

This is the percentage of graduates undertaking further study or in a professional job ("positive destinations"), in the annual survey by HESA six months after graduation. Because of the relatively small numbers in some departments, two years of data (2016 and 2017 graduates) are aggregated to make the scores more reliable. A low score on this measure does not necessarily indicate unemployment – some graduates may have taken jobs that are not categorised as professional work. The averages for each subject are given at the foot of each subject table in this chapter and in two tables in chapter 3 (see pages 52–55). Because individual percentages are rounded, some employment tables may add up to slightly more or less than 100%.

The Education table uses a fifth indicator: Ofsted grades, a measure of the quality of teaching based on the outcomes of Ofsted inspections of teacher training courses.

Note that in the tables that follow, when a figure is followed by *, it refers solely to data from 2015–16 because no data for 2016–17 are available.

The subjects listed below are covered in the tables in this chapter:

Accounting and Finance
Aeronautical and
    Manufacturing Engineering
Agriculture and Forestry
American Studies
Anatomy and Physiology
Animal Science
Anthropology and Forensic
    Science
Archaeology
Architecture
Art and Design
Biological Sciences
Building
Business Studies
Celtic Studies
Chemical Engineering
Chemistry
Civil Engineering
Classics and Ancient
    History
Communication and Media
    Studies
Computer Science
Creative Writing
Criminology
Dentistry
Drama, Dance and
    Cinematics

East and South Asian Studies
Economics
Education
Electrical and Electronic
    Engineering
English
Food Science
French
General Engineering
Geography and
    Environmental Sciences
Geology
German
History
History of Art, Architecture
    and Design
Hospitality, Leisure,
    Recreation and Tourism
Iberian Languages
Italian
Land and Property
    Management
Law
Librarianship and
    Information Management
Linguistics
Materials Technology
Mathematics
Mechanical Engineering

Medicine
Middle Eastern and
    African Studies
Music
Nursing
Other Subjects Allied to
    Medicine (see page 247
    for subjects included in
    this category)
Pharmacology and Pharmacy
Philosophy
Physics and Astronomy
Physiotherapy
Politics
Psychology
Radiography
Russian and East European
    Languages
Social Policy
Social Work
Sociology
Sports Science
Theology and Religious
    Studies
Town and Country Planning
    and Landscape
Veterinary Medicine

Accounting and Finance

Record numbers of students started degrees in accounting and finance in 2017, as enrolments grew for the third year in row. There were more than 7,000 entrants in accounting and close to 2,500 in finance, with more than five applications to every place in both subjects. Accounting was also one of the best bets for a place through clearing, with more than 1,000 students securing a place this way in 2017.

At the top of the table, Leeds has won back the leadership it lost to Strathclyde last year, moving up three places in the process. Glasgow, which has moved up five places in the new table, has the highest entry standards, benefiting from the conversion rate for Scottish qualifications in the UCAS tariff.

The most satisfied students are at Liverpool John Moores, which remains outside the top 20, having decided not to enter the Research Excellence Framework (REF) in this category.

Employment rates in the two areas come a surprisingly long way down the table of subjects – only 35th of 67 subject areas. Those who do find graduate jobs have starting salaries around the average for all subjects, at £22,000 in 2017. The table again shows huge variation in graduates' employment prospects. At Queen's Belfast, 94% of graduates went straight into a professional job or further study, but at six universities the proportion was 50% or less.

Some of the leading universities demand maths A-level and all welcome it, but there is considerable variation in entry standards, from over 200 points at three institutions to less than 100 at 14 others. About 130 universities and colleges expect to offer accounting or finance, either alone or in combination, in 2019.

Accounting and Finance	Teaching quality %	Student experience %	Research quality %	Entry standards (UCAS points)	Graduate prospects %	Overall score
1 Leeds	89.5	93.0	39.3	178	87.0	100.0
2 Strathclyde	71.5	75.1	44.3	211	89.5	97.5
3 Warwick	79.7	86.1	40.4	176	88.9	97.3
4 Bath	80.5	79.6	41.8	185	87.5	97.2
5 Glasgow	78.9	85.9	22.1	218	88.7	97.0
6 Loughborough	81.4	84.2	32.6	164	96.5	96.4
=7 Exeter	82.4	85.8	24.4	177	90.6	95.4
=7 Lancaster	80.5	83.6	42.6	149	88.9	95.4
9 Queen's, Belfast	80.5	79.9	32.7	162	94.0	95.1
10 Birmingham	81.6	81.1	29.1	160	91.8	94.3
11 Ulster	86.3	85.7	40.4	123	83.9	93.6
12 London School of Economics	55.4	58.1	52.3	203	93.6	93.1
13 Newcastle	81.8	81.9	20.7	156	93.1	92.9
14 Nottingham	75.2	77.3	32.6	161	90.3	92.8
15 Durham	77.6	80.0	23.1	162	90.8	92.2
16 Reading	79.8	77.4	29.3	147	87.9	91.7
=17 East Anglia	82.2	84.6	28.1	146	81.1	91.6
=17 Sussex	80.3	82.8	23.7	142	90.6	91.6
=17 York	78.9	80.5	24.0	172	—	91.6
20 Manchester	77.2	80.0	33.3	169	73.2	91.2

Accounting and Finance cont

	Teaching quality %	Student experience %	Research quality %	Entry standards (UCAS points)	Graduate prospects %	Overall score
21 Sheffield	78.5	80.3	26.8	147	86.6	91.1
=22 Liverpool John Moores	94.1	93.4	—	140	84.0	90.7
=22 Nottingham Trent	91.7	91.6	4.6	135	86.3	90.7
=22 Swansea	79.4	83.5	22.0	136	90.4	90.7
25 City	80.8	83.9	28.7	165	68.2	90.5
26 Liverpool	80.9	82.5	20.1	152	82.1	90.3
27 Aberdeen	66.8	73.6	24.9	180	88.0	90.1
28 Stirling	79.4	78.3	25.2	157	77.6	89.9
=29 Aston	85.9	87.0	19.7	138	73.4	89.3
=29 Bristol	72.2	76.2	32.1	174	70.8	89.3
=29 Kent	74.9	76.5	24.8	137	90.2	89.3
32 Robert Gordon	83.4	78.8	2.6	193	74.6	89.2
33 Heriot-Watt	75.2	76.8	18.8	160	83.6	89.0
34 Cardiff	75.4	76.2	32.0	153	73.6	88.8
35 Southampton	76.3	77.0	24.0	151	79.6	88.7
36 Dundee	77.7	77.6	12.1	167	79.1	88.2
=37 Queen Mary, London	68.4	71.9	31.3	154	81.9	88.1
=37 Surrey	79.2	81.3	15.8	170	69.3	88.1
=39 Edinburgh	68.1	74.6	25.8	175	74.8	87.8
=39 Northumbria	85.0	86.7	4.0	145	78.4	87.8
41 Royal Holloway, London	76.7	78.5	27.0	137	—	86.9
42 Aberystwyth	85.6	84.0	14.5	119	74.8	86.7
43 Gloucestershire	89.4	88.4	—	111	82.2	86.4
=44 Lincoln	84.7	83.8	4.8	117	83.6	86.2
=44 West of Scotland	87.3	85.0	2.9	143	70.4	86.2
46 Portsmouth	79.2	80.8	9.5	115	88.0	86.1
47 De Montfort	79.3	79.7	10.7	104	90.3	85.7
48 Derby	88.9	84.8	0.9	97	86.2	85.6
=49 Keele	83.0	80.3	10.2	115	79.0	85.3
=49 Oxford Brookes	87.5	91.8	5.1	116	69.7	85.3
=49 South Wales	91.6	90.0	0.2	119	68.9	85.3
=52 Essex	77.4	79.9	25.1	114	68.7	84.6
=52 Worcester	88.6	90.8	0.9	113	70.8	84.6
=54 Glasgow Caledonian	77.8	78.4	1.8	166	68.3	84.5
=54 Greenwich	84.9	85.7	3.3	137	65.4	84.5
=56 Chester	87.6	86.3	0.5	109	75.9	84.4
=56 Teesside	91.1	88.5	2.0	94	75.0	84.4
58 Buckingham	90.4	88.5	—	105*	71.7	84.2
=59 Coventry	83.7	84.9	1.6	118	75.0	84.0
=59 Liverpool Hope	88.1	90.1	—	100	74.3	84.0
61 Westminster	79.4	83.2	2.4	131	74.5	83.9
62 Edge Hill	79.0	81.2	—	133	77.1	83.8

63 Edinburgh Napier	75.9	77.2	2.3	147	75.2	83.7
64 West of England	82.4	85.2	5.5	115	71.1	83.6
=65 Bangor	80.5	83.8	23.4	122	53.7	83.4
=65 Leicester	67.2	70.3	24.3	126	77.5	83.4
=67 Huddersfield	76.9	75.8	4.1	130	77.3	83.1
=67 Plymouth	84.8	85.0	13.1	116	58.2	83.1
=69 Bradford	73.8	76.4	11.8	133	70.7	82.8
=69 Hertfordshire	83.0	85.3	0.9	112	72.1	82.8
=69 Hull	72.7	76.3	10.2	121	78.4	82.8
72 Birkbeck, London	81.2	82.9	16.1	86	71.0	82.5
73 Birmingham City	84.2	87.8	1.3	116	63.8	82.2
=74 Manchester Metropolitan	81.7	80.8	4.7	126	62.1	81.9
=74 Sheffield Hallam	86.2	86.9	0.6	118	59.4	81.9
76 Central Lancashire	87.1	88.8	4.4	125	50.0	81.8
77 London South Bank	82.0	83.5	2.1	91	75.7	81.6
78 Bolton	93.1	87.5	—	94	56.3	81.0
79 East London	85.1	90.8	0.8	101	59.7	80.9
80 Brunel	67.8	72.5	23.0	118	65.0	80.7
81 Sunderland	81.1	75.4	0.4	119	66.7	80.5
=82 Leeds Beckett	83.3	82.3	0.8	105	63.9	80.4
=82 Middlesex	74.9	76.7	10.5	108	67.7	80.4
=82 Staffordshire	88.6	92.1	2.6	109	46.7	80.4
85 Northampton	83.0	81.1	1.0	97	66.8	80.1
86 Salford	76.4	79.3	5.9	115	58.2	79.1
87 Buckinghamshire New	84.4	86.2	1.8	112	47.0	78.8
88 West London	80.4	82.0	—	111	56.7	78.7
89 London Metropolitan	80.7	80.8	0.6	91	63.6	78.4
=90 Kingston	76.6	79.8	9.2	127	43.9	78.1
=90 Solent	77.1	75.1	—	94	69.4	78.1
92 Chichester	79.0	79.5	—	109	57.4	78.0
93 Leeds Trinity	87.7	86.5	—	85	50.0	77.7
=94 Bournemouth	71.7	71.2	8.8	116	57.5	77.4
=94 Winchester	81.9	83.6	—	97	52.4	77.4
=96 Abertay	69.9	71.2	—	141	55.2	76.9
=96 Wolverhampton	80.1	79.1	2.4	87	57.1	76.9
98 Cardiff Metropolitan	72.0	77.4	—	111	60.0	76.8
99 Roehampton	64.1	67.1	4.5	110	69.0	75.9
100 Anglia Ruskin	81.5	75.9	3.4	84	48.4	75.1
101 Canterbury Christ Church	71.0	73.7	—	97	60.5	75.0
102 Brighton	66.3	65.0	6.5	108	59.9	74.8
103 Bedfordshire	69.3	76.8	3.1	82	54.1	73.2

Employed in professional job	53%	Employed in non-professional job and Studying	2%
Employed in professional job and studying	8%	Employed in non-professional job	18%
Studying	9%	Unemployed	10%
Average starting professional salary	£22,000	Average starting non-professional salary	£18,000

Aeronautical and Manufacturing Engineering

Most of the courses in this ranking focus on aeronautical or manufacturing engineering, but the category includes some with a mechanical title. In addition, manufacturing degrees often go under the rubric of production engineering. Although they do not feature in this table, degree apprenticeships at leading firms like Rolls-Royce provide an attractive alternative to a conventional degree in this area.

Both applications and enrolments for traditional degree courses in aeronautical engineering – now categorised by UCAS as Aerospace Engineering – have risen in each of the last five years, however, and are almost twice what they were in 2008. Demand for the smaller field of production and manufacturing engineering has been steadier, and only 625 students started courses in 2017.

The subjects share ninth place out of the 67 subject groups for starting salaries, but are not in the top 30 for the proportion of graduates going straight into professional jobs or further study. Almost 60% of the 2017 graduates went straight into high-level work, and at seventh-placed Newcastle over 95% either went into such jobs or continued studying.

Cambridge remains well clear at the top of the table overall, registering by far the best scores for research and entry standards. Imperial has lost second place after a relatively poor year for student satisfaction, and has been overtaken by Bristol. The University of the West of Scotland again has much the most satisfied students, as the only institution where nine out of ten undergraduates had a positive view both of teaching quality and the broader student experience.

Many universities demand maths and physics at A-Level, and give extra credit for further maths, computing and/or design technology. Entry grades are high at the leading universities, with Cambridge averaging almost 240 points per entrant and Imperial only four points less. Coventry and the West of Scotland remain the only post-1992 universities in the top 20.

Aeronautical and Manufacturing Engineering	Teaching quality %	Student experience %	Research quality %	Entry standards (UCAS points)	Graduate prospects %	Overall score
1 Cambridge	83.7	85.5	67.0	239	93.6	100.0
2 Bristol	83.7	86.1	52.3	209	78.0	92.1
3 Imperial College	66.2	71.0	59.6	235	86.2	91.6
4 Glasgow	80.6	80.8	47.2	200	82.8	90.8
5 Leeds	85.5	87.6	40.9	180	83.5	90.5
6 Nottingham	83.8	86.0	40.8	169	80.5	88.4
=7 Newcastle	74.1	76.9	30.2	—	95.2	88.2
=7 Southampton	75.1	77.1	52.3	189	78.7	88.2
9 Bath	74.3	76.7	37.4	194	85.9	88.0
10 Loughborough	77.2	80.8	41.8	167	84.1	87.4
11 Swansea	76.1	78.7	45.5	148	86.2	86.7
12 Sheffield	74.1	73.4	36.0	161	82.8	84.4
13 Strathclyde	69.5	72.0	37.2	201	73.2	83.8
14 Liverpool	76.0	81.4	32.1	146	80.1	83.4
15 Coventry	88.1	89.5	10.3	131	80.9	83.0
16 Manchester	68.1	75.9	35.1	174	77.4	82.9
17 Surrey	76.4	75.4	30.8	165	75.0	82.8

18 Brunel	73.5	78.0	23.7	153	82.1	82.4
19 West of Scotland	90.7	94.9	9.0	157*	65.6	81.9
20 Ulster	88.3	86.7	—	131	80.6	81.2
=21 Staffordshire	87.3	87.1	5.7	125	79.3	81.1
=21 Teesside	87.1	88.1	5.8	120	—	81.1
=23 Central Lancashire	83.2	81.4	7.1	138	—	80.7
=23 Queen's, Belfast	67.6	66.5	36.7	155	77.4	80.7
25 Plymouth	80.6	80.8	15.7	111	83.7	80.6
26 Hertfordshire	73.5	73.6	16.5	124	83.6	79.3
27 Portsmouth	75.8	78.6	9.1	103	88.9	79.2
28 Sussex	72.6	78.3	—	135	87.5*	79.1
29 Queen Mary, London	62.5	63.2	46.7	150	71.4	78.8
30 West of England	74.4	74.3	10.6	126	81.3	78.3
31 Salford	80.1	81.2	4.4	132	68.8	76.6
32 City	82.4	81.9	23.1	128	55.6	76.3
33 Aston	72.8	74.7	20.6	142	61.5	75.6
34 Sheffield Hallam	68.2	68.5	17.8	118	71.4	74.4
35 Wolverhampton	80.1	80.3	4.4	87	—	74.1
36 Buckinghamshire New	81.2	74.5	—	84*	74.1	73.6
37 Kingston	73.0	73.6	2.9	115	57.9	70.3
38 South Wales	67.6	66.7	—	118	65.0	70.0
39 Brighton	50.3	56.8	7.4	117	52.0	63.2

Employed in professional job	57%	Employed in non-professional job and Studying	1%
Employed in professional job and studying	2%	Employed in non-professional job	14%
Studying	15%	Unemployed	12%
Average starting professional salary	£26,000	Average starting non-professional salary	£17,000

Agriculture and Forestry

The numbers starting degrees in agriculture and forestry fell only slightly in 2017, but three of the 16 universities in last year's table – Glasgow, Lincoln and Plymouth – have now dropped out of it. Little more than 2,000 students took up agriculture in 2017, with another 110 starting courses in forestry or arboriculture, but this was still more than in any year up to 2014. However, the two subjects are in the bottom four for graduate prospects, with a 14% unemployment rate that is among the highest in the sector. Those who do find professional jobs – nearly half of the 2017 cohort – command salaries that are around average for all subjects, at £22,000.

Newcastle and Kent were the only universities to see 80% of their 2017 graduates go straight into highly-skilled employment or continue their studies. But Nottingham is the leader overall, as it was last year. It has the highest entry standards and good scores on the other measures, but neighbouring Nottingham Trent (NTU) is closing fast after moving up eight places to second. NTU has by far the most satisfied students in the table but is handicapped by a low research score. Neither university teaches agriculture in Nottingham – NTU has a specialist campus in Brackenhurst, while Nottingham students are taught on the university's biosciences campus at Sutton Bonnington.

With such low numbers taking the two subjects, this table tends to be volatile. Queen's Belfast, which recorded much the best score in the Research Excellence Framework, achieved last year's biggest rise, but is now back where it started. Only Nottingham occupies the same position as last year. There are two specialist institutions in the table: the Royal Agricultural University and Harper Adams, which is the leading modern university in the overall table but only ninth for agriculture and forestry. Unusually, 20 points cover nine of the 13 universities' average entry grades.

Agriculture and Forestry	Teaching quality %	Student experience %	Research quality %	Entry standards (UCAS points)	Graduate prospects %	Overall score
1 Nottingham	90.5	87.9	36.4	167	68.8	100.0
2 Nottingham Trent	95.3	93.7	4.1	164	69.8	96.8
=3 Newcastle	79.5	79.2	28.4	144	80.8	94.3
=3 Reading	79.0	77.0	50.7	134	75.9	94.3
5 Kent	83.1	84.7	—	156	80.5	93.6
6 Queen's, Belfast	66.6	65.8	56.3	143	78.9	93.5
7 Aberystwyth	82.6	83.9	38.2	142	63.7	92.9
8 Bangor	83.5	82.3	29.7	129	77.1	92.4
9 Harper Adams	83.3	83.6	5.7	132	74.5	89.0
10 Royal Agricultural University	79.7	79.5	2.1	125	54.1	82.0
11 Oxford Brookes	68.3*	65.9*	—	132	57.7	79.8
12 Cumbria	76.3	65.1	—	125	48.6	78.3
13 Greenwich	—	—	19.5	114	43.1	75.8

Employed in professional job	43%	Employed in non-professional job and Studying	2%
Employed in professional job and studying	5%	Employed in non-professional job	28%
Studying	8%	Unemployed	14%
Average starting professional salary	£22,000	Average starting non-professional salary	£18,000

American Studies

Applications for degrees in American Studies have halved since their heyday before £9,000 fees were introduced. Another decline in 2017 left only 325 students beginning degrees. Yet the American Studies table contains one more university – Manchester Metropolitan – than last year, and 54 institutions plan to offer the subject in 2019.

The subject has become a fixture in the bottom ten of our employment table. Those who find graduate-level work have average starting salaries of £20,000, but only a third of graduates in 2017 were in this happy position. Three out of ten graduates went on to take another course.

Birmingham is back on top of the American Studies table, after surrendering that position to Sussex last year. Birmingham benefits from the highest score in the table for graduate prospects and is only a point behind East Anglia and second-placed Manchester in terms of the highest entry standards.

Scores derived from the National Student Survey (NSS) have improved in the latest table, with three universities (led by Portsmouth) topping 90% for satisfaction with the quality of teaching. Hull and Winchester, the other two, also reached 90% in the sections of the NSS devoted to the broader student experience.

Degrees classified by UCAS as American studies include a variety of courses such as international relations and black studies. Most concentrate on the culture and politics of the USA and Canada. A growing number of courses offer the opportunity of a year at an American or Canadian university as part of a four-year degree. The leading universities are likely to expect English or history at A-level or the equivalent.

American Studies	Teaching quality %	Student experience %	Research quality %	Entry standards (UCAS points)	Graduate prospects %	Overall score
1 Birmingham	82.5	74.7	48.8	152	81.2	100.0
2 Manchester	—	—	49.1	153	65.2	97.7
3 Sussex	81.6	76.7	45.6	143	78.8	97.6
4 Kent	87.1	72.6	47.3	116	79.4	95.5
5 Nottingham	80.8	76.9	39.9	136	73.7	94.5
=6 East Anglia	77.0	72.6	33.1	153	60.4	91.6
=6 Portsmouth	91.3	87.1	32.2	103	70.0	91.6
8 Manchester Metropolitan	86.1	84.7	29.0	120	—	90.7
9 Swansea	89.5	84.4	18.5	123	70.2	90.6
10 Leicester	81.6	76.0	34.3	121	63.2	89.7
11 Hull	91.2	90.1	26.1	117	50.4	89.1
12 Winchester	90.5	90.9	—	121	76.2	88.2
13 Essex	79.3	71.2	46.9	100	58.2	87.7
14 Liverpool	—	—	33.4	—	39.3*	86.0
15 Keele	78.4	73.3	29.8	115	57.9	85.9
16 Goldsmiths, London	79.0	68.6	34.9	—	54.2	85.4
17 Canterbury Christ Church	87.2	76.7	16.3	103	41.3	81.2
18 York St John	87.2	83.3	—	100*	51.7	79.8
19 Derby	65.3	58.4	13.5	108*	30.7	72.0

Employed in professional job	32%	Employed in non-professional job and Studying	5%
Employed in professional job and studying	1%	Employed in non-professional job	27%
Studying	24%	Unemployed	11%
Average starting professional salary	£20,000	Average starting non-professional salary	£17,000

Anatomy and Physiology

Entry standards in anatomy and physiology dropped across the board in 2017, as universities expanded their intakes for the fifth year in a row despite receiving fewer applications. The numbers starting degrees topped 4,600 and there were still almost eight applications to the place, but one in ten secured entry through Clearing. Just one of the 46 universities in the table averaged less than 110 points on the UCAS tariff, but only two (compared with four in 2016) averaged more than 200 points.

The table covers a broad range of courses, including the biomedical science degrees that have been growing in popularity over recent years. Very few actually have the title of anatomy or physiology, but they include degrees in cell biology, neurosciences and pathology. Entry requirements often include at least two science subjects – usually biology and chemistry – although some post-1992 universities will accept just one science.

The top three universities for anatomy and physiology are unchanged since the last edition, with Cambridge just ahead of St Andrews and Newcastle. But there are big changes from there on. Cardiff enters the table in fourth place and Dundee has shot up 15 places to fifth. Derby's students are the most satisfied with the quality of teaching, despite its low position, while Cardiff has the top score for the broader student experience.

The subjects are in the top 20 for graduate prospects and are not much lower for starting salaries. Three universities – Northampton, St Andrews and the West of England all saw every graduate go straight into professional employment or continue their studies at the end of 2017. Two more universities have joined the table since last year, making it 50% larger than it was a decade ago. Older universities dominate the leading positions; Glasgow Caledonian is the only post-1992 institution in the top 20.

Anatomy and Physiology

		Teaching quality %	Student experience %	Research quality %	Entry standards (UCAS points)	Graduate prospects %	Overall score
1	Cambridge	—	—	52.5	242	84.0	100.0
2	St Andrews	90.3	91.0	37.6	178	100.0	98.7
3	Newcastle	89.5	91.2	47.8	160	91.8	96.4
4	Cardiff	90.7	92.9	33.3	154	—	94.1
5	Dundee	78.3	83.5	55.4	187	79.8	93.6
6	Loughborough	88.2	92.3	52.1	150	79.2	93.1
=7	Glasgow	77.5	81.3	33.4	199	84.7	92.4
=7	Oxford	—	—	50.9	208	76.3	92.4
9	University College London	73.6	73.5	55.4	191	78.7	91.6
10	Liverpool	90.5	91.8	31.7	148	83.3	91.5
11	Leeds	82.4	83.6	40.9	165	82.1	91.2
12	Salford	92.6	90.0	12.7	150	90.5	91.1
13	Glasgow Caledonian	91.1	82.7	8.1	143	97.5	90.4
14	Bristol	78.6	78.0	49.7	171	75.0	89.9
15	Swansea	79.0	77.6	44.7	156	—	89.7
16	Aberdeen	81.0	81.5	34.7	193	70.3	89.4
=17	Brighton	93.3	88.4	4.8	125*	95.3	89.0
=17	Queen Mary, London	81.7	88.0	26.1	148	85.7	89.0
19	Sussex	75.4	76.5	46.8	141	84.9	88.5
20	Huddersfield	82.8	77.5	7.8	132	99.7	87.7
21	Manchester	77.3	77.4	38.3	163	76.4	87.6
22	King's College London	75.4	74.5	38.0	163	78.4	87.4
23	Queen's, Belfast	72.9	75.0	33.3	156	85.0	87.2
=24	Central Lancashire	92.9	91.8	8.3	147*	74.4	86.6
=24	Northampton	83.5	78.1	—	128*	100.0	86.6
=26	Leicester	80.6	83.3	36.5	147	73.0	86.5

=26 St George's, London	77.3	74.7	20.0	131	94.4	86.5
28 Nottingham	77.1	73.2	26.5	159	77.5	85.5
=29 Manchester Metropolitan	84.9	82.9	12.0	136	82.2	85.4
=29 West of England	83.1	82.2	—	110*	100.0	85.4
31 Edinburgh	65.8	67.6	52.8	176	68.7	85.3
=32 Cardiff Metropolitan	85.0	82.8	—	112	93.8	84.6
=32 Portsmouth	81.6	74.7	8.1	131	89.5	84.6
34 Coventry	87.9	90.8	4.5	112	82.2	83.9
35 Plymouth	83.4	81.0	—	140	79.9	83.0
36 Reading	81.7	76.3	26.6	141	67.4	82.9
37 Keele	86.0	87.4	16.5	127	68.4	82.7
38 Bangor	83.3	80.7	—	133	77.8	81.9
39 Queen Margaret, Edinburgh	61.9	58.7	—	156	97.4	81.5
=40 Derby	95.9	92.6	1.6	101	68.8	81.3
=40 Westminster	83.0	87.1	21.2	111	68.6	81.3
42 Oxford Brookes	83.0	79.7	21.3	130	63.6	81.0
43 East London	81.2˙	82.9	—	115	79.7	80.6
44 Greenwich	77.1	81.0	2.2	123	—	79.7
45 Ulster	71.7	72.2	—	127	83.1	79.2
46 Anglia Ruskin	69.4	62.3	2.2	110	88.2	77.9

Employed in professional job	42%	Employed in non-professional job and Studying	2%
Employed in professional job and studying	4%	Employed in non-professional job	14%
Studying	31%	Unemployed	8%
Average starting professional salary	£22,000	Average starting non-professional salary	£15,600

Animal Science

Only 6% of graduates of 2017 animal science courses were unemployed at the end of the year, placing it among the ten best subjects on this measure. However, it remains rooted to the bottom of our employment table because it had by far the largest proportion of graduates – almost half – beginning their careers in lower-level jobs. Some universities' employment scores are worryingly low – below 5% in Edinburgh Napier's case and under 30% at five more. Yet, for the second year in a row, all the graduates of Middlesex's degree in veterinary nursing found professional employment or continued studying.

The Animal Science table was first published only four years ago and was a reflection of growing interest in the group of subjects under this heading. Extracted from the agriculture category, degree courses range from animal behaviour to equine science and veterinary nursing. Almost 2,700 started courses in 2017, about 10% of them finding a place through Clearing. Most degrees will require biology and probably chemistry.

Glasgow remains well clear at the top of the table, with by far the highest entry standards among the 18 universities in the ranking. Aberystwyth has moved up to second, with much the best scores for student satisfaction. It is the only university to reach 90% satisfaction for teaching quality or the broader student experience. Third-placed Reading registered the best results in the Research Excellence Framework, but only 12 of the 18 universities in the table entered.

Animal Science

	Teaching quality %	Student experience %	Research quality %	Entry standards (UCAS points)	Graduate prospects %	Overall score
1 Glasgow	72.1	76.7	42.3	213	66.7	100.0
2 Aberystwyth	90.4	90.6	38.2	124	65.7	93.2
3 Reading	77.7	78.9	50.7	138	56.3	92.1
4 Nottingham	70.4	69.3	36.4	157	75.4	91.0
5 Nottingham Trent	87.1	82.6	4.1	166	71.1	90.4
6 Liverpool	—	—	32.9	151	82.9	90.2
7 Middlesex	85.1	69.2	—	140	100.0	87.7
8 Lincoln	85.1	84.0	—	148	66.7	86.1
9 Bristol	76.9	69.4	33.2	147	28.6	84.6
10 Royal Veterinary College	84.4	84.2	—	143	56.1	84.0
11 Harper Adams	81.3	77.1	5.7	139	45.2	81.8
12 Greenwich	—	—	19.5	140	24.3	79.0
13 Chester	79.3	78.0	7.9	129	31.8	78.7
14 Plymouth	83.7	77.7	—	131	23.2	77.2
15 Anglia Ruskin	69.0	66.3	24.6	124	25.0	76.8
16 Oxford Brookes	68.3*	65.9*	21.3	—	26.7	75.6
17 Canterbury Christ Church	83.3	76.5	—	93	40.0	74.1
18 Edinburgh Napier	60.3	46.7	—	157	4.8	68.9

Employed in professional job	25%	Employed in non-professional job and Studying	4%
Employed in professional job and studying	2%	Employed in non-professional job	44%
Studying	18%	Unemployed	6%
Average starting professional salary	£19,000	Average starting non-professional salary	£17,056

Anthropology

The unexpected rise of anthropology since the introduction of £9,000 fees came to at least a temporary halt in 2017, as applications and enrolments dropped a little. But both were more than twice as high as they were in 2011 and there were still nearly six applications for every place. Although the numbers starting degrees remain below 2,000, the number of universities in the table continues to grow and 43 universities and colleges expect to offer the subject this year.

Some attribute the subject's rise in popularity to television series, but there has been no firm explanation. Much of the growth has come in joint Honours degrees, pairing the subject with everything from accountancy to linguistics or law. There are no subject-specific requirements for most degree courses, although some universities favour candidates who have taken sociology, biology or another science in the sixth-form.

Anthropology has tended to be the preserve of old universities, but there are seven post-1992 institutions in the latest table. Portsmouth is the only one to feature in the top ten and had by far the best graduate prospects in the table. Overall, however, Cambridge has recaptured the lead from Birmingham, which has dropped to third. Neither Cambridge nor second-placed Oxford had enough responses to the National Student Survey (NSS) for satisfaction scores to be published, but Cambridge had the highest entry standards in the table and good graduate prospects. East London's students are the most satisfied with the quality of teaching, while Brunel and Portsmouth tie for the best score on the sections of the NSS dealing with the broader student experience.

Employment prospects will be the main concern of those considering a degree in anthropology. It is only just outside the bottom ten for the proportion of graduates going straight into "professional" jobs or further study, and it ties with East and South Asian Studies for the unwanted distinction of the highest unemployment rate. The picture is a little better in the earnings table, but anthropology is still in the bottom 20, with average starting salaries in professional jobs of £20,000 in 2017.

Anthropology	Teaching quality %	Student experience %	Research quality %	Entry standards (UCAS points)	Graduate prospects %	Overall score
1 Cambridge	—	—	40.4	213	84.8	100.0
2 Oxford	—	—	38.8	205	79.1	98.3
3 Birmingham	82.9	78.0	50.9	140	81.0	96.3
4 London School of Economics	77.5	78.5	41.3	196	69.9	95.4
5 University College London	70.4	71.8	49.3	179	74.4	94.7
6 Portsmouth	91.6	90.3	32.2	107	91.7	94.1
7 Manchester	—	—	36.7	158	73.1	92.6
8 Exeter	72.1	72.0	41.0	167	77.4	92.5
9 St Andrews	92.4	85.5	25.0	199	54.8	92.1
10 SOAS London	—	—	31.1	157	75.6	92.0
11 Sussex	79.2	76.4	34.4	150	79.7	91.7
12 Durham	72.1	66.3	29.1	176	79.4	90.1
13 Brunel	94.2	90.3	29.3	131	63.9	89.9
14 Edinburgh	77.2	73.2	42.2	164	59.9	89.8
15 Aberdeen	81.4	78.5	31.8	182	55.3	89.3
16 Queen's, Belfast	83.0	78.5	49.0	151	42.4	88.3
=17 Kent	78.1	78.6	20.5	131	76.7	85.7
=17 Liverpool John Moores	89.5	84.6	15.1	140	65.1	85.7
19 East London	96.0	74.1	13.7	—	53.7	84.2
20 Leeds	79.1	79.3	—	153	80.8	83.7
21 Goldsmiths, London	70.7	65.5	34.5	133	53.7	81.3
22 Bournemouth	80.6	72.3	19.9	109	62.4	80.3
23 Wales Trinity St David	89.5	89.3	17.3	96	48.3	79.0
24 Oxford Brookes	79.5	77.5	17.3	125	49.3	78.4
25 Bristol	65.9	62.5	11.2	147	62.1	77.1
26 Roehampton	54.4	50.8	27.7	103	51.7	71.2

Employed in professional job	36%	Employed in non-professional job and Studying	2%
Employed in professional job and studying	3%	Employed in non-professional job	21%
Studying	24%	Unemployed	15%
Average starting professional salary	£20,000	Average starting non-professional salary	£17,063

Archaeology and Forensic Science

Only 450 students started single honours archaeology degrees in 2017, but over 50 universities and colleges plan to offer degrees in the subject in 2019. Most of the students covered by this table are actually taking courses classified as forensic and archaeological science, which saw 2,465 new enrolments. Taken as a whole, the subjects have now regained the levels of demand seen before £9,000 fees arrived. For most applicants, money is not the attraction – archaeology is back in the bottom ten in our earnings table. But graduates' immediate prospects have been improving – the subjects are just outside the top 50 in the employment table, with two-thirds of leavers going into graduate-level jobs or continuing their studies.

Cambridge remains top of the table and has the highest entry standards, while Dundee – holder of the best research grades – is now the nearest challenger. Further down the table, there have been some sharp rises, not least by Birmingham City, where unusually high levels of student satisfaction have helped the university to jump 40 places into a share of 16th place. Queen's Belfast has gone up 11 places and into the top ten, while both Nottingham Trent and Teesside have enjoyed rises of more than 20 places. The top graduate prospects were at sixth-placed Liverpool.

There are no specific subject requirements for a degree in archaeology, although geography, history and science subjects are all considered relevant. Entry standards are relatively low – only 13 of the 58 universities in the table average more than 150 points. More than 10% of those starting courses in 2017 came through Clearing.

Archaeology and Forensic Science	Teaching quality %	Student experience %	Research quality %	Entry standards (UCAS points)	Graduate prospects %	Overall score
1 Cambridge	—	—	47.2	213	84.8	100.0
2 Dundee	82.7	83.4	55.4	178	82.2	98.5
3 Oxford	—	—	42.9	196	81.6	97.5
4 Durham	88.1	82.6	41.2	176	73.6	94.9
5 University College London	88.8	85.4	51.4	146	73.6	94.2
6 Liverpool	—	—	33.5	150	85.7	93.7
7 Glasgow	82.9	82.9	16.4	195*	75.0	91.6
8 Exeter	84.5	81.7	33.6	154	77.0	91.4
9 Queen's, Belfast	93.7	91.3	36.9	127	72.1	91.2
10 York	83.6	79.2	35.1	148	78.1	90.9
11 Birmingham	85.8	77.1	40.3	146	72.6	90.5
12 Leicester	87.5	82.7	37.2	123	79.3	90.4
13 Southampton	84.7	80.8	43.5	141	70.8	90.3
14 Newcastle	86.0	82.7	25.8	147	78.5	90.1
15 Swansea	83.2	75.5	39.4	126	78.1	89.0
=16 Birmingham City	98.0	97.1	—	129	80.9	88.6
=16 Reading	90.7	81.1	44.7	128	62.3	88.6
18 Kent	81.3	79.7	33.1	144	72.2	88.3
19 Manchester	88.5*	82.6*	24.7	156	64.4	87.9
20 Sheffield	79.2	78.2	31.6	139	73.7	87.3
21 Huddersfield	89.3	88.7	—	140	82.6	87.2

22	Nottingham Trent	82.1	84.1	4.1	167	72.2	86.1
23	Bangor	88.1	80.6	24.3	126	—	86.0
24	Nottingham	81.4	80.2	23.7	142	68.4	85.7
25	Cardiff	86.8	80.0	31.1	124	63.8	85.3
26	Aberdeen	80.9	75.7	29.4	—	66.7	84.8
27	Teesside	88.1	86.4	—	125	79.5	84.6
28	Worcester	88.8	83.9	8.1	117	74.1	83.8
29	Robert Gordon	81.6	77.2	8.8	153	68.2	83.7
30	De Montfort	93.1	93.0	—	113	72.5	83.6
31	Bradford	73.4	70.1	23.6	120	80.3	83.5
32	Lincoln	80.8	84.1	—	128	80.3	83.2
33	Warwick	81.4	73.6	—	159	70.4	82.9
34	Derby	88.8	90.4	3.6	122	67.2	82.6
35	Coventry	84.5	88.1	—	127	71.7	82.3
36	West of Scotland	84.7	82.1	—	131	71.0	82.0
37	Central Lancashire	80.5	77.0	9.8	139	63.9	81.4
38	Wales Trinity St David	87.7	80.8	17.3	99	65.0	81.1
39	Hull	72.4	69.6	31.7	117	66.0	81.0
40	Keele	75.5	71.5	—	131	78.3	80.6
41	Edinburgh	72.0	65.7	20.9	179	48.1	80.4
42	Liverpool John Moores	78.4	80.5	—	147	62.0	79.9
43	Staffordshire	84.6	81.0	—	125	64.9	79.7
44	West of England	72.5	73.9	—	137	72.7	79.4
=45	Chester	91.1	82.3	15.4	102	52.7	79.0
=45	Greenwich	85.1	86.5	—	141	52.0	79.0
47	Bournemouth	75.4	77.4	19.9	123	56.0	78.7
48	Glasgow Caledonian	63.1	59.3	4.7	173	65.3	78.4
49	Abertay	62.0	67.7	—	188	57.1	77.8
50	Anglia Ruskin	75.0	72.7	24.6	107	56.6	77.5
=51	South Wales	79.9	80.6	—	132	56.1	77.4
=51	Winchester	70.8	71.4	7.5	100	76.2	77.4
53	West London	75.4	78.2	—	110	67.3	76.6
54	Manchester Metropolitan	79.4	78.8	—	149	44.7	76.1
55	Canterbury Christ Church	76.6	77.2	16.3	101	41.2	72.7
56	Wolverhampton	67.4	70.0	—	122	49.2	71.0
57	Cumbria	77.9	67.3	1.5	100	46.7	70.5
58	London South Bank	58.9	51.8	—	95	65.7	68.5

Employed in professional job	35%	Employed in non-professional job and Studying	5%
Employed in professional job and studying	3%	Employed in non-professional job	23%
Studying	25%	Unemployed	11%
Average starting professional salary	£19,185	Average starting non-professional salary	£16,536

Architecture

Architecture is not in the top 40 subjects for starting salaries in professional jobs, but graduates know that this soon changes. After five years at work, female architects earn 11% more than the average graduate and men 6% more. The workload on degree courses is above average – 16 hours a week, compared to 14 for all subjects – but initial employment prospects are good. Architecture has moved into the top 15 of the 67 subject groups for the proportion of graduates finding high-level work or continuing to study. Seven out of ten graduates went straight into a professional role in 2017 and the subject was close to the top ten for overall graduate prospects.

Qualification usually takes seven years, in which the first degree is but a step on the way. That is a considerable financial commitment, especially when course materials can add another £1,000 to the burden. Nevertheless, there were still close to six applications per place in 2017. The number of places rose for the third year in a row and is up by 20% since £9,000 fees were introduced.

The four leading universities for architecture remain the same for the third year in a row, although Bath is only half a point ahead of Cambridge at the very top. There is plenty of movement further down the table, notably by Coventry, which has jumped 20 places and into the top ten. Liverpool is another new entrant to the top ten, after a rise of seven places to seventh.

Bath has good scores on all the measures, but does not lead on any of them. The most satisfied students – both in relation to teaching quality and the broader student experience – are at the University of the West of England. Falmouth has a rare 100% employment record, while University College London posted the best grades in the Research Excellence Framework. The table contains one name that may be unfamiliar: Manchester School of Architecture is a joint enterprise between Manchester and Manchester Metropolitan universities.

There are no particular subjects required for entry to most degrees in architecture, although some universities prefer candidates with art A-level or equivalent, and most welcome maths. Entry standards at the leading universities are relatively high – more than 220 points average at Cambridge – but four of the bottom eight universities average less than 100 points on the UCAS tariff.

Architecture	Teaching quality %	Student experience %	Research quality %	Entry standards (UCAS points)	Graduate prospects %	Overall score
1 Bath	78.3	80.1	52.9	207	96.6	100.0
2 Cambridge	81.3*	76.5*	49.0	223	90.9	99.5
3 Sheffield	90.3	91.0	36.6	172	96.4	98.8
4 University College London	78.0	75.4	54.1	191	91.0	97.1
5 Strathclyde	83.8	76.7	23.0	207	93.5	95.6
6 Newcastle	74.8	76.2	43.7	177	89.9	93.5
7 Liverpool	84.4	81.4	43.5	145	86.5	93.1
8 Queen's, Belfast	81.6	76.6	35.2	153	91.1	92.3
9 West of England	96.5	97.3	10.6	141	86.0	92.0
10 Coventry	95.2	94.1	10.3	144	86.3	91.7
11 Cardiff	67.0	60.8	40.7	182	94.5	91.2
12 Kent	77.8	78.4	33.3	163	85.6	90.7
=13 Edinburgh	72.9	67.7	35.1	181	87.5	90.6
=13 Falmouth	94.5	92.1	—	111	100.0	90.6

15	Nottingham	78.5	76.8	14.8	174	90.1	89.9
16	Northumbria	87.7	89.8	5.9	171	82.3	89.8
17	Dundee	85.3	76.9	8.7	169	87.3	89.4
=18	Oxford Brookes	85.7	82.5	17.6	144	85.6	89.2
=18	Reading	79.0	77.0	40.0	142	—	89.2
20	Manchester School of Architecture	76.2	71.3	12.6	166	94.7	88.9
21	De Montfort	77.8	77.2	35.9	122	89.0	88.8
22	Solent	96.0	92.1	—	91*	92.6	87.7
23	Plymouth	86.0	82.2	13.2	122	88.3	87.6
24	Portsmouth	88.4	89.4	—	111	91.7	86.9
=25	Nottingham Trent	84.7	81.1	3.4	138	88.1	86.8
=25	Westminster	85.1	82.5	10.7	139	82.3	86.8
27	Ulster	76.8	69.1	28.6	122	88.2	86.5
=28	Robert Gordon	79.6	79.8	8.3	163	81.2	86.4
=28	University of the Arts London	80.3	78.0	—	149	90.6	86.4
=30	Cardiff Metropolitan	96.0	92.7	—	99	82.1	85.7
=30	University for the Creative Arts	83.6	82.6	3.4	136	84.6	85.7
32	Arts University, Bournemouth	88.8	84.7	2.4	126	82.2	85.6
33	Central Lancashire	90.8	86.9	3.0	121	77.8	84.9
34	Greenwich	84.9	78.1	2.0	134	82.5	84.6
35	Liverpool John Moores	83.6	81.2	4.9	138	78.8	84.5
36	Kingston	86.5	87.5	10.1	133	69.2	83.9
=37	Derby	79.6	76.8	6.7	117	86.6	83.8
=37	Norwich University of the Arts	95.4	81.7	—	118	73.7	83.8
39	Lincoln	76.9	73.5	3.2	126	89.6	83.7
40	London South Bank	79.8	72.0	19.6	103	82.6	83.2
41	Birmingham City	84.3	78.9	9.6	122	75.3	83.1
42	Edinburgh Napier	82.4	75.9	5.7	139	74.3	82.8
43	Sheffield Hallam	83.1	85.1	13.4	118	69.5	82.4
44	Leeds Beckett	85.1	79.5	5.6	117	74.1	82.1
45	Salford	72.8	72.0	19.6	119	75.6	81.1
46	Middlesex	85.7	81.5	13.3	128	60.0	80.9
47	Huddersfield	79.0	76.4	—	122	76.5	80.5
48	London Metropolitan	80.9	74.4	7.2	97	75.3	79.6
49	Northampton	86.9	77.0	—	77	78.6	79.5
50	Brighton	74.2	73.7	13.1	116	69.8	78.9
51	East London	81.8	80.8	8.1	113	63.0	78.7
52	Anglia Ruskin	73.3	71.5	5.2	98	78.6	78.1
53	Wolverhampton	75.7	74.5	5.6	116	60.9	76.0
54	Glasgow Caledonian	71.1	69.3	9.1	—	69.2	75.2
55	Ravensbourne	71.2	68.5	—	92	66.7	73.2

Employed in professional job	68%	Employed in non-professional job and Studying	0%
Employed in professional job and studying	4%	Employed in non-professional job	10%
Studying	9%	Unemployed	9%
Average starting professional salary	£20,000	Average starting non-professional salary	£16,640

Art and Design

Art and design are among the big recruiters in higher education, with over 117,000 students applying for places in 2017 and three more universities joining our table in the latest edition of the *Guide*. Indeed, two new universities – Leeds Arts and Ravensbourne – have been established since the last edition was published. The numbers enrolling in the larger design area have fallen for the last two years, but there were still almost 19,000 starters in 2017 and another 4,600 embarking on fine art degrees.

The subjects always feature in the lower reaches of the tables for employment and earnings, but artists and designers accept that they may have a period of lowly paid self-employment early in their career while they find a way to pursue their vocation. Only four universities, Lancaster, Portsmouth, Staffordshire and Bournemouth Arts, saw more than 80% of 2017 graduates find professional jobs or postgraduate courses. However, specialist arts universities and arts faculties of generalist institutions have increased their focus on employability in recent years, and only three of the 85 universities in the latest table dropped below 50% positive destinations, compared with 17 two years ago.

Newcastle is top of the table for the third year in a row, but this time it has to share that honour with Oxford. The two might have been separated if Oxford undergraduates had responded to the National Student Survey (NSS) in sufficient numbers for a score to be compiled. Bangor has the most satisfied students, both where teaching quality is concerned and in those sections of the NSS devoted to the broader student experience, but it remains just outside the top ten. Essex is the big mover among the leading universities, jumping 12 places to fifth in the new table.

Most courses in art and design are at post-1992 institutions, but older foundations fill the top 12 places. Higher entry standards are partly responsible, although most artists would argue that entry grades are of less significance than in other subjects. Selection in art and design rests primarily on the quality of candidates' portfolios and many undergraduates enter through a one-year Art Foundation course. Nottingham Trent is the highest-placed modern university, having moved up another two places following a big rise last year.

Art and Design	Teaching quality %	Student experience %	Research quality %	Entry standards (UCAS points)	Graduate prospects %	Overall score
=1 Newcastle	88.4	88.3	37.3	176	70.8	100.0
=1 Oxford	—	—	39.7	239	70.0	100.0
3 Lancaster	77.1	76.5	48.0	163	81.4	99.1
4 Loughborough	79.8	77.3	35.3	190	76.0	98.8
5 Essex	94.0	90.4	46.9	—	56.5	97.8
6 University College London	86.8	86.7	44.7	176	55.9	97.0
7 Glasgow	66.0	69.4	37.2	220	—	95.7
8 Ulster	80.9	73.7	57.2	133	66.5	94.8
9 Brunel	80.4	79.6	32.8	139	76.8	94.4
10 Dundee	83.0	80.2	39.9	172	56.0	94.2
11 Leeds	74.1	69.1	33.6	169	74.8	94.0
12 Bangor	96.8	93.0	—	133	75.0	93.7
13 Nottingham Trent	83.4	80.5	4.7	161	79.1	93.2
=14 Kingston	87.2	82.1	10.1	188	60.7	93.0
=14 West of England	91.0	88.6	15.0	160	60.3	93.0

16	Wales Trinity St David	86.2	79.7	39.2	111	70.4	92.9
=17	Goldsmiths, London	77.4	76.1	25.9	194	59.8	92.8
=17	Southampton	79.3	73.4	35.4	171	60.9	92.8
=19	Aberystwyth	86.9	81.6	21.6	119	76.0	92.5
=19	Portsmouth	86.2	81.7	—	126	88.3	92.5
=21	Bournemouth	86.7	87.0	15.0	123	76.1	92.4
=21	Robert Gordon	88.5	82.8	11.5	159	66.2	92.4
23	De Montfort	89.1	87.0	10.2	126	75.2	92.2
24	Staffordshire	87.5	81.9	2.3	123	85.1	92.1
25	Arts University, Bournemouth	79.1	75.1	2.4	168	80.4	92.0
26	Coventry	82.0	80.3	18.1	140	73.9	91.9
27	Manchester Metropolitan	78.4	76.4	9.7	175	71.6	91.7
=28	Kent	64.7	64.3	44.3	141	78.8	91.4
=28	Northumbria	85.3	84.3	13.3	158	63.4	91.4
30	Westminster	81.8	76.6	22.5	135	68.9	90.5
31	Oxford Brookes	88.8	87.6	10.4	172	50.4	90.2
=32	Edinburgh	74.6	69.2	27.9	164	64.0	90.0
=32	Sheffield Hallam	87.5	84.7	15.5	135	62.1	90.0
34	University for the Creative Arts	86.8	83.1	3.4	151	65.8	89.9
35	Heriot-Watt	70.9	67.0	31.1	162	66.1	89.7
=36	Leeds Arts	84.2	81.2	—	177	59.5	89.3
=36	Reading	73.2	69.2	38.9	136	64.8	89.3
38	Liverpool Hope	79.1	70.8	—	151	78.6	89.2
39	Lincoln	81.8	79.7	7.1	130	72.8	88.9
=40	Falmouth	82.1	74.2	3.0	130	76.5	88.5
=40	Salford	90.4	85.6	8.0	136	57.4	88.5
42	Central Lancashire	87.5	82.3	3.9	129	66.1	88.2
43	Birmingham City	86.7	82.7	9.6	137	58.9	88.0
44	Liverpool John Moores	81.7	76.1	7.2	151	62.5	87.7
=45	Buckinghamshire New	89.2	81.7	6.1	114	66.1	87.6
=45	Derby	81.1	77.4	5.1	130	70.7	87.6
47	Huddersfield	80.3	76.4	4.8	130	71.8	87.5
=48	Greenwich	85.9	79.4	3.5	136	62.9	87.3
=48	Teesside	82.0	79.4	2.9	116	74.3	87.3
50	Hull	83.7	81.1	11.2	127	61.5*	87.1
51	Norwich University of the Arts	81.4	76.8	5.6	151	60.5	87.0
52	South Wales	87.1	80.8	3.3	135	59.5	86.7
=53	University of the Arts London	76.5	71.1	8.0	151	64.9	86.6
=53	Winchester	87.6	85.7	—	107	67.9	86.6
55	London South Bank	76.7	70.2	12.8	103	78.5	86.4
56	Bath Spa	80.1	71.8	9.6	131	66.1	86.3
57	Anglia Ruskin	86.1	82.4	8.5	125	54.3	85.4
58	Hertfordshire	76.9	70.1	5.8	116	73.9	85.3
=59	Abertay	75.3	71.1	—	161	61.9	85.1
=59	Plymouth	76.7	74.8	14.7	148	53.8	85.1
=61	Solent	87.1	85.5	1.6	118	57.2	85.0

	Teaching quality %	Student experience %	Research quality %	Entry standards (UCAS points)	Graduate prospects %	Overall score
=61 Worcester	81.8	79.3	11.1	117	59.7	85.0
63 Brighton	80.9	74.6	13.1	137	53.6	84.9
64 Edinburgh Napier	70.8	74.5	—	168	61.2	84.8
65 Middlesex	80.3	76.6	13.3	118	58.8	84.7
66 Suffolk	92.0	79.2	—	117	54.5	84.4
=67 Cardiff Metropolitan	84.6	80.9	7.9	114	55.4	84.1
=67 Wolverhampton	82.7	78.9	8.9	107	60.3	84.1
69 Sunderland	80.8	71.5	9.8	127	56.8	83.8
70 Glyndŵr	85.1	74.2	7.8	127	52.1	83.7
71 Gloucestershire	80.6	78.3	—	126	59.2	83.5
72 Glasgow Caledonian	82.6	78.7	1.8	162	42.0	83.2
73 East London	74.6	72.0	9.8	126	59.7	83.0
74 Cumbria	77.5	71.1	6.1	140	54.3	82.9
75 West London	81.9	78.6	4.5	118	53.3	82.4
76 London Metropolitan	77.8	71.1	4.7	117	60.7	82.3
77 Ravensbourne	74.3	74.1	—	104	70.1	82.2
78 Chichester	67.1	63.2	—	134	70.0	81.8
79 Northampton	81.6	77.3	2.9	111	54.2	81.6
80 Bolton	81.4	75.2	—	124	52.2	81.4
81 Chester	69.8	63.5	6.2	121	64.2	80.9
82 Leeds Beckett	81.6	77.0	1.2	115	50.8	80.8
83 Canterbury Christ Church	84.9	76.9	7.3	108*	43.4	80.0
84 York St John	70.5	66.0	—	121	45.9	75.9
85 Bedfordshire	63.4	63.5	—	80	59.8	73.7

Employed in professional job	54%	Employed in non-professional job and Studying	2%
Employed in professional job and studying	1%	Employed in non-professional job	25%
Studying	8%	Unemployed	10%
Average starting professional salary	£19,000	Average starting non-professional salary	£15,808

Biological Sciences

The biological sciences have set a new record for the numbers starting degrees in five of the six years since £9,000 fees were introduced. The exception was in 2017, when enrolments for biology, botany, genetics and microbiology all fell slightly. But normal progress has been resumed in the current academic year, with 52,000 students embarking on courses across the group as a whole, confirming the subjects' status as the most popular sciences. Universities obviously expect the trend to continue since the table contains more than 100 universities for the first time.

Cambridge remains top for the 14th year in a row, but Oxford has slipped to third for the first time in that period, overtaken by Imperial College London. The average grades for entrants to Cambridge's Natural Sciences degree are among the highest in any subject, while Imperial has excellent graduate prospects. Students at Abertay are by some distance the most satisfied with the quality of teaching – it is the only institution to top 90% on either of our measures derived from the National Student Survey – but the university does not make the top 50, mainly because it has one of the lowest research grades.

Satisfaction rates are generally good – only nine universities dropped below 70% on teaching quality and eight on the broader student experience. Graduates are less enthusiastic, however: three years after graduation almost 40% of biologists wish they had chosen a different subject – one of the biggest proportions in the arts or sciences. Employment rates and graduate salaries have improved a little, but are still in the bottom half of all subjects. Four out of ten graduates stay on for a postgraduate qualification, either full or part-time.

Microbiology provides the stiffest competition at entry, with almost six applications to the place, but the leading universities' requirements can be tough across all the subjects in this category. Many will demand two sciences at A-level, or the equivalent – usually biology and chemistry – for any of the biological sciences.

Biological Sciences	Teaching quality %	Student experience %	Research quality %	Entry standards (UCAS points)	Graduate prospects %	Overall score
1 Cambridge	80.6*	77.4*	52.5	242	83.9	100.0
2 Imperial College	76.0	79.0	61.6	209	88.4	99.2
3 Oxford	—	—	50.9	217	83.9	98.0
4 Dundee	80.3	81.9	55.4	184	85.2	96.9
5 Lancaster	86.6	87.7	46.5	158	82.3	94.8
6 St Andrews	85.7	84.3	37.6	210	73.4	94.5
7 Sheffield	81.5	86.9	57.4	164	77.8	94.4
8 Warwick	83.8	86.4	37.1	160	86.9	94.1
9 York	85.2	85.2	41.9	176	77.4	93.6
=10 Exeter	85.1	85.4	39.7	177	77.8	93.5
=10 University College London	75.4	75.6	55.4	190	77.6	93.5
12 Bristol	82.3	83.8	46.8	179	76.1	93.4
13 Durham	76.7	76.0	32.9	205	80.7	92.6
14 King's College London	81.9	82.6	38.0	175	79.0	92.4
=15 Birmingham	83.1	80.0	38.1	161	81.6	92.0
=15 Glasgow	82.6	82.3	33.4	200	72.4	92.0
17 Strathclyde	72.5	77.7	52.2	183	76.6	91.9
18 Bath	76.7	81.3	31.5	182	82.6	91.7
19 Manchester	80.0	79.1	38.3	167	78.8	91.1
20 Nottingham Trent	84.2	84.9	24.1	141	87.2	90.8
=21 Kent	78.4	81.4	39.1	136	85.1	90.4
=21 Leeds	80.5	82.6	40.9	162	74.9	90.4
23 Southampton	83.5	85.5	34.2	154	76.5	90.3
24 Edinburgh	69.9	72.3	62.9	178	70.1	90.2
25 Aston	80.9	78.7	39.1	139	82.0	90.0
26 Aberdeen	82.8	82.4	34.7	185	66.8	89.6
27 Surrey	85.5	86.8	37.5	158	68.4	89.5

Biological Sciences cont

		Teaching quality %	Student experience %	Research quality %	Entry standards (UCAS points)	Graduate prospects %	Overall score
28	Swansea	82.6	85.5	38.6	137	75.9	89.3
29	Sussex	72.5	73.6	46.8	149	80.3	89.1
30	Aberystwyth	85.3	85.5	38.2	123	75.6	88.7
31	East Anglia	80.1	82.3	38.8	142	75.1	88.6
32	Portsmouth	85.5	82.7	24.3	111	84.5	87.9
33	Nottingham	77.5	78.9	26.5	156	77.2	87.5
34	Leicester	79.3	80.5	36.5	137	72.8	87.0
35	Glasgow Caledonian	79.2	80.1	8.1	171	78.0	86.7
36	Cardiff	78.6	75.3	33.3	154	71.2	86.6
37	Queen's, Belfast	70.8	72.8	47.3	145	72.7	86.4
=38	Birkbeck, London	77.4	75.2	41.0	96	83.0	86.2
=38	Liverpool	73.0	72.8	33.9	144	77.6	86.2
40	Keele	81.2	84.2	16.5	130	78.2	85.8
=41	Newcastle	75.2	76.4	28.4	152	72.7	85.5
=41	Stirling	75.6	78.2	49.0	164	56.9	85.5
43	Teesside	85.6	85.6	—	121	84.3	85.4
44	Lincoln	88.7	88.2	—	129	77.5	85.2
45	Gloucestershire	88.7	88.1	14.5	119	72.3	85.1
=46	Hull	77.8	77.5	31.7	124	74.3	85.0
=46	Royal Holloway, London	78.0	78.6	25.7	133	74.4	85.0
=48	Central Lancashire	85.0	82.1	8.3	135	75.8	84.9
=48	Essex	83.7	83.4	17.8	111	77.9	84.9
=50	Huddersfield	84.2	80.6	7.8	128	77.3	84.4
=50	Northumbria	74.7	78.5	14.0	137	79.9	84.4
52	Robert Gordon	73.6	77.9	4.9	166	77.0	84.2
53	Hertfordshire	86.4	87.4	10.9	106	74.7	83.7
=54	Abertay	92.0	84.2	4.3	133	67.2	83.6
=54	Queen Mary, London	69.5	75.2	26.1	143	74.3	83.6
56	Oxford Brookes	75.1	79.2	21.3	122	75.5	83.3
57	Westminster	76.0	79.9	21.2	122	74.3	83.2
58	Sheffield Hallam	84.0	85.0	10.4	116	72.9	83.1
=59	Brunel	76.5	73.7	18.2	136	72.9	82.9
=59	St George's, London	64.2	69.8	20.0	153	78.4	82.9
=61	Coventry	75.6	79.2	4.5	123	79.9	82.3
=61	Sunderland	81.5	79.2	7.5	113	76.8	82.3
=63	Queen Margaret, Edinburgh	82.0	77.2	—	142	72.7	82.2
=63	Reading	75.6	72.2	26.6	140	66.1	82.2
65	Plymouth	85.0	85.2	17.4	133	59.5	82.1
66	Staffordshire	86.3	84.7	—	105	75.7	82.0
=67	Derby	87.9	86.4	1.6	113	70.4	81.9
=67	Edinburgh Napier	85.5	84.7	8.9	161	55.2	81.9
=69	Chester	82.4	80.6	12.0	107	72.7	81.8

=69	Roehampton	78.8	81.6	20.6	103	71.7	81.8
=69	West of England	81.7	82.1	8.2	126	69.2	81.8
72	Edge Hill	84.6	84.4	6.2	122	67.7	81.6
73	Heriot-Watt	57.8	60.3	26.3	157	77.7	81.5
74	Ulster	73.4	77.5	—	125	81.1	81.4
=75	Liverpool John Moores	83.6	82.4	15.1	136	58.0	81.0
=75	Manchester Metropolitan	80.9	78.7	12.0	125	66.5	81.0
77	Bradford	76.5	74.2	9.5	115	75.6	80.8
=78	Salford	85.4	82.4	12.7	122	59.3	80.3
=78	West of Scotland	79.2	78.4	29.0	155	47.8	80.3
80	Bangor	79.2	79.0	31.5	139	50.1	80.1
81	Worcester	85.2	86.8	10.9	110	60.2	79.8
82	Bolton	85.3	81.3	—	108	68.0*	79.5
=83	Bath Spa	81.3	72.3	—	114	72.8	79.4
=83	Leeds Beckett	76.0	79.6	3.5	113	72.1	79.4
85	Bedfordshire	76.3	79.0	25.1	84	68.3	79.3
86	South Wales	82.9	80.9	—	127	63.4	79.2
=87	Greenwich	68.1	75.9	7.4	127	70.1	78.4
=87	London Metropolitan	72.9	71.7	—	111	76.6	78.4
89	East London	77.9	82.7	—	96	71.7	78.3
90	Cardiff Metropolitan	74.9	75.7	—	114	71.6	78.2
91	Wolverhampton	73.7	76.8	—	108	70.0	77.2
92	Kingston	78.0	77.7	2.6	110	62.6	76.7
93	Canterbury Christ Church	80.4	74.2	11.9	79	63.3	76.0
94	Royal Veterinary College	62.0	60.1	—	143	70.0	75.5
95	Brighton	79.0	69.7	4.8	105	59.7	75.2
96	Middlesex	56.2	68.9	10.0	114	72.2	75.1
=97	London South Bank	57.4	67.4	35.0	100	58.7	74.1
=97	Northampton	76.3	72.7	—	105	59.0	74.1
99	Liverpool Hope	41.0	41.0	—	128	93.6	74.0
100	Anglia Ruskin	79.6	77.8	2.2	106	49.5	73.3
101	Bournemouth	72.0	69.1	4.7	113	51.4	72.0

Employed in professional job	30%	Employed in non-professional job and Studying	3%
Employed in professional job and studying	2%	Employed in non-professional job	18%
Studying	35%	Unemployed	10%
Average starting professional salary	£21,000	Average starting non-professional salary	£16,000

Building

Applications and enrolments for degrees in building are recovering at last, but both are still down by more than a third since the recession of 2008, when the decline set in. Building is in the top ten subjects both for employment prospects and starting salaries in professional jobs – and yet there are still only four applications per place. Now there is the added complication of degree apprenticeships in construction as a potentially attractive alternative for those planning a career in the sector.

Almost 80% of those completing building degrees in 2017 went straight into graduate-level employment, and only five of the 35 universities in our table dropped below this mark. The same number, spread through the table, scored more than 95% for graduate prospects. Loughborough remains top for building, with University College London still in second place. Loughborough achieved the best grades in the Research Excellence Framework, while students on UCL's Project Management for Construction degree and those at Heriot-Watt have the highest entry grades. In general, entry requirements are lower than for most subjects – only 81 points at Derby.

The relatively low numbers of students on many building courses make for fluctuations in the scores, especially where satisfaction levels are concerned. Students at Derby were the most satisfied both with the quality of teaching and the broader student experience. Last year's top university for teaching quality, Nottingham Trent, is not in the top ten in the new edition.

Courses in this category include surveying and building services engineering, as well as construction. The table is dominated by post-1992 universities, although older foundations take five of the top six places.

Building	Teaching quality %	Student experience %	Research quality %	Entry standards (UCAS points)	Graduate prospects %	Overall score
1 Loughborough	75.3	79.6	58.3	150	96.4	100.0
2 University College London	72.4	77.5	54.1	164	92.9	99.2
3 Reading	79.1	76.3	40.0	137	96.6	95.9
4 Heriot-Watt	67.8	76.1	38.1	164	92.9	95.8
5 Ulster	85.0	85.8	28.6	133	94.1	94.8
6 West of England	91.2	91.2	10.6	129	92.9	92.7
7 Oxford Brookes	86.3	87.8	17.6	126	93.6	92.4
8 Robert Gordon	83.1	83.6	8.3	142	92.5	91.7
9 Nottingham	80.0	83.7	14.8	138	—	91.2
10 Sheffield Hallam	86.2	80.2	13.4	122	93.8	90.7
11 Nottingham Trent	80.9	79.6	3.4	129	96.3	89.8
12 Northumbria	74.5	77.1	5.9	140	90.4	88.4
13 South Wales	74.8	69.5	—	146	92.3	88.1
=14 Anglia Ruskin	88.0	87.1	5.2	120	85.4	87.4
=14 Liverpool John Moores	81.6	78.0	4.9	132	87.0	87.4
16 Edinburgh Napier	83.4	83.6	5.7	128	83.7	86.9
17 Salford	73.9	71.7	19.6	130	84.1	86.6
18 Aston	80.0	80.2	20.6	136*	75.0	86.5
19 Glasgow Caledonian	71.9	69.3	9.1	154	80.0	86.1
20 Portsmouth	80.1	75.9	—	108	95.1	85.8
21 Coventry	81.0	83.0	10.3	107	87.5	85.6
22 Leeds Beckett	78.9	77.2	5.6	107	90.0	84.8
23 Bolton	87.6	81.3	2.5	—	77.8	84.6
=24 London South Bank	59.6	60.4	19.6	111	95.5	84.3
=24 Wolverhampton	83.0	84.2	5.6	101	86.5	84.3
26 Plymouth	74.3	78.1	13.2	121	81.1	84.2
27 Central Lancashire	78.4	79.2	3.0	124	80.0	83.5

28 Derby	94.2	91.6	5.6	81*	81.3	82.8
29 Greenwich	67.0	60.9	2.0	134	83.3	81.9
30 Westminster	59.4	62.0	10.7	125	86.0	81.7
31 Brighton	68.6	75.6	—	102	88.9	81.0
32 Kingston	67.2	66.6	—	123	80.0	79.8
33 Wales Trinity St David	81.8	78.8	—	104	72.4	78.6
34 Birmingham City	59.5	60.5	2.7	125	79.2	78.3
35 East London	75.8	67.5	8.1	—	70.6	77.0

Employed in professional job	75%	Employed in non-professional job and Studying	0%
Employed in professional job and studying	4%	Employed in non-professional job	7%
Studying	5%	Unemployed	9%
Average starting professional salary	£26,000	Average starting non-professional salary	£17,316

Business Studies

The Business Studies table is the biggest in our *Guide*, with 121 universities – one more than last year. The various branches of business and management are the largest recruiters of undergraduates in the UK, with almost 57,000 students starting courses last autumn. For the second year in a row, fewer students embarked on degrees in the two areas as a whole, although the demand for management is still growing. Business and management also remain the biggest area in Clearing, with more than 4,000 students finding places through the service in 2017.

Some of the most famous business schools are absent from this ranking because they do not offer undergraduate courses. Manchester Business School provides Manchester's undergraduate courses, as well as MBAs and executive education. The top two in the table are unchanged since last year, with Oxford in the lead. It has the highest entry standards, while the London School of Economics, in 11th place, was the top scorer in the Research Excellence Framework. Only a little further down the table, there has been considerable movement, with Southampton jumping 28 places to 13th and Bristol up 30 places to 16th.

Student satisfaction levels have dipped since last year's introduction of more focused questions in the National Student Survey. Only four universities – none of them in the top 30 – satisfied more than 85% of final-year undergraduates on the quality of teaching. Trinity Saint David, in 91st place, produced the best score on this measure. Buckingham, in 47th place, did best for the broader student experience. Three years after graduation, almost 39% of respondents say they would have chosen a different subject. Disappointments in the graduate employment market may be partly responsible. Although nearly six out of ten graduates went straight into a professional job in 2017, the subjects are outside the top 40 overall. Salary levels for those who do find professional employment are much better – business studies is among a large group of subjects sharing 26th place.

Graduate prospects are less variable than in the last edition of the *Guide*. Only two universities, Exeter and Loughborough, saw 90% of graduates go straight into professional employment or postgraduate study, compared with four last year. There were also only two where the rate dropped below 50%, compared with six last year.

SOUTHALL AND WEST LONDON COLLEGE LEARNING CENTRE

Business Studies

		Teaching quality %	Student experience %	Research quality %	Entry standards (UCAS points)	Graduate prospects %	Overall score
1	Oxford	—	—	32.0	232	85.1	100.0
2	St Andrews	81.9	85.0	43.8	212	85.5	98.3
=3	Bath	82.0	83.7	41.8	187	83.2	95.8
=3	Warwick	79.6	85.3	40.4	188	86.2	95.8
5	Loughborough	82.7	87.9	32.6	164	92.5	95.4
6	Leeds	82.8	86.6	39.3	167	85.9	95.1
7	Lancaster	81.8	83.3	42.6	152	89.3	94.6
=8	Exeter	79.1	83.0	24.4	174	94.0	93.6
=8	Strathclyde	77.7	79.1	44.3	207	71.7	93.6
10	University College London	66.5	69.7	43.9	192	87.3	91.4
11	London School of Economics	63.1	64.1	52.3	193	85.4	90.7
12	East Anglia	80.5	83.7	28.1	148	80.7	90.3
13	Southampton	79.5	80.4	24.0	151	85.6	90.2
14	York	78.9	80.5	24.0	149	85.7	89.9
15	Durham	72.3	73.6	23.1	177	88.5	89.7
16	Bristol	75.0	73.9	32.1	176	77.3	89.4
17	King's College London	64.5	72.5	38.2	186	82.8	89.2
18	Aberdeen	73.7	77.9	24.9	178	78.6	89.1
=19	Birmingham	71.6	73.4	29.1	162	87.2	89.0
=19	Sheffield	74.1	79.9	26.8	143	87.7	89.0
=19	Stirling	78.6	79.0	25.2	162	76.5	89.0
22	Queen's, Belfast	80.3	77.2	32.7	147	75.1	88.9
=23	City	74.4	79.9	28.7	164	77.3	88.8
=23	Nottingham	71.4	74.4	32.6	157	84.8	88.8
25	Manchester	73.6	75.2	33.3	163	77.4	88.6
26	Liverpool	78.7	79.3	20.1	150	81.8	88.5
27	Reading	75.3	75.0	29.3	143	84.6	88.4
=28	Glasgow	64.3	71.8	22.1	192	86.7	88.0
=28	Nottingham Trent	81.9	82.5	4.6	143	87.0	88.0
30	Heriot-Watt	79.7	80.8	18.8	157	74.9	87.9
=31	Cardiff	74.3	76.5	32.0	153	76.0	87.8
=31	Newcastle	71.7	75.6	20.7	157	87.2	87.8
33	Kent	74.0	75.1	24.8	142	84.9	87.5
=34	Sussex	71.6	73.7	23.7	150	85.1	87.1
=34	Swansea	77.3	80.3	22.0	136	79.2	87.1
=34	Ulster	81.9	82.4	40.4	124	61.8	87.1
37	Aston	78.0	78.7	19.7	143	78.0	87.0
38	SOAS London	—	—	25.0	144	75.7	86.9
39	Harper Adams	85.9	84.0	—	126	81.3	86.3
40	Aberystwyth	84.6	82.8	14.5	114	75.4	86.0
41	Royal Holloway, London	71.6	74.7	27.0	147	75.4	85.6
42	De Montfort	80.0	81.1	10.7	109	84.1	85.4

43 Coventry	81.7	82.5	1.6	126	80.7	85.2
44 Robert Gordon	78.8	77.3	2.6	166	72.5	85.1
45 West of England	82.0	84.6	5.5	118	77.8	85.0
46 Edinburgh	66.5	70.7	25.8	168	73.8	84.8
47 Buckingham	85.2	88.3	—	108	76.8	84.7
48 Lincoln	77.8	79.0	4.8	126	82.5	84.6
49 Surrey	66.1	72.8	15.8	166	79.7	84.5
50 Bangor	77.1	79.5	23.4	125	69.0	84.4
51 Portsmouth	75.4	77.3	9.5	118	85.1	84.3
52 Dundee	75.2	72.4	12.1	164	68.7	84.0
53 Huddersfield	77.5	78.5	4.1	135	76.6	83.8
=54 Essex	75.1	77.7	25.1	112	72.3	83.7
=54 Oxford Brookes	77.1	78.4	5.1	127	78.7	83.7
56 Bournemouth	79.9	79.7	8.8	123	71.3	83.5
=57 Leicester	71.7	72.4	24.3	129	71.3	83.1
=57 Liverpool Hope	85.0	85.7	—	107	70.8	83.1
59 Queen Margaret, Edinburgh	79.0	77.7	—	141	72.0	83.0
60 Derby	82.9	78.5	0.9	111	75.7	82.9
=61 Glasgow Caledonian	77.3	79.1	1.8	179	56.6	82.7
=61 Gloucestershire	80.5	79.3	—	123	73.4	82.7
=61 Hull	75.5	74.7	10.2	122	75.9	82.7
=61 Queen Mary, London	67.1	68.9	23.5	147	72.5	82.7
65 Abertay	77.0	80.3	—	137	71.7	82.6
66 Edinburgh Napier	73.5	75.6	2.3	155	71.0	82.5
=67 Bradford	76.3	78.4	11.8	128	67.3	82.4
=67 West London	83.3	86.5	—	113	66.7	82.4
=69 Liverpool John Moores	76.7	78.0	—	142	70.8	82.3
=69 Plymouth	76.7	79.4	13.1	111	70.9	82.3
71 Chester	84.4	81.9	0.5	108	69.0	82.2
=72 Bath Spa	79.7	79.8	—	111	75.5	82.1
=72 Brunel	72.0	74.4	23.0	132	64.4	82.1
=74 Edge Hill	81.0	79.5	—	128	67.3	82.0
=74 Falmouth	74.8	70.3	—	106	89.8	82.0
76 Sheffield Hallam	79.8	78.5	0.6	117	72.6	81.9
77 Keele	76.1	77.8	10.2	118	69.3	81.8
=78 Manchester Metropolitan	75.9	77.1	4.7	128	70.8	81.7
=78 Worcester	82.9	81.7	0.9	113	66.3	81.7
=80 Hertfordshire	78.0	79.0	0.9	125	70.0	81.6
=80 Northumbria	72.9	75.4	4.0	140	71.4	81.6
82 Central Lancashire	76.6	76.4	4.4	128	69.4	81.5
83 Solent	80.4	80.4	—	107	71.2	81.3
=84 Birmingham City	79.9	81.3	1.3	123	63.5	81.1
=84 Leeds Trinity	86.5	87.7	—	92	62.2	81.1
86 Teesside	75.8	76.6	2.0	112	74.8	81.0
=87 Buckinghamshire New	84.6	84.1	1.8	114	56.4	80.8
=87 Suffolk	79.9	76.6	—	118	68.0	80.8

Business Studies cont

		Teaching quality %	Student experience %	Research quality %	Entry standards (UCAS points)	Graduate prospects %	Overall score
89	South Wales	78.5	77.5	0.2	134	62.3	80.6
90	Staffordshire	76.2	77.3	2.6	115	68.9	80.3
91	Wales Trinity St David	86.6	84.3	—	94	59.1	80.2
92	West of Scotland	74.5	75.0	2.9	144	59.6	79.9
93	Chichester	77.4	80.1	—	112	63.3	79.4
=94	Anglia Ruskin	82.0	79.0	3.4	95	61.2	79.3
=94	University of the Arts London	73.9	69.4	—	127	69.4	79.3
96	St Mary's, Twickenham	75.5	74.3	—	110	68.9	79.1
97	London Metropolitan	80.7	76.3	0.6	97	64.6	79.0
=98	Greenwich	75.0	75.3	3.3	133	57.4	78.9
=98	Sunderland	77.0	77.7	0.4	119	59.9	78.9
=100	Leeds Beckett	75.3	77.2	0.8	109	65.3	78.7
=100	Winchester	79.5	74.5	—	108	61.9	78.7
102	Birkbeck, London	70.5	70.5	16.1	107	64.6	78.6
103	Westminster	68.2	73.2	2.4	132	66.3	78.4
104	Royal Agricultural University	70.6	74.6	—	103	73.5	78.3
105	London South Bank	68.1	69.7	2.1	103	78.4	78.2
=106	Brighton	73.1	70.2	6.5	113	63.5	78.0
=106	Kingston	73.8	75.7	9.2	120	54.1	78.0
108	York St John	78.5	76.7	0.8	102	57.9	77.6
109	Salford	68.9	71.5	5.9	118	64.0	77.5
110	East London	77.7	78.3	0.8	103	55.7	77.3
111	Wolverhampton	79.9	79.7	2.4	98	51.6	77.1
112	Middlesex	69.3	72.7	10.5	115	57.1	76.9
113	Bolton	77.5	74.7	—	97	58.3	76.7
114	Cardiff Metropolitan	68.7	69.2	—	118	64.8	76.5
115	Northampton	74.5	72.5	1.0	100	56.7	75.7
116	Roehampton	67.6	71.4	4.5	102	62.1	75.5
117	Canterbury Christ Church	72.2	71.1	—	105	53.3	74.5
118	Bedfordshire	69.0	69.3	3.1	85	60.7	74.0
119	Glyndŵr	73.2	68.0	—	76	51.0	72.0
120	Cumbria	64.7	66.3	5.6	94	47.8	71.0
121	Newman	62.5	64.6	—	111	44.2	70.0

Employed in professional job	55%	Employed in non-professional job and Studying	2%
Employed in professional job and studying	3%	Employed in non-professional job	20%
Studying	10%	Unemployed	10%
Average starting professional salary	£22,000	Average starting non-professional salary	£17,971

Celtic Studies

For the second year in a row, fewer than 100 students took up places on full-time degrees in Celtic Studies in 2017. Enrolments were 50% down on the already small numbers when £9,000 fees were introduced, leaving only eight universities in the table. The ranking is split between four universities from Wales, which naturally major in Welsh, and the remaining four, which focus on Gaelic or Irish studies. Ironically, it is the only one from England that tops the table for the seventh year in a row. Cambridge has the highest entry grades and the best performance in the 2014 Research Excellent Framework.

The students who do opt for Celtic studies are overwhelmingly satisfied with the experience – no university scores less than 80% on either of the measures derived from the National Student Survey (NSS). Swansea is the leader on the sections of the NSS relating to the quality of teaching, and it ties with second-placed Bangor for satisfaction with other aspects of their course, although a low research score restricts the university to a share of fifth place overall,

Third-placed Cardiff had the best graduate prospects in a year when Celtic Studies registered the lowest unemployment of any group of subjects outside the health disciplines, contributing to a move of seven places up the employment table to 38th out of the 67 areas. Almost half of the 2017 graduates went on to take another course. Starting salaries for those in professional jobs were a different matter. Celtic studies remained in the bottom ten.

Celtic Studies	Teaching quality %	Student experience %	Research quality %	Entry standards (UCAS points)	Graduate prospects %	Overall score
1 Cambridge			54.0	197	81.8	100.0
2 Bangor	95.8	95.8	39.6	179	69.8	97.6
3 Cardiff	90.5	93.4	32.5	160	84.3	95.3
4 Aberystwyth	89.6	88.2	23.7	162	79.6	92.7
=5 Queen's, Belfast	93.6	92.3	53.6	134	39.3	92.0
=5 Swansea	96.6	95.8	19.4	140	68.6	92.0
7 Glasgow	80.0	82.9	41.1	—	75.0*	89.8
8 Ulster	94.2	90.6	35.7	116	51.7	89.5

Employed in professional job	23%	Employed in non-professional job and Studying		2%
Employed in professional job and studying	6%	Employed in non-professional job		25%
Studying	41%	Unemployed		3%
Average starting professional salary	£19,000	Average starting non-professional salary		n/a

Chemical Engineering

Applications for chemical engineering degrees have dropped by almost a quarter in two years, even though the subject remains among the top four subjects for starting salaries in professional jobs. The decline in the numbers starting courses has been less steep, however, and the 2017 total of 3,160 entrants was still almost double the 2008 figure. With enrolments for engineering as a whole dropping in the current academic year, a third successive decline is probable but, with almost six applications to the place, chemical, process and energy engineering remains in a relatively healthy state.

Degree courses normally demand chemistry and maths A-levels, or their equivalent, and often physics as well. Most courses offer industrial placements in the final year and lead to Chartered Engineer status. The subjects remain in the top 20 for graduate prospects, despite a high unemployment rate of 13%.

Cambridge has dropped off the top of the table for the first time in 16 years, overtaken by Imperial College London. But the two could not be closer: Cambridge has the highest entry standards (by a single point) and the top research score. It is ranked by QS among the top four universities in the world for chemical engineering – three places ahead of Imperial. The most satisfied students both with teaching quality and the broader student experience are those at Teesside, although the university is only 16th overall. Portsmouth, one place lower overall, saw an impressive 94% of 2017 leavers going straight into graduate-level employment or continuing to study, a total beaten only by Lancaster in eighth place.

Four out of five chemical engineers come with A-levels or equivalent rather than vocational qualifications, and average entry grades are the highest for any engineering subject – more than half of the 29 universities in the table average more than 150 points at entry. This helps produce engineering's largest proportion of Firsts and 2:1s.

Chemical Engineering	Teaching quality (%)	Student experience (%)	Research quality (%)	Entry standards (UCAS points)	Graduate prospects (%)	Overall score
1 Imperial College	80.8	86.0	59.6	233	89.7	100.0
2 Cambridge	83.7	85.5	62.0	234	86.2	99.9
3 Nottingham	83.6	86.2	40.8	173	90.7	94.3
4 Bath	80.8	87.8	37.4	205	80.2	92.3
5 Birmingham	72.6	77.1	47.0	185	88.5	92.1
6 Sheffield	81.1	85.3	36.8	158	86.2	90.7
7 Strathclyde	65.8	67.7	37.2	225	87.0	90.3
8 Lancaster	67.4	71.0	41.6	157	96.2	90.0
9 Leeds	73.1	78.1	30.7	191	87.1	89.7
=10 Manchester	68.5	73.5	48.4	187	82.2	89.3
=10 Swansea	72.2	76.8	45.5	141	90.0	89.3
12 Loughborough	75.1	84.2	41.8	159	81.4	88.7
13 University College London	63.2	70.0	44.6	187	84.5	88.0
14 Heriot-Watt	73.6	76.6	47.8	166	77.9	87.9
15 Newcastle	75.7	78.0	30.2	162	83.7	87.4
16 Teesside	87.3	90.7	5.8	113	86.3	85.1
17 Portsmouth	71.8	77.6	9.1	131	94.4	84.6
18 Queen's, Belfast	68.4	67.8	36.7	154	81.0	84.4
19 Surrey	79.7	84.1	30.8	153	65.3	82.8
20 Bradford	81.0	86.0	7.7	122	81.0	82.5
21 Aberdeen	70.0	74.3	28.4	165	69.6	81.5
22 Edinburgh	51.4	57.4	50.3	197	69.3	81.1
23 London South Bank	70.9	77.2	19.6	100	83.8	80.8

24 Aston	72.8	74.7	20.6	127	76.7	80.6
25 West of Scotland	70.4	75.6	9.0	161	75.0	80.2
26 Hull	65.6	70.8	16.5	111	86.7	80.0
27 Chester	80.8	80.6	7.1	100	—	79.9
28 Huddersfield	85.2	82.7	10.2	97	60.6	75.8
29 Wolverhampton	61.0	56.8	4.4	104	—	70.0

Employed in professional job	52%	Employed in non-professional job and Studying	1%
Employed in professional job and studying	2%	Employed in non-professional job	7%
Studying	24%	Unemployed	13%
Average starting professional salary	£27,500	Average starting non-professional salary	£18,000

Chemistry

A second year of decline in both applications and enrolments in 2017 confirmed that chemistry's extended period of rising popularity had come to an end. But entry standards at the leading universities remain high – six universities average more than 200 points. Some courses require maths as well as chemistry, and most successful candidates for the leading universities take more than one science at A-level.

Cambridge and Oxford (in that order) remain clear at the top of the table, although neither has student satisfaction scores because responses to the National Student Survey did not reach the 50% threshold for publication. Cambridge has the highest entry standards and the best research grades – 97% of the work submitted for the Research Excellence Framework was considered world-leading or internationally excellent. Both Cambridge and Oxford are among the top six universities in the world for chemistry, according to QS. The best scores on both of our measures derived from the NSS are at Aston, which has still dropped 12 places overall and out of the top 20. Kingston in 51st place equals Aston's score for student experience.

Chemistry is just outside the top 20 for graduate prospects and salaries in graduate-level employment. Only two universities (Nottingham Trent and King's College, London) saw 90% of 2017 graduates go straight into professional jobs or continue their studies, compared with four in the last edition. Only one university (Northumbria) dropped below 60% on this measure.

Chemistry is mainly old university territory, but Nottingham Trent has moved two places further up the top 20 this year. Nearly nine out of ten chemistry undergraduates come with A-levels or their equivalent. A total of 112 universities and colleges plan to offer the subject in 2019.

Chemistry	Teaching quality %	Student experience %	Research quality %	Entry standards (UCAS points)	Graduate prospects %	Overall score
1 Cambridge	—	—	70.3	242	84.0	100.0
2 Oxford	—	—	63.1	228	89.8	98.5
3 York	89.8	89.8	44.6	177	86.1	95.2
=4 Durham	80.1	78.5	49.1	216	85.6	94.7
=4 St Andrews	82.1	86.3	50.3	207	83.0	94.7
6 Liverpool	82.6	85.1	55.6	145	88.1	93.3

Chemistry cont

		Teaching quality %	Student experience %	Research quality %	Entry standards (UCAS points)	Graduate prospects %	Overall score
7	Warwick	81.2	83.8	50.8	173	84.4	92.8
8	Nottingham	82.9	84.5	48.5	155	86.9	92.7
9	Glasgow	81.8	81.6	41.1	201	82.6	92.6
10	University College London	75.7	75.2	56.0	189	83.9	92.2
11	Heriot-Watt	87.6	83.1	34.2	173	83.2	91.7
=12	Lancaster	86.6	79.0	37.5	153	85.7	91.1
=12	Surrey	87.1	90.4	30.8	161	82.7	91.1
14	Nottingham Trent	85.7	88.8	24.1	128	92.3	91.0
15	Bristol	77.7	81.7	56.6	183	77.6	90.9
16	Birmingham	83.1	84.0	37.3	162	82.8	90.5
17	Bath	78.5	81.5	43.0	171	82.1	90.2
18	Manchester	—	—	46.0	171	75.0	90.0
19	Edinburgh	79.8	77.8	48.4	180	76.9	89.6
20	Sheffield	84.4	86.6	38.9	151	78.4	89.1
=21	Imperial College	64.4	66.0	54.6	204	81.8	89.0
=21	Keele	85.8	87.6	41.1	121	81.4	89.0
23	Leeds	81.7	82.6	35.9	160	80.1	88.9
24	Aston	95.2	94.4	20.6	127	78.9	88.7
25	Leicester	84.9	85.1	32.8	127	83.6	88.6
26	Strathclyde	74.2	72.3	40.1	191	79.8	88.5
=27	Queen's, Belfast	82.0	79.1	34.7	150	80.8	88.1
=27	Southampton	81.4	81.5	50.7	153	74.2	88.1
29	Loughborough	83.4	84.7	23.9	147	82.4	88.0
30	Cardiff	74.9	78.1	30.9	142	84.7	86.8
31	Sussex	86.5	86.6	25.8	147	74.3	86.5
32	East Anglia	76.6	77.0	39.2	150	78.1	86.4
33	Bangor	79.6	83.9	19.1	129	84.6	86.2
34	Plymouth	85.2	83.8	25.3	119	79.5	85.9
35	King's College London	75.8	74.0	—	161	90.0	85.8
36	Newcastle	76.3	81.8	28.5	150	76.6	85.1
37	Sheffield Hallam	86.3	84.7	17.8	111	79.8	85.0
38	Huddersfield	84.3	80.4	11.0	110	84.7	84.8
39	South Wales	88.3	87.8	—	122	81.3	84.6
40	Reading	77.9	71.4	27.3	127	81.5	84.5
41	Greenwich	86.1	84.8	7.4	129	78.0	84.2
42	West of Scotland	81.7	68.7	29.0	124	77.8	83.9
43	Liverpool John Moores	78.8	78.1	6.0	134	83.3	83.8
44	Manchester Metropolitan	81.9	80.0	16.3	125	77.9	83.6
45	Kent	79.1	79.0	27.5	130	74.7	83.5
46	Bradford	75.6	78.6	9.5	111	86.8	83.4
47	Queen Mary, London	72.1	74.5	37.0	132	74.2	82.7
48	Aberdeen	73.5	74.0	31.6	167	67.0	82.0

=49 Hull		77.2	75.9	24.2	107	77.3	81.9
=49 London Metropolitan		80.5	79.1	—	110	82.6	81.9
51 Kingston		94.9	94.4	2.6	102*	62.9	80.0
52 Central Lancashire		62.5	68.1	11.7	125	83.9	79.8
53 Northumbria		84.3	83.4	14.0	128	59.7	78.5
54 Brighton		70.8	64.8	4.8	101	82.2	78.4

Employed in professional job	39%	Employed in non-professional job and Studying	2%
Employed in professional job and studying	2%	Employed in non-professional job	12%
Studying	34%	Unemployed	10%
Average starting professional salary	£22,500	Average starting non-professional salary	£16,653

Civil Engineering

Cambridge has regained the lead in civil engineering for the first time in three years, registering the highest entry standards and the best research grades. It is ranked by QS as the second best university in the world for the subject, with last year's leader, Imperial College London only one place behind. Imperial has been pipped by Glasgow in our table, however, thanks mainly to a rare 100% employment score by Glasgow's 2017 graduates.

Both applications and enrolments were steady in 2017, following two years of increases. Graduate prospects that are in the top ten for all subjects are one obvious attraction; 70% of leavers go straight into professional jobs, earning average salaries of £26,000, which are also in the top ten of the 67 subject groups.

The plentiful employment opportunities are reflected in the table, where 25 of the 55 universities saw at least nine out of ten graduates go straight into professional jobs or on to postgraduate study.

By contrast, only one university reached 90% in each of our student satisfaction measures. Ulster, which has enjoyed a 17-place rise into the top 20, was the top performer in the sections of the National Student Survey relating to teaching quality, whereas Aberdeen was the top scorer on the broader student experience.

Some of the top degrees in civil engineering are four-year courses leading to an MEng; others are sandwich courses incorporating a period at work. The leading departments will expect physics and maths A-levels, or their equivalent. Fewer than half of all civil engineering undergraduates are admitted with A-levels, however, reflecting the popularity of BTEC. Almost half of the universities in the table are post-1992 institutions, but none reaches the top 20.

Civil Engineering	Teaching quality %	Student experience %	Research quality %	Entry standards (UCAS points)	Graduate prospects %	Overall score
1 Cambridge	83.7	85.5	67.0	239	93.5	100.0
2 Glasgow	79.4	85.4	47.2	198	100.0	95.8
3 Imperial College	78.4	84.1	61.5	220	87.5	95.5
=4 Bath	78.4	78.1	52.9	196	97.5	94.6
=4 Southampton	82.5	87.1	52.3	181	93.5	94.6

Civil Engineering cont

		Teaching quality %	Student experience %	Research quality %	Entry standards (UCAS points)	Graduate prospects %	Overall score
6	Bristol	82.2	84.8	52.3	190	91.9	94.5
7	Aberdeen	89.2	90.0	28.4	159	95.7	92.8
8	Exeter	85.1	86.1	36.4	155	96.8	92.4
9	Sheffield	79.4	82.4	43.1	160	97.2	92.0
10	Edinburgh	77.0	80.0	50.3	187	85.7	91.0
=11	Cardiff	82.2	87.7	35.0	150	93.4	90.8
=11	Nottingham	84.3	86.2	40.8	157	87.8	90.8
=13	Birmingham	85.6	86.8	21.9	163	92.7	90.6
=13	Strathclyde	76.6	80.3	35.7	191	90.3	90.6
=13	Swansea	79.6	84.9	45.5	133	96.4	90.6
16	Heriot-Watt	80.3	80.5	47.8	175	84.7	90.5
17	Loughborough	83.0	87.2	26.9	151	95.3	90.4
18	Leeds	81.0	86.9	32.0	169	87.1	89.8
19	Ulster	90.2	89.6	28.6	118	92.6	89.7
20	Dundee	80.8	81.6	46.2	159	84.9	89.6
21	University College London	79.3	79.5	23.1	176	93.2	89.4
22	Manchester	78.2	80.2	36.4	170	88.5	89.3
23	Surrey	79.3	83.8	30.8	161	89.7	89.0
24	Liverpool	76.0	81.4	32.1	135	97.3	88.3
25	Newcastle	72.8	76.1	40.9	154	88.9	87.2
26	Queen's, Belfast	73.6	75.0	31.3	149	94.3	87.1
27	Northumbria	82.6	82.4	30.7	132	86.7	87.0
28	Teesside	87.1	83.1	5.8	135	92.6	86.9
29	West of Scotland	85.0	82.2	9.0	151*	88.5	86.7
30	Nottingham Trent	85.0	80.7	3.4	135	95.3	86.5
31	Coventry	85.4	87.6	10.3	123	90.8	86.4
32	Abertay	85.0	83.6	16.3	137	85.7	86.2
33	Bradford	80.7	84.3	17.8	120	91.9	85.8
34	Edinburgh Napier	79.1	82.3	7.7	143	91.2	85.5
=35	Central Lancashire	83.2	81.4	7.1	131	—	84.6
=35	Plymouth	80.6	80.8	15.7	117	90.0	84.6
37	Wolverhampton	86.4	88.1	—	93	92.3	83.9
38	Portsmouth	80.0	79.7	9.1	114	89.6	83.3
39	Anglia Ruskin	85.5	88.2	5.2	111	82.4	83.2
40	Greenwich	75.1	70.6	5.5	137	92.9	83.0
=41	Brunel	69.5	76.1	23.7	139	85.5	82.9
=41	Leeds Beckett	83.2	87.0	5.6	103	85.7	82.9
43	West of England	71.8	78.2	10.6	132	89.5	82.6
44	Salford	73.4	72.6	19.6	137	84.1	82.4
45	West London	85.3	79.9	—	122	81.0	82.0
46	Glasgow Caledonian	72.1	79.4	9.1	162	76.3	81.5
47	City	72.0	75.0	23.1	119	80.6	80.8

48 London South Bank	74.0	76.1	19.6	107	82.2	80.6
49 South Wales	81.1	83.6	—	122	76.0	80.3
50 Liverpool John Moores	70.3	72.9	—	144	83.3	79.9
51 Derby	75.3	80.2	6.7	91	85.3	79.6
52 East London	81.0	82.4	2.3	121	72.1	79.5
53 Kingston	80.5	80.5	2.9	123	66.1	77.9
54 Bolton	63.2	68.6	—	130*	59.1	71.3
55 Brighton	58.1	62.2	5.1	109	64.2	69.9

Employed in professional job	67%	Employed in non-professional job and Studying	1%
Employed in professional job and studying	3%	Employed in non-professional job	6%
Studying	14%	Unemployed	9%
Average starting professional salary	£26,000	Average starting non-professional salary	£15,808

Classics and Ancient History

The number of students starting classics degrees has risen (gradually) for six years in a row, with enrolments now in excess of 1,100. Applications are running at record levels and, while history degrees generally suffered a decline in demand in 2017, numbers are still up compared with the first year of £9,000 fees.

Independent schools dominate provision of Latin and Greek at A-level, producing some of the highest average grades of any subjects. However, most universities offering classics teach the subject from scratch, as well as to more practised students.

Cambridge has topped the table for 13 years in a row, although Oxford has lost second place to Durham for the first time in that period. Cambridge has the highest scores in the table for research and entry grades, while Glasgow, in sixth, just pips St Andrews for the best graduate prospects. The table has more movement than last year's – Leeds has moved up six places into the top ten, while Warwick has dropped 11 places from sixth.

Roehampton's students are again the most satisfied with the quality of teaching, although the university remains only one place off the bottom of the table because it was the only one of the 23 universities not to enter the Research Excellence Framework. Fourth-placed St Andrews does best on the other sections of the National Student Survey, but generally scores in classics have dropped a little this year. Several universities teach the subjects as part of a modular degree scheme, but not as a degree in its own right, while most providers now broaden their offering with degrees in classical studies or classical civilisation that range beyond Latin or Greek.

Graduate prospects for classicists showed a sharp decline last year, but have stabilised in the new edition.

Starting salaries in graduate-level employment are up one place to 37th, while the proportion going into such jobs or on to further study remains 43rd of the 67 subject groups. More than a third of graduates opt for postgraduate courses, but the unemployment rate of 11% was above average in 2017.

Classics and Ancient History

	Teaching quality (%)	Student experience (%)	Research quality (%)	Entry standards (UCAS points)	Graduate prospects (%)	Overall score
1 Cambridge	—	—	65.0	214	76.7	100.0
2 Durham	88.5	80.9	54.3	199	79.8	97.8
3 Oxford	—	—	58.3	207	79.3	97.3
4 St Andrews	89.9	87.3	43.2	187	83.9	96.9
5 Exeter	83.0	80.8	45.0	176	80.5	93.3
6 Glasgow	79.2	81.9	32.7	156	84.2	89.7
7 Birmingham	81.6	80.8	40.3	153	71.7	88.2
8 Nottingham	75.9	71.7	52.0	153	70.4	87.8
9 University College London	73.7	66.3	42.7	174	72.4	87.0
10 Leeds	85.5	83.6	29.1	155	67.4	86.4
=11 Bristol	—	—	42.2	184	71.3	86.0
=11 Liverpool	—	—	28.9	141	72.7	86.0
=11 Newcastle	76.0	71.9	44.7	150	69.1	86.0
14 Royal Holloway, London	89.4	79.4	20.4	141	73.2	85.8
15 King's College London	71.9	65.4	43.6	156	70.9	85.0
16 Kent	78.3	70.3	33.1	117	78.7	84.3
17 Warwick	72.5	66.7	45.0	158	64.2	84.0
18 Edinburgh	81.2	71.7	34.9	176	55.4	83.7
19 Reading	74.4	63.0	45.2	133	68.7	83.5
20 Manchester	—	—	31.0	145	65.0	83.2
21 Swansea	82.2	77.7	25.0	123	67.4	81.9
22 Roehampton	91.1	86.7	—	99	67.1	78.6
23 Wales Trinity St David	86.1	80.6	15.7	95*	45.7	73.9

Employed in professional job	33%	Employed in non-professional job and Studying	3%
Employed in professional job and studying	3%	Employed in non-professional job	20%
Studying	31%	Unemployed	11%
Average starting professional salary	£21,600	Average starting non-professional salary	£16,000

Communication and Media Studies

Loughborough is out on its own as the leader in Communication and Media Studies, having shared that distinction with Sheffield last year. Sheffield, which still does not have scores for student satisfaction because of a low response rate in the National Student Survey, has dropped four places in the new table, while Exeter has moved up the same number to second. Exeter, whose entry standards are exceeded only by Strathclyde in 14th place, has jumped almost 20 places in two years. Undergraduates at Queen's, Belfast, are the most satisfied with the quality of teaching.

Graduate prospects are the weak suit of many universities in these subjects – fewer than half of the 2016 graduates at 13 of the 97 universities in the table had professional jobs or places on a postgraduate course by the end of the year. Swansea, which is just outside the top ten overall after an 11-place rise, recorded an exceptional 92% score for graduate prospects. But the subjects were in the bottom ten on this measure nationally and seventh from bottom for starting salaries in professional jobs. The division of jobs into professional and non-graduate fields of employment hits communication and media studies harder than most other subjects. Academics in the field argue that it is normal for students completing media courses to take "entry level" work that is not classified as a graduate job.

Nevertheless, courses in media studies continue to confound the sceptics who believed that a combination of £9,000 fees and poor employment prospects would bring about the collapse in recruitment long predicted in the media itself. Although applications for journalism and media studies fell in 2017, enrolments both then and in the current academic year were well ahead of the period immediately before and after the introduction of £9,000 fees. The subjects used to be the preserve of post-1992 universities, but older institutions have been moving in and now occupy the top 17 places. Northumbria is the only modern university in the top 20.

Communication and Media Studies	Teaching quality %	Student experience %	Research quality %	Entry standards (UCAS points)	Graduate prospects %	Overall score
1 Loughborough	80.6	84.3	62.3	156	78.9	100.0
2 Exeter	85.2	79.2	46.2	184	71.4	99.6
3 Leeds	79.9	79.0	54.5	166	79.9	99.3
4 Lancaster	83.3	84.2	51.4	148	82.1	98.9
5 Sheffield	—	—	37.9	149	84.5	98.8
6 Warwick	85.0	84.8	61.7	166	55.4	97.3
7 Cardiff	79.2	80.5	55.4	152	75.3	97.0
8 Southampton	88.5	83.8	42.7	151	67.1	96.1
9 York	89.3	86.3	26.0	149	—	96.0
10 Newcastle	80.5	78.3	37.8	152	79.5	95.3
11 Swansea	83.9	82.9	18.5	132	92.0	94.3
12 Queen's, Belfast	92.5	85.5	38.3	159*	50.0	93.9
13 Stirling	82.1	79.3	36.0	173	58.9	93.5
=14 King's College London	76.3	68.7	55.8	168	55.9	92.6
=14 Strathclyde	73.4	78.3	39.4	193	53.3	92.6
16 Surrey	74.4	68.7	30.2	171	72.0	92.0
17 Keele	84.1	84.0	25.0	129	74.3	91.4
18 Northumbria	85.3	84.3	22.2	144	66.5	91.3
19 Leicester	72.0	74.0	46.1	129	78.3	91.2
20 East Anglia	76.9	72.3	43.8	144	64.5	90.6
21 City	69.6	71.4	30.9	153	77.8	90.4
22 Goldsmiths, London	71.6	65.4	60.0	142	62.7	90.3
23 Salford	81.8	77.5	36.9	132	62.6	89.8
24 Liverpool	—	—	27.5	135	68.2	89.6
=25 Glasgow Caledonian	79.1	73.4	15.2	178	57.9	89.3
=25 Kent	84.0	80.6	—	134	81.8	89.3
27 Nottingham Trent	82.9	80.8	10.0	135	72.8	88.8
28 De Montfort	81.0	79.0	31.2	106	75.4	88.7

Communication and Media Studies
cont

	Teaching quality %	Student experience %	Research quality %	Entry standards (UCAS points)	Graduate prospects %	Overall score
29 Royal Holloway, London	80.2	70.5	38.1	143	56.6	88.6
30 Sussex	66.7	67.5	43.6	135	72.3	88.1
31 Birkbeck, London	83.5	78.7	34.7	91	74.1	88.0
32 Liverpool John Moores	83.7	83.6	6.2	137	67.2	87.8
33 Staffordshire	83.6	81.8	6.7	105	81.3	87.1
=34 Liverpool Hope	85.6	83.7	—	100	84.8	87.0
=34 Portsmouth	84.2	81.9	12.8	106	75.5	87.0
36 West of England	84.9	81.1	18.6	109	67.8	86.8
37 Aberystwyth	86.1	78.9	9.2	123	66.8	86.7
38 Oxford Brookes	75.8	73.7	25.3	127	67.0	86.4
=39 Edinburgh Napier	74.8	74.9	9.5	165	59.5	86.3
=39 Lincoln	80.0	79.3	4.0	131	72.3	86.3
41 Westminster	72.9	69.9	28.3	128	69.0	86.2
42 Coventry	75.3	74.3	18.1	126	70.3	85.8
=43 Central Lancashire	82.4	81.0	7.9	125	64.6	85.6
=43 Manchester Metropolitan	73.7	71.5	29.0	132	61.9	85.6
45 Queen Mary, London	76.1	68.3	35.1	139	52.2	85.5
46 St Mary's, Twickenham	89.5	84.1	9.1	106	62.1	85.4
47 Plymouth Marjon	88.7	88.4	—	112	58.5	84.2
=48 Derby	82.1	74.8	13.5	112	64.2	84.1
=48 Roehampton	75.8	76.3	26.4	96	69.5	84.1
50 Birmingham City	82.2	76.2	6.0	124	62.2	84.0
=51 Queen Margaret, Edinburgh	69.2	65.1	14.0	152	62.9	83.8
=51 West of Scotland	75.5	68.7	11.3	151	56.0	83.8
53 Robert Gordon	74.6	67.3	7.5	156	57.3	83.7
54 Hull	79.7	80.2	11.2	119	59.4	83.6
=55 Bangor	84.0	80.6	24.7	125	38.9	83.1
=55 Bournemouth	73.9	73.8	15.1	129	60.1	83.1
57 Huddersfield	79.1	74.5	—	118	69.2	83.0
58 Gloucestershire	79.4	78.8	9.3	115	60.2	82.8
59 East London	84.7	83.2	13.9	107	51.7	82.7
=60 Brunel	69.6	72.6	23.0	110	67.5	82.6
=60 Ravensbourne	76.9	69.5	—	106	78.8	82.6
62 Solent	76.5	74.2	0.8	117	69.8	82.4
63 Sheffield Hallam	76.5	75.4	14.4	121	56.6	82.2
64 University for the Creative Arts	83.2	79.5	3.4	101	62.8	82.0
65 York St John	92.4	92.0	4.4	107	40.3	81.8
=66 Sunderland	74.1	70.1	13.0	112	64.4	81.6
=66 Teesside	76.9	72.5	2.9	100	73.6	81.6
68 Anglia Ruskin	85.4	81.0	26.4	101	40.4	81.5
=69 Bath Spa	71.3	68.7	13.9	122	62.2	81.3
=69 Canterbury Christ Church	78.0	73.6	7.3	105	64.2	81.3

=69	Edge Hill	77.4	77.0	10.2	126	50.9	81.3
72	Worcester	78.4	76.7	8.2	111	57.2	81.0
73	Chester	77.6	71.6	4.3	104	66.8	80.9
74	Leeds Trinity	79.7	76.4	3.9	101	62.9	80.8
=75	Kingston	79.9	75.1	15.7	111	49.5	80.7
=75	Winchester	74.7	74.5	15.8	115	54.0	80.7
77	University of the Arts London	75.8	71.4	—	117	64.3	80.6
78	Leeds Beckett	82.1	83.7	11.0	104	47.5	80.5
79	Falmouth	72.9	65.1	—	118	68.8	80.3
80	Middlesex	77.8	76.7	11.0	112	51.3	80.2
81	Greenwich	73.0	69.2	3.5	121	61.8	80.1
82	London South Bank	69.5	70.0	12.8	105	66.9	80.0
83	Wolverhampton	69.6	68.9	33.2	91	57.8	79.6
84	Chichester	83.5	83.2	—	118	40.7	79.1
85	Suffolk	83.4	68.2	—	122	45.5	78.8
86	Glyndŵr	74.8	62.7	7.8	105	58.7	78.2
87	Bedfordshire	79.5	78.1	8.2	85	52.0	77.6
88	Ulster	64.9	61.4	34.0	117	41.8	77.2
89	Northampton	77.2	70.4	—	98	55.4	77.0
90	South Wales	74.8	70.1	—	123	43.3	76.5
91	London Metropolitan	66.3	59.6	5.9	99	66.1	76.2
92	West London	64.3	57.7	4.5	115	61.9	76.1
93	Brighton	68.5	65.4	16.2	108	44.0	75.3
94	Wales Trinity St David	81.2	77.6	—	81	46.2	75.0
95	Cumbria	67.7	53.1	—	106	57.9	73.9
96	Buckinghamshire New	61.8	56.0	—	113	46.1	71.0
97	Bradford	69.5	62.1	—	123	27.8	70.9

Employed in professional job	49%	Employed in non-professional job and Studying		2%
Employed in professional job and studying	2%	Employed in non-professional job		27%
Studying	10%	Unemployed		10%
Average starting professional salary	£19,000	Average starting non-professional salary		£16,185

Computer Science

Five successive increases in the numbers starting degrees in computer science came to at least a temporary halt last autumn, but the enrolment was still close to record levels. Areas such as artificial intelligence and games design have taken off to such an extent that they attracted 13,000 applications between them in 2017, nearly five times the total in 2012, while computer science itself saw a 50% increase over the same period. Some of the leading universities demand maths at A-level, or the equivalent, while others want computing or computer science.

Overall, the subjects offer good prospects for graduates – they are close to the top 20 of the 67 subject groups, with two-thirds of leavers going straight into professional employment. The £25,000 average salary in such jobs puts computer science into a tie for 14th place. But the table shows the advantage of winning a place at one of the leading universities. All but one of the top ten universities registered positive destinations for at least 90% of graduates, whereas only two of the bottom ten reached 70%. Exeter and Bath had the best record in 2017, with 97% of graduates going straight into professional employment or continuing their studies.

The top five in the table are unchanged since last year. Cambridge, which has the highest entry standards, is rated in the top five in the world for computer science by QS, with Oxford only two places lower. However, it is Imperial College, which produced the best grades in the Research Excellence Framework and whose students were closest to Cambridge's on entry standards, that is second in our table. The undergraduates most satisfied with their teaching and broader student experience are at East London, which is only just in the top 60 overall.

Entry standards vary more widely than in most subjects, with average scores on the new UCAS tariff ranging from more than 200 points at five universities to less than 100 points at another five. A growing number of universities are also offering degree apprenticeships in the more popular areas of computer science.

Computer Science	Teaching quality %	Student experience %	Research quality %	Entry standards (UCAS points)	Graduate prospects %	Overall score
1 Cambridge	—	—	57.1	239	96.5	100.0
2 Imperial College	80.8	87.0	64.1	229	92.5	99.0
3 Warwick	85.4	85.4	54.8	197	94.6	96.9
4 Oxford	—	—	60.6	213	90.9	96.3
5 St Andrews	83.1	87.2	33.4	214	90.8	94.6
6 Leeds	86.8	81.4	41.6	171	94.7	93.3
7 Swansea	83.2	85.8	47.5	160	92.7	92.5
8 Durham	74.0	75.9	38.8	209	94.7	92.1
=9 Bath	80.9	80.9	33.3	177	97.0	91.9
=9 Glasgow	75.1	77.4	50.3	197	88.9	91.9
11 Birmingham	78.6	78.6	46.4	175	93.5	91.7
12 Exeter	78.3	85.6	40.7	160	97.1	91.5
13 Manchester	78.9	80.9	50.7	172	87.6	91.2
=14 Edinburgh	70.4	74.1	54.3	192	88.6	90.5
=14 Sheffield	79.3	81.1	51.1	154	89.7	90.5
16 University College London	65.9	70.6	62.7	195	89.4	90.4
17 Bristol	71.8	74.0	49.2	193	88.7	90.3
18 York	77.7	76.8	46.9	162	92.3	90.2
19 Nottingham	77.3	79.6	45.4	159	88.8	89.4
=20 Dundee	80.5	85.1	29.4	181	80.7	88.9
=20 Southampton	70.5	75.8	48.2	171	90.9	88.9
=20 Strathclyde	81.6	80.1	21.1	197	81.8	88.9
23 Loughborough	82.2	85.3	18.7	156	93.1	88.7
24 Newcastle	74.9	77.3	49.7	158	86.9	88.6
25 Royal Holloway, London	78.2	80.4	35.1	140	95.0	88.4
=26 King's College London	71.7	74.7	47.6	160	90.0	88.1
=26 Lancaster	69.7	74.4	44.8	158	94.5	88.1
28 Liverpool	—	—	40.5	140	87.6	88.0

29 Aberystwyth	82.4	80.7	38.4	120	92.5	87.8
30 Heriot-Watt	73.0	73.3	39.5	178	81.9	86.9
31 Cardiff	77.1	79.4	25.0	149	91.1	86.7
32 Surrey	72.7	73.7	25.3	156	90.4	85.4
33 Brunel	78.8	78.0	25.2	148	83.4	85.3
34 Kent	69.1	68.6	37.8	148	91.9	85.2
35 Liverpool Hope	83.6	83.2	8.8	110	93.2	84.4
36 East Anglia	68.1	69.8	35.9	149	87.7	84.0
37 Huddersfield	81.1	79.8	7.4	138	86.1	83.8
38 Sussex	71.6	69.3	21.6	149	90.6	83.7
39 Bangor	83.0	79.9	17.6	128	80.3	83.6
=40 Portsmouth	82.7	82.6	7.2	122	86.7	83.5
=40 Queen Mary, London	67.6	73.4	37.4	149	82.3	83.5
=42 Bath Spa	85.4	84.2	13.9	112	—	83.4
=42 Nottingham Trent	80.4	78.1	5.2	147	83.8	83.4
=42 West of England	81.3	80.3	5.9	135	85.3	83.4
=45 Abertay	80.2	74.7	3.4	172	78.0	83.3
=45 Aston	79.3	78.3	21.7	133	80.1	83.3
=45 Lincoln	79.8	81.8	13.6	133	81.5	83.3
48 Falmouth	88.0	86.8	—	110	84.6	83.1
49 Queen's, Belfast	65.9	69.0	29.5	151	88.4	83.0
50 Aberdeen	68.4	69.8	37.4	154*	79.2	82.9
=51 Leicester	70.2	69.7	30.2	135	87.0	82.7
=51 London South Bank	80.1	79.6	19.6	89	91.8	82.7
53 Wales Trinity St David	91.5	89.1	1.0	121	72.1	82.6
54 Robert Gordon	82.0	78.2	4.3	149	77.9	82.5
55 Plymouth	74.4	71.6	21.8	131	84.2	82.1
56 West London	88.4	86.2	1.2	103	79.5	81.7
=57 Oxford Brookes	72.5	73.8	13.0	134	86.5	81.6
=57 Staffordshire	79.6	75.6	0.4	125	88.4	81.6
59 East London	92.1	89.6	2.3	116	66.9	81.5
=60 Bournemouth	81.6	81.9	8.5	127	75.2	81.4
=60 Essex	67.2	69.2	34.3	122	86.2	81.4
=60 University of the Arts London	91.4	85.4	—	109	73.7	81.4
63 South Wales	86.2	84.5	3.6	132	69.6	81.3
64 Stirling	71.9	69.7	14.0	132	88.0	81.2
=65 Edge Hill	82.5	84.0	0.3	137	72.8	81.1
=65 Salford	76.2	78.5	15.3	132	76.2	81.1
67 Northumbria	84.0	80.8	4.0	147	67.1	81.0
68 Coventry	77.5	78.4	3.3	124	83.6	80.9
69 De Montfort	75.0	75.4	13.4	111	85.4	80.5
=70 Derby	77.6	73.3	5.0	123	83.6	80.4
=70 Sheffield Hallam	79.2	76.8	14.4	122	74.7	80.4
72 Edinburgh Napier	76.9	75.7	5.2	138	77.3	80.3
=73 Sunderland	85.4	79.9	1.8	122	71.2	80.0
=73 Ulster	77.4	75.2	16.6	128	72.1	80.0

Computer Science cont

		Teaching quality %	Student experience %	Research quality %	Entry standards (UCAS points)	Graduate prospects %	Overall score
75	York St John	86.3	78.8	—	112	75.0	79.9
76	Hull	70.9	68.0	22.2	121	82.4	79.8
=77	Liverpool John Moores	76.5	73.1	3.2	143	74.0	79.4
=77	Reading	68.4	64.3	16.3	143	81.1	79.4
=79	Manchester Metropolitan	77.6	75.0	5.6	131	73.6	79.2
=79	Teesside	77.5	71.9	3.4	127	77.9	79.2
81	Worcester	80.7	76.0	—	117	73.0	78.3
=82	Chester	85.3	71.7	1.3	110	71.3	78.1
=82	Gloucestershire	77.5	79.5	—	125	70.6	78.1
=82	Leeds Beckett	78.6	78.5	0.2	117	72.3	78.1
85	Greenwich	75.0	75.1	7.3	143	64.8	78.0
86	Glyndŵr	83.5	79.2	3.9	113	64.0	77.7
87	Glasgow Caledonian	71.4	67.6	4.0	156	69.1	77.6
88	City	68.0	71.1	21.8	143	64.3	77.5
89	Hertfordshire	66.5	71.8	7.8	122	79.9	77.2
90	Birmingham City	74.0	74.4	4.9	126	69.5	77.1
=91	Central Lancashire	72.6	69.6	—	140	71.2	76.9
=91	West of Scotland	78.8	72.7	3.2	132	63.2	76.9
93	Bradford	71.4	72.1	—	133	72.9	76.8
=94	Cardiff Metropolitan	69.4	72.1	—	121	78.7	76.7
=94	Keele	65.7	72.9	10.8	124	75.3	76.7
96	London Metropolitan	83.5	81.0	0.7	91	67.3	76.6
97	Suffolk	79.1	74.9	—	125	63.6	76.5
98	Solent	75.5	71.8	—	109	75.0	76.4
=99	Goldsmiths, London	68.0	67.2	29.2	134	59.9	76.3
=99	Kingston	77.3	74.9	5.3	111	66.7	76.3
101	Anglia Ruskin	79.7	76.2	—	103	67.4	76.0
102	Middlesex	74.9	75.3	14.2	123	53.6	75.1
103	Buckinghamshire New	85.3	81.1	—	97	54.9	74.9
=104	Birkbeck, London	67.0	66.9	28.7	106*	63.6	74.8
=104	Wolverhampton	71.0	75.5	—	94	75.0	74.8
106	Westminster	65.4	69.4	2.9	123	69.7	74.1
=107	Bolton	74.7	71.8	—	110	62.6	73.8
=107	Chichester	64.3	62.1	—	119	77.3	73.8
=107	Northampton	74.2	65.0	—	112	66.5	73.8
110	Brighton	70.3	69.5	6.4	113	62.8	73.5
111	Bedfordshire	70.7	70.1	9.1	86	61.4	71.8
112	Canterbury Christ Church	71.1	72.3	—	102	51.4	70.3

Employed in professional job	64%	Employed in non-professional job and Studying	1%
Employed in professional job and studying	2%	Employed in non-professional job	11%
Studying	11%	Unemployed	12%
Average starting professional salary	£25,000	Average starting non-professional salary	£16,500

Creative Writing

Creative writing is bottom of the salaries table and only one place off it for the proportion of graduates going straight into professional jobs or continuing their studies. But that has not stopped another three universities joining our table for the subject, as the numbers enrolling for creative writing degrees has continued to rise. Almost 900 students started courses in 2017 and over 100 universities and colleges plan to offer the subject in 2019. Many will be part of a joint honours programme or are still too small to qualify for our table, which is now in its fifth year. Creative writing is paired with subjects as diverse as law, dance and business, but more normally with English.

Lancaster has taken over from Warwick at the top of the table, thanks mainly to an outstanding 95% success rate for graduate prospects – a full ten percentage points ahead of its nearest challenger, London South Bank. Warwick has the highest entry grades and the best performance in the 2014 Research Excellence Framework, while Birmingham City, which has gone up 11 places and into the top ten, has much the most satisfied students. There are some big changes further down the table, with Bolton and Greenwich both jumping 25 places, to 12th and 23rd respectively.

With fewer than four applications to the place, entry standards are generally low – only seven of the 51 universities averaged more than 150 points on the new UCAS tariff. The table is largely composed of post-1992 universities, although the top eight are all older foundations. Most applicants recognise that professional employment will be uncertain and some are not even aiming for a full-time job on graduation. Nevertheless, creative writing – or imaginative writing, as it is known by UCAS – has been a significant, but little-noticed area of growth in higher education over recent years.

Creative Writing	Teaching quality %	Student experience %	Research quality %	Entry standards (UCAS points)	Graduate prospects %	Overall score
1 Lancaster	81.1	79.5	47.0	155	95.5	100.0
2 Warwick	79.3	70.8	59.8	189	66.7	99.6
3 Newcastle	88.0	81.8	54.3	153	—	99.2
4 Birmingham	82.7	79.8	37.0	165	81.0	97.1
5 Royal Holloway, London	84.3	77.5	49.9	147	75.7	96.4
6 Nottingham	72.8	70.9	56.6	167	61.7	94.1
7 Surrey	83.8	75.7	39.1	154	69.0*	93.8
8 Bangor	80.4	73.7	46.3	142	70.5	92.9
9 Birmingham City	96.1	91.2	30.9	104	69.2	91.1
=10 East Anglia	71.8	72.8	36.2	169	59.4	90.3
=10 Manchester Metropolitan	90.2	82.8	29.0	121	68.4	90.3
12 Bolton	95.6	85.7	14.4	—	60.0	90.2
13 Coventry	80.0	78.1	18.1	137	77.4	88.9
14 Plymouth	85.4	76.9	30.5	130	60.5	88.3
15 Queen's, Belfast	74.8	69.1	53.1	—	64.3	88.2
16 Aberystwyth	82.8	79.4	31.2	114	65.6	87.2
17 De Montfort	80.6	81.1	24.1	110	73.8	86.7

Creative Writing cont

		Teaching quality %	Student experience %	Research quality %	Entry standards (UCAS points)	Graduate prospects %	Overall score
18	Westminster	84.3	83.1	28.9	106*	62.3	86.1
19	Chester	88.4	89.3	10.7	109	65.6	85.5
20	St Mary's, Twickenham	90.9	81.8	14.6	111	61.8	85.4
21	London South Bank	86.9	81.8	12.8	86*	84.6	85.3
22	Derby	82.8	79.7	13.5	115	69.8	85.1
23	Greenwich	88.1	85.8	14.4	118	53.5	84.5
24	Brunel	70.5	67.9	30.9	127	64.3	84.4
25	Liverpool John Moores	79.1	75.4	17.9	138	52.6	84.0
26	Hull	84.1	75.1	22.7	113	57.6	83.9
27	Edge Hill	86.3	76.7	12.1	122	54.9	83.3
28	Portsmouth	70.3	64.9	17.1	116	80.4	83.1
29	Central Lancashire	84.9	80.8	9.9	118	56.6	82.9
30	Gloucestershire	87.6	79.7	9.3	116	54.2	82.6
31	Chichester	81.8	80.3	16.3	115	53.3	82.4
32	Liverpool Hope	80.2	76.8	26.9	104	—	82.1
33	West of England	66.2	69.3	35.4	134	46.3	81.9
34	Worcester	85.7	77.7	8.2	112	56.8	81.8
35	Salford	78.5	76.3	7.8	126	57.3	81.6
36	Bath Spa	69.3	63.3	23.5	118	64.5	81.2
37	Roehampton	77.5	73.8	20.8	110	54.0	81.0
38	Sheffield Hallam	86.8	84.3	14.6	119	35.1	80.9
39	Bedfordshire	92.7	84.8	45.8	82	17.6*	80.3
40	Winchester	81.4	76.3	—	123	54.2	80.0
41	Essex	62.9	57.3	37.7	133	—	79.8
42	Anglia Ruskin	93.8	80.3	16.3	89	40.0	79.6
43	Kingston	78.3	71.2	15.7	109	52.2	79.5
44	York St John	67.4	66.5	9.7	119	64.3	78.8
45	South Wales	81.2	71.5	12.8	109	43.2	78.0
46	Northampton	83.3	81.0	15.3	97	34.6	77.1
47	Falmouth	71.7	66.4	—	107	61.8	76.1
48	Bournemouth	74.2	65.0	15.1	122	33.3	75.8
49	Canterbury Christ Church	81.6	69.1	8.0	98	42.1	75.5
50	Middlesex	61.8	65.2	11.0	107*	56.5*	74.8
51	East London	80.0	75.9	—	94	32.2	72.3

Employed in professional job	27%	Employed in non-professional job and Studying	5%
Employed in professional job and studying	3%	Employed in non-professional job	30%
Studying	21%	Unemployed	13%
Average starting professional salary	£18,000	Average starting non-professional salary	£16,068

Criminology

The Criminology table has settled down since the last edition, when 11 universities joined in its second year of publication, one of them going straight to the top. That university was Lancaster, which remains the clear leader despite not registering the top score on any of the individual measures. Now Sheffield has joined in second place, thanks mainly to graduate prospects that are at least 20 percentage points ahead of practically all the other universities in the table. Salford is the only other newcomer, in 23rd place.

The data in this table previously appeared under sociology and law, but the growth in demand for degrees in criminology justified a ranking of its own. It remains an area of expansion, both for traditional degrees and degree apprenticeships, partly in response to moves towards a graduate-entry police force. No fewer than 154 universities and colleges plan to offer degrees in criminology this year, albeit in some cases only as part of a broader social science degree.

Sociology or psychology is welcomed by some departments, but there are no specific entry requirements for criminology degrees, apart possibly from GCSE maths, since the course is likely to involve the use of statistics. Third-placed Stirling has the highest entry standards and Kent the best research score. Students at Glyndŵr are by far the most satisfied with both the quality of teaching and the broader student experience, and the university has shot up 27 places as a result. It would almost certainly have been placed higher than 14th if it had entered the Research Excellence Framework in this subject.

Criminology remains in the bottom six subjects for the proportion of graduates going straight into professional employment or further study, but those who find professional jobs are paid an average of £20,000, placing the subject in the top 50 on this measure. Many criminology graduates eventually find employment in the police force, prison service, the Home Office, charities or law practices. Although the unemployment rate is a respectable 8%, more than a third of graduates start out in lower-level jobs.

Criminology	Teaching quality %	Student experience %	Research quality %	Entry standards (UCAS points)	Graduate prospects %	Overall score
1 Lancaster	86.9	87.5	51.4	150	74.5	100.0
2 Sheffield	73.0	74.8	26.8	147	95.5	94.9
3 Stirling	81.8	79.5	33.8	174	55.6	94.5
4 Swansea	83.3	82.5	20.4	152	74.4	94.2
5 Nottingham	80.1	77.0	43.5	144	68.2	93.9
6 Kent	77.3	75.8	59.0	125	69.4	93.3
7 Leeds	75.9	76.8	40.1	155	65.3	93.2
8 York	75.5	71.6	47.5	158	57.1	92.3
9 Southampton	75.4	73.4	52.8	148	55.0	91.8
10 Manchester	76.6	75.2	27.2	151	70.3	91.7
=11 Durham	73.9	69.5	28.7	158	71.8	91.6
=11 Portsmouth	85.6	83.4	12.1	128	78.8	91.6
13 Birmingham	76.3	71.1	40.1	145	—	91.0
14 Glyndŵr	96.8	96.5	—	118	66.7	90.8
15 Queen's, Belfast	82.3	77.9	39.3	139	48.8	89.9

Criminology cont

		Teaching quality %	Student experience %	Research quality %	Entry standards (UCAS points)	Graduate prospects %	Overall score
16	Liverpool Hope	88.9	85.4	8.6	114	73.7	89.6
17	Essex	74.1	73.3	44.3	112	73.3	89.2
=18	Lincoln	85.0	82.2	5.8	126	69.9	88.5
=18	Surrey	86.0	82.5	—	160	50.6	88.5
20	Sussex	74.5	71.1	27.9	140	64.7	88.4
21	Leicester	79.2	78.2	26.3	127	61.7	88.2
22	Nottingham Trent	78.5	78.0	5.1	131	74.9	87.8
23	Salford	83.3	79.0	27.7	123	55.0	87.7
=24	Edinburgh Napier	80.2	78.2	—	164	52.9	87.4
=24	Huddersfield	84.3	79.1	9.5	121	67.5	87.4
26	Gloucestershire	84.3	80.9	—	120	72.4	87.1
27	Sheffield Hallam	87.8	83.9	14.4	118	54.1	86.8
28	De Montfort	82.1	78.4	11.2	106	74.4	86.6
=29	Hull	78.6	72.6	14.3	117	73.0	86.5
=29	Northumbria	78.4	73.8	12.7	139	59.8	86.5
31	West of England	85.6	82.4	10.9	129	51.5	86.4
32	Coventry	84.6	82.1	—	121	66.1	86.2
33	Central Lancashire	77.1	73.7	11.8	136	61.8	86.1
34	Liverpool John Moores	75.3	74.0	5.8	140	66.4	86.0
35	Derby	89.6	84.7	2.4	113	58.9	85.9
=36	Birmingham City	77.1	77.5	3.8	131	63.8	85.2
=36	Solent	81.5	83.7	—	110	70.7	85.2
38	Abertay	79.8	74.6	5.0	158	43.4	85.0
39	Plymouth	80.5	79.2	16.0	117	55.5	84.8
40	Aberystwyth	78.0	70.2	14.3	110	69.3	84.6
41	Edge Hill	82.3	81.1	12.1	123	49.5	84.5
42	Brighton	79.5	76.7	12.4	113	58.2	83.7
=43	Greenwich	81.1	75.6	2.1	127	53.3	83.2
=43	Royal Holloway, London	78.0	77.8	—	137	50.7	83.2
45	Bradford	72.4	66.8	10.6	115	71.4	83.1
46	West London	72.2	75.5	—	114	74.2	82.9
=47	Teesside	74.0	71.3	15.0	105	65.5	82.5
=47	Westminster	75.9	78.1	—	121	60.3	82.5
=49	Cardiff	73.4	69.4	30.8	—	51.3*	82.4
=49	London Metropolitan	78.1	74.6	8.8	109	59.7	82.4
51	Manchester Metropolitan	72.7	70.4	6.9	129	56.1	81.9
52	Winchester	79.9	79.5	4.4	108	51.9	81.3
53	South Wales	77.4	68.5	15.4	131	37.5	81.0
=54	Kingston	80.4	76.0	—	108	54.3	80.8
=54	Middlesex	70.6	67.8	14.9	114	57.9	80.8
56	London South Bank	65.9	65.8	20.1	103	67.9	80.7
57	Leeds Beckett	82.7	79.6	6.4	108	40.3	80.1

58 Anglia Ruskin	87.9	82.0	5.4	90	43.2	80.0
59 Roehampton	70.0	69.6	—	102	66.0	78.8
60 Suffolk	76.9	72.1	—	104	45.1	77.2
61 Northampton	73.3	64.7	—	104	51.9	76.7
62 City	62.6	61.2	20.8	141	26.7	76.4
63 Canterbury Christ Church	73.5	71.6	3.2	105	38.9	75.8
64 Chester	74.2	67.8	0.3	103	41.3	75.3

Employed in professional job	34%	Employed in non-professional job and Studying	5%
Employed in professional job and studying	3%	Employed in non-professional job	31%
Studying	20%	Unemployed	8%
Average starting professional salary	£20,000	Average starting non-professional salary	£17,000

Dentistry

Dentists are the best-paid graduates to emerge from higher education and the most likely to find a professional job. Only medics matched the £31,000 average salaries paid to the 96% of those who found such work after graduating in 2017. There is no figure for less skilled work because virtually everyone who completes a degree goes on to become a dentist. None of the 15 undergraduate dental schools saw less than 96.6% of graduates going into professional jobs or further study. This measure is not used to determine positions so as not to exaggerate the impact of tiny numbers delaying their entry into the profession.

The numbers seeking places on degrees in dentistry were up slightly in 2017, but still 30% lower than they were at the start of the decade. There were more than eight applications to the place and entry standards are high – nowhere averages less than 170 points on the new UCAS tariff. Most schools demand chemistry and biology, and some also require maths or physics.

Most degrees last five years, although several universities offer a six-year option for those without the necessary scientific qualifications. The number of places has been increased in recent years to tackle shortages of dentists, but there are still more applications to the place than in any subject except medicine.

Scores in the subject are so close that the ranking changes frequently, but Glasgow has held on to the lead it assumed two years ago. Glasgow has the highest entry standards and good scores for student satisfaction and employment. Second-placed Queen's Belfast was one of four universities – with Dundee, Birmingham and Central Lancashire – to see every graduate go into professional employment or further study. But Queen's was pipped by Plymouth to the highest scores in the National Student Survey. Student satisfaction remains high at most of the dental schools. Fifth-placed Manchester produced the best results in the Research Excellence Framework, as it did in the 2008 assessments.

Dentistry

		Teaching quality %	Student experience %	Research quality %	Entry standards (UCAS points)	Graduate prospects %	Overall score
1	Glasgow	91.3	89.9	29.3	228	99.2	100.0
2	Queen's, Belfast	96.3	94.3	50.7	193	100.0	98.7
3	Dundee	90.8	86.8	22.1	220	100.0	95.7
4	Newcastle	93.0	89.6	43.6	184	98.5	93.3
5	Manchester	78.3	77.9	57.1	185	98.5	91.6
6	Cardiff	87.3	88.8	36.8	188	99.3	90.8
7	Leeds	83.6	88.0	31.7	187	99.1	88.2
8	Bristol	73.2	67.8	47.1	192	99.0	88.1
9	Plymouth	98.8	98.6	9.5	184	96.6	87.3
=10	King's College London	78.5	74.6	40.9	184	99.1	86.8
=10	Queen Mary, London	67.6	69.1	48.3	191	97.5	86.8
12	Sheffield	90.8	87.2	28.5	170	97.5	85.1
13	Birmingham	82.2	81.4	19.2	187	100.0	84.0
14	Liverpool	73.0	71.3	31.7	182	99.2	82.0
15	Central Lancashire	80.5	74.3	8.3	—	100.0	76.6

Employed in professional job	96%	Employed in non-professional job and Studying	0%
Employed in professional job and studying	2%	Employed in non-professional job	0%
Studying	1%	Unemployed	1%
Average starting professional salary	£31,000	Average starting non-professional salary	n/a

Drama, Dance and Cinematics

For the first time, our table for Drama, Dance and Cinematics contains more than 100 institutions, including several specialist universities and colleges. Four more institutions have joined in the latest edition, making ten newcomers in the last five years. Applications for all three subjects fell in 2017, although the numbers actually starting courses remained broadly stable. Enrolments in drama and cinematics are still well up on 2012, when £9,000 fees were introduced. There are now more than six applications to the place in drama, although rather fewer in the other subjects.

The subjects' popularity has never been reflected in high entry grades – quality of performance is a more important criterion on many courses. No university averages 200 points at entry and two average less than 100. Fourth-placed Glasgow has the highest score, at 195 points. Essex has taken over from Exeter at the top of the table, thanks mainly to the highest scores in both of our student satisfaction measures.

The Royal Conservatoire of Scotland again has by far the best of a generally poor set of employment figures, with 91% of leavers going straight in to professional jobs or further study. Overall, drama, dance and cinematics are in the bottom ten for graduate prospects, despite an unemployment rate of 9% that is no higher than in most subjects, and they are three from the bottom of the salaries table. As in other performing arts, freelancing and periods of temporary employment are common for new graduates – more than 30% started out in low-level jobs in 2017.

Drama, Dance and Cinematics	Teaching quality %	Student experience %	Research quality %	Entry standards (UCAS points)	Graduate prospects %	Overall score
1 Essex	94.0	90.5	37.7	143	85.4	100.0
2 Sussex	91.8	87.8	45.6	150	76.7	99.3
3 Exeter	81.1	82.8	46.3	172	75.3	98.8
4 Glasgow	72.7	74.3	53.9	195	68.5	98.4
=5 Central School of Speech and Drama	—	—	47.7	138	76.3	96.0
=5 Lancaster	85.4	87.9	48.0	154	64.6	96.0
=5 Sheffield	—	—	60.0	149	63.9	96.0
=5 Surrey	88.8	85.1	27.2	168	66.9	96.0
9 Birmingham	77.0	78.2	36.9	168	75.9	95.7
10 Queen Mary, London	83.4	77.0	68.4	150	56.8	94.9
11 Queen Margaret, Edinburgh	84.6	74.9	14.0	177	74.4	94.7
12 Manchester	—	—	58.6	163	56.5	94.5
13 Warwick	66.2	67.5	61.7	162	73.1	94.0
14 York	82.6	82.2	26.0	169	64.4	93.5
15 Royal Holloway, London	81.9	76.0	50.6	153	61.1	93.3
=16 Coventry	90.8	88.4	18.1	137	72.0	92.6
=16 Royal Conservatoire of Scotland	79.8	74.6	11.3	144	91.1	92.6
18 Arts University, Bournemouth	82.4	81.9	2.4	159	79.2	92.1
19 Kent	79.1	75.9	44.3	138	69.3	91.7
20 Edinburgh Napier	72.0	71.0	37.9	166	66.7	91.6
=21 Nottingham Trent	83.0	80.3	10.0	164	68.7	91.5
=21 Oxford Brookes	91.5	80.4	27.8	129	68.3	91.5
23 Aberystwyth	89.1	82.8	30.3	129	67.0	91.2
24 De Montfort	86.4	85.1	14.5	126	78.8	90.8
25 Goldsmiths, London	91.8	89.6	28.3	132	57.6	90.7
=26 Huddersfield	88.7	85.8	28.0	127	64.7	90.4
=26 Leeds	72.3	75.2	28.0	163	66.3	90.4
28 Bristol	65.7	61.8	48.7	181	56.2	90.3
29 East Anglia	71.7	77.3	43.8	172	49.5	90.2
30 Edinburgh	68.4	65.2	48.0	178	52.0	89.9
31 Birmingham City	91.9	88.7	11.6	131	63.2	89.3
32 Loughborough	75.3	75.6	32.4	149	62.5	89.1
=33 Hertfordshire	82.6	80.0	5.3	135	74.9	88.3
=33 Nottingham	77.1	72.9	45.8	141	54.5	88.3
35 Queen's, Belfast	76.8	79.1	38.3	139	55.7	87.9
36 Lincoln	87.1	83.4	6.5	133	63.2	87.2
37 Robert Gordon	89.3	83.5	11.5	—	52.9	87.1
38 Portsmouth	82.3	82.9	—	126	76.6	87.0
=39 Norwich University of the Arts	84.0	80.3	—	133	70.8	86.9
=39 Westminster	79.5	76.2	—	137	75.6	86.9
41 East London	85.6	81.9	11.2	126	64.5	86.8
42 Roehampton	76.9	73.6	46.6	123	55.5	86.4

Drama, Dance and Cinematics cont

		Teaching quality %	Student experience %	Research quality %	Entry standards (UCAS points)	Graduate prospects %	Overall score
43	Manchester Metropolitan	75.5	75.5	7.5	144	68.4	86.3
44	Liverpool Hope	78.7	78.9	3.0	124	77.3	86.2
=45	Reading	75.2	71.1	34.8	135	57.5	86.0
=45	Staffordshire	89.3	83.8	—	108	73.9	86.0
=47	Falmouth	80.2	77.5	6.2	122	73.4	85.7
=47	Middlesex	81.4	78.2	16.1	129	61.6	85.7
=47	Northumbria	84.7	83.1	13.3	150	44.7	85.7
=50	Derby	83.6	81.0	5.1	121	69.0	85.6
=50	Liverpool John Moores	86.5	82.7	—	139	57.4	85.6
52	University for the Creative Arts	78.3	73.1	3.4	134	69.3	85.1
=53	Gloucestershire	85.3	79.0	—	131	59.5	84.4
=53	Solent	88.7	80.9	—	119	62.3	84.4
55	Bedfordshire	89.2	87.4	5.6	106	61.7	84.3
=56	Hull	83.6	81.7	11.2	126	54.8	84.2
=56	St Mary's, Twickenham	86.9	78.2	9.1	131	51.8	84.2
58	Aberdeen	67.6	59.9	29.3	153	—	83.7
=59	Bath Spa	77.1	73.1	10.7	133	59.9	83.6
=59	Chichester	83.9	82.5	9.7	129	50.8	83.6
=59	Plymouth Marjon	92.7	87.3	—	116	52.6	83.6
62	Sunderland	82.1	82.3	4.2	127	57.0	83.4
=63	Edge Hill	79.2	79.0	3.8	134	56.6	83.2
=63	London South Bank	82.3	77.6	—	111	70.1	83.2
=63	University of the Arts London	76.3	69.6	—	143	61.7	83.2
66	Worcester	85.0	85.0	3.5	126	51.4	83.0
=67	Plymouth	81.0	79.1	20.2	125	48.2	82.9
=67	York St John	87.7	82.0	10.5	125	45.2	82.9
69	Ulster	90.8	85.2	40.0	115	27.2	82.8
70	Sheffield Hallam	86.6	82.9	14.4	125	42.4	82.6
=71	Central Lancashire	75.9	71.8	3.9	132	61.6	82.5
=71	Wolverhampton	91.0	88.2	—	112	51.5	82.5
=73	Brunel	74.5	66.1	32.6	128	49.5	82.4
=73	Chester	86.5	82.5	4.3	115	53.9	82.4
=73	West of England	78.8	74.8	—	137	56.4	82.4
76	Leeds Arts	85.6	83.5	—	134	43.2	81.8
77	West of Scotland	80.4	71.7	—	137	51.8	81.5
78	Teesside	82.5	82.6	2.9	120	51.9	81.4
=79	London Metropolitan	84.5	73.5	—	108	62.2	81.2
=79	Salford	81.1	76.5	7.2	132	45.4	81.2
81	South Wales	80.0	71.3	6.4	134	48.1	81.1
82	Wales Trinity St David	82.7	74.6	—	110	61.8	81.0
83	Northampton	83.9	77.6	—	126	48.0	80.7
84	Kingston	75.2	71.1	15.7	131	45.3	80.2

=85	Anglia Ruskin	78.4	78.5	16.9	117	43.5	79.8
=85	Brighton	75.9	65.2	13.1	125	50.7	79.8
=87	Greenwich	61.6	60.3	3.5	151	58.2	79.5
=87	West London	77.7	75.6	2.3	122	50.9	79.5
89	Winchester	77.7	75.1	11.2	121	43.9	79.1
90	Bournemouth	63.8	65.3	15.1	132	54.6	79.0
=91	Bolton	76.3	71.4	—	123	50.2	78.3
=91	Cardiff Metropolitan	77.4	82.5	—	125*	42.1	78.3
93	Leeds Beckett	75.3	74.9	1.7	118	50.0	78.1
94	Ravensbourne	66.3	58.4	—	116	69.7	78.0
95	Bishop Grosseteste	82.8	74.9	—	92	49.5	76.2
96	Canterbury Christ Church	74.5	69.7	15.2	104	43.7	76.1
97	Newman	67.5	68.3	9.6	117	45.8	75.7
98	Suffolk	65.1	54.8	—	138	42.1	74.1
99	Cumbria	71.7	66.4	—	115	41.9	74.0
100	Buckinghamshire New	67.5	64.8	—	110	40.8	71.9
101	Glyndŵr	72.0	58.1	—	88	45.9	70.5

Employed in professional job	49%	Employed in non-professional job and Studying	2%
Employed in professional job and studying	2%	Employed in non-professional job	29%
Studying	9%	Unemployed	9%
Average starting professional salary	£18,720	Average starting non-professional salary	£16,000

East and South Asian Studies

The apparent surge in interest in China, including the promotion of Mandarin in some sixth forms, has barely impacted on higher education. Indeed, the numbers starting degrees dropped in 2017 after a decline of almost a third in the number of applications. The total enrolling for East and South Asian Studies as a whole barely topped 500 and the numbers for all non-European languages fell again in 2018. Japanese is the main draw among East and South Asian subjects, although only 195 students started degrees in 2017.

Most undergraduates learn their chosen language from scratch, although universities expect to see evidence of potential in other modern language qualifications. East and South Asian studies are often included in broader modern languages or area studies degrees, but the School of Oriental and African Studies, in London, offers a range of languages, including Burmese, Indonesian, Thai, Tibetan and Vietnamese. South Asian Studies is available at only four universities.

Degrees in these subjects are afforded extra protection by the Government because of their small size and their economic and cultural importance. Cambridge retains the leadership of the table, registering the highest entry grades and the best employment score. None of the top three secured enough responses to the National Student Survey for student satisfaction scores to be published. Nottingham Trent, the only post-1992 university in the top ten, achieved the best scores on these measures.

The small numbers of graduates make for exaggerated swings in the employment and salaries tables. East Asian Studies ties with anthropology for the unwanted distinction of the highest unemployment rate – 15% – and is just outside the bottom ten for graduate prospects generally. But the subjects do much better in the comparisons of graduate earnings, sharing 26th place, with average starting salaries of £22,000 in professional jobs.

East and South Asian Studies	Teaching quality %	Student experience %	Research quality %	Entry standards (UCAS points)	Graduate prospects %	Overall score
1 Cambridge	—	—	45.0	215	88.9	100.0
2 Oxford	—	—	36.2	209	84.6	96.2
3 Manchester	—	—	48.9	161	67.2	95.3
4 Durham	76.8	79.8	34.6	178	—	92.8
5 Edinburgh	82.1	82.3	30.1	166	66.2	91.7
6 Leeds	78.7	70.7	30.6	160	68.6	89.5
7 Hull	84.3	78.4	22.7	130*	—	88.6
=8 Nottingham	69.8	57.9	27.3	159	82.4	87.4
=8 Nottingham Trent	86.1	85.3	10.0	113*	76.2	87.4
10 SOAS London	79.8	70.2	26.3	146	59.5	86.2
11 Sheffield	72.7	70.4	16.7	155	61.6	83.3
12 Oxford Brookes	82.6	74.1	—	134	59.0	81.4
13 Central Lancashire	80.4	79.8	—	121	54.5	79.6

Employed in professional job	45%		Employed in non-professional job and Studying	2%
Employed in professional job and studying	1%		Employed in non-professional job	21%
Studying	16%		Unemployed	15%
Average starting professional salary	£22,000		Average starting non-professional salary	£16,500

Economics

The numbers starting economics degrees have risen by almost a quarter since higher fees were introduced, following another significant increase in 2017. Consistently good prospects for graduates are an obvious attraction. The subject is sixth for starting salaries in professional jobs, reflecting the value that employers place on a subject that they see combining the skills of the sciences and the arts. It is just outside the top 20 for the proportion of leavers going straight into graduate-level work or continuing their studies.

Applications and enrolments are running at record levels and, with well in excess of six applications to the place, competition is stiff. Cambridge entrants average more than 230 points on the UCAS tariff, Oxford over 220 and another five universities average more than 200. Many of those considering a degree in economics underestimate the mathematical skills required. Most of the leading universities demand maths at A-level or its equivalent as part of offers that are consistently high. The range of entry scores has been widening, however, as more universities have joined the table: eight have averages of less than 100 points in the latest table.

Cambridge tops the table for the third year in a row, again registering the highest entry grades and the best graduate prospects. Economists from the leading universities invariably command some of the highest salaries on graduation. While the average salary for 2017 graduates in professional jobs was £27,000 by the end of the year, Cambridge economists averaged £37,000 at this point and £49,000 three years later.

The London School of Economics took the laurels in the Research Excellence Framework, while Hertfordshire in 41st place, had the best scores on both of the measures derived from the National Student Survey (NSS), just ahead of East London, in 62nd place.

Economics	Teaching quality %	Student experience %	Research quality %	Entry standards (UCAS points)	Graduate prospects %	Overall score
1 Cambridge	—	—	45.0	232	94.1	100.0
2 Oxford	—	—	58.0	222	84.3	99.5
3 Warwick	74.9	80.3	49.6	203	92.8	99.3
4 University College London	68.4	70.4	70.2	207	85.8	98.5
5 London School of Economics	61.9	60.7	70.7	214	89.8	97.5
6 St Andrews	78.0	82.3	23.6	207	92.5	96.4
7 Bath	73.7	78.7	41.8	191	90.8	96.3
8 Leeds	81.0	83.3	39.3	173	88.1	96.2
9 Nottingham	77.2	82.9	31.7	183	87.6	94.7
10 Loughborough	81.9	84.9	32.6	159	87.3	94.4
11 Strathclyde	74.4	76.9	44.3	199	79.4	94.3
12 Lancaster	78.7	79.7	42.6	151	87.4	94.1
13 Exeter	75.7	78.4	26.9	182	91.9	94.0
14 Durham	72.5	74.6	23.1	205	90.1	93.4
15 Bristol	68.4	71.3	43.6	185	83.6	92.3
=16 Essex	89.4	89.3	43.6	109	75.0	91.8
=16 Surrey	77.0	78.6	33.0	173	80.5	91.8
=18 Glasgow	68.4	74.8	26.4	180	89.3	91.0
=18 Liverpool	81.4	85.4	20.1	148	85.1	91.0
20 East Anglia	84.0	84.6	25.7	144	79.9	90.8
21 Royal Holloway, London	77.3	79.3	31.3	131	85.9	90.1
22 Birmingham	75.4	71.6	26.6	163	84.3	89.9
23 Aberdeen	72.9	77.1	16.0	183	85.1	89.8
24 Aston	78.4	75.3	19.7	132	91.8	89.6
=25 Heriot-Watt	77.3	83.3	18.8	144	85.7	89.5
=25 York	73.6	76.1	22.6	157	86.7	89.5
=27 Newcastle	70.7	75.7	20.7	155	90.7	89.4
=27 Nottingham Trent	88.0	88.4	4.6	125	87.6	89.4
29 Queen's, Belfast	78.6	80.4	32.7	147	74.8	89.0
30 Buckingham	91.1	90.1	—	116	86.0	88.6
=31 Edinburgh	68.7	73.0	30.2	180	77.3	88.4
=31 Manchester	73.0	73.6	26.8	164	79.7	88.4
=33 Queen Mary, London	71.6	74.3	31.3	159	78.6	88.3
=33 Stirling	75.0	75.5	25.2	153	80.4	88.3
35 Sheffield	72.2	76.7	16.6	152	85.7	87.7
36 Southampton	68.8	73.0	23.4	151	85.8	87.5

Economics cont

		Teaching quality %	Student experience %	Research quality %	Entry standards (UCAS points)	Graduate prospects %	Overall score
=37	Bangor	86.9	87.6	23.4	116	70.6	87.1
=37	Coventry	86.7	90.0	1.6	112	84.3	87.1
=37	Kent	75.6	79.6	14.6	142	82.8	87.1
40	Swansea	75.4	74.6	22.0	129	83.6	86.9
=41	Cardiff	71.7	72.4	32.0	152	74.8	86.8
=41	Hertfordshire	94.1	93.2	0.9	110	75.9	86.8
43	Dundee	77.8	74.0	12.1	152	80.7	86.7
44	Sussex	70.2	71.4	25.1	141	80.0	85.7
45	De Montfort	81.8	83.6	10.7	98	82.2	85.1
=46	King's College London	72.8	70.3	—	177	78.3	84.3
=46	Portsmouth	79.6	81.4	9.5	111	79.1	84.3
48	Reading	69.0	67.1	29.3	141	73.5	83.9
49	SOAS London	65.4	64.0	22.9	140	81.0	83.6
=50	Keele	83.7	83.1	10.2	112	69.6	83.2
=50	West of England	78.4	81.0	5.5	108	79.2	83.2
52	Plymouth	77.4	78.6	13.1	110	73.7	82.6
=53	Huddersfield	77.3	77.9	4.1	121	—	82.5
=53	London Metropolitan	93.6	85.6	—	103	65.4	82.5
55	Aberystwyth	84.3	80.5	14.5	101	66.7	82.2
56	Central Lancashire	84.4	83.5	4.4	118	66.7	82.1
57	Hull	73.4	67.4	10.2	119	79.7	82.0
=58	Leicester	66.2	69.8	21.4	133	73.4	81.8
=58	Manchester Metropolitan	78.1	72.3	4.7	122	75.0	81.8
60	Birmingham City	81.7	84.6	1.3	107	70.0	81.2
61	Oxford Brookes	74.1	70.9	5.1	121	76.4	81.1
62	East London	93.0	91.9	0.8	91	59.6	80.9
63	Sheffield Hallam	78.9	80.5	—	109	72.4	80.7
=64	Birkbeck, London	76.6	70.9	19.1	92	—	80.3
=64	Greenwich	80.6	80.2	3.3	117	65.2	80.3
66	Ulster	74.8	81.9	—	118	69.9	79.9
67	London South Bank	67.5	77.0	—	85	86.7	79.6
68	Goldsmiths, London	71.7	68.8	16.8	112	67.7	79.3
69	Leeds Beckett	82.4	83.6	0.8	103	63.0	79.2
=70	Cardiff Metropolitan	70.3	65.1	—	108	81.0	79.0
=70	Middlesex	80.3	78.7	10.5	98	61.5	79.0
72	City	68.5	72.5	15.1	137	59.7	78.4
73	Salford	65.9	69.7	5.9	112	72.4	77.5
74	Anglia Ruskin	81.8	78.5	3.4	82*	60.0	76.6
75	Brunel	67.0	67.8	9.9	112	65.7	76.5
76	Bradford	55.3	55.9	12.7	120	71.9	75.0
77	Northampton	77.0	78.8	—	93	50.8	73.4
78	Kingston	71.4	65.6	9.2	99	51.2	72.6

Employed in professional job	56%	Employed in non-professional job and Studying	1%
Employed in professional job and studying	5%	Employed in non-professional job	11%
Studying	16%	Unemployed	11%
Average starting professional salary	£27,000	Average starting non-professional salary	£18,000

Education

There were almost five women for every man who started a teacher training degree in 2017, which helps to explain the shortage of male teachers in primary schools. Degrees in the education category are not confined to teacher training; over 10,000 students every year embark on courses classified as Academic Studies in Education. But the BEd courses, which account for the rest of the education category, remain the most common route into primary teaching. Secondary school teachers are more likely to take the Postgraduate Certificate in Education, or train through the Teach First or Schools Direct programmes, which are not included in these statistics. Both applications and enrolments for BEd courses fell in 2017, but they are well above the levels seen when higher fees were introduced in 2012.

Entry standards are not high – even Cambridge does not average 200 points on the UCAS tariff – but there are approaching six applications to every place for teacher training. The ratio for other courses in the education category, which include training for early years and outdoor education, is much lower. Glasgow remains top of the Education table although it does not lead on any individual measure. All eight Scottish universities in the table appear in the top dozen places. They benefit from the UCAS tariff points for Scottish secondary qualifications – Strathclyde is well clear of Cambridge on this measure – but also have the top seven scores for graduate prospects.

Employment scores at different universities are influenced by the variations in demand for new staff between primary and secondary schools, as well as between different parts of the UK. Universities that specialise in primary training are at an advantage at the moment in terms of employment. Cambridge is an example of those that do not offer Qualified Teacher Status, but combine the academic study of education with other subjects. Some of the best-known education departments are absent from the table because they offer only postgraduate courses. University College London's Institute of Education, which is ranked top in the world in this field by QS, and Oxford, which achieved the top grades in the 2014 Research Excellence Framework, are two examples.

Students at the University of the West of Scotland, which has the best graduate prospects, are the most satisfied with the quality of teaching on their course, while those at Coventry delivered the top score for the broader student experience. The table includes Ofsted inspection data for universities in England. Nine institutions – all in the top 20 overall – tie for the best scores.

Morale is often said to be low in the teaching profession, but the official survey of graduates three years into their careers shows that those who studied education are among the least likely to wish they had taken a different subject. Competitive salaries in the early years of teaching may be one reason – education is just outside the top 20 of our 67 subject groups. The subject is also in the top 30 for the proportion going straight into professional jobs or continuing to study.

Education

		Teaching quality %	Student experience %	Research quality %	OFSTED Rating	Entry standards (UCAS points)	Graduate prospects %	Overall score
1	Glasgow	92.2	86.4	32.5	—	186	97.8	100.0
2	West of Scotland	95.2	90.4	7.5	—	178	99.1	97.6
3	Durham	88.0	80.6	38.9	4.0	162	89.4	96.3
4	Cambridge	—	—	36.6	4.0	187	82.4	96.0
=5	Manchester	90.7	87.4	46.0	4.0	137	77.0	94.5
=5	Stirling	83.0	77.2	29.2	—	175	96.0	94.5
=5	Royal Conservatoire of Scotland	88.4	78.7	—	—	191	97.4	94.5
8	Dundee	86.1	80.3	11.7	—	180	94.9	93.9
9	Strathclyde	81.0	76.8	19.8	—	194	89.0	93.4
10	Edinburgh	74.5	74.0	23.1	—	186	98.8	92.8
11	Aberdeen	80.1	73.3	7.6	—	187	94.9	91.6
12	Birmingham	73.3	73.5	40.9	4.0	152	83.8	91.3
13	Northumbria	85.1	83.3	—	4.0	144	90.7	89.9
14	Southampton	81.2	83.8	41.1	3.0	155	86.0	89.8
15	Coventry	92.6	92.7	18.1	—	117*	87.5	89.7
16	East Anglia	88.8	82.5	27.2	3.0	160	77.9	88.7
17	Brighton	86.2	81.3	1.6	4.0	127	88.4	88.4
18	St Mary's, Twickenham	87.2	85.8	1.8	4.0	116	88.6	88.2
19	Brunel	85.0	86.5	20.4	4.0	130	65.9	87.9
20	Winchester	87.2	87.1	2.2	4.0	123	77.4	87.3
=21	Keele	85.1	76.6	25.0	3.5	136	74.2	87.1
=21	Reading	84.2	81.3	25.8	3.0	136	88.0	87.1
23	York	77.5	74.9	43.3	3.0	138	80.6	86.4
=24	University College London	72.1	70.3	40.2	3.5	165	58.1	85.7
=24	Warwick	—	—	43.6	3.7	153	61.5	85.7
=24	West of England	91.8	91.6	5.3	3.0	134	80.1	85.7
27	Bangor	76.3	76.8	39.6	—	131	74.8	85.2
=28	Liverpool Hope	89.3	88.0	7.3	3.0	120	86.1	84.8
=28	Liverpool John Moores	83.7	82.2	3.0	3.5	143	72.1	84.8
30	Derby	86.5	83.2	1.1	3.4	127	80.1	84.7
31	Gloucestershire	82.0	79.1	—	3.7	122	81.2	84.4
32	Huddersfield	88.3	83.6	5.9	3.1	125	81.9	84.3
33	Nottingham Trent	79.8	77.6	2.6	3.3	155	76.3	84.2
34	Chester	82.2	81.3	1.4	3.7	122	76.2	84.1
35	Sheffield Hallam	82.0	82.0	2.0	3.7	127	72.1	83.9
=36	Birmingham City	86.7	83.4	1.8	3.0	128	84.8	83.7
=36	Roehampton	81.7	80.5	20.2	3.0	117	84.0	83.7
38	Plymouth	87.0	84.5	9.4	3.0	127	74.3	83.2
39	Sunderland	86.9	82.1	3.8	2.7	124	91.1	83.1
40	Sheffield	83.7	79.2	32.9	3.0	145	51.3	83.0
41	Bedfordshire	90.2	86.9	3.1	3.1	112	76.9	82.9
42	Edge Hill	79.8	77.9	1.4	3.0	134	85.2	82.3

43	De Montfort	80.0	80.7	11.2	—	111	80.7	82.1
44	Hertfordshire	87.7	84.2	—	3.0	121	76.6	82.0
45	Aberystwyth	88.9	85.5	—	—	122	65.6	81.9
46	Plymouth Marjon	83.3	78.8	—	3.3	129	70.8	81.8
47	Bath Spa	77.3	71.9	3.2	3.7	123	70.2	81.7
48	Leeds	71.8	71.1	31.6	3.0	151	59.0	81.4
49	York St John	75.9	75.5	1.5	3.3	122	81.6	81.3
=50	Oxford Brookes	86.9	82.6	3.3	2.7	130	73.6	81.0
=50	South Wales	87.5	82.9	—	—	129	60.9	81.0
=52	Canterbury Christ Church	84.3	78.8	2.8	3.0	122	74.2	80.9
=52	Leeds Trinity	85.2	84.1	—	3.0	109	78.7	80.9
=52	Middlesex	76.8	75.2	14.9	3.0	122	76.0	80.9
55	Chichester	76.2	76.9	—	3.0	124	84.3	80.5
56	Cumbria	80.1	73.7	0.4	3.0	118	83.6	80.4
57	East London	84.8	84.3	2.8	3.0	127	63.1	80.3
=58	Manchester Metropolitan	79.9	75.0	5.8	2.7	136	76.3	80.2
=58	Worcester	82.7	81.6	2.5	3.0	119	71.5	80.2
=60	Northampton	86.5	83.5	1.8	3.0	110	70.3	80.1
=60	Teesside	79.2	75.4	15.0	—	115	70.2	80.1
62	Greenwich	80.8	78.6	0.8	3.3	130	60.4	80.0
63	Wolverhampton	79.7	76.1	1.9	3.0	122	75.2	79.8
64	London South Bank	75.7	73.1	— —	3.0	113	88.2	79.6
=65	Hull	78.7	74.2	5.0	3.0	130	68.1	79.5
=65	Bishop Grosseteste	80.4	75.6	1.4	3.1	115	73.3	79.5
=67	Leeds Beckett	85.8	81.4	2.3	3.0	118	62.7	79.4
=67	Newman	78.9	77.4	2.2	3.0	127	70.0	79.4
69	Portsmouth	79.1	74.8		3.5	106	68.0	79.3
=70	Staffordshire	79.1	71.8	7.6	3.0	122	70.0	79.2
=70	Wales Trinity St David	88.1	83.8		—	117	56.4	79.2
72	Ulster	83.5	83.5	27.5	—	111	48.6	79.1
73	London Metropolitan	81.5	78.5	3.3	3.1	101	70.5	78.7
74	Anglia Ruskin	85.5	83.0	0.8	3.0	112	56.5	77.9
=75	Kingston	80.4	80.7	—	3.0	110	60.1	77.0
=75	Goldsmiths, London	75.8	68.4	17.4	3.0	107	61.5	77.0
77	Central Lancashire	74.8	67.6	—	—	124	68.7	76.8
78	Cardiff	63.6	58.1	35.3	—	138	56.5	76.2
79	Newcastle	64.2	59.8	33.1	—	125	—	74.6
80	Bolton	79.2	73.9	3.1	—	110	52.9	74.5
81	Cardiff Metropolitan	75.0	70.7	—	—	117	52.0	73.2
82	Glyndŵr	75.6	57.4	—	—	125	52.3	72.7

Employed in professional job	56%	Employed in non-professional job and Studying	2%
Employed in professional job and studying	2%	Employed in non-professional job	19%
Studying	16%	Unemployed	5%
Average starting professional salary	£22,500	Average starting non-professional salary	£15,933

Electrical and Electronic Engineering

The demand for places in electrical and electronic engineering dipped again in 2017, when other branches of the discipline were more stable. The numbers starting courses were still marginally lower than in the years before the introduction of higher fees, and engineering as a whole has suffered a further decline in 2018. Some natural applicants for electrical or electronic engineering have been diverted into courses such as computer science or games design and, at slightly below five applications to the place, selection is less competitive than in most other branches of engineering. A rise of five places has taken the subject to 14th in the overall table for graduate prospects and it is in the top eight for salaries in graduate-level jobs.

Cambridge has extended its lead in electrical and electronic engineering, with the best research grades and a clear advantage over second-placed Imperial College on entry standards. The QS rankings rate Cambridge in the top four universities in the world, with Imperial only one place lower. The scores are close together for much of the table, allowing some big moves. University College London is up eight places to sixth, while Loughborough has jumped ten places and into the top ten, for example. Further down the table, East London has come from outside the top 50 to 26th place. Students at Solent – which is 50th – are the most satisfied with the quality of teaching, whilst those at Anglia Ruskin, three places lower, score highest for the broader student experience.

Most of the top courses demand maths and physics at A-level, or the equivalent. Graduate prospects are excellent at the leading universities – indeed, 17 of the 66 universities in the table saw at least 90% of their 2017 graduates find professional work or continue their studies. However, the rate was below 70% at ten of the bottom 25 universities.

Electrical and Electronic Engineering	Teaching quality %	Student experience %	Research quality %	Entry standards (UCAS points)	Graduate prospects %	Overall score
1 Cambridge	83.7	85.5	67.0	239	93.5	100.0
2 Imperial College	77.6	80.8	65.0	222	92.8	96.5
3 Leeds	86.7	88.3	41.8	179	95.1	92.9
4 Glasgow	74.6	80.9	47.2	202	91.8	91.5
5 Strathclyde	81.3	81.3	41.7	208	86.6	91.4
=6 Southampton	76.0	78.0	53.3	191	90.7	91.2
=6 University College London	77.8	79.1	59.0	194	84.1	91.2
8 Nottingham	87.7	88.7	40.8	155	91.6	90.4
9 Exeter	82.1	81.5	36.4	161	94.2	88.9
10 Loughborough	85.4	87.8	23.8	165	91.6	88.2
11 Newcastle	81.0	81.1	39.4	159	89.5	87.8
12 Bath	77.5	81.5	28.6	176	90.8	87.3
13 Swansea	80.0	85.1	45.5	134	90.9	87.1
=14 Essex	88.2*	87.0*	34.3	126	91.3	86.9
=14 Manchester	78.0	81.8	37.0	170	85.9	86.9
16 Surrey	81.9	83.6	36.3	162	82.3	86.3
17 Bristol	67.4	70.1	52.3	176	85.6	86.1
18 Queen's, Belfast	70.3	67.3	47.3	147	96.1	85.9

19 Birmingham	76.3	76.5	32.1	161	91.0	85.8
20 Edinburgh	68.3	74.3	50.3	169	85.3	85.7
21 Heriot-Watt	74.4	73.3	47.8	164	82.7	85.6
22 Sheffield	72.8	76.4	42.6	157	87.7	85.4
23 York	89.7	86.4	21.4	146	83.4	85.2
24 Lancaster	68.4	73.9	41.6	163	87.5	84.6
25 Cardiff	78.0	83.8	30.2	155	83.3	84.3
26 East London	79.2	76.3	2.3	—	92.9	83.0
27 Liverpool	79.1	81.8	30.4	137	82.2	82.8
28 Kent	75.9	81.4	27.3	137	85.0	82.2
29 Plymouth	87.7	85.1	13.3	123	85.5	82.1
=30 Bangor	81.8	79.9	31.9	118	82.7	81.9
=30 Sussex	71.8	80.7	24.0	132	90.9	81.9
32 Aston	81.0	80.0	25.8	144	77.4	81.7
33 Portsmouth	82.2	82.9	7.2	122	93.2	81.6
34 Brunel	79.8	83.5	26.4	136	77.6	81.3
=35 Bedfordshire	84.8	83.3	9.1	—	76.9	81.1
=35 Central Lancashire	78.2	73.1	11.7	142	88.9	81.1
=35 Northumbria	74.3	70.9	30.7	145	81.0	81.1
38 Ulster	71.3	77.3	22.8	131	90.2	81.0
39 Coventry	85.7	86.0	10.3	129	80.8	80.8
40 Queen Mary, London	66.6	70.4	41.9	135	83.0	80.6
41 West of England	86.7	88.1	10.6	119	76.3	79.3
42 Aberdeen	78.3	75.1	28.4	156	65.0	79.0
43 Hertfordshire	90.7	85.8	16.5	122	67.3	78.9
44 Robert Gordon	74.5	77.2	8.8	163	75.0	78.7
45 Derby	83.2	79.6	6.7	125	79.5	78.5
46 London South Bank	78.5	80.9	19.6	124	74.1	78.1
47 Liverpool John Moores	69.5	71.8	8.7	133	89.2	78.0
48 Huddersfield	78.4	77.6	10.2	127	79.3	77.9
49 Glasgow Caledonian	79.0	76.4	4.7	154	71.3	77.4
50 Solent	92.9	85.9	—	92	78.4	77.3
51 Sheffield Hallam	69.5	72.7	17.8	123	82.2	76.9
52 Hull	63.9	66.2	16.5	122	86.7	75.9
53 Anglia Ruskin	90.8	95.6	9.1	—	50.0	75.2
54 Teesside	72.1	69.8	5.8	120	75.8	73.8
55 Staffordshire	73.1	71.9	5.7	96	81.8	73.7
56 Salford	73.8	70.2	4.4	134	68.6	73.4
57 Greenwich	77.0	74.6	7.5	—	65.8	73.2
=58 Brighton	70.3	67.1	7.4	130	71.4	73.1
=58 City	72.2	74.2	23.1	140	54.3	73.1
60 Birmingham City	75.1	74.0	—	131	67.5	72.9
61 De Montfort	63.5	60.1	12.5	123	78.6	72.8
62 Reading	69.3	51.4	16.3	133*	70.6	72.6
63 Westminster	75.3	65.8	2.9	128	66.7	72.1
64 Manchester Metropolitan	63.3	64.4	16.3	127	68.9	71.8

Electrical and Electronic Engineering cont	Teaching quality %	Student experience %	Research quality %	Entry standards (UCAS points)	Graduate prospects %	Overall score
65 South Wales	58.0	57.0	—	131	83.3	71.3
66 Sunderland	77.6	71.3	—	80*	66.7	68.9

Employed in professional job	64%	Employed in non-professional job and Studying	1%
Employed in professional job and studying	2%	Employed in non-professional job	10%
Studying	14%	Unemployed	9%
Average starting professional salary	£26,500	Average starting non-professional salary	£16,497

English

English is among the biggest recruiters of undergraduates, despite the fact that the subject is usually in the lower reaches of the tables for graduate prospects and for starting salaries in professional jobs. But the attractions of a degree in English appear to be on the wane – applications have dropped in six of the last seven years, falling by another 4% in 2017. Nevertheless, the table remains one of the largest in the *Guide*, with more than 100 universities. Entry standards are high at the leading institutions, although only three universities (led by Durham) average more than 200 points.

St Andrews and Durham shared the lead in last year's table, but St Andrews is out on its own in the latest edition, albeit by the smallest possible margin. For once, neither Oxford nor Cambridge is in the top three, York leapfrogging both of them to take third place. The best overall scores on our measures derived from the NSS were at Teesside, which is only just outside the top 30 overall, although it is pipped for satisfaction with teaching quality by Suffolk in lowly 95th position. English produces consistently good levels of student satisfaction, with many of the top performers in the bottom half of the table overall.

Queen Mary, University of London, which has dropped 20 places to 35th this year, produced much the best results in the Research Excellence Framework.

More than a third of English graduates go on to a postgraduate course, and unemployment has been no higher than average for all subjects for the last three years, although approaching three in ten graduates start out in lower-level jobs. Employment rates have improved recently, and the subject has climbed out of the bottom 20 this year. Seven universities saw fewer than half of their 2017 graduates go straight into professional work or further study, but there were 13 in this position in the last edition of the *Guide*.

English	Teaching quality %	Student experience %	Research quality %	Entry standards (UCAS points)	Graduate prospects %	Overall score
1 St Andrews	89.2	84.9	60.4	199	73.0	100.0
2 Durham	84.1	75.8	57.9	210	82.0	99.9
3 York	85.9	81.3	61.5	174	83.3	99.3
4 Oxford	—	—	50.7	204	76.6	98.4
5 Exeter	86.8	83.1	46.2	180	82.1	97.9

6 Cambridge	—	—	50.0	206	82.6	97.5
7 Aberdeen	92.3	90.2	46.3	179	66.5	96.7
8 Lancaster	86.0	84.4	47.0	160	81.0	96.3
9 Birmingham	86.8	83.3	37.0	166	81.3	95.5
10 Newcastle	83.3	80.1	54.3	160	76.9	95.2
11 Nottingham	78.3	76.0	56.6	167	78.9	94.6
12 Glasgow	78.4	75.0	52.0	182	73.5	93.8
13 Warwick	76.2	71.6	59.8	181	73.3	93.7
=14 Manchester	—	—	49.1	165	76.3	93.3
=14 Sheffield	—	—	42.2	154	79.2	93.3
=16 Surrey	87.9	77.5	39.1	160	72.7	93.2
=16 University College London	74.9	68.4	61.7	190	70.1	93.2
18 Loughborough	83.0	82.8	32.4	145	81.4	92.4
=19 Royal Holloway, London	83.4	79.0	49.9	148	70.7	92.3
=19 Sussex	81.0	78.2	45.6	151	75.6	92.3
21 King's College London	79.8	72.5	47.6	170	72.4	92.2
22 Aberystwyth	91.6	88.0	31.2	115	75.9	91.9
=23 Dundee	87.0	86.0	32.8	164	61.8	91.1
=23 Stirling	87.0	77.6	29.8	160	69.7	91.1
25 Leeds	79.9	75.6	38.6	164	72.6	91.0
=26 Bristol	73.6	66.7	30.0	191	81.4	90.9
=26 Kent	80.5	76.4	47.3	131	76.1	90.9
=28 Southampton	83.5	79.6	38.4	149	70.1	90.8
=28 Swansea	81.6	79.5	43.6	132	74.6	90.8
30 Nottingham Trent	86.9	83.1	30.0	135	71.8	90.5
31 Strathclyde	81.5	79.0	39.4	197	54.7	90.4
32 Teesside	93.8	90.5	15.6	103	77.9	90.3
33 Liverpool	—	—	47.8	140	68.8	90.1
34 Edinburgh Napier	91.2	85.5	37.9	167	47.4	89.9
=35 Plymouth	91.1	83.6	30.5	120	67.1	89.7
=35 Queen Mary, London	77.1	71.3	64.0	137	65.1	89.7
37 Huddersfield	90.0	83.0	29.9	123	67.0	89.4
38 Queen's, Belfast	81.3	76.1	53.1	148	58.6	89.3
=39 De Montfort	85.6	82.9	24.1	110	78.3	89.0
=39 West of England	89.0	87.5	35.4	113	63.9	89.0
41 Oxford Brookes	84.3	82.8	27.8	128	71.2	88.8
42 Leicester	79.1	74.9	45.4	127	70.9	88.7
43 Coventry	86.2	83.8	18.1	118	76.8	88.6
44 Liverpool Hope	78.8	79.4	26.9	105	86.5	88.5
=45 Birmingham City	91.8	89.0	30.9	114	59.0	88.3
=45 Cardiff	80.4	74.0	35.1	149	67.1	88.3
=47 Bolton	90.3	90.0	14.4	87*	76.7	87.8
=47 Northumbria	88.1	83.2	27.2	135	59.6	87.8
=49 Bangor	81.8	79.3	46.3	123	60.1	87.5
=49 Bedfordshire	83.5	84.6	45.8	85	67.9	87.5
=49 Edge Hill	87.3	81.2	12.1	122	73.9	87.5

English cont

		Teaching quality %	Student experience %	Research quality %	Entry standards (UCAS points)	Graduate prospects %	Overall score
=49	Lincoln	87.9	80.8	16.2	126	69.5	87.5
53	Edinburgh	69.5	70.7	43.6	171	65.5	87.3
54	Staffordshire	85.6	83.4	—	103	87.0	87.2
55	Manchester Metropolitan	85.5	80.0	29.0	123	62.5	86.8
=56	East Anglia	75.4	74.1	36.2	160	61.3	86.7
=56	Liverpool John Moores	86.8	80.9	17.9	129	65.1	86.7
58	Newman	89.8	88.9	9.6	101	70.2	86.5
59	Ulster	91.5	88.9	35.1	115	47.2	86.4
60	Salford	89.6	82.8	7.8	118	67.9	86.2
=61	Keele	79.5	75.3	29.8	129	66.8	86.1
=61	Reading	80.7	69.8	36.3	132	63.3	86.1
63	Essex	75.3	73.7	37.7	116	72.1	86.0
64	Greenwich	92.5	87.1	14.4	115	57.6	85.9
65	Portsmouth	81.8	79.1	17.1	105	75.6	85.7
66	Sunderland	83.6	80.5	15.3	98	75.6	85.6
=67	Birkbeck, London	87.6	79.6	36.7	85	60.6	85.3
=67	Brunel	81.6	76.5	30.9	123	61.1	85.3
=67	Hertfordshire	83.2	79.8	7.8	120	72.6	85.3
70	Solent	92.3	84.4	—	107	67.5	85.2
71	Wolverhampton	87.7	83.8	7.6	107	67.9	85.0
72	Leeds Trinity	91.3	90.1	6.2	95	64.0	84.8
73	Central Lancashire	88.1	84.4	9.9	114	62.1	84.7
74	Derby	87.5	83.0	13.5	117	59.7	84.6
75	London South Bank	86.9	81.8	12.8	86*	70.0	84.3
76	St Mary's, Twickenham	87.3	82.9	14.6	108	60.1	84.2
77	Buckingham	86.1	80.8	—	102	72.2	83.8
78	York St John	87.9	82.7	9.7	110	60.0	83.7
79	Aston	77.7	77.4	23.4	120	62.6	83.5
80	Roehampton	78.8	74.1	20.8	109	66.9	83.2
81	Sheffield Hallam	83.7	81.7	14.6	117	57.4	83.1
82	Bournemouth	83.1	76.6	15.1	122	58.8	83.0
=83	Bishop Grosseteste	91.1	74.5	6.7	89	64.5	82.8
=83	Chester	85.4	83.7	10.7	111	57.2	82.8
85	Westminster	80.4	76.8	28.9	106	57.1	82.7
86	Gloucestershire	82.7	79.8	9.3	115	60.6	82.5
87	Winchester	86.0	86.2	—	110	59.3	82.2
=88	Leeds Beckett	82.3	79.4	11.0	101	63.3	82.1
=88	Northampton	84.3	71.9	15.3	100	62.3	82.1
90	Hull	74.9	69.3	22.7	125	62.0	81.9
91	Bath Spa	76.6	70.1	23.5	118	59.2	81.5
92	Falmouth	78.9	68.8	—	118	71.1	81.4
93	South Wales	79.9	71.1	12.8	113	60.7	81.1

94 Worcester	80.7	70.4	8.2	104	65.5	81.0
95 Suffolk	94.8	88.2	—	109	41.2	80.8
96 Chichester	79.3	75.7	16.3	104	58.0	80.7
97 Kingston	80.6	74.1	15.7	103	56.8	80.4
98 Canterbury Christ Church	85.2	77.7	8.0	104	50.9	79.9
99 Cardiff Metropolitan	84.3	82.2	—	101	54.9	79.7
100 East London	80.3	71.6	13.7	96*	54.8	78.9
101 Goldsmiths, London	73.1	65.5	34.9	118	45.1	78.6
102 Brighton	80.6	74.6	16.2	106	43.7	78.0
103 Anglia Ruskin	74.8	71.1	16.3	98	53.4	77.5
104 Cumbria	86.9	76.7	—	103	42.0	77.2
105 Plymouth Marjon	82.9	74.3	—	96	48.5	76.7
106 Middlesex	67.4	55.4	11.0	111	51.1	73.5

Employed in professional job	34%	Employed in non-professional job and Studying	5%
Employed in professional job and studying	3%	Employed in non-professional job	23%
Studying	26%	Unemployed	8%
Average starting professional salary	£19,500	Average starting non-professional salary	£16,224

Food Science

Food science is well inside the top 30 subject groups for both salaries and employment. Only 735 students started courses in 2017, but this was still an increase of almost 10% on the previous year, and 40 universities and colleges are offering the subject this year. Degrees range from professional cookery to food manufacturing, nutrition, dietetics and food security. There are even specialist baking science degrees at London South Bank.

Leeds has taken over the leadership of the table from Surrey. The top five all score more than 90% for graduate prospects, but the best rate of all, for the third year in a row, is at Hertfordshire, which is 11th in the table but saw 97% of 2017 graduates go straight into professional employment or continue studying. Leeds has the highest satisfaction rate for the broad student experience, but the greatest satisfaction with teaching quality is at fifth-placed Glasgow Caledonian. Queen's Belfast registered the top score in the Research Excellence Framework.

Most of the universities offering food science are post-1992 institutions, but only three – Robert Gordon, Glasgow Caledonian and Plymouth – feature in the top ten. Others are making progress, however. Worcester has moved up 20 places and Abertay 16 to join the top 20. Entry standards are modest – the highest are at third-placed Robert Gordon, which averages 184 points, but that is 20 points clear of the next highest. The scores are more bunched than in most tables – no university averages less than 100 points, but only seven average more than 150.

Food Science

		Teaching quality %	Student experience %	Research quality %	Entry standards (UCAS points)	Graduate prospects %	Overall score
1	Leeds	88.7	93.5	36.8	162	92.8	100.0
2	Surrey	82.9	87.1	37.5	162	95.3	98.7
3	Robert Gordon	88.4	88.1	4.9	184	96.9	98.2
4	Queen's, Belfast	77.1	77.0	56.3	150	91.8	97.0
5	Glasgow Caledonian	93.1	88.2	8.1	—	94.7	95.8
6	Nottingham	77.7	79.8	36.4	153	85.1	93.4
7	Plymouth	92.0	91.8	17.4	156	73.1	92.5
8	Newcastle	81.2	84.0	28.4	151	80.3	92.1
9	Ulster	87.6	89.2	42.5	128	74.2	91.7
10	Reading	71.9	70.8	50.7	140	84.1	91.5
11	Hertfordshire	84.8	83.7	14.8	121	97.0	90.2
12	King's College London	62.2	59.5	46.8	161	78.0	89.2
13	Worcester	85.3	83.9	—	127	92.9	87.8
14	Coventry	82.0	79.9	—	132	93.5	87.6
15	Abertay	86.0	80.8	—	144	80.0	87.3
16	Leeds Beckett	84.5	86.2	—	131	86.1	87.1
17	Central Lancashire	81.0	79.0	8.3	137	80.9	86.5
18	Liverpool John Moores	86.9	88.9	6.0	142	61.7	85.1
19	Chester	71.3	72.6	12.0	125	88.9	84.5
20	Harper Adams	83.1	83.3	5.7	107	86.9	84.4
21	Bath Spa	91.8	85.2	—	127	68.3	84.1
22	Bournemouth	90.9	87.7	4.7	127	63.3	83.9
23	Teesside	83.8	83.5	—	110*	85.2	83.6
24	Manchester Metropolitan	84.5	80.0	12.0	123	67.4	83.3
25	Edge Hill	90.1	91.4	—	122	64.3	82.9
26	London Metropolitan	80.3	80.3	—	111	82.8	82.3
27	Huddersfield	74.2	62.8	—	137	81.0	82.2
28	Sheffield Hallam	80.8	77.5	3.7	122	73.1	82.1
29	Roehampton	77.7	79.0	20.6	106	72.0	81.8
30	Queen Margaret, Edinburgh	74.1	71.2	—	163	58.7	81.7
31	Royal Agricultural University	72.9	78.1	2.1	103*	91.7*	81.5
32	St Mary's, Twickenham	76.4	79.5	—	123	74.1	81.1
33	Greenwich	69.3	77.3	19.5	—	71.4	80.9
34	Oxford Brookes	85.0	86.1	3.0	121	57.7	80.3
35	Northumbria	62.4	74.4	14.0	140	64.8	80.0
36	Cardiff Metropolitan	73.4	74.0	—	116	78.9	79.9
37	Kingston	77.9	78.9	2.6	116*	65.2	78.8
38	Westminster	79.6	81.8	—	123	57.3	78.5
39	Liverpool Hope	80.0	75.7	—	104	61.9	76.2
40	Leeds Trinity	79.4	78.4	—	105*	59.6	76.1
41	London South Bank	55.9	48.3	—	102	60.0	67.8

Employed in professional job	54%	Employed in non-professional job and Studying	3%
Employed in professional job and studying	3%	Employed in non-professional job	16%
Studying	16%	Unemployed	8%
Average starting professional salary	£22,000	Average starting non-professional salary	£17,000

French

The long decline of modern languages continues. Only 360 students started single honours degrees in French in 2017 – less than half the number at the start of a decade in which enrolments have fallen every year. Another 2,450 students opted for broader language courses, many of which included French, but even these were down in 2018. Some universities have closed their language departments, but more than 70 of them are offering full-time undergraduate courses in or including French starting in 2019. It remains the most popular language at degree level, but a continuing decline at A-level suggests more tough times ahead.

Entry standards remain relatively high, however. In spite of the falling numbers, there were almost six applications to the place in 2017 and many of the candidates came from high-achieving independent schools. Six universities average at least 200 points on the UCAS tariff and only one dropped below an average of 110 points. Perhaps not surprisingly, nine out of ten undergraduates enter with A-levels or their equivalents, although many universities will teach the language from scratch, especially as part of joint degrees.

Four of the top five are unchanged since last year, with Cambridge well clear at the head of the table. Newcastle is the newcomer in this group, moving up nine places to third. Cambridge has the best research grades and Oxford's entry standards are surpassed only by Glasgow in 20th. Second-placed Lancaster again registers the best graduate prospects. For the second year in a row, it was the only university to see 90% of graduates find professional jobs or continue studying – over ten percentage points ahead of its nearest challenger. Portsmouth, just outside the top 30 overall, had the best scores in all aspects of the National Student Survey (NSS), with almost 98% approving of the quality of teaching. Nationally, French is in the top 30 for starting salaries in graduate-level jobs, but just in the bottom half for employment prospects.

French	Teaching quality %	Student experience %	Research quality %	Entry standards (UCAS points)	Graduate prospects %	Overall score
1 Cambridge	—	—	54.0	203	80.6	100.0
2 Lancaster	85.3	89.3	47.0	160	97.1	99.5
=3 Newcastle	91.5	90.6	36.3	173	80.7	95.9
=3 Warwick	85.4	81.9	45.2	168	84.3	95.9
5 Oxford	—	—	41.3	207	77.0	95.7
6 Durham	84.2	73.6	34.6	199	86.3	95.4
7 Surrey	90.6	89.8	39.1	167	76.2	94.6
8 Queen's, Belfast	81.7	80.8	53.6	158	78.3	94.5
9 Strathclyde	82.2	78.6	42.0	202	71.9	94.0
10 Exeter	82.3	81.8	35.1	175	84.5	93.6
11 Southampton	81.9	79.6	42.7	160	81.3	93.0

French cont

	Teaching quality %	Student experience %	Research quality %	Entry standards (UCAS points)	Graduate prospects %	Overall score
12 St Andrews	88.5	86.4	26.4	200	72.0	92.7
13 Manchester	—	—	48.9	156	78.2	92.6
14 Birmingham	81.8	78.5	33.7	163	82.5	91.5
15 Bangor	91.4	87.6	39.6	127	76.3	91.4
16 Reading	86.1	80.2	41.7	128	81.0	91.2
=17 Sheffield	76.9	75.6	41.2	149	84.8	91.1
=17 York	83.0	77.7	37.3	157	78.9	91.1
19 Liverpool	81.7	79.6	33.4	139	86.3	90.5
20 Glasgow	80.0	77.9	26.3	214	68.8	90.3
21 Cardiff	89.6	85.6	32.5	155	70.6	90.2
22 Stirling	81.8	74.9	29.8	173	78.2	90.0
=23 Bath	79.5	82.6	27.4	168	80.3	89.9
=23 Bristol	76.6	71.7	36.0	170	78.9	89.9
=25 Kent	76.9	77.3	41.9	129	84.1	89.7
=25 Nottingham	76.5	73.7	39.4	149	81.5	89.7
27 Leeds	82.0	81.5	30.6	163	74.8	89.4
28 King's College London	70.4	68.7	42.1	167	77.0	88.7
29 Royal Holloway, London	81.5	69.3	48.3	143	68.1	88.6
30 University College London	67.4	59.5	43.7	185	73.6	88.2
31 Portsmouth	97.9	94.0	32.2	101*	66.7*	87.6
32 Edinburgh	73.1	71.4	30.3	180	71.7	87.0
33 Leicester	92.4	93.0	16.9	142	68.5	86.7
34 Aberdeen	66.5	72.2	29.3	200	70.0	86.6
35 Heriot-Watt	66.8	62.8	26.3	189	73.2	84.9
36 Aberystwyth	81.9	77.5	16.6	115	83.1	84.0
=37 Hull	87.1	82.8	22.7	115	69.8	83.9
=37 Queen Mary, London	83.2	78.6	35.1	133	58.0	83.9
39 Chester	80.5	81.6	17.3	113	75.2	82.3
40 Swansea	72.4	66.0	22.8	116	83.4	82.2
41 Manchester Metropolitan	90.4	90.5	29.0	124	45.5	81.8
=42 Aston	85.2	78.8	23.4	128	56.2	81.1
=42 Nottingham Trent	87.4	85.0	7.6	117	70.0	81.1
44 Oxford Brookes	90.7	84.8	—	128	68.0	80.6
45 Ulster	77.4	70.9	22.4	127*	50.0	76.8
46 Edinburgh Napier	70.9	71.5	—	159	57.9	75.0
47 Coventry	76.0	77.9	—	114	58.1	73.2
48 Westminster	66.3	69.1	2.0	115	57.1	70.5

Employed in professional job	48%	Employed in non-professional job and Studying	2%
Employed in professional job and studying	3%	Employed in non-professional job	18%
Studying	19%	Unemployed	10%
Average starting professional salary	£22,000	Average starting non-professional salary	£17,500

General Engineering

There have been changes at the top of the general engineering table where Cambridge has regained its leading position pushing, Bristol into second place after one year at the top. Bristol registered the best graduate prospects and a level of satisfaction with the quality of teaching, beaten only by the West of England in 15th place. Cambridge leads on the sections of the National Student Survey relating to the broader student experience and has the highest entry grades. Oxford has the best research score and has risen from fifth to third, pushing Imperial College into fourth position. There is movement further down the table, too, with Central Lancashire going up 16 places to 15th and Ulster rising 11 places to 17th position

The numbers starting general engineering courses rose slightly in 2017, taking the figure to the highest in a decade. The same may not be true of the current academic year, since enrolments for engineering as a whole are down. Although they do not yet draw as many applications as mechanical engineering, the general courses attract students who are looking for maximum career flexibility. It may also help that general engineering has become a fixture in the top five of the graduate earnings table, with median salaries of £27,500 in professional jobs. The subject has been dropping in the overall employment table, however. Having been in the top ten only three years ago, it is now only just inside the top 20.

The popularity of general engineering courses is reflected in the addition of three universities – Hull, Wolverhampton and Middlesex – to the latest table. More than half of the top 15 universities saw at least 90% of their 2017 graduates go straight into professional jobs or continue their studies. Most of the leading universities will require both maths and physics at A-level, with further maths, design technology and/or computing welcome additions.

General Engineering	Teaching quality %	Student experience %	Research quality %	Entry standards (UCAS points)	Graduate prospects %	Overall score
1 Cambridge	83.7	85.5	67.0	239	93.5	100.0
2 Bristol	87.5	84.4	52.3	220	97.4	98.8
3 Oxford	—	—	68.7	234	88.3	95.3
4 Imperial College	83.3	84.4	60.1	214	84.6	95.2
5 Glasgow	79.4	85.4	47.2	213	93.1	94.8
6 Sheffield	80.3	83.6	51.4	172	91.4	92.6
7 Nottingham	84.4	76.8	40.8	—	90.0	92.1
8 Heriot-Watt	77.4	78.7	47.8	196	—	91.7
9 Durham	75.1	75.0	39.4	219	88.7	91.0
10 Warwick	76.9	79.0	47.2	169	89.2	90.0
11 Exeter	68.9	74.8	36.4	173	96.7	88.4
12 King's College London	69.6	81.4	56.6	168	—	87.9
13 Lincoln	80.1	78.0	12.4	—	90.9*	87.5
14 Swansea	75.8	80.8	45.5	132	86.4	86.9
=15 Central Lancashire	76.6	79.3	7.1	152	92.3	84.8
=15 West of England	89.9	85.0	10.6	123	81.9	84.8
17 Ulster	83.6	82.6	22.8	117	79.5	83.6
18 Leicester	75.7	77.4	34.4	134	79.1	83.4

General Engineering cont

		Teaching quality %	Student experience %	Research quality %	Entry standards (UCAS points)	Graduate prospects %	Overall score
19	Greenwich	77.5	76.9	5.5	—	84.6*	83.2
20	Bournemouth	84.3	82.5	8.5	122	81.7	82.8
21	Aberdeen	72.4	76.4	28.4	146	—	82.7
22	Bradford	81.0	85.0	7.7	129	79.6	82.1
23	Liverpool	76.0	81.4	32.1	164*	65.5	82.0
24	Cardiff	68.5	79.9	30.2	147	77.4	81.8
25	Derby	83.8	79.8	6.7	109	—	81.4
=26	Aston	72.8	74.7	20.6	128	81.3	80.9
=26	Liverpool John Moores	72.8	62.1	14.2	133	88.5	80.9
28	Queen Mary, London	69.6	60.0	46.7	145	69.2	79.8
29	London South Bank	69.1	66.3	19.6	111	87.5*	79.6
=30	City	71.3	74.9	23.1	125	67.0	77.2
=30	Glasgow Caledonian	72.9	72.1	4.7	151	69.9	77.2
=32	Coventry	75.2	71.5	10.3	94	76.7	76.8
=32	Hull	65.6	70.8	16.5	134	—	76.8
34	Wolverhampton	68.4	68.1	—	102	80.6	74.9
35	Middlesex	76.1	78.6	—	112	62.4	74.0
36	West of Scotland	68.4	67.9	9.0	—	69.2	73.2
37	Edinburgh Napier	65.1	68.9	—	136	63.1	71.9
38	Northampton	60.3	51.9	—	84	77.8	69.5

Employed in professional job	59%	Employed in non-professional job and Studying	0%
Employed in professional job and studying	2%	Employed in non-professional job	9%
Studying	18%	Unemployed	12%
Average starting professional salary	£27,500	Average starting non-professional salary	£16,380

Geography & Environmental Sciences

Geography and environmental sciences are holding their own in terms of applications and enrolments, as they continue to benefit from strong interest in 'green' issues among young people. There were small increases in the numbers starting degrees in 2017, continuing a trend that has seen the annual intake for human geography grow by a third since higher fees were introduced in 2012. Physical geography and the courses categorised by UCAS as the "science of terrestrial and aquatic environments" have seen more modest increases.

The subjects' attractions do not seem to be related to immediate career prospects since geography and environmental science are outside the top 40 in the employment table. They fare a little better in the comparison of earnings, although the average starting salary of £21,505 in professional jobs is still below the mean for all subjects.

Durham has swapped places with Cambridge to take first place in the table, while Oxford has been pushed into fourth place by St Andrews. Oxford has the highest entry grades, while Bristol was the top university in the Research Excellence Framework (REF). Liverpool Hope, which was one of two universities with a 90% score for graduate prospects in last year's guide, is the only one this year. Staffordshire has the highest levels of satisfaction on both of the measures derived from the National Student Survey, but only just finishes in the top 40 because it did not enter the REF in this category and has one of the lowest entry scores.

Physical geography courses may give preference to candidates with a science or maths A-level in addition to geography, while for environmental science, most of the leading universities will ask for two from biology, chemistry, maths, physics and geography at A-level or the equivalent. Both entry scores and graduate prospects vary widely in this table, and are influenced by which branch of geography is offered, as well as by the university.

Geography and Environmental Sciences	Teaching quality %	Student experience %	Research quality %	Entry standards (UCAS points)	Graduate prospects %	Overall score
1 Durham	85.2	81.9	55.0	199	85.0	100.0
2 Cambridge	—	—	57.3	208	83.3	99.7
3 St Andrews	90.4	89.9	44.2	197	77.2	99.0
4 Oxford	—	—	41.1	212	80.4	98.8
5 Bristol	80.4	80.5	61.3	185	84.8	98.4
6 Lancaster	81.6	82.6	46.5	166	87.3	96.2
7 Glasgow	85.2	84.9	42.4	180	78.3	95.9
8 Exeter	80.3	80.6	43.7	172	82.6	94.7
9 Birmingham	81.5	82.3	42.0	157	85.8	94.6
=10 Aberystwyth	91.8	89.4	38.6	117	83.8	94.2
=10 Leeds	81.0	82.7	42.3	161	82.9	94.2
12 London School of Economics	70.3	68.9	46.9	192	87.7	93.9
13 Newcastle	83.2	83.7	43.1	151	80.5	93.7
14 Loughborough	87.7	89.8	24.3	148	83.3	93.4
15 Manchester	82.7	83.4	36.6	162	77.9	92.9
16 University College London	77.1	77.0	52.3	175	73.3	92.8
=17 Nottingham	80.7	79.9	39.6	156	81.2	92.7
=17 Royal Holloway, London	88.1	85.2	45.8	137	72.4	92.7
=17 Southampton	84.3	83.8	45.8	153	71.8	92.7
=17 Stirling	83.3	84.0	30.3	180	73.8	92.7
21 Swansea	81.4	84.0	39.4	132	80.2	91.3
22 Cardiff	82.0	83.2	36.8	153	73.3	91.1
23 Sussex	81.6	80.5	35.8	145	76.6	90.7
24 Liverpool Hope	89.2	87.5	1.6	109	94.6	90.1
25 Dundee	76.4	79.1	28.3	172	74.8	89.8
=26 Aberdeen	74.7	74.5	38.2	181	68.3	89.4
=26 East Anglia	80.0	79.9	47.4	142	66.6	89.4
28 Nottingham Trent	92.4	91.9	4.1	128	76.8	89.3
29 Sheffield	78.1	80.4	31.1	149	75.0	89.1
30 Liverpool	81.7	83.1	26.3	140	74.8	89.0
31 York	80.6	78.1	23.9	143	77.2	88.6
32 Hull	87.1	84.3	31.7	112	70.4	88.2

	Teaching quality %	Student experience %	Research quality %	Entry standards (UCAS points)	Graduate prospects %	Overall score
=33 Edinburgh	72.9	70.3	38.2	172	69.3	88.1
=33 Queen Mary, London	78.8	77.2	45.1	128	69.7	88.1
35 Leicester	77.2	80.4	29.7	131	77.0	87.9
=36 Portsmouth	88.7	85.2	14.9	111	76.3	87.7
=36 Queen's, Belfast	81.7	84.4	36.9	133	63.7	87.7
38 Manchester Metropolitan	90.3	89.1	14.9	116	69.6	87.4
=39 Coventry	92.3	90.2	2.0	117	73.8	87.3
=39 Staffordshire	96.8	94.7	—	96	74.4	87.3
41 Reading	78.8	75.3	35.0	134	70.4	87.2
42 Keele	90.9	90.2	16.4	119	63.1	86.7
=43 Ulster	92.2	91.0	17.2	110	62.7	86.5
=43 Winchester	90.9	84.6	7.5	114	—	86.5
45 Bangor	81.9	81.9	31.5	123	65.4	86.3
46 Plymouth	86.3	84.4	25.8	111	65.4	86.0
47 Greenwich	79.8	82.6	7.4	127*	79.2	85.9
48 Chester	91.1	89.1	6.4	112	67.5	85.8
49 Gloucestershire	89.6	87.9	14.5	120	60.4	85.4
50 King's College London	69.1	69.4	40.0	160	64.0	85.2
51 Northumbria	84.3	85.0	15.4	131	61.2	84.8
52 West of England	89.6	88.7	6.4	113	63.8	84.6
53 Hertfordshire	85.8	85.0	—	105	75.5	84.3
54 Birkbeck, London	75.7	72.1	34.7	104	72.0	84.2
55 Derby	80.9	82.5	3.6	108	78.3	84.1
56 South Wales	95.6	87.3	—	124	49.8	82.9
=57 Liverpool John Moores	84.2	80.3	—	127	65.5	82.8
=57 Worcester	89.0	88.3	8.1	105	57.8	82.8
59 Salford	83.8	78.3	16.7	109	61.5	82.5
=60 Leeds Beckett	83.7	86.9	5.6	107	61.8	82.0
=60 Sheffield Hallam	81.4	80.1	13.4	116	60.7	82.0
62 Edge Hill	81.1	81.4	6.2	113	62.0	81.2
63 Bournemouth	79.9	79.5	19.9	116	54.3	81.1
64 Central Lancashire	80.9	79.6	9.8	118	56.5	80.6
65 Oxford Brookes	74.1	75.3	17.3	124	58.8	80.4
66 Kingston	79.4	69.1	6.9	92	72.7	80.3
67 Solent	82.6	84.1	—	89*	62.5	79.5
68 Northampton	83.2	74.9	7.7	99	57.7	79.3
69 Cumbria	78.4	71.8	1.5	114	63.2	79.1
70 Brighton	83.5	77.4	5.1	102	51.0	78.0
71 Bath Spa	79.5	77.7	—	110	53.3	77.5
72 Canterbury Christ Church	79.9	77.5	—	99	48.1	75.6
73 St Mary's, Twickenham	65.3	57.6	—	96	56.0	71.2

Employed in professional job	39%	Employed in non-professional job and Studying	3%
Employed in professional job and studying	3%	Employed in non-professional job	19%
Studying	26%	Unemployed	11%
Average starting professional salary	£21,505	Average starting non-professional salary	£16,643

Geology

Entry standards in geology have dropped in this edition of the *Guide*, reflecting a continuing decline in applications. Only three universities, compared with six last year, reached an average of 200 points on the UCAS tariff and, throughout the table, the average was down by seven points. There had been a 14% fall in applications the previous year, with a further decline in 2017 taking the total well below the level seen in the year when £9,000 fees were introduced. The number starting courses has also fallen, although there were still five applications to the place.

Imperial College, still at the top of the table, was one of the places where the average entry points dipped below 200, but it achieved the best research grades and has good scores across the board. Cambridge recorded among the highest grades in any subject (242 on average) but the top three are unchanged compared with last year. Some of the leading universities expect candidates to have two scientific or mathematical subjects at A-level, or the equivalent.

Only Celtic Studies has a higher proportion of graduates continuing their studies than Geology. More than 40% took this route in 2017, helping the subject to finish in the top half of the table for graduate prospects. Birkbeck, University of London, had the best score on this measure and has entered the table in fourth place overall.

Newcastle, which has jumped 15 places into the top ten, has the highest scores on all aspects of the National Student Survey. Only Imperial comes within four points of it on these measures. Portsmouth is the leading post-1992 university in the table as a whole, two places outside the top 20.

Geology	Teaching quality %	Student experience %	Research quality %	Entry standards (UCAS points)	Graduate prospects %	Overall score
1 Imperial College	93.6	90.8	59.6	195	87.6	100.0
2 Cambridge	—	—	58.0	242	84.0	99.2
3 Oxford	—	—	52.1	221	82.2	96.2
4 Birkbeck, London	87.3	83.2	43.6	—	91.7	96.0
5 St Andrews	86.2	86.3	44.2	206	75.0	92.8
6 Exeter	89.1	85.6	45.7	168	77.9	91.9
7 Durham	77.5	78.1	42.2	173	91.2	91.6
=8 Newcastle	94.0	93.1	35.4	137	—	91.3
=8 Southampton	81.4	83.8	58.3	151	79.1	91.3
10 Leeds	86.9	88.6	41.9	166	78.0	91.0
11 Bristol	80.5	80.8	55.8	174	73.4	90.4
12 Birmingham	80.8	80.9	38.6	150	81.9	88.2
13 East Anglia	82.8	75.4	47.4	143	77.5	88.1
14 Royal Holloway, London	78.6	76.2	43.4	128	81.5	86.6
=15 Liverpool	—	—	30.3	139	72.0	86.5

Geology cont

		Teaching quality %	Student experience %	Research quality %	Entry standards (UCAS points)	Graduate prospects %	Overall score
=15	Manchester	78.6	78.4	44.5	151	73.7	86.5
17	Aberdeen	74.1	80.3	38.2	156	78.7	86.2
18	University College London	75.1	75.2	47.9	177	67.9	86.1
19	Glasgow	72.0	74.7	38.5	179	73.3	85.3
20	Leicester	81.8	79.5	37.2	139	71.6	84.8
21	Bangor	82.3	84.2	31.5	103	79.2	84.1
22	Portsmouth	83.3	76.3	19.8	112	85.9	83.9
23	Cardiff	79.6	82.3	21.3	143	75.0	83.1
24	Edinburgh	65.7	65.8	38.2	195	68.3	82.7
25	Derby	87.6	89.8	3.6	111	81.7	82.4
26	Hull	83.6	84.2	31.7	109	66.7	81.6
27	Keele	82.1	75.9	12.2	114	78.6	80.6
28	Aberystwyth	74.5	63.0	34.9	97	79.3	80.4
29	Plymouth	82.8	78.0	25.3	120	62.4	79.3
30	Brighton	82.7	80.3	5.1	99	55.1	73.0
31	Edge Hill	64.8	62.4	—	104	67.7	69.9
32	Kingston	64.4	53.8	6.9	94	68.8	69.7
33	South Wales	83.5	84.0	—	94	43.0	69.4

Employed in professional job	31%	Employed in non-professional job and Studying	3%
Employed in professional job and studying	2%	Employed in non-professional job	15%
Studying	38%	Unemployed	10%
Average starting professional salary	£21,000	Average starting non-professional salary	£16,575

German

Degree courses in German have struggled to attract students for almost 20 years. The number of applications in 2017 was less than half the total at the start of the decade. The introduction of £9,000 fees undoubtedly contributed to falling numbers, but there has been a worldwide decline in the language that has been worrying the German government, as well as academic linguists. Many students learn the language through broader modern languages degrees, but German has suffered more than other languages from the decline in the numbers taking courses in the sixth-form, or even earlier. Only 125 students started single honours degrees in German in 2017, and the numbers taking languages have dropped again in the current academic year.

Lancaster has toppled Cambridge from top of the table for German, a position it had held for 12 years. Oxford has the highest entry standards and Cambridge the best score from the Research Excellence Framework, while St Andrews registered the best graduate prospects. The best scores for teaching quality and student satisfaction are to be found further down the table: Nottingham Trent, in the bottom ten, heading both the measures derived from the National Student Survey. Chester, the highest-placed of just three post-1992 universities in the ranking, was nearest challenger on satisfaction levels. Southampton, Swansea, Herriot Watt and Cardiff have enjoyed big rises into this year's top 20, while UCL has plummeted 25 places from ninth place in the last edition.

Most universities in the table offer German from scratch as well as catering for those who took the subject at A-level. Employment prospects are better than in other modern languages, although the small numbers mean that the differences can be slight from year to year. German is in the top 30 for the proportion of graduates going into professional jobs or onto postgraduate courses, but 11 places lower in the salary table.

German	Teaching quality %	Student experience %	Research quality %	Entry standards (UCAS points)	Graduate prospects %	Overall score
1 Lancaster	91.4	91.6	47.0	—	85.7	100.0
2 Cambridge	—	—	54.0	203	80.6	99.8
3 Oxford	—	—	41.3	205	79.3	95.4
=4 King's College London	92.6	86.0	42.1	164	79.6	95.1
=4 Warwick	89.6	89.8	45.2	177	74.1	95.1
6 Newcastle	92.8	90.2	36.3	178	78.2	95.0
7 Durham	84.2	73.6	34.6	199	86.3	94.8
8 St Andrews	81.3	77.7	26.4	201	89.7	93.9
9 Sheffield	—	—	41.2	147	85.6	93.6
10 Exeter	82.3	81.8	35.1	175	84.5	93.1
11 Birmingham	81.4	84.6	33.7	—	85.6	92.9
12 Southampton	82.3	79.7	42.7	181	76.0	92.8
13 Nottingham	86.1	79.0	39.4	141	86.4	92.6
14 Manchester	—	—	48.9	154	80.4	92.0
15 Cardiff	86.9	86.4	32.5	144	83.9	91.6
16 Leeds	86.5	88.3	30.6	161	79.1	91.3
17 Glasgow	78.4	77.1	26.3	200	—	90.6
18 Liverpool	88.3	88.2	33.4	140	—	90.3
19 Heriot-Watt	84.2	81.2	26.3	189	74.6	90.0
20 Swansea	92.3	90.2	22.8	119	86.2	89.8
21 Chester	96.3	92.9	17.3	—	70.9	89.6
=22 Aberystwyth	89.8	85.4	16.6	—	78.3*	89.2
=22 Bath	79.9	77.5	27.4	161	83.3	89.2
24 Reading	74.4	76.9	41.7	119	86.1	88.7
25 Kent	78.2	83.8	41.9	128	77.4	88.6
26 Bristol	80.0	78.8	36.0	175	68.7	88.4
27 Portsmouth	91.1	86.9	32.2	110	76.4	88.0
28 Nottingham Trent	97.8	94.9	7.6	—	69.6	87.8
29 York	81.9	73.9	37.3	145	—	87.6
30 Queen Mary, London	86.8	73.6	35.1	121	76.7	87.3
31 Aston	81.5	81.3	23.4	136	80.3	86.5
32 Royal Holloway, London	72.2	68.9	48.3	—	70.2*	84.7
33 Bangor	78.7	81.3	39.6	120	65.9	84.3
34 University College London	67.7	58.8	43.7	182	59.5	83.5

	Teaching quality %	Student experience %	Research quality %	Entry standards (UCAS points)	Graduate prospects %	Overall score
35 Edinburgh	73.4	74.3	30.3	179	59.4	83.2
36 Hull	90.5	89.3	22.7	118	58.2	81.9
37 East Anglia	83.6	80.5	—	143	76.3	81.3

Employed in professional job	50%	Employed in non-professional job and Studying		2%
Employed in professional job and studying	4%	Employed in non-professional job		17%
Studying	20%	Unemployed		8%
Average starting professional salary	£21,000	Average starting non-professional salary		£18,000

History

Four years of growth in applications for history came to an end in 2016, and there was a further drop of 11% in the following year. The demand for places was back below the levels seen before the arrival of £9,000 fees, and the decline has now produced a small drop in the numbers starting degrees. The subject is in the bottom 20 for employment, with more than a quarter of graduates starting out in low-level jobs. History is 40th in the earnings table, although surveys have suggested that historians often rise to the top later in their careers.

Durham and Cambridge took it in turns to lead the history table for seven years, but Cambridge is now top for the fourth time in a row, while Durham has slipped one more place to third, overtaken by Oxford. Cambridge has the highest entry standards and recorded the top score in the 2014 Research Excellence Framework (REF). The leading scores for our other measures are all to be found outside the top 20. Liverpool Hope, for example, has by far the best graduate prospects.

History illustrates some of the paradoxes surrounding the National Student Survey (NSS), especially where teaching quality is concerned. The top eight universities for student satisfaction with teaching quality – and 17 of the top 20 – are all post-1992 institutions; yet the top 20 in our table, even including the NSS results, are older foundations. Suffolk scored 100% for satisfaction with teaching quality and also has the best score for the broader student experience, but only 27% of graduates went straight into professional employment or a postgraduate course – like last year, the lowest score in this table and most others.

Employment scores are disappointing at many universities in the table, although still an improvement on last year. Eleven of the 95 institutions saw less than half of those graduating in 2017 go into professional jobs or start postgraduate courses by the end of the year.

History	Teaching quality %	Student experience %	Research quality %	Entry standards (UCAS points)	Graduate prospects %	Overall score
1 Cambridge	—	—	56.3	211	80.9	100.0
2 Oxford	—	—	56.1	208	81.9	97.1
3 Durham	84.5	73.6	41.4	208	86.2	96.1
4 St Andrews	87.3	83.4	46.7	198	71.7	95.6

5 Sheffield	83.1	82.0	53.7	159	78.5	93.9
6 Lancaster	87.9	80.4	37.0	161	83.4	93.5
7 York	84.0	77.6	43.3	173	79.6	93.2
8 Birmingham	83.9	79.2	48.8	163	76.6	93.0
9 Exeter	79.3	75.1	45.6	183	80.1	92.8
10 University College London	78.2	69.3	51.9	186	77.9	92.6
11 Loughborough	91.1	91.0	22.5	150	82.2	92.3
12 Warwick	79.3	74.6	51.7	175	74.8	92.2
13 Leeds	82.9	79.9	43.6	169	74.0	92.0
14 London School of Economics	74.8	68.4	46.8	189	79.5	91.4
15 Glasgow	80.8	74.3	47.7	185	67.2	91.3
16 Sussex	84.8	78.5	41.3	140	79.9	91.0
17 Nottingham	81.2	76.9	36.9	161	81.3	90.9
18 Manchester	—	—	39.8	162	71.2	90.6
19 Southampton	80.3	75.4	50.6	151	71.9	90.2
=20 East Anglia	84.2	77.9	47.4	147	68.0	90.1
=20 Kent	83.5	77.4	41.3	136	79.0	90.1
22 Lincoln	90.8	85.8	25.9	124	79.7	90.0
23 Dundee	85.5	82.1	30.4	172	64.9	89.5
=24 Bristol	—	—	40.6	186	70.9	89.4
=24 Strathclyde	81.3	73.5	42.0	198	56.0	89.4
=26 Queen Mary, London	82.7	78.6	43.7	147	67.3	89.1
=26 Royal Holloway, London	84.1	76.9	40.6	139	72.3	89.1
28 Aberdeen	81.6	80.4	36.1	169	64.7	88.9
29 Newcastle	81.6	76.6	29.0	161	75.5	88.7
30 Portsmouth	89.5	87.6	32.2	107	73.4	88.5
=31 Hertfordshire	83.6	80.6	46.7	108	72.9	88.4
=31 King's College London	76.9	66.9	45.3	163	71.7	88.4
=33 Keele	85.1	81.7	32.8	122	76.1	88.3
=33 Liverpool	—	—	38.9	140	67.2	88.3
35 Liverpool Hope	88.5	83.4	15.7	105	87.3	87.6
=36 Brunel	89.7	77.8	32.4	121	68.4	87.5
=36 Swansea	83.4	81.8	25.0	132	76.8	87.5
38 Cardiff	84.4	77.0	31.4	145	68.0	87.4
39 Liverpool John Moores	91.5	88.0	15.9	130	68.3	87.2
40 Stirling	84.0	79.9	28.5	166	56.9	86.8
=41 Northumbria	88.1	83.0	30.7	127	61.8	86.7
=41 Queen's, Belfast	80.7	77.4	46.3	147	55.5	86.7
=43 Aberystwyth	85.9	82.5	19.5	123	75.2	86.5
=43 Edinburgh	71.5	67.3	46.9	178	61.5	86.5
45 Teesside	86.0	77.8	27.9	101	78.9	86.4
=46 Huddersfield	89.2	79.0	22.3	112	71.8	86.0
=46 Hull	85.7	81.9	26.1	117	70.3	86.0
=48 Bangor	88.2	84.2	24.3	128	61.3	85.9
=48 SOAS London	—	—	20.8	137	71.7	85.9
50 Coventry	89.6	86.2	5.6	117	77.2	85.6

History cont

	Teaching quality %	Student experience %	Research quality %	Entry standards (UCAS points)	Graduate prospects %	Overall score
=51 Leicester	79.0	76.0	34.3	132	66.2	85.2
=51 Oxford Brookes	81.7	78.4	35.0	129	61.5	85.2
53 Plymouth	94.0	88.0	22.6	109	53.1	84.8
54 Roehampton	86.5	82.5	21.4	101	71.1	84.7
55 Central Lancashire	91.9	88.3	12.0	114	60.7	84.4
56 Newman	89.7	83.6	12.0	108	68.8	84.3
57 Northampton	91.0	83.8	21.5	104	59.6	84.2
58 Chichester	92.9	84.3	15.8	106	60.6	84.1
=59 Birkbeck, London	78.3	71.3	48.4	104	61.9	84.0
=59 Essex	81.5	78.2	34.8	107	64.0	84.0
=59 Reading	81.5	70.3	35.4	133	58.2	84.0
62 De Montfort	78.7	74.3	23.4	111	78.2	83.9
63 Nottingham Trent	82.3	78.3	17.5	131	66.1	83.6
64 Sheffield Hallam	88.8	82.9	38.3	109	42.3	83.4
65 Manchester Metropolitan	84.8	81.6	18.0	122	61.8	83.3
66 Derby	93.0	86.9	13.5	104	55.7	83.1
67 Ulster	89.8	83.4	24.0	110	48.2	82.6
68 West of England	86.8	81.1	28.9	116	46.9	82.5
69 East London	77.2	76.2	13.9	—	72.2	82.2
70 Leeds Trinity	95.3	84.0	10.3	88	55.7	81.9
=71 Goldsmiths, London	79.4	71.0	34.5	122	50.6	81.3
=71 Winchester	85.9	80.8	19.1	108	53.4	81.3
73 Canterbury Christ Church	91.3	85.4	16.3	94	48.9	81.1
74 St Mary's, Twickenham	90.7	81.6	11.0	97	54.3	80.8
75 Edge Hill	80.3	75.5	23.6	115	54.1	80.5
76 Westminster	81.1	77.4	11.8	106	64.1	80.3
77 Staffordshire	87.4	81.8	—	89	67.6	80.1
78 Wales Trinity St David	90.6	80.9	17.3	94	45.4	79.9
79 Chester	84.9	80.8	9.1	112	52.3	79.6
=80 Anglia Ruskin	87.1	86.4	15.3	96	45.7	79.5
=80 Gloucestershire	80.7	85.8	11.2	113	52.7	79.5
=80 South Wales	89.2	77.0	15.8	123	37.6	79.5
=83 Leeds Beckett	82.9	82.9	11.0	98	56.3	79.4
=83 Salford	80.5	74.5	—	116	68.3	79.4
85 Bath Spa	79.0	71.6	8.3	109	65.6	79.0
86 Suffolk	100.0	97.4	—	100	27.3	78.8
87 Bishop Grosseteste	78.7	67.3	7.0	93	71.7	78.2
=88 Wolverhampton	85.3	76.2	18.8	95	44.4	78.1
=88 Worcester	77.4	67.2	19.5	109	56.4	78.1
90 York St John	87.9	79.8	—	104	50.4	78.0
91 Sunderland	82.0	73.8	7.7	97	53.9	77.0
92 Greenwich	73.4	62.7	8.6	125	59.8	76.5

93 Brighton	79.9	72.2	13.1	103	41.9	75.4
94 Kingston	80.1	77.2	—	101	42.1	74.0
95 Bradford	63.8	58.9	12.7	—	72.0*	73.6

Employed in professional job	31%	Employed in non-professional job and Studying	4%
Employed in professional job and studying	3%	Employed in non-professional job	22%
Studying	29%	Unemployed	10%
Average starting professional salary	£21,000	Average starting non-professional salary	£16,497

History of Art, Architecture and Design

Almost 60 institutions are offering history of art at degree level this year and our table continues to grow, with Aberystwyth joining in second place. It has the best graduate prospects – almost ten percentage points ahead of its nearest challenger, Cambridge, which tops the table overall for the fourth year in a row. Cambridge is the only one of the 29 universities in the table to occupy the same position as last year.

Entry standards are high. Oxford, in fourth place, is the only university to average 200 points, but most average well over 150. Plymouth, only six places off the bottom of the table, has the highest scores on both of our measures derived from the National Student Survey, although it has to share that distinction with Liverpool John Moores in the sections relating to the broader student experience. The Courtauld Institute, an independent college of the University of London based in Somerset House, and previously the only specialist institution to top any of our league tables, had the best results in the Research Excellence Framework, when 95% of its submission was rated as world-leading or internationally excellent. It is now down to eighth place in the table, however, after a drop of five places.

Employment levels have improved, lifting the subjects into the top 50 of the 67 subject groups. Cambridge and Aberystwyth were the only universities where 80% of the 2017 graduates went straight into professional jobs or postgraduate study, but just one, compared with four last year, slipped below 50% on this measure. The relatively small numbers taking degrees in the history of art, architecture or design can make for considerable volatility in the statistics, but it remains inside the top 50 in the latest salaries table.

History of Art, Architecture and Design	Teaching quality %	Student experience %	Research quality %	Entry standards (UCAS points)	Graduate prospects %	Overall score
1 Cambridge	—	—	49.0	195	84.4	100.0
2 Aberystwyth	85.9	82.5	21.6	—	93.6	97.9
3 St Andrews	87.4	83.6	42.1	188	75.4	97.3
4 Oxford	—	—	39.7	210	77.8	96.4
5 York	83.8	77.7	53.2	148	77.9	94.6
6 Birmingham	84.0	79.2	43.7	151	79.4	94.1
7 Manchester	—	—	54.0	154	67.4	93.9
8 Courtauld	78.1	72.3	66.0	171	67.2	93.8
9 Warwick	79.2	74.7	53.0	167	71.4	93.1

History of Art, Architecture and Design cont

		Teaching quality %	Student experience %	Research quality %	Entry standards (UCAS points)	Graduate prospects %	Overall score
10	SOAS London	–	–	40.9	158	69.2	92.3
11	University College London	78.6	69.6	44.7	186	68.8	92.2
12	East Anglia	84.1	78.0	36.9	161	68.4	91.9
13	Leeds	82.8	79.6	30.0	166	71.1	91.7
14	Exeter	79.7	75.7	35.1	180	67.7	91.4
15	Sussex	84.8	78.5	25.2	144	79.2	91.3
16	Aberdeen	81.9	80.2	36.1	–	65.5	90.5
17	Oxford Brookes	81.7	78.4	35.0	142	72.5	90.4
18	Kent	83.1	76.8	44.3	135	65.1	90.1
=19	Glasgow	80.9	74.8	37.2	172	59.3	89.9
=19	Manchester Metropolitan	84.8	81.6	9.7	162	–	89.9
21	Nottingham	81.3	77.2	30.9	152	68.8	89.7
22	Leicester	80.3	76.6	42.0	125	73.0*	89.6
23	Plymouth	94.0	88.0	14.7	114	63.3	88.9
24	Liverpool John Moores	91.5	88.0	7.2	–	50.0*	88.4
25	Bristol	–	–	28.3	175	59.0	87.9
26	Essex	81.5	77.9	46.9	114	–	87.6
27	Goldsmiths, London	79.4	71.0	25.9	164	54.3	86.2
28	Edinburgh	72.0	67.5	27.9	162	68.0	86.0
29	Brighton	80.4	72.7	13.1	102	40.0	78.2

Employed in professional job	37%	Employed in non-professional job and Studying	3%
Employed in professional job and studying	2%	Employed in non-professional job	23%
Studying	26%	Unemployed	9%
Average starting professional salary	£20,280	Average starting non-professional salary	£16,000

Hospitality, Leisure, Recreation & Tourism

This group of subjects covers a variety of courses directed towards management in the leisure and tourism industries, mainly delivered at modern universities. Taken together with sports studies, it remains close to the top 20 for applications, although the numbers have dropped for three successive years and are down by a quarter since the years immediately before £9,000 fees were introduced. Because so many graduates begin their careers in low-level jobs, the subjects are never far from the foot of the employment table. They are fifth from bottom in the new edition. The subjects do better in the earnings table, but are still in the bottom 20.

Entry standards are modest – only five universities average more than 150 points on the UCAS tariff. They are led by second-placed Strathclyde with 214 points. However, the overall leader, for the fourth year in a row, is Birmingham, which produced by far the best results in the Research Excellence Framework, when 90% of its submission was considered world-leading or internationally excellent. Portsmouth, in 19th place, has the best graduate prospects, one of only three universities to see eight out of ten graduates go straight into professional employment or onto a postgraduate course. The proportion was below one in three at three universities.

Many of the courses included in this category teeter on the edge of eligibility for our table because student numbers are low. As a result, there is more churn than in other subject groups – four universities have dropped out this year, while two have joined. Only seven of the 59 institutions in the latest table are pre-1992 universities, but they include five of the top ten.

Students at tenth-placed Sunderland are the most satisfied with the quality of teaching, just ahead of those at fourth-placed Lincoln, who gave the best ratings for the broader student experience. More than 100 universities and colleges are offering courses in one or more of the hospitality, leisure, recreation and tourism subjects in 2019.

Hospitality, Leisure, Recreation and Tourism	Teaching quality %	Student experience %	Research quality %	Entry standards (UCAS points)	Graduate prospects %	Overall score
1 Birmingham	87.4	88.6	63.7	158	73.9	100.0
2 Strathclyde	76.0	80.6	44.3	214	54.5	95.4
3 Manchester	91.6	90.3	—	155	77.6	90.3
4 Lincoln	95.4	97.3	11.4	121	78.7	90.2
5 Ulster	91.1	93.7	31.0	120	63.0	88.9
6 Staffordshire	90.4	91.3	19.1	143	56.8	87.8
7 Liverpool John Moores	77.1	82.5	45.3	140	54.1	87.5
8 Surrey	70.7	73.9	33.6	169	57.8	87.2
9 Edinburgh	66.0	71.0	26.1	177	65.6	87.0
10 Sunderland	95.6	93.1	2.4	115	69.3	85.6
11 Central Lancashire	86.4	87.0	5.1	143	61.0	84.8
12 Coventry	83.4	84.7	1.6	135	70.6	84.4
13 Leeds Beckett	85.1	83.9	12.6	120	64.9	83.7
14 Edge Hill	79.1	78.3	7.7	145	—	83.5
15 Oxford Brookes	81.3	84.8	5.1	139	63.5	83.4
16 Glasgow Caledonian	86.5	84.4	15.2	145	44.6	83.2
17 Huddersfield	81.1	82.2	—	132	70.6	82.9
18 Winchester	80.8	77.9	—	118	77.5	82.2
=19 Falmouth	92.2	89.5	—	110	63.0	82.1
=19 Portsmouth	71.8	73.4	8.1	116	83.2	82.1
=19 Sheffield Hallam	82.9	80.6	8.5	121	64.5	82.1
22 De Montfort	81.8	71.9	—	126	74.1	82.0
23 Bournemouth	77.4	77.6	9.0	124	67.9	81.7
24 Manchester Metropolitan	80.9	80.6	4.7	129	63.0	81.6
25 Hertfordshire	85.3	81.7	0.9	120	65.6	81.5
=26 Gloucestershire	71.3	76.1	6.0	117	80.5	81.4
=26 West of Scotland	78.2	72.3	9.1	143	57.7	81.4
=28 Solent	81.5	77.9	0.6	122	69.1	81.2
=28 University of the Arts London	74.1	69.9	—	141*	71.4	81.2
30 London South Bank	70.6	65.7	35.0	114	62.0	81.1
31 Greenwich	80.5	78.5	3.3	134	59.6	80.8
32 Robert Gordon	81.5	76.4	2.6	138	56.6	80.6

		Teaching quality %	Student experience %	Research quality %	Entry standards (UCAS points)	Graduate prospects %	Overall score
=33	Chichester	85.8	79.4	—	113	65.5	80.4
=33	Derby	87.4	83.6	0.9	123	55.2	80.4
=33	Queen Margaret, Edinburgh	78.5	79.0	—	124	67.1	80.4
=33	Westminster	71.9	72.9	10.7	144	58.1	80.4
37	Arts University, Bournemouth	71.3	68.5	—	121	81.6	80.2
38	Liverpool Hope	82.3	87.0	10.9	103	57.7	79.6
39	Chester	86.8	79.0	6.6	112	54.4	79.4
40	Aberystwyth	78.7	80.8	14.5	113	53.3*	79.0
41	Edinburgh Napier	73.8	73.0	2.3	150	51.8	78.8
42	Plymouth	78.9	78.7	13.1	114	52.9	78.6
43	Canterbury Christ Church	78.0	79.4	19.0	102	53.4	78.3
44	Salford	72.0	69.6	5.9	124	63.2	78.1
45	Brighton	77.3	72.0	10.9	123	51.8	77.9
46	East London	85.5	75.8	0.8	105	57.9	77.6
47	Northampton	84.8	80.4	—	111	53.0	77.5
48	Wolverhampton	77.4	73.3	5.6	120	53.2	77.1
49	West London	79.8	79.0	—	112	53.5	76.5
50	Cardiff Metropolitan	67.4	69.0	7.7	120	56.5	75.5
51	Bedfordshire	81.5	82.5	6.7	89	47.0	74.4
52	South Wales	73.1	61.8	10.8	—	52.4	74.0
53	London Metropolitan	78.0	71.9	—	103	51.9	73.9
54	Wales Trinity St David	80.2	78.7	—	96	48.8	73.7
55	Middlesex	76.2	76.9	10.5	116	32.7	73.4
56	Buckinghamshire New	74.8	70.6	0.9	112	47.3	73.3
57	St Mary's, Twickenham	84.9	80.0	4.8	100	32.3	72.7
58	Cumbria	63.7	61.8	3.2	125*	45.7	71.4
59	Anglia Ruskin	72.4	75.8	3.4	—	30.0	67.7

Employed in professional job	48%	Employed in non-professional job and Studying	2%
Employed in professional job and studying	1%	Employed in non-professional job	31%
Studying	7%	Unemployed	10%
Average starting professional salary	£20,000	Average starting non-professional salary	£17,000

Iberian Languages

Spanish had been showing signs of bucking the downward trend for language degrees, but two years of modest growth in enrolments came to an end in 2017, when fewer than 300 students started single honours degrees. Applications were down by 15%, taking them back below 2,000. Those statistics do not capture the much larger number of students who learn the language as part of a broader modern languages programme, but even they continued to decline both in 2017 and 2018. The table also includes Portuguese, but not one student has started a single honours degree in the language since 2012. Nevertheless, Portuguese will still be available – either alone or as part of a modern languages degree – at 23 universities in 2019. It can be combined with Czech, Russian, philosophy or theatre (among other subjects) at Bristol.

Cambridge has a clear lead at the top of the table, with Lancaster moving up one place to become its nearest challenger. Oxford, which has slipped two places to sixth, has the highest entry grades, but Cambridge produced the top results in the Research Excellence Framework. Lancaster has by far the best graduate prospects, with 96.7% of graduates going straight into professional employment or further study. Only Aberystwyth comes within ten percentage points. Chester, only six places off the bottom of the table, has the top scores for student satisfaction – unusually high ones at that – although Newcastle, which has moved up five places to third overall, is not far behind.

Iberian Languages are tied with French and nine other subjects for 26th place on graduate salaries in professional jobs. They are in the bottom half for overall graduate prospects, although most universities offering the languages have a reasonable employment record. Only three fell below 60% for the proportion of graduates going straight into professional jobs or further study. Only seven of the 48 in this year's table are post-1992 universities, none of them reaching the top 30. Portsmouth comes closest.

Iberian Languages	Teaching quality %	Student experience %	Research quality %	Entry standards (UCAS points)	Graduate prospects %	Overall score
1 Cambridge	—	—	54.0	203	80.6	100.0
2 Lancaster	82.8	80.0	47.0	152	96.7	97.5
3 Newcastle	93.1	91.9	36.3	171	82.5	96.9
4 Durham	84.2	73.6	34.6	199	86.3	95.7
5 Surrey	89.6	82.7	39.1	165	—	94.6
6 Oxford	—	—	41.3	214	72.7	94.4
7 Exeter	82.3	81.8	35.1	175	84.5	93.9
8 Glasgow	79.4	78.2	26.3	204	85.6	93.7
9 Queen's, Belfast	81.6	82.1	53.6	150	74.2	93.0
10 Southampton	85.1	85.2	42.7	147	77.6	92.6
=11 St Andrews	82.8	81.5	26.4	186	79.8	92.0
=11 Strathclyde	75.4	71.7	42.0	203	73.1	92.0
13 Heriot-Watt	84.2	81.2	26.3	189	77.0	91.8
14 Manchester	—	—	48.9	149	70.7	91.6
15 Aberystwyth	82.3	78.8	16.6	—	88.7*	91.4
16 York	83.3	83.6	37.3	153	75.0	90.8
17 Bristol	76.6	71.7	36.0	168	81.2	90.4
18 University College London	76.6	67.9	43.7	182	71.3	90.1
19 Leeds	77.9	78.9	30.6	164	79.7	89.7
20 Kent	81.8	81.4	41.9	127	77.0	89.6
21 King's College London	74.4	69.9	42.1	165	76.0	89.5
=22 Bath	77.4	79.6	27.4	170	79.2	89.4
=22 Queen Mary, London	89.8	83.8	35.1	137	70.4	89.4
=22 Sheffield	82.5	77.6	41.2	145	72.1	89.4

Iberian Languages cont

		Teaching quality %	Student experience %	Research quality %	Entry standards (UCAS points)	Graduate prospects %	Overall score
=25	East Anglia	83.6	80.5	33.1	143	75.0	88.9
=25	Nottingham	75.7	68.8	39.4	154	78.4	88.9
27	Birmingham	78.8	77.2	33.7	168	70.2	88.3
28	Bangor	88.6	86.0	39.6	130	63.4	88.0
29	Edinburgh	73.5	73.8	30.3	183	71.1	87.5
30	Royal Holloway, London	74.8	74.2	48.3	147	66.7	87.4
31	Warwick	72.9	66.9	45.2	162	—	87.3
32	Aberdeen	70.1	84.6	29.3	176	71.0*	87.1
=33	Portsmouth	85.5	89.2	32.2	110	72.5	87.0
=33	Stirling	74.6	71.9	29.8	161	76.0	87.0
35	Manchester Metropolitan	90.5	91.4	29.0	115	65.1	86.2
36	Cardiff	79.6	78.7	32.5	143	68.6	86.1
37	Hull	90.1	88.5	22.7	108	71.0	85.5
38	Liverpool	73.7	70.4	33.4	138	74.2	85.1
39	Swansea	89.5	86.8	22.8	113	66.8	84.6
40	Aston	84.1	83.0	23.4	129	67.4	84.4
41	Leicester	88.5	89.1	16.9	132	63.6	84.1
42	Reading	76.6	68.3	41.7	124	—	83.7
43	Chester	94.5	92.5	17.3	110	59.3	83.1
44	Northumbria	79.8	79.9	—	136*	74.2*	80.8
45	Coventry	64.8	70.4	18.1	109	77.8	78.8
46	Nottingham Trent	86.6	87.6	7.6	126	53.7	78.7
47	Ulster	74.0	72.5	22.4	123*	49.6	76.0
48	Westminster	73.0	69.2	2.0	127	63.6	75.2

Employed in professional job	47%	Employed in non-professional job and Studying	2%
Employed in professional job and studying	3%	Employed in non-professional job	21%
Studying	18%	Unemployed	10%
Average starting professional salary	£22,000	Average starting non-professional salary	£17,000

Italian

There was a 50% increase in the numbers starting degrees in Italian in 2017 – but that still amounted to only 30 students – less than half the total before £9,000 fees were introduced. Even allowing for the much larger numbers of undergraduates who include Italian in broader language programmes or as one or more modules in another subject, demand is worryingly low. Forty universities offered the language in 2016, but only 23 are doing so in 2019, almost all of them as part of a modern languages degree. Most students have no previous knowledge of Italian, although they are likely to have taken another language at A-level.

Cambridge, which did best in the Research Excellence Framework, is well clear at the top of the table, while second-placed Oxford has the highest entry grades. Edinburgh and Bristol have both entered the top ten after big rises. Nottingham Trent has the highest levels of student satisfaction in both of the measures derived from the National Student Survey, while Birmingham was well clear of the field on graduate prospects, with 95% of those completing courses in 2017 going straight into professional jobs or continuing to study.

The small numbers of students can make for exaggerated swings in the graduate employment statistics. Italian has dropped 18 places and out of the top 50 in the latest employment table, although it does better in the comparison of graduate salaries. Entry standards remain surprisingly high, given the small numbers of applicants. Only one of the 16 universities with enough students to compile an entry score (Portsmouth) averages less than 120 points on the UCAS tariff. There is a high response rate and scores have generally been good in the National Student Survey. Only one university (University College London) failed to satisfy at least three quarters of final-year undergraduates on the quality of teaching.

Italian

		Teaching quality %	Student experience %	Research quality %	Entry standards (UCAS points)	Graduate prospects %	Overall score
1	Cambridge	—	—	54.0	203	80.6	100.0
2	Oxford	—	—	41.3	217	76.6	95.3
3	Manchester	—	—	48.9	151	84.1	95.2
4	Durham	84.2	73.6	34.6	199	86.3	94.6
5	Exeter	82.3	81.8	35.1	175	84.5	92.8
6	Birmingham	78.1	74.1	33.7	165	95.1	92.2
7	Kent	85.6	85.1	41.9	123*	87.0	92.0
8	Warwick	84.0	78.3	45.2	163	72.1	91.8
9	Edinburgh	81.0	79.5	30.3	183*	75.4	89.9
10	Bristol	76.6	71.7	36.0	169	75.5	88.4
11	University College London	62.7	55.9	43.7	187	81.6	88.0
12	Portsmouth	91.4	86.9	32.2	110	76.1	87.9
13	Leeds	85.9	85.6	30.6	161	64.8	87.7
14	Bath	77.4	81.9	27.4	146	83.7	87.4
15	Cardiff	86.8	82.5	32.5	141	66.0	86.8
16	Bangor	86.4	80.6	39.6	—	56.4*	86.6
=17	Nottingham Trent	94.5	95.1	7.6	—	60.7	85.3
=17	Reading	84.7	80.6	41.7	125	58.1	85.3
19	Royal Holloway, London	78.9	68.6	48.3	—	56.1*	84.1

Employed in professional job	44%	Employed in non-professional job and Studying	2%
Employed in professional job and studying	3%	Employed in non-professional job	22%
Studying	16%	Unemployed	12%
Average starting professional salary	£21,000	Average starting non-professional salary	£17,400

Land and Property Management

Graduate salaries and employment levels in land and property management are among the best of any group outside the health professions. Over 80% of graduates go straight into professional employment, helping the subjects to a top-ten position for graduate prospects, and starting salaries of £25,000 in those jobs place land and property management 14th on that criterion. Like last year, there were too few graduates in lower-level jobs to compile a national average.

The subject table reflects those high employment rates: over 94% of graduates at third-placed Reading found high-level work or continued to study, and only one university dropped below 80% on this measure. The table is still less than half the size it was in 2006, however, with no representation from Scotland or Wales. Nevertheless, more than 20 universities and colleges are offering courses in this area in 2019. They include degrees in woodland ecology and conservation, and property management and valuation, as well as the real estate degrees that are the largest recruiters. Cambridge has a predictably big lead, with the best research score and entry grades that are nearly 60 points ahead of the next highest in the table. Oxford Brookes has the most satisfied students and has gone up three places to second overall since last year.

The subjects have acquired a reputation for recruiting disproportionate numbers from independent schools, but property firms donated more than £500,000 to support a 'Pathways to Property' scheme to try to widen participation. Those who take the courses appear to enjoy the experience: although there are no outstandingly high scores from the National Student Survey, only one university in the table recorded less than 70% satisfaction with the teaching or broader student experience.

Land and Property Management	Teaching quality %	Student experience %	Research quality %	Entry standards (UCAS points)	Graduate prospects %	Overall score
1 Cambridge	78.3*	72.4*	49.0	203	89.7	100.0
2 Oxford Brookes	85.9	83.6	17.6	135	92.4	95.8
3 Reading	71.1	71.7	40.0	146	94.4	94.7
=4 Nottingham Trent	82.0	82.7	3.4	122	93.3	92.6
=4 Ulster	78.5	79.8	28.6	110	90.0	92.6
6 Sheffield Hallam	79.7	78.7	13.4	112	92.1	91.7
7 Birmingham City	81.9	82.5	2.7	110	90.9	91.1
8 Westminster	67.4	72.6	10.7	115	84.2	85.9
9 Greenwich	76.4	75.3	2.0	134	70.0	84.9

Employed in professional job	79%	Employed in non-professional job and Studying	0%
Employed in professional job and studying	3%	Employed in non-professional job	5%
Studying	5%	Unemployed	9%
Average starting professional salary	£25,000	Average starting non-professional salary	n/a

Law

Already one of the most popular choices for higher education, law is one of the few subjects to have enjoyed increased enrolments for the current academic year. The numbers starting degrees passed 26,000 in 2017, as applications set another record. Entry standards reflect this: only in medicine do so many universities make such testing demands. Eight of the 102 universities in the table average at least 200 points and more than a third average more than 150 points. However, so many universities now offer law that there are still nine where the average was below 100 points in 2017.

Cambridge has extended its already considerable lead over Oxford at the top of the table, although neither leads on any individual measure. Glasgow benefits from the UCAS conversion rate for Scottish secondary qualifications in registering the highest entry standards, while Lancaster has the best score for graduate prospects. The students who are most satisfied with the quality of teaching are at Gloucestershire, just outside the top 30, and the best rate in the sections of the National Student Survey devoted to the broader student experience is at Bolton, which is not in the top 60. Both universities were handicapped by not entering the Research Excellence Framework in law.

Law has broken into the top 20 in the employment table but it is only 55th out of the 67 subjects for early career earnings, which average (just) less than £20,000 in professional jobs. Only about half of all graduates go on to practise law, and training contracts for those who do keep the median in graduate-level jobs relatively low. Those in lower-level employment are only £3,000 worse off, although the later rewards in professional jobs can be considerable. Aspiring solicitors in England go on to take the Legal Practice Course, while those aiming to be barristers take the Bar Vocational Course, so it is no surprise that 45% of all law graduates are engaged in postgraduate study six months after completing a degree. Note that in Scotland, most law courses are based on the distinctive Scottish legal system, which also has different professional qualifications.

Law	Teaching quality %	Student experience %	Research quality %	Entry standards (UCAS points)	Graduate prospects %	Overall score
1 Cambridge	—	—	58.7	225	89.8	100.0
2 Oxford	—		51.8	208	83.9	94.6
3 University College London	75.8	67.7	57.7	206	89.2	94.5
4 London School of Economics	71.2	67.9	64.5	209	85.8	93.7
5 Aberdeen	83.7	84.6	20.9	198	90.2	92.9
6 Glasgow	74.7	78.5	33.8	233	84.5	92.6
7 Durham	79.6	75.9	32.8	209	86.0	92.2
8 Dundee	87.0	86.0	16.3	184	89.4	92.1
9 Edinburgh	74.0	76.0	40.8	198	85.4	91.2
10 Leeds	82.7	87.7	40.1	169	79.2	91.1
=11 Kent	81.7	83.8	43.9	148	84.6	90.9
=11 Nottingham	74.6	74.4	45.2	181	86.3	90.9
13 Bristol	75.8	71.5	50.5	188	79.3	90.3
14 King's College London	69.1	67.9	39.2	205	87.0	89.8
15 Strathclyde	69.9	68.6	29.4	214	88.5	89.6
16 Stirling	86.8	85.3	19.4	172	80.1	89.2
17 Lancaster	70.4	71.6	38.9	152	93.5	88.8

Law cont

	Teaching quality %	Student experience %	Research quality %	Entry standards (UCAS points)	Graduate prospects %	Overall score
18 York	76.5	78.2	30.3	175	81.7	88.2
19 Exeter	77.3	75.8	21.4	173	86.9	88.0
20 Glasgow Caledonian	82.3	79.6	1.8	182	86.0	87.2
21 Queen's, Belfast	69.0	67.7	40.3	153	87.6	86.8
=22 East Anglia	77.0	78.3	26.5	162	80.7	86.7
=22 Swansea	82.8	81.5	20.4	135	83.8	86.7
24 Sheffield	73.0	73.2	31.9	152	85.8	86.6
25 Warwick	67.1	67.6	41.9	181	80.1	86.4
26 Birmingham	72.7	70.1	33.6	158	83.2	86.2
27 Heriot-Watt	77.9	82.6	18.8	165*	79.2	86.1
28 Reading	75.3	73.3	31.2	144	82.8	85.8
=29 Newcastle	73.4	71.7	25.4	177	80.0	85.7
=29 Southampton	78.0	74.2	18.2	152	84.8	85.7
=31 Aberystwyth	85.5	84.2	14.3	112	84.8	85.5
=31 Gloucestershire	91.9	83.7	—	114	86.4	85.5
=33 Abertay	84.7	70.0	1.2	152	88.0	85.3
=33 London South Bank	82.1	84.2	20.1	94	87.9	85.3
35 Manchester	—	—	27.2	168	85.2	85.2
36 Leicester	77.4	79.5	26.4	144	77.4	85.0
=37 Portsmouth	74.3	73.6	32.2	125	84.3	84.9
=37 Queen Mary, London	73.3	71.3	23.7	169	79.7	84.9
=37 Sussex	73.4	72.4	23.3	150	84.2	84.9
40 Bangor	84.6	81.0	12.0	133	78.0	84.3
41 Nottingham Trent	82.4	80.2	2.3	142	82.7	84.0
42 Ulster	83.7	79.7	48.5	128	58.9	83.9
43 Robert Gordon	79.6	75.8	3.9	167	79.3	83.8
=44 Buckingham	79.8	77.8	—	115	92.8	83.7
=44 Liverpool	—	—	19.6	147	83.0	83.7
46 Cardiff	70.7	68.6	27.2	158	78.8	83.6
47 Lincoln	81.3	81.7	5.0	121	84.2	83.4
=48 Aston	82.3	79.2	19.7	140	71.3	83.3
=48 Birkbeck, London	74.5	71.2	37.9	113	78.5	83.3
=48 Keele	70.5	71.8	30.5	115	85.2	83.3
=51 Plymouth	81.7	80.6	16.0	121	76.3	82.9
=51 West London	87.0	89.4	—	102	80.8	82.9
53 Greenwich	88.1	84.2	2.1	133	71.5	82.4
54 Edge Hill	86.5	85.1	12.1	119	70.1	82.3
=55 Hull	75.8	74.3	12.6	123	82.0	82.0
=55 SOAS London	69.4	69.9	26.7	150	75.7	82.0
57 Sheffield Hallam	84.0	83.6	14.4	118	70.6	81.9
58 Edinburgh Napier	85.3	82.1	—	169	64.9	81.8
59 South Wales	85.9	84.2	—	124	73.8	81.7

=60	Coventry	82.0	79.7	5.6	113	78.1	81.4
=60	Manchester Metropolitan	78.5	76.0	14.9	124	75.0	81.4
=62	Bolton	87.1	89.7	—	100	75.0	81.3
=62	Bradford	77.6	76.9	11.8	126	76.5	81.3
=62	De Montfort	79.2	79.3	5.2	108	81.9	81.3
65	Northumbria	80.1	80.2	2.5	135	74.9	81.2
66	Essex	68.6	68.8	31.6	116	76.6	80.5
67	Huddersfield	77.0	76.6	—	127	78.8	80.2
68	Derby	80.8	75.9	2.4	102	80.0	80.1
=69	Solent	87.7	86.8	—	96	71.4	80.0
=69	Teesside	78.1	73.5	15.0	112	74.0	80.0
=71	Liverpool John Moores	72.8	66.9	2.7	136	82.2	79.9
=71	Staffordshire	82.1	75.9	—	112	77.1	79.9
73	Brunel	68.8	69.7	20.3	132	75.6	79.8
=74	Chester	74.2	74.2	—	108	85.3	79.7
=74	St Mary's, Twickenham	79.4	81.2	—	110	76.8	79.7
76	West of England	77.6	78.4	3.5	116	74.1	79.2
77	Middlesex	67.2	70.4	21.4	107	79.1	79.0
=78	Brighton	80.3	78.1	6.5	112	69.5	78.7
=78	East London	77.0	74.5	8.6	109	73.8	78.7
80	Birmingham City	78.4	81.3	2.8	118	69.7	78.6
=81	Central Lancashire	75.8	77.0	5.3	132	68.5	78.4
=81	Sunderland	76.5	68.3	0.7	104	81.2	78.4
83	Surrey	64.4	62.7	8.5	159	76.2	78.3
84	Westminster	71.4	71.2	7.5	116	76.4	78.0
=85	Bedfordshire	87.4	87.4	3.6	74	66.2	77.8
=85	Salford	76.9	72.9	5.9	119	69.9	77.8
=87	Hertfordshire	74.8	73.9	—	105	76.0	77.3
=87	Northampton	77.2	79.1	—	95	74.0	77.3
89	Cumbria	90.9	79.9	—	81	64.0	77.1
90	London Metropolitan	75.5	68.1	0.3	85	81.2	76.9
91	Bournemouth	63.9	60.7	8.8	116	82.4	76.8
92	Oxford Brookes	71.2	69.1	5.1	122	70.1	76.2
93	Anglia Ruskin	85.5	83.4	5.2	94	57.3	76.1
=94	City	71.6	69.0	9.1	141	62.1	76.0
=94	Wolverhampton	78.6	77.4	2.7	101	65.2	76.0
96	Leeds Beckett	74.5	79.8	—	102	66.1	75.2
97	Liverpool Hope	64.9	55.0	—	96	84.4	74.4
98	West of Scotland	76.8	72.0	—	134	54.1	73.9
99	Winchester	73.9	68.2	—	105	62.1	73.0
100	Canterbury Christ Church	82.6	77.4	3.2	115	45.2	72.8
101	Kingston	64.9	66.0	—	108	64.5	71.4
102	Buckinghamshire New	64.5	71.9	—	97	60.3	70.3

Employed in professional job	33%	Employed in non-professional job and Studying	5%
Employed in professional job and studying	6%	Employed in non-professional job	14%
Studying	34%	Unemployed	8%
Average starting professional salary	£19,998	Average starting non-professional salary	£17,000

Librarianship and Information Management

Only three universities are left in the table for librarianship and information management – a third of the number a decade ago and two less than last year. None of them has a degree specifically in librarianship, which is now normally studied at Masters level; indeed, some postgraduate training is required to enter the profession after completing a first degree. Most of the courses in this category focus on broader information services. Only 175 students started undergraduate programmes in 2017, although this was 55 more than in the previous year.

As in other subjects with small enrolments, there can be huge swings in the national statistics. Librarianship and Information Management has dropped 23 places from last year's position on the verge of the top 20 for the proportion of graduates in professional jobs or further study, but is sharing 14th place in the earnings table, with median salaries of £25,000 in graduate-level jobs. There are real contrasts among universities in our table, with the top two scoring around 90% for graduate prospects, but the third less than 50%. Yet it is third-placed Manchester Metropolitan that has the highest scores for all aspects of student satisfaction.

Loughborough, which heads the table for the fifth year in succession, has much the highest entry standards, although it could not match the graduate prospects at second-placed Northumbria. Leeds, which has dropped out of the table this year, was the star of the Research Excellence Framework.

Librarianship and Information Management	Teaching quality %	Student experience %	Research quality %	Entry standards (UCAS points)	Graduate prospects %	Overall score
1 Loughborough	79.4	82.6	45.1	156*	89.0	100.0
2 Northumbria	73.8	76.3	21.0	124*	92.3	91.9
3 Manchester Metropolitan	81.3	84.3	4.7	131	46.4	91.4

Employed in professional job	55%	Employed in non-professional job and Studying	1%
Employed in professional job and studying	4%	Employed in non-professional job	19%
Studying	9%	Unemployed	12%
Average starting professional salary	£25,000	Average starting non-professional salary	£16,881

Linguistics

Applications for courses in linguistics dipped in 2017 after reaching record levels in the previous year. There was only a small drop in the numbers starting degrees, however, and 70 universities are offering courses classified by UCAS as linguistics in 2019. In its pure form, linguistics examines how language works, and can lead to work in speech therapy or the growing field of teaching English as a foreign language. The subject has fared much better than might have been expected since the introduction of £9,000 fees, with both applications and enrolments running well ahead of the levels seen a decade ago.

Almost three-quarters of the students are female. There are about five applications for each place and entry standards are comparatively high, with 11 of the top 15 universities averaging more than 150 points on the UCAS tariff. Second-placed Cambridge has the top scores for entry standards and graduate prospects, but neither it nor Oxford has published scores from the latest National Student Survey because the two universities did not reach the 50% response rate required. Cambridge had the lowest satisfaction rates in the entire table on the last occasion that a score could be produced, and this was enough to keep Oxford at the top overall. Edinburgh, in eighth place, has the best research score. Students at Bangor, in 14th place, are the most satisfied with the quality of teaching, while those at the University of the West of England, which is in the bottom ten, gave the highest rating to the broader student experience.

Linguistics has dropped 11 places and out of the top 50 in the employment table but does a little better in the comparison of earnings, sharing 47th place with eight others. Almost one graduate in three starts off in lower-level employment, and only Cambridge and Essex saw eight out of ten of those completing a linguistics degree go straight into professional work or onto a postgraduate course in 2017.

Linguistics	Teaching quality %	Student experience %	Research quality %	Entry standards (UCAS points)	Graduate prospects %	Overall score
1 Oxford	—	—	41.3	209	77.4	100.0
2 Cambridge	—	—	54.0	215	87.9	98.4
3 Lancaster	84.4	81.9	47.0	156	78.3	96.7
4 Aberdeen	90.1	86.9	46.3	143	72.7	95.9
5 Manchester	76.8	77.2	48.9	152	79.8	94.7
6 Newcastle	84.5	80.1	36.3	171	69.1	93.8
7 Kent	83.4	82.5	41.9	133	78.5	93.5
8 Edinburgh	81.7	80.8	57.7	164	56.6	93.4
9 Warwick	76.7	75.3	45.2	169	—	93.2
10 Leeds	91.7	85.9	30.6	157	65.8	93.1
11 King's College London	81.2	81.0	42.1	157	69.0	92.9
12 Sheffield	—	—	42.2	142	76.0	92.6
13 SOAS London	91.8	83.3	26.0	160	60.9	91.0
14 Bangor	93.9	87.0	39.6	131	55.6	90.4
=15 Queen Mary, London	80.3	72.7	50.3	124	69.6	90.2
=15 University College London	69.3	74.5	43.7	169	66.3	90.2
17 Manchester Metropolitan	87.1	82.7	29.0	126	71.7	89.9
18 Roehampton	92.0	85.4	21.8	101	77.4	89.0
19 Glasgow	78.4	75.0	26.3	—	75.0*	88.9
20 York	76.0	72.0	37.3	142	68.9	88.5
21 Huddersfield	85.1	83.0	29.9	116	69.2	88.1
22 Central Lancashire	84.5	79.3	15.2	124	77.8	87.8
23 Essex	72.8	69.3	36.0	117	80.4	87.6
24 West of England	90.4	91.4	9.5	121	65.1	86.2
25 Cardiff	80.4	74.0	35.1	—	59.3*	85.3
26 Nottingham Trent	86.0	81.8	10.0	120	69.6	85.1
27 Wolverhampton	82.0	76.2	12.8	113	69.6	83.4
28 York St John	86.0	81.0	9.7	111	60.0	81.8
29 Salford	84.5	80.0	4.8	110	53.3*	78.8

Linguistics cont	Teaching quality %	Student experience %	Research quality %	Entry standards (UCAS points)	Graduate prospects %	Overall score
30 Reading	65.2	57.5	25.8	138	—	78.7
31 Hertfordshire	71.9	71.6	—	112	69.2	78.2
32 Westminster	81.6	72.5	2.0	102	51.9	75.8
33 Ulster	74.2	72.8	22.4	122	33.7	75.3
34 Brighton	64.7	64.5	16.2	103	47.7	72.6

Employed in professional job	39%	Employed in non-professional job and Studying	3%
Employed in professional job and studying	3%	Employed in non-professional job	26%
Studying	22%	Unemployed	7%
Average starting professional salary	£20,000	Average starting non-professional salary	£16,354

Materials Technology

Courses in this table cover four distinct areas: materials science, mining engineering, textiles technology and printing, and marine technology. The various subjects are highly specialised and attract relatively small numbers – fewer than 700 started courses in all of these areas combined in 2017 – with applications and enrolments rising slightly from 2016. Although there are only 15 universities in the table – two more than last year – more than 50 institutions are offering courses in this area in 2019. The leading universities demand chemistry and sometimes also physics, maths or design technology at A-level or its equivalent.

Cambridge remains well ahead of the rest at the top of the table, with much the highest scores for entry standards and research: only 3% of the university's submission to the Research Excellence Framework was considered less than world-leading or internationally excellent. However, Loughborough has the best graduate prospects and the top scores on both of the measures derived from the National Student Survey – successes that have helped the university rise one place to third, just behind Oxford.

Materials technology has slipped two places in the salaries table but is still 14th, with an average that reached £25,000 in 2017, and it is only eight places lower for graduate prospects after a big rise last year. More than half went straight into professional jobs, while nearly three in ten continued their studies, either full or part-time. Entry standards are relatively high, with only one university averaging (slightly) less than 120 points on the UCAS tariff.

Materials Technology	Teaching quality %	Student experience %	Research quality %	Entry standards (UCAS points)	Graduate prospects %	Overall score
1 Cambridge	78.5*	81.2*	78.3	242	84.0	100.0
2 Oxford	—	—	70.8	236	93.4	99.0
3 Loughborough	96.1	93.7	41.8	173	95.9	97.0
4 Imperial College	70.9	80.1	62.3	216	82.8	93.6
5 Sheffield	82.4	88.2	41.0	162	95.7	92.5

6 Exeter	93.3	89.0	36.4	144	87.8	91.1
7 Birmingham	81.7	81.3	49.3	166	83.7	90.5
8 Swansea	83.6	84.0	45.5	130	95.0	90.3
9 Manchester	81.4	79.9	36.4	177	74.6	87.3
10 Queen Mary, London	63.3	67.6	40.0	147	76.4	80.7
11 De Montfort	91.2	83.6	12.5	124	65.8	80.2
12 Birmingham City	88.4	82.8	—	123	77.3	80.1
13 Sheffield Hallam	74.6	77.2	17.8	121	76.1	78.8
14 Buckinghamshire New	84.8	74.1	—	138	55.0	74.7
15 Huddersfield	64.3	55.0	10.2	118	46.9	66.6

Employed in professional job	49%	Employed in non-professional job and Studying	2%
Employed in professional job and studying	2%	Employed in non-professional job	11%
Studying	24%	Unemployed	11%
Average starting professional salary	£25,000	Average starting non-professional salary	£18,000

Mathematics

Maths continues to grow in popularity, another record enrolment in 2017 meaning that universities have added more than 1,000 places in the subject since the start of the decade. Including statistics and joint honours degrees, the number of applications is now well over 50,000 a year. Our table reflects this, with four more universities joining in the latest edition.

Entry standards are high: the top four in this year's table all average more than 220 points and the top seven plus two others at least 200. The scores are boosted by the fact that most successful candidates for the leading universities have taken two A-levels in the subject, as well as two or three others. But the table also covers a wide spread of entry scores: 16 universities average less than 120 points and four of them less than 100.

Maths is often cited as one of the subjects most likely to lead to a lucrative career, and our earnings table seems to bear this out. The subject is one of five sharing 14th place for average salaries in professional jobs six months after graduation. However, it is still outside the top 20 in the table based on the proportion of graduates going straight into such jobs or embarking on another course. Three in ten continue their studies after graduation, while just under half find high-level employment.

Cambridge remains ahead of Oxford at the top of the table. Cambridge leads on entry grades, while Oxford produced the best results in the Research Excellence Framework. The best scores on the other measures are surprisingly widely spread through the table. Chichester, which is 59th out of the 73 universities, has the best graduate prospects, for example, with over 96% positive destinations. South Wales, the leading post-1992 university in a creditable 21st place, is the clear leader in the sections of the National Student Survey (NSS) devoted to teaching quality, with a record 99.3% satisfaction level. It is just behind De Montfort, in 26th place, in the remaining sections of the NSS. Mathematicians appear to be more satisfied with the quality of teaching than their peers in almost any other subject – only four of 73 institutions dropped below 70% on this measure.

Mathematics

	Teaching quality %	Student experience %	Research quality %	Entry standards (UCAS points)	Graduate prospects %	Overall score
1 Cambridge	—	—	60.7	242	88.9	100.0
2 Oxford	—	—	67.5	228	90.6	99.1
=3 Imperial College	77.9	81.9	59.7	225	84.5	96.4
=3 St Andrews	82.0	79.2	44.2	234	88.5	96.4
5 Durham	78.6	77.0	44.0	218	86.4	94.0
6 Warwick	77.1	75.4	55.8	208	83.6	93.8
7 University College London	76.1	75.3	42.0	203	90.2	93.0
8 Lancaster	81.4	82.1	45.8	162	88.2	92.8
9 Heriot-Watt	83.2	82.1	42.3	177	83.0	92.2
10 Manchester	82.5	81.6	44.3	184	79.1	91.7
11 Loughborough	86.9	86.7	31.0	159	84.0	91.3
12 Southampton	83.0	82.7	41.9	170	80.4	91.2
13 Birmingham	82.2	83.4	34.1	174	83.9	91.1
14 Edinburgh	73.4	75.8	43.7	198	84.0	90.9
15 Strathclyde	79.3	81.0	34.6	191	82.5	90.8
16 Nottingham	78.4	78.6	44.8	178	81.1	90.6
17 Glasgow	78.4	81.4	41.4	205	74.5	90.4
18 Exeter	77.8	82.2	37.9	174	82.2	90.0
19 Leeds	77.5	77.7	42.0	171	80.8	89.5
20 Bath	73.1	71.9	35.7	196	85.0	89.4
21 South Wales	99.3	95.8	10.1	126	79.0	89.2
22 Dundee	82.1	79.0	48.2	159	73.8	89.1
23 Bristol	69.9	69.0	57.3	194	76.0	89.0
24 Sheffield	—	—	34.0	156	82.2	88.9
25 Aberystwyth	94.9	90.4	19.4	124	78.2	88.6
26 De Montfort	94.0	96.0	—	102	90.0	88.0
27 Kent	76.1	77.7	28.2	136	89.1	87.4
=28 London School of Economics	66.7	66.0	28.7	210	85.7	87.3
=28 Queen's, Belfast	74.0	72.9	25.0	162	88.8	87.3
30 Cardiff	79.7	82.8	31.6	165	74.1	87.1
31 Sussex	75.5	75.5	28.5	135	89.0	87.0
32 York	81.9	79.3	27.0	159	76.6	86.9
33 Surrey	80.3	78.8	31.5	164	74.4	86.8
34 Nottingham Trent	86.8	87.5	18.4	133	77.7	86.6
35 Newcastle	79.6	81.7	32.0	158	73.0	86.4
=36 Coventry	83.8	85.3	9.4	125	86.7	86.2
=36 Essex	74.0	78.8	34.3	122	85.3	86.2
=38 Northumbria	88.1	88.2	16.7	135	74.3	86.0
=38 Salford	87.1	90.6	4.4	104	87.5	86.0
40 Aberdeen	74.8	78.1	32.0	170	74.4	85.9
=41 East Anglia	79.7	79.7	33.7	148	72.3	85.7
=41 Royal Holloway, London	83.5	83.5	35.5	137	68.4	85.7

43 Swansea	75.8	76.4	20.7	139	84.0	85.1
=44 Keele	84.9	84.1	19.5	129	74.8	85.0
=44 Stirling	81.1	79.2	14.0	161	76.6	85.0
46 Portsmouth	85.1	83.4	11.2	107	84.2	84.9
47 Reading	77.3	72.7	35.3	131	76.5	84.7
48 King's College London	69.6	67.2	37.1	163	76.2	84.2
49 Hull	79.9	71.0	24.2	122	79.9	83.9
50 Liverpool John Moores	81.8	79.9	3.2	129	80.7	83.0
=51 Hertfordshire	80.8	80.9	20.2	103	76.8	82.8
=51 Leicester	72.0	75.3	25.0	134	77.7	82.8
=51 Wolverhampton	85.9	89.2	—	110	77.6	82.8
54 Aston	77.0	80.7	21.7	130	72.9	82.7
=55 Greenwich	85.6	85.4	5.1	124	71.9	82.3
=55 Liverpool	—	—	29.8	142	72.9	82.3
=55 London Metropolitan	86.8	92.6	13.5	75	73.7	82.3
58 Central Lancashire	80.1	75.6	19.8	130	71.4	82.2
59 Chichester	72.5	77.5	—	86	96.3	81.7
60 Liverpool Hope	71.6	76.1	8.8	104	88.0	81.5
61 Queen Mary, London	71.8	71.7	30.3	138	69.7	81.3
62 Brunel	75.4	73.9	25.8	117	71.2	81.0
=63 City	80.4	82.6	30.2	120	57.7	80.5
=63 Oxford Brookes	82.5	78.4	13.9	140	62.3	80.5
65 Plymouth	89.8	87.6	9.3	130	55.8	80.4
66 Manchester Metropolitan	89.6	86.6	5.6	119	59.8	80.1
67 Chester	73.8	77.3	7.1	111	78.8	80.0
68 Sheffield Hallam	67.0	77.3	17.8	113	74.4	79.0
69 Middlesex	72.4	80.4	14.2	103	—	78.4
70 West of England	78.8	72.1	10.6	121	65.8	78.3
71 Brighton	82.0	77.2	6.4	107	63.1	77.6
72 Derby	74.8	71.0	5.0	99	74.5	77.4
73 Kingston	80.3	82.2	—	93	58.0	74.9

Employed in professional job	45%	Employed in non-professional job and Studying	1%
Employed in professional job and studying	4%	Employed in non-professional job	13%
Studying	26%	Unemployed	11%
Average starting professional salary	£25,000	Average starting non-professional salary	£17,472

Mechanical Engineering

Mechanical engineering is by far the biggest branch of engineering, attracting twice as many applicants as any of the other subjects, even after a marginal decline in 2017. It is just outside the top ten for all degree choices. The introduction of higher fees only increased the subject's popularity, as students looked for a sure route to well-paid employment. Although there was also a decline in enrolments in 2017, numbers had still grown by more than 50% from a decade ago. It is not hard to see why. Mechanical engineering is among the top 15 subjects for early career prospects and in the top six for starting salaries in graduate-level employment. Almost two-thirds of graduates go straight into such jobs.

Cambridge and Imperial College London share the lead in mechanical engineering this year. Cambridge, last year's leader, is ranked in the top three in the world for the subject by QS, with Imperial also in the top ten. Cambridge has the highest entry standards, the top research score and the best graduate prospects. But Imperial draws level with higher satisfaction rates in both of the measures derived from the National Student Survey. Student satisfaction with the quality of teaching is relatively low nationally, compared with other subjects, however. Northampton has the best scores in both of our satisfaction measures and is the only university to reach 90% on teaching quality.

More than 130 universities and colleges are offering mechanical engineering in 2019. Most of the leading universities demand maths – preferably with a strong component of mechanics – and another science subject (usually physics) at A-level or its equivalent. With more than six applications to the place, entry standards are high at the leading universities, five of which averaged more than 200 points in 2017. Even so, three institutions averaged less than 100 points.

Mechanical Engineering	Teaching quality %	Student experience %	Research quality %	Entry standards (UCAS points)	Graduate prospects %	Overall score
=1 Cambridge	80.1	86.1	67.0	239	93.5	100.0
=1 Imperial College	88.0	90.8	59.6	230	91.1	100.0
3 Bristol	75.4	78.6	52.3	211	89.3	93.2
4 Leeds	82.2	85.8	40.9	195	86.1	92.1
5 Bath	80.4	82.8	37.4	199	89.0	91.9
=6 Loughborough	82.5	84.4	41.8	168	87.8	90.8
=6 Southampton	72.9	77.7	52.3	183	89.6	90.8
8 Heriot-Watt	77.6	79.3	47.8	181	86.3	90.4
9 Swansea	81.6	84.5	45.5	145	90.1	90.1
10 Nottingham	81.3	82.9	40.8	168	86.5	89.9
11 Lancaster	78.3	82.9	41.6	166	87.9	89.6
12 Glasgow	70.2	73.1	47.2	204	85.5	89.4
13 Sheffield	76.1	83.8	36.0	168	89.9	89.1
14 Birmingham	78.3	75.1	37.7	167	90.5	88.9
15 Strathclyde	70.3	72.9	37.2	220	83.5	88.6
16 Surrey	81.8	78.7	30.8	167	86.6	88.1
=17 Edinburgh	64.9	72.5	50.3	188	84.4	87.3
=17 University College London	62.2	70.0	44.6	199	88.0	87.3
19 Cardiff	73.3	81.4	30.2	162	87.9	86.5
20 Coventry	85.0	87.3	10.3	138	91.5	86.3
=21 Northampton	96.9	91.4	4.1	109*	—	85.9
=21 Ulster	86.0	84.2	22.8	129	86.0	85.9
23 Exeter	66.9	73.0	36.4	170	88.3	85.7
24 Newcastle	72.3	76.4	30.2	153	87.7	85.1
25 Manchester	75.0	76.8	35.1	176	75.5	84.9
26 Huddersfield	82.1	82.3	10.2	126	92.2	84.4
=27 Liverpool	72.6	75.6	32.1	142	86.5	84.3

=27	Teesside	87.8	86.3	5.8	126	87.1	84.3
29	Dundee	72.4	72.9	34.1	170	77.1	83.8
30	Queen's, Belfast	65.2	69.6	36.7	147	85.8	82.9
31	Aberdeen	77.0	78.8	28.4	161	71.3	82.7
32	De Montfort	84.4	87.0	12.5	112	82.9	82.6
33	London South Bank	81.2	75.2	19.6	124	83.7	82.5
34	Portsmouth	82.9	82.3	9.1	113	86.4	82.2
35	Sunderland	85.8	82.5	8.8	114	80.8	81.5
=36	Greenwich	67.5	69.6	29.5	142	82.5	81.2
=36	Plymouth	78.2	74.1	15.7	124	83.6	81.2
=38	Queen Mary, London	62.6	72.6	46.7	134	75.7	80.7
=38	West of England	80.6	80.7	10.6	119	80.7	80.7
40	Aston	72.6	71.4	20.6	140	80.0	80.5
41	Sussex	72.8	77.3	24.0	124	78.3	80.3
42	Derby	78.2	70.9	6.7	131	84.1	80.2
=43	Northumbria	66.6	71.7	30.7	142	75.5	79.7
=43	Oxford Brookes	70.7	68.1	13.9	144	82.3	79.7
45	Lincoln	80.1	78.0	—	118	84.0	79.6
46	Brunel	67.8	75.2	23.7	144	75.3	79.5
47	Hull	72.4	71.9	16.5	121	81.3	79.1
48	Central Lancashire	72.2	66.7	7.1	131	84.4	78.6
49	Manchester Metropolitan	75.2	74.9	16.3	125	73.8	78.4
50	Liverpool John Moores	72.4	72.5	4.7	136	80.3	78.3
51	Robert Gordon	65.9	71.6	8.8	163	75.8	78.1
52	West of Scotland	69.6	67.2	9.0	144	79.2	77.9
53	Salford	75.9	77.7	4.4	135	73.0	77.8
=54	Anglia Ruskin	83.5	81.6	9.1	90	73.0	77.4
=54	Harper Adams	76.6	72.3	—	110	82.8	77.4
56	Sheffield Hallam	70.1	71.8	17.8	114	76.9	77.2
=57	Bradford	64.9	71.7	7.7	113	86.4	77.0
=57	Hertfordshire	68.6	69.2	16.5	114	79.3	77.0
=57	South Wales	67.9	66.5	—	119	88.9	77.0
60	Wales Trinity St David	82.6	75.3	1.0	84	75.0	75.5
61	Solent	81.0	75.1	—	115	66.7	75.1
62	City	79.2	78.3	23.1	124	48.3	74.3
63	Chester	69.3	66.5	7.1	108	—	73.1
64	Staffordshire	70.7	63.5	5.7	110	70.3	72.9
65	Birmingham City	68.3	71.0	—	111	70.1	72.5
66	Brighton	69.1	71.9	7.4	112	63.1	72.1
67	Glasgow Caledonian	68.3	73.7	4.7	137	54.5	71.4
68	Kingston	70.6	74.8	2.9	115	57.3	71.0
69	Bolton	63.1	61.8	—	95	58.8	66.6

Employed in professional job	62%	Employed in non-professional job and Studying	1%
Employed in professional job and studying	2%	Employed in non-professional job	10%
Studying	15%	Unemployed	10%
Average starting professional salary	£27,000	Average starting non-professional salary	£17,500

Medicine

New medical schools are opening this year at Edge Hill, Lincoln and Sunderland, adding to the 500 additional places that were made available to study the subject in the current academic year. The first year of expansion helped to spark an 8% increase in applications, reversing a three-year decline. There were still almost nine applications to the place in 2017 and the highest entry standards in any subject. Sixteen of the 33 schools in the table average 200 points or more at entry and none less than 180. In spite of this – and the fact that you can only apply to four medical schools – medicine is in the top eight subjects for the volume of applications. Nearly all schools demand chemistry and most biology. Physics or maths is required by some, either as an alternative or addition to biology. Universities will want to see evidence of commitment to the subject through work experience or voluntary work. Almost all schools interview candidates, and several use one of the two specialist aptitude tests (*see* chapter 2).

The subject carries unique prestige and shares top place in the employment table. Employment scores for individual schools are not used in the ranking (although they are still shown for guidance) to avoid small differences distorting positions in a subject where virtually all graduates become junior doctors or researchers. Thirteen schools reported full employment in 2017, and none dropped below 97%. The average starting salary of £31,000 for junior doctors was matched only by dentists.

Oxford has topped the table for the last eight years, but Cambridge has slipped to fifth place for the first time in that period, overtaken by Swansea and Imperial this year. Keele has risen the most, jumping six places into sixth position, while Glasgow remains in second place. Plymouth, although outside the top 20, has the highest satisfaction rating for the quality of teaching, while Brighton and Sussex, in 17th place, does best in the remaining sections of the National Student Survey. There was little to choose between the top scorers in the Research Excellence Framework, but Lancaster produced the best results.

Undergraduates have to be prepared to work long hours, particularly towards the end of the course, which will usually be five years long. Many students are now opting for the postgraduate route into the medical profession instead, although this is even longer.

Medicine	Teaching quality %	Student experience %	Research quality %	Entry standards (UCAS points)	Graduate prospects %	Overall score
1 Oxford	89.5	88.1	48.9	221	97.0	100.0
2 Glasgow	83.9	83.9	42.3	239	99.8	99.2
3 Swansea	89.2	84.6	44.7	—	100.0	97.2
4 Imperial College	79.4	83.0	54.6	214	99.3	97.0
5 Cambridge	73.0	66.1	52.0	235	98.8	96.7
6 Keele	91.1	90.8	50.0	195	99.6	95.6
7 Newcastle	87.9	86.4	44.8	207	99.8	95.0
8 Queen Mary, London	86.4	89.2	40.2	214	99.3	94.7
9 Exeter	88.2	90.1	41.6	207	99.6	94.3
=10 Aberdeen	86.9	89.3	20.2	242	99.4	93.5
=10 Dundee	81.5	85.6	25.1	243	100.0	93.5
12 Lancaster	88.9	83.8	55.2	178	100.0	92.6

13 University College London	68.6	71.1	53.3	215	99.5	92.3
14 Bristol	82.6	77.0	47.5	198	100.0	91.3
15 Edinburgh	68.3	64.5	49.8	218	98.7	91.0
16 Queen's, Belfast	89.1	88.2	34.6	196	99.7	89.5
17 Brighton and Sussex Medical School	92.2	92.8	34.3	189	100.0	89.4
18 East Anglia	89.3	89.8	31.8	198	99.4	89.1
19 Sheffield	88.8	88.6	36.5	189	100.0	88.7
20 Leeds	86.8	87.7	32.1	198	100.0	88.3
21 St Andrews	83.3	89.2	19.8	220	98.2	87.8
22 Cardiff	77.0	77.8	34.5	201	100.0	85.9
23 Plymouth	92.9	92.1	23.1	189	100.0	85.6
24 Birmingham	77.5	77.7	31.5	203	99.8	85.5
25 Nottingham	72.6	71.8	36.8	202	100.0	85.1
26 Leicester	79.1	78.2	33.3	193	99.4	84.5
27 King's College London	64.8	63.5	48.3	189	99.3	83.3
28 Hull-York Medical School	78.9	74.2	36.2	185	100.0	83.2
29 Manchester	73.0	70.0	34.6	197	99.7	83.1
30 Southampton	69.9	68.6	35.6	193	100.0	81.7
31 St George's, London	75.8	74.7	22.4	200	99.8	80.8
32 Liverpool	64.2	61.6	31.7	180	99.8	75.1
33 Warwick	63.5	60.7	26.2	—	100.0	72.4

Employed in professional job	95%	Employed in non-professional job and Studying	0%
Employed in professional job and studying	1%	Employed in non-professional job	0%
Studying	3%	Unemployed	1%
Average starting professional salary	£31,000	Average starting non-professional salary	n/a

Middle Eastern and African Studies

This is one of the smallest categories in the *Guide* in terms of the numbers taking degrees. Only 100 students started courses in Middle Eastern and African Studies combined in 2017, although larger numbers will have included modules from this group in a broader area studies degree. Arabic shared in a small increase in enrolments for non-European languages, although this has not continued into the current year. The subjects enjoy some official protection because they are classed as "vulnerable" and of national importance. It is just as well because applications remain well down on the norm before the introduction of £9,000 fees.

Cambridge and St Andrews share top place in the table, although neither university leads on any of the individual measures. Oxford has the highest entry standards and the best graduate prospects, but is restricted to fourth place because it had the lowest levels of student satisfaction in the table when its undergraduates last responded to the National Student Survey in sufficient numbers for a score to be published. Cambridge and Manchester also failed to reach the 50% threshold in the latest survey. Although bottom of the table overall, Westminster has the top scores in both of our measures of satisfaction. Birmingham, only one place higher, did best in the Research Excellence Framework.

Again, the small numbers can make for big swings in the national statistics. A £2,160 rise in the average starting salary in professional jobs has taken Middle Eastern and African Studies into the top 20 in this year's earnings table, but the subjects have dropped seven places to 37th for graduate prospects, with an unemployment rate that reached 14% at the end of 2017, one of the highest figures for any subject. Applicants for courses in Arabic or African languages are not expected to have previous knowledge of the language, although they would normally be expected to demonstrate an aptitude for learning other languages.

Middle Eastern and African Studies	Teaching quality %	Student experience %	Research quality %	Entry standards (UCAS points)	Graduate prospects %	Overall score
=1 Cambridge	—	—	45.0	215	88.9	100.0
=1 St Andrews	82.0	79.0	46.7	190	—	100.0
3 Durham	82.9	75.9	34.6	180	88.5	96.7
4 Oxford	—	—	36.2	223	89.6	94.0
5 Edinburgh	72.0	70.4	30.1	167	89.2	91.6
6 Exeter	69.9	73.5	36.0	167	76.7	89.9
7 Manchester	—	—	48.9	147	75.0	89.0
8 SOAS London	80.0	71.8	26.3	148	76.0	88.2
9 Leeds	74.5	73.1	30.6	160	69.2	87.4
10 Birmingham	74.1	67.2	50.9	137	57.1	86.7
11 Westminster	86.0	89.7	11.3	106	66.7	82.8

Employed in professional job	43%	Employed in non-professional job and Studying	2%
Employed in professional job and studying	3%	Employed in non-professional job	14%
Studying	24%	Unemployed	14%
Average starting professional salary	£24,000	Average starting non-professional salary	£15,000

Music

Four years of healthy increases in applications for music degrees came to an abrupt halt in 2017 with a decline of almost 5,000. However, the numbers starting courses are still running at almost twice the level of a decade ago. The expansion of provision has meant that there are now fewer than four applications per place. Entry grades are relatively low at most universities –19 of the 79 universities in this year's table average less than 120 UCAS points – although music grades and the quality of auditions carry more weight in selecting students. Nine out of ten degree applicants come with A-levels, and most university departments expect music to be among them, although they may accept a distinction or merit in Grade 8 music exams.

The character of courses varies considerably, from the practical and vocational programmes in conservatoires to the more theoretical degrees in some of the older universities, and everything from creative sound design and new media to sonic arts elsewhere. No fewer than 181 universities, colleges and other providers are offering undergraduate courses in 2019.

Durham has retained the lead it established two years ago, although this time it does not top any individual measure. Southampton is close behind, having jumped eight places to second.

The most satisfied students are at Ulster, which scored over 97% in both of our measures derived from the National Student Survey. The Royal Academy of Music has this year's best employment score, with an impressive 93.4% of graduates going straight into professional work or postgraduate study in 2017. The four leading specialist institutions are all in the top six on this measure.

Music invariably finishes ahead of the other performing arts in the employment table, although it is still only just outside the bottom 20 overall. The 7% unemployment rate is one of the best in the table, but 28% of leavers were in non-graduate occupations six months after graduation. Music has slipped back into second to last place in this year's earnings table, however.

Music	Teaching quality %	Student experience %	Research quality %	Entry standards (UCAS points)	Graduate prospects %	Overall score
1 Durham	81.4	74.1	64.9	213	90.8	100.0
2 Southampton	91.9	89.6	70.7	168	85.5	99.4
3 Manchester	—	—	56.3	210	80.7	97.6
4 Birmingham	82.6	81.6	50.7	193	86.3	96.1
5 Oxford	—	—	66.3	199	73.4	95.7
6 Glasgow	84.2	82.2	46.0	208	77.6	95.4
=7 Cardiff	91.2	90.6	47.0	173	74.1	94.0
=7 Royal Holloway, London	84.7	80.5	55.0	191	72.8	94.0
9 Nottingham	89.3	84.8	55.4	168	73.5	93.5
10 Edinburgh	81.7	78.0	48.0	214	69.5	93.4
11 Leeds	80.6	77.9	44.2	188	82.6	93.0
12 Bristol	84.2	81.5	48.0	192	70.6	92.5
13 Cambridge	—	—	48.0	202	89.0	91.6
14 Sheffield	—	—	60.0	146	72.3	89.7
15 Aberdeen	79.5	75.2	32.0	193	72.7	89.2
16 York	81.5	82.9	37.1	167	74.3	89.0
17 Edinburgh Napier	91.6	86.6	—	184	75.4	88.2
18 King's College London	78.0	67.7	43.5	170	72.9	87.6
19 Surrey	79.1	75.4	27.2	178	74.9	87.4
20 Bangor	91.0	87.5	24.7	140	71.7	86.8
21 Liverpool Hope	92.9	84.5	15.5	117	86.7	86.7
22 Newcastle	72.7	66.9	40.8	169	75.9	86.4
23 SOAS London	—	—	60.0	131	58.3	86.3
24 City	88.9	84.2	34.0	154	60.0	86.1
25 Ulster	97.3	97.7	40.0	129	50.3	85.9
26 Royal College of Music	83.8	81.4	10.9	126	92.6	85.8
27 Royal Northern College of Music	83.7	84.9	12.3	124	88.9	85.3
28 Oxford Brookes	79.7	86.4	30.2	140	72.9	85.1
=29 Birmingham City	90.4	82.8	11.6	136	76.4	84.9
=29 Royal Conservatoire of Scotland	74.8	73.5	11.3	160	87.1	84.9
31 Royal Academy of Music	74.1	65.4	23.9	135	93.4	84.7
=32 Coventry	85.1	83.4	18.1	130*	77.8	84.5
=32 Keele	86.5	87.8	41.7	121	62.6	84.5

Music cont

		Teaching quality %	Student experience %	Research quality %	Entry standards (UCAS points)	Graduate prospects %	Overall score
34	Goldsmiths, London	77.8	70.7	51.1	132	67.7	84.3
35	Huddersfield	83.4	80.1	28.0	123	73.6	83.7
36	London South Bank	90.3	85.9	12.8	112	76.9*	83.2
37	Queen's, Belfast	75.7	72.0	38.3	159	60.6	83.1
38	Greenwich	81.5	78.0	—	163	75.0	83.0
39	Brunel	77.4	74.1	32.6	136	67.7	82.2
40	Chester	80.4	73.6	4.3	139	81.4	82.0
=41	Hull	85.6	84.0	11.2	138	64.9	81.6
=41	Lincoln	88.8	84.7	6.5	123	—	81.6
43	Bath Spa	82.2	81.1	10.7	133	71.0	81.4
44	Staffordshire	82.5	80.0	—	113	86.4	81.2
45	Sussex	67.3	65.6	30.2	145	75.0	81.1
46	Kent	66.0	59.0	44.3	129	72.7	80.1
47	Falmouth	83.4	72.1	6.2	114	79.2	80.0
48	De Montfort	75.9	69.2	14.5	120*	80.0	79.9
49	Salford	84.4	81.2	7.2	141	59.7	79.6
50	Liverpool	—	—	31.4	146	53.4	79.5
51	West of Scotland	75.8	66.2	11.3	157	64.8	79.3
52	Sunderland	88.9	73.2	4.2	128	64.0	79.1
=53	Derby	91.7	81.9	6.7	131	50.7	78.4
=53	Hertfordshire	79.5	79.4	5.3	119	70.9	78.4
55	University of the Arts London	86.7	70.1	—	102	73.7	77.4
56	Solent	91.9	87.7	—	111	51.6	76.4
57	York St John	81.3	77.9	10.5	108	60.3	76.1
58	Central Lancashire	77.2	73.2	3.9	111	69.3	75.9
59	Anglia Ruskin	83.8	79.5	16.9	108	51.6	75.8
60	West London	70.1	68.4	2.3	130	70.6	75.7
=61	East London	84.5	82.7	11.2	122	45.8	75.6
=61	Middlesex	74.9	71.0	16.1	118	60.1	75.6
63	South Wales	76.5	70.8	6.4	122	63.0	75.5
64	Wolverhampton	85.3	81.8	—	114	53.8	75.1
65	Winchester	68.7	67.4	11.2	128	64.3	75.0
66	Manchester Metropolitan	73.4	64.7	7.5	123	64.2	74.7
67	Brighton	76.7	73.4	13.1	135	46.0	74.3
68	Northampton	87.0	82.0	—	106	51.7	74.2
69	Leeds Beckett	82.1	77.8	1.7	127	48.4	74.1
=70	Bournemouth	71.8	66.3	15.0	116*	58.8	73.8
=70	Chichester	73.0	69.4	9.7	139	50.1	73.8
72	Plymouth	66.2	56.9	20.2	119	63.0	73.5
73	Gloucestershire	74.3	65.5	—	130	57.9	73.2
74	Kingston	81.6	79.5	—	107	52.4	73.0
75	Canterbury Christ Church	75.4	66.0	15.2	116	47.1	72.1

76 Plymouth Marjon		80.4	72.6	—	115	46.7	71.5
77 Westminster		59.6	51.9	22.5	113	56.3	69.8
78 Edge Hill		58.7	52.3	3.8	136	—	67.7
79 Cumbria		58.6	53.3	—	133	39.1	64.6

Employed in professional job	41%	Employed in non-professional job and Studying	3%
Employed in professional job and studying	5%	Employed in non-professional job	25%
Studying	19%	Unemployed	7%
Average starting professional salary	£18,500	Average starting non-professional salary	£16,380

Nursing

The scrapping of bursaries for nursing degrees prompted a 20% decline in applications in 2017. The total was 20,000 less than at any time in the previous five years. But, since nursing is by far the most popular subject in the UCAS system, there were plenty of applicants to go round and the numbers starting courses were still the second-highest on record, after only a small drop. The chances of winning a place were also the highest in recent years. With no sign of bursaries returning, the trend may well continue in 2019.

Entry requirements were already comparatively low, considering the demand for places. Almost two-thirds of nursing students arrive without A-levels, many of them upgrading other health-related qualifications. Although only two universities averaged less than 120 points (by one point) on the UCAS tariff in 2017, just six others topped 160 points. The highest aggregates were Glasgow's 197 points and Edinburgh's 185. The two Scottish rivals have swapped places at the top of the table again this year, with Glasgow taking over the leadership. A little further down, Ulster has moved up 15 places to tenth.

Ironically, it is the bottom university of the 71 in the table – Bolton – where students are the most satisfied with both the quality of teaching and other aspects of the student experience. Bolton suffers for not entering the Research Excellence Framework (REF) in nursing, but it also has by far the lowest score for graduate prospects, 25 percentage points behind the rest. Nine universities, including Suffolk, in 69th place, saw all their 2017 graduates go straight into professional jobs or further study. Nursing is in the top three for graduate destinations, but only 26th for salaries in professional jobs.

Portsmouth, another of the universities with a 100% employment record, as well as student satisfaction exceeding 90%, remains the highest-placed post-1992 university, at 14th. Southampton, in equal 10th place, produced much the best results in the REF, when 94% of its work was rated as world-leading or internationally excellent.

Nursing	Teaching quality %	Student experience %	Research quality %	Entry standards (UCAS points)	Graduate prospects %	Overall score
1 Glasgow	93.0	91.7	42.3	197	96.2	100.0
2 Edinburgh	81.2	75.8	53.4	185	100.0	98.4
3 Manchester	84.9	81.2	57.1	151	97.7	95.0
4 Liverpool	91.5	89.1	35.3	140	100.0	94.1

Nursing cont

		Teaching quality %	Student experience %	Research quality %	Entry standards (UCAS points)	Graduate prospects %	Overall score
5	Keele	94.0	92.1	20.9	147	100.0	93.9
6	Birmingham	85.6	85.2	37.0	150	99.3	93.8
7	Surrey	82.7	81.5	37.5	158	98.3	93.7
8	Bangor	81.2	71.5	34.7	163	99.3	93.5
9	Leeds	81.2	74.4	31.7	161	99.8	93.3
=10	Southampton	72.2	71.1	65.7	140	99.2	92.6
=10	Ulster	88.3	90.3	27.7	139	99.7	92.6
12	Queen Margaret, Edinburgh	89.4	87.2	1.5	165	98.2	92.2
13	City	92.3	89.4	20.5	142	96.7	91.7
14	Portsmouth	92.5	87.9	24.3	128	100.0	91.6
15	Swansea	79.8	78.1	14.5	165	98.3	91.5
16	Huddersfield	83.8	80.2	13.2	153	99.3	91.2
17	East Anglia	75.0	72.6	24.9	160	99.0	91.1
18	Coventry	90.7	87.8	4.5	143	99.4	90.8
19	Lincoln	83.1	80.0	22.6	139	100.0	90.7
=20	Northumbria	82.8	77.2	14.0	148	99.6	90.5
=20	Queen's, Belfast	79.2	78.1	34.7	137	98.8	90.5
22	West of Scotland	89.7	85.3	29.0	125	97.8	90.4
23	Manchester Metropolitan	86.5	85.3	12.0	138	99.6	90.2
=24	Hull	85.3	78.2	16.7	144	97.8	90.1
=24	Nottingham	75.4	68.6	31.4	146	99.2	90.1
=26	King's College London	72.3	67.7	34.6	148	98.1	89.7
=26	York	70.7	65.0	40.2	153	96.3	89.7
28	Essex	86.7	72.8	—	152	99.4	89.6
=29	Cardiff	68.5	59.1	36.8	152	99.0	89.5
=29	Leeds Beckett	88.5	84.3	3.5	136	100.0	89.5
31	South Wales	81.4	79.7	2.2	152	99.1	89.4
=32	Dundee	86.1	85.2	22.1	123	98.8	89.2
=32	Staffordshire	89.9	84.7	—	136	99.4	89.2
=32	Stirling	76.4	68.5	34.1	135	99.0	89.2
=35	Birmingham City	81.6	76.0	1.5	153	98.4	89.0
=35	Chester	82.0	77.9	12.0	138	99.5	89.0
=35	Derby	81.3	79.3	7.3	141	100.0	89.0
38	Liverpool John Moores	80.9	79.0	6.0	149	97.4	88.7
=39	Middlesex	82.7	78.6	10.0	137	99.1	88.6
=39	Salford	83.9	80.9	3.8	141	98.6	88.6
41	Glasgow Caledonian	80.0	76.6	8.1	141	98.9	88.4
=42	West of England	84.4	84.1	8.2	133	98.1	88.3
=42	Worcester	89.3	87.1	2.6	128	98.6	88.3
44	Oxford Brookes	81.8	78.3	3.0	139	98.8	88.0
=45	Bedfordshire	82.6	75.4	25.1	119	99.0	87.9
=45	Plymouth	78.4	70.8	9.5	144	98.3	87.9

=47	Edge Hill	90.3	87.4	2.0	134	94.7	87.7
=47	Hertfordshire	83.8	79.4	4.0	132	99.1	87.7
=47	Sheffield Hallam	79.1	76.1	3.7	142	98.5	87.7
=47	Teesside	85.5	80.7	2.4	134	97.6	87.7
51	London South Bank	79.6	76.9	13.7	124	99.9	87.4
52	Northampton	81.7	75.7	1.6	137	98.8	87.3
53	Bournemouth	82.9	77.5	4.7	131	98.7	87.2
54	Bradford	70.9	71.1	9.5	148	98.1	87.1
55	De Montfort	81.4	78.3	13.0	131	95.9	86.9
=56	Greenwich	80.0	77.0	2.2	132	98.5	86.6
=56	Robert Gordon	81.2	72.9	4.9	127	99.4	86.6
=56	West London	85.6	82.2	2.5	132	95.2	86.6
59	Anglia Ruskin	82.0	77.7	3.1	127	98.6	86.5
60	Wolverhampton	81.3	77.9	11.0	136	93.8	86.4
61	Canterbury Christ Church	80.3	72.7	2.2	129	99.3	86.3
62	Cumbria	79.0	76.5	0.7	131	98.6	86.2
63	Kingston/St George's, London	76.1	74.2	2.6	128	100.0	85.9
64	Central Lancashire	71.3	69.8	8.3	135	97.7	85.4
65	Buckinghamshire New	87.0	86.4	1.0	129	91.3	85.2
66	Brunel	68.4	74.5	18.2	—	96.3	84.9
67	Brighton	73.3	66.4	4.8	127	98.7	84.6
68	Sunderland	81.9	83.2	7.5	121	90.0	83.4
69	Suffolk	66.1	60.8	—	126	100.0	83.0
70	Edinburgh Napier	61.9	58.6	5.3	119	96.2	80.6
71	Bolton	96.8	93.8	—	130	66.5	77.8

Employed in professional job	94%	Employed in non-professional job and Studying	0%
Employed in professional job and studying	1%	Employed in non-professional job	1%
Studying	1%	Unemployed	2%
Average starting professional salary	£22,000	Average starting non-professional salary	£18,000

Other Subjects Allied to Medicine

The withdrawal of NHS bursaries has hit applications in virtually all the subjects in this group, which includes audiology, complementary therapies, counselling, health services management, health sciences, nutrition, occupational therapy, optometry, ophthalmology, orthoptics, osteopathy, podiatry and speech therapy. Physiotherapy and radiography now have rankings of their own. As in nursing, however, universities upped the offer rate in 2017 to the point where there were increases in enrolments for medical technology and some of the smaller subjects.

Most of the institutions in the table are post-1992 universities, but only Oxford Brookes, Glasgow Caledonian and Robert Gordon feature in the top 20. Strathclyde remains at the head of the table, without topping any of the individual measures, while Southampton, the star performer in the Research Excellence Framework (REF), is up six places to second. Exeter has enjoyed an even more spectacular rise, jumping from 30th to 12th place this year. Students at Oxford Brookes are the most satisfied with the quality of teaching, while Robert Gordon has the best scores in the other sections of the National Student Survey. Cambridge, not surprisingly, has much the highest entry grades, but did not enter the REF in the relevant category and is only seventh in the table as a result.

The choice of specialism naturally affects graduate employment rates, which range from better than 90% positive destinations at 28 of the 80 universities in the table to less than 60% at three others. Leeds and Kingston (for the second and third year in a row respectively) reached 100%, as did Swansea, Sunderland and Wolverhampton. Overall, the subjects are just outside the top ten for employment prospects, with two-thirds of graduates going straight into professional jobs and only 6% unemployed. As a group, the subjects are level with nursing for median salaries in professional jobs, inside the top 30.

Subjects allied to Medicine	Teaching quality %	Student experience %	Research quality %	Entry standards (UCAS points)	Graduate prospects %	Overall score
1 Strathclyde	83.5	78.7	52.2	217	92.9	100.0
2 Southampton	83.2	81.7	65.7	152	97.8	97.2
3 University College London	74.5	84.3	48.4	187	93.5*	95.6
=4 Leeds	86.2	91.3	31.7	160	100.0	95.5
=4 Manchester	83.2	78.8	57.1	157	95.0	95.5
6 Lancaster	84.1	86.6	55.2	161	87.5	95.1
7 Cambridge	—	—	—	242	84.0	94.7
8 Cardiff	86.1	85.1	36.8	155	97.5	94.5
9 East Anglia	86.4	87.7	24.9	168	96.2	94.2
10 Dundee	79.3	75.9	31.3	188	95.5	94.0
11 Liverpool	91.9	92.6	35.3	133	94.9	93.9
12 Exeter	82.9	79.0	41.1	174	87.8	93.4
13 Aston	82.7	81.0	39.1	147	98.7	93.2
14 Birmingham	87.0	86.2	31.5	166	87.9	93.1
15 Reading	80.3	78.9	42.3	171	85.7	92.2
16 Newcastle	77.2	78.9	47.8	168	84.9	91.9
17 Oxford Brookes	94.9	93.2	3.0	143	97.4	91.7
18 City	89.6	86.4	20.5	145	94.2	91.6
19 Glasgow Caledonian	84.9	86.4	8.1	183	88.4	91.3
20 Robert Gordon	92.1	93.9	4.9	163	87.5	91.2
21 Swansea	72.0	70.4	44.7	142	100.0	90.2
=22 Sheffield	76.3	79.8	38.3	154	87.5	89.8
=22 Surrey	77.4	84.3	37.5	157	83.5	89.8
=22 West of Scotland	86.2	84.3	29.0	143	85.7	89.8
25 Warwick	81.6	85.0	25.3	162	82.9	89.6
26 Plymouth	84.8	81.2	9.5	150	96.1	89.5
27 Birmingham City	90.4	86.7	1.5	142	95.5	89.4
28 Teesside	91.8	91.0	2.4	147	87.5	89.0
29 Hull	85.3	77.9	16.7	—	88.9	88.6
30 Queen Mary, London	75.7	76.5	48.3	144	—	88.4
31 King's College London	77.8	74.3	34.6	154	—	88.3

32 Northampton	91.3	88.4	1.6	136	90.6	88.1
33 Kingston	77.9	78.9	2.6	—	100.0*	88.0
34 South Wales	84.2	80.7	2.2	149	94.0	87.8
35 Ulster	84.8	84.3	27.7	138	79.2	87.4
36 Sunderland	75.5	72.8	7.5	—	100.0	86.9
=37 Bedfordshire	82.6	75.4	25.1	109*	96.2	86.6
=37 Portsmouth	85.8	83.3	24.3	135	78.3	86.6
=39 Manchester Metropolitan	81.9	79.5	12.0	168	76.9	86.5
=39 West of England	86.5	86.4	8.2	134	85.4	86.5
41 Huddersfield	82.8	78.8	13.2	133	90.2	86.4
42 De Montfort	86.5	85.9	13.0	122	87.1	86.3
=43 Derby	89.3	84.0	7.3	133	83.6	86.2
=43 London Metropolitan	80.3	80.3	5.2	—	90.0*	86.2
45 Bradford	81.3	79.7	9.5	135	89.6	85.8
=46 London South Bank	82.7	76.4	13.7	125	91.1	85.7
=46 Sheffield Hallam	88.0	86.9	3.7	134	82.8	85.7
48 Lincoln	82.1	81.0	22.6	132	78.8	85.2
=49 Cardiff Metropolitan	88.5	84.8	3.6	136	77.8	84.6
=49 Wolverhampton	69.8	67.5	11.0	138	100.0	84.6
51 Coventry	83.6	85.7	4.5	129	83.4	84.4
=52 Anglia Ruskin	87.6	85.5	3.1	112	86.6	84.2
=52 Greenwich	83.3	79.7	2.2	135	84.7	84.2
=52 Hertfordshire	84.0	82.8	4.0	126	85.4	84.2
=52 Worcester	92.4	85.7	2.6	122	78.3	84.2
56 Northumbria	68.5	64.9	14.0	157	90.0	84.1
57 Brighton	88.8	85.4	4.8	131	75.5	84.0
58 Liverpool John Moores	79.7	80.0	6.0	144	80.5	83.8
=59 Bournemouth	79.1	73.2	4.7	136	88.1	83.7
=59 Nottingham	86.1	75.6	31.4	144	60.0	83.7
=61 Central Lancashire	84.9	81.6	8.3	128	77.8	83.4
=61 Salford	84.8	83.0	3.8	137	76.0	83.4
63 Queen Margaret, Edinburgh	75.0	69.2	6.7	155	83.1	83.3
64 Brunel	54.8	65.1	18.2	163	94.4	83.2
65 York St John	80.2	80.0	1.9	132	84.1	83.1
66 Bangor	78.3	77.8	34.7	133	64.6	82.7
67 Glyndŵr	80.8	75.7	3.6	129*	83.8	82.6
68 St Mary's, Twickenham	72.8	75.3	4.8	138	86.0	82.3
69 Canterbury Christ Church	72.9	66.4	2.2	121	90.4	80.4
70 Leeds Beckett	82.7	83.1	3.5	107	76.7	80.3
71 Plymouth Marjon	85.1	75.2	—	129	69.2	79.9
72 Staffordshire	85.3	86.5	—	100	75.0	79.8
73 Essex	84.4	85.1	—	103	73.6	79.4
74 Cumbria	59.7	61.0	0.7	132	94.0	78.6
75 Middlesex	67.3	67.6	10.0	119	79.7	77.9
76 Chester	76.1	73.8	12.0	108	70.7	77.8
77 East London	81.2	81.8	7.6	110	62.3	77.5

Subjects allied to Medicine cont	Teaching quality %	Student experience %	Research quality %	Entry standards (UCAS points)	Graduate prospects %	Overall score
78 Westminster	74.0	70.5	21.2	116	57.1	76.1
=79 Newman	77.6	77.3	—	120	58.9	75.5
=79 Wales Trinity St David	81.1	75.3	—	117*	57.6	75.5

Employed in professional job	62%	Employed in non-professional job and Studying	2%
Employed in professional job and studying	3%	Employed in non-professional job	10%
Studying	16%	Unemployed	6%
Average starting professional salary	£22,000	Average starting non-professional salary	£16,000

Pharmacology and Pharmacy

Pharmacology and pharmacy are quite different courses, leading to different careers. Departments in England are evenly split between those specialising in the two disciplines, with only four covering both. While the MPharm degree, which is the only direct route to professional registration as a pharmacist, takes four years, pharmacology is available either as a three-year BSc or as an extended course. The MPharm is now offered at 30 institutions, while another 18 are running a BSc in the subject or as part of a broader degree. Most degrees in either area require chemistry and another science or maths at A-level or the equivalent.

Applications for the group as a whole, which includes toxicology degrees, were down for the sixth year in a row in 2017, having dropped 25% in that time. However, as in other health subjects, changes in the offer rate have ensured that the numbers starting courses have not fluctuated to the same extent. Enrolments in 2017 were within ten of the previous year, but there were fewer than 5.4 applications per place, compared with seven in 2011. Entry standards have fallen accordingly, with eight universities averaging less than 120 points, although that has not stopped three more universities joining the table.

Cambridge remains top of the table, the university's normal high entry standards making the difference. Bristol remains in second, sharing the position with Ulster. Queen's, Belfast, which produced the best results in the Research Excellence Framework, is in fourth. Bristol tops the rating for student satisfaction with teaching standards whilst Keele, in 12th has the highest score for the overall student experience.

The employment table does not suggest subjects that should be struggling to attract applicants – pharmacology and pharmacy remain seventh out of 67 subject groups, with 82% of graduates going straight into professional jobs and only 3% unemployed. At four universities – Ulster, Lincoln, Kent and Reading – the employment rate was 100%. The earnings table is a different matter, however: partly because of the training structure for pharmacists, the subjects are seldom in the top 40. In the latest edition, they remain in the bottom ten.

Pharmacology and Pharmacy

	Teaching quality %	Student experience %	Research quality %	Entry standards (UCAS points)	Graduate prospects %	Overall score
1 Cambridge	—	—	52.5	242	84.0	100.0
=2 Bristol	92.8	91.8	47.0	175	90.2	98.0
=2 Ulster	92.1	93.0	42.5	154	100.0	98.0
4 Queen's, Belfast	84.3	84.2	60.0	163	97.6	97.4
5 Nottingham	82.3	84.8	51.2	174	98.7	97.0
6 Glasgow	81.9	81.4	33.4	207	92.9	95.5
7 Strathclyde	68.7	75.2	52.2	218	94.6	95.0
=8 Leeds	88.6	91.5	40.9	162	88.5	94.9
=8 Manchester	79.3	81.4	57.1	161	95.1	94.9
10 Bath	79.1	79.2	56.2	162	96.5	94.8
11 Cardiff	83.1	84.3	36.8	166	97.7	94.6
12 Keele	92.5	94.8	20.9	146	95.4	94.2
13 Aston	86.6	83.9	39.1	136	98.0	93.7
14 Birmingham	86.6	86.5	19.2	155	99.4	93.2
15 Lincoln	89.6	93.5	22.6	122	100.0	92.9
=16 East Anglia	76.4	79.1	38.1	164	99.2	92.8
=16 Reading	86.8	80.7	34.2	131	100.0	92.8
18 Dundee	81.4	81.0	55.4	—	88.9	92.6
19 Kent	—	—	42.3	126	100.0	92.5
20 University College London	69.8	77.3	51.3	177	93.6	92.3
21 King's College London	74.9	81.6	46.8	158	92.1	91.8
22 Newcastle	83.1	80.9	47.8	181	75.0	91.6
23 Liverpool	89.2	89.8	31.7	150	80.3	91.2
24 Robert Gordon	76.0	76.9	4.9	187	99.4	90.2
25 Aberdeen	80.7	75.0	34.7	173	81.0	89.6
26 Portsmouth	82.7	83.9	24.3	120	95.6	89.3
27 Bradford	81.3	84.0	9.5	131	97.2	88.4
28 Sunderland	81.9	83.5	7.5	131	95.2	87.8
29 De Montfort	80.0	82.8	13.0	119	97.9	87.6
30 Huddersfield	77.3	80.5	13.2	126	99.2	87.5
31 Wolverhampton	79.8	79.2	11.0	134	94.1	87.1
32 Central Lancashire	71.5	72.1	8.3	158	98.7	86.8
33 Brighton	77.3	80.4	4.8	127	99.2	86.6
34 Hull	83.7	82.5	16.7	—	81.1*	86.5
35 Liverpool John Moores	73.5	76.2	6.0	137	99.6	86.2
36 Hertfordshire	81.4	80.1	10.9	112	92.2	85.7
=37 Greenwich	77.1	81.0	2.7	127	92.6	84.9
=37 Sussex	75.4	76.5	8.0	148	—	84.9
39 Queen Margaret, Edinburgh	90.6	79.2	1.5	134	75.0	84.4
=40 Glasgow Caledonian	79.4	82.9	8.1	154	72.2	83.8
=40 Westminster	83.0	87.1	21.2	111	73.1	83.8
42 Kingston	81.8	83.9	2.6	118	83.5	83.7

Pharmacology and Pharmacy cont

	Teaching quality %	Student experience %	Research quality %	Entry standards (UCAS points)	Graduate prospects %	Overall score
43 Queen Mary, London	67.9	62.0	40.2	145	–	83.2
44 Coventry	74.4	83.4	4.5	116	88.5	83.1
45 East London	89.4	85.8	7.6	92	59.8	79.2
46 London Metropolitan	75.6	76.7	5.2	105	62.9	76.3
47 Anglia Ruskin	69.4	62.3	3.1	74*	–	71.9

Employed in professional job	72%	Employed in non-professional job and Studying	1%
Employed in professional job and studying	10%	Employed in non-professional job	4%
Studying	10%	Unemployed	3%
Average starting professional salary	£19,000	Average starting non-professional salary	£16,640

Philosophy

Philosophy continues to grow in popularity; both applications and enrolments rose in 2017 and are now – perhaps surprisingly – higher than in the years before £9,000 fees were introduced. There was another 5% increase in applications in 2017, even though the subject is in the bottom 20 for the proportion of graduates going straight into professional jobs or continuing to study. A third take the postgraduate route, but the 13% unemployment rate is one of the highest among the 67 subject groups. Those in professional employment are paid relatively well, however. Although no longer in the top 20, median salaries of £22,000 are firmly in the top half of the table.

Oxford remains on top of the philosophy table, with the highest entry standards and the best grades in the Research Excellence Framework. Newcastle has shot up 13 places to take third position, just behind Cambridge. But the highest levels of student satisfaction are at Bangor, in 29th place, which managed unusually high scores of around 98% in both of the measures derived from the National Student Survey. The best graduate prospects in 2017 were at the London School of Economics, fractionally ahead of Winchester. Both institutions saw 90% of philosophers go straight into professional jobs or postgraduate courses. However, the proportion was below 50% at four of the 52 universities in the table.

Relatively few philosophy undergraduates studied the subject at A-level – some departments actively discourage it. Degrees can require more mathematical skills than many candidates expect, especially when there is an emphasis on logic in the syllabus. There is wide variation in entry standards, with both Oxford and Cambridge averaging more than 200 points, but two universities dropping below 100 and another six averaging less than 110 points.

Philosophy	Teaching quality %	Student experience %	Research quality %	Entry standards (UCAS points)	Graduate prospects %	Overall score
1 Oxford	–	–	61.3	214	84.4	100.0
2 Cambridge	–	–	51.6	208	83.3	99.3
3 Newcastle	86.9	86.5	54.3	148	84.8	97.5

4 Birmingham	85.5	81.0	52.8	155	85.7	97.0
5 St Andrews	86.0	84.2	52.7	191	68.5	96.9
6 University College London	77.8	69.5	55.6	192	81.4	96.1
7 London School of Economics	72.4	67.2	48.6	198	90.5	95.6
8 Exeter	80.0	77.2	41.0	178	84.4	94.7
9 Warwick	80.4	78.7	47.7	177	73.2	93.8
10 Durham	77.8	73.6	30.1	191	80.6	92.3
11 Bristol	—	—	40.9	186	71.1	92.0
12 Southampton	87.6	81.8	31.7	151	75.1	91.9
13 Sussex	82.9	80.7	34.2	143	82.9	91.8
14 Manchester	—	—	31.9	163	74.3	91.3
15 Sheffield	—	—	48.3	153	72.8	90.8
16 Aberdeen	85.0	84.6	39.1	156	62.4	90.6
17 Leeds	81.4	80.7	39.5	160	66.3	90.4
18 Royal Holloway, London	80.1	78.5	30.5	140	84.7	90.3
=19 Edinburgh	75.0	71.5	49.7	166	68.9	90.2
=19 York	80.4	78.3	30.7	153	78.5	90.2
21 Lancaster	70.4	66.8	53.0	145	78.2	89.2
22 Stirling	86.5	74.7	22.7	167	64.7	88.6
23 Winchester	91.1	86.0	—	112*	90.0	88.1
24 King's College London	71.3	66.2	53.9	176	57.6	87.9
25 Cardiff	83.3	77.5	36.3	136	64.5	87.8
26 Keele	90.6	88.9	23.7	118	65.0	87.7
27 Nottingham	79.2	75.2	28.2	146	73.0	87.6
28 Liverpool Hope	95.3	90.6	—	104	77.3	86.7
29 Bangor	98.5	97.9	—	128	59.2	86.6
30 Liverpool	76.4	71.2	28.4	133	78.2	86.4
31 Birkbeck, London	76.9	69.8	37.4	110	78.0	86.0
=32 Bath Spa	90.7	86.3	—	110	80.0	85.9
=32 Essex	79.8	75.3	44.0	109	65.3	85.9
34 Queen's, Belfast	78.9	74.0	40.3	143	53.1	85.2
=35 Glasgow	76.2	72.5	18.9	172	62.2	84.9
=35 Hertfordshire	77.3	72.0	32.9	104	76.4	84.9
=37 East Anglia	80.6	73.3	28.6	137	56.8	83.9
=37 Kent	73.7	71.0	31.0	118	72.7	83.9
=39 Central Lancashire	92.8	86.2	8.3	101	60.9	83.4
=39 St Mary's, Twickenham	90.1	80.4	7.0	113	64.0	83.4
41 Nottingham Trent	88.5	85.8	10.0	128	53.1	83.1
42 Dundee	80.0	73.9	27.7	156	41.5	82.2
43 Oxford Brookes	85.2	80.7	8.4	123	58.9	82.1
44 Anglia Ruskin	86.4	84.6	—	86	72.7	81.4
=45 Manchester Metropolitan	83.5	72.7	12.5	122	58.1	81.2
=45 Roehampton	83.1	68.7	—	107	77.6	81.2
=47 Hull	87.9	80.0	10.5	111	48.8	80.2
=47 Reading	75.1	61.6	28.6	127	55.8	80.2
49 West of England	86.3	85.6	18.6	120	36.9	80.0

Philosophy cont	Teaching quality %	Student experience %	Research quality %	Entry standards (UCAS points)	Graduate prospects %	Overall score
50 Brighton		80.9	72.1	13.1	102	59.7	79.2
51 Gloucestershire		77.1	63.2	6.9	127	58.3	77.9
52 Leeds Trinity		78.3	73.3	—	94	48.0	73.7

Employed in professional job	35%	Employed in non-professional job and Studying	4%
Employed in professional job and studying	3%	Employed in non-professional job	19%
Studying	26%	Unemployed	13%
Average starting professional salary	£22,000	Average starting non-professional salary	£17,000

Physics and Astronomy

Physics degrees have among the highest entry grades in the university system, with eight of the 47 institutions in our latest table averaging at least 200 points and another ten at least 170. Only one university drops below 110 points, the equivalent of BBC at A-level. St Andrews leads the table pushing Cambridge, into second place for the first time in more than a decade. Cambridge still has the highest entry standards, its 2017 entrants averaging over 240 points. Overall, there are almost six applications to the place. Most universities demand physics and maths at A-level for both physics and astronomy, as well as good grades overall.

The long decline in the numbers taking physics in the sixth-form and at university was being reversed before higher fees arrived. But eight successive increases in the numbers starting physics degrees came to a halt in 2016 and, while growth had resumed 12 months later, this does not appear to have been repeated in the current academic year. The much smaller numbers taking astronomy or astrophysics also grew in 2017, with more than 30 universities offering the subjects. The "Brian Cox effect" has been credited for the current popularity of both physics and astronomy, in recognition of the engaging Manchester University professor's many television appearances.

St Andrews' strength in the National Student Survey helps to lift it to first place with the highest scores in the sections on teaching quality, while Swansea did best in the sections relating to the broader student experience. Cambridge, which is in the top four universities in the world for physics, according to QS, produced the best grades in the Research Excellence Framework.

More than 40% of those completing degrees in physics or astronomy stay on for a postgraduate course, helping the subjects to a place in the top 20 for graduate prospects. They are higher still in the earnings table, average salaries of £26,000 six months after graduation taking physics and astronomy into the top ten. Three universities, compared with none in the last edition of the table, saw 90% of graduates go straight into professional jobs or continue studying in 2017. Eighth-placed Birmingham again had the top rate, and only at Dundee did the proportion of positive destinations drop below 60%.

Physics and Astronomy

		Teaching quality %	Student experience %	Research quality %	Entry standards (UCAS points)	Graduate prospects %	Overall score
1	St Andrews	93.2	90.8	51.0	224	90.8	100.0
2	Cambridge	—	—	55.7	242	84.0	97.7
3	Oxford	—	—	52.1	239	90.4	96.5
4	Durham	80.0	76.4	46.2	228	89.2	94.6
5	Nottingham	89.1	89.1	48.3	174	84.0	93.8
6	Warwick	84.7	82.7	46.1	198	84.9	93.4
7	Lancaster	89.9	86.9	37.6	180	88.8	93.2
8	Birmingham	83.7	84.1	33.8	196	91.9	92.7
9	Leeds	86.6	86.8	41.8	168	85.5	91.8
10	Southampton	84.1	85.3	44.1	163	84.3	91.0
11	Manchester	—	—	44.9	204	81.6	90.7
12	Bath	78.8	78.6	40.0	198	84.8	90.5
=13	Glasgow	76.2	77.9	42.0	202	83.1	90.2
=13	Heriot-Watt	92.1	88.6	44.1	167	72.7	90.2
15	Surrey	83.9	82.1	39.6	165	84.5	89.9
16	Edinburgh	76.6	72.6	48.7	209	76.9	89.8
17	Bristol	75.9	75.0	43.7	184	84.7	89.4
=18	Exeter	79.6	83.0	42.4	178	80.4	89.3
=18	Swansea	91.4	93.5	33.0	142	81.7	89.3
20	University College London	68.5	70.3	45.1	199	87.1	89.2
21	Strathclyde	83.5	84.1	45.3	193	67.5	88.4
22	Imperial College	55.7	58.5	49.6	231	87.6	88.2
23	York	82.2	77.5	35.8	163	83.3	87.9
=24	Cardiff	81.2	83.1	34.9	158	79.4	86.8
=24	Leicester	81.9	78.9	40.8	142	79.6	86.8
=24	Liverpool	—	—	31.5	155	82.2	86.8
27	Queen's, Belfast	80.3	78.0	44.4	157	73.7	86.4
28	Sheffield	80.6	81.0	36.8	163	75.9	86.2
29	King's College London	76.5	77.1	35.8	164	80.2	85.9
30	Royal Holloway, London	77.7	80.4	31.5	146	84.4	85.7
31	Aberdeen	71.2	65.7	32.0	186	82.9	85.0
32	Loughborough	83.6	83.4	19.0	146	83.7	84.7
33	Keele	86.5	83.0	31.8	123	76.8	84.6
34	Sussex	81.5	79.7	24.7	138	79.5	83.4
=35	Kent	80.8	82.0	30.7	132	75.5	83.3
=35	Nottingham Trent	88.6	86.6	20.1	128	76.1	83.3
37	Hertfordshire	82.8	79.8	20.2	123	83.3	83.0
38	West of Scotland	83.7	78.5	19.1	155	72.7	82.0
39	Queen Mary, London	74.6	73.7	27.6	135	80.1	81.9
40	Northumbria	85.2	85.6	30.7	128	61.1	80.7
41	Aberystwyth	82.7	85.9	12.4	112	80.0	80.6
42	Dundee	86.2	88.4	34.1	167	46.4	80.3

Physics and Astronomy cont		Teaching quality %	Student experience %	Research quality %	Entry standards (UCAS points)	Graduate prospects %	Overall score
43 Portsmouth		75.7	72.2	21.8	112	77.4	78.8
44 Salford		87.1	88.8	4.4	112	72.6	78.4
45 Hull		75.3	67.6	24.2	114	68.9	76.7
46 Central Lancashire		67.3	71.1	19.8	109	64.3	73.0

Employed in professional job	38%	Employed in non-professional job and Studying	1%
Employed in professional job and studying	3%	Employed in non-professional job	10%
Studying	38%	Unemployed	11%
Average starting professional salary	£26,000	Average starting non-professional salary	£16,500

Physiotherapy

More than 95% of physiotherapy graduates go straight into professional jobs – enough to take the subject into the top five in this year's employment table and close to the top 20 for graduate salaries. Applications are well above the level before £9,000 fees arrived and the numbers starting courses rose again in 2017. As a result, almost 60 universities and colleges are offering undergraduate courses in physiotherapy, or a related subject such as osteopathy or chiropractic, starting in 2019. Most of the leading courses demand biology A-level or equivalent, but some may also want another science or maths. The Chartered Society of Physiotherapy accredits all degrees in the subject in the UK.

Robert Gordon's meteoric rise to the top of the physiotherapy table has not been sustained, despite high satisfaction levels and one of 11 maximum scores for graduate prospects. Southampton, the previous leader and the holder of the best results in the Research Excellence Framework, is back on top. Physiotherapy students are among the most satisfied in any subject; only seven of the 34 universities in the table fell below 80% approval for the quality of teaching. Bournemouth, which has shot up 17 places and into the top ten, managed 99% satisfaction for teaching quality and 98% for the broader student experience. Even this was not the year's biggest rise: Central Lancashire is up 18 places to seventh and East Anglia 22 places to a share of third position.

The ranking is in its sixth year, the subject having appeared previously as part of the table for "other subjects allied to medicine". Entry standards have been rising and vary less than in most subjects. Although three universities average more than 200 points, only East London, at the bottom of the table, averages less than 140 points. Two-thirds of the universities in the table are post-1992 institutions, but only four feature in the top ten.

Physiotherapy	Teaching quality %	Student experience %	Research quality %	Entry standards (UCAS points)	Graduate prospects %	Overall score
1 Southampton	83.0	79.5	65.7	181	100.0	100.0
2 Robert Gordon	98.0	95.5	4.9	201	100.0	98.1
=3 Cardiff	90.7	92.9	36.8	163	98.7	96.3

=3	East Anglia	80.1	74.5	24.9	207	97.0	96.3
5	Nottingham	77.1	73.2	40.6	171	98.3	95.1
6	Birmingham	72.3	69.9	63.7	174	94.6	94.8
7	Central Lancashire	92.9	91.8	8.3	163*	100.0	94.6
8	Liverpool	90.5	91.8	35.3	145	98.4	94.5
9	Worcester	98.8	95.9	2.6	156	100.0	94.2
10	Bournemouth	99.1	98.3	4.7	147	100.0	93.7
11	Glasgow Caledonian	91.1	82.7	8.1	202	93.3	93.6
12	Bradford	96.9	96.0	9.5	158	97.7	93.5
13	Keele	86.0	87.4	20.9	148	98.9	93.1
=14	Brunel	84.3	85.8	18.2	149	99.0	92.8
=14	Salford	92.6	90.0	3.8	148	100.0	92.8
16	Coventry	87.9	90.8	4.5	155	99.3	92.7
17	Manchester Metropolitan	84.9	82.9	12.0	165	97.0	92.3
=18	Leeds Beckett	88.0	83.3	3.5	150	100.0	92.2
=18	Teesside	86.9	87.0	2.4	150	100.0	92.2
20	Oxford Brookes	83.0	79.7	3.0	155	100.0	92.1
21	Ulster	71.7	72.2	27.7	150	98.8	91.9
22	Sheffield Hallam	93.4	88.2	3.7	150	97.9	91.8
23	West of England	83.1	82.2	8.2	150	98.8	91.6
24	Kingston/St George's, London	77.3	74.7	2.6	158	100.0	91.5
25	Hertfordshire	89.0	92.4	4.0	154	96.9	91.4
26	Plymouth	83.4	81.0	9.5	159	96.7	91.2
27	Huddersfield	82.8	77.5	13.2	144	98.6	91.1
=28	King's College London	75.4	74.5	34.6	179	90.2	90.5
=28	Queen Margaret, Edinburgh	61.9	58.7	1.5	193	96.8	90.5
30	Northumbria	88.7	89.3	14.0	160	91.9	89.8
31	Brighton	93.3	88.4	4.8	142	95.1	89.6
32	York St John	85.9	87.7	1.9	147	94.6	88.8
=33	Cumbria	39.6	27.9	0.7	146	100.0	85.0
=33	East London	81.2	82.9	7.6	127	91.2	85.0

Employed in professional job	72%	Employed in non-professional job and Studying	1%
Employed in professional job and studying	10%	Employed in non-professional job	4%
Studying	10%	Unemployed	3%
Average starting professional salary	£22,100	Average starting non-professional salary	£16,575

Politics

The numbers starting politics degrees have risen for five years in a row – ever since the fees went up – and applications have grown by 50% in that time. Even after considerable expansion of provision, there are still almost six applications to every place. Graduate salaries may be one slightly surprising reason. Like last year, politics is among the top 20 subjects for starting salaries in professional jobs, which averaged £23,000 in 2017. The subject is mid-way in the employment table, after an improvement on the last edition.

There is a new leader of the politics table for the second year in a row, Warwick moving up two places with good scores across the board but without leading on any individual indicator. St Andrews, last year's leader, has dropped to third after a decline in graduate prospects. Second-placed Oxford has the highest entry standards, while Essex, in eighth place, was well ahead of the field in the Research Excellence Framework, with 87% of its work considered world-leading or internationally excellent. Most of the highest scores from the National Student Survey are to be found much further down the table, however. Undergraduates at Central Lancashire, which is just outside the top 40, are the most satisfied with the quality of teaching, while Wolverhampton, a new entrant to the table in 59th place, has the top rating for the broader student experience.

Both entry standards and graduate prospects show considerable variation among the 83 universities in the table. Six universities average more than 200 points at entry, while another 12 average less than 100. The London School of Economics, in sixth place overall, was the only university to see 90% of leavers go straight into professional employment or postgraduate study in 2017, but another 18 topped 80%. Only four universities, compared with eight last year, were under the 50% mark for graduate prospects, but another nine were below 60% on this measure.

Politics	Teaching quality %	Student experience %	Research quality %	Entry standards (UCAS points)	Graduate prospects %	Overall score
1 Warwick	82.8	81.6	52.7	189	84.4	100.0
2 Oxford	—	—	61.1	215	83.4	99.7
3 St Andrews	89.7	82.9	38.4	209	72.3	98.3
4 Cambridge	—	—	38.2	213	84.8	97.5
5 University College London	70.4	71.8	57.0	187	85.0	96.4
6 London School of Economics	66.0	61.5	54.6	202	90.8	96.2
7 Lancaster	80.4	76.1	53.0	153	81.7	95.5
8 Essex	80.3	81.1	69.6	111	79.5	95.3
=9 Exeter	79.0	76.5	29.8	175	85.5	93.7
=9 Strathclyde	80.4	77.2	41.6	201	65.8	93.7
11 Sheffield	72.6	75.4	48.3	156	85.3	93.6
12 Loughborough	87.1	84.3	22.5	146	86.6	93.5
13 York	80.1	76.2	36.9	157	83.1	93.3
=14 Bath	73.4	73.8	27.4	180	89.6	92.9
=14 Birmingham	82.1	77.5	31.1	157	82.6	92.9
16 Aberystwyth	87.0	84.5	40.2	124	76.5	92.6
17 Durham	72.4	67.2	27.0	202	83.4	92.1
18 Bristol	77.2	72.2	30.4	183	75.5	91.2
19 Glasgow	78.1	73.1	30.5	193	69.6	91.0
20 Newcastle	80.6	77.7	22.0	156	81.2	90.5
21 Nottingham	75.2	70.9	30.8	163	81.4	90.4
22 Edinburgh	67.9	68.3	44.5	169	76.9	90.1
23 Portsmouth	84.1	82.6	32.2	106	81.1	90.0
=24 Leeds	75.6	74.5	25.1	164	80.4	89.9
=24 Manchester	—	—	28.4	165	78.6	89.9

26 King's College London	74.1	71.4	29.0	185	73.2	89.8
=27 Kent	82.7	79.4	27.8	140	73.5	89.4
=27 Southampton	76.1	73.8	37.0	143	75.8	89.4
=29 Keele	85.5	86.5	24.0	119	76.1	89.3
=29 Sussex	75.3	69.7	33.6	142	81.8	89.3
=31 East Anglia	80.6	76.6	35.5	140	69.9	89.0
=31 Stirling	80.5	78.8	33.8	150	66.8	89.0
33 Dundee	80.7	81.6	10.8	158	79.1	88.8
34 Royal Holloway, London	75.6	72.1	30.5	137	78.0	87.9
35 Aston	76.5	74.5	38.6	122	73.4	87.7
=36 Aberdeen	77.7	77.2	18.4	177	67.0	87.5
=36 SOAS London	—	—	30.5	169	61.7	87.5
38 Brunel	81.7	77.1	32.4	112	71.2	87.0
39 Greenwich	90.0	87.6	8.6	118	71.7	86.8
40 Reading	71.8	65.0	37.0	138	75.4	86.7
41 Central Lancashire	95.9	86.5	12.0	—	52.2	86.6
=42 Birkbeck, London	76.9	73.5	31.3	98	81.9	86.5
=42 Queen Mary, London	75.1	69.9	28.1	140	73.9	86.5
44 Queen's, Belfast	78.3	71.6	35.0	142	63.1	86.4
45 Plymouth	88.3	83.4	25.8	108	63.6	86.3
46 Swansea	78.8	78.5	18.5	121	76.1	85.8
47 Surrey	78.5	78.2	12.5	159	66.8	85.4
48 Cardiff	72.4	64.9	30.4	142	71.3	85.1
49 Liverpool Hope	82.0	83.5	7.0	115	76.6	84.9
=50 Nottingham Trent	83.1	81.2	5.1	123	73.9	84.5
=50 West of England	86.9	84.4	13.8	119	61.8	84.5
52 Coventry	85.7	82.3	5.6	112	72.5	84.3
=53 Liverpool	—	—	12.0	137	69.3	84.2
=53 Oxford Brookes	78.8	74.9	17.8	125	70.1	84.2
=53 Westminster	84.5	83.7	14.3	105	68.2	84.2
56 Leicester	73.7	69.1	20.0	123	76.7	84.0
57 Northumbria	83.6	78.1	12.7	130	62.5	83.6
58 De Montfort	82.9	78.5	10.7	101	74.2	83.5
59 Wolverhampton	94.0	91.3	—	96	64.0	83.4
60 City	77.0	78.0	24.6	123	61.7	83.3
61 Bradford	74.1	72.3	12.7	117	77.9	83.0
62 Manchester Metropolitan	88.2	81.4	18.0	124	50.3	82.9
63 Hull	78.0	66.9	10.8	122	74.8	82.7
64 East London	86.5	86.7	13.7	97	60.1	82.5
65 Leeds Beckett	87.3	81.7	—	99	68.4	81.8
66 Lincoln	71.4	76.0	7.7	115	76.8	81.5
67 London Metropolitan	86.3	80.5	1.2	98	65.5	80.9
=68 Bournemouth	77.2	71.1	15.1	111	—	80.7
=68 Sheffield Hallam	82.7	75.0	14.4	108	57.8	80.7
70 Ulster	80.0	78.3	20.9	113	51.5	80.5
71 Huddersfield	70.2	63.5	9.5	120	73.7	79.7

Politics cont

		Teaching quality %	Student experience %	Research quality %	Entry standards (UCAS points)	Graduate prospects %	Overall score
72	West of Scotland	75.9	67.8	—	140	58.1	78.1
73	Salford	69.1	58.7	4.8	117	72.0	77.5
74	Winchester	84.3	83.4	—	107	45.8	76.8
75	Kingston	78.1	72.0	—	99	59.0	76.2
=76	Canterbury Christ Church	88.5	81.7	3.2	99	37.2	75.8
=76	Northampton	82.0	76.6	—	85	54.6	75.8
78	Middlesex	70.8	66.2	14.9	96	—	75.7
79	Goldsmiths, London	66.8	63.0	16.8	106	54.8	74.8
80	Chichester	67.9	63.3	15.8	91	—	73.7
81	Chester	77.7	71.3	—	97	47.9	73.4
82	Derby	60.6	59.3	13.5	100	59.8	72.9
83	Brighton	66.8	55.1	13.1	96	41.7	69.6

Employed in professional job	40%	Employed in non-professional job and Studying	3%
Employed in professional job and studying	3%	Employed in non-professional job	19%
Studying	24%	Unemployed	11%
Average starting professional salary	£22,000	Average starting non-professional salary	£16,500

Psychology

The psychology table is the biggest in the *Guide*, with three more universities joining this year, bringing the total to 117. Despite a small drop in 2017, psychology was one of only three subjects to attract more than 100,000 applications. That decline was not enough to stop a fifth successive rise in the number of students starting degrees in the subject, 50% more than in 2008. Psychology's popularity endures in spite of poor performances in the graduate employment market: it is only just outside the bottom ten for the proportion of graduates with "positive destinations", and for average starting salaries in professional-level jobs. Although most subjects in the table have higher levels of unemployment, nearly a third of graduates begin their careers in low-level jobs.

Most undergraduate programmes are accredited by the British Psychological Society, which ensures that key topics are covered, but the clinical and biological content of courses still varies considerably. Some universities require maths and/or biology A-levels among three high-grade passes, but others are much less demanding. The contrast is obvious in the ranking, with 25 universities averaging at least 160 points at entry but another 16 falling below 110 points. Cambridge has the highest entry grades in the table, but Oxford remains top. Exeter, which has moved up four places to seventh, has the best graduate prospects and is one of only five universities where more than 80% of 2017 graduates found professional employment or continued studying.

Ninth-placed Loughborough achieved the highest scores in the Research Excellence Framework. Bolton, just outside the top 50 despite a string of awards for its psychology degrees, has the highest levels of satisfaction with the quality of teaching. Birmingham City in a lowly

70th place has the best scores in the sections of the National Student Survey devoted to other aspects of the student experience. Satisfaction levels are high at most universities in the table, as they have been in previous years.

Psychology	Teaching quality %	Student experience %	Research quality %	Entry standards (UCAS points)	Graduate prospects %	Overall score
1 Oxford	87.4*	86.8*	58.6	212	78.4	100.0
2 Bath	84.8	87.6	56.2	194	82.1	98.5
3 St Andrews	88.5	88.5	45.4	197	71.2	95.6
4 Cambridge	72.4*	67.5*	57.5	217	78.3	94.8
5 King's College London	83.3	82.9	54.1	178	—	94.3
6 University College London	75.9	77.9	57.0	187	76.6	93.7
7 Exeter	78.4	82.1	43.3	176	83.6	93.5
8 York	85.4	86.6	46.7	162	76.1	93.1
9 Loughborough	81.9	84.3	62.3	160	71.4	92.7
=10 Cardiff	85.2	82.6	55.7	168	68.6	92.4
=10 Lancaster	85.3	86.3	38.5	154	81.5	92.4
12 Newcastle	81.1	81.2	50.0	166	75.3	92.1
13 Bristol	69.9	72.8	49.4	178	83.1	91.6
14 Warwick	79.4	85.6	43.1	170	70.4	90.4
15 Durham	76.3	76.4	37.1	188	73.4	90.2
16 Glasgow	64.9	74.8	52.9	187	75.4	90.0
17 Surrey	82.3	87.4	22.0	167	76.4	89.6
18 Swansea	74.2	75.2	44.7	147	83.1	89.4
19 Strathclyde	85.5	84.3	23.5	200	60.3	89.1
20 Sussex	75.7	76.4	42.3	149	79.5	88.9
=21 Edinburgh	67.9	76.2	52.8	186	66.8	88.7
=21 Sheffield	78.8	81.4	38.8	148	76.2	88.7
=23 Nottingham Trent	85.9	87.4	19.3	144	78.0	88.5
=23 Southampton	78.6	78.2	47.8	161	67.0	88.5
25 Royal Holloway, London	83.6	85.2	37.8	150	68.6	88.4
26 Kent	72.5	81.5	38.8	148	79.3	88.2
27 Nottingham	73.8	78.9	36.4	164	72.9	87.6
28 Aberdeen	81.2	82.0	38.7	156	65.8	87.5
29 Birmingham	59.7	65.4	55.8	166	78.7	87.3
30 Bangor	84.5	85.5	32.0	132	72.0	87.1
31 Leeds	75.3	81.5	33.0	167	66.5	86.5
32 Queen's, Belfast	83.7	84.6	40.2	151	56.3	85.8
33 Liverpool	78.4	79.1	34.6	144	69.0	85.7
=34 Essex	78.5	80.9	41.0	116	73.3	85.5
=34 Stirling	70.8	71.1	40.1	162	68.8	85.5
=36 East Anglia	75.8	80.3	33.2	155	66.4	85.4
=36 Portsmouth	80.2	81.4	21.0	122	79.9	85.4
38 Manchester	73.5	76.3	44.9	155	63.5	85.3

Psychology cont

		Teaching quality %	Student experience %	Research quality %	Entry standards (UCAS points)	Graduate prospects %	Overall score
39	Staffordshire	88.2	88.4	8.2	121	74.2	84.7
40	De Montfort	86.4	88.4	11.2	110	75.9	84.2
41	Lincoln	86.3	87.5	7.9	133	70.0	84.1
=42	Birkbeck, London	79.2	81.2	59.9	118	53.7	83.6
=42	Leicester	83.0	83.6	29.6	132	60.9	83.6
44	Aston	71.1	73.8	39.1	136	69.3	83.5
45	West London	88.4	84.7	7.6	113	74.0	83.4
46	Liverpool Hope	85.0	84.8	5.5	113	75.9	82.9
=47	Abertay	79.0	79.0	15.1	156	62.0	82.6
=47	Coventry	79.2	82.1	7.8	119	77.5	82.6
49	Northumbria	78.9	80.8	18.7	139	64.8	82.5
=50	Buckingham	84.2	81.3	—	138	69.7	82.3
=50	Reading	71.5	68.2	42.3	146	61.2	82.3
52	Bolton	91.2	86.6	3.6	119	64.5	82.0
=53	Dundee	75.4	79.8	22.7	159	56.7	81.9
=53	London South Bank	81.2	83.1	8.6	101	78.3	81.9
=55	Edge Hill	83.6	80.6	18.8	130	61.0	81.8
=55	Glasgow Caledonian	77.6	76.5	8.1	184	55.1	81.8
57	Plymouth	81.7	83.4	33.8	127	53.6	81.6
=58	Central Lancashire	76.5	76.9	12.2	126	72.4	81.4
=58	Huddersfield	80.0	77.6	9.5	122	72.0	81.4
=58	West of Scotland	87.7	85.6	9.4	142	54.5	81.4
=61	Keele	82.2	84.2	17.7	121	62.3	81.3
=61	Oxford Brookes	80.8	84.8	18.1	129	60.2	81.3
=63	Aberystwyth	89.9	87.3	—	111	66.3	81.0
=63	Roehampton	80.3	80.2	26.4	110	63.9	81.0
65	Gloucestershire	79.2	78.8	—	125	73.8	80.8
66	Goldsmiths, London	77.6	74.2	40.4	129	52.8	80.6
=67	Derby	85.2	83.3	8.4	113	64.3	80.4
=67	Ulster	82.3	82.6	23.2	120	56.9	80.4
69	Teesside	73.7	74.5	15.0	106	76.2	80.1
=70	Birmingham City	89.1	88.6	—	120	58.7	79.9
=70	Edinburgh Napier	77.7	80.3	5.3	162	54.7	79.9
=72	Hull	70.2	67.9	26.8	124	67.4	79.6
=72	Liverpool John Moores	73.5	74.2	7.8	140	66.5	79.6
=74	Manchester Metropolitan	80.5	78.0	12.0	126	60.6	79.5
=74	Sunderland	88.4	85.5	7.5	114	57.0	79.5
76	Queen Margaret, Edinburgh	73.9	75.2	8.6	137	64.9	79.3
=77	Chester	86.7	83.9	7.9	121	54.3	78.9
=77	West of England	85.3	85.1	8.2	127	52.5	78.9
79	City	72.5	74.1	24.1	135	56.9	78.8
=80	Hertfordshire	76.2	77.7	6.0	108	70.8	78.6

=80	Worcester	83.2	85.2	7.1	116	57.7	78.6
82	Wolverhampton	80.2	81.7	—	101	69.4	78.2
83	East London	77.2	75.9	8.3	99	70.4	78.1
=84	Bedfordshire	81.9	79.6	25.1	89	58.6	78.0
=84	Brunel	70.7	70.1	26.6	126	59.0	78.0
=84	Chichester	88.5	86.1	10.3	103	52.9	78.0
87	York St John	81.6	85.4	11.0	120	52.2	77.9
88	Heriot-Watt	63.6	60.4	26.9	151	59.3	77.7
89	Bath Spa	80.6	75.0	—	117	63.7	77.5
90	Sheffield Hallam	79.4	80.3	3.7	119	58.5	77.3
91	Bradford	72.7	74.6	9.5	127	60.5	77.1
92	Greenwich	80.5	75.5	6.7	128	53.5	76.9
93	Cardiff Metropolitan	77.8	77.2	—	117	61.9	76.7
=94	Cumbria	83.1	80.1	—	82	67.3	76.5
=94	Middlesex	72.4	73.2	7.6	115	64.2	76.5
=94	Salford	79.6	73.4	3.8	123	56.7	76.5
97	Queen Mary, London	56.1	61.8	26.1	141	63.3	76.2
=98	St Mary's, Twickenham	82.6	80.8	4.8	121	49.3	76.0
=98	Suffolk	75.8	73.2	—	127	59.0	76.0
=100	Bournemouth	77.2	77.8	13.0	112	53.4	75.9
=100	Leeds Trinity	83.4	80.5	—	103	57.3	75.9
102	London Metropolitan	76.0	71.6	—	108	65.1	75.7
103	Westminster	66.2	66.3	9.3	117	67.4	75.6
104	South Wales	77.9	73.3	0.9	130	53.7	75.5
105	Solent	76.2	77.7	—	105	60.5	75.1
=106	Newman	79.4	82.8	0.8	114	51.3	75.0
=106	Wales Trinity St David	86.3	84.4	—	101	49.6	75.0
108	Winchester	76.6	78.9	6.5	114	51.0	74.6
109	Kingston	78.2	76.9	6.5	107	51.0	74.1
110	Anglia Ruskin	78.8	77.8	12.6	104	43.9	73.2
111	Leeds Beckett	74.7	78.1	6.5	108	48.1	72.9
112	Canterbury Christ Church	73.1	73.3	2.2	114	49.8	72.4
113	Northampton	78.1	77.4	0.4	104	47.3	72.2
114	Buckinghamshire New	78.9	80.1	—	100	44.4	71.5
115	Bishop Grosseteste	63.1	58.8	—	111	62.3	71.0
116	Brighton	68.9	67.3	12.4	119	42.5	70.8
117	Glyndŵr	38.8	39.3	3.6	136*	59.0	65.4

Employed in professional job	30%	Employed in non-professional job and Studying	6%
Employed in professional job and studying	5%	Employed in non-professional job	26%
Studying	24%	Unemployed	9%
Average starting professional salary	£19,500	Average starting non-professional salary	£16,500

Radiography

Radiography was among the top six subjects for graduate prospects in 2017. An impressive 95% of graduates went straight into professional jobs and just 3% were unemployed six months after completing a degree. The subject has slipped slightly in the earnings table, but it is still 24th for salaries in those professional jobs. Diagnostic courses usually involve two years of studying anatomy, physiology and physics followed by further training in sociology, management and ethics, and the practice and science of imaging. The therapeutic branch covers much of the same scientific content in the first year, but follows this with training in oncology, psycho-social studies and other modules. Degrees require at least one science subject, usually biology, among three A-levels or the equivalent.

The table is in its sixth year, radiography having been listed previously among "other subjects allied to medicine" in the *Guide*. Bangor, which has the highest entry qualifications, is top for the fourth year in succession. It was one of seven institutions to record 100% employment among its radiographers in 2017. Leeds, Robert Gordon, Bradford, Cumbria, Salford and Derby were the others. Derby, which has moved up to fourth place, had the most satisfied students in both of our measures derived from the National Student Survey. Exeter, which remains in second place, was the clear leader in the Research Excellence Framework.

The scores for graduate prospects reflect the subject's elevated position in the employment table. City and Ulster were the only universities where fewer than nine out of ten graduates went straight into professional jobs or further study – and both of them scored at least 86%, enough to register the top graduate prospects in some subjects. Entry grades are not high, but they have been rising: only two universities averaged less than 120 points in the latest survey.

Radiography	Teaching quality %	Student experience %	Research quality %	Entry standards (UCAS points)	Graduate prospects %	Overall score
1 Bangor	84.1	74.8	34.7	194	100.0	100.0
2 Exeter	80.3	80.4	42.4	176	99.0	98.6
3 Leeds	91.6	86.6	31.7	165	100.0	98.4
4 Derby	95.9	94.9	—	160	100.0	95.0
=5 Cardiff	84.4	84.0	36.8	140	97.7	94.5
=5 Liverpool	88.1	86.4	35.3	138	97.2	94.5
=5 Robert Gordon	91.3	90.4	4.9	158	100.0	94.5
8 Cumbria	95.5	92.2	0.7	154	100.0	94.3
9 Teesside	92.4	90.2	2.4	145	97.3	91.8
=10 Bradford	81.0	81.2	9.5	138	100.0	91.4
=10 Glasgow Caledonian	81.8	72.6	8.1	166	95.5	91.4
12 Salford	90.6	83.3	3.8	130	100.0	91.3
13 West of England	91.9	89.3	8.2	133	96.8	91.0
14 Sheffield Hallam	91.9	89.1	3.7	148	94.5	90.8
15 Queen Margaret, Edinburgh	80.3	85.5	1.5	151	97.2	90.4
16 Birmingham City	85.6	81.8	1.5	137	98.2	90.1
17 Hertfordshire	82.8	84.7	4.0	134	95.9	88.8
18 London South Bank	76.9	68.7	13.7	119	98.4	88.3

19 Portsmouth	59.5	53.7	24.3	149	95.3	88.0
20 Suffolk	80.2	80.5	—	127	96.2	87.2
21 Ulster	75.1	78.0	27.7	147	86.4	87.1
22 City	88.7	89.1	20.5	129	87.0	87.0
23 Canterbury Christ Church	74.8	68.9	2.2	113	98.0	85.7
24 Kingston/St George's, London	60.3	51.6	2.6	131	94.7	83.2

Employed in professional job	94%	Employed in non-professional job and Studying	0%
Employed in professional job and studying	1%	Employed in non-professional job	2%
Studying	1%	Unemployed	3%
Average starting professional salary	£22,125	Average starting non-professional salary	n/a

Russian and Eastern European Languages

Both applications and enrolments for degrees in Russian and East European languages rose in 2017, but only 55 students actually embarked on single honours programmes – half the total in 2009. Many others are learning Russian as part of a broader modern languages programme, but these have also been in decline, enrolments dropping by another 10% in the current academic year. Only 13 universities are advertising single or dual honours Russian degrees in 2019.

As in other subjects, the small numbers inevitably make for exaggerated swings in the statistics. Russian dropped ten places in last year's employment table but is up 13 places to 25th this year. Half of all graduates went straight into professional employment in 2017 and another 27% continued studying. The unemployment rate – the highest in any subject in 2016 – had almost halved in a year. Yet average starting salaries in professional jobs had dropped by £3,000, taking the subjects 22 places down the earnings table.

Top for the fifth year in a row, Cambridge has the highest entry standards and the best research score, taking it well clear of Oxford in second place. Glasgow, in 5th place, has much the best graduate prospects, nine percentage points better than any other university. Four of the 16 universities in the table have no scores for student satisfaction, due to the boycott of the National Student Survey (NSS) in those institutions. Portsmouth, the only post-1992 university in the table, has the top scores in both of the measures derived from the NSS.

Most undergraduates learn Russian or another Eastern European language from scratch. Despite the small numbers, entry standards remain high throughout the table: the top two average more than 200 points on the UCAS tariff and only Portsmouth has an average of less than 130 points.

Russian and Eastern European languages	Teaching quality %	Student experience %	Research quality %	Entry standards (UCAS points)	Graduate prospects %	Overall score
1 Cambridge	—	—	54.0	203	80.6	100.0
2 Oxford	—	—	41.3	201	85.7	94.9
3 Durham	81.5	73.6	34.6	199	86.3	93.5
4 Exeter	82.3	81.8	35.1	175	84.6	92.4
5 Glasgow	84.1	78.9	26.3	169*	96.9	92.1

Russian and Eastern European languages cont	Teaching quality %	Student experience %	Research quality %	Entry standards (UCAS points)	Graduate prospects %	Overall score
6 Leeds	82.7	85.5	30.6	162	87.1	91.1
7 Birmingham	78.1	74.8	33.7	165	87.9	90.2
8 Manchester	—	—	48.9	154	68.2	90.0
9 University College London	74.6	68.8	43.7	173	72.6	89.1
10 St Andrews	80.8	80.4	26.4	186	76.7*	89.0
11 Nottingham	78.9	70.7	39.4	130*	85.7	88.2
12 Sheffield	—	—	41.2	139	58.6	87.8
13 Portsmouth	91.1	86.9	32.2	110	76.1	87.4
14 Bristol	72.5	70.7	36.0	166	72.7	86.2
15 Edinburgh	75.5	75.5	30.3	174	55.7*	83.3
16 Bath	69.9	61.2	27.4	159*	73.9*	82.0

Employed in professional job	50%	Employed in non-professional job and Studying	4%
Employed in professional job and studying	0%	Employed in non-professional job	13%
Studying	23%	Unemployed	10%
Average starting professional salary	£21,000	Average starting non-professional salary	£16,000

Social Policy

The London School of Economics has regained its accustomed place as the clear leader in social policy, having had to share the position with Strathclyde last year. The LSE is in the bottom four for student satisfaction with the quality of teaching, but its research score is 15 percentage points ahead of its nearest challenger, Kent. Now second, Strathclyde's social policy programmes, which are offered mainly as joint degrees at undergraduate level, are still too new to have graduates, but the students' entry standards are the highest in the table. Bath, which has the best graduate prospects, has moved 13 places to third position. Students at Staffordshire, in 26th place, are the most satisfied with the quality of teaching, while Coventry received the top rating for the broader student experience.

The demand for places on social policy degrees fluctuated in the aftermath of £9,000 fees, but both applications and enrolments grew for the third year in a row in 2017. There were fewer than four applications for every place, however. Nevertheless, there are four new universities in the latest table, taking the total to 45, and 77 universities and colleges plan to offer the subject in 2019. Entry standards are generally modest: only three universities average more than 180 points on the UCAS tariff, while another three dropped below 100 points.

Nationally, the subject is in the bottom ten for employment, with almost three graduates in ten starting out in low-level jobs. This is reflected in the table for social policy, where at six universities, less than half of the graduates found professional work or continued studying, and only five universities reached 80% on this measure. The picture is only a little more positive in the comparison of starting salaries in graduate-level jobs, where social policy shares 47th place with seven other subjects.

Social Policy

	Teaching quality %	Student experience %	Research quality %	Entry standards (UCAS points)	Graduate prospects %	Overall score
1 London School of Economics	69.3	74.0	74.9	183	87.4	100.0
2 Strathclyde	78.7	77.0	31.9	195	—	96.2
3 Bath	80.0	70.3	43.4	156	90.4	95.1
4 Bangor	92.1	89.8	39.6	146	72.1	94.7
5 Edinburgh	76.4	74.8	53.4	191	57.5	93.3
6 Leeds	81.4	78.8	47.6	154	72.7	93.1
7 Birmingham	80.4	75.6	40.1	145	82.7	92.6
8 Coventry	94.4	95.4	5.6	—	70.6	92.5
9 Loughborough	78.0	70.8	40.6	158	75.6	91.4
=10 Bristol	70.0	67.9	47.9	155	80.8	91.1
=10 Swansea	88.9	85.3	22.7	135	78.8	91.1
12 Nottingham	77.4	73.8	43.5	140	77.5	90.5
13 Kent	77.6	72.5	59.0	126	72.2	90.1
14 Stirling	81.1	78.7	33.8	162*	62.5	89.8
15 Glasgow	73.6	70.5	41.8	169	61.2	88.8
16 York	72.0	72.7	47.5	125	78.4	88.4
17 Liverpool Hope	88.2	82.8	8.6	122	83.3	88.2
18 Bolton	96.0	88.0	1.0	—	60.0*	87.8
19 Southampton	77.8	64.8	52.8	137	—	87.3
20 Queen's, Belfast	78.0	74.5	26.2	144	69.0	86.8
21 Cardiff	74.7	75.1	30.8	142*	65.6	86.0
22 Aston	74.8	66.5	38.6	120	75.8	85.8
23 Salford	83.5	81.3	27.7	118	66.1	85.7
24 West of Scotland	90.4	84.5	9.4	—	57.1	85.6
25 Sheffield	67.6	71.3	26.8	144	73.1	85.1
26 Staffordshire	96.5	93.1	—	100*	69.2	84.6
27 Keele	81.4	79.2	25.0	130	58.5	84.4
28 Edge Hill	82.3	81.1	5.7	121	—	82.3
29 De Montfort	72.6	68.1	11.2	120	74.1	81.1
=30 Central Lancashire	71.6	68.0	11.8	135	65.9	81.0
=30 Lincoln	81.9	79.4	5.8	117	62.5	81.0
32 Anglia Ruskin	90.8	80.7	5.4	102	58.8	80.8
33 Chester	87.8	77.1	0.3	111	60.0	80.2
34 Wolverhampton	86.3	81.9	—	114	54.6	79.5
35 Northampton	78.4	75.7	—	137	47.9	78.2
36 Ulster	78.0	77.4	39.2	109	33.9	78.1
37 Middlesex	73.3	71.6	14.9	111	55.9	77.5
38 Birmingham City	69.9	68.6	3.8	122	62.2	77.3
39 London Metropolitan	68.1	70.4	8.8	110	63.7	76.9
40 Bedfordshire	82.0	82.4	16.3	91	45.0	76.6
41 Wales Trinity St David	83.3	82.2	—	94	53.5	76.5
42 Plymouth	80.4	79.2	16.0	—	37.3	76.2

Social Policy cont

	Teaching quality %	Student experience %	Research quality %	Entry standards (UCAS points)	Graduate prospects %	Overall score
43 Canterbury Christ Church	73.5	71.6	3.2	—	48.3*	74.1
44 Brighton	71.0	66.6	12.4	114	37.5	72.6
45 Goldsmiths, London	56.5	56.4	13.5	99	—	66.8

Employed in professional job	35%	Employed in non-professional job and Studying	3%
Employed in professional job and studying	4%	Employed in non-professional job	26%
Studying	21%	Unemployed	11%
Average starting professional salary	£20,000	Average starting non-professional salary	£16,224

Social Work

The Frontline programme, modelled on Teach First, is trying to attract graduates of other subjects to train as social workers but, for the moment, social work degrees remain the main route into the profession. Near-record numbers of students are taking them, even though applications have dropped from 80,000 to 52,500 over the last decade. A combination of falling demand and increasing provision has seen the number of applications per place drop from more than seven in 2010 to four in 2017. Although Goldsmiths averages less than 100 points at entry, only Edinburgh and Glasgow Caledonian average more than 170 points.

Edinburgh has held on to the top place in Social Work that it won last year, one of five Scottish universities in the top ten. Second-placed Stirling has a rare 100% employment score but does not have enough students taking social work for average entry grades to be published. Edinburgh is not top on any individual measure but is second both for research and for entry standards, where, surprisingly, it trails Glasgow Caledonian by a single point. Kent produced the best results in the Research Excellence Framework but remains outside the top 20 because of low student satisfaction.

Nineteen of the 78 universities in the table did not enter the assessments. Bolton has the highest levels of satisfaction with the quality of teaching – and has moved up more than 20 places to the verge of the top ten as a result – but it is another university without enough students to compile entry standards. Students at Kingston, outside the top 40, are the most satisfied with the broader student experience.

Remarkably, social work does better in the comparison of earnings in professional jobs than in the table based on overall graduate prospects. A median salary of £26,000 in graduate-level employment places it in the top ten of the 67 groups, whereas it is only just in the top 30 for the proportion of graduates going straight into such jobs or continuing to study. Unemployment is relatively low, at 8%, but one graduate in five started out in low-level employment in 2017. A total of 22 universities saw positive destinations for at least 90% of their 2017 graduates, but the rate was under 60% at seven others.

Social Work

		Teaching quality %	Student experience %	Research quality %	Entry standards (UCAS points)	Graduate prospects %	Overall score
1	Edinburgh	87.1	78.5	53.4	174	78.3	100.0
2	Stirling	89.6	77.1	33.8	—	100.0	98.6
3	Nottingham	83.0	79.7	43.5	151	94.3	97.4
4	Lancaster	71.0	69.7	51.4	165	93.2	97.3
5	Queen's, Belfast	81.2	85.0	39.3	145	96.2	96.3
6	Dundee	93.1	90.4	31.1	145	84.2	95.5
7	Bath	85.5	83.1	43.4	160	72.0	95.0
8	Glasgow Caledonian	85.3	77.1	8.1	175	89.7	94.7
9	Bedfordshire	92.2	89.6	16.3	—	87.1	94.3
10	Strathclyde	81.3	76.3	31.9	168	78.4	94.2
11	Bolton	96.0	88.0	1.0	—	89.5	93.6
12	East Anglia	73.1	63.2	45.8	148	92.9	93.5
13	Leeds	77.0	74.7	47.6	159	72.8	93.2
14	York	73.8	61.8	47.5	139	95.8	93.0
=15	Plymouth	85.4	78.1	16.0	155	88.8	92.9
=15	Robert Gordon	82.3	74.9	18.0	153	93.6	92.9
17	Birmingham	73.2	70.4	40.1	152	87.7	92.8
18	East London	89.3	85.2	10.6	146*	90.8	92.5
19	London South Bank	87.6	82.5	20.1	138*	90.4	92.0
20	West of England	80.4	82.3	10.9	144	96.5	91.3
21	West of Scotland	84.4	80.3	9.4	145	90.9	90.7
22	Sussex	83.8	69.4	27.9	142	84.0	90.6
=23	Kent	66.1	63.4	59.0	134	85.8	90.5
=23	Swansea	74.4	72.9	22.7	148	90.7	90.5
25	Salford	87.8	83.7	27.7	132	80.4	90.4
26	Ulster	83.4	79.8	39.2	118	87.3	90.2
27	Middlesex	83.6	78.6	14.9	146	82.9	89.7
28	Lincoln	86.4	77.4	5.8	133	94.2	88.9
29	Portsmouth	81.5	76.9	12.1	140	87.9	88.8
=30	Hull	81.0	74.8	14.3	134	90.6	88.5
=30	Nottingham Trent	85.4	81.8	5.1	152	77.4	88.5
32	De Montfort	83.5	79.6	11.2	126	93.1	88.2
33	Central Lancashire	86.2	81.5	11.8	142	76.3	88.0
34	Bournemouth	90.3	83.3	4.7	123	91.1	87.9
35	Derby	91.9	87.5	5.6	129	80.9	87.6
36	Oxford Brookes	88.1	84.1	—	135	85.2	87.5
37	Anglia Ruskin	83.2	77.9	5.4	128	93.3	87.3
38	Birmingham City	86.0	82.2	3.8	139	80.4	87.1
39	Hertfordshire	79.4	75.3	4.0	135	91.7	87.0
40	Brunel	62.7	50.1	28.5	156*	81.8	86.3
41	London Metropolitan	85.6	84.2	8.8	118	86.3	86.0
42	Kingston/St George's, London	92.3	91.0	—	124	78.5	85.9

Social Work cont

		Teaching quality %	Student experience %	Research quality %	Entry standards (UCAS points)	Graduate prospects %	Overall score
43	Liverpool John Moores	84.2	86.8	5.8	151	63.4	85.8
=44	Brighton	80.3	66.0	12.4	120	92.1	85.4
=44	Huddersfield	78.0	74.0	9.5	143	76.9	85.4
46	Liverpool Hope	82.4	78.0	8.6	122	84.0	84.9
47	Northumbria	79.2	78.7	12.7	145	64.5	84.4
=48	Keele	49.7	49.3	25.0	146	95.8	84.3
=48	Staffordshire	84.7	79.6	—	109	95.0	84.3
50	Teesside	66.6	61.5	15.0	133	89.4	84.0
51	Suffolk	80.0	75.0	—	133*	81.7	83.9
=52	Coventry	84.1	83.0	5.6	128	73.0	83.8
=52	Sheffield Hallam	81.9	83.1	—	121	84.2	83.8
=52	Solent	78.6	75.5		122	90.0	83.8
55	Manchester Metropolitan	78.1	77.7	6.9	138	64.6	82.1
=56	Edge Hill	77.6	77.1	5.7	125	74.1	81.7
=56	Winchester	81.7	77.9	—	121	77.0	81.7
58	Chichester	87.6	88.0	—	123	64.0	81.4
=59	Cardiff Metropolitan	81.4	73.9	—	124	73.6	81.1
=59	Greenwich	89.5	87.0	2.2	—	56.2	81.1
61	Leeds Beckett	89.4	88.7	6.4	120	57.0	81.0
62	South Wales	80.8	72.7	15.4	127	59.7	80.7
63	Buckinghamshire New	86.4	78.8	—	105	78.1	80.4
64	Gloucestershire	78.3	73.9	—	113	80.5	80.0
65	Wolverhampton	77.6	76.1	—	120	71.1	79.3
=66	Canterbury Christ Church	76.7	72.7	2.2	118	72.4	79.1
=66	Sunderland	81.6	79.4	1.9	127	57.8	79.1
68	Plymouth Marjon	89.1	88.0	—	109*	61.0	78.9
69	Newman	76.4	75.4	2.2	136	54.9	78.5
70	Bangor	85.5	80.9	—	124	52.4	78.0
71	Bradford	60.9	64.5	10.6	133	67.6	77.9
=72	Essex	77.0	70.8	—	109	75.7	77.8
=72	Northampton	70.9	64.2	—	125	72.1	77.8
74	West London	56.7	50.8	—	140*	80.0	77.7
75	Chester	74.6	64.7	0.3	124	65.5	77.1
=76	Cumbria	80.4	68.1	—	122	56.0	76.2
=76	Goldsmiths, London	68.3	59.3	13.5	92	83.9	76.2
78	Worcester	71.4	66.8	—	123	63.5	76.0

Employed in professional job	59%	Employed in non-professional job and Studying	2%
Employed in professional job and studying	3%	Employed in non-professional job	18%
Studying	10%	Unemployed	8%
Average starting professional salary	£26,000	Average starting non-professional salary	£16,000

Sociology

Applications to study sociology have risen more than 12,000 in four years, and universities have responded to the subject's renaissance by providing 3,000 additional places. For the first time, more than 8,000 students started sociology degrees in 2017, prompting even more universities and colleges to offer the subject. The Sociology table now contains 94 institutions, and 128 universities and colleges are advertising degrees or foundation degrees in 2019. Immediate job prospects cannot be responsible for the boom: sociology has dropped into the bottom three for the proportion of graduates finding professional work or continuing their studies. Less than a third of sociologists found such work, while considerably more started out in low-level jobs. Those who did find professional work did rather better, but their median salary of £20,000 was only just in the top 50 of the 67 subject groups.

Cambridge remains top of the table, with the highest entry standards and the best graduate prospects. It was one of six universities where more than 80% of sociologists went straight into professional jobs or began postgraduate courses. But the proportion was under 40% at five others. The best performance in the Research Excellence Framework was at Kent, just outside the top ten. As in the 2008 assessments, the sociology panel was no respecter of reputations: the London School of Economics is only eighth on this measure while Cambridge is well outside the top ten. The most satisfied students, on both of our measures derived from the National Student Survey, are at Anglia Ruskin, which is only just inside the top 50 overall. Even in the top ten, there have been some big changes: Lancaster is up 19 places to third, while the London School of Economics has risen ten places to ninth, despite being handicapped by its usual low satisfaction scores.

Degree courses starting in 2019 will include subjects such as urban studies, women's studies and some communication studies, as well as sociology itself, and a large number of institutions teach the subject as part of a combined studies or modular programme. Entry standards are moderate: nine of the 94 universities in the table average less than 100 points on the UCAS tariff and another 35 less than 120 points.

Sociology	Teaching quality %	Student experience %	Research quality %	Entry standards (UCAS points)	Graduate prospects %	Overall score
1 Cambridge	—	—	39.2	213	84.8	100.0
2 Bath	87.5	84.3	43.4	165	83.9	99.3
3 Lancaster	86.9	87.5	51.4	149	82.8	99.0
=4 Bristol	85.3	78.6	46.7	160	78.4	97.0
=4 Exeter	85.5	82.8	41.0	162	78.9	97.0
6 Loughborough	91.3	87.5	40.6	153	69.2	96.4
7 Glasgow	79.4	74.6	41.8	198	70.3	96.2
8 Edinburgh	77.4	72.2	48.8	177	65.6	93.6
9 London School of Economics	68.8	65.5	45.2	179	80.7	93.0
10 Surrey	86.0	82.5	30.2	158	63.4	92.2
11 Kent	77.0	74.7	59.0	124	73.7	92.0
12 Leeds	75.9	76.8	47.6	154	67.5	91.9
13 Manchester	76.6	75.2	50.4	153	64.3	91.6
14 Durham	78.9	77.9	28.7	168	66.3	90.9

Sociology cont

		Teaching quality %	Student experience %	Research quality %	Entry standards (UCAS points)	Graduate prospects %	Overall score
15	King's College London	77.8	74.3	42.2	154	—	90.7
=16	Nottingham	80.1	77.0	43.5	139	64.9	90.5
=16	Stirling	80.0	78.3	33.8	168	57.8	90.5
18	York	75.5	71.6	45.1	138	73.5	90.4
19	Lincoln	88.3	82.2	—	123	85.7	89.1
20	Sheffield	75.2	78.6	26.8	135	78.0	89.0
21	Portsmouth	84.6	82.1	32.2	107	70.8	88.7
=22	Bangor	83.9	81.7	39.6	123	57.1	88.6
=22	Liverpool Hope	88.9	85.4	8.6	121	73.9	88.6
24	Newcastle	75.9	76.9	30.3	144	66.9	88.2
25	Southampton	74.4	72.4	52.8	139	55.6	88.1
=26	Aberdeen	79.2	76.3	31.0	175	45.8	88.0
=26	Birmingham	72.3	67.0	31.1	149	74.1	88.0
28	Aston	78.4	75.2	38.6	125	63.0	87.5
=29	Coventry	84.6	82.1	5.6	113	82.0	87.4
=29	Warwick	67.4	66.6	31.7	153	75.3	87.4
31	Liverpool	—	—	24.5	136	69.3	87.1
32	Essex	74.1	73.3	44.3	112	67.9	86.8
33	Keele	80.9	77.2	25.0	117	66.5	86.2
34	Abertay	82.5	80.7	5.0	161	56.3	86.1
35	Queen's, Belfast	81.0	76.7	26.2	137	55.1	86.0
=36	Huddersfield	85.5	78.5	9.5	113	72.2	85.9
=36	Oxford Brookes	81.9	79.8	17.8	122	65.2	85.9
38	Sussex	70.6	66.8	29.7	138	70.2	85.7
=39	Leicester	79.2	78.2	18.4	124	63.0	84.9
=39	Queen Margaret, Edinburgh	85.0	84.8	—	129	63.3	84.9
41	Cardiff	73.4	69.4	30.8	140	58.3	84.8
=42	Glasgow Caledonian	82.8	72.1	12.7	179	39.1	84.7
=42	Gloucestershire	84.3	80.9	14.5	108	64.1	84.7
=42	Newman	89.0	79.5	2.2	117	63.6	84.7
=42	Nottingham Trent	81.9	82.1	5.1	129	64.2	84.7
46	Northumbria	78.4	73.8	12.7	132	64.9	84.4
47	Edinburgh Napier	80.2	78.2	5.3	152	55.7	84.3
48	Anglia Ruskin	93.5	88.5	26.4	87	44.6	84.2
49	West of England	85.6	82.4	10.9	118	55.8	84.0
=50	Robert Gordon	77.5	81.9	4.9	153	53.5	83.7
=50	Salford	83.3	79.0	27.7	113	48.2	83.7
=52	De Montfort	82.1	78.4	11.2	107*	65.0	83.4
=52	Ulster	81.2	79.3	39.2	113	40.6	83.4
54	Central Lancashire	78.5	74.9	11.8	112	67.7	83.1
=55	Derby	89.6	84.7	13.5	100	50.0	83.0
=55	Plymouth	83.9	79.3	16.0	109	55.0	83.0

57	Roehampton	71.7	71.6	24.9	104	71.4	82.9
=58	East London	86.1	80.5	13.7	114	48.3	82.6
=58	Teesside	74.0	71.3	15.0	117	68.5	82.6
=60	Bedfordshire	81.7	80.6	16.3	93	61.8	82.4
=60	St Mary's, Twickenham	82.7	86.7	—	107	62.2	82.4
62	Sheffield Hallam	87.8	83.9	14.4	118	40.3	82.3
63	Bradford	72.4	66.8	10.6	121	72.2	82.0
64	Wolverhampton	87.7	86.8	—	93	59.4	81.9
65	Edge Hill	82.3	81.1	5.7	123	50.7	81.7
=66	Hull	78.6	72.6	14.3	113	57.9	81.5
=66	West of Scotland	75.9	71.1	9.4	141	53.4	81.5
68	Northampton	89.4	80.5	—	99	55.6	81.3
69	Birmingham City	77.5	76.4	3.8	122	56.5	80.6
=70	Brunel	73.1	66.5	26.0	117	52.2	80.3
=70	Goldsmiths, London	70.6	66.2	33.4	120	48.2	80.3
72	Greenwich	81.1	75.6	—	135	46.3	80.2
73	Royal Holloway, London	78.0	77.8	—	132	50.0	80.1
=74	Liverpool John Moores	74.0	73.1	5.8	132	54.1	80.0
=74	Sunderland	84.5	77.0	1.9	114	48.7	80.0
76	Manchester Metropolitan	72.7	70.4	14.9	119	55.9	79.9
=77	Bournemouth	79.0	81.1	4.7	107	53.3	79.7
=77	London Metropolitan	78.1	74.6	—	85*	73.0	79.7
79	Leeds Beckett	82.2	79.8	6.4	98	51.8	79.6
80	Staffordshire	76.4	70.0	—	101	68.8	79.3
81	Westminster	75.9	78.1	—	109	57.7	78.9
82	Bath Spa	78.1	72.1	13.9	119	37.4	77.9
=83	Buckinghamshire New	79.6	79.6	—	104	47.7	77.7
=83	Middlesex	70.6	67.3	14.9	116	50.5	77.7
85	Winchester	79.9	79.5	4.4	100	42.5	77.1
86	Brighton	74.2	68.8	12.4	109	44.5	76.7
87	Chester	74.2	67.8	6.4	107	50.3	76.6
88	Kingston	80.4	76.0	—	97	44.3	76.2
89	Suffolk	76.0	70.7	—	124	38.9	75.8
90	City	62.6	61.2	20.8	129	39.8	75.0
91	Worcester	77.5	78.6	—	108	32.4	74.5
92	London South Bank	65.9	65.8	20.1	88	50.0	74.4
=93	Canterbury Christ Church	73.5	71.6	—	97	44.8	73.9
=93	South Wales	68.5	52.8	—	112	55.9	73.9

Employed in professional job	30%	Employed in non-professional job and Studying	5%
Employed in professional job and studying	2%	Employed in non-professional job	32%
Studying	21%	Unemployed	10%
Average starting professional salary	£26,000	Average starting non-professional salary	£16,400

Sports Science

Sports science has been one of the big growth areas of UK higher education over the past decade, with a 50% increase in undergraduate entrants. It is now among the top ten subjects for applicants, and over 190 universities and colleges – nearly 30 more than last year – are offering courses. Both applications and enrolments for sport and exercise science degrees dipped in 2017 but seem to have recovered in the current academic year.

The UCAS category of sport and exercise science covers more than 40 specialisms, from sports therapy to equestrian sport studies and marine sport technology. Many courses contain more science and less physical activity than some candidates expect. Essex, for example, requires maths or one of the sciences at A-level. Many universities now offer sports scholarships for elite performers, but most are not tied to a particular course and, officially at least, do not allow normal entry requirements to be waived.

All the universities at the top of the table have excellent sports facilities and successful teams, but it is their performance in sports degree courses and research that counts here. Competition is as fierce as it would be in a major championship. Bath and Exeter are tied for first place, without leading on any individual measure, and less than one point covers the top four universities. Birmingham, in third place, had much the best grades in the Research Excellence Framework, while Loughborough, the most famous name in university sport, is up to fourth.

The most satisfied students are at Aberystwyth – clearly when it comes to the quality of teaching and tied with Manchester Metropolitan in terms of the broader student experience. Aberdeen has the highest entry grades, while the best graduate prospects are at Essex. Sports science has one of the lowest unemployment rates, at 6%, and is in the top 40 for graduate prospects, but it has dropped into the bottom five for starting salaries in professional jobs.

Sport Science	Teaching quality %	Student experience %	Research quality %	Entry standards (UCAS points)	Graduate prospects %	Overall score
=1 Bath	84.2	83.5	54.0	172	82.5	100.0
=1 Exeter	81.3	87.6	50.8	172	84.8	100.0
3 Birmingham	85.0	83.1	63.7	154	81.7	99.4
4 Loughborough	83.1	86.8	52.1	164	83.3	99.2
5 Glasgow	80.6	83.1	42.3	180	83.6	98.7
6 Leeds	83.2	86.0	50.5	159	72.1	95.6
7 Nottingham	87.2	79.2	31.4	165	—	95.5
8 Durham	80.5	80.4	28.7	171	82.2	95.3
=9 Essex	85.9	90.9	25.8	137	86.5	94.9
=9 Liverpool John Moores	84.3	84.3	45.3	156	72.8	94.9
=9 Surrey	86.0	84.5	33.6	156	—	94.9
12 Aberdeen	85.8	83.0	34.7	198	60.0	94.7
=13 Edinburgh	73.2	75.8	26.1	180	81.3	93.5
=13 Nottingham Trent	89.9	88.6	7.3	162	78.1	93.5
15 Swansea	82.8	84.1	38.8	139	78.6	93.4
16 Portsmouth	87.3	87.1	8.1	144	83.3	92.4
=17 Bangor	88.5	89.3	30.6	148	67.6	92.3

=17	East Anglia	84.8	88.9	27.2	152	71.3	92.3
19	Stirling	78.0	79.3	33.6	157	73.4	91.6
20	Aberystwyth	94.1	91.1	23.5	118	74.0	91.5
21	Staffordshire	89.8	87.2	19.1	125	76.6	90.9
22	Coventry	87.5	87.7	4.5	146	77.2	90.7
23	Suffolk	91.4	88.6	—	149	71.9	90.0
24	Liverpool Hope	90.7	89.5	10.9	118	78.0	89.8
25	Roehampton	80.8	78.9	20.6	116	85.4	89.4
26	London South Bank	79.8	70.8	35.0	115	81.6	89.1
27	Manchester Metropolitan	89.8	91.1	12.0	129	69.7	89.0
28	Sheffield Hallam	86.9	83.3	8.5	142	70.9	88.7
29	Chester	89.6	88.4	6.6	118	75.4	88.3
=30	Abertay	80.2	81.8	8.9	153	70.8	88.1
=30	Ulster	78.2	77.8	31.0	146	65.9	88.1
32	Edge Hill	86.4	86.0	7.7	147	65.5	87.8
=33	Brunel	71.9	72.9	46.4	139	66.7	87.7
=33	Lincoln	78.3	77.2	11.4	143	75.9	87.7
=33	Robert Gordon	74.5	73.5	4.9	163	75.9	87.7
36	St Mary's, Twickenham	84.0	82.2	4.8	130	75.4	87.3
37	Brighton	84.3	82.4	10.9	144	65.9	87.2
38	Gloucestershire	82.0	81.4	6.0	136	73.7	87.1
39	Middlesex	75.5	71.5	10.0	132	81.7	86.7
=40	Kent	69.9	67.8	21.0	146	75.9	86.4
=40	Plymouth Marjon	92.6	90.9	—	137	59.9	86.4
42	Bradford	72.6	67.0	9.5	156	75.0	86.2
43	Cardiff Metropolitan	79.7	83.3	7.7	142	67.8	86.1
=44	Chichester	82.0	83.8	15.2	127	67.1	85.9
=44	Strathclyde	84.5	82.4	—	192	46.7	85.9
46	Wolverhampton	85.0	82.8	5.6	124	69.7	85.7
=47	Buckinghamshire New	85.6	84.8	0.9	115	74.1	85.6
=47	Edinburgh Napier	78.3	82.0	5.3	158	62.2	85.6
=47	Huddersfield	83.3	76.5	—	135	72.2	85.6
=50	Salford	86.9	86.1	3.8	126	65.8	85.4
=50	West of Scotland	79.3	81.5	9.1	145	64.2	85.4
=50	Winchester	86.6	84.7	—	109	75.5	85.4
53	Worcester	80.9	79.8	4.9	128	72.3	85.3
=54	Northumbria	75.2	75.2	4.4	154	67.8	85.0
=54	South Wales	86.7	84.3	10.8	132	59.2	85.0
56	Hull	84.4	84.4	14.2	130	59.7	84.9
=57	Central Lancashire	81.4	78.1	5.1	132	67.8	84.6
=57	Glyndŵr	76.8	73.5	3.6	129	76.2	84.6
=57	London Metropolitan	86.6	82.0	—	102	76.3	84.6
60	Bournemouth	78.3	78.2	9.0	131	68.8	84.5
=61	East London	78.9	74.6	7.6	124	71.8	84.1
=61	Oxford Brookes	79.5	74.1	3.0	139	67.6	84.1
=61	Solent	78.8	78.9	0.6	132	70.6	84.1

Sport Science cont	Teaching quality %	Student experience %	Research quality %	Entry standards (UCAS points)	Graduate prospects %	Overall score
=64 Leeds Beckett	78.0	78.7	12.6	131	64.3	83.8
=64 Wales Trinity St David	86.6	86.5	–	104	70.7	83.8
=66 Hertfordshire	78.5	76.2	0.9	122	73.7	83.6
=66 Newman	88.8	84.7	2.8	121	60.0	83.6
68 Canterbury Christ Church	86.8	85.4	19.0	121	52.6	83.5
69 Bedfordshire	78.4	77.7	6.7	108	73.7	83.1
=70 Kingston	91.4	86.7	2.6	105	60.9	82.9
=70 York St John	81.5	83.2	5.5	122	62.9	82.9
72 Leeds Trinity	83.1	86.2	0.8	109	66.7	82.6
=73 Derby	77.3	73.5	1.7	127	68.3	82.3
=73 Teesside	79.1	77.0	2.4	120	67.7	82.3
75 Sunderland	79.9	79.8	2.4	135	59.2	82.2
=76 Anglia Ruskin	76.7	77.9	–	120	69.8	82.0
=76 Greenwich	67.6	66.3	7.4	145	68.8	82.0
78 Bolton	80.5	77.6	–	107	68.7	81.3
79 Northampton	78.9	76.0	–	112	48.9	76.3
80 Cumbria	62.3	54.8	3.2	124	63.4	75.6
81 Bishop Grosseteste	65.5	61.2	–	108*	51.2	71.8

Employed in professional job	39%	Employed in non-professional job and Studying	4%
Employed in professional job and studying	5%	Employed in non-professional job	23%
Studying	23%	Unemployed	6%
Average starting professional salary	£19,000	Average starting non-professional salary	£16,000

Theology and Religious Studies

By no means all those taking degrees in theology or religious studies go into the church, but the vocation has helped to maintain relatively healthy graduate employment records. More than 40% go on to a postgraduate course, either full or part-time, and another third go straight into professional work, taking the subjects (just) into the top half of the employment table. Even in the earnings table, the subjects are in the top 40, with average starting salaries in professional jobs of £21,500 at the end of 2017.

Just over 1,000 students began degrees in theology or religious studies in 2017 – slightly fewer than in the previous year and about a third down on the period before higher fees were introduced. Applications have followed a similar downward path, and 2018 saw the closure of Heythrop College, part of the University of London, after 400 years of teaching theology. There are now little more than four applications to the place nationally. There are still 36 universities in the table, however, and many more offering the subject as part of a broader degree. Religious studies can be combined with maths or music at Glasgow, film and media at Stirling, or applied psychology at Trinity Saint David.

The top two in the table remain unchanged from last year, with Cambridge extending its lead over Durham. Cambridge has the best graduate prospects and (with Oxford) the highest entry standards, while Durham produced the best results in the Research Excellence Framework. Competition is particularly keen in Scotland, which has three universities in the top ten. They are led by St Andrews, in sixth place. Chester, the only post-1992 university in the top 20, has the highest levels of satisfaction in both measures taken from the National Student Survey.

Theology and Religious Studies	Teaching quality %	Student experience %	Research quality %	Entry standards (UCAS points)	Graduate prospects %	Overall score
1 Cambridge	—	—	44.6	202	90.4	100.0
2 Durham	85.3	77.3	56.6	182	85.5	97.4
3 Exeter	88.5	86.7	38.9	172	87.7	95.9
4 Bristol	—	—	36.0	171	89.3	94.6
5 Oxford	—	—	46.7	202	77.2	93.6
6 St Andrews	93.4	92.1	28.9	189	68.6	93.4
=7 Aberdeen	92.3	89.8	39.9	158	73.7	93.2
=7 Birmingham	89.4	84.8	36.2	148	86.1	93.2
9 Lancaster	79.8	80.3	53.0	153	78.1	91.9
10 Edinburgh	84.7	81.5	43.2	163	75.0	91.8
11 Nottingham	82.9	79.2	43.9	148	78.6	90.8
12 Sheffield	—	—	25.3	144	89.2	90.4
13 Leeds	82.5	82.2	44.4	152	73.2	90.2
14 Glasgow	92.9	84.7	21.4	—	72.0	89.1
15 Liverpool Hope	93.7	91.7	17.7	105	82.2	87.7
16 SOAS London	83.6	72.7	34.1	139	74.4	87.0
17 Manchester	—	—	37.2	143	63.4	86.0
18 King's College London	72.5	65.7	37.1	154	66.7	83.6
19 Chester	95.5	93.3	11.1	113	61.7	83.5
20 Cardiff	75.2	70.5	33.5	141	63.9	82.6
21 Bath Spa	92.4	89.7	8.3	120	61.8	82.5
22 Queen's, Belfast	81.6	80.3	—	147	74.3	82.3
23 Winchester	89.6	86.4	18.0	107	62.0	82.0
24 St Mary's, Twickenham	83.1	74.3	9.4	114	77.5	81.7
25 Roehampton	81.0	77.5	24.3	100	71.4	81.5
26 Kent	68.2	69.3	44.1	120	64.6	80.9
27 Chichester	91.5	84.1	—	108	67.3	80.5
28 Newman	88.4	84.4	3.5	102	65.9	79.6
29 Canterbury Christ Church	87.9	74.6	16.3	101	58.7	79.0
30 Bishop Grosseteste	77.1	63.4	—	102*	86.1	78.4
31 York St John	83.5	75.9	4.8	109	64.6	78.0
32 South Wales	93.4	89.2	—	106	50.0	77.6
=33 Gloucestershire	82.3	70.1	6.9	124	52.9	76.2
=33 Wolverhampton	83.6	77.8	—	92	65.4	76.2

Theology and Religious Studies cont	Teaching quality %	Student experience %	Research quality %	Entry standards (UCAS points)	Graduate prospects %	Overall score
35 Wales Trinity St David	76.0	63.3	30.0	123	40.0	75.0
36 Leeds Trinity	76.2	63.7	9.9	96	57.6	73.3

Employed in professional job	32%	Employed in non-professional job and Studying	5%
Employed in professional job and studying	3%	Employed in non-professional job	18%
Studying	33%	Unemployed	8%
Average starting professional salary	£21,500	Average starting non-professional salary	£15,912

Town and Country Planning and Landscape

Three universities dropped out of the table for town and country planning and landscape last year and another one has gone in the latest edition, but applications recovered in 2017, almost reaching 4,000 for the first time in the current decade. Many students considering a career in these areas opt for a postgraduate course, but nearly 1,000 started out as undergraduates.

Almost two-thirds of graduates in the planning and landscape groups go straight into professional jobs, placing the subjects in the top 12 in the employment table. They are also in the top 20 for starting salaries in graduate-level employment. The subject table reflects these successes, with five of the top seven universities seeing at least nine out of ten graduates go straight into professional jobs or further study in 2017. At University College London and Edinburgh, the rate was 100%.

UCL has gone up two places to overtake Cambridge, which has been the perennial leader of the table and still has by far the highest entry standards. Ulster's students are the most satisfied with the quality of teaching, just ahead of those at Queen's Belfast, which has much the highest rating in the other sections of the National Student Survey.

Entry standards are lower on landscape and garden design courses, where there are only three applications to the place, than for planning, where the ratio is closer to five per place. But only six of the 24 universities in the table average more than 150 points. More than 40 universities and colleges are offering courses in landscape or garden design in 2019, some of them as an element of a broader degree in geography or architecture. Over 70 expect to run courses in various areas of planning, including disaster management and emergency planning, rural enterprise and land management, and coastal safety management.

Town and Country Planning and Landscape	Teaching quality %	Student experience %	Research quality %	Entry standards (UCAS points)	Graduate prospects %	Overall score
1 University College London	79.9	82.8	54.1	175	100.0	100.0
2 Cambridge	78.3*	72.4*	49.0	203	89.7	98.5
3 Queen's, Belfast	94.3	94.3	35.2	130	93.3	95.5
4 Loughborough	74.8	75.5	58.3	154	87.5	93.9
5 Birmingham	76.9	80.3	42.0	138	97.9	92.9

6	Edinburgh	75.1	71.1	35.1	155	100.0	92.7
7	Sheffield	77.5	80.5	36.6	143	96.2	92.4
8	Cardiff	83.7	76.4	36.8	141	85.5	91.0
9	Reading	79.0	77.0	40.0	146	—	90.7
10	Gloucestershire	91.8	91.0	20.6	116	91.7	90.5
11	Heriot-Watt	62.3	62.8	38.1	172	89.7	89.0
12	Liverpool	82.4	83.7	26.3	129	—	88.2
13	Ulster	94.5	89.9	28.6	114	70.2	87.5
=14	Newcastle	72.3	72.6	43.7	124	85.7	87.3
=14	West of England	85.1	86.6	10.6	119	91.4	87.3
16	Dundee	84.5	76.3	8.7	—	85.2*	87.2
17	Manchester	71.3	75.3	36.5	145	74.1	86.1
18	Glasgow Caledonian	67.9	70.9	9.1	172	80.6	84.7
19	Birmingham City	86.2	76.5	2.7	106	77.8	81.0
20	Leeds Beckett	86.5	86.5	5.6	105	68.8	80.7
21	Manchester Metropolitan	76.2	71.3	9.7	—	75.0*	80.6
22	Oxford Brookes	71.2	69.0	17.6	117	76.9	80.2
23	Westminster	83.3	82.4	10.7	133	50.0	79.2
24	Greenwich	73.3	70.9	2.0	—	66.7	75.8

Employed in professional job	58%	Employed in non-professional job and Studying	2%
Employed in professional job and studying	6%	Employed in non-professional job	11%
Studying	16%	Unemployed	8%
Average starting professional salary	£23,000	Average starting non-professional salary	£17,000

Veterinary Medicine

Only medicine itself has higher entry standards than veterinary medicine, where successful candidates had an average of almost 200 points on the UCAS tariff in 2017. However, after the fourth successive drop in applications, at all but one of the seven veterinary schools in our table (the Royal Veterinary College) this represented a fall in average entry grades compared with the previous year. The number of applications per place was down to little more than six, compared with nine in 2013. An eighth veterinary school opened that year, at the University of Surrey, but there is still insufficient data to include it in this table.

The number of places in veterinary medicine is centrally controlled. Most courses demand high grades in chemistry and biology, with some accepting physics or maths as one alternative subject. Cambridge and the Royal Veterinary College also set applicants a specialist aptitude test that is used by a number of medical schools. Few candidates win places without evidence of practical commitment to the subject through work experience, either in veterinary practices or laboratories. The norm for veterinary science degrees is five years, but the Cambridge course takes six years and both Bristol and Nottingham offer a "gateway" year. Edinburgh and the Royal Veterinary College (RVC) also run four-year courses for graduates. There are no degrees in the subject in Wales or Northern Ireland, or in the post-1992 universities, although a number of them and several colleges offer veterinary nursing.

Edinburgh and Glasgow have retained first and second positions in the subject table, with the RVC rising two places to third. Glasgow has the highest entry grades, but Edinburgh performed best in the Research Excellence Framework. Nottingham, in fifth place, again has much the most satisfied students both for the quality of teaching and the broader student experience.

Veterinary medicine is another of the rankings in which employment scores have been removed from the calculations that determine universities' positions. The scores are still shown in the table, but the review group of academic planners consulted on the *Guide* agreed that employment rates in the subject were so tightly bunched that small differences could distort the overall ranking. Veterinary medicine is in the top three subjects for earnings in professional jobs and fourth in this year's employment table.

Veterinary Medicine	Teaching quality %	Student experience %	Research quality %	Entry standards (UCAS points)	Graduate prospects %	Overall score
1 Edinburgh	89.2	85.3	46.8	205	96.1	100.0
2 Glasgow	87.8	82.3	42.3	221	99.2	99.5
3 Royal Veterinary College	84.7	83.9	40.8	191	99.0	92.3
4 Cambridge	66.5*	63.2*	43.1	214	95.7	91.4
5 Nottingham	96.3	95.1	36.4	178	98.1	91.0
6 Liverpool	—	—	32.9	174	98.2	86.0
7 Bristol	80.2	83.1	33.2	187	98.1	85.6

Employed in professional job	94%	Employed in non-professional job and Studying	0%
Employed in professional job and studying	0%	Employed in non-professional job	1%
Studying	2%	Unemployed	3%
Average starting professional salary	£30,000	Average starting non-professional salary	n/a

14 Applying to Oxbridge

Oxbridge (as Oxford and Cambridge are called) not only dominates UK higher education; the two universities are recognised as among the best in the world – the top two, according to the Times Higher Education global ranking. But that is not why they merit a separate chapter in this *Guide*.

The two ancient universities have different admissions arrangements from the rest of the higher education system. Although part of the UCAS network, the deadline for applications is three months earlier than for other universities, you can only apply to one or the other, and selection is in the hands of the colleges rather than the university centrally. Most candidates apply to a specific college, although you can make an open application if you are happy to go anywhere.

There have been reforms to the admissions system at both universities in recent years, in order to make the process more user-friendly to those who do not have school or family experience to draw upon. Most significantly, Cambridge has reintroduced 'pre-interview written assessments' in most subjects, with tests on the day of interview in the rest. Both universities have also changed the way applicants are matched to colleges. Candidates are now distributed around colleges more efficiently, regardless of the choices they make initially.

There is little to choose between the two universities in terms of entrance requirements, although Cambridge's are generally slightly higher, and a formidable number of successful (and even unsuccessful) applicants have the maximum possible grades. However, that does not mean that the talented student should be shy about applying: both have fewer applicants per place than many less prestigious universities, and admissions tutors are always looking to extend the range of schools and colleges from which they recruit. For those with a realistic chance of success, there is little to lose except the possibility of one wasted space out of five on the UCAS application.

Most successful candidates do not regret their choice. Research by the Higher Education Policy Unit found that Oxbridge students were more satisfied than those at other Russell Group universities. Three-quarters, compared with less than half elsewhere, felt that their course provided good value for money. They worked harder and received better and more timely feedback from academics.

Overall, there are about five applicants to every place at Cambridge and six at Oxford, but there are big differences between subjects and colleges. As the tables in this chapter show, competition is particularly fierce in subjects such as medicine and law, but those qualified to read earth sciences or modern languages have a much better chance of success. The pattern is similar to that in other universities, although the high degree of selection (and self-selection) that precedes an Oxbridge application means that, even in the less popular subjects, the field of candidates is certain to be strong.

Both have done their best to live down their socially exclusive image, but many sixth-formers still fear that they would be out of their depth at Oxbridge, socially as well as academically. In fact, the state sector produces about 60% of entrants to Oxford and Cambridge – albeit only 40% from non-selective schools – and the dropout rate is lower than at almost any other university. The 'champagne set' is still present and its activities are well publicised, but most students are hard-working, high achievers with the same concerns as their counterparts on other campuses.

Diversity

Both universities and their student organisations have put a great deal of effort into trying to encourage applications from state schools, and many colleges have launched their own campaigns. But the two universities finished bottom of our new widening participation table and their admissions figures remain controversial. Six of Cambridge's colleges admitted fewer than ten black British students between 2012-16, while a quarter of Oxford's colleges failed to admit even one such student in three years.

Some colleges set relatively low standard offers to encourage applicants from the state sector who may reveal their potential at interview. Some admissions tutors will give the edge to well-qualified candidates from comprehensive schools over those from highly academic independent schools because they consider the former to have made a greater achievement in the circumstances. Others stick with tried and trusted sources of good students. The independent sector still enjoys a degree of success out of proportion to its share of the school population.

Cambridge: The Tompkins Table 2018

College	2018	2017	2016	College	2018	2017	2016
Christ's	1	2	3	Clare	16	13	18
Pembroke	2	4	2	Sidney Sussex	17	17	16
Trinity	3	1	1	Magdalene	18	16	9
Peterhouse	4	10	8	Fitzwilliam	19	21	23
King's	5	8	14	Downing	20	20	12
Jesus	6	14	7	St Edmund's	21	22	28
Churchill	7	5	11	Newnham	22	23	21
St John's	8	3	5	Girton	23	24	27
Emmanuel	9	6	4	Robinson	24	25	22
St Catharine's	10	19	17	Hughes Hall	25	26	29
Selwyn	11	9	15	Murray Edwards	26	29	25
Trinity Hall	12	15	13	Homerton	27	28	24
Queens'	13	7	6	Lucy Cavendish	28	18	26
Gonville & Caius	14	11	19	Wolfson	29	27	20
Corpus Christi	15	12	10				

Choosing the right college

Simply in terms of winning a place at Oxford or Cambridge, choosing the right college is not quite as important as it used to be. Both universities have got better at assessing candidates' strengths and finding a suitable college for those who either make an open application or are not taken by their first-choice college. At Oxford, subject tutors from around the university put candidates into bands at the start of the selection process, using the results of admissions tests as well as exam results and references. Applicants are spread around the colleges for interview and may not be seen by their preferred college if the tutors think their chances of a place are better elsewhere. More than a quarter of successful candidates are offered places by a college other than the one to which they applied.

Cambridge relies on the 'pool', which gives the most promising candidates a second chance if they were not offered a place at the college to which they applied. Those placed in the pool are invited back for a second round of interviews early in the New Year. The system lowers the stakes for those who apply to the most selective colleges – typically around 20% of offers come via the pool. Cambridge still interviews more than 80% of applicants, whereas the system at Oxford has resulted in more immediate rejections in some subjects. Overall around 60% of Oxford applicants are interviewed, but there is great variation by subject.

Most Oxbridge applicants still apply direct to a particular college, however, not only to maximise their chances of getting in, but because that is where they will be living and socialising, as well as learning. Most colleges may look the same to the uninitiated, but there are important differences. Famously sporty colleges, for example, can be trying for those in search of peace and quiet.

Thorough research is needed to find the right place. Even within colleges, different admissions tutors may have different approaches, so personal contact is essential. The tables in this chapter give an idea of the relative academic strengths of the colleges, as well as the varying levels of competition for a place in different subjects. But only individual research will suggest

Oxford: The Norrington Table 2018

College	2018	2017	2016	College	2018	2017	2016
St John's	1	6	12	St Peter's	16	29	28
Magdalen	2	11	3	University	17	8	4
St Catherine's	3	26	10	Exeter	18	25	25
Merton	4	2	1	Queen's	19	5	30
New College	5	1	18	Mansfield	20	15	29
Jesus	6	18	14	Lady Margaret Hall	21	14	23
Brasenose	7	7	7	Somerville	22	23	16
Wadham	8	13	6	Keble	23	12	17
Balliol	9	10	8	St Anne's	24	19	26
Trinity	10	9	5	Pembroke	25	3	13
Christ Church	11	17	24	Lincoln	26	30	19
Oriel	12	20	2	Hertford	27	22	20
St Hilda's	=13	28	27	St Hugh's	28	21	22
Worcester	=13	4	9	St Edmund Hall	29	24	21
Corpus Christi	15	16	15	Harris Manchester	30	27	11

Oxford applications and acceptances by course

Arts	Applications			Acceptances			Acceptances to Applications %		
	2017	2016	2015	2017	2016	2015	2017	2016	2015
Ancient and modern history	104	92	77	23	22	18	22	24	23
Archaeology and anthropology	94	97	93	19	18	27	20	19	29
Classical archaeology and ancient history	85	108	79	22	19	20	26	18	25
Classics	293	325	291	116	121	111	40	37	38
Classics and English	37	40	42	13	8	11	35	20	26
Classics and modern languages	28	26	24	7	6	6	28	23	40
Computer science and philosophy	82	75	45	14	10	5	17	13	11
Economics and management	1,317	1,116	1,127	80	83	87	6	7	8
English	938	1,025	1,044	224	235	227	24	23	22
English and modern Languages	85	100	128	20	17	24	24	17	19
European and Middle Eastern languages	63	39	41	16	11	17	25	28	42
Fine art	246	251	255	28	27	28	11	11	11
Geography	405	347	321	77	70	82	19	20	26
History	971	1,003	1,004	214	227	237	22	23	24
History and economics	121	130	114	16	15	13	13	12	11
History and English	89	81	72	16	11	9	18	14	13
History and modern languages	109	109	87	28	24	18	26	22	21
History and politics	417	355	317	52	45	41	12	13	13
History of art	126	123	137	14	14	14	11	11	10
Law	1,501	1,403	1,298	192	211	195	13	15	15
Law with law studies in Europe	278	269	279	28	25	31	10	9	11
Mathematics and philosophy	108	111	100	16	18	14	15	16	14
Modern languages	436	483	491	159	159	173	36	33	35
Modern languages and linguistics	74	90	70	26	29	23	35	32	33
Music	175	188	195	69	71	72	39	38	37
Oriental studies	155	167	163	44	44	40	28	26	25
Philosophy and modern languages	48	61	60	17	17	17	35	28	28
Philosophy and theology	141	129	103	32	29	23	23	22	22
Physics and philosophy	131	108	104	13	12	16	10	11	15
Philosophy, politics and economics (PPE)	1,983	1,820	1,691	249	248	239	13	14	14
Theology	99	93	117	30	31	35	30	33	30
Theology and oriental studies	8	9	3	2	3	2	25	33	66
Total Arts	**10,747**	**10,373**	**9,972**	**1,876**	**1,880**	**1,875**	**17.4**	**20.8**	**18.6**

where you will feel most at home. For example, women may favour one of the few remaining single-sex colleges (Murray Edwards, Newnham and Lucy Cavendish at Cambridge). Men have no such option.

The ranking of colleges in the Tompkins Table (see page 282) is not officially endorsed by

Oxford applications and acceptances by course cont

Sciences	Applications			Acceptances			Acceptances to Applications %		
	2017	2016	2015	2017	2016	2015	2017	2016	2015
Biochemistry	731	558	511	108	103	98	15	18	19
Biological sciences	568	512	541	113	114	114	20	22	21
Biomedical sciences	370	339	266	37	39	31	10	12	12
Chemistry	601	659	750	184	174	189	31	26	25
Computer science	427	384	335	36	27	30	8	7	9
Earth sciences (Geology)	122	92	110	31	31	31	25	34	28
Engineering sciences	904	890	1,029	170	177	154	19	20	15
Experimental psychology	295	251	257	51	49	51	17	20	20
Human science	185	177	254	30	28	27	16	16	11
Materials science (including MEM)	167	155	145	31	35	32	19	23	22
Mathematics	1,371	1,333	1,145	185	189	176	13	14	15
Mathematics and computer science	306	226	199	33	28	29	11	12	10
Mathematics and statistics	190	210	229	13	17	16	7	8	7
Medicine	1,544	1,675	1,375	152	154	146	10	9	11
Physics	1,231	1,124	1,064	178	186	184	15	17	17
Psychology and philosophy (PPL)	189	186	195	42	30	33	22	16	17
Total Sciences	**9,191**	**8,771**	**8,405**	**1,394**	**1,381**	**1,341**	**15.1**	**17.1**	**16.0**
Total Arts and Sciences	**19,938**	**19,144**	**18,377**	**3,270**	**3,261**	**3,216**	**16.4**	**18.9**	**17.5**

Cambridge University, but Oxford University now produces the Norrington Table (see page 283). Sanctioned or not, both tables give an indication of where the academic powerhouses lie – information which can be as useful to those trying to avoid them as to those seeking the ultimate challenge. Although there can be a great deal of movement year by year, both tables tend to be dominated by the rich, old foundations. Both tables are compiled from the degree results of final-year undergraduates. A first is worth five points; a 2:1, three; a 2:2, two; a third, one point. The total is divided by the number of candidates to produce each college's average.

In both universities, teaching for most students is based in the colleges. In practice, however, in the sciences this arrangement holds good only for the first year. One-to-one tutorials, which are Oxbridge's traditional strength for undergraduates, are by no means universal. Teaching groups remain much smaller than in most universities, and the tutor remains an inspiration for many students.

The applications procedure
Both universities will have a UCAS deadline of 15 October 2019 (at 6pm) for entry in 2020 or deferred entry in 2021. For Cambridge, you may then take admissions tests at the beginning of November at your school or college, or other authorised centre, while other subjects will continue to administer tests when you attend for interview. The Cambridge website lists the

Cambridge applications and acceptances by course

Arts, Humanities and Social Sciences	Applications			Acceptances			Acceptances to Applications %		
	2017	2016	2015	2017	2016	2015	2017	2016	2015
Anglo-Saxon, Norse and Celtic	49	65	59	19	21	20	38.8	32.3	33.9
Archaeology	56	–	–	26	–	–	46.4	–	–
Architecture	430	360	384	37	44	49	8.6	12.2	12.8
Asian and Middle Eastern studies	114	121	121	32	38	43	28.1	31.4	35.5
Classics	172	146	136	84	78	74	48.8	53.4	54.4
Classics (4 years)	50	32	45	18	11	15	36.0	34.4	33.3
Economics	1,005	1,183	1,136	155	164	160	15.4	13.9	14.1
Education	95	105	80	34	31	31	35.8	29.5	38.8
English	763	726	714	212	190	197	27.8	26.2	27.6
Geography	324	322	345	90	97	108	27.8	30.1	31.3
History	591	607	625	181	199	197	30.6	32.8	31.5
History and Mod Lang	77	–	–	20	–	–	26.0	–	–
History and Politics	195	–	–	40	–	–	20.5	–	–
History of art	109	102	101	23	26	23	21.1	25.5	22.8
Human, social and political sciences	932	1,070	1,012	166	182	208	17.8	17.0	20.6
Land economy	276	248	246	56	56	50	20.3	22.6	20.3
Law	1,161	1,048	1,015	219	217	208	18.9	20.7	20.5
Linguistics	96	113	88	33	38	27	34.4	33.6	30.7
Modern and medieval languages	404	385	387	180	176	173	44.6	45.7	44.7
Music	136	130	151	65	61	63	47.8	46.9	41.7
Philosophy	270	200	203	45	48	46	16.7	24.0	22.7
Theology and religious studies	91	100	87	39	43	41	42.9	43.0	47.1
Total Arts, Humanities and Social Sciences	**7,396**	**7,063**	**6,935**	**1,774**	**1,720**	**1,733**	**24.0**	**24.4**	**25.0**

Sciences	2017	2016	2015	2017	2016	2015	2017	2016	2015
Computer science	867	719	642	105	99	91	12.1	13.8	14.0
Engineering	2,296	2,351	2,089	334	337	312	14.5	14.3	14.9
Mathematics	1,456	1,312	1,308	257	256	247	17.7	19.5	18.9
Medical sciences	1,341	1,274	1,300	257	269	265	19.2	21.1	20.4
Natural sciences	2,809	2,943	3,036	629	618	652	22.4	21.0	21.5
Psych and behavioural sciences	379	497	392	59	75	61	15.6	15.1	16.0
Veterinary medicine	248	228	251	59	60	64	23.8	26.3	26.0
Total Science and Technology	**9,396**	**9,687**	**9,018**	**1,700**	**1,737**	**1,692**	**18.1**	**17.9**	**18.1**
Total	**16,792**	**16,750**	**15,953**	**3,474**	**3,457**	**3,425**	**20.7**	**20.6**	**21.5**

Note: the dates refer to the year in which the acceptances were made.
Mathematics includes mathematics and mathematics with physics. Medical sciences includes medicine but does not include the graduate course in medicine.

subjects setting the pre-interview assessments, which may include reading comprehension, problem-solving test, or thinking skills assessment, in addition to a paper on the subject itself. At Oxford, a number of subjects (but not all) also require applicants to take a written test, either before or at the time of interview. In addition, once Cambridge receives your UCAS form, you will be asked to complete an online Supplementary Application Questionnaire (SAQ) by 22 October in most cases. For international applications to Cambridge, you must also submit a Cambridge Online Preliminary Application (COPA), by 20 September or 15 October, depending on where interviews are held; check the Cambridge website for full details.

You may apply to either Oxford or Cambridge, but not both in the same admissions year, unless you are seeking an Organ award at both universities. Interviews take place in December for those short-listed (for international applicants, Cambridge holds some interviews overseas while Oxford holds some interviews over the internet, though medicine interviewees must come to Oxford, as must EU interviewees). Applicants will receive either a conditional offer or a rejection early in the new year.

For more information about the application process and preparation for interviews, visit **www.undergraduate.study.cam.ac.uk/** or **www.ox.ac.uk/admissions/undergraduate**.

Oxford College Profiles

Balliol

Oxford OX1 3BJ   01865 277758   www.balliol.ox.ac.uk
Undergraduates: 380   Postgraduates: 295   undergraduate@balliol.ox.ac.uk

Balliol is one of the oldest and most academic colleges at the university, usually featuring in the top ten of the Norrington Table. Last year it ranked ninth. Famous as the alma mater of many prominent post-war politicians, and more recently of former Foreign Secretary, Boris Johnson, Balliol has maintained a strong presence in university life and is usually well represented in the Union and most other societies. Balliol students recently voted unanimously to establish a scholarship for a student with refugee status. The college has surprisingly spacious grounds for its Broad Street location, with the occasional concrete block nestled in among the elegant traditional buildings. It has an impressive medieval library, which allows students 24-hour access to over 70,000 books and periodicals. Balliol has cultivated an attractively cosmopolitan atmosphere with a thriving music and drama scene. It is also one of the few colleges with a fully functional theatre, the Michael Pilch Studio. Undergraduates are offered guaranteed accommodation in college for their first and final years. Graduate students are usually lodged in beautiful Holywell Manor, a ten-minute walk from the main site. Hall food is of good quality and comparatively cheap, and the JCR has its own student-run café, Pantry. The student-run bar, one of the cheapest in Oxford, is home to the 'Balliol Blue' cocktail, which is infamous with students across the university.

Brasenose

Oxford OX1 4AJ   01865 277510 (admissions)   www.bnc.ox.ac.uk
Undergraduates: 365   Postgraduates: 242   admissions@bnc.ox.ac.uk

Nestled beside the Radcliffe Camera, Brasenose has an advantageous city-centre position. The alma mater of David Cameron, the college was one of the first to admit women in the 1970s, and now has a near-even split. At 'BNC', as the college is often known, sport isn't taken too seriously and is usually more about participation, for instance with its annual sports day between staff and students. Diversity is also a recent focus, with Brasenose celebrating cultural events like St. David's Day & Holi and putting up portraiture of BME, LGBTQ+ and female alumni. Named after the door knocker on the 13th-century Brasenose Hall, the college has a pleasant, intimate atmosphere conducive to study and maintained its high place on the Norrington Table this year, placing seventh. Law, PPE, and History are traditional strengths, and the recently renovated library is open 24-hours – there is also a separate law library. The annexe at Frewin Court near the Oxford Union means nearly all undergraduates can live in college rooms, and postgraduates are offered accommodation at the St Cross Hollybush Row sites. Student welfare is well supported: Brasenose regularly falls at the top end of student satisfaction surveys, with morale-boosting college counsellors and yoga classes on offer, amongst other activities.

Christ Church

Oxford OX1 1DP   01865 276196 (admissions)   www.chch.ox.ac.uk
Undergraduates: 432   Postgraduates: 196   admissions.officer@chch.ox.ac.uk

The college, founded by Cardinal Wolsey in 1525, boasts the largest quad in Oxford, complete with an ornamental pond full of koi carp, donated by the Empress of Japan. Its imposing buildings attract near-permanent crowds of visiting tourists, and stern bowler-hatted porters guard the doors, setting the tone of 'ChCh' as one of the most academic, traditional colleges in Oxford. Around half of offers tend to be made to state school pupils, which leaves Christ Church with one of the higher proportions of private school students. The 18th-century library is palatial (although it is a listed building, and therefore not open 24 hours a day) and is supplemented by a separate law library. Accommodation, provided for all three years, is rated by students as excellent and includes flats off Iffley Road, as well as a number of wood-panelled shared sets (double rooms), and more modern rooms in the college's Blue Boar quad. 'Oxmas', when the college places huge Christmas trees in the quads, is a highlight. A three-course dinner in the famous 'Hogwarts' hall costs less than £3, providing exceptional value. The college has a formal approach to dining, with informal and formal sittings taking place every night, and twice-termly Guest Dinners. Christ Church's chapel is the cathedral of the Diocese of Oxford, and the college backs onto the enchanting Christ Church Meadows, filled variously with walkers, college rowing teams, and a herd of English Longhorn cows.

Corpus Christi

Oxford OX1 4JF   01865 276693 (admissions)   www.ccc.ox.ac.uk
Undergraduates: 249   Postgraduates: 100   admissions.office@ccc.ox.ac.uk

Corpus is one of Oxford's smallest colleges, giving it a tight-knit support network. It is naturally overshadowed by its gigantic neighbour, Christ Church, but makes the most of its intimate, friendly atmosphere and exquisite beauty. Although the college has only around 350 students including postgraduates, it has an admirable 24-hour library, and its original 16th century library is still in use. Academic expectations are high and English, Classics, PPE and Medicine are especially well-established. Corpus can offer accommodation to all its undergraduates, one of its many attractions to those seeking a smaller community in Oxford. Because of the college's small size, sports teams usually pair up with other colleges. The college is also one of the most generous with bursaries, giving travel, book and vacation grants at an almost unparalleled level across the university. The MBI Al-Jaber Auditorium is a large, modern and pleasant space built into a bastion of the medieval city wall and is used for music and drama, as well as for parties, art exhibitions and film screenings. Corpus's drama club, 'The Owlets', is highly regarded in Oxford. The college hosts an annual charity 'Tortoise Fair' every summer, where around 1500 people come to hear live music and watch the famous inter-college tortoise race.

Exeter

Oxford OX1 3DP   01865 279661 (academic secretary)   www.exeter.ox.ac.uk
Undergraduates: 334   Postgraduates: 212   admissions@exeter.ox.ac.uk

Exeter boasts one of the most spectacular views of the city from its Fellows' Garden, overlooking Radcliffe Square and All Souls' College. Nestled between the High Street and Broad Street, Exeter is right in the heart of town. Most undergraduates are guaranteed three years of college accommodation, although many second-year students currently live out. The rooms are graded in price, but tend to be of good standard. The Cohen Quad development, located offsite on Walton Street, opened last year and provides a further 90 ensuite bedrooms in a stunning state-of-the-art building. Exeter students are known to be lively and outspoken, and the student-run charity, ExVac, is a big part of the JCR's identity. Notable alumni include Edward Burne-Jones and Phillip Pullman. The college also boasts a number of other societies. The John Ford Society exists to fund dramatic ventures; the Fortescue Society to talk about the law; the PPE Society to bring in high-profile speakers. The annual arts festival, in partnership with neighbours Lincoln and Jesus, brings a week of live music, theatre and poetry to Turl Street during Hilary Term.

Harris Manchester

Oxford OX1 3TD   01865 271009 (admissions)   www.hmc.ox.ac.uk
Undergraduates: 108   Postgraduates: 145   admissions@hmc.ox.ac.uk

As the university's only college for mature students (21 or older), Harris Manchester can seem a little distant from the undergraduate community. Students are proud, however, of its close-knit, friendly atmosphere. Founded in Manchester in 1786 to provide education for non-Anglican students, Harris Manchester finally settled in Oxford in 1889 after spells in both York and London. A full college since 1996, its central location with fine buildings and grounds in Holywell Street is very convenient for the Bodleian, and the college also has an excellent library with the best student-to-book ratio in the university. The college also offers a number of grants of up to £18,500 for second undergraduate degrees. Due to its small size, Harris Manchester offers a more limited number of degree courses, and has fewer clubs and societies than other colleges. Students are rarely left wanting though, as they can often join larger colleges' clubs. All college accommodation is on the main site and rooms are available for the first and final year. Graduate accommodation is awarded by ballot, and there is no accommodation for couples or families. Food is included in the college fees, which means self-catering is not an option, but its food is excellent, if expensive. The college has renovated most of its accommodation on the main site and a new building opened in 2017, providing a further eight ensuite student rooms, a lecture hall, new music practice rooms and a gym.

Hertford

Oxford OX1 3BW   01865 279404 (admissions)   www.hertford.ox.ac.uk
Undergraduates: 414   Postgraduates: 293   undergraduate.admissions@
                                                       hertford.ox.ac.uk

Though tracing its roots to the 13th century, Hertford is determinedly modern. The college was one of the first to admit women and is popular with state school applicants, thanks to its strong commitment to access. Hertford offers a £1000 bursary to students from low income families and was the first college to become a living wage employer, further cementing its progressive reputation. The Principal, Will Hutton, a former editor of The Observer, has helped foster a dynamic atmosphere since his appointment in 2011. His popular panel discussions draw large audiences and focus on a range of topical issues. Past events include a discussion on the Leveson inquiry with Hugh Grant. The college can lodge undergraduates for the entire course of their study. All first years live in the main college site, with its iconic Bridge of Sighs and its proximity to popular pubs The Turf Tavern and The King's Arms. Second and third years live in Abingdon House and Warnock House annexe near Folly Bridge. Music is very strong at Hertford, with a Jazz Band, Wind Band, Choir and Orchestra. Hertford has a fun reputation, hosting regular bops (college parties) at the gay club Plush. Open mic nights and lunchtime recitals are popular. The quality of food in hall is variable, with street food pop-ups a recent feature.

Jesus

Oxford OX1 3DW   01865 279721 (admissions)   www.jesus.ox.ac.uk
Undergraduates: 346   Postgraduates: 198   admissions.officer@jesus.ox.ac.uk

Alma mater to T.E. Lawrence and Harold Wilson, Jesus consistently ranks highly for student satisfaction. It is known for being one of the friendliest colleges. Founded by Elizabeth I at the request of a Welsh churchman in 1571, the college continues to maintain strong links with the country. Welsh students form 15% of the student body, the college runs a summer school for Welsh students, and chalk drawings of Welsh dragons sit proudly at the entrances to staircases in Second Quad. Tucked away on a small site off Turl Street, Jesus houses a 24-hour library, music rooms, and a bar. Off site, the college has squash courts and extensive playing fields with hockey, cricket, football and rugby pitches, grass tennis courts, netball courts, a boathouse, and a sports pavilion. The college also has an orchestra shared with St Peter's, and a non-selective choir. Accommodation is almost universally excellent and relatively inexpensive. Self-catering flats in north and east Oxford have enabled every graduate to live in throughout his or her Oxford career. The college offers a number of generous bursaries and grants, including a book grant and a vacation grant. Jesus holds a shared ball with Somerville every three years, with the next in 2019.

Keble

Oxford OX1 3PG   01865 272708 (admissions)   www.keble.ox.ac.uk
Undergraduates: 425   Postgraduates: 330   admissions@keble.ox.ac.uk

Keble is one of Oxford's most distinctive colleges, built of brick in unmistakably extravagant Victorian Gothic style. Its main quad has been likened to a castle – and to lasagne. With over 400 undergraduates and 330 full-time graduates, it is one of the biggest colleges in Oxford, and with guaranteed accommodation for undergraduates for three years, its vibrant community spirit provides Keble students with a coveted social life. Thanks to a £25 million grant, the largest donation in Keble's history, the new H B Allen Centre is now home to the first of 230 graduate students – doubling the previous capacity. The site will also boast a 120-seat lecture theatre and an exhibition space. The college's sporting record remains exemplary, with rugby and rowing traditional strengths. The men's first team won the Summer Eights river headship in 2018, and the topic of celebratory boat-burning stoked fierce debate in the JCR. The college also has a thriving music society and is a hub for university drama, with its O'Reilly Theatre and its Arts Week every Hilary term. English is a particular strong suit in this arts-supporting college. The college hall, where students wear gowns three nights a week, is one of the most impressive in the university, and the Keble Cafe in the O'Reilly Theatre building is perfect for socialising and study. The annual Keble Ball is one of the most popular and best value black tie events in Oxford, selling out in minutes every year. Keble is usually ranked around the middle of the Norrington Table, although it dropped to 23rd place last year.

Lady Margaret Hall

Oxford OX2 6QA   01865 274310 (admissions)   www.lmh.ox.ac.uk
Undergraduates: 401   Postgraduates: 210   admissions@lmh.ox.ac.uk

Lady Margaret Hall, Oxford's first college for women, has been co-educational since 1978 and now enjoys an equal gender balance. For many students, LMH's comparative isolation – the college is three-quarters of a mile north of the city centre – is a real advantage, providing spacious and green grounds and welcome refuge from tourists. For others it means a long journey to central facilities. The college's beautiful gardens back onto the Cherwell River, allowing LMH to have its own punt house and tennis courts. LMH also boasts a theatre and gym. It has a 24-hour library, with particularly strong collections in the arts and humanities and individual study booths prized among finalists seeking solitary working conditions. Accommodation is guaranteed for first, second and third-year students since the opening of the Pipe Partridge Building, which also houses a new JCR, dining hall and lecture theatre. The Clore Graduate centre and Donald Fothergill building, opened in 2016, provide just over 40 ensuite study bedrooms for graduate students. The recent appointment of former Guardian editor Alan Rusbridger as Principal has boosted the college's star power, and LMH's strong reputation in PPE is evident in its notable alumni and students – Benazir Bhutto, the former Prime Minister of Pakistan, and Nobel Peace Prize winner Malala Yousafzai.

Lincoln

Oxford OX1 3DR   01865 279836 (admissions)   www.lincoln.ox.ac.uk
Undergraduates: 304   Postgraduates: 300   admissions@lincoln.ox.ac.uk

Lincoln's ivy-covered medieval buildings and famous library (a converted Queen Anne church) combine to produce a delightful environment in which to spend three years. The college's relaxed atmosphere is justly celebrated and city-centre accommodation is provided for all undergraduates. Lincoln is known for having the best hall food in Oxford, and for the popular Deep Hall bar. Graduate students are housed a few minutes' walk away in Bear Lane, or at sites close to the science park and on Little Clarendon Street. Lincoln has one of the largest number of scholarships available for graduate students and rewards undergraduates who perform well in examinations. Its laid-back and friendly atmosphere is reflected in Lincoln's position on the Norrington Table – 26th out of 30 this year. The recently refurbished Garden Building is a stylish addition, providing much needed space for music practice, dining and teaching. The Oakeshott room is a popular venue for screenings and performances and hosted many of the shows in this year's Turl Street Arts Festival.

Magdalen

Oxford OX1 4AU   01865 276063 (admissions)   www.magd.ox.ac.uk
Undergraduates: 386   Postgraduates: 236   admissions@magd.ox.ac.uk

Perhaps the most beautiful Oxford college, Magdalen is known around the world for its tower, its deer park and its May Morning celebrations. C. S. Lewis is said to have dreamt up Narnia whilst on a walk around the awe-inspiring grounds. In recent years, the college has worked hard to shake off its public school image, with a recent exhibition in the hall celebrating its diversity. Undergraduates tend to be studious and competitive. The college consistently performs strongly in the Norrington Table, coming second this year, and has won University Challenge a record four times. In 2016, the Longwall library at Magdalen re-opened after a £10.5 million refurbishment, providing three times the number of reader spaces. First-year students are accommodated in the Waynflete Building and all undergraduates can be housed in college for the full length of their course. After three years of rent freezes, accommodation prices are now more level with other colleges than in the past. Over 25% of students receive some type of financial support during their studies, ranging from travel grants to funding for creative projects. The college has had a lot of sporting success on the river in recent years and punting from Magdalen's tourist-laden punt house is popular during the summer. Drama is strong, and the well-regarded Magdalen Players host a production in the gardens every summer.

Mansfield

Oxford OX1 3TF   01865 270920 (admissions)   www.mansfield.ox.ac.uk
Undergraduates: 235   Postgraduates: 168   admissions.officer@mansfield.ox.ac.uk

Formally becoming an Oxford college in 1995, Mansfield is fairly central, with its attractive Victorian buildings close to the science park, English faculty and social science library. Its proximity to the University Parks facilitates collegiate sporting enthusiasm. Taking less than 100 undergraduate students per year, the community is close-knit and the atmosphere relaxed. Mansfield has a strong representation of state school students – 88% of its undergraduate intake in 2017 – and many of its students are from black and ethnic minority communities. All undergraduates can live in college accommodation, either on-site or in an annexe in east Oxford. First-year postgraduates are also housed by the College in off-site accommodation. The College has four 24-hour libraries, an unusually high number. The JCR and Crypt Cafe are popular for socialising and casual study, as is the sun terrace during the summer months. The recently completed Hands building provides additional accommodation, a new lecture building and a home for the Law faculty's Bonavero Institute of Human Rights.

Merton

Oxford OX1 4JD   01865 286316 (admissions)   www.merton.ox.ac.uk
Undergraduates: 297   Postgraduates: 241   undergraduate.admissions@
                                                       merton.ox.ac.uk

Founded in 1264 by Walter de Merton, Bishop of Rochester and Chancellor of England, Merton is one of Oxford's oldest and most prestigious colleges. It has an enduring reputation for academic excellence – and a strict administration to go with it – reflected in its position usually at or near the top of the Norrington Table. After a surprise fall to 27th place three years ago, it is now in fourth place. The medieval library is the envy of other colleges, but surprisingly is not open 24 hours a day. Accommodation is some of the cheapest in the university, of good standard and offered for all three years. Merton's food is well-priced and among the best; formal hall is served six times a week. The college provides generous bursaries and grants to students, and has a free gym. Merton's many diversions include the Merton Floats, its dramatic society, the Bodley Club for literary speakers, and an excellent Winter Ball every three years. Its choir and the organ have an ever-growing reputation. The college recently established a scheme inviting local school girls to form a choir at the college, enabling them to participate in Merton's musical tradition.

New College

Oxford OX1 3BN   01865 279272 (admissions)   www.new.ox.ac.uk
Undergraduates: 416   Postgraduates: 357   admissions@new.ox.ac.uk

New College is very academic, topping the Norrington Table in 2017 and coming fifth last time. In spite of its name, the college is extremely old – founded in 1379 by William of Wykeham – large and much more relaxed than most expect behind its daunting facade. It is a bustling place, as proud of its excellent music and its bar as of its academic prestige. Musical students flourish here thanks to the choir, orchestra and chamber groups. There is a band room and a new music building on Mansfield Road is currently under construction. Traditionally poor at attracting state school students, the college has been making efforts to change this with its new 'Step Up' access initiative. All first, second and fourth-year students can live in college and most third years live out in private accommodation. Over 90% of the rooms are ensuite and many have recently been equipped for disabled access. New College boasts an enchanting common room and the gardens are a memorable sight, especially the other-worldly mound in the heart of the college. The grounds provide the perfect setting for the Commemoration Ball, held every three years, with the next in summer 2019. The college also hosts an annual boat party in London, which is popular with students from across the university. Students also benefit from summer access to the college chalet (shared with Balliol and University) near Mont Blanc. The college is currently planning a new tower, which has caused tension with neighbouring Mansfield College due to its height and location.

Oriel

Oxford OX1 4EW   01865 276522 (admissions)   www.oriel.ox.ac.uk
Undergraduates: 316   Postgraduates: 202   admissions@oriel.ox.ac.uk

Although it is nicknamed 'Toriel' due to the strong presence of its students in the Union and Conservative Association, Oriel is a friendly, centrally-located college. It is known for its unusual portico in the main quad – and more recently, for the controversial statue of Cecil Rhodes, which looks out onto the High Street. Behind this, however, are some impressive achievements. The college is traditionally described as having "a strong crew spirit", reflecting its traditions on the river; in the 2018 Torpids competition, Oriel achieved a rare Double Headship, with both the women's and men's crews coming Head of the River. Academically, the college usually falls at the top end of the Norrington Table, coming 12th for 2018. Oriel has a strong sporting reputation and, apart from the boathouse, facilities include an impressive sports ground, squash courts and multiple gyms. Meal and rent costs are some of the lowest in Oxford. Accommodation is variable, but is guaranteed for the duration of an undergraduate course and extensive (mainly graduate) accommodation is provided one mile away off the popular Cowley Road. Several flats have been completed recently, providing some limited facilities for couples. The annual Garden Play is a highlight of Trinity Term, with an active chapel choir and a visiting musician fleshing out their programme of cultural activities.

Pembroke

Oxford OX1 1DW   01865 276412 (admissions)   www.pmb.ox.ac.uk
Undergraduates: 366   Postgraduates: 238   admissions@pmb.ox.ac.uk

Tucked away off St Aldate's, Pembroke is a welcoming and inclusive community with a growing state school intake. Blending traditional and modern architecture, its relaxed atmosphere contrasts with its neighbour Christ Church. History is a traditionally strong subject, with several students winning university-wide prizes over the years. However, the college usually lingers towards the bottom end of the Norrington Table. Pembroke is able to accommodate all undergraduates after an elegant new quad was opened in April 2013, and the Sir Geoffrey Arthur Building on the river, ten minutes' walk away, offers excellent facilities. Students are active in drama and music and there is a Trinity term musical each year. The college often hosts talks and panels by high-profile media figures. Food is among the most expensive in Oxford and students living on-site must pre-pay for a minimum of six dinners a week at a rate of £315 per term. Rowing is strong, with Pembroke men and women traditionally performing well and several going on to represent the university crews.

Queen's

Oxford OX1 4AW   01865 279161   www.queens.ox.ac.uk
Undergraduates: 333   Postgraduates: 181   admissions@queens.ox.ac.uk

With its beautiful neo-Classical dome and bell-tower, Queen's is one of the more striking sights of the High Street. Its academic record is a little less striking, with a patchy performance on the Norrington Table. All Queen's students are offered accommodation throughout their degree, with first-years housed on the main site, and subsequent year groups housed in annexes around central Oxford. The main site is beautiful, and the facilities are excellent, with many of the rooms ensuite. The two refurbished squash courts are said to be the best in Oxford and the college has a gym, and a lecture theatre used for concerts and film screenings. The Upper Library is one of the finest reading rooms in Oxford, and the New Library was completed in 2017. Queen's provides generous book and travel grants, and has active sport, drama, and music societies. The Trinity Term garden play is a highlight of the calendar. Queen's is fully catered and therefore has limited kitchen access, but the food is reasonably priced. The beer cellar is one of the most popular in the university and the JCR facilities are better than average; the daily JCR afternoon tea is a must.

St Anne's

Oxford OX2 6HS   01865 274840 (admissions)   www.st-annes.ox.ac.uk
Undergraduates: 428   Postgraduates: 283   admissions@st-annes.ox.ac.uk

Occupying a spacious site in the north of the city, St Anne's makes up in community spirit what it lacks in sandstone grandeur. The ship-shaped dining hall, with its skylight and absence of portraits, serves up some of the best food in Oxford thanks to 'Chef of the Year', Ray Killick. The new library and academic centre on Woodstock Road is an impressive sight with 2000 books added to its shelves every year. The college coffee shop, STACS, is quaint and popular with students wanting to take a break. The college has recently had a strong presence in the university journalism scene. Its men's and women's football teams won tournaments last year. A 10-15 minute cycle from the Bodleian, accommodation is guaranteed to undergraduates for three years, and the college also operates an equalisation scheme, giving grants to students wishing to live out. Postgraduates are housed in Summertown, a five-minute cycle away. St Anne's students benefit from a number of internships, CV clinics and career workshops organised by the college. Usually placed in the bottom half of the Norrington Table, the college focuses on student welfare and support rather than rigorous competition and maintains a friendly atmosphere. It has the highest proportion of female undergraduates at 55%, and Tom Ilube, named the most influential British person of African-Caribbean origin in 2017, was elected as an advisory fellow.

St Catherine's

Oxford OX1 3UJ   01865 271703 (admissions)   www.stcatz.ox.ac.uk
Undergraduates: 502   Postgraduates: 442   admissions@stcatz.ox.ac.uk

St Catherine's strikes an immediate chord with those seeking to avoid the uniformity of some other colleges. Arne Jacobsen's modernist design for 'Catz', one of Oxford's youngest and largest undergraduate colleges, has attracted much attention for its spacious site (including a rare car park) and laid-back atmosphere. The student body describes itself as "Oxford without the stereotypes." Close to the Law, English and Social Science faculties, the university science park and the pleasantly rural Holywell Great Meadow, St Catherine's is a lot nearer to the city centre than it feels. The Wolfson library is open until midnight. Rooms are small but tend to be warmer than in other, more venerable, colleges, and are now available on site for first, second and third-year students. Catz has the largest bar in Oxford and their 'bops' are always very popular. There is an excellent theatre, as well as an on-site boathouse, gym and squash courts. Like many of the larger colleges, sporting success is high – the men's rugby team topped the league last year, with the women's football team also placing highly. The College has increased welfare support with a College Counsellor and the JCR has created a fund for transgender students in college. Six portraits of female college members have been commissioned and are due to be hung in the library's (currently all male) collection. The college is a hub for university drama and hosts the annual Cameron Mackintosh Chair of Contemporary Theatre, whose incumbents have included Arthur Miller, Claude-Michel Schönberg and Sir Ian McKellen. With around 500 such students currently, St Catherine's has the highest undergraduate population in Oxford.

St Edmund Hall

Oxford OX1 4AR   01865 279009 (admissions)   www.seh.ox.ac.uk
Undergraduates: 407   Postgraduates: 315   admissions@seh.ox.ac.uk

Dating back to the 13th century, St Edmund Hall – 'Teddy Hall' – has one of Oxford's smallest college sites but one of its most populous. The college offers all first year undergraduates accommodation in its medieval quads a stone's throw from the Bodleian. The sporting culture is vigorous, with the men's rugby and basketball teams securing victory in last year's Cuppers tournaments. It is also becoming increasingly known for creative writing, with a Writer in Residence, annual journalism prizes, weekly student-run writers' workshops and an annual publication. High-achieving students can apply to the Masterclass Fund for up to £1000 per year to fund advanced coaching in their area of interest. Academically, Teddy Hall tends to yo-yo between the middle and the bottom of the Norrington Table. Last year, it came in 29th out of 30 colleges. Accommodation is offered for two years for undergraduates and there is an annexe at Norham Gardens, close to the University Parks. The food is more expensive than most colleges but the quality is very high.

St Hilda's

Oxford OX4 1DY   01865 286620 (admissions)   www.st-hildas.ox.ac.uk
Undergraduates: 398   Postgraduates: 181   admissions@st-hildas.ox.ac.uk

Although the college, founded in 1893, lasted more than 100 years as an all-female institution, the governing body voted in 2006 to admit men. There are now equal numbers of males and females. The college prides itself on its commitment to fostering an inclusive and laid-back atmosphere, introducing the post of Class Liberation Officer to support working class students. The college is on the rise academically, jumping from 28th to 13th place last year.

Like the other originally female colleges, St Hilda's boasts an impressive library, which is particularly well stocked for English. The college has beautiful riverside gardens, allowing students to go punting from the college site, and is close to the lively social scene of hip Cowley Road. Some visitors mistake the college for the Magdalen School, which is next door, and there are more teenagers in the area than around other colleges. St. Hilda's has a purpose-built music building and recording studio, and the drama society puts on termly plays in the college theatre. Accommodation is guaranteed to first years and finalists, and the common room and student-run bar have been renovated and enlarged. Rooms offer some of the best river views in Oxford, with the city's spires as a backdrop. St. Hilda's is known for its liberal leanings, its spacious, light-filled buildings, and its annual ball, which prides itself on being the most affordable in Oxford.

St Hugh's

Oxford OX2 6LE   01865 274910 (admissions)   www.st-hughs.ox.ac.uk
Undergraduates: 424   Postgraduates: 435   admissions@st-hughs.ox.ac.uk

St Hugh's, alma mater of Prime Minister Theresa May, is well-liked for its relaxed atmosphere and spacious grounds. Originally founded to admit only women, St Hugh's was criticised by students in 1986 when it began admitting men, but there is now an equal male/female ratio and it has a large student body. It is a bicycle ride from the city centre, or a manageable 25-30 minutes on foot, although this is far enough to make it the butt of student jokes about its distance from town. It is an ideal college for those seeking a place to live and study away from the madding crowd, and its gardens provide the perfect backdrop for the springtime outdoor cinema. Despite having one of the biggest and best libraries, open 24 hours, academic pressure remains comparatively low. St Hugh's guarantees on-site accommodation to undergraduates for the duration of their degree, although the standard of rooms is variable. The quality of food is high, with themed formal dinners on special occasions, and meals are subsidised. The college also boasts an on-site café and a comfortable JCR. The Dickson Poon Building, a recently constructed Chinese studies centre, provides an additional place to work and socialise. The college enjoys extensive grounds and there is space for a croquet lawn and tennis courts, as well as areas for Frisbee and football.

St John's

Oxford OX1 3JP   01865 277317 (admissions)   www.sjc.ox.ac.uk
Undergraduates: 397   Postgraduates: 241   admissions@sjc.ox.ac.uk

St John's is one of Oxford's powerhouses in academics, sport, and student life, excelling in almost every field and boasting arguably the most beautiful gardens in the university. Founded in 1555 by a London merchant, it is Oxford's wealthiest college by some distance, and makes the most of its resources by providing guaranteed college accommodation at a subsidised rate for all its undergraduates as well as generous book grants and prizes. The St John's Discount Scheme, which gives students discounts at many Oxford shops and eateries, is the envy of other colleges. St John's topped the Norrington Table last year, and is located on a large, quiet site off the attractive St Giles'. Modernist architecture proliferates more than would be expected, tucked away behind the imposing front quads, and most students are housed in these blocks. Academic standards are high, and students benefit from the impressive library and recently renovated study spaces and attached café. The college has a strong sporting tradition with a particular strength in women's rowing, as well as a chapel choir, drama society and orchestra. As befits such an all-round strong college, entry is fiercely competitive.

St Peter's

Oxford OX1 2DL   01865 278863 (admissions)   www.spc.ox.ac.uk
Undergraduates: 355   Postgraduates: 208   admissions@spc.ox.ac.uk

Opened as St Peter's Hall in 1929, St Peter's has been an Oxford college since 1961. Its eclectic mix of medieval, Georgian and 19th-century buildings are in the city centre and close to most of Oxford's main facilities, including the enormous new Westgate shopping centre. Though still young, St Peter's is well represented in university life and generally hovers in the middle of the Norrington Table. History teaching is particularly good and the college Master, Mark Damazer, former controller of BBC Radio 4, regularly invites high-profile speakers. Accommodation is available for students in their first and third years, varying from traditional rooms in college to new purpose-built rooms a few minutes' walk away. The facilities are impressive, including a recently upgraded JCR and a popular student bar (one of the few that is entirely student run). Formal hall is held twice a week and meals are on a pay-as-you-go basis. The JCR hosts popular open mic nights every two weeks, along with a roster of other cultural activities. Linton Quad and the chapel have undergone recent refurbishment, and the new Hubert Perrodo building has won multiple design awards. The college has a proud sporting heritage, being particularly strong at rugby and rowing.

Somerville

Oxford OX2 6HD   01865 270619 (admissions)   www.some.ox.ac.uk
Undergraduates: 426   Postgraduates: 221   secretariat@some.ox.ac.uk

Named after the astronomer Mary Somerville, Somerville was one of the first two colleges at Oxford founded to admit women. Members celebrated the news that the pioneering academic would become the first woman, other than a royal, to grace a British bank note. Since 1994, Somerville has admitted men and women equally, while retaining its pioneering and inclusive ethos. Alma mater to Margaret Thatcher, Indira Gandhi and Nobel prize winner Dorothy Hodgkin, Somerville is one of the most international and diverse colleges. Rooms in college, just off the attractive St Giles' and close to the Ashmolean Museum and Taylor Institution, are provided for three years to most undergraduates and all first-year postgraduates. Somerville welcomes state school applicants and drew nearly two-thirds of its UK undergraduate intake from that sector last year. There are kitchens in all buildings and subsidised food in hall. There are a number of clubs, from the excellent chapel choir to a baking society and the Boat Club. There is also a new Arts Budget in place to fund various creative projects. Somerville usually ranks towards the bottom of the Norrington Table, coming in at 22nd last year. The 24-hour library is one of largest. Students dominate university journalism and Somerville secured its third President of the Oxford Union in 2016.

Trinity

Oxford OX1 3BH   01865 279860 (admissions)   www.trinity.ox.ac.uk
Undergraduates: 289   Postgraduates: 137   admissions@trinity.ox.ac.uk

Architecturally impressive with enviable lawns, Trinity is one of Oxford's least populous – but most popular – colleges. The college admits some 80 undergraduates each year and is among the strongest academically. It usually finishes in the top ten of the Norrington Table. It is ideally located on Broad Street, next to Blackwell's bookshop and the Weston Library, a short stroll from the University Parks and the science park. Whilst members are active in all walks of university life, the college has its own debating and drama societies. The Trinity Players stage at least two productions a year, including one on the signature Trinity lawn which is popular across the university. Facilities are impressive, with a well-stocked college gym and squash courts. Trinity Boat Club and the chapel choir are the largest societies. Journalism is popular, and students produce a termly newsletter called The Broadsheet. Usually, all undergraduates are given a room on the main site in their first and second years, with the majority of third and fourth-years living on charming Woodstock Road in the north of the city. Trinity Students rate the food highly for both its quality and price. Its lavish white-tie Commemoration Ball, every three years, has one of the biggest budgets in Oxford and sells out in minutes.

University

Oxford OX1 4BH 01865 276677 (admissions) www.univ.ox.ac.uk
Undergraduates: 381 Postgraduates: 238 admissions@univ.ox.ac.uk

'Univ', as it is popularly known, was the first Oxford college to boast an alumnus in the Oval Office when Bill Clinton, a Rhodes Scholar in the late 1960s, became President of the USA. Centrally located on the High Street, the college is one of three claiming to be Oxford's oldest, and has made a significant effort to shake off its public school image and become "the friendly college" with its recent access initiatives. It has a generous bursary scheme, and travel grants are available for study trips abroad. Academic expectations are high and the college prospers in most subjects, especially Law, PPE, and the sciences. First and third years are housed on-site, with second years living in a comfortable annexe in Summertown. A newly-refurbished block provides double beds, kitchens and ensuites for students who snag rooms there – by random ballot – as well as widespread disabled access. University is particularly well represented on the river, with men's and women's crews, of which there are many, doing well in recent years, and a state-of-the-art boathouse (built after an arson attack on the previous one in 1999). The college also has access to a chalet in the foothills of Mont Blanc, with reading parties welcome in the summer. Multiple 24-hour libraries and close proximity to the Bodleian make University ideal for bookish students. Beyond the libraries, the chapel choir is excellent, and students put on a well-attended Revue every Hilary Term.

Wadham

Oxford OX1 3PN 01865 277545 (admissions) www.wadham.ox.ac.uk
Undergraduates: 474 Postgraduates: 241 admissions@wadham.ox.ac.uk

Wadham is best known among students for its progressive and liberal atmosphere and its leftist politics, although it boasts a large and imposing site to rival the most touristic of colleges. The JCR – or student union (SU) as it has rebranded itself – is famously active, although the breadth of political opinion is greater than its left-wing stereotype suggests. The college is very strong on admitting students from state schools, partly due to its successful Student Ambassador Scheme. Its gardens are beautiful and host Shakespeare performances each summer. The college has a good 24-hour library, with a well-stocked Persian history section. Although weekday dinners are served in the 17th-century hall, Wadham is the only college with no gowned formal hall sittings. Undergraduates are guaranteed accommodation on-site in their first year and final year, and in other years they are offered accommodation in two modern college-owned complexes roughly a mile from the centre of town. Highlights in the social calendar are Queer Week, a riotous celebration of LGBTQIA culture, and Wadstock, the college's open-air spring music festival. Student welfare is a big priority at Wadham. The Student Union has four welfare officers, along with a women's officer, an LGBTQIA officer, a people of colour and racial equality officer, a disabled students officer and a trans rep. The women's rowing team was second in the top division after three years at the head of the river, and the men's 1st VIII was fifth. The college also contributes to the local community through a new scheme which delivers food that is not eaten in hall to a local homeless centre.

Worcester

Oxford OX1 2HB   01865 278391 (admissions)   www.worc.ox.ac.uk
Undergraduates: 429   Postgraduates: 185   admissions@worc.ox.ac.uk

Worcester is to the west of Oxford what Magdalen is to the east: a spacious contrast to the urban rush of the city centre. The college's subtle exterior conceals a delightful environment, including some striking Baroque architecture, extensive gardens, medieval cottages, and a lake. It is one of Oxford's most popular colleges due to its beauty, academic reputation, and student satisfaction. The college gardeners even post horticultural updates to their own blog and the Buskins dramatic society makes use of the beautiful grounds, with annual summer Shakespeare performances in the gardens. Worcester has a great reputation for sport; it is the only college with its sports grounds on-site. Arts Week is an annual highlight and includes a delightful mix of plays, concerts and recitals. Provost Jonathan Bate, a renowned Shakespeare scholar, encourages Worcester's unparalleled arts activities. Accommodation, guaranteed for three years and graded by price, is within the college grounds, or less than 300 metres away in comfortable rooms with kitchen access. The stylish, multi-million pound Sultan Nazrin Shah Centre opened last year, providing extra lecture theatres and rehearsal space. The college boasts good quality food, and has a formal sitting every night. Like Magdalen and New, it hosts a Commemoration Ball every three years, a highlight of the Oxford social calendar. Students hold a "Worcester in the Park" event every summer term, with music and Pimm's.

Cambridge College Profiles

Christ's

Cambridge CB2 3BU   01223 334900   www.christs.cam.ac.uk
Undergraduates 420   Postgraduates: 200   admissions@christs.cam.ac.uk

Through a gate on Saint Andrew's Street you will find the tranquillity of Christ's College, over whose quads have passed the feet of illustrious alumni including Charles Darwin, John Milton and more recently Sacha Baron Cohen, of *Borat* fame. In front of the college is the bustle of Cambridge's main shopping centre, while behind lies Christ's Pieces with its popular tennis courts and lawns. Rooms are allocated on a ballot basis, but students who achieve first-class exam results are given preference. About 40% of rooms are ensuite (including small, single bedrooms in New Court and large, doubles in Second Court). There are also more traditional rooms and sets (a study room and bedroom) in the college's beautiful First Court. Some second years are accommodated in houses on Jesus Lane, a five-minute walk away. The Visual Arts Centre, student theatre and well-attended student film group keeps Christ's culturally vibrant. On the sports front, it is particularly strong on the football pitch and is one of only five Oxbridge colleges to have its own swimming pool, which is thought to be the oldest still in use in the UK. Celebratory students jump into the pool after their final exams. The college is strong academically and came first in last year's Tompkins table with over a third of graduates achieving a first. The previous year it was second.

Churchill

Cambridge CB3 0DS   01223 336202   www.chu.cam.ac.uk
Undergraduates 487   Postgraduates: 310   admissions@chu.ac.uk

Churchill is a little way out of town but closest to the West Cambridge Site, which houses many of the University's science departments. It's one of the largest college campuses and though the brutalist architecture may not be to everyone's taste, Churchill has some of the best facilities: a gym, theatre-cum-cinema, music room and recording studio, squash and tennis courts, grass pitches and the largest dining hall in Cambridge. A new court, housing 68 ensuite rooms (reputed to be the plushest undergraduate accommodation in town), was completed in 2016, as was a new boathouse. Over 40% of the college's rooms are now ensuite. Churchill is one of the least traditional colleges: students are welcome to walk on the grass and they don't wear academic gowns when dining formally in hall. It is also one of the few not to charge a fixed bill for catering in addition to meal charges – a move popular with Churchillians. It has a very diverse student body, with one of Oxbridge's highest state undergraduate intakes – 76.5% in the latest application cycle – and a relatively large number of postgraduate and overseas students. The college performs well academically (seventh in the Tompkins Table), a success sometimes attributed to what students have called its 'dangerously comfortable' library.

Clare

Cambridge CB2 1TL   01223 761612   www.clare.cam.ac.uk
Undergraduates 496   Postgraduates: 297   admissions@clare.cam.ac.uk

Clare, with its central location on the Backs and elegant courts and gardens, is popular with applicants. Amongst the oldest colleges, it has a strong reputation for music and a world-renowned choir. The bar in Clare Cellars, often plays host to DJ and live music nights that draw students from across the university. For accommodation, Old Court offers a traditional experience, while

Memorial Court, across the river, is close to the University Library and both humanities and science departments. The Colony, closer to the boathouse on the slopes of Castle Hill, is made up of large houses converted into student lodgings. All first years live in Memorial, Thirkill or Lerner Court, a modern living space opened in 2008. The college has an enthusiastic boat club with the highest participation rate in Cambridge, and very good sports facilities just beyond the university's botanic garden (a ten-minute cycle ride away). It has a thriving music society as well as regular recitals. Clare is evenly balanced in terms of arts and sciences, and at Tripos over a quarter of finalists achieved Firsts. It also has a good gender split – at last count it was almost 50:50 among undergraduates. An arts-heavy list of alumni includes David Attenborough and the journalist Matthew Parris.

Corpus

Cambridge CB2 1RH   01223 338056   www.corpus.cam.ac.uk
Undergraduates 280   Postgraduates: 220   admissions@corpus.cam.ac.uk

For those who prefer a more intimate atmosphere, Corpus is one of Cambridge's smallest colleges with an undergraduate population that hovers just below 300. Steeped in history it is the only Oxbridge college to have been founded by townspeople – in 1352 – and is home to the oldest court in either of the universities, which has been in continuous use since the 14th century. That said, there is plenty that is up-to-date. Accommodation is varied: some are housed in ancient college rooms where walking to the bathroom may mean a quick trip outside, others are accommodated away from, but close to, the main college site, in the Beldam, Bene't Street and Botolph Court buildings. The college has its own gym, playing fields and an open-air swimming pool, in Leckhampton, just over a mile away. All undergraduate students are guaranteed accommodation, although rooms are allocated on the basis of exam results, which is not always popular. Many in Cambridge know Corpus for its unusual clock, donated by alumnus and inventor John C Taylor in 2008, which sits on the corner of Trumpington Street outside the eponymous Taylor Library, which is housed, along with the all-important college bar, in Kwee Court. To expand the sports offering, Corpus joins up with King's and Christ's to form collaborative 'CCK' sports teams. It also has a small but much-used theatre, the Corpus Playroom, where students from across the university stage plays and comedy nights.

Downing

Cambridge CB2 1DQ   01223 334826   www.dow.cam.ac.uk
Undergraduates 420   Postgraduates: 220   admissions@dow.cam.ac.uk

Downing students are rightly proud of the spacious quadrangle around which the college's neoclassical architecture is set. It opens onto a paddock where many a summer garden party livens up exam term. The college was originally founded for the study of law and natural sciences in 1800. It is still popular with scientists, lawyers and geographers thanks to its fall-out-of-bed-and-into-lectures proximity to their faculties, but it is now home to an eclectic body of students studying all subjects. Extra-curricular strengths lie on the sports field (Downing is known as a fearsome opponent on both the rugby field and the river) and in the arts thanks to the Howard Theatre, a 160- seat space, a vibrant Drama Society that hosts a yearly festival of student writing, and the new Heong Gallery dedicated to modern and contemporary art that opened in 2016. All students, both graduate and undergraduate, can be housed on the main site, which helps to foster a solid sense of community. The accommodation, which is relatively expensive, has been described as 'hotel standard' – undergraduate rooms often come with double beds and ensuite bathrooms.

Emmanuel

Cambridge CB2 3AP   01223 334290   www.emma.cam.ac.uk
Undergraduates 470   Postgraduates: 220   admissions@emma.cam.ac.uk

'Emma' as Emmanuel is fondly known, prides itself on an open, friendly atmosphere that is underpinned (though you may not realise it) by a strong academic ethic. It regularly comes in the top ten in the Tompkins Table, ninth in the most recent ratings, and has fielded a couple of successful University Challenge teams. Students love it for its central location, busy and cheap bar, well-subsidised accommodation – which includes a free weekly load of washing in the rent – and the spacious grounds where ducks roam and barbecues are held in summer. Founded by Puritans in the 1580s, it tries to maintain a forward-thinking and egalitarian atmosphere. It has a relatively even gender split, a female master and two thirds of the current undergraduate intake hails from the state sector. Societies and sports focus more on inclusion than competition with a diverse array of activities. But Emma does enjoy sporting success; last year one student became the champion inter-college wind-surfer and a cohort of students won the Team Racing Cuppers. Its understated, yet beautiful, Christopher Wren chapel hosts a number of concerts organised by the music society. Other clubs include Mountaineering Society and Emmanuel Real Ice Cream Society. As one of the better-endowed colleges, Emmanuel offers a number of bursaries and scholarships.

Fitzwilliam

Cambridge CB3 0DG   01223 332030   www.fitz.cam.ac.uk
Undergraduates 440   Postgraduates: 320   admissions@fitz.cam.ac.uk

Founded in the 19th century to increase access to Cambridge, Fitzwilliam is proud of its heritage as a college committed to widening participation. It moved to its current location in the grounds of a Regency estate in 1963, and while it doesn't have the archetypal ancient architecture, the college gardens are some of the most beautiful and well-tended in town. If you climb to the top of its library, designed by award-winning architect Edward Cullinan, you are at the highest point in the city. The atmosphere is one of a tight-knit community and students are accommodated throughout their degrees in one of 400 rooms or in houses minutes from the main campus. The friendly feel is helped by the busy coffee shop where students and staff alike indulge in renowned homemade cakes. As well as extensive renovations to its central building and dining hall, the accommodation of 'Fitz', as the college is fondly known, has also been modernised. All first-year rooms are semi-ensuite, equipped with a shower and washbasin, and most of the student kitchens contain ovens – many of the older colleges provide students with basic 'gyp rooms' that only contain fridges and hobs. On the academic front, Fitz ranges from mid-Tompkins Table to around 20th place, and it does well on the sports field – recent success includes winning the inter-college cricket two years on the trot – thanks to its well-kept pitches, five minutes away, and a new gym.

Girton

Cambridge CB3 0JG   01223 338972   www.girton.cam.ac.uk
Undergraduates 500   Postgraduates: 280   admissions@girton.cam.ac.uk

Girton is as far to the west of Cambridge as Homerton is to the east, but for some the distance out of town is a good reason to apply. Its grounds, which include lawns, orchards, sports pitches and courts, majestic brick buildings and an indoor swimming pool, amount to some 50 acres. Girton students either live on this tranquil campus, in rooms that range from atmospheric Victorian bedrooms to modern ensuites in Ash Court, or they live off-site in college-owned houses or the recently opened Swirles Court, located on the university's new North West

Cambridge Development at Eddington. Founded as a women's college in 1869, it was the first to go co-educational and now has an equal gender balance that recently has been slightly weighted in favour of men. There is still an all-female corridor, which women students can favour in the accommodation ballot. Being out of town fosters a familial feel and many at Girton would consider themselves Girtonian first and Cambridge students second. Academically, Girton tends towards the bottom of the ratings, but this may be mostly to do with its vibrant extra-curricular scene. It is known for the arts and has its own museum, dark room for photography and permanent 'Peoples' Portraits' exhibition.

Gonville & Caius

Cambridge CB2 1TA   01223 332413   www.cai.cam.ac.uk
Undergraduates 560   Postgraduates: 250   admissions@cai.cam.ac.uk

It is hard to believe that Gonville & Caius (pronounced 'keys') is steps away from Cambridge's main thoroughfare and market place. It is one of the oldest colleges, having been founded as Gonville Hall in 1348. Unlike other colleges, Caius has Formal Hall, a three-course meal served in the ancient dining hall, every night of the week. Any students who wish to attend have to wear the college's blue formal gown – though often with jeans or sports kit underneath. Caius has a unique dining policy: undergraduates have to pay up-front for 36 dinners a term, around four per week. Unpopular with some, this tradition creates a strong community, with students generally returning to college for meals. Caius has some great, functional accommodation in the Stephen Hawking Building, which offers modern, ensuite rooms – named in honour of the physicist who was a Fellow of the college for over 52 years – and in Harvey Court, which was renovated in 2011. But there are also more traditional rooms and sets in the central, historic Old Courts, just steps away from Kings Parade. A brand new boathouse and gym has been welcomed by rowers and the college holds imaginative events for potential applicants such as its pioneering 'Women in Economics' day. New academic prizes for sixth formers were launched in 2017. Among an impressive line-up of alumni, the college boasts no fewer than 14 Nobel Laureates. It generally sits in the upper half of the Tompkins table, although currently middling in 14th place, and for those keen on study, the library is a treat. It used to be the university library and is set under the arched roof of the Cockerell Building just outside.

Homerton

Cambridge CB2 8PH   01223 747252   www.homerton.cam.ac.uk
Undergraduates 550   Postgraduates: 500   admissions@homerton.cam.ac.uk

Homerton celebrated the 250th anniversary of its foundation in the east London district of that name last year, but it remains the newest Cambridge College, because it only moved to Cambridge in 1894 and formally became a college in 2010. It is the largest in Cambridge; it has around 1,500 students – half undergraduates and half graduates – who live on a large, landscaped site in the southeast of the city. Close to the railway station, it is a 15-minute cycle ride from town. The benefit is space. Accommodation is made up of largely ensuite study bedrooms of a high standard. The college also has tennis courts, a gym, a squash court and a football pitch. There is an orchard and extensive lawns that can be walked on – Homerton students are quick to talk of the college's friendly and unstuffy atmosphere. It still holds a feeling of history in its striking neo-Gothic Great Hall, built in 1889, which is used for daily student meals and for candlelit formal dinners. This is set to be updated with a £7m project for a new, more capacious dining hall. It has a near 50:50 gender split and hosts all courses except architecture. It is also home to the largest number of students studying the education Tripos, in line with its history as a teaching training college. The arts abound and honorary fellows include Dame Carol Ann Duffy, Sir Andrew Motion and Dame Evelyn Glennie.

Hughes Hall

Cambridge CB1 2EW   01223 334897   www.hughes.cam.ac.uk
Undergraduates 90   Postgraduates: 600   admissions@hughes.cam.ac.uk

Hop off the train and walk down Cambridge's vibrant Mill Road, and tucked away you will find Hughes Hall. Founded in 1885, Hughes Hall is the oldest graduate college in the University of Cambridge. It welcomes applications for postgraduate courses and applications for undergraduate courses from students over 21 in all subjects. Two-thirds of the students come from outside the UK, and the college has a flair for science, law and business. Although just around the corner from a busy high street, the college has a peaceful setting around the University's cricket ground, with the two terraces above the dining hall providing a great view. Hughes Hall has a strong record on the sports pitch and on the river. In 2017, four students competed at the World Rowing Championships, and the year before, one Hughesian rowed in the Rio Olympics. Students taking courses of three years or longer are given priority for accommodation, and first-year-students are generally given rooms on the central site. In 2016, 85 new single ensuite rooms were built along with a bike store and study rooms in the Gresham Court building. The college also has a number of flats and studios for students in established long-term relationships, but these tend to be in high demand.

Jesus

Cambridge CB5 8BL   01223 339455   www.jesus.cam.ac.uk
Undergraduates 510   Postgraduates: 380   undergraduate-admissions@jesus.cam.ac.uk

Jesus is the envy of many a Cantabrigian for its spacious grounds near both the river and the centre of town. Its red brick buildings are iconic and many date back to Jesus' founding in the 1500s. Its chapel is believed to be the oldest university building in Cambridge. But the college has also modernised: a development at West Court has student common rooms, a games room, a café and a popular bar and terrace. It also has on-site football, rugby and cricket pitches as well as three squash courts and five tennis courts. As one of the biggest colleges it is home to an eclectic population that is as strong on the sports field as it is in music and art. All undergraduates are accommodated for every year of their degree, not just the first three – this is particularly convenient for medical students. The much-loved grounds often host modern sculpture exhibitions – the college's collection contains work by the likes of Antony Gormley and John Bellany – and students are allowed to roam on most of the grass. In summer, Jesus holds a hotly-touted May Ball – popular with first years because of its 'party hard' atmosphere. Despite all that is going on, students still find time for their degrees and Jesus regularly features in the top half of the Tompkins Table, coming 6th in 2018.

King's

Cambridge CB2 1ST   01223 331255   www.kings.cam.ac.uk
Undergraduates 430   Postgraduates: 280   undergraduate.admissions@kings.cam.ac.uk

King's is the Cambridge of TV programmes and postcards. The iconic chapel, home to the widely-broadcast Christmas Carol service, and elegant facades back onto the River Cam, giving King's an enviable location that is ideal for both arts and science students – and popular with tourists. Despite its appearance and the fact that it was originally founded in 1441 as a college for boys from Eton, King's is proudly the most anti-establishment of the colleges. It hosts an 'affair' rather than a May Ball that is highly popular and always has a left-field theme. It has done away with the Fellows' 'High Table' in the dining hall and hangs a hammer and sickle flag in its bar – though its presence there is hotly debated each year. A relatively high state school intake -72% of its offers were made to maintained sector students in the last application cycle – is aided by the college actively seeking out those from disadvantaged backgrounds. Accommodation ranges from the archetypally Cambridge (think mullioned windows overlooking the river) to ensuite rooms in newer hostels. It has climbed up the Tompkins Table, coming fifth last year. The college has a strong, literary legacy, and two of its alumni, Zadie Smith and Fiona Mozley, have been on the Man Booker shortlist. On the sports field, it joins up to some success with Corpus Christi and Christ's.

Lucy Cavendish

Cambridge CB3 0BU   01223 332190   www.lucy-cav.cam.ac.uk
Undergraduates 120   Postgraduates: 290   admissions@lucy-cav.cam.ac.uk

Unlike any other Oxbridge college, Lucy Cavendish – Lucy to its members – takes only female students over the age of 21. This encourages a slightly more staid and studious atmosphere than other colleges, but one that is highly supportive. Founded in 1965 by female academics who believed that opportunities for women at the university were too restricted, Lucy holds strong to its founding remit. Guest speakers in recent years have included Dame Margaret Hodge, Dr Lorna Williamson, novelists Nicci Gerrard and Sean French and the French Ambassador, Sylvie Berman. Accommodation is provided for all students either in college or in nearby houses, close to those of St Edmund's and Fitzwilliam, making for easy intermingling with these other 'hill' colleges. The active students' union arranges frequent Formal Hall swaps and bops. The college has a growing reputation for sport. In recent years, it has provided two consecutive captains for the Blues female rugby team, two players for the Blues football team and three rowers in the University Boat Club. The Lucy Cavendish Boat Club persuades a third of the student community to give rowing a try at some point. The college is also known for its Fiction Prize, which has helped to launch the publishing career of many successful authors including Gail Honeyman and Laura Marshall.

Magdalene

Cambridge CB3 0AG   01223 332135   www.magd.cam.ac.uk
Undergraduates 339   Postgraduates: 212   admissions@magd.cam.ac.uk

Magdalene rejoices in the longest river frontage of any Cambridge college and is renowned for its ancient and beautiful grounds. Students are often found revising on 'The Beach' during the summer exam term. It is one of the smaller colleges but this means that students tend to know each other. Magdalene has a reputation for being more traditional than some: it famously hosts one of the university's few white-tie balls every two years, and has one of the cheapest formal halls in Cambridge. It also has its own punts. The college's sports pitches are shared with St John's, both have a sporty reputation, and Magdalene also has its own Eton Fives court. Students live in the main college courts, in the 'Village' on the other side of Magdalene Street, or in college-owned houses a few minutes' walk away. Students from different year groups are housed together. The college's most famous alumnus, Samuel Pepys, is immortalised in the Pepys Building that houses a collection of 3,000 of the diarist's books and manuscripts preserved on their original shelves. Magdalene tends toward the middle of the Tompkins ratings and came 18th in the last list. Its renowned studious Master, former Archbishop of Canterbury Rowan Williams who arrived in 2013, has done much to raise its academic profile. In March 2017 a big fundraising campaign was announced in aid of more undergraduate bursaries, a new library and art gallery, and renovation of the Pepys Building.

Murray Edwards

Cambridge CB3 0DF   01223 762229   www.murrayedwards.cam.ac.uk
Undergraduates 360   Postgraduates: 170   admissions@murrayedwards.cam.ac.uk

One of Cambridge's three colleges for women, Murray Edwards is possibly the most gregarious of them. It is informal, relaxed and students spend as much time mingling with those from other colleges in town as taking advantage of their calm and spacious campus at the top of Castle Hill. It hosts a renowned garden party during May Week to which tickets sell quickly, and the Saturday brunch, served up in 'The Dome' dining hall is legendary – it has been voted best in Cambridge. It does much to promote women in the workplace, most notably running a programme on academic leadership and career development called Gateway that runs once a week during term. It also has a strong population of women in STEM subjects and a high state school intake – around 70% at last count. Its laid-back atmosphere extends to the gardens where students can grow herbs and vegetables as well as, unusually for a Cambridge college, walk on the grass. Sport is strong and everything from climbing to hockey is catered for. The college often provides Blues players to the university teams. Murray Edwards is also home to the second largest collection of women's art in the world, which is includes work by Barbara Hepworth, Tracey Emin and Paula Rego.

Newnham

Cambridge CB3 9DF   01223 335783   www.newn.cam.ac.uk
Undergraduates 370   Postgraduates: 290   admissions@newn.cam.ac.uk

Newnham was founded for women to attend lectures at Cambridge in 1871 – though it was another 77 years before they were admitted as full members of the university – and it prides itself on academic excellence and creating a supportive atmosphere for women to achieve their potential. Seminars in conjunction with organisations such as Women of the Year are common. Alumni include Germaine Greer, who is still a fellow at the college, Sylvia Plath, Diane Abbott, Mary Beard and Emma Thompson. Newnham came 22nd in the Tompkins Table last year – though this still meant that a fifth of students achieved a First. For arts students it is ideally located for the Sidgwick Site and for those who like to socialise, Newnham often joins up with nearby Selwyn for socials, formals and for its choir (Newnham has no chapel). The grounds of the college are much loved by Newnhamites and stretch to 18-acres including sports pitches, tennis courts and an on-site arts centre known as 'The Old Labs'. This year, Newnham students can enjoy 90 new ensuite rooms, as well as a new Porters' Lodge, gym, café and rooms for conferences and supervisions. The college's new build is named after Cambridge's first ever female professor: Dorothy Garrod.

Pembroke

Cambridge CB2 1RF   01223 338154   www.pem.cam.ac.uk
Undergraduates 430   Postgraduates: 295   admissions@pem.cam.ac.uk

Duck your head through the gate of Pembroke College at the corner of Pembroke and Trumpington Streets and you'll find yourself in an historic oasis. Given its position, Pembroke is surprisingly large and has extensive gardens and a Christopher Wren chapel. Though most famous for its poets, including Ted Hughes and Edmund Spenser, Pembroke has been excelling in the sciences of late, hosting panels with business leaders and, in 2015, a cohort of its engineers won a prestigious national competition. Loyal Pembroke students love the college for the cheap rents (although, it is said that, for some rooms, the rents reflect the quality), a lively café and facilities that include a gym and a bowling green. While performing well academically – last year Pembroke came second in the Tompkins Table – there is a strong extra-curricular ethos too. There are dozens of clubs and societies, including the Pembroke College Music Society, the Stokes Scientific Society, Pembroke Politics and the drama group the Pembroke Players, who regularly take productions to the Edinburgh Festival. In sport, the college is strong in football, hockey and rowing. Last year, both the men's and women's football first teams had division-winning, unbeaten seasons and both reached the Cuppers final. It is well-endowed (hence the cheap rents) and in 2015 Pembroke received what is thought to be the largest bequest ever given to a Cambridge college.

Peterhouse

Cambridge CB2 1RD   01223 338223   www.pet.cam.ac.uk
Undergraduates 260   Postgraduates: 206   admissions@pet.cam.ac.uk

It may be Cambridge's most diminutive college – hovering around 260 undergraduates in recent years – but Peterhouse's influence belies its size and it boasts five Nobel Prize winners. It is also Cambridge's oldest college and remains home to some quirky traditions and a famously old-world formal hall. Only 54% of the most recent intake is from state schools, but the college enjoys a good gender balance and welcomed its first female master in 2016. It is one of the richer colleges, has a roster of travel grants and academic awards and accommodation standards are high. Students are housed either on site or no more than five minutes away for all years of their degree. Rooms are allocated on a points-based system that accounts both for academic progress and extra-curricular achievements. Though it doesn't have its own sports ground, Peterhouse does have its own squash court and a recently-built gym. It also has one of Cambridge's wilder outdoor spaces known as The Deer Park, no deer but many students roaming in summer. Peterhouse is well located for both the science and arts faculties and is particularly strong in the arts. It has two libraries, the Perne and the Ward, which provide plenty of quiet space away from the busier atmospheres of faculty libraries.

Queens'

Cambridge CB3 9ET   01223 335540   www.queens.cam.ac.uk
Undergraduates 500   Postgraduates: 500   admissions@queens.cam.ac.uk

Queens' (make sure you get the apostrophe in the right place in comparison to its Oxford counterpart) is a bustling college that has a central location spanning both sides of the River Cam with the Mathematical Bridge attributed to Sir Isaac Newton joining the two. It has the third largest colleges population and, especially in the new courts, has a lively, outgoing feel. Drama is popular thanks to the active BATS dramatic society and sport is strong – Queens' tends to provide a number of players to Blues teams and has sports clubs covering everything from chess to water polo. It also has a well-attended biennial May Ball that has welcomed renowned bands including Kaiser Chiefs and Bastille. The college has an eclectic mix of architecture that dates from its founding in 1448 right through to the present day. Accommodation in the Dokett building has just been reopened with ensuite facilities. First year students are housed in the Cripps Building, while second and third year students are allocated their accommodation through a ballot system. Students also have the option of sharing a set of rooms, rather than having their own single bedsit. Queens' is particularly strong in the sciences (thanks to bursaries and awards available in those subjects) and performs well at Tripos, generally ranking within the upper half of the Tompkins Table.

Robinson

Cambridge CB3 9AN	01223 339143	www.robinson.cam.ac.uk
Undergraduates 386	Postgraduates: 172	apply@robinson.cam.ac.uk

Though occasionally ribbed for the austere redbrick architecture, Robinson students are a loyal lot and the college has made a virtue of its appearance: The Red Brick Café is envied by many and Brickhouse, the student theatre company makes good use of its outdoor space. The (also red brick) chapel is renowned for its fantastic acoustic and organ. It may not be the most architecturally beautiful college, but it does have a rolling programme of refurbishment that has resulted in very good facilities even if rents are not as well subsidised as some. There is a big focus on the quality of food and 'The Garden Restaurant' (the canteen) is renowned as one of the best in Cambridge. For those who want to focus on academe it is conveniently situated just behind the University Library and minutes away from the arts faculties on the Sidgwick Site and the Maths, Physics and Materials Science buildings. Robinson often wields strong football, netball and rugby teams. The sports grounds, shared with Queens', Selwyn and King's, are less than a mile from the main site. Robinson tends to rest in the second half of the Tompkins Table (it was 24th in the latest) but has been as high as 3rd. It recently faced criticism for admitting only five disadvantaged students between 2016 and 2018, meaning that just 1.8% of UK-based students were from disadvantaged areas. But despite having a high private school intake in the last admissions cycle – only 48% of students came from the maintained sector – the college is known for its sociable, friendly atmosphere.

Selwyn

Cambridge CB3 9DQ	01223 335896	www.sel.cam.ac.uk
Undergraduates 400	Postgraduates: 250	admissions@sel.cam.ac.uk

Selwyn sits on the other side of the River Cam from the city centre and enjoys a roomy location just behind the Sidgwick Site, which makes the lecture commute an easy two-minute walk for arts and humanities students. The only gripe about its location is that it's a ten-minute walk to the nearest cash point and supermarket. It was among the first colleges to admit women and typically has an even gender balance – there were 62 men and 61 women in the most recent undergraduate intake. Selwyn also has a relatively large contingent of state-educated undergraduates, in the latest admissions cycle, 71% of offers were made to students from the maintained sector. All are accommodated for all years of their degrees in what is likely to be, thanks to an extensive refurbishment programme, an ensuite room. Academically Selwyn comes in the middle of the university's rankings – 11th in the latest Tompkins Table – but music is strong and the college choir's album "*The Eternal Ecstasy*" was featured on Classic FM and spent three weeks in the specialist charts. On the sports front, long-standing clubs known as the Hermes and Sirens fund grants for various teams and the college recently christened a new rowing boat.

Sidney Sussex

Cambridge CB2 3HU   01223 338872   www.sid.cam.ac.uk
Undergraduates 350   Postgraduates: 275   admissions@sid.cam.ac.uk

Sidney Sussex, which was founded in 1596, is located, happily for students, just opposite the entrance to the city centre's main supermarket. It's a short cycle ride in one direction to the river, a two-minute walk to the main student theatre, the ADC, and a five-minute walk to the natural science faculties. Sidney is one of the smaller colleges, but, because of its little, centrally located site, many students are housed in one of 11 nearby hostels. However, there are some atmospheric rooms to be had in the main buildings, a few of which include ensuite facilities. Sidney is a musical college with an award-winning chapel and a recently inaugurated organ. Also in the chapel, more bizarrely, is buried Oliver Cromwell's head (he was among the college's first students). The college bar is a social hub, thanks to its affordability and rowdy 'bops'. Food is also well reviewed and the college chefs scooped numerous awards in the 2017 university-wide culinary competition. Sports teams are more enthusiastic than wildly competitive and grounds are shared with Christ's, a ten-minute cycle ride away.

St Catharine's

Cambridge CB2 1RL   01223 338319   www.caths.cam.ac.uk
Undergraduates 440   Postgraduates: 220   undergraduate.admissions@caths.cam.ac.uk

Despite its unusual open court frontage 'Catz', as St Catharine's is fondly known, is one of the least assuming of the colleges strung along Cambridge's famous King's Parade. It is mid-sized but boasts two libraries, thanks to the remit for learning instilled by its original benefactor, Robert Woodlark. St Catharine's has a high state school intake, in the last application cycle 76% of offers were made to students from the maintained sector. Catz students live on site in first year before moving out to the popular St Chad's complex in second year, where accommodation is split into flats with octagonal bedrooms. St Chad's is near the Sidgwick Site – useful for arts students looking to wake up as late as possible before lectures. Recent improvements include the McGrath Centre, which houses an auditorium, junior common room and bar, and a refurbished boathouse and hockey pitch. St Catharine's came 10th in the Tompkins Table in 2018 and its students are enthusiastic on the extra-curricular front. It fields strong rowing and hockey teams, and in the tradition of one of its most illustrious alumni, Sir Peter Hall, the drama troupe, The Shirley Society, is popular.

St Edmund's

Cambridge CB3 0BN   01223 336086   www.st-edmunds.cam.ac.uk
Undergraduates 117   Postgraduates: 450   admissions@st-edmunds.cam.ac.uk

Having recently celebrated its 50th year as a mainly graduate college, St Edmund's – known as 'Eddies' – enjoys a reputation as one of Cambridge's most international colleges with a student body that, though male-heavy, hails from almost 80 different countries. Undergraduates must be 21 or more on entry. It is also renowned for providing numerous sportsmen and women to the university's Blues teams and, last year, a team of four who broke the world record for the longest continual row. St Edmund's location up on the 'hill' near Fitzwilliam and Murray Edwards gives the college a buzzing atmosphere and it is known as one of the most social of the graduate colleges. Work is still done and last year, Eddies enjoyed its best exam term record yet. Accommodation and food are on the expensive side as it doesn't enjoy the big endowments of some of the larger colleges, but there are a good variety of rooms on offer from ensuites in the recently built Brian Heap building to maisonettes a short walk away for couples and small families. St Edmund's is unique among Cambridge colleges in having a Catholic chapel and also takes a relaxed approach to traditions. There is no Fellows' high table in hall for example.

St Johns

Cambridge CB2 1TP   01223 338703   www.joh.cam.ac.uk
Undergraduates 569   Postgraduates: 325   admissions@joh.cam.ac.uk

St John's and Trinity enjoy a friendly rivalry: both are large, rich and architecturally beautiful colleges and they are next-door neighbours. St John's is home to Cambridge's famous Bridge of Sighs and a stunning chapel whose tower is the highest building in town. Thanks to a large undergraduate body St John's is a diverse place, though it is particularly renowned for its prowess on the sports field. The 'Red Boys' team is the dominant force in inter-college rugby – they won the league three years in a row – and 'Maggie', as the college boat club is familiarly known, fielded the most successful men's boat in the May 'Bumps' competition. St John's endowments mean that it can support a wide range of activities from launching its own record label – The Gentlemen of St John's singers tour worldwide – to financial initiatives which aim to help students from low income backgrounds. For the academically ambitious, first-class results are also rewarded with grants from £400 to £600. Accommodation standards are high and the food in the buttery is regularly delicious and well subsidised. St John's also hosts a May Week Ball that is known as one of the most fabulous. On the night, punts fill the river near the college to watch the legendary fireworks display.

Trinity Hall

Cambridge CB2 1TJ   01223 332535   www.trinhall.cam.ac.uk
Undergraduates 382   Postgraduates: 229   admissions@trinhall.cam.ac.uk

'Tit Hall', as Cambridge's fifth oldest college is known, is tucked behind its more grandiose neighbours, Trinity and Clare, allowing it to enjoy a less tourist-heavy river frontage. That's not to say it's not picturesque and its small size allows its 380 or so undergraduates to get to know each other quickly. It is also ideally located for a wander into town as well as short cycle rides to the Sidgwick Site for the arts faculties and the University Library. Thanks to its endowments Tit Hall is one of the richer colleges, which means that accommodation is cheap and facilities are good. All first-years are housed on the central site, where the cafeteria, coffee shop, bar, library, chapel and main music room are also located. But the college also has some swanky new off-site accommodation. A block with double ensuite rooms called 'WYNG Gardens' opened recently and the rooms at the Wychfield site, ten-minutes away, have been newly refurbished. The college is both sporty and musical; the chapel choir's most recent recording received gilded reviews. Trinity Hall rose to 12th place in the most recent Tompkins Table and the modern Jerwood Library is a much-loved study space for students. Alumni include the eminent scientists Stephen Hawking and David Thouless as well as the Olympic medal-winning cyclist Emma Pooley.

Trinity

Cambridge CB2 1TQ   01223 338422   www.trin.cam.ac.uk
Undergraduates 695   Postgraduates: 350   admissions@trin.cam.ac.uk

The largest of all Oxbridge colleges, Trinity was established in 1546 and occupies extensive grounds that span the River Cam. Its famous Wren Library contains everything from the Capell collection of Shakespeariana to the earliest manuscript of Winnie-the-Pooh. Like its neighbour St John's, Trinity is well endowed – the wealthiest of all the colleges – which allows it to provide high quality and cheap accommodation. The college admitted just 11 students from low participation postcodes over the past three years, meaning that 2.9% of the student body came from a disadvantaged area. But its ample resources make lots of bursaries available to its undergraduate population. The Tudor-Gothic buildings of New Court have been renovated to provide 169 student rooms and nearly half the college's accommodation is now ensuite. Since 1997, Trinity has not come below eighth in the Tompkins Table, but there is much else besides work. A two-storey gym and netball, football, rugby and cricket pitches, minutes from the main gate, mean that sports are easy to enjoy. Hockey pitches, badminton, tennis and squash courts are also available and the college punts are a popular choice on summer afternoons. The chapel is home to an active choir who recently completed a tour of Australia and Hong Kong. In 2017 the JCR was refurbished and now has a 65-inch TV with Sky Sports and Netflix. It's a wonder work gets done, but students say that the college takes on a studious atmosphere in exam term. Trinity has recently expanded its access and outreach programmes and while some say it is too big and the tourists too many, others revel in the choice this allows.

Wolfson

Cambridge CB3 9BB 01223 335918 www.wolfson.cam.ac.uk

Undergraduates 168 Postgraduates: 300 ugadministrator@wolfson.cam.ac.uk

Established as University College in 1965, Wolfson took its current name from a generous grant from the Wolfson Foundation just eight years after it was founded. It is first and foremost a college for graduate students but also welcomes 150 or so mature undergraduates each year. All are guaranteed three years of accommodation. The community is varied with students from over 90 countries and aged from 21 to over 70 (the average age is 25). It's a forward-thinking place with famously little distinction between fellows and students (there is no 'high table' in hall for example) and a President rather than a Master. The current President is the eminent scientist, Professor Jane Clarke. The 1970s buildings are not the town's most beautiful but the gardens are an oasis of calm and it is close to the River Cam's picturesque banks. It is also not far from the Sidgwick Site and the University Library, though the city centre is about a 20-minute walk. On site the college has one of the university's best gyms as well as a basketball-cum-tennis court. In celebration of its 50th anniversary in 2015, Wolfson managed to raise £7 million in donations. Students are seeing the benefit in grants and modernisation.

15 University Profiles

This chapter provides profiles of every university that appears in *The Times and Sunday Time*s league table. In addition there are profiles for the biggest supplier of part-time degrees, the Open University, and for University College Birmingham, the only institution which did not release data for use in the table. However, we do not have separate profiles for specialist colleges, such as the Royal College of Music (**www.rcm.ac.uk**) or institutions that only offer postgraduate degrees, such as Cranfield University (**www.cranfield.ac.uk**). Their omission is no reflection on their quality, simply a function of their particular roles. A number of additional institutions with degree-awarding powers are listed at the end of the book with their contact details.

The federal University of London (**www.london.ac.uk**) is by far Britain's biggest conventional higher education institution, with more than 120,000 students. The majority study at colleges in the capital, but such is the global prestige of the university's degrees that over 50,000 students in 180 different countries take University of London International Programmes. The university, which celebrated its 175th anniversary in 2011, consists of 18 self-governing colleges, the Institute in Paris and the School of Advanced Study, which comprises ten specialist institutes for research and postgraduate education (details at **www. sas.ac.uk**). City University joined the university in 2016. The university does not have its own entry in this chapter, but the following colleges do: Birkbeck, City, Goldsmiths, King's College London, London School of Economics and Political Science, Queen Mary, Royal Holloway, SOAS and University College London. Contact details for its other constituent colleges are given on page 584.

Guide to the profiles
The profiles contain valuable information about each university. You can find contact details, including postal address, telephone number for admission enquiries, email or web addresses for admissions and prospectus enquiries, web addresses for the university and the students' union, and the dates of forthcoming open days, where available. In addition, each profile provides information under the following headings:

» **_The Times and Sunday Times_ rankings:** For the overall ranking, the figure in bold refers to the university's position in the 2020 *Guide* and the figure in brackets to the previous year. The information is taken from the main league table (see chapter 1 for explanations and sources), apart from that taken from our new Social Inclusion table which is included for the first time (see chapter 6).

» **Undergraduates:** The number of full-time undergraduates is given first followed by part-time undergraduates (in brackets). The figures are for 2016–17, and are the most recent from the Higher Education Statistics Agency (HESA).

» **Postgraduates:** The number of full-time postgraduates is given first followed by part-time postgraduates (in brackets). The figures are for 2016–17, and are the most recent from HESA.

» **Mature students:** The percentage of undergraduate entrants who were 21 or over at the start of their studies in 2017. The figures are from UCAS.

» **International students:** The number of undergraduate overseas students (both EU and non-EU) as a percentage of full-time undergraduates. The figures are for 2016–17, and are from HESA.

» **Applications per place:** The number of applicants per place for 2017, from UCAS.

» **Accommodation:** The information was obtained from university accommodation services, and their help is gratefully acknowledged.

» **Where do students come from:** For an explanation of the data contained here please see the explanation in the introduction to chapter 6. This data is not used in the ranking of universities but gives a broad indication of their social mix.

Tuition fees

Details of tuition fees for 2019–20 are given wherever possible. At the time of going to press, a number of universities had not published their international fees for 2019–20. In these cases, the fees for 2018–19 are given. Please check university websites to see if they have managed to give updated figures. Fees for 2019–20 will not be published until late summer 2019, although at universities in England, those for UK students have been limited to a maximum of £9,250 by the Government.

While EU students who started courses in 2018 were given a guarantee that UK rather than International fees would apply to them, the situation for entrants after that year was unclear at the time of going to press (see chapter 4). It is of the utmost importance that you check university websites for the latest information.

Every university website gives full details of the financial and other support the university provides to its students, from scholarships and bursaries to study support and hardship funds. Some of the support will be delivered automatically but most will not, and you must study the details on the websites, including methods of applying and deadlines, to get the greatest benefit out of your university. In addition, in England the Office for Students (**www.officeforstudents.org.uk**) publishes "Access Agreements" for every English university on its website. Each agreement outlines the university's plans for fees, financial support and measures being taken to widen access to that university and to encourage students to complete their courses.

University of Aberdeen

Aberdeen is our Scottish University of the Year and was also one of five shortlisted for the UK award. Sir George Boyne, an Aberdonian and double graduate of the university who took over last year as principal and vice-chancellor, will be hoping to build on Aberdeen's 14-place rise in the table. He has promised to make the university "inclusive, inter-disciplinary and international in reach and quality". Boyne was formerly pro-vice chancellor of the University of Cardiff, where he was head of the College of Arts, Humanities and Social Sciences. He will want to reverse the 25% fall in the number of undergraduate entrants seen in 2017.

The university hopes to recruit more international students, but an internal report said that many of its historic buildings would need upgrading first. Aberdeen is already investing £377m on its Aberdeen campuses, but the report said another £68m would be needed to avoid "significant risks".

Aberdeen is the fifth-oldest university in the UK, a fusion of two ancient institutions, the first of which was established in 1495. The original King's College premises are the focal point of an attractive campus, complete with cobbled main street and Georgian buildings, about a mile from the city centre. The futuristic Sir Duncan Rice Library, named after the principal who commissioned it, cost £57m and has been named among the most beautiful in the world.

Medicine is one of the university's principal strengths. The highly-regarded medical school is based at Foresterhill, a 20-minute walk away from the King's College campus, where the university shares Europe's largest health campus with NHS Grampian, placing researchers, scientists, clinicians and patients together on one site. A new building for the Rowett Institute, the university's nutrition and health research centre, is the latest addition. Buses link the two campuses with the Hillhead residential complex.

The university won funding last June for an additional 30 medical student places a year, specifically to train extra doctors specialising in general practice. Last year, Aberdeen won a Queen's Anniversary Prize – the highest honour available – for its contribution to health services research over the past 40 years. The university's researchers pioneered the combination of clinical and economic research in order to assess which medical treatments are the most effective for use in the NHS.

Aberdeen is building its presence overseas, too, chiefly through a joint venture in Qatar, where it has become the first UK university to offer bachelor's degrees, initially in business management and accountancy and finance.

In Scotland, there are still only 14,500 students, a third of whom come from the

---

King's College
Aberdeen AB24 3FX
01224 272 090
study@abdn.ac.uk
www.aberdeen.ac.uk
www.ausa.org.uk
Open days 2019:
see website

The Times and The Sunday Times **Rankings**

Overall Ranking: 26 (last year: 40)

Teaching quality	79.6%	69
Student experience	79.9%	=42
Research quality	29.9%	44
Entry standards	182	=12
Graduate prospects	80.9%	=39
Good honours	85.4%	16
Expected completion rate	89.5%	41
Student/staff ratio	15.4	=55
Services and facilities	£2,369	45

north of the country. About one in six is from England among a total of 120 nationalities. Entry standards are once again in the top 20 in the UK, but a contextualised admissions policy encourages lower offers for applicants from schools with generally poor results. There is also a Children's University, which provides a range of accredited activities to encourage primary and secondary school children to engage in educational and active extracurricular pursuits.

New undergraduates are paired with current students, often on the same course, under the Students4Students scheme, to help them settle in and get the most from university life. There is a menu of "enhanced study" options designed to broaden undergraduate degrees. Students can incorporate a language, business or computing into their degree, or choose from a range of cross-disciplinary programmes. The aim is to give graduates broader knowledge and more intellectual flexibility, and Aberdeen's last institutional review praised the "transformative" effect of curriculum reforms, as well as the quality of online learning resources, personal tutoring and employability initiatives.

In tune with its location, the university is particularly strong in disciplines related to the oil and gas industries. At its own underwater research facility, Oceanlab, at Newburgh, north of Aberdeen, engineers lead the world in creating systems capable of operating at depths of up to 11,000 metres. The university's expertise is spread much more widely, however.

Three quarters of the work submitted for the 2014 Research Excellence Framework was rated as world-leading or internationally excellent. The university was placed top in the UK for environmental and soil science and in the top three for psychology and English.

Students find the city lively and welcoming, if expensive: the JobLink service provides a good selection of part-time employment. Aberdeen was named as the safest city in Scotland in 2017 by a consulting firm which ranked 230 cities.

The university's ICT network has more than 1,600 computers for student use. All new undergraduates are guaranteed housing – an important benefit in a city with the highest rents in Scotland. A £22m Aquatic Centre, with 50-metre pool and ten-metre diving board, opened in 2014, completing the Aberdeen Sports Village, which includes a full-size indoor football pitch

Good train connections, including several direct services to London each day, and a busy airport make Aberdeen's location less remote. Few universities can offer such outstanding scenery and natural facilities for outdoor pursuits.

Tuition fees

» Fees for Scottish/EU students 2019–20   £0–£1,820
RUK fees   £9,250 (capped at £27,750 for 4-year courses)
» Fees for International students 2019–20   £15,300–£19,300
Medicine   £40,500
» For scholarship and bursary information see
www.aberdeen.ac.uk/study/undergraduate/finance.php
» Graduate salary   £22,500

Student numbers

Undergraduates	9,742	(466)
Postgraduates	2,529	(1,411)
Applications/places		19,120/2,295
Applications per place		8.3
Overall offer rate		76.9%
International students		31.3%

Accommodation

University provided places: 3,204 (catered 7%)
Catered costs: £147 per week
Self-catered: £99–£142 per week
First years guaranteed accommodation
www.abdn.ac.uk/accommodation

Where do the students come from?

State schools (non-grammar)	76.1%	Working-class homes	25%	Black ethnic minority	2.6%
Grammar schools	3.5%	Deprived areas	3.7%	Disabled	5.7%
Independent schools	20.4%	All ethnic minorities	10.1%	Mature (over 21)	16.8%

Abertay University

Abertay was the first university to introduce the minimum access thresholds recommended by Scotland's Commission on Widening Access for the 2019 intake of students onwards. The scheme identifies the minimum academic standard and subject knowledge needed to complete a programme.

In business management, for example, this could mean three C-grade Highers, rather than the standard offer of four Bs, where promising applicants attend a school or college with little tradition of progress to higher education, have spent significant time in care, live in an area of deprivation, or have parents or guardians who did not go to university. The university scores well for state-school admissions and the proportion of mature learners in our new social inclusion ranking.

More than a third of the undergraduates arrive from colleges rather than schools, and 96% are from some part of the state sector, almost exclusively from comprehensive schools.

With fewer than 4,000 students, Abertay promises a more personal experience than undergraduates receive at most universities. It is based in the centre of Dundee, with all the teaching and learning buildings within five minutes' walk of each other. They are modern and functional, such as the innovative White Space facility, the university's flagship creative learning and working environment, where students study alongside industry professionals who are working on real commercial or broadcast projects.

New laboratories costing £3.5m opened in 2017, supporting teaching and research in food, forensics and biomedical science. Students were consulted on the design of the labs, which include Scotland's only Consumer Experience Laboratory for use by the university's highly-rated Division of Food and Drink. Another £4m has been spent refurbishing the Bernard King library, named after a former principal, which has 250 computer workstations.

Abertay, best known for computer arts and game design, has reshaped its portfolio of courses, having introduced mandatory interdisciplinary courses for all undergraduates and Scotland's first accelerated degrees. It dropped the least popular of its traditional programmes.

The seven fast-track honours degrees include ethical hacking and computer arts, which can be taken in three years, rather than the norm of four north of the border. The final two years consist of 45 weeks rather than the usual 30. Other subjects available in this format – unique so far in Scotland – include business studies, game design and production, sports development, and food and consumer science.

Further reforms have included quicker responses to assessed work, with students submitting work electronically and receiving

Kydd Building
Bell Street
Dundee DD1 1HG
01382 308 000
sro@abertay.ac.uk
www.abertay.ac.uk
www.abertaysa.com
Open days 2019:
see website

The Times and The Sunday Times Rankings

Overall Ranking: =105 (last year: 98)		
Teaching quality	79.2%	=71
Student experience	77%	=86
Research quality	5.1%	=92
Entry standards	157	35
Graduate prospects	73.4%	=83
Good honours	70.4%	=85
Expected completion rate	74.9%	123
Student/staff ratio	18.5	=112
Services and facilities	£1,905	96

their feedback and marks the same way. Grading was simplified, and students guaranteed to have lectures and seminars in the same place at the same time every week. An improvement in the outcome for the wider student experience is a welcome dividend.

They are part of a move towards more problem- and work-based approaches to learning, focusing on real-world issues and teamwork. All courses can be taken on a part-time basis, and many programmes aim to offer students the chance to spend at least 30% of their time in industry.

The changes helped to reverse five years of decline in undergraduate enrolments in 2017. The demand for places is strongest in computer arts and games design, the area for which the university is best known and where it claims to be the world leader.

Abertay introduced the UK's first degree in ethical hacking and cyber-security, and has a partnership with Perfect World Education, in China, to deliver a master's degree in Beijing. Sony chose the university as the site for the largest teaching laboratory in Europe for its PlayStation consoles, and Abertay hosts the national Centre for Excellence in Computer Games Education. All games students become members of UKIE (UK Interactive Entertainment) and gain access to a bespoke programme of industry mentorship and support.

Graduates include David Jones, the creator of the Grand Theft Auto video game series, and more recently the founders of independent games studio Puny Astronaut, who last year secured a six-figure deal to bring their first game to market.

The university hosts the Dundee Academy of Sport, launched in partnership with Dundee and Angus College – a venture using sport as a vehicle for learning.

The city has seen considerable investment recently, including the development of its waterfront, centred on the £80m V&A Dundee design museum, which opened last year. The *Wall Street Journal* ranked it alongside Shanghai, Madagascar and the Faroe Islands as one of world's ten "hot destinations". Dundee has a large student population and the cost of living is modest – a study by the website GoCompare rated Abertay the most affordable university in the UK.

A 500-bed student village allows all first-years who want accommodation to be guaranteed a place, and about 10% of students benefit from support which includes bursaries for students from the rest of the UK whose family income is below £34,000.

Tuition fees

» Fees for Scottish/EU students 2019–20	£0–£1,820
RUK fees	£9,250
» Fees for International students 2019–20	£14,000–£14,800
» For scholarship and bursary information see	
www.abertay.ac.uk/study-apply/money-fees-and-funding	
» Graduate salary	£20,500

Student numbers

Undergraduates	3,252	(205)
Postgraduates	176	(213)
Applications/places	5,010/1,040	
Applications per place	4.8	
Overall offer rate	88.7%	
International students	14.2%	

Accommodation

University provided places: 500 (catered 0%)
Self-catered: £62–£125 per week
First years guaranteed accommodation
www.abertay.ac.uk/life/accommodation

Where do the students come from?

State schools (non-grammar)	95.4%	Working-class homes	33.8%	Black ethnic minority	0.9%
Grammar schools	0.6%	Deprived areas	8.8%	Disabled	7.8%
Independent schools	4.0%	All ethnic minorities	6.2%	Mature (over 21)	35.7%

Aberystwyth University

Now a double winner of our University of the Year for Teaching Quality title, the government has backed this assessment of Aberystwyth with a gold award in its Teaching Excellence Framework (TEF). Aber had opted out of the initial round of TEF rankings published in 2017.

The high levels of student satisfaction that won the university our award for two years running have now helped secure the TEF outcome. The adjudication panel found "outstanding levels of stretch" ensuring that all students were significantly challenged to achieve their full potential. Substantial investment in elearning was another plus point, as was the integrated approach to Welsh-language teaching.

The university has been making great strides up our league table, after a slump to 79th position in 2015, despite implementing cuts to address a growing deficit. A plan to save £11.4m over two years has seen a restructuring of departments with the eventual loss of up to 100 jobs. Lower student numbers were partly responsible for the deficit, with tuition income falling by £2.4m.

Although applications and enrolments have now steadied, numbers of new undergraduates are down by almost a third on the last year before higher fees were introduced, despite an offer rate that is among the highest in the UK.

New courses are still being introduced, however. Degrees in computer science, modern languages, and psychology and education took their first students last year. Three-year science degrees are already being offered as four-year programmes, including a year in industry, and there is a range of four-year integrated master's degrees, which reach postgraduate levels of study without the need to source additional funding.

Important capital developments are also under way. Aber is investing more than £20m in restoring the iconic Old College building, which will include performance and gallery space and a centre for entrepreneurs and new businesses, as well as a cafe and community rooms. It will also house a university museum and a science centre with interactive displays alongside a planetarium and 4D facility, highlighting the university's links with the European Space Agency.

The university's strategic plan promises further improvements in the student experience. A £1m refurbishment of the Hugh Owen Library on the Penglais campus was completed last year and the Arts Centre's 300-seat theatre has undergone a refit. The Welsh medium hall of residence is set to reopen in September this year with en-suite accommodation for 200 students, following a £12m refurbishment.

Penglais
Aberystwyth SY23 3FL
01970 622 021
ug-admissions@aber.ac.uk
www.aber.ac.uk
www.abersu.co.uk
Open days 2019:
see website

The Times and The Sunday Times Rankings
Overall Ranking: =48 (last year: =47)

Teaching quality	86.5%	1
Student experience	84.1%	3
Research quality	28.1%	46
Entry standards	119	=100
Graduate prospects	78.2%	56
Good honours	67.3%	=104
Expected completion rate	83.2%	85
Student/staff ratio	16.6	=83
Services and facilities	£1,838	102

Several more campus developments are planned. A £40.5m Innovation and Enterprise Campus, on the university's Gogerddan site, will feature a biorefining centre, future food centre, analytical science laboratories and a seed processing and biobank facility. There are plans, too, for a veterinary hub for research to protect both animal and human health, with backing from the European Regional Development Fund through the Welsh government.

Scores in the 2014 Research Excellence Framework showed improvement on the previous assessments, with the departments of international politics, geography and earth science, and the Institute of Biological, Environmental and Rural Sciences (Ibers) doing particularly well. The institute, which serves 1,500 undergraduate and research students, gives Aber the widest range of land-related courses in the UK.

The attractive seaside location remains a draw for applicants, although travel to other parts of the UK is slow. The two campuses are about a mile apart, with teaching facilities and residential accommodation within walking distance of each other. But it was announced last year that a branch campus in Mauritius, which lost £1m in its first two years after struggling to recruit students, is set to close.

About a third of Aber's students are from Wales, and Welsh-medium teaching is thriving. More than 95% of the undergraduates are state educated – 91% in comprehensive schools — a higher proportion than expected given the mix of subjects. The Student Welcome Centre continues to offer advice on everything from money problems to learning difficulties long after undergraduates have enrolled.

There is self-catering accommodation for more than 3,300 students, with a central hub that includes social and learning facilities. Three university libraries are complemented by the National Library of Wales, which gives free access to students. An app brings together a range of study-related services on a single screen, allowing students to check what lectures and seminars they have, access their AberLearn virtual learning pages, look at local bus timetables and see what public computers are available.

The Students' Union (AberSU) was named the best Higher Education Students' Union in Wales for 2017 and has the largest entertainment venue in the region. Sports facilities are good and well used. As well as a refurbished fitness centre, there are two sports halls and outdoor facilities include a swimming pool, 400-metre running track, 50 acres of playing fields and specialist facilities for water sports.

Tuition fees

» Fees for UK/EU students 2019–20   £9,000
» Fees for International students 2019–20   £13,600–£15,200
» For scholarship and bursary information see
   www.aber.ac.uk/en/undergrad/money-matters
» Graduate salary   £18,720

Student numbers

Undergraduates	6,069	(1,256)
Postgraduates	601	(529)
Applications/places		8,940/1,965
Applications per place		4.5
Overall offer rate		98.5%
International students		14.8%

Accommodation

University provided places: 3,500 (catered 4%)
Catered costs: £116 per week
Self-catered: £85–£136 per week
First years guaranteed accommodation
www.aber.ac.uk/en/accommodation

Where do the students come from?

State schools (non-grammar)	90.8%	Working-class homes	33.8%	Black ethnic minority	0.6%
Grammar schools	4.4%	Deprived areas	12.5%	Disabled	9.7%
Independent schools	4.8%	All ethnic minorities	6.1%	Mature (over 21)	11.9%

Anglia Ruskin University

Anglia Ruskin's was the only one of five new medical schools ready to take its first students last year. A £20m building on the Chelmsford campus and a 20-year history as the east of England's largest provider of nursing, midwifery and allied health courses gave the university a head start on the rest.

The medical school is the first to open in Essex and it is hoped that up to half of the 100 places each year will go to students from the region, who will also stay to practise there when they qualify.

The new school came hard on the heels of the opening of Anglia's Science Centre. The £45m development, on the university's Cambridge campus, offers impressive new facilities for students and researchers in psychology, animal biology, and biomedical science and forensics. These include a 200-seat bioscience laboratory, a 300-seat lecture theatre and expanded space for postgraduate students.

However, the expansion of degree apprenticeships, promised in a new strategy launched on the 25th anniversary of Anglia Ruskin's becoming a university, may prove to be equally significant. There are some 800 apprentices in the current academic year, and the university plans to almost double this number by September. A dozen new programmes will include B2B sales,

civil engineering, and senior leadership, as well as others for police officers and digitech business analysts.

Anglia Ruskin has a history of providing innovative courses: the BOptom (Hons) was the first qualification of its kind in the UK and the hearing aid audiology course was among the first to lead directly to registration. Each undergraduate has an adviser to help compile a degree package, looking at the chosen subject from different points of view to maximise future job prospects.

The university scores well for student perceptions of teaching quality and for their wider university experience – comfortably the strongest areas in our survey – but its overall ranking has fallen again this year. It gained a silver award in the new Teaching Excellence Framework, winning praise for its support for students at risk of dropping out and for employers' contributions to the curriculum.

Anglia Ruskin won an award for its work with 2,000 businesses, which attempts to instil entrepreneurial values in both students and staff. The university has an innovative scheme placing graduates with the region's small firms – usually the companies that are least likely to take on those emerging from higher education.

There are more than 35,000 students on campuses in Chelmsford, Cambridge and Peterborough, as well as in the City of London, where the focus is on business courses.

Bishop Hall Lane
Chelmsford CM1 1SQ
01245 686 868
answers@anglia.ac.uk
www.anglia.ac.uk
www.angliastudent.com
Open days 2019:
see website

The Times and The Sunday Times **Rankings**
Overall Ranking: 122 (last year: 113)

Teaching quality	82.4%	=30
Student experience	79.1%	=54
Research quality	5.4%	=90
Entry standards	106	=127
Graduate prospects	68.3%	108
Good honours	71.3%	=80
Expected completion rate	79.2%	=109
Student/staff ratio	18.2	=106
Services and facilities	£1,520	125

There is also a partnership with the College of West Anglia, which allows some 10,000 students to take Anglia Ruskin degree courses in King's Lynn, Wisbech and Milton, on the outskirts of Cambridge.

The university has spent £100m on campus improvements in the past six years, adding facilities such as medical science SuperLabs, mock hospital wards, computer gaming suites and paramedic skills labs.

The numbers taking up places had been steady since the introduction of £9,000 fees, but there was a 16% fall in new enrolments in 2017. Nearly all the undergraduates attended state schools or colleges and almost 40% were from the four poorest socioeconomic groups at the time of the last survey.

Some world-leading research was identified in all five faculties in the 2014 Research Excellence Framework. The best performances were in music, drama and the performing arts. Health subjects also did well, alongside media studies, geography and environmental science. The Global Sustainability Institute is building an international reputation for its research, and Anglia Ruskin is aiming to make sustainability an important part of every student's experience.

The social scene naturally varies between campuses, but all are within an hour of London by train. There is no formal guarantee of accommodation for new entrants, other than international students, but most are offered one of the 2,300 residential places if they apply by the end of August. September is usually not too late, but there may be a waiting list.

The university offers a range of sporting facilities, including an on-campus sports centre with a well-equipped gym in Chelmsford. In Cambridge, there is also a gym on campus and work has begun on a £5m redevelopment of its nearby outdoor sports ground to add two new full-size, floodlit artificial pitches, including a 3G pitch. There will be a new pavilion with changing rooms, spectator viewing and a warm-up gym plus three grass pitches for football and rugby. In Peterborough, Anglia Ruskin students have access to Vivacity's clubs. There are also leisure centres and a lido.

Tuition fees

» Fees for UK/EU students 2019–20   £9,250
  Foundation courses   £7,750
» Fees for International students 2018–19   £12,500–£14,500
» For scholarship and bursary information see
  www.anglia.ac.uk/student-life/help-with-finances
» Graduate salary   £22,000

Student numbers

Undergraduates	15,566 (2,560)
Postgraduates	1,897 (2,221)
Applications/places	18,070/2,645
Applications per place	6.8
Overall offer rate	73.5%
International students	12.8%

Accommodation

University provided places: 2,306
Self-catered: £94–£169 per week
First years accommodated on first-come-first-served basis
www.anglia.ac.uk/student-life/accommodation

Where do the students come from?

State schools (non-grammar)	92.4%	Working-class homes	38.9%	Black ethnic minority	15.7%
Grammar schools	4.0%	Deprived areas	16.6%	Disabled	5.7%
Independent schools	3.6%	All ethnic minorities	31.3%	Mature (over 21)	53.1%

Arts University Bournemouth

The Arts University Bournemouth (AUB) has consolidated its previous rise of 13 places in our table, assisted by the best employment record of any of its specialist arts university peers.

Its successes in the graduate employment market also helped AUB to a gold rating in the Teaching Excellence Framework. The judging panel praised the high levels of stimulation and challenge in small classes and regular contact with tutors.

Professionals are engaged in the delivery of courses so that students develop the relevant skills to succeed in employment, while physical and digital resources were said to be of the highest quality, providing a professional work environment for students.

The accolades continued last year with the presentation of a Queen's Anniversary Prize for "distinguished degree level education in costume design for the UK's leading creative industries". The citation noted the achievements of AUB alumni in Oscar nominations and extensive involvement in high-profile television productions such as *Downton Abbey* and *Sherlock*, as well as in live theatre. More prosaically, AUB's foundation diploma courses were rated as outstanding by Ofsted.

There are almost five applications for every place, despite a drop in demand in 2017, making AUB one of the most selective universities in the country. It has operated as a specialist institution since 1885 and offers degrees in acting, architecture, dance, event management and film production, as well as art and design subjects. The university describes its courses as having a "highly practical streak" designed to give students an edge in a competitive creative world.

The university has a Skillset Media Academy in partnership with Bournemouth University, offering eight accredited courses in areas from animation to make-up for media and performance. The two institutions also bid successfully to become a Screen Academy, through which Skillset recognises excellence in film and the broader screen-based media.

Plans have been approved for an Innovation Studio for student and alumni start-up companies on the main campus in Poole.

Recent developments include the opening of the first drawing studio to be built at a UK art school for 100 years. The Photography Building opened in 2015, with flexible teaching spaces and IT suites, while the Gallery showcases work by students and other contemporary artists, hosting talks, events and film nights to support the exhibition programme.

The Enterprise Pavilion on campus helps to develop, attract and retain new creative businesses in the southwest.

The purpose-built library includes the Museum of Design in Plastics, which holds more than 12,000 artefacts of predominantly

Wallisdown
Poole BH12 5HH
01202 363 228
admissions@aub.ac.uk
www.aub.ac.uk
www.aub.ac.uk/life-aub/
students-union
Open days 2019:
see website

The Times and The Sunday Times **Rankings**
Overall Ranking: =51 (last year: 51)

Teaching quality	80.7%	=54
Student experience	78.5%	=65
Research quality	2.4%	119
Entry standards	161	=28
Graduate prospects	80.5%	46
Good honours	67.5%	101
Expected completion rate	89.3%	42
Student/staff ratio	15.7	=61
Services and facilities	£1,786	109

20th- and 21st-century mass-produced design and popular culture. The items are selected specifically to support the academic courses taught at the university.

Laser-cutting machinery and a 3D printer feature among the high-tech equipment available to students.

Only 12 staff were entered for the 2014 Research Excellence Framework, in which 43% of their work was rated as world-leading or internationally excellent. Students and staff liaise on an innovative programme of professional practice and research, with different disciplines encouraged to work together.

Many AUB academics have links to and experience in the creative industries, while the careers service provides students with subject-specific and generic advice on future employment. Industry liaison groups and visiting tutors keep the university abreast of developments in the creative industries, and alumni return regularly as lecturers.

A low dropout rate is a point of particular pride for AUB. Although it has slipped above 6% in the latest projection, that is still well below the university's benchmark figure. Seven out of ten entrants last year were expected to receive some form of financial assistance. Current support for students includes bicycle vouchers, funding for educational visits and hardship loans.

More than 700 residential places are either run by the university or endorsed by it, with 300 more rooms to come in halls that are under construction on campus. There is a register of approved housing at the website www.aubstudentpad.com and accommodation days in July and August help current and prospective students to find potential housemates. Priority for the allocation of university places goes to overseas students and those with disabilities or other medical conditions. But plans for expansion at the campus in Poole should enable it to take at least some more students.

AUB has no sports facilities of its own but provides a subsidy for its students to access the extensive facilities and clubs at neighbouring Bournemouth University. The town has a large, cosmopolitan student population and one of the most vibrant club scenes outside London. The capital is less than two hours away by regular train and coach services or via good motorway links.

Tuition fees

» Fees for UK/EU students 2019–20   £9,250
Foundation years £6,000

» Fees for International students 2019–20   £13,250–£16,950

» For scholarship and bursary information see www.aub.ac.uk/apply/funding

» Graduate salary   £18,000

Student numbers		
Undergraduates	3,177	(19)
Postgraduates	72	(46)
Applications/places	6,415/1,275	
Applications per place	5.0	
Overall offer rate	57.1%	
International students	16.0%	

Accommodation

University provided places: 739 (catered 0%)
Self-catered: £145–£175 per week
No accommodation guarantee
www.aub.ac.uk/apply/accommodation

Where do the students come from?

State schools (non-grammar)	95.1%	Working-class homes	30.4%	Black ethnic minority	2.6%
Grammar schools	1.1%	Deprived areas	10.6%	Disabled	12.7%
Independent schools	3.8%	All ethnic minorities	11.9%	Mature (over 21)	10.4%

University of the Arts London

The University of the Arts London (UAL) is the biggest university of its type in Europe and among the top six institutions in the world in the QS subject ranking for art and design, which relies heavily on academic reputation. It is also one of the biggest risers in our table this year.

Student satisfaction remains stubbornly low in London and in some specialist arts universities in particular — a combination that does UAL no favours — while immediate graduate prospects are notoriously uncertain in its fields. However, the university has taken imaginative (and often expensive) initiatives to improve both the student experience and graduate employability, with the latter seeing a 35-place rise in our rankings.

UAL will soon be unrecognisable from the group of colleges that came together as the London Institute 30 years ago and received university status in 2004. A new campus will be ready for the London College of Fashion (LCF) at the Queen Elizabeth Olympic Park next year, forming part of the East Bank arts quarter alongside the V&A and Sadler's Wells.

Another new campus is being developed for the London College of Communication, near its existing premises at Elephant and Castle, while Central Saint Martins (CSM) already occupies a prize-winning building at King's Cross. The £200m development brought CSM together on one site for the first time, and its grade II listed former granary was voted the world's best higher education building of the year.

The redevelopment of the Camberwell College of Arts campus is now complete, adding galleries, refectory, workshops, studios and a new library, as well as a 264-room hall of residence.

Chelsea College of Arts, the other member of the original grouping, already had a new base next to the Tate Gallery when the university was formed. Wimbledon College of Arts joined in 2006, bringing an international reputation in theatre design and the UK's largest school of theatre. A new Total Performance School there brings together all the main performance disciplines, enabling students to work in teams to design, perform and manage theatre and other live events to a professional level.

The constituent colleges continue to use their own names and enjoy considerable autonomy. The university as a whole now has 14,000 undergraduates, almost 80% of whom study art and design. Entry is highly competitive: even during three years of falling demand for places, only 30% of applicants received offers. There has been a recovery, with a 1.6% increase in applications, bucking the national trend.

A Creative Attributes Framework, drawn up in consultation with leading employers such as John Lewis, Estée Lauder and Bafta, is designed to ensure that all UAL's courses enable students to develop the qualities they will need to succeed in the creative industries. Students have access to

272 High Holborn
London WC1V 7EY
020 7514 6000
http://enquiries.arts.ac.uk
www.arts.ac.uk
www.arts-su.com
Open days 2019:
see website

The Times and The Sunday Times Rankings

Overall Ranking: =94 (last year: 115)

Teaching quality	76.3%	=109
Student experience	70.9%	=126
Research quality	8.0%	73
Entry standards	139	54
Graduate prospects	72.2%	=91
Good honours	65.8%	=116
Expected completion rate	84.1%	=75
Student/staff ratio	14.4	29
Services and facilities	£1,805	107

the largest specialist careers centre in the country for art and design, while the pioneering Fashion Technology: Emerging Futures programme supports graduates early in their careers.

In September 2017 UAL also opened notjustashop to sell products and artwork designed by its alumni, with the profits helping to support the enterprise programme for students and graduates.

This is a university like no other. Where else would the university chancellor – artist Grayson Perry – take to the stage for last summer's graduation ceremonies in a couture gown containing 220,000 hand-stitched pearl beads held together with 6kg of lurex? The garment was designed by UAL fashion textile knit student Yuxuan Yang after Perry challenged students to design his ensemble for graduation. Assisted by fellow student Gemma Maarten and 92 other LCF students, the gown was the product of countless beading parties held over several weeks.

UAL performed well in the 2014 Research Excellence Framework, when 83% of the work submitted was considered world-leading or internationally excellent. All of it reached one of the top two categories for its external impact. The university is a partner in the newly established Institute of Coding, announced by prime minister Theresa May at the World Economic Forum in Davos last year. UAL is one of 25 university partners in the organisation, which aims to ensure employers and individuals can access the skills they need in the global digital economy.

Equally impressively for prospective applicants, across the years, half of all the shortlisted artists for the Turner Prize have been UAL graduates. The Business of Fashion named CSM as the best college in the world for undergraduates – and London College of Fashion as fourth best – in its most recent ranking.

One example of the close relationship with the creative industries is a five-year investment by fashion giant Kering to develop a joint curriculum in sustainability. Around one third of the undergraduates come from the four poorest socioeconomic groups, while 94% attended state schools or colleges.

The colleges vary considerably in character and facilities, although a single students' union serves them all. The university's student hub provides a central place for students to work, socialise and share ideas, as well as being the location for student services such as housing and careers. UAL has 13 halls of residence spread around the colleges. Househunting workshops help those who have to rely on the scattered private housing market.

Tuition fees

» Fees for UK/EU students 2019–20 Foundation courses from £5,420	£9,250
» Fees for International students 2019–20	£19,930
» For scholarship and bursary information see www.arts.ac.uk/study-at-ual/student-fees-funding	
» Graduate salary	£19,200

Student numbers

Undergraduates	14,567	(194)
Postgraduates	2,774	(755)
Applications/places	27,935/4,160	
Applications per place	6.7	
Overall offer rate	30.2%	
International students	46.8%	

Accommodation

University provided places: 3,500 (catered 0%)
Self-catered: £119–£297 per week
No accommodation guarantee
www.arts.ac.uk/study-at-ual/accommodation

Where do the students come from?

State schools (non-grammar)	91.6%	Working-class homes	33.1%	Black ethnic minority	8.6%
Grammar schools	2.0%	Deprived areas	7.1%	Disabled	17.4%
Independent schools	6.4%	All ethnic minorities	29.8%	Mature (over 21)	20.1%

Aston University

Aston has been sliding down our league table, slipping back this time even in areas of traditional strength such as student satisfaction and graduate job prospects. Indeed, the university has now dropped out of the top 50 – a surprising contrast to its position well inside the top 30 a decade ago. Aston's popularity with students is undimmed, however, with applications and enrolments remaining far above the levels seen before the introduction of £9,000 fees.

A portfolio of job-oriented degrees with work experience as standard is the main attraction. The university finishes higher in our new social inclusion rankings than it does in our academic league table. No university has a larger proportion of ethnic students.

For the first time, medicine is among the options for undergraduates in the current academic year. The medical school has been taking postgraduates since 2015, but the first undergraduate cohort is made up of international applicants and local students on the innovative Sir Doug Ellis Pathway to Healthcare programme who achieved the entry criteria. The aim is to be the most socially inclusive medical school in the UK, with up to 40% of students from low-income families.

The strategic involvement of professional bodies and employers in course design and delivery was among the qualities that brought Aston a gold rating in the Teaching Excellence Framework. The panel was impressed by the way in which employability skills were embedded through an integrated placement year, pre-entry masterclasses, the Talent Bank placement matching service, and the Aston professional mentoring scheme.

A glowing testimonial also described "outstanding physical and digital resources that are actively and consistently used by students" and "personalised provision with the highest levels of engagement and commitment, including bookable personal tutoring sessions and a substantial number of trained student peer mentors".

Entrants this year will have access to a new students' union at the heart of the campus, which now features open green spaces and a remodelled Chancellor's Lake. Located close to the centre of Birmingham, the university has replaced its 1970s buildings with modern teaching facilities and conveniently-placed student accommodation.

A £215m programme of improvements includes an impressive library and a new home for the highly-rated business school, which accounts for almost half of all Aston's students. The school has announced a new partnership with the French business school, Kedge, to collaborate on teaching and research. Among the benefits will be access to the Kedge campus in Suzhou, China, for Aston students.

Aston Triangle
Birmingham B4 7ET
0121 204 3000
ugadmissions@aston.ac.uk
www.aston.ac.uk
www.astonsu.com
Open days 2019:
see website

The Times and The Sunday Times **Rankings**

Overall Ranking: 56 (last year: 46)

Teaching quality	79.0%	=78
Student experience	78.3%	=70
Research quality	25.8%	49
Entry standards	137	58
Graduate prospects	79.1%	52
Good honours	81.3%	=26
Expected completion rate	90.7%	33
Student/staff ratio	20.1	125
Services and facilities	£1,937	92

Once a college of advanced technology, Aston also remains strong in engineering and the sciences. A partnership between the school of engineering and applied science, and Capgemini, a global consulting, technology and outsourcing company, was responsible for the UK's first degree apprenticeships. There are now 340 students taking nine programmes, which range from digital technology solutions to nuclear engineering and supply chain leadership and management.

A further 11 traditional degrees ranging from international business and Mandarin Chinese to biochemistry and a series of joint degrees with history, have also been launched. Seven out of ten students undertake work experience, often abroad, and many later secure graduate jobs at the scene of their placement. The university is already in the top four on this measure and is aiming to offer placements on every course by 2020. Aston's was voted the best placement service at the National Undergraduate Employability Awards and the university also won the award for the best employer engagement with the careers service.

Aston has been concentrating on improving the student experience and boosting research performance. It did well in the latest assessments of research, doubling the proportion of work in the top two categories to 80%. Life and health sciences led the way, with business and management, politics and engineering also producing good results. New research centres in enterprise, healthy ageing, Europe, and neuroscience and child development proved their worth, and research funding is at record levels. Aston was also one of a dozen universities to be awarded a prestigious Regius Professorship to celebrate the Queen's 90th birthday. Aston's is in pharmacy, another of the university's strengths.

The MyAston mobile app, used regularly by 80% of students, gives access to course materials and other information. The completion of the Aston student village brought the number of residential places on campus past the 3,000 mark, maintaining the guarantee of accommodation for all first-year students who make Aston their firm choice on their UCAS application.

The Woodcock Sport Centre, which includes a grade II listed swimming pool and a sports hall with indoor courts and team sports facilities, is the centrepiece of the sporting offer.

Tuition fees

- » Fees for UK/EU students 2019–20 £9,250
- » Fees for International students 2019–20 £14,600–£18,500
  Medicine £37,000
- » For scholarship and bursary information see www.aston.ac.uk/study/undergraduate/student-finance
- » Graduate salary £21,500

Student numbers

Undergraduates	10,111	(926)
Postgraduates	1,469	(1,104)
Applications/places	16,270/2,420	
Applications per place	6.7	
Overall offer rate	84%	
International students	17.8%	

Accommodation

University provided places: 3,000 (catered 7%)
Self-catered: £131–£137 per week
First years guaranteed accommodation
www.aston.ac.uk/accommodation/

Where do the students come from?

State schools (non-grammar)	87.2%	Working-class homes	42.1%	Black ethnic minority	15.2%
Grammar schools	7.7%	Deprived areas	9.8%	Disabled	3.0%
Independent schools	5.1%	All ethnic minorities	72.4%	Mature (over 21)	4.5%

Bangor University

Bangor has always benefited from levels of student satisfaction that are among the highest in Wales and now close to the top 20 in the UK. But its National Student Survey (NSS) scores have been higher in the past; the fall has contributed to a dip in its overall ranking.

The NSS successes were the prime reason Bangor was the only university in Wales to achieve a gold award in the first round of the Teaching Excellence Framework. The panel commented favourably on the personalised support for students and strategic approach to assessment, as well as the very good physical and virtual learning resources. Welsh/English bilingual learning was another area to attract praise.

Bangor also opened a £20m science park on Anglesey last year, bringing together businesses from the ICT, science and research sectors with staff and students from the university. There is outline planning consent for more building, which could include a £100m thermal and hydraulic testing facility.

The highly-rated School of Ocean Sciences is located just across the Menai Straits, but the other 22 academic schools are all within walking distance of each other in Bangor. The small coastal city is rated as one of the cheapest – and safest – places in the UK in which to study. Much of the university estate has been redeveloped or modernised in recent years.

Applications have dipped a little recently, but undergraduate enrolments have been broadly steady. Most students come from outside Wales, but around 20% speak Welsh and one of the halls of residence is for Welsh-speakers and learners of the language.

A peer guiding scheme arranges for second- and third-year students to mentor new arrivals and arrange social activities for them. Bangor also has a flourishing international exchange programme, which gives students the option of studying overseas for one extra year in a wide variety of destinations.

A raft of new degrees includes professional Welsh (Cymraeg proffesiynol). Geography with environmental forestry is also offered alongside physical geography and oceanography, and law with Chinese. The Study Skills Centre helps with the transition to university and provides continuing academic support.

In addition, the Bangor Employability Award accredits co curricular and extracurricular activities, such as volunteering and part-time work, that are valued by employers. The university maintains formal links with Horizon Nuclear Power and Siemens Healthcare Diagnostics to provide skilled graduates in specific fields.

There is a pioneering dyslexia service, which offers individual and group support

College Road
Bangor LL57 2DG
01248 383 717
applicantservices@bangor.ac.uk
www.bangor.ac.uk
www.undebbangor.com
Open days 2019:
see website

The Times and The Sunday Times **Rankings**

Overall Ranking: =63 (last year: 55)

Teaching quality	83.3%	=19
Student experience	81.5%	=21
Research quality	27.2%	48
Entry standards	134	61
Graduate prospects	67.8%	111
Good honours	69.3%	=92
Expected completion rate	88.2%	=47
Student/staff ratio	16.7	=85
Services and facilities	£1,747	113

throughout students' courses. More than 9% of undergraduates receive a disability allowance – well above the sector average. More than 95% of the students come from state schools or colleges, many of them from areas of low participation in higher education. The university's Talent Opportunities Programme, which operates in schools across North Wales, targets potential applicants from families in lower socioeconomic groups who have little or no history of going to university.

Bangor finished among the top 50 universities in the 2014 Research Excellence Framework, with half of the schools rated in the top 20 in the UK, leisure and tourism, languages and psychology leading the way.

The university has almost 3,000 residential places – enough to guarantee accommodation to new entrants who apply by the end of July. The 600-bed student village has a cafe, shop, laundrette, student lounges, outdoor recreation and games area, a mini cinema and performance and music space.

Bangor's Pontio arts and innovation centre (the name means "to bridge" in Welsh) connects town and gown with a cinema, theatre and restaurants. At the time of its opening Professor John Hughes, Bangor's vice-chancellor, said it would be "transformational" for the university and region, and placed Pontio firmly in the community tradition that saw quarrymen in the 19th century put part of their weekly wages towards the establishment of a college. Bangor's School of Lifelong Learning continues the tradition with courses across North Wales.

Social life for most students is concentrated mainly on the students' union, housed in the centre. Its clubs and societies, which are free to students, were voted the best in the UK for two years in succession. Bangor's main sports centre has a two-storey gym, including 50 cardiovascular machines, a six-platform Olympic lifting area, two sports halls, an aerobics studio, cycling studio, gymnastics hall, climbing wall and squash courts, and gym membership is included in halls fees. The region's spectacular scenery, with its outdoor sporting opportunities from Snowdonia to the sea, is among the university's attractions.

Tuition fees

» Fees for UK/EU students 2019–20 £9,000
» Fees for International students 2018–19 £12,750–£14,800
» For scholarship and bursary information see www.bangor.ac.uk/courses/undergrad/study-with-us/undergraduate-funding
» Graduate salary £20,000

Student numbers

Undergraduates	8,029	(588)
Postgraduates	1,509	(1,143)
Applications/places		9,560/2,075
Applications per place		4.6
Overall offer rate		93.8%
International students		21.2%

Accommodation

University provided places: 2,960 (catered 0%)
Self-catered: £80–£134 per week
First years guaranteed accommodation
www.bangor.ac.uk/studentlife/accommodation.php.en

Where do the students come from?

State schools (non-grammar)	89.3%	Working-class homes	34.9%	Black ethnic minority	1.6%
Grammar schools	6.5%	Deprived areas	15.3%	Disabled	9.3%
Independent schools	4.2%	All ethnic minorities	7.7%	Mature (over 21)	22.7%

University of Bath

Bath will welcome a period away from the limelight after finding itself at the centre of the storm over vice-chancellors' pay. Dame Glynis Breakwell's £468,000 salary was the highest at any university until she stepped down last August. The protracted controversy, which prompted the resignation of four MPs from the university's court, is thought to have affected student recruitment. A leaked email from Bath's head of admissions early in the 2018 recruitment cycle said that the university was "underperforming", while its main competitors had seen increases in applications.

Applications were already down in 2017, although there were still more than seven for each place. A gold award in the Teaching Excellence Framework came too late in the admissions cycle to influence most potential entrants, but the judging panel found that students from all backgrounds achieved consistently outstanding outcomes. Employer involvement and alumni mentoring help to develop the skills valued in the labour market and there is extensive professional accreditation across the curriculum, the panel said, while final-year dissertations and projects round off consistent and frequent engagement of students with developments from the forefront of research, scholarship and professional practice.

The university is in the top five for graduate prospects and invariably close to that ranking in our overall institutional league table. Almost two thirds of undergraduates take a work placement or study abroad as part of their degree. Student entrepreneurship is actively encouraged through a number of initiatives and projects.

Bath celebrated its 50th anniversary in 2016 with the opening of the £4.5m Virgil Building, a city centre student hub and professional services building, which has learning space, a cafe and access to student support services such as the careers service, students' union and skills centre. The university's 200-acre campus is on the edge of Bath, but the new development acknowledges that – particularly beyond the first year – many students base themselves in the city, a world heritage site and thriving social centre.

Three new buildings are under construction on the campus. The Milner Centre for Evolution is an £8.5m research development for the evolutionary sciences, a £34.5m residential development will add almost 300 places with a cafe and communal spaces, while the expansion of the Sports Training Village will double the number of exercise stations and provide more group space. A BSc in sport, management and coaching is planned this year, as is a new degree in criminology.

The sports facilities are outstanding and include a 50-metre Olympic Legacy swimming

Claverton Down
Bath BA2 7AY
01225 383 019
ask-admissions@bath.ac.uk
www.bath.ac.uk
www.thesubath.com
Open days 2019:
June 21, 22,
September 14

The Times and The Sunday Times Rankings
Overall Ranking: 13 (last year: 12)

Teaching quality	79.0%	=78
Student experience	80.7%	=31
Research quality	37.3%	24
Entry standards	186	10
Graduate prospects	87.5%	5
Good honours	86.2%	14
Expected completion rate	95.1%	11
Student/staff ratio	15.8	=66
Services and facilities	£2,486	37

pool, indoor running track, multipurpose sports hall, eight indoor tennis courts and indoor facilities for athletics, shooting, fencing and judo. There is even a revamped bobsleigh and skeleton start area, as used by Lizzy Yarnold, the double Olympic gold medallist, and her predecessor Amy Williams. They are among numerous graduates and elite users of the Sports Training Village to win medals at recent Olympic and Commonwealth games. But all students are encouraged to use the university's facilities through clubs for everything from ultimate frisbee to Latin and ballroom dancing. Bath also pioneered sports scholarships a quarter of a century ago, and there will be a range of them available this year.

Research is thriving: nearly a third of Bath's submission to the 2014 Research Excellence Framework was judged to be world-leading, with 87% in the top two categories. The university is the lead institution in the new National Institute of Coding, which is charged with improving the digital skills of the nation. The research grants and contracts portfolio is worth over £130m and there are 25 international strategic partnerships with top-ranked institutions worldwide.

Bath is a highly-internationalised university, with more than 30% of students coming from outside the UK, representing over 100 nationalities. A third of the 16,000 students are postgraduates. The modern campus has pleasant grounds with a grass amphitheatre and lake, as well as conveniently-placed amenities. The Edge, the arts, education and events centre, has a theatre, performance studio, rehearsal studios, three galleries and a cafe for use by the university and the wider community.

The university owns or manages more than 4,500 residential places, enabling it to accommodate all new entrants and more than a quarter of all undergraduates. More than one in four undergraduates come from independent schools and the university has one of the lowest intakes of students from comprehensive schools, just 55.5%, ranking Bath 122 out of 132 institutions in our guide.

Students generally like the city, and many take advantage of the nightlife of nearby Bristol, which is only a few minutes away by public transport. The popular students' union won an award for being one of the best developed and well managed in the UK. The university's support services include an up-to-date virtual learning environment and centralised provision of advisory services.

Tuition fees

» Fees for UK/EU students 2019–20 £9,250
   Foundation courses £7,710
» Fees for International students 2019–20 £16,600–£20,700
» For scholarship and bursary information see
   www.bath.ac.uk/study/ug/fees
» Graduate salary £26,000

Student numbers

Undergraduates	12,774	(99)
Postgraduates	2,423	(1,613)
Applications/places		27,555/3,535
Applications per place		7.8
Overall offer rate		80.1%
International students		29.2%

Accommodation

University provided places: 4,874 (catered 23%)
Catered costs: £180–£215 per week
Self-catered: £70–£210 per week
First years guaranteed accommodation
www.bath.ac.uk/groups/student-accommodation

Where do the students come from?

State schools (non-grammar)	55.5%	Working-class homes	18.2%	Black ethnic minority	1.8%
Grammar schools	17.1%	Deprived areas	5.5%	Disabled	5.5%
Independent schools	27.4%	All ethnic minorities	15.1%	Mature (over 21)	3.0%

Bath Spa University

Three years of sharp decline in rankings, during which the university has dropped 45 places in our table, are among the factors behind successive falls in applications to Bath Spa. The continuing reduction in the number of 18-year-olds and the national decline in demand from mature and part-time students contributed to another drop of more than 5% last year. The university is planning 14 new degrees for 2019, ranging from creative writing and publishing, drawing, and forensic psychology to festivals and events to stimulate demand.

The numbers actually starting degrees at Bath Spa remain much higher than in the years following the introduction of £9,000 fees, however. An attractive location and imaginative branding as "the university of creativity, culture and enterprise" proved popular with students. Styling itself as a liberal arts university, Bath Spa was the driving force behind the Global Academy of Liberal Arts (Gala), bringing together a diverse range of institutions from around the world.

With one eye on the recent decline in student satisfaction – previously one of Bath Spa's strengths in our table – Professor Susan Rigby, the new vice-chancellor, has been charged with "renewing the university's commitment to the student experience". For the current academic year, students have been given the option of a "professional placement year" on all undergraduate programmes which do not already offer it. Bath Spa is also launching a range of degree apprenticeships, starting with four programmes last year and adding another dozen from September, when there could be 350 apprentices.

The university is making progress on a massive capital project, converting a former factory close to the River Avon into a new campus for the Bath School of Art and Design. The first phase of the refurbished grade II listed building is due to open this year with modern teaching facilities, workshop, studio and gallery space, as well as a cafe and art shop. The new campus will also improve the cycle route and pedestrian pathway which runs alongside the Avon. The university has already spent £6m on specialist facilities for the school at the Sion Hill campus, which is also within walking distance of the city centre and where there is a student village of 550 study bedrooms.

The main Newton Park campus is four miles outside the World Heritage city, in grounds landscaped by Capability Brown in the 18th century, with a handsome Georgian manor house owned by the Duchy of Cornwall as its centrepiece. Historic buildings blend sympathetically with modern facilities, following a £70m redevelopment that was completed in 2014. The Creative Writing Centre is housed in the 14th-century gatehouse,

Newton Park
Newton St Loe
Bath BA2 9BN
01225 875 875
admissions@bathspa.ac.uk
www.bathspa.ac.uk
www.bathspasu.co.uk
Open days 2019:
see website

The Times and The Sunday Times Rankings
Overall Ranking: =103 (last year: 94)

Teaching quality	79.1%	=75
Student experience	74.8%	=104
Research quality	7.9%	=74
Entry standards	122	92
Graduate prospects	66.9%	114
Good honours	74.6%	=59
Expected completion rate	85.3%	67
Student/staff ratio	19.9	123
Services and facilities	£1,851	101

a scheduled ancient monument. There is also a postgraduate centre at Corsham Court, a 16th-century manor house near Chippenham.

Despite a setting that would seem to be a magnet for applicants from independent schools, 94% of the UK intake is state educated, and about a third were from working-class homes in the last survey. Two thirds of the students are female, reflecting the arts and social science bias in the curriculum, and a quarter of all students are over 25.

Bath Spa took silver in the government's Teaching Excellence Framework. The awarding panel was impressed by the personalised teaching, the availability of a personal tutor, peer mentoring, and independent study that provide "rigour and stretch". The panel also found that the investment in physical and digital resources, supported by a team of learning technologists, demonstrably enhances student engagement.

All students have the opportunity to collect a Global Citizenship award by completing a module that covers a range of cross-cutting issues with relevance to all subjects in the arts, humanities and sciences. Bath Spa also offers a pre-entry year for international undergraduates with language tuition, academic instruction and information on UK history and culture, as well as the opportunity to become involved in community projects. International students now comprise 15% of the university's intake.

Bath Spa became a university only in 2005, but the history of its predecessor colleges goes back 160 years, and it boasts some famous alumni, including Body Shop founder Anita Roddick and Turner Prize winner Sir Howard Hodgkin. It enjoyed its best-ever research assessments in 2014, when more than half of a relatively small submission was rated as world-leading or internationally excellent. The university received an 86% increase in research funding as a result. It had strengthened its research capacity in key areas such as creative writing and art and design through the appointment of high-profile professors including Fay Weldon and Gavin Turk.

Tuition fees

» Fees for UK/EU students 2019–20	£9,250
Foundation courses	£7,950
» Fees for International students 2018–19	£12,900–£13,900
» For scholarship and bursary information see	
www.bathspa.ac.uk/students/student-finance	
» Graduate salary	£18,000

Student numbers

Undergraduates	6,158	(93)
Postgraduates	967	(761)
Applications/places	12,210/2,265	
Applications per place	5.4	
Overall offer rate	87.8%	
International students	9.7%	

Accommodation

University provided places: 2,147 (catered 0%)
Self-catered: £69–£242 per week
First years guaranteed accommodation
www.bathspa.ac.uk/accom

Where do the students come from?

State schools (non-grammar)	89.2%	Working-class homes	33.1%	Black ethnic minority	2.1%
Grammar schools	4.4%	Deprived areas	13.1%	Disabled	10.9%
Independent schools	6.4%	All ethnic minorities	9.1%	Mature (over 21)	15.7%

University of Bedfordshire

A strategic plan for the university, adopted in 2017, sets out to establish Bedfordshire as a leading university for expanding higher education opportunities. A top ten ranking in our new social inclusion table suggests this is realistic. Targets include annual increases in the number of white working-class men enrolling as students and maintaining the university's already high participation rates among ethnic communities. A new foundation year for students without the necessary qualifications for degree-level study and a big expansion in degree apprenticeships are among the measures expected to achieve these goals.

Bedfordshire also plans to expand its activities through partnerships in London, Birmingham and internationally. One example is a new partnership with Middle East University in Jordan that will make it the first UK university to offer undergraduate degrees in that country. Closer to home, a new community charter sets out plans to work with partners across the region.

There is a commitment to improving the learning experience of Bedfordshire students over the next three years. This includes opening a new building on the university's original Luton campus devoted to teaching and research in science, technology, engineering and maths. A parallel programme of course development will expand the options available to students in computing and introduce provision in mechanical engineering, automotive engineering, pharmacy and optometry. Almost 80 new programmes are being offered, many of them adapting existing degrees to include professional practice or foundation years.

In addition, the six apprenticeship programmes are being expanded, almost doubling the number of students they can accommodate. New offerings are being developed for food industry technical professionals, cyber security professionals, quantity surveyors, enterprise computing professionals, senior leaders, operations and departmental managers, and HR consultants.

A new healthcare simulation suite has opened on the Luton campus, replicating a general hospital ward, and including an operating theatre, pre-op, post-op and critical care areas, as well as neo-natal facilities. A seven-floor library costing £46m opened on the campus in 2016, with 916 study spaces, laptops for loan, 530 PCs and a cafe. A study hub offers advice and guidance on academic and study skills.

The university has a campus in Bedford and a newer one in Milton Keynes, which was developed in partnership with the local authority. The Bedford campus is in a leafy setting 20 minutes' walk from the town centre, where there is a 280-seat auditorium and a

University Square
Luton LU1 3JU
0300 330 0073
admissions@beds.ac.uk
www.beds.ac.uk
www.bedssu.co.uk
Open days 2019:
see website

The Times and The Sunday Times Rankings
Overall Ranking: 121 (last year: 108)

Teaching quality	81.6%	=42
Student experience	79.7%	=44
Research quality	7.0%	=78
Entry standards	97	132
Graduate prospects	70.6%	98
Good honours	63.5%	127
Expected completion rate	72.8%	=125
Student/staff ratio	17.6	=100
Services and facilities	£2,157	75

students' union, as well as accommodation for 600 students.

Bedford is home to the education and sport faculty, with around 2,500 students, making it the UK's largest provider of physical education teacher training, as well as a national centre for other subjects. Another 1,000 students take subjects such as performing arts, law and business management.

However, most of Bedfordshire's students remain on the university's town-centre site in Luton, where there is also a £40m student halls complex and a well-equipped media arts centre. The Putteridge Bury campus, a neo-Elizabethan mansion on the outskirts of Luton, doubles as a management centre and conference venue, while nursing and midwifery students in the growing faculty of health and social sciences are based at the Butterfield Park campus near Luton, or at the Oxford House site in Aylesbury, Buckinghamshire.

Bedfordshire achieved a silver award in the first national Teaching Excellence Framework. The university has been praised for its successes in widening participation, not only in enrolling students from groups that are under-represented in higher education, but also in helping them to achieve good results.

Almost all the undergraduates are state educated, and more than half come from the four lowest socio-economic classes. Close to half of undergraduates are 21 or over on entry and nearly one in five students comes from outside the EU. This year's entrants from the UK and EU will receive a welcome package of £450 to spend on books or university services.

The university more than doubled the number of academics it entered for the 2014 Research Excellence Framework. It was rewarded with one of the biggest increases in funding for research at any university. Almost half of the work submitted for assessment was placed in the top two categories, with social work and social policy, health subjects and English producing particularly good results.

Both Luton and Bedford have their share of pubs, clubs and restaurants, and London is 30–40 minutes away by train. Bedfordshire was named among the top six universities for its environmental record in the People & Planet Green League. It was the first university in England to promise not to invest in the fossil fuel industry, following a national student campaign, and is Fairtrade-accredited. There are good sports facilities in Bedford and Luton, where there are also student discounts for non-university facilities.

Tuition fees

» Fees for UK/EU students 2019–20   £9,250
    Foundation courses   £7,500
» Fees for International students 2019–20   £12,350
» For scholarship and bursary information see
    www.beds.ac.uk/howtoapply/money
» Graduate salary   £20,000

Student numbers

Undergraduates	**8,837 (2,024)**
Postgraduates	**1,837 (1,302)**
Applications/places	**11,800/1,610**
Applications per place	**7.3**
Overall offer rate	**86.5%**
International students	**17.4%**

Accommodation

University provided places: 1,937 (catered 0%)
Self-catered: £97–£199 per week
First years guaranteed accommodation
www.beds.ac.uk/student-experience2/living-at-bedfordshire/accommodation

Where do the students come from?

State schools (non-grammar)	97.6%	Working-class homes	50.1%	Black ethnic minority	34.0%
Grammar schools	1.3%	Deprived areas	10.9%	Disabled	5.0%
Independent schools	1.1%	All ethnic minorities	60.9%	Mature (over 21)	56.4%

Birkbeck, University of London

Birkbeck joined our league table in 2017 because a fast rise in full-time courses made comparisons with other universities more valid than before, even though its classes are taught in the evening. But the essentially part-time nature of the student experience still places Birkbeck at a disadvantage, leaving it surprisingly close to the bottom of the table, despite its undoubted excellence.

Few universities can claim to do more to widen access to higher education and it features in the top ten of our new table that measures social inclusion.

However, low spending on student facilities, for example, compared with residential universities and the fact that its undergraduates are more likely to pause their education, often returning at a later date, hit the institution hard in our main academic rankings.

Until recently, all Birkbeck's courses were part-time and it still describes itself as "London's evening university", but the option of a more intensive format enables students to complete a degree in three years and qualify for the full package of loans. It has been so popular that there was an increase of almost 13% in applications last year, while most other universities saw a decline. A range of foundation-year courses for students without the qualifications for degree-level study helped to boost its popularity.

Most undergraduate programmes are now available on a full-time basis. Eleven new degrees were launched last September, including three options for studying intercultural communication, three for maths and three for molecular biology. There are also new offerings in archaeology and geography, and culinary industry management.

The switch to full-time courses was triggered by the nationwide collapse in part-time enrolments, but the option of studying for four years, rather than three, remains open. Birkbeck is also offering degree apprenticeships in chartered management, digital and technology solutions, laboratory science and senior leadership.

Birkbeck was placed in the silver category in the government's Teaching Excellence Framework. The panel was impressed by the range of initiatives to help students who would not otherwise be in higher education to graduate successfully. Programmes supported students from diverse backgrounds, the panel said, enabling them to achieve their full potential through a curriculum that is at the forefront of research.

Birkbeck is ranked just outside the top 300 universities in the world by QS. More than 80% of its eligible academics were entered for the 2014 Research Excellence Framework and their results placed the college in the top 30 of all UK institutions. Almost three quarters of

Malet Street
London WC1E 7HX
020 3907 0700
studentadvice@bbk.ac.uk
www.bbk.ac.uk
www.bbk.ac.uk/su
Open days 2019:
see website

Edinburgh
Belfast
Cardiff
LONDON

The Times and The Sunday Times Rankings
Overall Ranking: 128 (last year: 122)

Teaching quality	77.3%	=101
Student experience	73.9%	=113
Research quality	34.6%	35
Entry standards	102	=129
Graduate prospects	69.0%	103
Good honours	57.2%	130
Expected completion rate	64.3%	132
Student/staff ratio	15.8	=66
Services and facilities	£1,189	132

the work submitted was rated world-leading or internationally excellent, with psychology and environmental science in the top six nationally.

Founded in 1823 as a mechanics' institute, Birkbeck is part of the University of London and based near Senate House, the university's headquarters in Bloomsbury. It has its own degree-awarding powers if it chose to exercise that right but, for the foreseeable future, will continue to award University of London degrees.

The college expanded beyond central London for the first time in 2013, sharing a five-storey building in Stratford with the University of East London. University Square Stratford is the first joint project of its kind in the capital, and Birkbeck offers courses in law and business, as well as a BSc in community development and public policy and a foundation degree in computing, information technology and web development. Birkbeck is part of the £40m Institute of Coding, launched this year to plug the digital skills gap.

Birkbeck graduates enjoy high average starting salaries, partly because almost 70% are mature students, many of them returning to already successful careers. A professional in-house recruitment service, Birkbeck Talent, links employers with students and graduates for both employment opportunities and paid internships.

Birkbeck welcomes applications from people without traditional qualifications and continues to attract non-traditional learners of all ages and backgrounds. Because mature students tend to apply late in the application process, 45% of undergraduates arrive through clearing. Those who have taken A-level or an equivalent qualification recently are made offers based on the UCAS tariff, but others are assessed by the college on the basis of interviews and/or short tests.

The My Birkbeck student centre acts as a front door to all the college's support services, from help in choosing courses and submitting applications to information about financial support and study skills.

Almost £20m has been spent improving the college's buildings. The latest improvements added new group study areas in the Torrington Square library, and Birkbeck now has access to more classrooms in Senate House. The students' union has also been redeveloped and rebranded.

Most Birkbeck students already live in the capital, but those in full-time study looking for accommodation have access to the University of London Housing Service. The college also has an agreement with the accommodation group Unite that entitles Birkbeck students to apply for places in its halls of residence.

Tuition fees

» Fees for UK/EU students 2019–20	£9,250
Foundation courses	£6,935
» Fees for International students 2019–20	£6,325–£13,675
» For scholarship and bursary information see	
www.bbk.ac.uk/student-services/financial-support	
» Graduate salary	£24,960

Student numbers

Undergraduates	3,030 (4,980)
Postgraduates	1,254 (3,653)
Applications/places	4,505/790
Applications per place	5.7
Overall offer rate	n/a
International students	10.5%

Accommodation

www.bbk.ac.uk/student-services/accommodation

Where do the students come from?

State schools (non-grammar)	87.8%	Working-class homes	42.8%	Black ethnic minority	n/a
Grammar schools	2.4%	Deprived areas	n/a	Disabled	6.6%
Independent schools	9.8%	All ethnic minorities	n/a	Mature (over 21)	69.0%

University of Birmingham

Winning a place at Birmingham has become significantly more difficult, with only 330 more entrants from 6,000 additional applications in 2017. It was the fifth year in a row that applications had risen, helped initially by the university starting the trend for unconditional offers — a boon for sixth formers, but the bane of many teachers who then have to keep students motivated to work for their A-levels knowing the outcomes are irrelevant.

Most subjects at Birmingham now operate the scheme, which guarantees places to all those who are predicted better than three As at A-level, as long as they make Birmingham their first choice. Prospective students also have access to an online "offer calculator" to give them a better idea of whether they are likely to secure a place.

Birmingham's popularity has been buoyed further by a gold award in the Teaching Excellence Framework. The judging panel found an "outstanding learning environment", with the university investing effectively in staffing and physical resources. A strategic focus on the development and delivery of relevant, research-informed teaching was said to be highly valued by employers.

The university is mid-way through a £600m building programme, which has included a new library costing £60m and a residential development adding 178 places to Birmingham's extensive accommodation stock. The Green Heart programme, which is creating 12 acres of parkland at the centre of the campus, is set to be finished by the time the next academic year begins, as is a new building with 200 study spaces, a moot room and interpreting suite. Another teaching and learning building is due to open early in 2020.

Birmingham was the original "redbrick" university. The 230-acre campus in leafy Edgbaston is dominated by a 300ft clock tower, one of the city's best-known landmarks, and boasts its own railway station. Dentistry is located in the city centre, while part of the School of Education is in Selly Oak, a mile from the Edgbaston campus. Drama is also located there, along with the BBC Drama Village, which is part of a strategic alliance between the university and the corporation.

There is also a new campus in Dubai, where the first students enrolled last year, taking courses in business, economics, computer science, mechanical engineering, and teacher education. Other subjects will be added as the campus develops. Birmingham will be the only Russell Group university among 26 with bases in Dubai's International Academic City.

Birmingham did well in the 2014 Research Excellence Framework, when more than 80% of its submission was rated as world-leading or internationally excellent. The university was ranked in the top five for philosophy, history,

**Edgbaston
Birmingham B15 2TT**
0121 414 3344
www.birmingham.ac.uk
www.guildofstudents.com
Open days 2019:
see website

The Times and The Sunday Times Rankings		
Overall Ranking: 14 (last year: 15)		
Teaching quality	79.2%	=71
Student experience	78.2%	73
Research quality	37.1%	26
Entry standards	166	=22
Graduate prospects	85.8%	=10
Good honours	85.8%	15
Expected completion rate	94.5%	13
Student/staff ratio	14.8	=39
Services and facilities	£2,840	17

classics, theology and religion, area studies, chemical engineering, and sport, exercise and rehabilitation studies. This performance took it into the top 20 for research quality and has helped to maintain its accustomed place in our top 20 overall.

Students have welcomed an increased focus on employability, successful alumni offering mentoring and the university's provision of bursaries to support work experience and internships in the UK and overseas. Three quarters of the undergraduates undertake work experience as part of their course. The university is a recent winner of our University of the Year for Graduate Employment.

Birmingham is launching its first degree apprenticeship course in the current academic year, a four-year BSc in computer science and digital technology in collaboration with PwC. There are also new degrees in English and film, sociology and criminology, aerospace engineering, and mechatronic and robotic engineering, as well as a five-year MPharm.

The numbers recruited from the poorest social groups have been rising gradually. The A2B (Access to Birmingham) programme, which encourages students from the West Midlands whose families have little or no experience of higher education to apply to university, is being extended to students in other parts of England. The university's Nationwide Contextual Offer scheme, introduced in 2017, reduces standard offers by one grade for those from areas of low participation in higher education or from schools with below-average GCSE grades.

The sports facilities are some of the best in the country and include an outdoor pursuits centre by Coniston Water in the Lake District. A £55m sport and fitness centre, opened in 2017, boasts Birmingham's first 50-metre swimming pool, a large multi-sports arena, squash court complex and gym. The Active Lifestyle Programme attracts 4,000 students to 150 different courses.

Campus facilities include a medical practice and a comprehensive student services hub, as well as a nightclub. Most of the halls and university flats are conveniently located in an attractive parkland setting near the main campus. There are almost 5,200 university-owned beds, and accommodation in the private sector is also plentiful. Some 1,700 privately-owned places are "endorsed" by the university. The campus is less than three miles from the city centre, which has become increasingly attractive to young people, but the area around the university has plenty of shops, pubs and restaurants.

Tuition fees

» Fees for UK/EU students 2019–20	£9,250
» Fees for International students 2019–20	£16,740–£23,460
Medicine & Dentistry	£38,100
» For scholarship and bursary information see	
www.birmingham.ac.uk/undergraduate/fees/index.aspx	
» Graduate salary	£23,000

Student numbers

Undergraduates	21,537	(904)
Postgraduates	7,086	(5,309)
Applications/places		55,340/6,475
Applications per place		8.5
Overall offer rate		81.8%
International students		23.5%

Accommodation

University provided places: 6,890 (catered 23%)
Catered costs: £127–£197 per week
Self-catered: £88–£169 per week
First years guaranteed accommodation
www.birmingham.ac.uk/accommodation

Where do the students come from?

State schools (non-grammar)	67.3%	Working-class homes	22.8%	Black ethnic minority	4.7%
Grammar schools	14.8%	Deprived areas	7.1%	Disabled	5.4%
Independent schools	17.9%	All ethnic minorities	27.2%	Mature (over 21)	4.9%

Birmingham City University

Birmingham City (BCU) has completed a £260m development programme with the opening of a striking new home for the Royal Birmingham Conservatoire, specialist laboratories for new courses in sport and life sciences, an experimental learning space and a new building for education. The programme has enabled the university to concentrate most of its activities onto two campuses in the city centre and nearby Edgbaston, following the closure of the original Perry Barr campus last year.

The City Centre campus, close to the eventual HS2 rail terminus, houses all student support services as well as business, law, social science and English. The highly-regarded courses in art and design and media are also based there, and the university occupies part of the Millennium Point building, helping to create Birmingham's Eastside learning quarter. The new conservatoire building will be a particular draw, with five performance spaces, including a 500-seat concert hall.

The City South campus, in Edgbaston, has a prize-winning library, IT suites, recreational space and teaching facilities that have been enhanced by new features such as an altitude chamber and anti-gravity treadmill. The world-renowned School of Jewellery is based in the city's Jewellery Quarter, while the Bournville campus hosts a college offering preparatory courses for overseas students to support the university's international ambitions. These include the establishment of the Birmingham Institute of Fashion and Creative Art in Wuhan, China, in partnership with Wuhan Textile University.

BCU has thrived since changing its name from the University of Central England in 2007. Enrolments have risen for seven years in a row, increasing the size of the undergraduate intake by a quarter and placing BCU among the top 20 universities in terms of the volume of applications attracted.

All BCU's degrees were "refreshed" in 2017 to give students the most relevant practical experience to boost their prospects in the graduate employment market. Work placements are available on most courses and employability skills are built into the curriculum through the Graduate+ scheme.

The university is also expanding its portfolio of degree apprenticeships from the existing five programmes, with plans to add another 12, including nursing, architecture, accounting, teaching and a postgraduate programme in engineering. There will also be seven new traditional degrees starting this year, including filmmaking, global sport management, policing and media production. BCU's black studies degree, launched in 2017, was the first of its kind in Europe.

University House
15 Bartholomew Row
Birmingham B5 5JU
0121 331 6295
admissions@bcu.ac.uk
www.bcu.ac.uk
www.bcusu.com
Open days 2019:
see website

BIRMINGHAM •

The Times and The Sunday Times **Rankings**

Overall Ranking: =87 (last year: 105)

Teaching quality	82.3%	33
Student experience	80.3%	=35
Research quality	4.3%	=99
Entry standards	128	=73
Graduate prospects	76.8%	63
Good honours	68.6%	99
Expected completion rate	83.6%	=79
Student/staff ratio	18.1	105
Services and facilities	£2,026	83

There are strong links with business and the professions, including pioneering work in green technology, which is attracting support from national and regional partners. The new STEAMhouse centre, which opened last May, encourages collaboration between the science, technology, engineering, arts and maths (Steam) sectors. Experimental workshops focus on product development, collaborative making and societal challenges, led by industry, with subscription-based access to fabrication facilities and £2,500 grants offered to selected small firms and sole traders to cover materials for early-stage prototyping.

BCU made a relatively small submission to the 2014 national research assessments, but 60% of the work reached the top two categories and almost 90% was judged to have delivered "outstanding" or "very considerable" external impact.

The university offers a range of scholarships and bursaries to encourage undergraduates to stay on for postgraduate study. In addition, all UK and EU undergraduate students starting courses in 2019 will receive at least £150 towards course materials and other costs which may be a barrier to study. The prize-winning Student Academic Partners scheme spawned a formal agreement between the university and the students' union to improve the student experience. The student inquiry service, Ask, handles all student queries either in person at helpdesks, over the phone or online. Students have access to learning tools such as Shareville – a virtual learning environment where they can engage with real-life scenarios.

Six out of ten students come from the West Midlands, many from ethnic minorities and more than 40% are from the poorest socio-economic groups. The university is working with schools in the region to encourage more young people to go on to higher education. Many students enter through the network of associated further education colleges, which run foundation and access programmes. A new suite of foundation year courses to prepare students without the necessary qualifications for entry to degree programmes was launched in 2017.

The university owns or manages more than 2,750 residential places – enough to guarantee accommodation for first years whose homes are more than ten miles from their place of study, if they apply before the deadline. The city's student scene is highly rated and has become a draw for many young applicants.

Tuition fees

- » Fees for UK/EU students 2019–20 £9,250
  Foundation courses £6,165
- » Fees for International students 2019–20 £12,300–£22,000
- » For scholarship and bursary information see
  www.bcu.ac.uk/student-info/finance-and-money-matters
- » Graduate salary £21,000

Student numbers

Undergraduates	17,492	(2,148)
Postgraduates	2,222	(2,268)
Applications/places		33,985/5,070
Applications per place		6.7
Overall offer rate		72.2%
International students		12.3%

Accommodation

University provided places: 2,759 (catered 0%)
Self-catered: £119–£144 per week
First years guaranteed accommodation
www.bcu.ac.uk/student-info/accommodation

Where do the students come from?

State schools (non-grammar)	97.2%	Working-class homes	46.9%	Black ethnic minority	16.3%
Grammar schools	0.5%	Deprived areas	14.1%	Disabled	5.3%
Independent schools	2.3%	All ethnic minorities	52.5%	Mature (over 21)	26.5%

Birmingham, University College (UCB)

University College Birmingham (UCB) is the only university that meets the criteria for inclusion in our main league table that is missing from it this year. UCB is unique among UK universities in having a third of its students taking further education programmes, some of them enrolling at 16. The university believes that would place it at a disadvantage in league tables such as ours, so it has again instructed the Higher Education Statistics Agency not to release its data. Consequently, UCB does not appear in our main league table or any of the subject tables.

Student satisfaction levels have fallen, but UCB already has a Silver rating in the Teaching Excellence Framework (TEF). The panel was impressed by the strong vocational focus in UCB's curriculum design, with work placements and professional accreditation a common feature on many courses. It found that students were stretched and there were "appropriate" contact hours, personalised learning through individual and group tutorials, and effective support services.

Nevertheless, applications dropped by almost 20% in 2017, although a higher offer rate ensured that the numbers starting degrees did not follow suit. Over 93% of applicants were offered places. The numbers enrolling at higher education level are only marginally greater than when full university status arrived in 2013.

Unlike other promoted colleges, UCB chose not to change its name in order to preserve its identity. It was the largest of a dozen colleges to become universities in 2013, with more than 5,000 higher education students and nearly 2,500 taking further education courses. The university traces its history back more than 100 years to the foundation of a Municipal Technical School offering cookery and household science courses. It has had degree awarding powers since 2007, although many degrees are still accredited by the University of Birmingham.

The core subjects are hospitality, tourism, business, sport and education. The most recent Ofsted inspection rated the further education provision as outstanding, while about two thirds of higher education students receive degrees from the University of Birmingham. UCB has an international reputation in hospitality and tourism, with about a third of the students coming from outside the UK. Two restaurants staffed by the university's students are open to the public, as well as to students and staff.

Based in the city centre, UCB is located close to the International Convention Centre, Symphony Hall and the Library of Birmingham, as well as the main shopping areas. The main campus is at Summer Row,

University College Birmingham
Summer Row
Birmingham B3 1JB
0121 604 1000
admissions@ucb.ac.uk
www.ucb.ac.uk
www.ucbguild.org.uk
Open days 2019: see website

The Times and The Sunday Times **Rankings**
Data not supplied

five minutes' walk from New Street station. UCB is investing £100m in new teaching and residential facilities. The first phase of development in Birmingham's historic Jewellery Quarter – a short walk from the main campus – opened in 2014. The second has now been granted planning permission and is due to open in September this year. The new red brick building, designed to celebrate the architectural heritage of the area, will include three lecture theatres, modern teaching spaces, a high performance strengthening and conditioning suite for sports studies, a gym and a student diner.

Existing specialist teaching facilities include high-quality training kitchens, a full bakery and a £2m Food Science and Innovation Suite. The university focuses on giving students an advantage in the highly competitive graduate job market. Many courses include full or half-year industrial placements, including overseas opportunities in the USA, Hong Kong, Canada and Europe. As well as arranging placements, the expanded careers and employability team, hired@UCB, helps students to develop skills such as communication, teamwork, problem solving and time management.

UCB has one of the most socially diverse student bodies in the country – more than half are from a black or minority ethnic background. Student ambassadors promote further and higher education to young people from a range of backgrounds. Almost all the undergraduates are state educated and more than half come from the four poorest socio-economic groups. Retention rates have been improving, but the TEF panel commented on the below-benchmark rates for some groups.

More than 1,000 students can be accommodated in UCB's halls of residence, and accommodation can be offered to all years and programmes of study. The Maltings halls are ten minutes' walk from UCB and Cambrian Hall is only 150 yards from the main campus. Both offer among the best value in the Midlands.

The Spa offers hairdressing salons, beauty therapy suites, a sports therapy clinic, a multi-gym, and a fitness assessment suite. There is also a gym and sports hall at The Maltings site, as well as a new multipurpose community hub with specialised work and dining spaces. It includes a 'beanbag' cinema area and a dance studio.

Tuition fees

» Fees for UK/EU students 2019–20	£9,250
» Fees for International students 2019–20	£10,300
Foundation course	£8,200
» For scholarship and bursary information see www.ucb.ac.uk/our-courses/undergraduate/ fees-funding-and-scholarships/	

Student numbers

Total	**7,500**
International	**900**

Accommodation

University provided places: 1,000+ (0% catered)
Self-catered: £98–£117 per week
No guarantee but all first years offered accommodation
www.ucb.ac.uk/student-life/accommodation/
accommodation.aspx

Where do the students come from?

Data not supplied

Bishop Grosseteste University

A gold award in the government's Teaching Excellence Framework (TEF) helped Bishop Grosseteste (BGU) to another increase in applications – the third in succession – taking demand to record levels. Still one of the smallest universities, it will not meet its target of 4,500 students this year, but undergraduates obviously like the personal touch in the current environment. BGU's score for satisfaction with the quality of teaching runs well ahead of its overall ranking, which is sharply down this year.

The TEF panel found an outstanding learning environment and students who are frequently engaged with developments from the forefront of research, scholarship or working practice. Course design and assessment practices ensure that all groups of students are challenged to achieve their full potential, the panel added. BGU is in the top ten for the proportion of academics holding a teaching qualification – three quarters, compared with the national average of less than half.

Based on an attractive, leafy campus in Lincoln, not far from the cathedral and castle, BGU has been training teachers since 1862. Named after a theologian and scholar who was Bishop of Lincoln in the 13th century, BGU is still proudly associated with the Church of England, although it welcomes students of all faiths and none. It describes itself as a church university within the Anglican tradition.

The campus has been gearing up for a larger intake. New teaching and learning facilities, attached to one of the two on-campus halls of residence, opened last year. The former college canteen and dining room had already been turned into teaching accommodation, with a £2.2m extension doubling the available space and creating a new landmark building for the university.

Other developments have seen the campus theatre upgraded to double as a cinema. The Venue is home to the Lincoln Film Society and is open to staff, students and the public. The library has been extended and now houses the student advice and learning development teams, as well as library services.

The portfolio of courses covers a range of arts and social sciences, with more new subjects planned in the next few years, but teacher training still dominates. Ofsted rates the courses for early years, primary and secondary teachers as "good". The inspectors praised the high quality of training and effective partnerships between the university and schools, adding that "university tutors' involvement in current educational research provides a sharp edge to the training programme." BGU's introduction of courses

---

Longdales Road
Lincoln LN1 3DY
01522 583 658
enquiries@bishopg.ac.uk
www.bishopg.ac.uk
www.bgsu.co.uk
Open days 2019:
June 8, July 12

Belfast
Edinburgh
LINCOLN
London
Cardiff

The Times and The Sunday Times Rankings
Overall Ranking: 113 (last year: 95)

Teaching quality	80.8%	=51
Student experience	74.8%	=104
Research quality	2.1%	121
Entry standards	112	=118
Graduate prospects	72.9%	=85
Good honours	66.4%	109
Expected completion rate	91.5%	31
Student/staff ratio	22	129
Services and facilities	£1,833	103

leading to Early Years teacher status has meant that BGU now trains teachers of every age group, including adults.

More than 60% of BGU's students come from the East Midlands, 44% from Lincolnshire itself. Their backgrounds reflect the socioeconomic make-up of the county, with eight out of ten fitting one or more of the government's widening participation categories. Almost one in five comes from an area with little tradition of higher education. The expansion of the university is intended to include more students from such areas, as well as more mature students taking work-based courses and more postgraduates and research students. BGU has added four new Masters degrees in English literature, history, theology and health and social care leadership, as part of this process.

Only 11 staff entered the 2014 Research Excellence Framework, but some work was classed as world-leading or internationally excellent in education, English and history, the three subjects in which the university was assessed. The university has opened the Lincolnshire Open Research and Innovation Centre (Loric) to assist local business, the public and third sector organisations. A new executive dean has been appointed to head the centre and extend the university's research capability and capacity.

BGU has more than 200 residential places of its own on campus and another 148 elsewhere that it manages or endorses. Rooms are allocated on a first-come, first-served basis, but the university guarantees to find approved accommodation for all first-year and international students.

The university's sports hall caters for a variety of different sporting activities and fitness classes and there is a well-appointed fitness suite. Ten acres of sports fields are close by. The city of Lincoln is one of the fastest-growing in the UK, with relatively low living costs. It may not compete with the big conurbations for youth culture, but it has a growing student population and a range of bars and nightclubs to serve it.

Tuition fees

- » Fees for UK/EU students 2019-20   £9,250
  Foundation courses   £6,935
- » Fees for International students 2018-19   £11,500
- » For scholarship and bursary information see
  www.bishopg.ac.uk/fees-funding
- » Graduate salary   £22,000

Student numbers

Undergraduates	1,741	(21)
Postgraduates	340	(123)
Applications/places		1,605/590
Applications per place		2.7
Overall offer rate		86.8%
International students		0.6%

Accommodation

University provided places: 365 (catered 0%)
Self-catered: £85–£137 per week
First years guaranteed accommodation
www.bishopg.ac.uk/student/accommodation/

Where do the students come from?

State schools (non-grammar)	96.1%	Working-class homes	44%	Black ethnic minority	0.7%
Grammar schools	2.8%	Deprived areas	22.9%	Disabled	13.1%
Independent schools	1.1%	All ethnic minorities	1.4%	Mature (over 21)	36.3%

University of Bolton

Bolton is planning to more than double the number of students it educates by next year, when it hopes to have 20,000 on its campuses. It will be a tough challenge, with applications falling by more than the national average both last year and in 2017. But the university plans to work more closely with other educational institutions in the region and increase links with businesses. An alliance with Bolton College is already in place.

Preparing for this growth, the university has moved into Bolton Central, its new flagship building in the centre of Bolton, which will be used as the base for the new Institute of Management. The new National Centre for Motorsport Engineering opened in 2017, hosting Bolton's Centre for Advanced Performance Engineering. The university has its own professional motor racing team, run in conjunction with a motorsports company, and offers degrees in automotive performance engineering and motorsport technology. Students work and learn alongside engineers and mechanics from the team, as well as the university's mechanical engineering lecturers.

Future plans include a £40m village for 850 students, replacing two existing halls that are further from the town centre campus and have a smaller capacity. A collaboration with the council and local NHS produced the Bolton One development, a £31m health, leisure and research centre on the main campus. It boasts a multi-sports hall, climbing wall and a sports and spinal injuries clinic, as well as a 25-metre competition swimming pool and a therapeutic hydrotherapy pool, fitness suite and community gym. The former sports hall is being transformed into a Creative Industries and Technologies Centre.

Other recent developments include a £10m facility for science and engineering and the formation of a new health sciences faculty to teach biomedical sciences and subjects allied to health and dentistry. A partnership with the owners of ten dental practices in the north of England enabled Bolton to offer well-equipped practice and new clinical simulation facilities for degrees in advanced dental nursing and dental hygiene and therapy, as well as a diploma of higher education for clinical dental technicians.

A silver rating in the Teaching Excellence Framework (TEF) was "the best news Bolton has ever had", according to Professor George Holmes, the vice-chancellor. The TEF panel commended the university on an institutional culture that facilitates, recognises and rewards excellent teaching, as well as providing excellent support for students from disadvantaged backgrounds. The university ranks in our top five for both social inclusion and student satisfaction with the quality of teaching.

Deane Road
Bolton BL3 5AB
01204 903 903
study@bolton.ac.uk
www.bolton.ac.uk
www.boltonsu.com
Open days 2019:
see website

The Times and The Sunday Times **Rankings**
Overall Ranking: 126 (last year: 124)

Teaching quality	85.6%	4
Student experience	82%	=14
Research quality	2.9%	115
Entry standards	114	=113
Graduate prospects	57.4%	131
Good honours	59.4%	129
Expected completion rate	68.9%	130
Student/staff ratio	14.7	=35
Services and facilities	£1,352	130

The university is planning to increase the number of degree apprenticeship programmes from three to eight, while other career-focused programmes range from sport rehabilitation to dental technology and special effects. But it is the university's psychology courses – ranked just outside our top 50 – that have been winning plaudits most recently. The criminological and forensic psychology degree, which includes the opportunity to take counselling certificates, received the top award for innovative programmes from the British Psychological Society.

General engineering was one of two areas to see a majority of their work rated as world-leading or internationally excellent in the 2014 Research Excellence Framework. The best results were in English, and almost a third of the university's submission reached the top two categories. Among the distinctive research features is a Centre for Islamic Finance.

The university traces its roots back 193 years to one of the country's first three mechanics institutes. Bolton exceeds all the access measures designed to widen participation in higher education: over half of the full-time undergraduates are from working-class homes and the proportion from areas without a tradition of higher education is among the highest in the UK, at more than 20%. More than a third of undergraduates study part-time – a significant proportion at a time when part-time numbers have plummeted nationally. The downside is that the projected dropout rate is also one of the highest in the UK, at more than 24%.

Bolton has partner colleges in several Asian countries and a branch campus in the United Arab Emirates. The Ras al-Khaimah campus offers a range of undergraduate and postgraduate courses identical to those taught in the UK. The £1m development near Dubai is designed to take 700 students. Those at Bolton have the opportunity to study in the UAE for part of their degree course.

The town of Bolton has a growing range of student-orientated facilities and is only 20 minutes from Manchester by train.

Tuition fees

» Fees for UK/EU students 2019–20	£9,250
» Fees for International students 2019–20	£12,450
» For scholarship and bursary information see www.bolton.ac.uk/study/undergraduate/feesfunding	
» Graduate salary	£18,500

Student numbers

Undergraduates	4,292	(936)
Postgraduates	448	(748)
Applications/places		5,165/975
Applications per place		5.3
Overall offer rate		72.8%
International students		7.5%

Accommodation

University provided places: 384 (catered 0%)

Self-catered: £80 per week

First years guaranteed accommodation

www.bolton.ac.uk/study/undergraduate/accommodation/

Where do the students come from?

State schools (non-grammar)	98.7%	Working-class homes	52.5%	Black ethnic minority	15.8%
Grammar schools	0.9%	Deprived areas	25.6%	Disabled	11.5%
Independent schools	0.4%	All ethnic minorities	38.2%	Mature (over 21)	48.3%

University of Bournemouth

Bournemouth has arrested its decline in our league table, rising one place a year after it dropped out of the top half of the table and saw applications fall by more than 10%. Student satisfaction has recovered, but lower staffing levels and a poor year for graduate prospects prevented it making further progress.

The university was placed in the silver category in the government's Teaching Excellence Framework, with the panel impressed that all undergraduates were offered work placements and most took them up. The panel also noted that most staff hold a teaching qualification and that there is strong support for peer-assisted learning, which is offered to all first-year undergraduates, providing advice and mentoring from more experienced undergraduates.

The university is completing a £200m programme of new buildings and equipment, and plans more spending. The Bournemouth Gateway Building, on the Lansdowne campus, is scheduled to open in September for the new academic year, providing a new home for the faculty of health and social sciences. The Poole Gateway building, on the main Talbot campus, should open a year later, with specialist facilities for the faculties of science and technology and media and communications.

The media courses that are Bournemouth's best-known feature already enjoy impressive resources, including a motion-capture facility for real-time animation, which is used in teaching and available for use by outside companies. The university hosts the National Centre of Computer Animation and graduates have worked on award-winning films such as *Star Wars: The Force Awakens* and *Ex Machina*. New degrees start this month in computer animation and games design, visual effects, games design and engineering, and digital creative industries.

There has also been investment in health courses, with degrees in biomedical sciences and medical science planned for this year, as well as others in operating department practice, cyber-psychology and psychology with forensic investigation. Tourism and hospitality management is another successful area at the university, with the department designated as a centre of excellence by the World Tourism Organisation.

Bournemouth's decision to invest £1m a year on academic appointments and the fusion of teaching and research paid off in the 2014 Research Excellence Framework, in which 60% of its entry was judged to be world-leading or internationally excellent. It was one of the biggest proportions at any post-1992 university and a considerable improvement on previous results. The university's Fusion Fund continues to promote "the combination

Fern Barrow
Talbot Campus
Poole BH12 5BB
01202 961 916
futurestudents@bournemouth.ac.uk
www.bournemouth.ac.uk
www.subu.org.uk
Open days 2019:
see website

***The Times and The Sunday Times* Rankings**
Overall Ranking: 78 (last year: 79)

Teaching quality	78.6%	=86
Student experience	77.2%	=83
Research quality	9.0%	=65
Entry standards	123	=88
Graduate prospects	68.7%	=106
Good honours	78.9%	=39
Expected completion rate	84.1%	=75
Student/staff ratio	17	=92
Services and facilities	£2,278	58

of inspirational teaching, world-class research and the latest thinking in the professions".

The university has been increasing its use of education technology, which enables part-time students to study from home or the workplace, reducing the amount of time they need to spend on campus. It invested £6m in a new Virtual Learning Environment, which gives all students access to a range of services and enables academics to track the performance of undergraduates, design courses, create content and grade assignments. Most students take advantage of personal development planning, both online and with trained staff.

There is a growing emphasis on international activity, with 2,600 overseas students from about 120 countries. The Global Horizons Fund helps students and staff to travel abroad for study, research, or work or life experience. For international students arriving at the university, Bournemouth International College provides preparatory courses in English and study skills.

The university's subject mix and its seaside location, between the Jurassic Coast and the New Forest national park, attract more middle-class students than most post-1992 universities, although almost 95% of undergraduates attended state schools. Applicants from low-income families and/or areas with little tradition of higher education are made offers below the published tariff.

Foundation degrees are delivered in partner colleges in Dorset, Somerset and Wiltshire, as well as on the main campus. Top-up courses are available for those who wish to turn their qualification into an honours degree.

Sports facilities have been improving since refurbishment of the gym, with the addition of a multipurpose large studio. The university does not own any residential accommodation, but controls or approves 3,700 places – enough to guarantee accommodation to first-year undergraduates who apply by early July. The Bournemouth Gateway development will add another 550 rooms.

The university finished just outside the top ten in the 2017 People & Planet league of environmental performance and has an EcoCampus gold award, as well as holding Fairtrade status.

Tuition fees

» Fees for UK/EU students 2019–20   £9,250
  Foundation degrees   £6,000
» Fees for International students 2019–20   £13,750–£14,500
» For scholarship and bursary information see
  www1.bournemouth.ac.uk/study/undergraduate/
  fees-funding
» Graduate salary   £21,909

Student numbers

Undergraduates	13,521 (2,619)
Postgraduates	1,774 (2,286)
Applications/places	23,150/3,885
Applications per place	6.0
Overall offer rate	79.7%
International students	13.0%

Accommodation

University provided places: 3,700 (catered 2%)
Catered costs: £178–£208 per week
Self-catered: £104–£192 per week
First years guaranteed accommodation
www1.bournemouth.ac.uk/why-bu/accommodation

Where do the students come from?

State schools (non-grammar)	90.0%	Working-class homes	31.4%	Black ethnic minority	4.6%
Grammar schools	4.7%	Deprived areas	12.0%	Disabled	8.7%
Independent schools	5.4%	All ethnic minorities	15.7%	Mature (over 21)	19.1%

University of Bradford

Originally one of the ten colleges of advanced technology, Bradford still describes itself as a "technology university", marketing itself as the only one in the north of England. It has settled on three strategic themes: advanced healthcare, innovative engineering and sustainable societies, and is aiming to be a world leader in its areas of strength.

The strategy suffered a setback when Bradford was not included among the five new medical schools opening in 2019, but it remains highly rated in other health subjects. The Wolfson Centre for Applied Healthcare Research, a joint project with the University of Leeds and Bradford Teaching Hospitals NHS Foundation Trust, is under construction, and facilities for physiotherapy and optometry have opened in recent years.

The developments are part of an estates plan that will eventually cost £260m and include new and upgraded teaching facilities and a large-scale refurbishment of the library, which won a Green Gown award for its insulation and natural ventilation. The university was a pioneer of environmental initiatives in higher education, and four years ago was rated the greenest university in the country and eighth in the world for its sustainable architecture and innovative technologies.

The university's modernisation plan is keeping it at the forefront of that movement. Bradford is the only university in the world with three Breeam (Building Research Establishment Environmental Assessment Method) "outstanding" rated buildings, while the "ecoversity" programme addresses issues of sustainable development in all the university's practices, including the curriculum.

Just outside the top ten in our new social inclusion rankings, Bradford was placed in the silver category in the government's Teaching Excellence Framework, with the panel finding that students were stretched to achieve their full potential and acquire the knowledge, skills and understanding that are most highly valued by employers. The independent assessors also praised a "strategic and systematic commitment to diversity and social mobility that enables the majority of students, including a very high number from BME backgrounds, to achieve excellent outcomes".

Always one of the most diverse of the pre-1992 universities, Bradford draws more than half of its UK undergraduates from the four poorest socio-economic groups, while just over 20% are international, many of them taught in partner institutions in Singapore, Brunei, Malaysia, Pakistan and India.

Bradford remains a small university, with only 11,000 students, but it is planning for gradual growth. More than a dozen new degrees, from mechanical engineering

Richmond Road
Bradford BD7 1DP
0800 073 1225
enquiries@bradford.ac.uk
www.bradford.ac.uk
www.bradfordunisu.co.uk
Open days 2019:
see website

The Times and The Sunday Times Rankings
Overall Ranking: 98 (last year: =75)

Teaching quality	74.7%	120
Student experience	75.6%	=99
Research quality	9.2%	=63
Entry standards	130	=66
Graduate prospects	82.8%	25
Good honours	77.3%	47
Expected completion rate	82.1%	95
Student/staff ratio	16.8	90
Services and facilities	£2,021	85

to sociology, are now offered. One is in applied peace and conflict studies, a new offering from perhaps the university's best-known feature, the Division of Peace Studies, which merged with the Centre of International Development. Another strength is the management school, whose distance learning MBA is ranked in the top 20 in the world by the Financial Times. The faculties of management, law and social sciences have merged to encourage innovation and interdisciplinary work.

Many honours degrees offer work experience or placements, which regularly rank Bradford in our top 30 for graduate prospects. The university is also developing a portfolio of degree apprenticeships, with four already on offer and another three planned this year, in management and chemistry, as well as one for advanced clinical practitioners. Bradford is leading a £13m programme to create a Digital Health Zone for the city to develop new healthcare products and links with practitioners.

An online portal is available to applicants and new students to smooth their transition to higher education. Computer-assisted learning is increasing in many subjects, making use of unusually extensive IT provision and a wireless network.

The university entered less than a quarter of eligible academics for the 2014 assessments of research, but their work produced good results. Almost three quarters of it was rated in the top two categories, with allied health, management and archaeological science producing particularly good grades.

The compact, lively campus is close to the city centre, with only management on a different site, two miles away in a 14-acre parkland setting. The conveniently placed sports facilities have a gym, climbing wall and sports hall. Bradford was awarded £500,000 by the Premier League and the Football Association for a sports hub for students and the local community with a floodlit, 3G football pitch, four tennis courts, refurbished changing pavilion and conditioning suite.

Places in halls are reasonably priced and all have internet connections. Rents for private housing are among the lowest in any university city. The university has particularly good provision for disabled students, who account for almost 10% of its population.

Tuition fees

- » Fees for UK/EU students 2019–20 £9,250
- » Fees for International students 2019–20 £12,190–£18,901
- » For scholarship and bursary information see www.bradford.ac.uk/fees-and-financial-support/tuition-fees
- » Graduate salary £20,020

Student numbers

Undergraduates	7,414	(631)
Postgraduates	829	(2,086)
Applications/places	12,530/1,795	
Applications per place	7.0	
Overall offer rate	84.8%	
International students	14.6%	

Accommodation

University provided places: 1,026 (catered 0%)
Self-catered: £110–£119 per week
First years guaranteed accommodation
www.bradford.ac.uk/student/accommodation/

Where do the students come from?

State schools (non-grammar)	93.7%	Working-class homes	58.3%	Black ethnic minority	9.0%
Grammar schools	4.3%	Deprived areas	15.6%	Disabled	9.2%
Independent schools	2.0%	All ethnic minorities	72.2%	Mature (over 21)	22.0%

University of Brighton

Every course at Brighton was reviewed for the start of the academic year in 2018. The university-wide curriculum review was not popular with all students — those in art and humanities protested at the removal of some modules — but the institution insists that the aim is to introduce contemporary approaches, while ensuring courses are inclusive, accessible and have fair and equitable workloads for all students.

Now in our bottom ten, Brighton earned a silver in the government's Teaching Excellence Framework. The judging panel complimented the university on close working relationships with professional bodies, employers and community groups and its personalised learning and support, particularly for students from diverse backgrounds during pre-entry and the first year.

Brighton is going ahead with plans to invest up to £200m in its campuses but is pursuing a cautious strategy in anticipation of harder times ahead for universities after Brexit. Professor Debra Humphris, the vice-chancellor, has ruled out increasing the number of students above the current 21,000, partly to take the pressure off the local housing market.

However, work started last year on the £60m transformation of the university's largest campus at Moulsecoomb. This will deliver 400 rooms in new halls of residence, an academic building, students' union and fitness facilities by the summer of 2020 with a further 400 student bedrooms by the following summer.

A new £14m Advanced Engineering building has opened on the campus, and the university is investing £1.5m a year in upgrading its other teaching and learning spaces. This includes a £600,000 improvement to its arts and humanities library in the current year.

The campus in Hastings has closed, with several courses transferring to Brighton or the Eastbourne site. Other courses will continue to be validated by the university and taught in Hastings at the University Centre established by East Sussex College Group.

The Eastbourne campus has a modern library and extensive leisure and sports facilities. Sport science laboratories and 354 en-suite residential places have been added there, and improvements made to the learning resources centre, lecture theatres and refectory. In central Brighton, facilities for photography, moving image and film and screen studies have been upgraded. There have also been improvements to the College of Arts and Humanities, on the Grand Parade campus, which hosts the national Design Archives.

Education students, as well as those taking languages and literature courses, are taught on the Falmer campus, on the outskirts

Mithras House
Lewes Road
Brighton BN2 4AT
01273 644 644
enquiries@brighton.ac.uk
www.brighton.ac.uk
www.brightonsu.com
Open days 2019:
see website

The Times and The Sunday Times **Rankings**
Overall Ranking: 123 (last year: 112)

Teaching quality	77.3%	=101
Student experience	73.4%	116
Research quality	7.9%	=74
Entry standards	118	=105
Graduate prospects	67.2%	112
Good honours	69.3%	=92
Expected completion rate	85.5%	=64
Student/staff ratio	18.2	=106
Services and facilities	£1,497	127

of Brighton, which also has a £7.3m sports centre. The site also houses the medical school, one of the first to be awarded to a post-1992 university. Run jointly with the University of Sussex, the school now trains almost 140 doctors a year. Its headquarters has also provided a new base for applied social sciences such as criminology and applied psychology.

The teaching facilities are designed to build real-life skills, and include a radio station and TV studio, a podiatry hospital, physiotherapy clinic, flight simulator, rapid prototyping facilities, industrial textile rooms, and a clinical skills and simulation suite for nursing students. Brighton is also in the top ten of the People & Planet league of environmental performance.

The university has always engaged in imaginative regional initiatives. It has the largest university multi-academy trust in the country, with 15 academies across Sussex. It also has a well-established programme of degree apprenticeships in health and social care. This year there may be more than 400 apprentices, with construction and built environment, digital technology and town planning added to the options.

More than nine out of ten degrees include a placement or the option of a sandwich year. The four-year fashion textiles degree, for example, offers work placements in America, France and Italy, as well as Britain. Last year

Ceoworld, the New York and UK-based business magazine, ranked Brighton 13 out of 110 fashion schools globally.

Brighton was in the top quarter for the impact of its submission to the 2014 Research Excellence Framework. Two thirds of its work was placed in one of the top two categories — a big improvement on 2008, when it was already among the most successful of the post-1992 universities.

The fashionable seaside location is a draw for students, who revel in Brighton's famously lively social scene. The university has a cosmopolitan atmosphere, with more international students and a more middle-class UK intake than most post-1992 universities, although 94% of undergraduates come from state schools.

Efforts to widen the intake further include well-established progression partnerships with schools in the region and cash bursaries of £500 for those with a household income of less than £25,000, with larger awards for care leavers.

Tuition fees

- » Fees for UK/EU students 2019–20 £9,250
- » Fees for International students 2019–20 £13,284–£14,460
  Medicine (2018–19) £30,450
- » For scholarship and bursary information see
  www.brighton.ac.uk/studying-here/fees-and-finance/
  index.aspx
- » Graduate salary £22,000

Student numbers

Undergraduates	14,872 (2,743)
Postgraduates	1,578 (2,460)
Applications/places	32,125/4,135
Applications per place	7.8
Overall offer rate	79.6%
International students	12.9%

Accommodation

University provided places: 2,679 (catered 43%)
Catered costs: £180 per week
Self-catered: £135–£160 per week
First years guaranteed accommodation
www.brighton.ac.uk/accommodation-and-locations/Index.aspx

Where do the students come from?

State schools (non-grammar)	89.8%	Working-class homes	34.2%	Black ethnic minority	5.9%
Grammar schools	4.7%	Deprived areas	12.5%	Disabled	9.6%
Independent schools	5.5%	All ethnic minorities	21.8%	Mature (over 21)	24.6%

University of Bristol

Reducing the standard offer for English and history by a grade, trimming the GCSE demands for medicine, and removing the requirement for maths A-level for management, to attract a broader intake, helped Bristol to a 13% rise in applications, one of the biggest at any university last year. In all subjects, students in "aspiring" state schools — those with below-average progression to higher education — or those living in such areas, are now made offers two grades below the norm, a very real attempt to improve social inclusion in an institution that lies fifth from bottom in our new ranking in this area.

Bristol pioneered "contextual admissions" almost two decades ago and has spent £18m on recruiting and supporting students from disadvantaged backgrounds. But still little more than half the UK undergraduates come from comprehensive schools. The new initiative includes making offers to five "high potential" students from every school or college in Bristol. Eligibility for the scheme is based on head teachers' assessment of potential and progress, rather than examination results alone.

The other key priority for the university is to enhance its student wellbeing and mental health services, after six students took their own lives in a single year. Some elements of the reforms have been controversial, such as the removal of hall tutors, but there has been major investment in a school-based Student Wellbeing Service and central facilities such as the Students' Health and Counselling Services. The aim is to "reach out to help our students rather than wait to be asked".

A revamped curriculum launched in 2017 offers Bristol undergraduates the choice of courses in innovation and enterprise, global citizenship or sustainable futures, as well as focusing on "core academic skills". Bristol Futures is designed to enable students to develop the qualities to thrive in a changing labour market, while the university improves its facilities and eventually adds a new campus in the city.

The plans include a transformation of the main university precinct, with a new library, more teaching, study and shared spaces, a student resource hub and improved sports facilities. A "global lounge" will serve as a hub for intercultural activity on campus and consolidate services for international students. The £300m enterprise campus, to be built next to Temple Meads station and focus on digital technologies, now has planning permission. It will include a new student village and is expected to open in 2021-22.

Having added over 2,000 places to its intake of new undergraduates in six years, Bristol now has around 18,000 undergraduates and nearly 6,000 postgraduate students — and intends to grow further. Almost 30 new undergraduate

Senate House
Tyndall Avenue
Bristol BS8 1TH
0117 394 1649
choosebristol-ug@bristol.ac.uk
www.bristol.ac.uk
www.bristolsu.org.uk
Open days 2019:
see website

The Times and The Sunday Times Rankings
Overall Ranking: =19 (last year: =16)

Teaching quality	75.7%	113
Student experience	74.1%	111
Research quality	47.3%	6
Entry standards	184	11
Graduate prospects	80.6%	=44
Good honours	89.3%	7
Expected completion rate	95.6%	8
Student/staff ratio	13.6	23
Services and facilities	£2,139	77

programmes are planned for this year, including a foundation year in the arts and humanities for those without the necessary qualifications for degree study. More than half of the new degrees are joint honours with English or history and a modern language.

The 2014 Research Excellence Framework confirmed Bristol's place among the leading universities in the UK. It ranked alongside Oxford in the top four and was rewarded for entering more than 90% of its eligible staff — a higher proportion than Oxford. Eighty-three per cent of its research rated as world-leading or internationally excellent. Among the many successes, geography consolidated its position as the leader in its subject, while the entire submissions in clinical medicine, health subjects, economics and sport and exercise sciences were placed in the top categories for their external impact.

However, the university had to settle for silver in the Teaching Excellence Framework, although the panel said: "Bristol's world-leading research is translated into education in which independent learning is encouraged." Low levels of satisfaction with assessment and feedback were the university's undoing, as has often been the case in our league table, although it has moved back into our top 20 recently, a minimum requirement for a university of Bristol's international standing.

There are 5,500 residential places for undergraduates, who must apply by July 31 and have Bristol as their firm choice to be guaranteed a room. There is an impressive sports complex with a well-equipped gym at the heart of the university precinct, which is currently under refurbishment to expand provision by 30%. The careers centre has also been upgraded. The students' union houses one of the city's biggest live music venues as well as a cafe, bars, theatre and swimming pool.

Bristol possesses a vibrant youth culture and, as one of the country's most prosperous cities, offers job opportunities to students and graduates alike. The university merges into the centre, its famous gothic tower dominating the skyline from the junction of two of the main shopping streets. Bristol was chosen by *The Sunday Times* as the best city in the UK in which to live in 2017. Most students enjoy life there and — although the cost of living can be high — many stay on after graduation.

Tuition fees

» Fees for UK/EU students 2019–20 £9,250
» Fees for International students 2019–20 £18,100–£22,300
  Dentistry £36,100; Medicine £31,800 (2018-19);
  Veterinary science £29,100
» For scholarship and bursary information see
  www.bristol.ac.uk/fees-funding
» Graduate salary £25,000

Student numbers

Undergraduates	17,190	(439)
Postgraduates	4,658	(1,304)
Applications/places	43,355/5,415	
Applications per place	8.0	
Overall offer rate	71.3%	
International students	22.4%	

Accommodation

University provided places: 5,500 (catered 33%)
Catered costs: £149–£179 per week
Self-catered: £90–£172 per week
First years guaranteed accommodation
www.bristol.ac.uk/accommodation/undergraduate/aspx

Where do the students come from?

State schools (non-grammar)	50.5%	Working-class homes	14.7%	Black ethnic minority	2.2%
Grammar schools	14.0%	Deprived areas	5.2%	Disabled	5.1%
Independent schools	35.5%	All ethnic minorities	16.0%	Mature (over 21)	5.6%

Brunel, University of London

Brunel managed an 18% increase in new undergraduates in 2017 at a time when some of its competitors were finding it hard to recruit. A quarter of them came through clearing, a route that is likely to continue to provide opportunities. The institution's longer-term aim is to be "at the pinnacle of technological universities in the UK" and in the top tier internationally.

About £400m has been spent on the single campus in northwest London to further that ambition, with another £150m being invested over a five-year period. Engineering and sports facilities are seeing the bulk of the spending, but a £50m learning and teaching centre is planned for next year. A new "green" building for science, technology, engineering and mathematics opened recently.

Some well-known figures have joined the academic staff over the years, with Benjamin Zephaniah taking up his first academic position as chairman of creative writing, and Will Self becoming professor of contemporary thought. Brunel alumni Jo Brand and Lee Mack have helped to establish the first Centre for Comedy Studies Research.

A raft of new courses, from film production to global challenges, enrolled their first students last year. Chemical engineering and entrepreneurship and innovation are going through the approval process to be added this year. Brunel was placed in the silver category in the government's Teaching Excellence Framework, the judging panel complimenting the university's analytical approach to addressing attainment gaps within the institution's diverse student body. The university is one of the most socially inclusive in Britain: about 60% of the students come from the black or minority ethnic communities and almost a third are from low-income households.

Health is a growing focus for the university. The new Brunel Partners Academic Centre for Health Sciences, for example, is working with two NHS foundation trusts in an attempt to revolutionise the way health and social care is delivered. There is also a new Centre for Health Effects of Radiological and Chemical Agents.

Brunel is benefiting from increased research funding since its good performance in the 2014 Research Excellence Framework. More than 60% of a large submission was rated as world-leading or internationally excellent, with sports sciences achieving the best results and ranking in the top five departments in the UK. Brunel did particularly well in the new assessments of the external impact of research.

The university has taken a number of steps to improve the student experience and graduates' career prospects, both of which

Uxbridge
UB8 3PH
01895 265 265
course-enquiries@brunel.ac.uk
www.brunel.ac.uk
https://brunelstudents.com
Open days 2019:
see website

The Times and The Sunday Times Rankings
Overall Ranking: 76 (last year: 59)

Teaching quality	73.8%	121
Student experience	74.4%	109
Research quality	25.4%	50
Entry standards	132	=63
Graduate prospects	70.9%	=94
Good honours	75.1%	57
Expected completion rate	87.1%	=54
Student/staff ratio	16.4	=78
Services and facilities	£2,370	44

have been among its traditional strengths. The Brunel Educational Excellence Centre provides students with opportunities to enhance their academic skills and encourages innovative teaching, while the Professional Development Centre focuses on employability, bringing together the award-winning Placement and Careers Centre, modern foreign languages and the Innovation Hub. The Brunel+ award recognises non-academic activities that may appeal to employers.

The impressive library and Brunel's world-class sports facilities have accounted for much of the investment on campus, which retains the original 1960s architecture, but with the addition of striking new buildings and landscaping. The sports facilities are among the best at any university and have been used by some of the world's top athletes, including Jamaican sprinters Usain Bolt and Yohan Blake.

More than 50 sports and activities clubs include American football, cheerleading, rock climbing and snowboarding, while the campus gym has four training zones. The multimillion-pound Indoor Athletics Centre on campus includes a 130-metre sprint straight, pole vault, high jump and long/triple jump facilities. There is also a bespoke strength and conditioning gym for elite student athletes. The Sports Park, just outside the campus, boasts a 400-metre athletics track with tennis and netball courts, pitches for football, rugby and hockey and a Football Association-registered 3G pitch.

Student accommodation has been transformed as part of the campus improvements. With the refurbishment of existing halls of residence and further construction there are now more than 4,600 places for new first-year, full-time students — enough to enable Brunel to be among the few universities to guarantee accommodation even to those from the local area and those arriving through clearing, as long as they apply by the end of August.

The university's location in Uxbridge, northwest London, is not the most glamorous in the capital, but it is little more than an hour from the West End by public transport. The self-contained campus is a rarity for a London university and is the centre of many students' social lives. A public bike scheme, introduced last summer, links the university, Uxbridge town centre and the local hospital.

Tuition fees

- » Fees for UK/EU students 2019–20 £9,250
- » Fees for International students 2019–20 £15,400–£18,720
- » For scholarship and bursary information see www.brunel.ac.uk/study/undergraduate-fees-and-funding
- » Graduate salary £23,000

Student numbers

Undergraduates	9,547	(293)
Postgraduates	2,392	(896)
Applications/places	21,295/2,495	
Applications per place	8.5	
Overall offer rate	80.5%	
International students	26.5%	

Accommodation

University provided places: 4,816 (catered 0%)
Self-catered: £111–£157 per week
First years guaranteed accommodation
www.brunel.ac.uk/life/accommodation

Where do the students come from?

State schools (non-grammar)	89.9%	Working-class homes	43.3%	Black ethnic minority	18.4%
Grammar schools	5.8%	Deprived areas	4.1%	Disabled	7.1%
Independent schools	4.3%	All ethnic minorities	69.5%	Mature (over 21)	11.0%

University of Buckingham

Buckingham is aiming to become the country's first drug-free university, by changing the culture to one with an emphasis on drugs education, peer pressure not to take drugs and encouraging alternatives to drugs and excessive alcohol for relaxation and enjoyment.

It has also declared itself Europe's first "positive university" — tackling the challenge of student mental health proactively and embedding positive psychology and resilience into the curriculum to enable staff and students to be happier, feel more engaged with learning and develop a purpose in their lives. All tutors are trained in the subject and every student will have a module focusing on positive relationships, engagements, meaning and achievement.

Regularly rated at or near the top for student satisfaction with teaching quality and the student experience, Buckingham was named The Sunday Times and The Times University of the Year for Teaching Quality in 2015 and received a gold award in the first Teaching Excellence Framework. Students value the tutorials of no more than ten undergraduates and the open access to academics and teaching staff.

There is also a growing market for the two-year degrees that Buckingham pioneered more than 40 years ago, which has seen the university take more students at a time when others were struggling to recruit.

Except in medicine, where the fees are £36,500 a year, Buckingham's UK and EU undergraduates pay a total of £25,200 for their two-year course — marginally less than on conventional, three-year degrees, but saving a year's living costs and enabling swifter entry to the labour market. The extended academic year, which makes the university's accelerated degrees possible, involves four nine-week terms and still allows for 13 weeks of vacation.

Undergraduates can begin courses in January or September. Just over half of the students are from overseas, but the proportion from Britain is growing. They have the option of a three-year degree in the humanities, and other schools are now following suit.

Students from the five counties nearest to the university — Buckinghamshire, Bedfordshire, Northamptonshire, Hertfordshire and Oxfordshire — are eligible for a reduction of £2,000 a year on their fees. Others who take out government maintenance loans of more than £5,000 qualify for bursaries of £1,100 and there are £2,000 scholarships (except in medicine) for those who achieve at least AAB at A-level.

For many years Britain's only private university, Buckingham is still the only one in our main league table, now well established in the top 50. It would finish higher if it had taken part in the Research Excellence Framework (REF). Buckingham has a

Hunter Street
Buckingham MK18 1EG
01280 820 313
admissions@buckingham.ac.uk
www.buckingham.ac.uk
Open days 2019:
see website

The Times and The Sunday Times Rankings
Overall Ranking: 43 (last year: =47)

Teaching quality	84.9%	8
Student experience	83.2%	8
Research quality	n/a	
Entry standards	128	=73
Graduate prospects	81.5%	33
Good honours	68.7%	98
Expected completion rate	84%	78
Student/staff ratio	11.3	4
Services and facilities	£2,344	48

number of research groups and more than 170 research students. It is refurbishing property to accommodate the Humanities Research Institute and plans to enter the REF in future.

There are still little more than 2,500 students, but current building plans, backed by a £70m fundraising programme, would allow for expansion. The new £8m Vinson Centre for Liberal Economics and Entrepreneurship, opened last year, includes a social study centre, cinema, coffee shop and lecture theatre, as well as hosting an enterprise hub for the region.

A development plan for the Buckingham riverside campus includes a new school of law and students' union in the old Tanlaw Mill. The proposals also include a sports centre and floodlit pitch for university and public use. Planning permission is under way to construct 150 new student rooms on campus to maintain the university's guarantee of accommodation for first-year students as the institution grows.

Buckingham's most prestigious development has been the opening of the UK's first private not-for-profit medical school, where the first students will qualify next year. The course, which has seen a 45% increase in applications in two years, is 4½ years long, modelled on the University of Leicester's MBChB (Bachelor of Medicine and Bachelor of Surgery) programme and is mainly attracting international students.

A new £8.5m clinical training centre opened at Milton Keynes University Hospital last year and the riverside campus plans include an extension for the school's headquarters. The education school is based at Whittlebury Hall, near Towcester, and the university also has a base in London to host lectures and other activities.

A degree in security and intelligence studies will launch this year, and Buckingham is developing new degrees and partnerships in podiatry and dentistry in the next few years. From this year, students will be able to take French or Spanish as minor options while choosing other subjects in which to major.

The main campus, which has been judged one of the safest in England and Wales, includes a bar and a fitness centre, with the Radcliffe Centre, which hosts internal and external events, nearby. The university's size and semi-rural location make for a very different student experience from the norm, but Buckingham does, different, rather well as its fees and term dates demonstrate. The town of Buckingham is pretty, with a good selection of pubs and restaurants, plus Milton Keynes and Oxford are nearby.

Tuition fees

» Fees for UK/EU students 2019–20		£12,600
» Fees for International students 2019–20		£17,400
Medicine		£36,500
» For scholarship and bursary information see		
www.buckingham.ac.uk/admissions/fees		
» Graduate salary		£20,000

Student numbers

Undergraduates	1,258	(56)
Postgraduates	1,111	(93)
Applications/places		1,090/160
Applications per place		6.8
Overall offer rate		n/a
International students		37.5%

Accommodation

University provided places: 548 (catered 0%)
Self-catered: £93–£235 per week
First years guaranteed accommodation
www.buckingham.ac.uk/life/accommodation

Where do the students come from?

State schools (non-grammar)	69.4%	Working-class homes	25%	Black ethnic minority	n/a
Grammar schools	5.8%	Deprived areas	n/a	Disabled	4.1%
Independent schools	24.8%	All ethnic minorities	n/a	Mature (over 21)	40.9%

Buckinghamshire New University

Bucks New has made gains in our league table and it was one of six universities to have a bronze rating upgraded to silver in the latest Teaching Excellence Framework. The judging panel was impressed by the provision of personalised learning through small class sizes, the development of individual action plans to support progression to employment, the embedding of skills in the curriculum and "live briefs" co-designed with students to address real world problems.

The university is not one that has struggled to fill its places. Indeed, its 2017 enrolment set a new record, with 500 students more than in the year before £9,000 fees were introduced. It has been adapting its portfolio of employment-related courses and is embarking on a big expansion of its degree apprenticeships, moving from eight to 14 programmes this year with up to 600 students. The new areas will include training for social workers, specialist community and public health nurses, police constables and production managers.

Bucks New specialises in degree programmes and professional qualifications serving the creative and cultural industries, management and the public sector. Travel and aviation courses, for example, provide the opportunity to study for a professional pilot's licence while also carrying out university studies. There are some of the UK's only music management courses, as well as film and television production.

The university was one of the first to offer a degree in policing and is also among the leading providers of nursing qualifications in the southeast, offering adult, child and mental health pre-qualifying nursing, as well as post-registration courses. Bucks New won the *Student Nursing Times*'s 2018 teaching innovation of the year award for its training with dementia simulation. Its use of a moulage specialist who is skilled in applying mock — and often gorily realistic — injuries in its simulation laboratories had previously won a *Guardian* award for teaching innovation.

Nursing is taught in Uxbridge and there is a new and innovative campus for higher education and professional development in Aylesbury, which hosts programmes taught by the university and Aylesbury College. The main campus is in High Wycombe, where more than 5,000 students are based, and which has seen more than £100m of investment over a ten-year period.

The prize-winning Gateway building transformed the town-centre campus with improved teaching, social and administrative space. Other learning areas and informal spaces have also been added in High Wycombe, where a student village of more than 400 ensuite bedrooms a short walk from the campus brings the total number of

Queen Alexandra Road
High Wycombe HP11 2JZ
01494 522 141
admissions@bucks.ac.uk
www.bucks.ac.uk
www.bucksstudentsunion.org
Open days 2019:
March 16 (Nursing only, Uxbridge); March 30;
June 15

The Times and The Sunday Times Rankings
Overall Ranking: 117 (last year: 126)

Teaching quality	83.5%	16
Student experience	81.0%	=25
Research quality	1.5%	124
Entry standards	112	=118
Graduate prospects	68.8%	105
Good honours	56.6%	131
Expected completion rate	76.2%	121
Student/staff ratio	16.0	=71
Services and facilities	£2,327	50

residential places offered by Bucks New to 885. This ensures new students are guaranteed a place, even if they come through clearing.

The university prides itself on its links with local business and private sector employers, who help to shape the curriculum as well as providing placement opportunities. The social work academy, for example, is run in partnership with Buckinghamshire county council, where the university's academics support the continuing professional development of qualified social workers and managers.

A new Life Sciences Innovation Centre won £1.3m of development funding last year. Based at Stoke Mandeville Hospital and High Wycombe, it will support the development of innovative products focused around a range of clinical areas including health and wellbeing, prevention and public health.

Bucks New was awarded university status in 2007 but has been celebrating the 125th anniversary of its foundation as a science and art school from the products of a local tax on beer and spirits. Research is focused on the needs of business, commerce and industry, as well as the public and voluntary sectors. However, the university is in the bottom three in our table for research quality, having entered only 24 staff for the 2014 Research Excellence Framework.

There are now some 9,000 students, two thirds of whom are full-time undergraduates, four in ten of them over 21 years old on entry.

They all receive a unique and valuable package of free activities through the students' union's Big Deal programme, which has been running for several years. The programme entitles all students to free entertainment, recreational activities, events and sport. However, there are no scholarships or bursaries at Buckinghamshire New University for the first time in the current academic year because the university has decided to pursue widening participation through other measures.

Sporting opportunities are plentiful, with clubs for 30 sports and links with professional clubs in the region. The university's gym is one of the best exercise facilities in the area, with app-based, high definition, touch-screen cardio machines, top-of-the-range resistance stations and interactive exercise equipment.

The Human Performance, Exercise and Wellbeing Centre, opened in 2016, has a three-lane running track with 3D motion-capture technology, along with a sports injury and physiotherapy clinic. High Wycombe has a range of student pubs and clubs and is within easy reach of London.

Tuition fees

- » Fees for UK/EU students 2019–20 £9,250
- » Fees for International students 2018–19 £10,500
- » For scholarship and bursary information see www.bucks.ac.uk/applying-to-bucks/undergraduate/fees-and-funding
- » Graduate salary £22,000

Student numbers

Undergraduates	6,220	(1,632)
Postgraduates	328	(691)
Applications/places		10,655/2,165
Applications per place		4.9
Overall offer rate		88.9%
International students		8.6%

Accommodation

University provided places: 885 (catered 0%)
Self-catered: £111–£185 per week
First years guaranteed accommodation
www.bucks.ac.uk/life-at-bucks/accommodation

Where do the students come from?

State schools (non-grammar)	93.9%	Working-class homes	46.2%	Black ethnic minority	19.8%
Grammar schools	2.5%	Deprived areas	9.0%	Disabled	4.3%
Independent schools	3.6%	All ethnic minorities	43.0%	Mature (over 21)	33.7%

University of Cambridge

Cambridge may have been overtaken by Oxford in some of the research-driven world rankings, but it remains top of our league table for the sixth year in a row, recognising the special qualities of its undergraduate education. It is top in just under half of our subject tables and ahead of all-comers on entry standards, completion rates, research quality and spending on student facilities.

Cambridge remains among the top six universities in all the main international rankings and also received a gold rating in the first edition of the government's Teaching Excellence Framework. The panel said the tutorial system enabled students to engage with world-leading scholars and to receive ongoing personalised feedback on their academic progress, as well as undertaking research alongside leaders in their field.

Candidates require predictions of A*AA at A-level in arts subjects and A*A*A in the sciences just to get through the first stage of the selection process, although candidates may be made a lower offer if their school or personal circumstances are thought to disadvantage them. Then there are Cambridge's own entrance tests, which, depending on the subject, take place either on the day of an interview, or in advance.

There may be fewer than five applicants to the place, but only one in three receives a conditional offer. Nine out of ten entrants have at least three A grades at A-level, or the equivalent.

As at Oxford, the selection process is endlessly controversial. By 2017, the proportion of places going to state-educated applicants had almost reached 63% — but only 40.1% once fully selective grammar schools are stripped out — well below the national average for Cambridge's courses and entry grades.

It was also revealed that only 58 black students had been admitted in 2017, although this represented a third of all black students reaching Cambridge's normal entry requirements. The university is third bottom of our new social inclusion ranking.

Unlike other Russell Group institutions, Cambridge has not expanded its undergraduate intake significantly. The £1bn North West Cambridge development will enable it to take more postgraduates and house more staff, as well as providing private housing. Even the university's first excursion into degree apprenticeships, with Lloyds Bank, Greggs Bakery and British Airways, will be at postgraduate level.

In the city centre, Cambridge possesses some of the most ancient and iconic buildings at any university. But huge sums have been spent modernising the facilities and the university has raised a £600m bond to continue the process. Recent additions include the £26m Maxwell Centre, on the West Cambridge site, where research scientists from industry will occupy

Cambridge Admissions Office
Fitzwilliam House
Cambridge CB2 1QY
01223 333 308
admissions@cam.ac.uk
www.cam.ac.uk
www.cusu.co.uk
Open days 2019:
July 4, 5

The Times and *The Sunday Times* **Rankings**

Overall Ranking: 1 (last year: 1)

Teaching quality	n/a	
Student experience	n/a	
Research quality	57.3%	1
Entry standards	225	1
Graduate prospects	86.8%	7
Good honours	92.6%	2
Expected completion rate	98.6%	1
Student/staff ratio	11.0	3
Services and facilities	£3,708	1

laboratory and desk space alongside Cambridge research groups. The university is raising more money to create new professorships and continue developing its biomedical campus and the West Cambridge site.

Cambridge entered 95% of eligible academics for the most recent Research Excellence Framework — no university involved a higher proportion — and 87% of their work was rated as world-leading or internationally excellent. It achieved the UK's best results in aeronautical and electronic engineering, business and management, chemistry, classics and clinical medicine.

The application system has been simplified somewhat, with candidates no longer required to complete an initial Cambridge form, as well as their UCAS form. However, they are sent the Supplementary Application Questionnaire, after they have submitted their UCAS form, covering the applicant's academic experience in more detail. The tripos system was a forerunner of the currently fashionable modular degree, allowing students to change subjects (within limits) midway through their courses. Students receive a classification for each of the two parts of their degree.

Choosing a college is an additional complication for those not familiar with Cambridge. Making the right choice is crucial, both to maximise the chances of winning a place and to ensure an enjoyable three years if you are successful. Applicants can take pot luck with an open application if they prefer not to opt for a particular college. But, though the statistics show that this route is equally successful, only a minority risks it.

Most teaching is now university-based, especially in the sciences, and a shift of emphasis towards the centre has been taking place more generally.

Sports facilities are predictably excellent, both at individual colleges and in the £16m sports centre, which features a large sports hall and a strength and conditioning wing.

Cambridge is not for everyone, however bright. The amount of high-quality work to be crammed into eight-week terms can prove a strain, but few drop out, such is the rigour in the selection process in the first place. Most students relish the experience — although for the past two years they have not elected to tell us quite how much by boycotting the National Student Survey completed by all other universities bar Oxford. Graduates reap the rewards in their careers, the upper echelons of many professions having a disproportionate number of Cambridge graduates.

Tuition fees

- » Fees for UK/EU students 2019–20 £9,250
- » Fees for International students 2019–20 £20,157–£30,678
  Medicine £52,638
- » For scholarship and bursary information see www.undergraduate.study.cam.ac.uk/fees-and-finance
- » Graduate salary £27,000

Student numbers		
Undergraduates	12,022	(321)
Postgraduates	6,444	(1,168)
Applications/places		17,235/3,475
Applications per place		5.0
Overall offer rate		31.2%
International students		33.8%

Accommodation

See: http://www.undergraduate.study.cam.ac.uk/why-cambridge/student-life/accommodation

College websites provide accommodation details

See Chapter 14 for individual colleges

Where do the students come from?

State schools (non-grammar)	40.1%	Working-class homes	10.2%	Black ethnic minority	2.1%
Grammar schools	22.5%	Deprived areas	4.4%	Disabled	4.6%
Independent schools	37.4%	All ethnic minorities	21.3%	Mature (over 21)	4.3%

Canterbury Christ Church

Applications to Canterbury Christ Church have dropped by more than a third in three years, but a higher offer rate has kept enrolments broadly stable. Now the university is hoping to revive the demand for places with a £150m campus development plan and a raft of new courses.

Seven new degrees took their first students last year, with the option of a foundation year added to 27 more, and the single degree apprenticeship will become ten in a year's time if all are approved. The proposed new areas for apprenticeships include journalism, policing, teaching and manufacturing engineering.

The opening of a new building for the arts marked the start of the transformation plan, providing the latest digital facilities that will be used by a number of the new courses. A multimillion-pound centre for science, engineering, technology and health opens in 2020, and will be home to the Kent and Medway Engineering, Design, Growth and Enterprise (Edge) Hub, as well as containing specialist health facilities.

Christ Church and the University of Kent have been approved to open the county's first medical school in 2020, offering 100 places on five-year Bachelor of Medicine and Bachelor of Surgery programmes.

The conversion of Canterbury's 19th-century prison for residential and teaching accommodation is the final development in the 15-year plan. Demolition work has already started outside the main building. At the heart of the extended site is the Abbey Square, a new public space framed by steps that double up as seating.

Christ Church also has campuses in Chatham and Broadstairs, and a postgraduate centre in Tunbridge Wells. The purpose-built campus at Broadstairs offers subjects ranging from commercial music to digital media, photography, and early childhood studies, while the recently expanded Medway site at Chatham's historic dockyard specialises in education and health programmes.

The majority of the students, however, are in Canterbury, on a world heritage site where Christ Church already has a prize-winning library and student services centre. All campuses are interconnected by a high-speed data network.

The former Church of England college achieved university status in 2005, and is one of the region's largest providers of courses and research for the public services, with teacher training courses that are highly rated by Ofsted, and strong programmes in health and social care, nursing and policing.

Seven out of ten undergraduates are female, partly the result of the subject mix, with its emphasis on health subjects and education. There are now almost 17,000

North Holmes Road
Canterbury CT1 1QU
01227 928 000
admissions@canterbury.ac.uk
www.canterbury.ac.uk
https://ccsu.co.uk
Open days 2019:
June 9, (Canterbury);
June 22 (Medway)

The Times and The Sunday Times **Rankings**
Overall Ranking: 118 (last year: 111)

Teaching quality	80.0%	65
Student experience	75.4%	101
Research quality	4.5%	98
Entry standards	111	121
Graduate prospects	64.7%	=119
Good honours	70.7%	84
Expected completion rate	79.5%	=107
Student/staff ratio	15.2	=50
Services and facilities	£1,913	93

students, more than half of whom come from Kent, while nearly 1,000 of the rest are from continental Europe or further afield. The university remains a Church of England foundation and has the Archbishop of Canterbury as its chancellor.

Almost half of Canterbury Christ Church's submission to the 2014 research assessments was placed in the top two categories, resulting in one of the biggest percentage increases in funding at any university. A life sciences industry liaison laboratory at Discovery Park in Sandwich, provides students with first-class facilities for science and research, and acts as an added resource for local businesses.

Another high-profile addition is the UK Institute for Migration Research, as is the Institute of Medical Sciences, which builds on the university's work in stem cell research and minimally-invasive surgery.

Engineering is one of the areas of most development, as the university works with employers to introduce courses that respond to real-world opportunities and produce more creative — and diverse — graduates. Christ Church is one of a growing number of universities around the world to adopt the CDIO (conceive, design, implement and operate) curriculum to foster creativity in engineering. There will be regional centres co-located with engineering and technology firms to complement the new hub.

Bucking the trend of recent years, Christ Church has moved from three terms to a semester-based system with teaching spread over two extended periods. The university believes that this will give students more opportunity to immerse themselves in their course with in-depth study and dedicated time set aside to develop their academic, personal and employability skills. Positive feedback from current students has helped in the design of these changes.

Sports facilities are good for those on the Canterbury campus and there is enough residential accommodation to guarantee a place for first-years who apply by the end of July. Canterbury is now a thriving student centre, and Christ Church contributes to the cultural life of the city with the Sidney Cooper Gallery and St Gregory's Centre for Music, a historic concert venue.

Tuition fees

» Fees for UK/EU students 2019–20	£9,250
Foundation courses	£6,575
» Fees for International students 2019–20	£11,900
Foundation courses	£8,500
» For scholarship and bursary information see www.canterbury.ac.uk/study-here/fees-and-funding/undergraduate-fees-and-funding	
» Graduate salary	£22,000

Student numbers

Undergraduates	10,283	(2,111)
Postgraduates	1,127	(1,679)
Applications/places		11,420/2,620
Applications per place		4.4
Overall offer rate		85.1%
International students		4.8%

Accommodation

University provided places: 1,825 (catered 0%)
Self-catered: £118–£167 per week
First years guaranteed accommodation
www.canterbury.ac.uk/accommodation

Where do the students come from?

State schools (non-grammar)	93.2%	Working-class homes	39.8%	Black ethnic minority	17.6%
Grammar schools	4.5%	Deprived areas	17.3%	Disabled	6.4%
Independent schools	2.3%	All ethnic minorities	26.0%	Mature (over 21)	34.5%

Cardiff University

A new five-year strategy aims to establish Cardiff as one of the top 20 universities in the UK and in the top 100 in the world. Both targets are ambitious, but Cardiff is moving rapidly up our table, having won our Welsh University of the Year award in 2017. Boasting two Nobel laureates on staff, it is the only member of the Russell Group of research-led universities in Wales and the only Welsh representative in the top 150 of the world rankings.

Enrolments are close to record levels, although they fell slightly in 2018 after a more significant fall in applications. Demand from European students has declined since the Brexit referendum, but there are still 7,500 students from outside the UK.

Other elements of the new strategy include a renewed focus on the university's civic mission and a goal to work with colleges, educational partners and all schools in Wales to improve the nation's educational attainment. Cardiff also aims to offer all undergraduates work placements as part of their degree and to help more students to spend time abroad during their studies. The university's Global Opportunity Centre co-ordinates study, work and volunteering options around the world.

New BSc degrees on offer include maths or business management with Welsh, both featuring a professional placement year.

A new home has opened for the highly-regarded School of Journalism, Media and Culture, alongside BBC Cymru Wales. It is the latest phase of a £600m development plan, the university's largest in a generation. A £50m Centre for Student Life will open this year at the heart of the Cathays Park campus, providing a central hub for student support services, as well as flexible social learning spaces, a 550-seat lecture theatre and shops. Other projects include a £40m programme to refurbish lecture theatres, classrooms and seminar rooms, a £300m Innovation Campus and a Translational Research Centre working with industry to develop medical diagnostic tools and therapies.

Cardiff was rated silver in the government's Teaching Excellence Framework. The panel praised "excellent" personalised support by tutors and the direct engagement of students with developments at the forefront of research, scholarship and professional practice. Discipline-relevant research training was found to enrich the learning experience for undergraduates.

An earlier audit by the Quality Assurance Agency complimented the university on its "powerful academic vision and well-developed and effectively articulated mission to achieve excellence in teaching and research".

Cardiff's main base is in the civic centre around Cathays Park. It has five healthcare schools at the Heath Park campus, a 53-acre

Cardiff
CF10 3AT
029 2087 4455
enquiry@cardiff.ac.uk
www.cardiff.ac.uk
www.cardiffstudents.com
Open days 2019:
July 5

The Times and The Sunday Times Rankings
Overall Ranking: 32 (last year: 35)

Teaching quality	78.5%	=89
Student experience	77.3%	=81
Research quality	35.0%	34
Entry standards	155	37
Graduate prospects	81.7%	=30
Good honours	78.9%	=39
Expected completion rate	92.4%	=24
Student/staff ratio	13.5	=21
Services and facilities	£2,267	59

site shared with the University Hospital of Wales and the university's joint venture Cardiff Medicentre, where spinout businesses such as Q5 Healthcare are developing innovative diagnostic tools. The School of Dentistry has some of the UK's most modern training facilities including a new simulation suite.

One undergraduate in seven comes from an independent school – the highest proportion in Wales – but there are extensive efforts to widen participation. Bursaries of £1,000 are available to undergraduates from low-income families. The projected dropout rate is comfortably the lowest in Wales.

The new Residences Life programme helps students to transition smoothly to higher education, ensuring that they feel part of their new community, while the Student Mentoring Scheme matches new entrants with established undergraduates from the same academic school to discuss topics including study techniques, budgeting and module choices.

Cardiff's results in the 2014 Research Excellence Framework were excellent, with 87% of its submission rated world-leading or internationally excellent, and in the UK's top three for impact. Civil and construction engineering gained top billing. However, it suffered in our research ranking by entering only 62% of eligible staff, 12 percentage points below any other Russell Group institution. The university slipped out of the top 50 in this year's Reuters ranking of the most innovative universities in Europe but was still only just outside the top ten UK institutions in the list.

The library has extensive electronic resources and speedy self-service provision. The university has 5,346 residential places for undergraduates, guaranteeing a place to all applicants who make Cardiff their first choice. The main residential site at Talybont boasts a sports training village, and there is also a city-centre dance studio and fitness suite, as well as 33 acres of outdoor facilities. The University's Cardiff Half Marathon is the second largest race of its type in the UK, and last year incorporated the first Commonwealth Half Marathon Championships.

Students find Cardiff relatively inexpensive, with a good range of nightlife and cultural venues.

Tuition fees

»	Fees for UK/EU students 2019–20	£9,000
»	Fees for International students 2019–20	£15,080–£19,950
	Medicine	£36,308
»	For scholarship and bursary information see www.cardiff.ac.uk/fees	
»	Graduate salary	£22,000

Student numbers

Undergraduates	19,412 (3,673)
Postgraduates	5,239 (3,273)
Applications/places	34,590/5,500
Applications per place	6.3
Overall offer rate	79.0%
International students	23.8%

Accommodation

University provided places: 5,346 (catered 6%)
Catered costs: £122–£147 per week
Self-catered: £108–£137 per week
First years guaranteed accommodation
www.cardiff.ac.uk/residences

Where do the students come from?

State schools (non-grammar)	76.5%	Working-class homes	23.8%	Black ethnic minority	2.7%
Grammar schools	8.8%	Deprived areas	10.8%	Disabled	5.7%
Independent schools	14.7%	All ethnic minorities	15.3%	Mature (over 21)	11.2%

Cardiff Metropolitan University

Proudly "ambitious and competitive", Cardiff Met is aiming to become one of the UK's top 50 universities by 2022-23. That will require a rise of some 60 places in our table.

The new Cardiff School of Technologies will welcome its first students this year, offering courses in digital media, data science and informatics, design technologies, electronics and systems engineering, and working closely with employers to fit their skill requirements. Teaching will begin on the central Llandaff campus, but it is hoped that the school will transfer to a new campus in the city centre by 2022, recruiting 2,000 new students by 2024.

This year the school is planning to launch Cardiff Met's first degree apprenticeships in cyber-security, data science and software engineering, with 45 places available.

Cardiff Global, launched last year, is expected to add to the current total of more than 7,000 international students, most of whom are taught in partner institutions overseas, as well as developing international research links. The scheme also encompasses Cardiff Open Colleges, which will build on the university's partnerships with schools and further education colleges to deliver clear paths to university entry, promote the expansion of Welsh medium provision and foster civic engagement.

Rating Cardiff Met silver in the Teaching Excellence Framework, assessors praised personalised learning, including its Welsh language offering. An enhanced personal tutor system has been introduced, giving students greater access to academic support, advice and guidance. Course design is informed by a significant focus on employability, the panel added, producing good outcomes for a range of student groups including those from black and minority ethnic communities, disadvantaged and mature students.

Graduate employability is one of the main priorities in Cardiff Met's strategy. Each academic school now has its own careers consultants with sector-specific knowledge and students can get professional help without an appointment, any day of the week. There is a programme of skills workshops, employer visits and one-to-one advice to put students at the head of the job-hunting pack. The university's first large-scale Graduate Careers Fair attracted more than 80 local, regional and national employers, and is now an annual fixture.

The Centre for Entrepreneurship supports a growing number of student start-up businesses, offering free desk space and access to mentors.

The university entered only a small team of its academics – 35 out of 381 – for the 2014 Research Excellence Framework but

200 Western Avenue
Llandaff
Cardiff CF5 2YB
askadmissions@cardiffmet.ac.uk
www.cardiffmet.ac.uk
www.cardiffmetsu.co.uk
Open days 2019:
see website

The Times and The Sunday Times Rankings
Overall Ranking: 108 (last year: 90)

Teaching quality	77.7%	=99
Student experience	77.9%	=76
Research quality	3.9%	108
Entry standards	126	=82
Graduate prospects	65.9%	116
Good honours	65.2%	123
Expected completion rate	79.5%	=107
Student/staff ratio	16.5	=81
Services and facilities	£2,599	=26

scored well, with 80% of its work rated in the top two categories denoting world-leading or internationally excellent quality. The university has since received a Queen's Anniversary Prize for the use of design and related 3D digital scanning technologies for maxillofacial reconstructive surgery.

In 2015 Cardiff Met celebrated the 150th anniversary of its founding as the Cardiff School of Art. For many years it was called the University of Wales Institute Cardiff, changing to its present name in 2011. Pending new developments, there are now two campuses, rated as the most environmentally friendly in Wales. The well-equipped, modern School of Art and Design is on the Llandaff campus, which also hosts the School of Management, as well as engineering, food science and health courses.

The Cyncoed campus, which houses education and sport, has a modern student centre and is the main centre of social activity, particularly for first-years. Construction of a 25-metre swimming pool, fitness suite, sports hall and squash courts will begin this year.

Cardiff Met is one of Britain's leading centres for university sport, producing more than 300 international representatives in 30 sports. Its teams have done justice to excellent existing facilities including a new sports arena and the £7m National Indoor Athletics Centre, winning university championships in archery, gymnastics, squash, weightlifting and judo. There is a thriving sports club scene and about 2,000 students take sport and dance-related courses.

Undergraduate applications have fallen for four years in a row, but enrolments edged up in 2017 and were close to record levels. Students from Wales account for two thirds of the 10,000 Cardiff-based students, half of whom are from the city or the Vale of Glamorgan.

The campuses are close to the city centre and linked by the Met Rider bus service during term-time. The halls of residence are a mile from the main campus on the Plas Gwyn Residential Campus, where there are enough places to accommodate just over half of the first-years. Apart from those with relevant medical conditions, only care-leavers and those who are under 18 at the start of term are guaranteed places.

Tuition fees

» Fees for UK/EU students 2019–20	£9,000
» Fees for International students 2018–19	£12,000
» For scholarship and bursary information see	
www.cardiffmet.ac.uk/study/finance/Pages/default.aspx	
» Graduate salary	£19,000

Student numbers

Undergraduates	8,084	(707)
Postgraduates	1,239	(964)
Applications/places		9,280/2,185
Applications per place		4.2
Overall offer rate		87.2%
International students		16.2%

Accommodation

University provided places: 1,650 (catered ?
Catered costs: £160–£171 per week
Self-catered: £112–£121 per week
www.cardiffmet.ac.uk/accommo⌐

Where do the students come from?

State schools (non-grammar)	93.5%	Working-class homes	38.4%
Grammar schools	1.4%	Deprived areas	20.3%
Independent schools	5.1%	All ethnic minorities	13

University of Central Lancashire

UCLan has 200 students taking degree apprenticeships — more than most universities — but by September this year it expects to have no fewer than 2,000. A dozen new programmes will account for most of this spectacular growth, ranging from two for nuclear technicians and engineers to others for police constables, social workers and nursing associates.

The pace of these developments does not signal a retreat from conventional degree programmes, however. Another 26 started on the Preston and Burnley campuses last year, with paramedic science, clinical psychology and film, media and popular culture among the new offerings. The first 15 UK students are due to be admitted to UCLan's medical degree. The School of Medicine opened in 2015 but until now, government quotas restricted the intake to self-funded international students. They will continue to be charged the full cost — now £38,000 a year — but their British counterparts will pay the normal £9,250 fee.

UCLan includes dentistry, pharmacy and astrophysics in a surprisingly wide portfolio of more than 200 undergraduate programmes. The Dental School was one of the few to open in the last 100 years, while the architecture degree was the first for a decade. As part of the university's £200m campus masterplan, an Engineering and Innovation Centre is due to open this year. The £32m building will be an integrated hub for teaching, research and knowledge exchange, dedicated to reclaiming Lancashire's role as a national centre for advanced manufacturing and encouraging more women to choose a career in engineering.

The university is in the top ten in the UK for the number of undergraduates it educates, despite a drop of almost 1,000 new enrolments in two years, as applications have fallen by a quarter. UCLan has made fewer offers, partly in order to preserve its entry standards, although it stresses that its commitment to widening participation in higher education means that it remains keen to attract entries from students with non-traditional qualifications.

UCLan ranks just outside our top 30 for social inclusion. Some 45% of the undergraduates come from the four lowest socio-economic classes. Every undergraduate programme includes the option of a foundation year for those without the necessary qualifications for degree-level study, while large numbers take external programmes delivered in further education colleges.

With more than 38,000 students and staff across all its campuses, UCLan is one of Britain's biggest universities. It dominates the centre of Preston and brings more than £200m a year into the local economy. There are also

Preston PR1 2HE
01772 892 444
uadmissions@uclan.ac.uk
www.uclan.ac.uk
www.uclansu.co.uk
Open days 2019:
see website

The Times and The Sunday Times Rankings
Overall Ranking: =105 (last year: 93)

Teaching quality	78.6%	=86
Student experience	76.5%	93
Research quality	5.6%	=87
Entry standards	130	=66
Graduate prospects	76.9%	62
Good honours	70.4%	=85
Expected completion rate	78.9%	112
Student/staff ratio	16.4	=78
Services and facilities	£1,875	99

smaller campuses in Cyprus and Mauritius. Closer to home, the Burnley campus gives local students the opportunity to gain qualifications without leaving home. The campus hosts a collaboration with Cisco Systems for advanced manufacturing, incorporating robotics, computer vision, non-destructive testing and component assembly.

The university's roots stretch back to 1828 and it has established partnerships with a variety of high-profile organisations. There is a longstanding collaboration with Nasa, for example, one recent research venture enabling UCLan scientists to help in the discovery of the first known system of seven Earth-size planets around a single star. There is also sector-leading stroke research with the Department of Health and work on nutritional science with the Bill and Melinda Gates Foundation. There was some world-leading research in all 16 subject areas that were assessed in the 2014 Research Excellence Framework. The undergraduate research internship scheme enables students from all disciplines to work on research projects for up to ten weeks.

UCLan also pioneered a scheme involving collaboration between a police force and a university with its partnership with Lancashire constabulary. This sees forensic experts and students working alongside each other in researching, investigating and delivering forensic science services. The project cemented the development of the Lancashire Forensic Academy, based at police headquarters in Hutton, with facilities including up-to-date research laboratories and equipment, teaching and training suites, crime scene houses, plus accommodation and conferencing spaces.

A strong focus on entrepreneurship has established a range of business incubation facilities for students and graduates. The university is consistently in the UK's top three for the number of graduate start-ups, with 77% still trading after three years. The university works with a wide variety of industrial partners and many undergraduate programmes are directly linked to them. All students can take advantage of work placements and other opportunities to enhance their employability.

The sports facilities are excellent and UCLan has entered 37 teams into the British Universities and Colleges Sport (BUCS) league for 2019–20. Preston offers a generally safe student environment and lower cost of living than Liverpool or Manchester but is only 50 minutes away from either city by public transport.

Tuition fees

» Fees for UK/EU students 2019–20 £9,250

  Foundation courses £5,550

» Fees for International students 2019–20 £12,450–£13,450

  Medicine £38,000

» For scholarship and bursary information see

www.uclan.ac.uk/study_here/fees_and_finance/index.php

» Graduate salary £20,000

Student numbers

Undergraduates	**16,165**	**(3,285)**
Postgraduates	**1,476**	**(3,234)**
Applications/places		**21,640/3,695**
Applications per place		**5.9**
Overall offer rate		**81.4%**
International students		**10.3%**

Accommodation

University provided places: 1,716 (catered 0%)

Self-catered: £72–£115 per week

www.uclan.ac.uk/accommodation/index.php

Where do the students come from?

State schools (non-grammar)	96.8%	Working-class homes	45.1%	Black ethnic minority	5.0%
Grammar schools	1.6%	Deprived areas	21.6%	Disabled	5.3%
Independent schools	1.6%	All ethnic minorities	23.1%	Mature (over 21)	35.7%

University of Chester

Chester will be hoping that a big expansion in its portfolio of degree apprenticeships can arrest a decline in applications, which fell by a fifth in three years and were down again by almost 10% at the official deadline for courses beginning last year.

New apprenticeships in digital and technology solutions, electrical and electronic engineering, mechanical engineering and process control engineering are planned for this year to add to those for chartered managers, business leadership, healthcare assistant practitioners and nursing associates. This will almost treble the number of places available since 2017. There will also be new honours degrees in microbiology, pharmacology, acting, primary education and musical theatre.

The university has blamed the withdrawal of NHS bursaries for part of the decline. It has made a multi-million-pound investment in Marris House, in Birkenhead, on the Wirral, to educate student nurses in skills laboratories resembling hi-tech hospital wards. They will be able to practise skills on virtual reality equipment before taking hospital or community placements. There are also new biology laboratories on the Parkgate Road Campus in Chester for the Faculty of Medicine, Dentistry and Life Sciences.

Chester was rated silver in the Teaching Excellence Framework, commended for its development of employability skills. More than two thirds of undergraduates take work-based learning modules. Chester was found to have an "embedded culture of valuing, recognising and rewarding good teaching", with more than two thirds of the academic staff holding Higher Education Academy fellowships. The panel acknowledged the investment made in high-quality teaching and learning facilities, as well as its relationship with student representatives.

About a quarter of the undergraduates are aged at least 21 on entry and two thirds are female. Nearly all are state-educated, and more than a third have working-class roots. Progression agreements guarantee interviews to students at a number of local colleges, subject to certain conditions, but there is no reduction in entry requirements.

Completion rates had been improving but have now slipped back compared with the national average for Chester's courses and entry qualifications. The university more than doubled the number of submissions made to the 2014 Research Excellence Framework compared with the 2008 assessments. Some research in all but one of 15 subject areas was judged to be world-leading or internationally excellent.

Chester's parent institution, the UK's first purpose-built teacher training college, was

---

Parkgate Road
Chester CH1 4BJ
01244 511 000
enquiries@chester.ac.uk
www.chester.ac.uk
www.chestersu.com
Open days 2019:
March 16

The Times and The Sunday Times Rankings
Overall Ranking: 73 (last year: =61)

Teaching quality	83.2%	21
Student experience	79.9%	=42
Research quality	4.1%	=102
Entry standards	115	=111
Graduate prospects	70.1%	102
Good honours	65.8%	=116
Expected completion rate	82.6%	=90
Student/staff ratio	15.3	=53
Services and facilities	£2,838	18

established in 1839 by leading figures in the Church of England including William Gladstone, who later became prime minister. The church connection remains with two chapels and other faith spaces for students, and Ofsted has rated its teacher training "outstanding".

By the time the college gained university status in 2005 it was offering a broad range of courses and had also expanded geographically. It began at Parkgate Road, a 32-acre site where three new biology laboratories have iPad Minis set in their workbenches to allow students to collect and record data, as well as to have access to lecturers' screencasts.

Parkgate Road, in manicured gardens, is only a short walk from the centre of Chester and boasts an upgraded library and new sports facilities including a sprint track, floodlit sports pitch and tennis courts as well as fitness suites and a dance studio. It is one of five campuses in Chester, including Queen's Park, once the headquarters of the army's wartime Western Command and now the Faculty of Business and Management.

The Riverside campus, set in the former County Hall, hosts an Innovation Centre for student and graduate entrepreneurs. Kingsway is home to the creative arts faculty with rehearsal studios for the performing arts and contemporary facilities for art and photography, a metal casting foundry and sound and video editing suites.

Just outside Chester – and accessible by a shuttle bus – is the Thornton Science Park, in the former Shell research facility, where academia and industry collaborate on new intelligent energy technologies.

The Warrington Campus, which has nine halls of residence, focuses on the public services and creative industries. It has high-quality production facilities and the university cultivates links with the BBC in Salford to inspire students looking ahead to media careers. The library has tripled in size and there is a business centre for students and local firms to share. The site also has an arts venue that regularly attracts up-and-coming acts.

The picturesque walled city of Chester has much to offer outside the student union social scene.

Tuition fees

» Fees for UK/EU students 2019–20		£9,250
Foundation courses		£7,850
» Fees for International students 2018–19		£11,950
» For scholarship and bursary information see		
http://www1.chester.ac.uk/study/undergraduate/finance		
» Graduate salary		£20,000

Student numbers

Undergraduates	9,539 (1,620)
Postgraduates	1,171 (2,995)
Applications/places	20,075/3,225
Applications per place	6.2
Overall offer rate	83.8%
International students	5.7%

Accommodation

University provided places: 1,905 (catered 30%)
Catered costs: £117–£164 per week
Self-catered: £83–£149 per week
www.chester.ac.uk/accommodation

Where do the students come from?

State schools (non-grammar)	93.8%	Working-class homes	33.9%	Black ethnic minority	3.1%
Grammar schools	3.6%	Deprived areas	20.7%	Disabled	7.4%
Independent schools	2.7%	All ethnic minorities	9.8%	Mature (over 21)	23.5%

University of Chichester

Chichester's new Engineering and Digital Technology Park, which opened last year, represents a radical departure for the university, which up until now has been associated mainly with the arts, social sciences, education and sport.

Costing £35m, it is designed to attract an additional 500 students a year and boost the local economy. The park, which has the support of 40 companies and received funding from the Local Enterprise Partnership, is the mainstay of the university's plan for gradual growth from the current 5,500 students.

The new engineering degrees, which are among 18 to have welcomed their first students in the current academic year, have an industry-led curriculum on the CDIO (Conceiving, Designing, Implementing, Operating) model that is being adopted by a growing number of universities. Students will have access to a welding floor, fabricating laboratory, 3D printers and an engineering centre. The park will also house the Department of Creative and Digital Technologies, with a sound stage big enough to hold an orchestra, television production studio, special effects room and media operation centre.

Among the new programmes are nationally-funded bridging courses for health and social care, and maths for engineering. Other new degrees include sport tourism, product design and data science. Chichester is also planning to expand its range of degree apprenticeships, which it has been offering since 2016. There will be up to 200 places in 2019, with new programmes planned for social workers, academics and engineers, subject to approval.

The university dates back to 1839 with the founding of a college named after William Otter, the Bishop of Chichester. This became a teacher training college for women and later merged with the Bognor Regis College of Education. The Bishop Otter campus in Chichester itself commemorates the education-minded clergyman and an ongoing link to the Church of England. Women still take up two thirds of the available places.

Chichester was placed in the silver category in the government's Teaching Excellence Framework, with the panel regarding student satisfaction levels as outstanding. It found that the student experience was "tailored to the individual, maximising rates of retention, attainment and progression, with particularly outstanding support for students from disadvantaged groups."

The university is a former double winner of our University of the Year for Student Retention and continues to have a dropout rate considerably lower than the level expected for a university with Chichester's courses and student profile. A dropout rate

Bishop Otter Campus
College Lane
Chichester PO19 6PE
01243 816 002
admissions@chi.ac.uk
www.chi.ac.uk
www.ucsu.org
Open days 2019:
see website

Edinburgh
Belfast
Cardiff   London
CHICHESTER

The Times and The Sunday Times Rankings
Overall Ranking: =94 (last year: 72)

Teaching quality	80.2%	63
Student experience	79.1%	=54
Research quality	6.4%	82
Entry standards	125	84
Graduate prospects	64.6%	121
Good honours	69.4%	91
Expected completion rate	88.2%	=47
Student/staff ratio	15.1	=47
Services and facilities	£1,531	124

below 7% is almost half the national average for its courses and entry qualifications.

The TEF panel also commented favourably on the embedding of employment skills in the curriculum, although Chichester was not in the top 100 on this measure in our table.

Stellar performances in the National Student Survey have been a feature of the university's annual showing in our guide, although there has been a recent decline in this area. There was also a 12% fall in applications in 2017, although only a marginal decline in the numbers taking up places.

Chichester achieved university status as one of a new band of institutions that were expected to focus on teaching rather than research. But it was given the power to award research degrees in 2014 and entered a quarter of its eligible staff for the Research Excellence Framework. There were good results in music, drama and performing arts, English and sport. The Mathematics Centre has an international reputation and has become a focal point for curriculum development in Britain and elsewhere. The PE teacher training course is one of the largest in the country and is highly rated by Ofsted.

Residential places are roughly equally divided between the two campuses, enabling Chichester to guarantee accommodation to anyone applying before the January UCAS deadline and making the university their first choice. There is a university bus service

linking the two and there are students' union bars at each.

Sports facilities are excellent and were recently further improved with a £2m investment. A running track was added on the Chichester campus and a multi-use sports dome houses netball or tennis and provides an all-weather facility to support teaching on sports courses. The Tudor Hale Centre for Sport includes well-equipped laboratories, fitness suite, sport injury clinic and teaching clinic. The university runs a gifted athlete programme.

The small cathedral city of Chichester is known for its theatre and as a yachting venue, while Bognor is popular for sailing and windsurfing. Both offer a good supply of private housing and some student-oriented bars. Much of the surrounding countryside has been designated an area of outstanding natural beauty.

Tuition fees

»	Fees for UK/EU students 2019–20	£9,250
»	Fees for International students 2019–20	£13,000
»	For scholarship and bursary information see www.chi.ac.uk/study-us/fees-finance	
»	Graduate salary	£19,200

Student numbers

Undergraduates	4,247	(404)
Postgraduates	380	(510)
Applications/places	6,410/1,280	
Applications per place	5.0	
Overall offer rate	75.7%	
International students	3.0%	

Accommodation

University provided places: 1,174 (catered 36%)
Catered costs: £131–£169 per week
Self-catered: £101–£142 per week
First years guaranteed accommodation
www.chi.ac.uk/accommodation

Where do the students come from?

State schools (non-grammar)	95.4%	Working-class homes	31.9%	Black ethnic minority	2.2%
Grammar schools	1.7%	Deprived areas	18.4%	Disabled	9.0%
Independent schools	2.9%	All ethnic minorities	6.9%	Mature (over 21)	16.5%

City, University of London

City has regained some of the ground it lost in 2017 in an unexpected plunge of 25 places down our league table. But the university is still not in the top 80 for graduate prospects, one of its traditional strengths, when it was in the top 20 three years ago. Applications seem not to have been affected, however: City was one of the few universities to see an increase in the demand for places last year, with additional pathways for business studies proving popular and new degrees in English and history recruiting well.

More facilities have been added at the highly-regarded Cass Business School, where an extra floor has been given over to open plan space and meeting rooms. This year a seven-storey building for the City Law School is due to open on the Northampton Square campus in Islington. More than £140m has been invested in new developments since 2012.

City has a silver rating in the Teaching Excellence Framework, with the panel commenting approvingly on the strong engagement with students and the students' union, as well as the university's focus on excellent assessment and feedback. There are ambitious targets for further improvements in the quality of work over the next ten years, while also increasing in size.

The university hopes that its London location and international approach will help position City "well within" the top 300 universities in the world and the top 30 in the country. Both are achievable but will require a change of gear.

Joining the University of London in 2016 has helped City to underline both its location and its quality. Applications were already rising significantly when City joined and enrolments have been healthy. Over the next four years, growth will be focused on subjects that have momentum, particularly through new and joint degrees and shared pathways.

A main entrance complex has been opened, with social spaces, a coffee shop, seating areas and exhibition space. The complex includes a 240-seat lecture theatre, along with a students' union space, informal learning and quiet study areas, cafeteria, internal courtyard and multifaith area.

An older building on campus has recently been renovated to provide PC labs, social and breakout spaces, a mezzanine balcony, improved access and external landscaping. The changes are being made with sustainability in mind: City has been in the top ten of the People & Planet University League of environmental performance for the past three years.

Once a college of advanced technology, the university now has more than a quarter of its students taking business courses, and nearly

Northampton Square
London EC1V 0HB
020 7040 8716
ugadmissions@city.ac.uk
www.city.ac.uk
www.citystudents.co.uk
Open days 2019:
see website

The Times and The Sunday Times Rankings
Overall Ranking: 68 (last year: =75)

Teaching quality	77.8%	=97
Student experience	78.8%	=61
Research quality	21.4%	52
Entry standards	142	=49
Graduate prospects	73.4%	=83
Good honours	71.8%	=77
Expected completion rate	87.2%	=52
Student/staff ratio	17.9	=102
Services and facilities	£2,352	47

as many taking health and community subjects, with the remainder studying law, computing, mathematics, engineering, journalism and the arts. There are strong links with business and the professions. Courses have a practical edge, and many of the staff hold professional, as well as academic, qualifications. About 400 professionals — most of them City graduates — take part in the prize-winning mentoring scheme each year.

The university attracts international students from more than 150 countries and many of them spend a year of their course abroad. At the same time, City has a better record than most of its peer group for widening participation in higher education, with approaching half of its undergraduates coming from low-income groups.

The Cass Business School is one of City's great strengths, ranking among the top 50 such institutions in the world. The school, which is based in the heart of the financial district and offers an MBA that is ranked fifth globally for entrepreneurship by the *Financial Times*, has built up an impressive cadre of visiting lecturers.

The university's law school was the first in the capital to offer a "one-stop shop" for legal training, from undergraduate to professional courses, and the journalism department, housed within the arts and social sciences school, is also highly regarded.

City entered little more than half of its eligible academics in the 2014 Research Excellence Framework, but three quarters of its submission was rated as world-leading or internationally excellent, with the best results produced by music and business.

The redeveloped sports centre, situated between the campus and the business school, is the largest university sports facility in central London. The 3,000 square metres of floor space at CitySport is available to students, staff and the local community. At its heart is the Saddlers sports hall, which meets Sport England standards and has seating for up to 400 spectators, and the centre also has a separate fitness area.

City has only 741 privately operated residential places, but guarantees accommodation for new entrants who accept an offer by the end of June.

Tuition fees

- » Fees for UK/EU students 2019–20   £9,250
- » Fees for International students 2019–20   £14,570–£18,000
- » For scholarship and bursary information see www.city.ac.uk/study/fees-and-funding
- » Graduate salary   £25,000

Student numbers

Undergraduates	9,243	(829)
Postgraduates	6,677	(2,654)
Applications/places		23,895/2,585
Applications per place		9.2
Overall offer rate		68.2%
International students		39%

Accommodation

University provided places: 741 (catered 5%)
Catered costs: £268–£277 per week
Self-catered: £156–£223 per week
First years guaranteed accommodation
www.city.ac.uk/accommodation/undergraduate

Where do the students come from?

State schools (non-grammar)	86.4%	Working-class homes	46%	Black ethnic minority	15.0%
Grammar schools	5.8%	Deprived areas	4.5%	Disabled	3.8%
Independent schools	7.8%	All ethnic minorities	71.6%	Mature (over 21)	16.8%

Coventry University

Undergraduate applications for courses starting last year were up by 8% against a downward national trend, making Coventry a deserving winner of our award as University of the Year for Student Experience. The university is also a three-time winner of our Modern University of the Year title.

The opening of a new "no-frills" campus in east London was one explanation, but there were gains across the university's four constituent parts. The original university in the centre of Coventry hosts most of the students, and the institution has opened university colleges on the main campus, in Scarborough, the City of London (mainly for international students), and now in Barking and Dagenham.

Fees at the university colleges, where students sacrifice some of the facilities normally associated with full-time higher education for a lower-cost degree, stand at £7,329 for science and engineering courses and £6,200 a year for classroom-based subjects. The model is proving popular and may be tried in other locations.

Coventry has been perhaps the most enterprising university in the UK since higher fees were introduced in 2012. As well as opening in new locations, it is spending £500m on its main campus and has transformed its portfolio of courses and tightened operations, introducing a popular ten-day guarantee for marking students' work.

The changes have brought spectacular increases in student satisfaction and a charge up the league tables. Coventry became, for a time, the most successful post-1992 university in our table and remains in the top 50 overall. It ranks just outside the top 30 for social inclusion in our new table.

The university was rated gold in the government's Teaching Excellence Framework. The panel found "consistently outstanding" student support services, especially for those from disadvantaged backgrounds, aiding retention and progression. There was also an exemplary approach to exposing students to the forefront of scholarship, research and professional practice, the panel said.

Coventry's £500m capital programme is by far the largest in its history. A new science and health building opened last year, with healthcare simulation facilities, an indoor running track and a biomedical sciences "superlab". A £73m residential development welcomed students, adding 1,500 places minutes from the campus. The university is also redeveloping a large city centre site that will be vacated by the council when it moves to new offices this year.

Undergraduates value the opportunity to make their own assessments of academics, who receive awards for excellent

---

Priory Street
Coventry CV1 5FB
024 7765 7688
studentenquiries@coventry.ac.uk
www.coventry.ac.uk
www.coventry.ac.uk/cuc
for University Colleges
www.cusu.org
Open days 2019:
see website

Edinburgh
Belfast
COVENTRY
Cardiff
London

The Times and The Sunday Times Rankings
Overall Ranking: =46 (last year: 44)

Teaching quality	83.4%	=17
Student experience	83.6%	5
Research quality	3.8%	=109
Entry standards	127	=80
Graduate prospects	80.9%	=39
Good honours	73.5%	=65
Expected completion rate	86.0%	60
Student/staff ratio	14.6	=33
Services and facilities	£2,305	53

teaching. The Centre for Academic Writing offers advice on essays and theses, while the Sigma "maths and stats" support centre offers a seven-day drop-in service, with specialist help available for dyslexics.

The Add+vantage scheme covers a wide range of skills to improve employability and the International Centre for Transformational Entrepreneurship helps students to start up and grow a business, aiming to "forge the next generation of great business thinkers".

New honours degree subjects include games art, food safety and applied global marketing. The university is also planning a big expansion of degree apprenticeships, increasing the number of places from 171 to 750 by September. New roles will include financial advisers, paralegals, HR consultants and nursing associates.

The university's concentration on teaching and learning may help to explain its failure to reach the top 100 for research. Only 13% of eligible staff were entered for assessment in the Research Excellence Framework, and 60% of their work was considered world-leading or internationally excellent overall. In health subjects, 94% of work submitted was judged in the top two categories.

Coventry is now investing £100m to increase its research capacity and performance, with new centres focusing on areas of strength. The Institute for Advanced Manufacturing and

Engineering, for example, is a "faculty on the factory floor" where university researchers and Unipart engineers work together on product development.

A new National Transport Design Centre, at the university's technology park, has research and teaching facilities aimed at bridging a projected shortfall in design skills across the UK. The university has long been a leading centre for automotive design, building on the city's car-building history, which continues today with Jaguar Land Rover.

The university traces its origins back to 1843 at its 33-acre campus near Coventry Cathedral. As well as its £20m turreted library, the institution's showcase features include a £55m engineering and computing building with an ethical hacking lab, Harrier Jump Jet and wind tunnel used for undergraduate study.

Students enjoy a relatively low cost of living with plenty of student-oriented nightlife. The buzz around Coventry will only grow as it prepares to hold the UK City of Culture title in 2021.

Tuition fees

» Fees for UK/EU students 2019–20 (£6,200–£7,329 at University Colleges)	£9,250
» Fees for International students 2018–19 (£9,000–£10,700 at University Colleges)	£12,600–£14,850
» For scholarship and bursary information see www.coventry.ac.uk/study-at-coventry/finance	
» Graduate salary	£22,000

Student numbers

Undergraduates	23,310 (2,395)
Postgraduates	3,848 (2,139)
Applications/places	34,190/5,855
Applications per place	5.8
Overall offer rate	83.8%
International students	33.7%

Accommodation

University provided places: 5,365 (catered 8%)
Catered costs: £143–£150 per week
Self-catered: £116–£190 per week
First years are given priority
www.coventry.ac.uk/accommodation

Where do the students come from?

State schools (non-grammar)	92.3%	Working-class homes	41.7%	Black ethnic minority	20.6%
Grammar schools	4.4%	Deprived areas	11.7%	Disabled	4.0%
Independent schools	3.3%	All ethnic minorities	52.9%	Mature (over 21)	18.3%

University for the Creative Arts

Students at our Modern University of the Year have the advantage of being able to develop their employability prospects at its Business School for the Creative Industries. The school is marketed as the first of its kind in the UK. It complements the portfolio of degrees in subjects students might expect to find at a specialist arts institution, with its remit of fostering the "innovative, high-level business and practical understanding" needed to embrace the challenges and opportunities of the creative industries.

Based in Epsom, the school offers a range of courses combining creative development with business approaches, capitalising on the university's links with a diverse range of companies and cultural institutions. Business management and marketing are among the degrees added for the current academic year, although the University of the Creative Arts (UCA) is not neglecting the arts, with plans to add acting and make-up and hair design.

UCA's 25-place rise in our table this year is the biggest of any institution and a ranking of 33= matches the highest ever for a modern university. Gains have been made in most indicators, notably a UK top-ten ranking for teaching quality.

The university recorded the biggest rise at any UK institution in the proportion of students awarded first or upper second-class degrees in 2017 — more than nine percentage points. Applications went up slightly last year, against the national trend, but they remain well short of the totals in the years before £9,000 fees were introduced.

The four campuses in Canterbury, Epsom, Farnham and Rochester have seen extensive developments, the latest of which is a £4m Film and Media Centre at Farnham. The new facility offers high-quality performance and music technology, including a black box film studio, dubbing theatre, recording studio, rehearsal space and a 250-seat lecture theatre. UCA has built a strong reputation in the film world, producing more than 20 Oscar and Bafta winners.

Farnham is the largest campus, with more than 2,000 students taking subjects ranging from advertising, animation and computer games technology to film production, journalism, music composition and technology. An acting and performance course is based at Farnham Maltings, where students can learn from a network of theatre professionals, as well as performance and rehearsal spaces. It is also the campus that can accommodate the lowest proportion of first-years, however – 55%, compared with 75% at Epsom and 100% at Rochester.

UCA Farnham
Falkner Road
Farnham GU9 7DS
01252 892 883
enquiries@uca.ac.uk
www.uca.ac.uk
http://ucasu.com
Open days 2019:
February 20; June 15

The Times and The Sunday Times Rankings
Overall Ranking: =33 (last year: 58)

Teaching quality	84.4%	10
Student experience	80.7%	=31
Research quality	3.4%	113
Entry standards	142	=49
Graduate prospects	72.7%	89
Good honours	74.1%	=62
Expected completion rate	83.6%	=79
Student/staff ratio	13.2	=17
Services and facilities	£2,657	25

The Epsom campus specialises in fashion, graphics and music courses, as well as housing the business school, and offers further education courses in general art, design and media. At Rochester, a purpose-built campus overlooking the River Medway, there is a full range of art and design courses, covering fashion, photography, computer animation and jewellery making. Students taking UCA's popular television production course are based at Maidstone Studios, the largest independent studio complex in the UK.

The modern Canterbury site close to the city centre focuses on architecture, but there are also degrees in fine art, interior design, graphic design, and illustration and animation and it houses a 3D fabrication lab and games design suites. The Canterbury School of Architecture is the only such school to remain within a specialist art and design institution.

Architecture aside, the university offers four-year degrees, incorporating a foundation year, as well as the three-year format. Students can also take a two-year extended diploma that can be topped up to produce an honours degree. All students are encouraged to develop an international perspective and to collaborate with those from parallel disciplines.

UCA was awarded silver in the government's Teaching Excellence Framework. The panel praised the high levels of personalised learning, which help to develop independence. It added that course design

and assessment, with good use of student feedback, allows students to be stretched. It added that this was reinforced by a successful partnership with the students' union.

A creative enterprise and development team aims to ensure that students are highly employable, entrepreneurial in their outlook and equipped to become freelancers or to start a business within their chosen sector. Many staff are practitioners as well as academics, and the founding colleges, which date back to Victorian times, have produced famous graduates such as the artist Tracey Emin and the fashion designers Karen Millen and Dame Zandra Rhodes, who is also the university's chancellor.

The most recent Research Excellence Framework rated almost two thirds of the small submission of work by UCA world-leading or internationally excellent. Ninety per cent of this reached the top two categories for its impact.

Tuition fees

» Fees for UK/EU students 2019–20	£9,250
» Fees for International students 2019–20	£14,800
»For scholarship and bursary information see www.uca.ac.uk/life-at-uca/fees	
» Graduate salary	£18,000

Student numbers

Undergraduates	4,592	(1,248)
Postgraduates	180	(160)
Applications/places		6,535/1,145
Applications per place		5.7
Overall offer rate		71.7%
International students		12.6%

Accommodation

University provided places: 982 (catered 0%)
Self-catered: £78–£161 per week
www.uca.ac.uk/accommodation

Where do the students come from?

State schools (non-grammar)	92.3%	Working-class homes	39%	Black ethnic minority	8.3%
Grammar schools	4.0%	Deprived areas	11.7%	Disabled	13.4%
Independent schools	3.7%	All ethnic minorities	24.6%	Mature (over 21)	15.7%

University of Cumbria

One of Cumbria's seven campuses is Britain's only one located in a national park – at Ambleside in the Lake District. Here the university runs the country's biggest programme of outdoor education courses and provides a base for conservation and forestry degrees.

The largest campus, at Lancaster, has been redeveloped and Cumbria is now focusing on improving its two sites in Carlisle, extending the library at its Institute of Arts and expanding IT capacity. New laboratories for Stem subjects (science, technology, engineering and maths) have already opened.

A growing university is a key component of the county's economic strategy, to attract skilled young people to the region and to revitalise the city of Carlisle at the same time. The university's applications and enrolments have fallen for the past three years, however.

Cumbria is only just outside the bottom five in our league table, despite improvements in staffing levels and student satisfaction with the quality of teaching. Having dropped six places previously, it has failed to make up lost ground.

Cumbria is also one of 14 universities in the bronze category of the government's Teaching Excellence Framework. The university suffered for a low graduate employment rate in highly-skilled jobs, although it pointed out that these are in short supply regionally, compared with the national average. It also noted that 76% of its academics hold teaching qualifications, compared with 44% nationwide, reflecting the university's commitment to excellence in teaching and learning.

The university promises students a high degree of personal support, and has stepped up its efforts. Having offered training on suicide prevention and awareness for all staff working with students, it has now recruited mental health case workers for its campuses in Ambleside, Carlisle and Lancaster. Student ambassadors, who are studying mental health nursing or have a particular interest in the issue, also work to increase awareness.

Established in 2007, Cumbria now has campuses in London, Workington and Barrow-in-Furness as well as Lancaster, Ambleside and its two bases in Carlisle. There are still only 8,600 students, however, fewer than 3,000 of them male.

Almost all the undergraduates are state-educated and the proportion from areas where few people have gone on to higher education in the past is one of the highest in England. More than a third of the undergraduates are 21 or more on entry, although only a quarter come from Cumbria itself. This commitment to widening participation results in a ranking just outside the top 40 for our new table measuring social inclusion in Britain's universities.

Head Office
Fusehill Street
Carlisle CA1 2HH
01228 616 234
enquirycentre@cumbria.ac.uk
www.cumbria.ac.uk
www.ucsu.me
Open days 2019:
see website

The Times and The Sunday Times Rankings
Overall Ranking: 125 (last year: 125)

Teaching quality	77.2%	=103
Student experience	71.5%	124
Research quality	1.2%	125
Entry standards	120	=94
Graduate prospects	73.6%	=77
Good honours	61.1%	128
Expected completion rate	83.5%	82
Student/staff ratio	16.7	=85
Services and facilities	£1,550	123

Significant investment in a ten-year plan for the university has brought improvements including a 220-seat lecture theatre at the Lancaster campus in a new teaching building. The campus has a gymnastics centre and fitness suite and has built a student centre and well-equipped library as well as extensive accommodation.

New residential blocks opened in 2017 in Ambleside, where the Institute for Leadership and Sustainability, part of the business school, is developing a portfolio of short courses and specialisms to make the best use of its unique setting.

The Workington campus has dedicated facilities for the nuclear graduate programme while the centre in Barrow is at Furness College, and specialises in nursing and health practitioner courses. The London campus, in the East End, provides an urban setting for training teachers, police officers and health professionals.

Cumbria's headquarters are in Carlisle, where the larger of the two sites, Brampton Road, is in parkland close to the River Eden. The second campus, Fusehill Street, is closer to the city centre and boasts an innovative multimedia learning resource centre and a sports centre with a four-court sports hall and well-equipped fitness room. The new laboratories on campus here are enabling Cumbria to expand its science portfolio into chemistry and biomedical science.

The creative arts produced by far the best results in the 2014 Research Excellence Framework, with 90% of the submission judged to have world-leading or internationally excellent impact. But, overall, Cumbria is just two places off the bottom of our research ranking, having entered only 27 academics (8% of those eligible) for assessment. Almost 30% of the work of this small group was placed in the top two categories, however.

The university is a partner in both the National College for Nuclear and the Project Academy for Sellafield, helping to provide specialist education and training in delivering decommissioning, reprocessing and nuclear waste management. Cumbria was shortlisted for a Green Gown award for reducing water use.

Tuition fees

» Fees for UK/EU students 2019–20	£9,250
Foundation courses	£6,000
» Fees for International students 2019–20	£10,500–£15,500
» For scholarship and bursary information see	
www.cumbria.ac.uk/study/student-finance/undergraduate	
» Graduate salary	£22,000

Student numbers

Undergraduates	4,666	(2,228)
Postgraduates	784	(957)
Applications/places	6,435/1,185	
Applications per place	5.4	
Overall offer rate	82.9%	
International students	3.3%	

Accommodation

University provided places: 1,153 (catered 0%)
Self-catered: £67–£120 per week
First years guaranteed accommodation
www.cumbria.ac.uk/student-life/accommodation/

Where do the students come from?

State schools (non-grammar)	95.5%	Working-class homes	41.9%	Black ethnic minority	2.1%
Grammar schools	1.5%	Deprived areas	22.9%	Disabled	7.2%
Independent schools	3.0%	All ethnic minorities	8.9%	Mature (over 21)	35.8%

De Montfort University

 De Montfort University (DMU) is our first University of the Year for Social Inclusion, combining a top-20 ranking in our new table with a strong record in the graduate jobs market and high levels of student satisfaction.

The university has moved into our top 20 for graduate opportunities, and its employment record was a significant factor behind a gold rating in the government's Teaching Excellence Framework. The panel said: "De Montfort delivers consistently outstanding teaching, learning and outcomes for its students."

DMU has put its considerable emphasis on employability behind its #DMUworks scheme to help students "think, feel and get work-ready while they're still at university". The programme connects the university's work placements, internships and volunteering with training and business-insider visits — and promises lifelong support for graduates in the workplace.

Student satisfaction has also been rising sharply, taking DMU into the top 20 for the broad student experience last year and into the top 40 for undergraduates' perceptions of teaching quality. Applications are running at near-record levels and enrolments are up by more than a quarter since higher fees were introduced.

Opened in 1870 as the Leicester School of Art, later Leicester Polytechnic, DMU has large-scale improvements in prospect under its £136m campus development plan. The latest phase has seen an award-winning transformation of a busy road into a public space with gardens and seating, connecting the centre of Leicester with the River Soar. The Vijay Patel Building, which brought all art and design courses together for the first time, was named as the region's best new educational building. As well as the Leicester School of Art, it features design, architecture and photographic facilities and the city's largest display space, The Gallery.

DMU has also opened a new business school in the Great Hall of Leicester Castle and the university has spent £3m on redeveloping the campus centre, where the students' union is based.

New degrees planned for this year include cyber-security, paramedicine and energy engineering. At the same time, DMU is increasing its portfolio of degree apprenticeships, adding programmes for four technology subjects, architecture and policing, which will take the number of apprentices to 200.

DMU's Leicester Media School has teamed up with Channel 4 to offer an MA in investigative journalism, aiming to equip graduates for the world of hard-hitting current affairs.

The DMUglobal programme aims to provide the most comprehensive programme of overseas study at any UK university to open

The Gateway
Leicester LE1 9BH
0116 250 6070
enquiry@dmu.ac.uk
www.dmu.ac.uk
www.demontfortsu.com
Open days 2019:
January 12

The Times and The Sunday Times **Rankings**
Overall Ranking: 65 (last year: =67)

Teaching quality	82.1%	=34
Student experience	81.7%	17
Research quality	8.9%	=68
Entry standards	113	=116
Graduate prospects	83.8%	=20
Good honours	71.3%	=80
Expected completion rate	83.6%	=79
Student/staff ratio	19.4	=119
Services and facilities	£2,181	69

students' minds to other cultures and make them employable across the world. Every undergraduate course includes at least one module offering international experience through a network of overseas universities and businesses. More than 1,000 students from many different courses went to New York in 2016 to take part in DMU's biggest study trip.

The university has also forged an innovative partnership with the United Nations, launching a campaign to do more for the worldwide refugee crisis last year. DMU is committed to sticking to the UN's 17 Sustainable Goals in its teaching, research and student activities.

Closer to home, students can participate in the award-winning Square Mile programme which taps into DMU's academic expertise and student volunteer network to aid community projects locally, across the UK and abroad. Under the hashtag #DMUlocal, about 2,500 students and staff provide aid through work placements or volunteering.

DMU has a proud record for widening access to higher education, with more than 40% of undergraduates coming from working-class homes, and a strong reputation for supporting disabled students. It is also one of seven institutions chosen for a new project to boost the results of black and ethnic minority students. The dropout rate for all undergraduates is below 12%, marginally less than the national average for the university's courses and entry qualifications.

Almost 60% of the university's research was judged to be world-leading or internationally excellent in the 2014 Research Excellence Framework. Longstanding partnerships with Hewlett-Packard and Deloitte are examples of strong links with business and industry, which feed into innovative training and research collaborations.

Students have access to extensive sports facilities including a 25-metre swimming pool and an £8m leisure centre. Almost £1m has been spent on coaching and support for teams and there are partnerships with Leicester City football club, Leicester Tigers rugby club, Leicestershire cricket and Leicester Ladies hockey club.

Leicester is one of the UK's most diverse cities, where students can thrive in a vibrant atmosphere. The city has had £3bn poured into regeneration projects since 2008. Rents in the private sector are low and there are almost 3,800 residential places within walking distance of the city centre.

Tuition fees

» Fees for UK/EU students 2019–20	£9,250
Foundation courses	£6,000
» Fees for International students 2019–20	£12,750–£15,500
» For scholarship and bursary information see www.dmu.ac.uk/study/undergraduate-study/ fees-and-funding-2018/fees-and-funding-2018.aspx	
» Graduate salary	£20,000

Student numbers

Undergraduates	17,694 (1,431)
Postgraduates	2,034 (2,044)
Applications/places	26,505/5,160
Applications per place	5.1
Overall offer rate	84.9%
International students	15.8%

Accommodation

University provided places: 3,779 (catered 0%)
Self-catered: £97–£178 per week
First years get priority for accommodation
www.dmu.ac.uk/study/undergraduate-study/
accommodation/accommodation.aspx

Where do the students come from?

State schools (non-grammar)	94.9%	Working-class homes	43.1%	Black ethnic minority	21.8%
Grammar schools	2.3%	Deprived areas	14.9%	Disabled	10.6%
Independent schools	2.8%	All ethnic minorities	52.8%	Mature (over 21)	15.4%

University of Derby

Derby has continued its steady rise up our table after taking a gold award in the Teaching Excellence Framework. The TEF panel was impressed by Derby's new teaching and learning strategy, with its emphasis on technology-enhanced learning. There was praise for the university's engagement with employers and the personalised learning offered to students, with academic support tailored to the needs of the individual.

Enrolments are running at record levels, after only a small dip in applications in 2017. In particular, Derby bucked the national trend by increasing the demand for nursing — a key area for the university. While applications dropped by 18% across the UK, Derby attracted a 25% increase in enrolments on its adult nursing degree and a 50% increase for mental health nursing. The university attributes this success to its ability to raise the number of placements it was offering.

The College of Health and Social Care has been restructured to give nursing a school of its own to reflect the growing numbers and ensure that teaching reflects changing employment demands. Training courses for teaching nursing will be open to international applications this year.

Across the university, students are attracted by the emphasis on "real-world learning", with facilities that include a simulated hospital and working radiography suite; replica crime scenes; industry-standard kitchens and a fine dining restaurant; computer games suites; a commercial spa and salon; a law court and a 58-acre Outdoor Leadership Centre. The university's Institute for Innovation in Sustainable Engineering supports advanced manufacturing with 3D printing and advanced testing with industrial partners such as Rolls-Royce.

Derby is planning a big expansion in degree apprenticeships, moving from five to 34 programmes by September 2019, with 500 apprentices. Subject areas include engineering, management, digital technologies, procurement and supply, express logistics, data science, surveying and marketing. There will also be two new traditional degrees, in geography and geology with environmental hazards.

Derby has invested £150m on its campuses in ten years. A £12.5m building for science, technology, engineering and maths (Stem subjects) opened in 2017, to follow a £10.8m sports centre and the Derby Law School building. Another £7m was spent on creating the campus in Chesterfield for nursing, engineering, IT and business innovation.

The Markeaton Street site in Derby hosts arts, design, engineering and technology courses, while those studying in health and social care are based at Britannia Mill, ten minutes' walk

---

Kedleston Road
Derby DE22 1GB
01332 591 167
askadmissions@derby.ac.uk
www.derby.ac.uk
www.derbyunion.co.uk
Open days 2019:
March 23 (Derby & Buxton);
April 17, June 8, July 13,
August 7 (Derby); June 8
(Buxton); June 15 (Chesterfield)

The Times and The Sunday Times **Rankings**

Overall Ranking: 75 (last year: 81)

Teaching quality	83.8%	=13
Student experience	80.0%	=40
Research quality	2.5%	118
Entry standards	119	=100
Graduate prospects	76.2%	65
Good honours	66.5%	108
Expected completion rate	82.2%	=93
Student/staff ratio	15.1	=47
Services and facilities	£2,015	86

away. The university's main campus is two miles from the city centre and caters for most of the other subjects including business, computing, science, humanities, education and law. The students' union, multifaith centre and main sports facilities are on this site. It also houses clinical skills facilities, including a purpose-built iDXA (a high-resolution digital scanner that provides full-body composition and bone density images) suite. The 550-seat Derby Theatre in the centre completes the university estate in the city. The three Derby bases are linked by free shuttle buses.

As well as the Chesterfield site, a further campus in Buxton is based in the former Devonshire Royal Hospital and offers courses in spa, outdoor recreation and hospitality management, as well as further education programmes. The domed building houses a training restaurant, a beauty salon and a health spa among its teaching facilities. The university also provides a foundation degree in spa management, taught at the London School of Beauty and Make-up in the capital.

All undergraduates can have access to their personal tutor whenever they need it and Derby guarantees that 85% of its classes contain fewer than 30 students. Course representatives sit on all senior management committees and the Institute for Learning Enhancement and Innovation works with academic staff to ensure that students receive the best possible learning experience.

Links with local industry help to prepare students for the workplace with placements available at Microsoft and IBM and internships at car manufacturers including Porsche, Bentley, Rolls-Royce and Toyota.

Derby entered just 19% of its eligible academics for the 2014 Research Excellence Framework, when nearly 30% of its submission reached one of the top two categories.

About half of all degree entrants qualify for a bursary of up to £1,000 a year, with more available for those from Derbyshire, and all full-time undergraduates receive a £100 ecard for books or other study resources.

The university spent £30m in five years to maintain its guarantee of accommodation for all first-years, and now has more than 2,500 places.

The sports centre has a 70-station fitness gym, squash courts, sports hall, climbing wall and adjacent outdoor pitches.

Tuition fees

- » Fees for UK/EU students 2019–20   £9,250
- » Fees for International students 2019–20   £13,250–£14,250
- » For scholarship and bursary information see www.derby.ac.uk/study/fees
- » Graduate salary   £20,800

Student numbers

Undergraduates	**11,056** (3,126)
Postgraduates	**1,137** (2,265)
Applications/places	**19,760/3,340**
Applications per place	**5.9**
Overall offer rate	**87.1%**
International students	**7.7%**

Accommodation

University provided places: 2,596 (catered 0%)
Self-catered: £105–£139 per week
First years guaranteed accommodation
www.derby.ac.uk/campus/accommodation/

Where do the students come from?

State schools (non-grammar)	95.2%	Working-class homes	38.6%	Black ethnic minority	8.7%
Grammar schools	2.3%	Deprived areas	23.3%	Disabled	7.8%
Independent schools	2.5%	All ethnic minorities	22.8%	Mature (over 21)	30.2%

University of Dundee

Dundee is well established in our top 30, with outstanding scores for student satisfaction and sustained success in the graduate jobs market. The combination also helped to secure a gold rating in the government's Teaching Excellence Framework.

Life sciences continue to be the jewel in Dundee's crown, helping to build a global reputation. Work on biological sciences topped the table in the 2014 Research Excellence Framework and the same year the university opened its £50m Discovery Centre to promote interdisciplinary collaboration.

A new joint degree programme with the National University of Singapore will allow students in biological and biomedical sciences to divide their study time between Scotland and Singapore, earning a qualification from both institutions. Dundee already has similar joint degree arrangements with Wuhan University and other institutions in China.

Two thirds of Dundee's students are from Scotland and nearly one in ten from Northern Ireland. Undergraduate applications from international students went up by almost 7% last year and a new International College on the main campus, offering preparatory courses before starting a degree, is expected to attract more.

Undergraduate applications overall have reached record levels, rising by more than 20% in three years. Consistently strong graduate employment results are one important draw. Dundee claims to send more graduates into the professions than any other institution in Scotland. Most degrees include a career planning module and an internship option.

Dundee is also stepping up its programme of graduate-level apprenticeships offered in partnership with business. The total of 90 places in six areas in the current academic year will rise to 220, with additional training in business management, IT and engineering.

Dundee last year became the first Scottish university to join the CMS collaboration at Cern, the European Organisation for Nuclear Research, building on expertise in the fields of materials, mechanical and civil engineering and computing. Civil engineering at the university was classed in the top three in the most recent Research Excellence Framework, while maths and general engineering were in the top ten.

Since 2016 Dundee has established a School of Business and introduced a liberal arts model for its School of Humanities, allowing students the option of studying several subjects throughout their degree instead of requiring them to specialise.

The leading architect Sir Terry Farrell designed the university's £200m redevelopment on its compact city campus, completed in 2005.

Nethergate
Dundee DD1 4HN
01382 383 838
contactus@dundee.ac.uk
www.dundee.ac.uk
www.dusa.co.uk
Open days 2019:
see website

The Times and The Sunday Times **Rankings**

Overall Ranking: 27 (last year: 23)

Teaching quality	83.0%	24
Student experience	82.0%	=14
Research quality	31.2%	42
Entry standards	174	16
Graduate prospects	81.7%	=30
Good honours	81.2%	28
Expected completion rate	87.1%	=54
Student/staff ratio	14.5	=30
Services and facilities	£2,203	=64

The medical school, in 20 acres of parkland, is a couple of miles offsite, and nursing and midwifery students are based 35 miles away in Kirkcaldy. The university's highly-rated design courses are taught at the Duncan of Jordanstone College of Art. The university is a key participant in the Dundee-based V&A project to improve design in Scotland.

Dundee has invested £6m in its campus network to provide advanced technology for online learning, supporting all courses, and improving connections for gaming and streaming in response to student feedback. The online portal MyDundee provides information during the application process and to prepare for the academic year.

Fees for UK students from outside Scotland are capped at a total of £27,750 for a four-year degree, while those with a household income of less than £20,000 receive bursaries of £2,000 a year. Dundee has a proud record in widening participation in higher education, boasting the largest increase of any university in the proportion of students admitted from the most deprived 40% of Scottish postcodes — accounting for more than 30% of the national figure.

At the heart of the approach is the successful Access Summer Schools — offering both physical and digital courses — which had a record 400-strong cohort in 2017 in their 25th year of operation. So far, the summer schools have helped 2,100 students to take up degree courses at Dundee University alone.

Dundee students benefit from some of the lowest costs of living of any university city in the UK. There is lively nightlife and one of Scotland's most active students' unions, plus excellent sports facilities where athletes trained for the 2014 Commonwealth Games in Glasgow. Within walking distance there are two multi-court sports halls, tennis courts and a top-of-the-range fitness and conditioning suite — so no excuse not to get in shape. A pool and outdoor facilities are only ten minutes' walk away and the university's Institute of Sport and Exercise runs a programme of 55 classes. Dundee's sports science laboratories are accredited for research and support for elite athletes.

Tuition fees

» Fees for Scottish/EU students 2019–20   £0–£1,820
  RUK fees £9,250 (capped at £27,750 except architecture, dentistry and biomedicine)
» Fees for International students 2019–20   £16,450–£19,950
  Medicine £43,000; Dentistry £44,650 (clinical years)
» For scholarship and bursary information see
  www.dundee.ac.uk/study/tuition-fees
» Graduate salary   £22,200

Student numbers

Undergraduates	9,206	(1,382)
Postgraduates	1,841	(2,959)
Applications/places		22,560/2,720
Applications per place		8.3
Overall offer rate		60.4%
International students		14.5%

Accommodation

University provided places: 1,587 (catered 0%)
Self-catered: £126–£150 per week
First years guaranteed accommodation
www.dundee.ac.uk/accommodation

Where do the students come from?

State schools (non-grammar)	86.1%	Working-class homes	29.1%	Black ethnic minority	1.7%
Grammar schools	6.9%	Deprived areas	6.9%	Disabled	5.0%
Independent schools	7.1%	All ethnic minorities	9.1%	Mature (over 21)	22.2%

Durham University

Durham was the highest-ranked of six universities upgraded to a gold award in the Teaching Excellence Framework this year. The TEF panel noted that rates of continuation and progression to highly-skilled employment or further study were exceptionally high – the university is in our top 20 for both. Durham also won praise for "rigorous monitoring procedures, which are part of an institutional culture that facilitates, recognises and rewards excellent teaching".

The university is investing £1bn over ten years in digital and physical resources, as well as enough high-quality appointments to improve staffing levels, as it seeks to grow from the current 15,000 students to 21,500 by 2027. All the growth will come in the small cathedral city of Durham, following the transfer of medical and other health students from the Stockton campus to Newcastle University. Stockton now houses a foundation college for international students.

The speed and scale of expansion led to proposals that some business and law students in the coming academic year would face lectures at 8am until new — and larger — facilities are completed that will allow students to be taught in greater numbers at one time. However, after an outcry from students and staff the proposed early starts for around 1,000 students were scrapped.

A new Centre for Teaching and Learning is due to open this September, containing a wide range of learning environments and technologies, including classrooms that will allow students to share courses in real time with others from peer institutions around the world. From the same month, a new education laboratory will be available to encourage innovation in teaching and assessment.

The Ogden Centre for Fundamental Physics, designed by Studio Daniel Libeskind, opened in 2017, and £25m is being spent to upgrade the university's IT programmes. By next year, there will also be new buildings for mathematical sciences and computer science. Further ahead, there will be a new waterside building for the business school and remodelled and repurposed accommodation for the arts and humanities.

The third-oldest university in England, Durham is determined to maintain its character, as one of the few collegiate universities in the UK. Undergraduates currently apply to one of 13 colleges, all of which are mixed, and which range in size from 300 to 1,300 students. They are the focal point of social life, although all teaching is undertaken in central academic departments. There are significant differences in atmosphere and student profile, ranging from the historic University College, in Durham Castle, to Collingwood College's modern buildings on the outskirts of the city.

Part of the university's strategy is to house at least half of all students in college

---

The Palatine Centre
Stockton Road
Durham DH1 3LE
0191 334 6128
admissions@durham.ac.uk
www.dur.ac.uk
www.durhamsu.com
Open days 2019:
see website

The Times and The Sunday Times **Rankings**
Overall Ranking: 7 (last year: 5)

Teaching quality	78.8%	=82
Student experience	75.9%	97
Research quality	39.0%	16
Entry standards	198	8
Graduate prospects	84.9%	17
Good honours	90.8%	=3
Expected completion rate	96.1%	=4
Student/staff ratio	14.9	=41
Services and facilities	£2,888	16

accommodation by 2027. To meet this objective the university is planning four to six new colleges in partnership with private sector developers. The first two, accommodating 1,000 students, are scheduled to open in 2020.

Durham has slipped out of the top five in our league table this time, dropping two places, but it remains inside the top 100 in both the QS and Times Higher Education world rankings. Its planned expansion is intended to ensure that it has the critical mass to remain competitive, especially in its strongest subjects, and maximise its contribution to the region.

A member of the Russell Group since 2012, Durham had four fifths of the work it submitted to the Research Excellence Framework judged world-leading or internationally excellent. More than a quarter of the subjects were in the top five nationally. Anthropology, archaeology, chemistry, classics, education, English, law, music, physics and theology led the way.

The university's blueprint promises a more diverse student intake. Only Oxford, St Andrews and Cambridge have a less socially inclusive student population, according to our new ranking. Durham's proportion of undergraduates from independent schools was more than 37% in 2016. A planned increase in the household income for students to be eligible for bursaries from £25,000 to almost £43,000 would increase the proportion receiving some financial support by up to 40%.

Sports facilities are excellent, and Durham is among the premier universities in national competitions. Its performance programme covers 16 sports and there are national centres in cricket, fencing, lacrosse, rugby union, tennis and rowing. Three quarters of students take part in sport on a regular basis, and 550 teams compete across 18 sports.

Durham has been ranked second in the British Universities and Colleges Sport league table since 2011. The first phase of an integrated sports park, at Maiden Castle, on the banks of the River Wear, is due to open in September, with a new rubber crumb sports pitch and upgraded hockey pitches.

The university introduced new safety measures for those socialising in Durham after three students drowned in the River Wear after nights out in the city in the space of 14 months. A programme praised by the Royal Society for the Prevention of Accidents includes improvements to riverside lighting and barriers, safety information, late-night taxis and a revised alcohol policy. For those looking for nightlife, or just a change of scene, Newcastle is a short train journey away.

Tuition fees
- » Fees for UK/EU students 2019–20 £9,250
- » Fees for International students 2019–20 £19,250–£24,300
- » For scholarship and bursary information see www.dur.ac.uk/study/ug/finance
- » Graduate salary £25,000

Student numbers

Undergraduates	13,455	(218)
Postgraduates	3,539	(1,183)
Applications/places	28,895/4,460	
Applications per place	6.5	
Overall offer rate	74.2%	
International students	27.5%	

Accommodation

University provided places: 6,005 (catered 70%)
Catered costs: £189–£207 per week
Self-catered: £133–£149 per week
First years guaranteed accommodation
www.dur.ac.uk/undergraduate/live/colleges/

Where do the students come from?

State schools (non-grammar)	46.4%	Working-class homes	14.2%	Black ethnic minority	1.3%
Grammar schools	16.5%	Deprived areas	6.4%	Disabled	5.3%
Independent schools	37.1%	All ethnic minorities	12.5%	Mature (over 21)	5.7%

University of East Anglia

The University of East Anglia (UEA) has seen applications drop by more than a quarter in two years, despite significant progress in our league table. The university blames the latest decline of 12% on a combination of factors, including the removal of NHS funding for pre-registration health courses, higher entry requirements for its law courses, and more competition for applicants in medicine.

UEA is expanding the options available to applicants. No fewer than 23 new degrees launched last year, many incorporating a placement year or year abroad. The new programmes include physics with a foundation year for students lacking the necessary qualifications to take the subject at degree level, and a range of joint honours degrees with education as one of the subjects.

Among the facilities awaiting entrants this year will be a new £30m building with teaching laboratories for students in science, technology, engineering and maths (Stem) subjects. The ground floor will also include social space and generic teaching space for 500 students. The university has already spent a similar amount on student accommodation, adding 915 places to its residential stock.

UEA remains in our top ten this year for spending on student services and the proportion of good honours degrees it awards.

Although not a measure specifically in our table, the proportion of first-class degrees has risen by 172% in five years, with one student in three receiving one. The university has defended the rise by explaining that it has invested an extra £20m a year and employed 400 more staff, reducing the number of students per academic from 18 to 13, over a similar period. If a first-class degree is your target, UEA offers one of the surest routes to achieving this.

The university was initially placed in the silver category in the government's Teaching Excellence Framework — an outcome UEA successfully appealed and got upgraded to gold. The independent panel applauded the university's "strategic approach to personalised learning, which secures high levels of commitment to studies." It also found that investment in high-quality physical and digital resources has had a demonstrable impact on the learning experience.

These include a media suite in the faculty of arts and humanities with recording studios, radio drama studio, IT teaching suite, digitisation lab, break-out rooms and edit suites and a £19m medical education and research building. The Enterprise Centre helps to develop students' entrepreneurial skills.

Health studies have been among UEA's fastest-developing areas in recent years. The newly-opened £80m Quadram Institute brings together food science, gut biology,

Norwich Research Park
Norwich NR4 7TJ
01603 591 515
admissions@uea.ac.uk
www.uea.ac.uk
www.uea.su
Open days 2019:
July 6

The Times and The Sunday Times **Rankings**		
Overall Ranking: 15 (last year: 13)		
Teaching quality	79.0%	=78
Student experience	78.5%	=65
Research quality	35.8%	32
Entry standards	153	38
Graduate prospects	77.1%	60
Good honours	87.8%	9
Expected completion rate	90.6%	=34
Student/staff ratio	13.4	=19
Services and facilities	£3,005	12

human health and disease, capitalising on the world-class bioscience cluster based on the Norwich Research Park.

Environmental science is traditionally the flagship school. The Climatic Research Unit and the government-funded Tyndall Centre for Climate Change Research, which has a hub in Shanghai, are among the leaders in the investigation of climate change. But social work and pharmacy produced even better results in the 2014 Research Excellence Framework, when 82% of all the work submitted by the university was placed in one of the top two categories.

Art history has the benefit of the Sainsbury Centre for the Visual Arts, perhaps the greatest resource of its type on any British campus. The centre houses a priceless collection of modern and tribal art in a building designed by Sir Norman Foster. Many of the original 1960s buildings on campus are listed, including the iconic Denys Lasdun-designed Ziggurat accommodation blocks.

The #AskUEA online platform is one of many improvements to the university's web presence and gives prospective students the chance to pose their own questions about university life. Once at UEA, students can bring any inquiries to four learning and teaching hubs; one for postgraduates, another for nursing and two for undergraduates in the other academic schools.

Most undergraduates have the opportunity of work experience as part of their course.

The university has sharpened its focus on employability in the curriculum and introduced an internship programme for recent graduates to work for between four and 12 weeks at a business in the eastern region.

An extensive building and refurbishment programme is under way on the 320-acre campus on the outskirts of Norwich, which has been awarded a Green Flag for its high environmental standards and the quality of its facilities. These include the refurbished students' union and the gymnastics centre that forms part of excellent facilities in UEA's Sportspark. It includes an Olympic-size swimming pool and fitness centre, five sports halls, 20 badminton courts, five squash courts, martial arts and dance studio, and a climbing wall.

Norwich, with its mixture of ancient architecture and contemporary culture, has been voted one of the best small cities in the world.

Tuition fees

» Fees for UK/EU students 2019–20	£9,250
» Fees for International students 2019–20	£15,600–£19,800
Medicine	£30,600
» For scholarship and bursary information see www.uea.ac.uk/study/undergraduate/finance	
» Graduate salary	£21,909

Student numbers

Undergraduates	12.033	(226)
Postgraduates	3,150	(1,786)
Applications/places		21,475/3,365
Applications per place		6.4
Overall offer rate		80.4%
International students		22.9%

Accommodation

University provided places: 4,597 (catered 0%)
Self-catered: £73–£156 per week
First years guaranteed accommodation
www.uea.ac.uk/study/undergraduate/accommodation

Where do the students come from?

State schools (non-grammar)	78.6%	Working-class homes	25.0%	Black ethnic minority	5.4%
Grammar schools	12.1%	Deprived areas	13.0%	Disabled	8.1%
Independent schools	9.2%	All ethnic minorities	19.6%	Mature (over 21)	12.9%

University of East London

The introduction of nursing at degree level helped UEL to outperform its peer group with an 8% rise in applications last year. The university acknowledges that the government's cap on nursing places will limit the number of students it can recruit, but other new offerings are also proving popular. Subjects from business management to chemistry, marketing and general engineering have been made available with a foundation year to bring students up to speed.

Second in London for student satisfaction (behind St Mary's Twickenham), UEL was given a positive verdict on its teaching and the broader student experience by more than 80% of final-year undergraduates. Overall, UEL is still well outside the top 100 in our table, but it has made considerable progress since it finished bottom in our 2016 listing.

The university remains, however, one of only 14 in our table at bronze level in the government's Teaching Excellence Framework. While some were upgraded to silver last year, UEL did not make a new submission.

East London puts civic engagement at the heart of its strategic vision, giving students the opportunity to get involved in real-life projects that make a difference in communities at local — and global — level. There is a particular focus on helping refugees get to grips with their rights and opportunities for support and mental healthcare through an online hub.

The university is in the top ten in our new table for widening participation in higher education. More than half of the undergraduates come from working-class homes and two thirds are drawn from East London's large ethnic minority populations.

They can benefit from a boost from the Noon Centre for Equality and Diversity in Business, which assists black, Asian, and minority ethnic students to prepare for a successful career in business. Almost 1,000 businesses take part in mentoring programmes and/or offer accredited placements within a work-based learning initiative.

More than 40% of students are 21 or older on entry – many choosing to start courses in February rather than in the autumn. A guidance unit advises local people considering returning to education. New Beginnings courses of up to ten weeks show prospective mature students what degree study involves and give successful participants access to a range of courses.

Every undergraduate at UEL receives a free Samsung tablet, pre-loaded with core etextbooks, as part of the university's efforts to cater for a student population where more than half are the first in their family to experience higher education. Another £3m was invested in new helpdesks in the student support hubs at both the Docklands and Stratford campuses.

Docklands Campus
University Way
London E16 2RD
020 8223 3333
study@uel.ac.uk
www.uel.ac.uk
www.uelunion.org
Open days 2019:
see website

The Times and The Sunday Times Rankings
Overall Ranking: =115 (last year: 114)

Teaching quality	81.4%	=44
Student experience	80.1%	=38
Research quality	7.2%	77
Entry standards	114	=113
Graduate prospects	65.3%	=117
Good honours	63.9%	126
Expected completion rate	73.3%	124
Student/staff ratio	17	=92
Services and facilities	£2,449	38

The student charter urges undergraduates to adopt the "35-hour attitude", which means studying for at least 35 hours a week and handing in assignments on time. UEL has a Centre for Student Success, working closely with employers to provide up-to-date information about the skills and experience they prize the most. The new YourWay programme combines online learning with the benefits of having a coach to keep students on track, leading to qualifications designed in conjunction with employers.

World-class research doubled in the 2014 Research Excellence Framework compared with the 2008 assessments, with 62% of the work submitted reaching the top two categories. For the impact of its research in psychology, UEL was ranked first equal in England.

UEL's waterside campus, in the shadow of Canary Wharf, was the first new campus in London for 50 years. Stratford, the original headquarters, has been the focus of recent development and is now the location for a joint venture with Birkbeck, University of London, offering subjects including law, performing arts, dance, music and information technology as daytime or evening courses. The Clinical Education Building at the campus hosts London's only degree course in podiatry.

There are almost 1,200 bed spaces on the Docklands campus — enough to guarantee accommodation to all new students who live more than an hour away, although about one in five who would like university accommodation has to be refused. Social life for many students revolves around the Docklands campus, although Stratford has more to offer since its post-Olympics transformation. Catering facilities at both main bases were revamped last summer, as new high street brands were brought in to provide more variety for students.

UEL itself has built on the legacy of the 2012 Olympics, when it hosted the United States team at SportsDock, a £21m centre at the Docklands campus. The institution's high-performing sports programme offers £2m in scholarships and bursaries and has trained competitors including Rio Olympics sprinter Adam Gemili. The university has signed a partnership with the London Lions basketball club, which will manage UEL's basketball provision and offer degree opportunities to its players.

Tuition fees

» Fees for UK/EU students 2019–20	£9,250
» Fees for International students 2018–19	£11,880
» For scholarship and bursary information see www.uel.ac.uk/fees-and-funding	
» Graduate salary	£20,020

Student numbers

Undergraduates	8,778	(932)
Postgraduates	1,663	(1,844)
Applications/places		14,060/2,325
Applications per place		6.0
Overall offer rate		83.5%
International students		9.1%

Accommodation

University provided places: 1,170 (catered 0%)
Self-catered: £148–£190 per week
www.uel.ac.uk/accommodation

Where do the students come from?

State schools (non-grammar)	96.3%	Working-class homes	54.7%	Black ethnic minority	33.7%
Grammar schools	1.4%	Deprived areas	9.0%	Disabled	6.4%
Independent schools	2.3%	All ethnic minorities	67.2%	Mature (over 21)	44.5%

Edge Hill University

To those not familiar with modern universities, Edge Hill may have been the most surprising name on the list of five new medical schools announced last year. But the institution in Ormskirk, Lancashire, has been confounding sceptics since it became a university in 2005 and is among the top dozen post-1992 universities in our table.

Rated gold in the Teaching Excellence Framework – one of only three in the northwest to achieve the top award in its first year – it was commended for its academic support, assessment and feedback, the biggest bugbear for most universities. The panel noted that "students from diverse backgrounds achieve consistently outstanding outcomes". Almost all Edge Hill's students are state-educated and the projected dropout rate is much better than the university's benchmark. An award-winning student finance support package rewards achievement as well as encouraging students to complete their studies, rather than simply offering incentives for enrolling.

The medical school will open its doors this year, with an initial intake of foundation-year students. The first degree in medicine will begin in 2020, by which time the university promises "outstanding" facilities in partnership with local health care providers. The Faculty of Health and Social Care is already one of the largest in the northwest and has well-established postgraduate medical degrees. Dr John Cater, the vice-chancellor, said the new school would be "distinctive, with a strong focus on widening access, community medicine, general practice and psychiatry".

Edge Hill has a reputation for helping students from low-participation backgrounds and hopes to provide an access route for non-traditional entrants to medical school. The university also has longstanding programmes to support mature students changing direction into health or education studies.

Almost £300m has been invested in the 160-acre campus over the past ten years. The £27m Catalyst building opened last summer, bringing together library, careers and student services and providing more than 1,000 study spaces, as well as social areas. The £13m Technology Hub opened in 2017, with biotechnology laboratories, big data servers and a virtual reality suite available to students and employers alike. In the past ten years the university has added new residences to ensure that all first-years can be guaranteed accommodation and more senior students can also be housed on campus.

Edge Hill has been training teachers since the 19th century and remains the UK's largest provider of secondary teacher training and courses for classroom assistants. It offers a broad portfolio of other courses,

---

St Helens Road
Ormskirk L39 4QP
01695 650 950
admissions@edgehill.ac.uk
www.edgehill.ac.uk
www.edgehill.org.uk
Open days 2019:
see website

The Times and The Sunday Times Rankings
Overall Ranking: 59 (last year: =61)

Teaching quality	82.9%	25
Student experience	81.1%	24
Research quality	4.9%	=94
Entry standards	131	65
Graduate prospects	77.2%	59
Good honours	71.9%	=74
Expected completion rate	85.4%	66
Student/staff ratio	15.2	=50
Services and facilities	£2,191	68

expanded this year with the addition of degrees in health subjects such as paramedic practice and nutrition, and in food science, plant science and geoenvironmental hazards. New offerings are planned in global public health, sports therapy, robotics and artificial intelligence, and politics and criminology from this year.

The withdrawal of NHS bursaries for health courses contributed to falls in applications and enrolments in 2017, and applications were down again last year by more than the national average. But the university expects to fill all its available places.

All undergraduates on arts and science programmes have the option of a sandwich year in industry or a year studying abroad to boost employability. Every student has a personal tutor, as well as access to counsellors and financial advice. The Solstice elearning centre is a national centre of excellence for teaching and learning, with a particular focus on learning in the workplace. Three quarters of all graduates leave with professional accreditation.

The university's £17m flagship building, Creative Edge, houses industry-standard equipment and resources for those studying media, film, animation, advertising and computing. It hosts the Institute for Creative Enterprise, which provides an interface between academic research and the creative industries, where students can take up opportunities to work on live TV and secure work placements.

Edge Hill is only just in our top 100 for research, although results improved in all six subject areas submitted to the 2014 Research Excellence Framework, with its best performances in English, sport and media studies.

One of the largest running tracks in Europe features in the university's sports provision, which includes a £30m sports centre with eight courts, a swimming pool and an 80-station fitness suite — as well as a steam room, sauna and cafe.

The students' union is housed in the spacious Student Hub, where there are open access computers as well as social space, shopping and dining facilities. All first-years can be housed in university accommodation and new facilities will increase places available for students throughout their courses.

Tuition fees

»	Fees for UK/EU students 2019–20	£9,250
	Foundation courses	£6,165
»	Fees for International students 2019–20	£12,000
»	For scholarship and bursary information see	
	www.edgehill.ac.uk/studentservices/moneyadvice	
»	Graduate salary	£22,000

Student numbers

Undergraduates	10,341 (1,275)
Postgraduates	1,136 (2,466)
Applications/places	18,145/3,080
Applications per place	5.9
Overall offer rate	78.7%
International students	1.6%

Accommodation

University provided places: 2,486 (catered 7%)
Catered costs: £109 per week
Self-catered: £74–£124 per week
First years guaranteed accommodation
www.edgehill.ac.uk/study/accommodation

Where do the students come from?

State schools (non-grammar)	96.7%	Working-class homes	39.1%	Black ethnic minority	2.2%
Grammar schools	1.9%	Deprived areas	21.7%	Disabled	6.8%
Independent schools	1.4%	All ethnic minorities	7.2%	Mature (over 21)	26.2%

University of Edinburgh

Edinburgh continues to rank higher in world rankings than it does in our league table, where it is hampered by poor scores for student satisfaction. It is now in the top 20 in the world in the QS World University Rankings, which place a greater emphasis on research. The university has capitalised on its global reputation by developing a joint institute in China with Zhejiang University, one of Asia's leading research institutions, which offers four-year degrees in biomedical sciences taught entirely in English.

Scores for undergraduates' perception of teaching quality still leave Edinburgh close to the bottom of the table on this measure, while scores for the student experience are not a lot better. However, applications are the second highest at any UK university, with the volume growing by more than than 50% after six successive increases. The university has responded by increasing the intake by nearly 2,000 places over the same period, but it is still only able to make offers to fewer than 40% of applicants.

Edinburgh plans to invest £1.5bn over the next decade on new buildings and other improvements, partly in order to produce a "highly satisfied student body with a strong sense of community".

The 125-year-old landmark students' union building is being redeveloped in a £75m project, and there are plans to upgrade the library and add more teaching rooms and space for student societies.

Edinburgh is also spending £8m on a new health and wellbeing centre, to house an expanded range of counselling and disability services. The university had already announced a new personal tutor system and a peer support scheme and has introduced the Edinburgh Teaching Award, a two-year qualification for staff.

Six new degrees will come on stream this year, including acoustics and musical technology, anatomy and development, agricultural economics and Portuguese. The university's strategic vision includes a commitment to enable undergraduates to develop as researchers and to give them the opportunity to draw on expertise outside their core discipline.

More than a quarter of the undergraduates come from outside the UK. Of Edinburgh's British intake, almost a third were privately educated. Selection guidelines aim to look beyond grades to consider candidates' potential, giving particular weight to references and personal statements. Measures to broaden the intake include an extensive summer school programme and support for students in the transition to higher education. There is also a range of bursaries, some worth up to £8,500 a year, to reduce the costs to English, Welsh or

33 Buccleuch Place
Edinburgh EH8 9J
0131 650 4360
https://www.sra.is.ed.ac.uk/
comms/enquiry/
www.ed.ac.uk
www.eusa.ed.ac.uk
Open days 2019:
see website

EDINBURGH
Belfast
London
Cardiff

The Times and The Sunday Times Rankings
Overall Ranking: 28 (last year: 24)

Teaching quality	72.8%	=125
Student experience	72.4%	119
Research quality	43.8%	10
Entry standards	182	=12
Graduate prospects	77.5%	57
Good honours	86.5%	11
Expected completion rate	92.0%	28
Student/staff ratio	12.6	12
Services and facilities	£2,195	67

Northern Irish undergraduates, who pay the full £9,250 fee for all four years of their degrees.

Top Scottish university in the 2014 Research Excellence Framework, Edinburgh submitted work that was judged to be 80% world-leading or internationally excellent. The university led the field in the UK for sociology, earth systems and environmental sciences, including geography, as well as computer science and informatics.

Researchers at the university were awarded the prestigious Queen's Anniversary Prize in 2017 for contributions over the past 40 years to improvements in women's health in fields including contraception, fertility, stillbirth and breast cancer. Another team of Edinburgh researchers has started a medical therapeutics company to develop treatments for age-related macular degeneration, a common cause of blindness.

Most of the university's buildings border the historic Old Town. Two miles to the south, the BioQuarter is a collaboration between the university and public bodies in a bid to consolidate Scotland's reputation as a world leader in biomedical science. The new £100m Rosalind Franklin Institute will bring together scientists and engineers from across the UK to develop new treatments for chronic disease.

The university is at the heart of the city. Its St Cecilia's Hall – Scotland's oldest purpose-built concert venue – has reopened after a two-year, £6.5m redevelopment. The McEwan Hall, another iconic building, has been renovated to combine ceremonial and conference spaces and reopened in 2017 after a two-year closure.

Edinburgh's sports facilities are among the best in the UK, producing past Olympic champions such as the cyclist Sir Chris Hoy and the rower Dame Katherine Grainger. The university has an outdoor centre 80 miles away in a beautiful Highland setting. In and around the city there is a network of gyms for student use, where membership packages start at just £1.15 a week. Students have a choice of 64 sports clubs and can take part in the full spectrum of sports fixtures from informal games to competitive tournaments.

There are more than 6,000 residential places – more than enough to guarantee a room for first-year students. Students thrive in the world-renowned cultural capital.

Tuition fees

» Fees for Scottish/EU students 2019–20   £0–£1,820
  RUK fees   £9,250
» Fees for International students 2019–20 £19,800–£32,100
  Medicine   £32,100–£49,900 (clinical years)
» For scholarship and bursary information see
  www.ed.ac.uk/student-funding
» Graduate salary   £22,510

Student numbers

Undergraduates	20,592 (1,048)
Postgraduates	7,824 (2,444)
Applications/places	62,480/6,385
Applications per place	9.8
Overall offer rate	50.4%
International students	36.0%

Accommodation

University provided places: 6,219 (catered 31%)
Catered costs: £186–£249 per week
Self-catered: £93–£169 per week
First years guaranteed accommodation
www.accom.ed.ac.uk/

Where do the students come from?

State schools (non-grammar)	60.2%	Working-class homes	18.7%	Black ethnic minority	0.6%
Grammar schools	6.2%	Deprived areas	4.1%	Disabled	5.4%
Independent schools	33.6%	All ethnic minorities	10.2%	Mature (over 21)	6.7%

Edinburgh Napier University

Edinburgh Napier is relying on its successful international activities to take it close to its target of 20% growth over five years.

The numbers starting courses in its home city have fallen, but the university is the largest UK provider of higher education in Hong Kong, teaching more than 3,000 students there each year, and now has 4,500 students taking its courses around the world and another 1,300 learning online. It has partners in Switzerland and several Asian countries, including China and India.

There are still fewer than 14,000 students on Napier's three Edinburgh campuses. The university promises them an "excellent personalised student experience", but satisfaction levels have plunged over recent years. Napier has dropped 50 places in both of the measures derived from scores in the National Student Survey, and is now in the bottom six for perceptions of teaching quality, scoring exactly the same as city neighbour, the University of Edinburgh.

Graduate prospects have improved markedly in the latest edition of this guide and there has been some progress in other areas. But the decline in student satisfaction has driven a fall of four places that leaves Napier as the lowest-ranked university in Scotland once again. Napier has lost the best part of 30 places in our table inside two years.

The university has embarked on an £84m investment in new teaching and research facilities, however. The aim is to create spaces that are more fluid than traditional classrooms to accommodate different styles of learning and teaching. There will still be lecture theatres, but their role will be reduced. Some additional facilities will be provided, but many of the new environments will be existing classrooms redesigned to promote interaction and embrace technology.

Napier has already spent £1m on such spaces for more than 300 students on its Merchiston campus and has added a new Cyber Academy training and cyberattack simulation suite and expanded computer games laboratory. Further investment will improve students' social and dining spaces over the next two years including the addition of a rooftop cafe.

There are similar intentions to extend the Sighthill campus before the relocation of the engineering school by 2022.

Engineering is currently based at Merchiston, but the campus is to be redeveloped as a hub for computing and the creative industries, with fully soundproofed music studios and a broadcast journalism newsroom.

The university runs Screen Academy Scotland in partnership with Edinburgh College of Art (now part of the University of

Sighthill Court
Edinburgh EH11 4BN
0333 900 6040
studentrecruitment@napier.ac.uk
www.napier.ac.uk
www.napierstudents.com
Open days 2019:
see website

EDINBURGH
Belfast
London
Cardiff

The Times and The Sunday Times Rankings
Overall Ranking: 120 (last year: 116)

Teaching quality	72.8%	=125
Student experience	72.3%	120
Research quality	4.6%	=96
Entry standards	150	40
Graduate prospects	73.8%	=74
Good honours	74.7%	58
Expected completion rate	81.5%	=98
Student/staff ratio	18.8	115
Services and facilities	£1,796	108

Edinburgh), reflecting the institution's strong reputation in film education. The creative arts produced the most successful of Edinburgh Napier's entries for the 2014 Research Excellence Framework.

The Sighthill campus is home to the schools of nursing, midwifery and social care, and life, sport and social sciences. It has a five-storey learning resource centre, an environmental chamber and biomechanics laboratory, and a large simulation and clinical skills centre with mock hospital wards and a high dependency unit simulator.

Integrated sports facilities feature a well-equipped fitness centre and a sports hall, as well as the BT Sport Scottish Rugby Academy. The business school is at the Craiglockhart campus, once a hospital for shell-shocked First World War soldiers. The building blends history and modernity, featuring a glass atrium and cybercafe and displaying the War Poets Collection, by Siegfried Sassoon and Wilfred Owen.

Many of Edinburgh Napier's courses include a work placement. The Confident Futures programme is said to be unique in higher education, using workshops to improve students' confidence and help them to develop skills, attributes and attitudes that will enhance their chances of being successful both while at university and in their careers.

For the growing numbers choosing to start their own businesses, Bright Red Triangle, the university's student enterprise service, offers free office space and advice to students and alumni. Edinburgh Napier has supported 350 start-ups in the past ten years.

There are fully networked libraries on each campus and a multimedia language laboratory and adaptive learning centre for students with special needs.

To minimise dropout rates, the university uses its students to mentor newcomers. Support begins with bridging programmes and pre-term introductions to staff and continues with summer top-up courses and workshops in employability skills and personal development.

Widening participation is high on the list of priorities, with a third of the undergraduates over 20 at entry. However, the university only ranks 90th in our new table measuring social diversity on campus. More than 2,000 students join Napier through "articulation routes", using their college qualifications to gain direct entry into year two or three of a degree course.

Tuition fees

» Fees for Scottish/EU students 2019–20   £0–£1,820
  RUK fees   £9,000 (capped at £27,000 for 4-year courses)
» Fees for International students 2019–20   £12,845–£14,925
» For scholarship and bursary information see
  www.napier.ac.uk/study-with-us/undergraduate/fees-and-finance
» Graduate salary   £22,440

Student numbers			Accommodation
Undergraduates	**9,341**	**(1,182)**	University provided places: 1,500 (catered 0%)
Postgraduates	**1,183**	**(1,204)**	Self-catered: £95–£151per week
Applications/places		**21,015/2,825**	First years guaranteed accommodation
Applications per place		**7.4**	www.napier.ac.uk/study-with-us/accommodation
Overall offer rate		**69.3%**	
International students		**19.1%**	

Where do the students come from?

State schools (non-grammar)	92.5%	Working-class homes	31.1%	Black ethnic minority	1.9%
Grammar schools	2.0%	Deprived areas	9.2%	Disabled	4.7%
Independent schools	5.5%	All ethnic minorities	7.7%	Mature (over 21)	33.5%

University of Essex

Essex set itself the target of reaching the top 25 in our table and achieved it two years ahead of schedule when it was still celebrating a gold award in the Teaching Excellence Framework (TEF) in 2017. It has fallen slightly since, although applications were up for the fourth year in a row last year, at a time when other universities were seeing demand fall. Not surprisingly, perhaps, enrolments are the highest in the university's history, more than 40% above the level when £9,000 fees were introduced.

The TEF panel found that student feedback was being used to develop rigorous and stretching teaching that is tailored to student needs. It said: "Students from all backgrounds achieve outstanding outcomes with regards to continuation and progression to highly-skilled employment or further study, notably exceeding the university's benchmark."

The Quality Assurance Agency has also praised the university's employability initiatives. The award-winning Frontrunners scheme arranges on-campus paid work experience for students. Other opportunities include an extensive internship programme, and work placements are integral to many courses. The Big Essex Award recognises students' extracurricular activities, volunteering and work experience and Essex Abroad supports those studying, working or volunteering overseas. Language tuition is free, and Essex mainly exempts tuition fees for a full year abroad or a placement year.

The original 1960s buildings on Essex's 200-acre parkland campus are gradually being replaced. The £13m Science, Technology, Engineering and Maths (Stem) Centre opened last year and includes a versatile, 180-seat wet laboratory for the biological sciences and a 200-seat learning space to encourage students from across the faculty of science and health to work collaboratively. The building also has social space and a cafe.

A new £12m Sports Arena, the size of three basketball courts, and 634 rooms in a new residential development awaited last year's entrants. Other contemporary facilities include a "zero carbon" business school, a student centre and a library extension.

Essex's student population is unusually diverse for a pre-1992 university, with high proportions of mature and international students. More than a third of undergraduates are from working-class homes and 96% were state-educated. An active outreach team works with schools to encourage progression to university. Essex ranks an excellent 41st in our new table measuring social diversity.

Degrees in childhood studies, tourism management, creative producing (theatre and film), and business economics are among new courses. The university is also considering

Wivenhoe Park
Colchester CO4 3SQ
01206 873 666
admit@essex.ac.uk
www.essex.ac.uk
www.essexstudent.com
Open days 2019:
June 15 (Colchester)

The Times and The Sunday Times **Rankings**
Overall Ranking: 29 (last year: 22)

Teaching quality	80.4%	=58
Student experience	79.7%	=44
Research quality	37.2%	25
Entry standards	117	=107
Graduate prospects	74.3%	72
Good honours	78.8%	41
Expected completion rate	86.2%	=58
Student/staff ratio	16.3	=76
Services and facilities	£3,408	5

an expansion of degree apprenticeships, to add to existing opportunities in computer science and electronic engineering, and adult and mental health nursing. A professional work placement has been introduced as part of several masters courses.

The social sciences are Essex's greatest strength, putting the institution among the world's top 40 in the QS rankings for both politics and sociology. The university received the only Regius professorship in political science in the awards to mark the Queen's diamond jubilee. It achieved the best results in the 2014 Research Excellence Framework (REF) in politics and was in the top ten for economics and art history. The university moved into the top 25 in our research ranking, with almost 80% of a large submission rated world-leading or internationally excellent.

Wivenhoe House, the original centrepiece of the university on the main campus near Colchester, includes a four-star hotel run by the Edge Hotel School. A second modern campus in Southend offers courses in business, health and the arts and its accommodation complex houses a gym and fitness studio. The Forum knowledge, learning and culture hub at the heart of the Southend campus houses a public and academic library, learning facilities, cafe and gallery, and has a floor reserved for student use. In addition, the university estate includes the East 15 Acting School on the Loughton campus.

An active students' union and good social and sporting facilities set over some 40 acres of land keep students engaged. Provision has been further enhanced by the new Sports Arena's 12 extra courts for badminton, three each for basketball and netball, and five new courts for volleyball. All the facilities are also open to the public.

The number of student sports club members has doubled to 4,000 in recent years, while another 2,400 students take part in drop-in sessions. All first-years are guaranteed a place in university accommodation, which has been voted some of the best in the UK. Some ground-floor flats have been adapted for disabled students. All the campuses are within easy access of London — or the atmospheric north Essex coastline if you prefer to get away from it all.

Tuition fees

» Fees for UK/EU students 2019–20   £9,250
» Fees for International students 2019–20   £15,000–£17,000
» For scholarship and bursary information see
  www1.essex.ac.uk/fees-and-funding
» Graduate salary   £20,000

Student numbers

Undergraduates	10,513	(774)
Postgraduates	2,087	(1,210)
Applications/places		20,415/3,050
Applications per place		6.7
Overall offer rate		75.7%
International students		30.3%

Accommodation

University provided places: 2,063 (catered 0%)
Self-catered: £82–£180 per week
First years guaranteed accommodation
www1.essex.ac.uk/accommodation/default.aspx

Where do the students come from?

State schools (non-grammar)	90.8%	Working-class homes	38.3%	Black ethnic minority	22.3%
Grammar schools	5.3%	Deprived areas	12.8%	Disabled	4.3%
Independent schools	3.9%	All ethnic minorities	44.4%	Mature (over 21)	14.5%

University of Exeter

After dropping out of our top ten for the first time in seven years in the last edition of the guide, Exeter is moving in the right direction again now. A decline in student satisfaction – especially in relation to the quality of teaching — was the main cause of the blip. The university has generally been among the leaders in the National Student Survey and received a gold award in the Teaching Excellence Framework. The awarding panel complimented Exeter on the contact hours and class sizes provided for students, the involvement of business, industry and professional experts in its teaching, and the outstanding environment in which it takes place.

Applications dropped for the first time in a decade in 2017, but there was another record enrolment, as the number of entrants passed the 6,000 mark for the first time. Exeter has added more than 1,500 places to its annual intake of undergraduates since higher fees were introduced, while also increasing its entry standards significantly. The proportion of applicants receiving a conditional offer of a place is one of the highest rates in the UK, partly because since joining the Russell Group in 2012, the university has been attracting better-qualified applicants.

Exeter has spent some £380m on campus improvements, expanding its facilities to cope with the growing number of students.

The latest additions are student hubs on all the campuses, giving students somewhere to eat, socialise and study, as well as to access help and information close to their lectures and tutorials. The £100m Penryn campus in Cornwall houses the £30m environment and sustainability institute with its renewable energy teaching and research centre.

Exeter and Falmouth University share the Penryn campus, which has a joint students' union. It is the base for the Exeter business school and the home of Exeter degrees in biosciences, geography, geology, clean energy, English, history, politics and mining engineering. The Exchange, a £10m learning, teaching and research hub, serves them all.

The main Streatham campus, close to the centre of Exeter and one of the most attractive settings for any university, hosts course provision for the majority of students as well as study bedrooms in the £130m student residences on site. A £1.2m digital humanities laboratory serves to examine, preserve and analyse historical, literary and visual material. Holding it all together is the £48m Forum building, which features an extended library, student services centre, technology-rich learning spaces and auditorium, as well as social and retail facilities.

The nearby St Luke's campus houses the medical school, which has a health education and research centre at the Royal Devon and Exeter Hospital. Also at St Luke's are the

Streatham Campus
Stocker Road
Exeter EX4 4QD
0300 555 6060 or 01392 723 044
https://www.exeter.ac.uk/enquiry/
www.exeter.ac.uk
www.exeterguild.org
Open days 2019:
see website

The Times and The Sunday Times Rankings
Overall Ranking: 12 (last year: 14)

Teaching quality	80.6%	56
Student experience	80.9%	28
Research quality	38%	18
Entry standards	176	15
Graduate prospects	85.5%	13
Good honours	86.3%	13
Expected completion rate	95.4%	9
Student/staff ratio	16.1	=74
Services and facilities	£2,745	19

Graduate School of Education and the sport and health sciences school. A £10m donation from billionaire Exeter alumnus Dennis Gillings and his wife Mireille will enable a neuro-imaging centre to be developed at the medical school. It is expected to accelerate the diagnosis of and treatment of dementia.

Exeter recorded much-improved results in the 2014 assessments of research. More than 80% of a large submission was rated as world-leading or internationally excellent, with clinical medicine, psychology and education producing particularly good results.

More than 30% of Exeter's undergraduates come from independent schools — a much higher proportion than the national average for the university's subjects and entry qualifications, although this figure has been coming down. Students from disadvantaged backgrounds and schools with poor results are made lower offers to encourage fair access. New campus-based degrees planned for this year include neuroscience, art history and visual culture, a degree apprenticeship in digital technology solutions, and a four-year integrated Masters in nursing

Exeter has a global outlook including a research partnership with the University of Queensland to focus on the interdisciplinary themes of environmental sustainability, healthy ageing, and physical activity and nutrition. Students can choose from a range of four-year programmes "with international study" and some three-year degrees include the option of a year abroad. All students are offered tuition in foreign languages and career management skills are built in, too. The university's Career Zone scheme helps boost student employability and access to internships and the Exeter Award provides official recognition of extracurricular activities. The university has one of the highest numbers of student volunteers at any UK institution.

More than £20m has been invested in sports facilities in recent years, providing some of the best in the country. The Sports Park on the main campus includes a 200-station gym, and Exeter is one of the few UK universities to have indoor tennis facilities to national competition standards. There is no shortage of student-oriented bars and clubs in the city.

Tuition fees

- » Fees for UK/EU students 2019–20 £9,250
- » Fees for International students 2019–20 £17,600–£22,500
  Medicine £35,000
- » For scholarship and bursary information see
  www.exeter.ac.uk/undergraduate/money/matters
- » Graduate salary £23,000

Student numbers

Undergraduates	18,139	(123)
Postgraduates	3,487	(1,428)
Applications/places		41,000/5,660
Applications per place		7.2
Overall offer rate		89.7%
International students		25.3%

Accommodation

University provided places: 5,682 (catered 21%)
Catered costs: £166–£251 per week
Self-catered: £87–£178 per week
First years guaranteed accommodation
www.exeter.ac.uk/accommodation

Where do the students come from?

State schools (non-grammar)	56.2%	Working-class homes	15.5%	Black ethnic minority	2.0%
Grammar schools	13.3%	Deprived areas	7.7%	Disabled	6.9%
Independent schools	30.6%	All ethnic minorities	11.1%	Mature (over 21)	6.5%

Falmouth University

Falmouth has dropped down our league table in the past two years, having been the leading arts university and just outside the top 50 overall. But it still earned a gold rating in the Teaching Excellence Framework (TEF) in 2017 and enjoys enduring popularity with prospective undergraduates. Although applications have declined for the past two years, enrolments remain at record levels – twice what they were a decade ago.

The TEF panel was particularly impressed with students' personalised learning, partly through individual timetabling and a "data-driven approach to monitoring contact and teaching patterns". It also complimented the university on stretching students and ensuring that they acquire the knowledge, skills and understanding most highly valued by employers.

The university traces its origins to 1902 when it was established as the Falmouth School of Art. Its two campuses — at Falmouth and Penryn — have benefited from investment of more than £100m in the past decade. Its second base, Penryn, is shared with the University of Exeter and has a unique joint students' union, FXU.

Falmouth is only just outside the top ten in this year's Times Higher Education student experience survey, gaining its highest marks for the campus environment, library and other facilities. But it fares much less well in the National Student Survey, used by this guide to rate teaching quality and the student experience.

There are still only about 5,000 students studying subjects including architecture, digital media and creative writing, graphic design and fashion. Photography has a long and celebrated history at Falmouth and the university claims to have some of the best teaching facilities in Europe, as well as an in-house photo agency helping to make the ambitions of students and alumni bear fruit.

The university still regards itself as a specialist art institution, but degrees now include acting, business entrepreneurship and marketing. Some courses make unconditional offers for the most promising applicants. The portfolio of business degrees expanded for the current academic year, with six new offerings combining business with data analytics, entrepreneurship, financial technology, digital marketing, management and development management.

About 60% of the undergraduates are female, although men are marginally more likely to receive an offer. Each new arrival is offered a student mentor for a year to support them during their transition to university life. The university has an internal teaching qualification for staff to promote high standards.

More than nine out of ten undergraduates are state-educated. Those with a family income

Woodlane
Falmouth TR11 4RH
01326 213 730
applicantservices@falmouth.ac.uk
www.falmouth.ac.uk
www.fxu.org.uk
Open days 2019:
see website

The Times and The Sunday Times **Rankings**

Overall Ranking: 84 (last year: 69)

Teaching quality	80.5%	**57**
Student experience	74.6%	**=107**
Research quality	4.6%	**=96**
Entry standards	121	**93**
Graduate prospects	77.0%	**61**
Good honours	72.6%	**71**
Expected completion rate	88.4%	**45**
Student/staff ratio	18.4	**=109**
Services and facilities	£1,456	**128**

of less than £42,675 receive up to £200 a year to spend on course materials. Students from Cornwall qualify for an extra £500 a year.

Falmouth merged in 2008 with Dartington College of Arts, in south Devon, adding a range of performance-related courses to its portfolio. These courses are now taught at the purpose-built Academy of Music and Theatre Arts (Amata) at Penryn, where there are extensive media facilities, including a 3-D printer and stereoscopic projector. The animation and visual effects department is part of the Cross Channel Film Lab, which aims to develop innovative visual effects for use in low-budget feature film production. As well as teaching facilities, Amata provides an arts venue attracting performers from all over the world.

Students at Penryn have use of a 117-seat cinema, motion capture studio, video editing suites and specialist animation software. For performing arts courses there are fully sprung dancefloors, rehearsal studios and theatre space, while the Falmouth campus near the town centre has an impressive graphic design building with open-plan studios, design labs, a 150-seat lecture theatre and photography facilities. The campus also features subtropical gardens and a popular cafe, opened in 2016.

University programmes using the Team Academy model encourage students to set up a business while they study, with a focus on the "learning and leisure" market to capitalise on Cornwall's tourist attractions and landmarks. The Launchpad scheme for graduate entrepreneurs has an emphasis on technology companies, creating new digital businesses to meet identified market demand in just one year.

There are residential places on both campuses, enabling the university to guarantee all full-time first-years accommodation as long as they apply by the deadline. Penryn added a new sports centre in 2016 as well as gym facilities; the university's seaside location means there are plenty of opportunities to try watersports.

Students make full use of Cornwall's coastline and rugged moors during their time in the wild southwest. Paid work is plentiful in the tourist trade and nightlife is lively during the holiday season. The bright lights of London — and other European cities — are closer than you might think, with good rail links.

Tuition fees

» Fees for UK/EU students 2019–20	£9,250
Foundation courses	£6,700
» Fees for International students 2019–20	£15,000
» For scholarship and bursary information see www.falmouth.ac.uk/tuition-fees	
» Graduate salary	£18,000

Student numbers

Undergraduates	5,067	(17)
Postgraduates	120	(179)
Applications/places	6,440/1,860	
Applications per place	3.5	
Overall offer rate	61.2%	
International students	9.6%	

Accommodation

University provided places: 2,170 (catered 0%)
Self-catered: £106–£189 per week
First years guaranteed accommodation
www.falmouth.ac.uk/facilities/university-accommodation

Where do the students come from?

State schools (non-grammar)	90.6%	Working-class homes	27.6%	Black ethnic minority	0.8%
Grammar schools	3.1%	Deprived areas	10.9%	Disabled	15.3%
Independent schools	6.3%	All ethnic minorities	6.4%	Mature (over 21)	12.6%

University of Glasgow

Glasgow has continued to climb our table, following its success in 2017 as our Scottish University of the Year after jumping nine places and into the UK top 20. Only St Andrews is placed higher in Scotland. The university also saw a record number of applications in 2017, accepting almost 1,000 more of a largely Scottish intake than was the case only three years previously.

One of the biggest education infrastructure projects in Scotland's history is now taking shape in Glasgow. Demolition has started on the former Western Infirmary site, adjoining the main campus, where about £430m will be spent over the next four years as the first stage of a wider £1bn ten-year investment. The university sees this as a "pivotal step" in the creation of world-class learning and teaching, and research and community facilities, which it expects to transform the city's West End.

A learning and teaching hub for 3,000 students will contain formal and informal learning spaces, a lecture theatre and technology-enhanced areas where students can work. There will also be new buildings for arts, social sciences, the health and wellbeing institute, and the science and engineering college, as well as a research and innovation hub housing large-scale interdisciplinary projects and incubator space for spin-out collaborations with industry.

On its existing sites, Glasgow has an imaging centre of excellence at the Queen Elizabeth University Hospital where undergraduates have the benefit of a £25m centre for teaching and learning. Extensive work has also taken place on the Garscube campus, four miles out of the city, which houses the veterinary school and outdoor sports facilities.

The university enjoys the rare distinction of having been established by papal bull, beginning its existence in the chapterhouse of Glasgow Cathedral in 1451. Since 1871 it has been based on the Gilmorehill campus in the city's fashionable West End. Teaching and learning facilities costing £35m have been created at the redeveloped Kelvin Hall, which offer improved access to the collections of the university's art gallery and museum, the Hunterian.

There is also a campus at Dumfries that takes liberal arts and teacher education degrees to southwest Scotland. More than £13m has been invested in improved sporting and social facilities there.

Unusually for a university of its type, Glasgow exceeds its benchmarks for widening participation in higher education, although it does not perform well in our new table on social inclusion. Almost two thirds of the students still come from Scotland — many from Glasgow and the surrounding area.

University Avenue, Glasgow G12 8QQ
0141 330 2000
ruk-undergraduate-enquiries
  @glasgow.ac.uk;
scot-undergraduate-enquiries
  @glasgow.co.uk;
student.recruitment@glasgow.ac.uk
www.glasgow.ac.uk
www.guu.org.uk;
www.qmunion.org.uk
Open days 2019: June 13

The Times and The Sunday Times **Rankings**

Overall Ranking: 17 (last year: 20)

Teaching quality	79.1%	=75
Student experience	79.6%	47
Research quality	39.9%	12
Entry standards	201	7
Graduate prospects	85.3%	16
Good honours	84.1%	21
Expected completion rate	88.6%	44
Student/staff ratio	14.9	=41
Services and facilities	£2,316	52

The university operates a number of access initiatives, including the Top-Up programme, which has been working with schools in the west of Scotland since 1999, and Talent Scholarships, which are worth £1,000 a year to academically able Scots from poor backgrounds.

One of Scotland's two representatives in the Russell Group, the university is in the top 100 in both the Times Higher Education and QS world rankings. It moved into the top dozen universities in the UK for research after a much-improved performance in the 2014 assessments, ranking in the UK top ten in 18 subjects. The best results came in architecture, agriculture, veterinary science and chemistry.

Glasgow is hoping to extend its global reach, having opened a joint graduate school with Nankai University in China and set up partnerships with institutions in Canada, Hong Kong and America. It has had a branch in Singapore for seven years, working with the Singapore Institute of Technology to deliver a joint engineering and mechatronics degree programme. Even on its home campus, more than a quarter of the undergraduates are from outside the UK.

Glasgow has a history of innovation: it was the first university in Britain to have a school of engineering and the first in Scotland to have a computer. More recently, it appointed Scotland's first Gaelic language officer and the country's first chair of Gaelic. The £20m Stratified

Medicine Scotland Innovation Centre at the Queen Elizabeth University Hospital campus involves a consortium of universities, NHS Scotland and industry partners.

Almost half of the university's applications are for broad arts or sciences degrees, rather than specific subjects, reflecting the popularity of a flexible system that allows students to delay choosing a specialism until the end of their second year. The internship hub facilitates more than 350 paid opportunities each year, including 150 on-campus internships.

Most students like the combination of campus and vibrant city, with the added bonus that Glasgow has been rated among the most cost-effective locations in which to study. Undergraduates have the choice of two students' unions, plus a sports union supporting more than 50 clubs and activities. Union facilities include a nightclub and cafe bars.

Tuition fees

» Fees for Scottish/EU students 2019–20   £0–£1,820
    RUK fees   £9,250 (capped at £27,750 for 4-year courses)
» Fees for International students 2019–20   £16,300–£21,020
    Medicine £45,170 (clinical years); Dentistry £42,170;
    Veterinary £29,250
» For scholarship and bursary information see
    http://www.gla.ac.uk/study/undergraduate/fees
» Graduate salary   £22,800

Student numbers

Undergraduates	18,005 (2,418)
Postgraduates	6,349 (1,842)
Applications/places	35,160/4,935
Applications per place	7.1
Overall offer rate	71.3%
International students	28.8%

Accommodation

University provided places: 3,419 (catered 7%)
Catered costs: £161–£178 per week
Self-catered: £96–£157 per week
First years guaranteed accommodation
(if more than 1hr 20mins away)
www.gla.ac.uk/myglasgow/accommodation

Where do the students come from?

State schools (non-grammar)	78.8%	Working-class homes	21.4%	Black ethnic minority	0.8%
Grammar schools	6.3%	Deprived areas	4.2%	Disabled	3.3%
Independent schools	14.8%	All ethnic minorities	8.1%	Mature (over 21)	15.1%

Glasgow Caledonian University

Improved levels of student satisfaction have helped Glasgow Caledonian (GCU) to a rise of eight places in our latest league table. Like other universities north of the border, it benefits from the conversion rate for Scottish secondary qualifications in the UCAS tariff — putting it in the top 25 for entry grades, above institutions such as Nottingham and Loughborough.

GCU describes itself as the University for the Common Good, a philosophy which extends into the curriculum, focusing on four attributes to equip students to serve their communities effectively. They involve active and global citizenship, an entrepreneurial mindset, responsible leadership and self-confidence.

The university is part of the Changemaker Campus network set up by social entrepreneurs Ashoka, striving to establish a global reputation for delivering social benefit and impact through education, research and social innovation. It helped to found the African Leadership College in Mauritius, where the first students embarked on GCU degrees in 2017.

In 2010 the university co-founded the Grameen Caledonian College of Nursing in Bangladesh, and past affiliations have been set up with an engineering college in Oman and universities and colleges in China, India and South America.

Now Glasgow Caledonian has become the first foreign university to be granted a charter to award its own degrees in New York. The powers relate to the university's portfolio of research-based master's programmes in fashion and business, which was launched in 2013, when GCU opened the first UK campus in the city. The university was also the first from Scotland to open a campus in London, again for fashion postgraduates.

The Glasgow campus was the first campus to be named as "cycle friendly" by Cycle Scotland and is also a platinum-award winning eco-friendly campus. The centrepiece of a £32m redevelopment is the Heart of the Campus, completed in 2016, with a striking glass reception area.

Although it is ranked 91st in our new table on social diversity, widening participation in higher education has always been one of the university's main aims, and it has recruited some heavy-hitters to support the project. Sir Alex Ferguson has pledged £500,000 to a bursary programme. The singer Annie Lennox was appointed chancellor last year, succeeding Professor Muhammad Yunus, the Nobel laureate and anti-poverty campaigner.

The university's Caledonian Club works with children as young as three years old and their families in Glasgow and London. More than a third of the undergraduates are from working-class homes and about three quarters are the first in their family to attend

Cowcaddens Road
Glasgow G4 0BA
0141 331 8630
https://www.gcu.ac.uk/enquire/
www.gcu.ac.uk
www.gcustudents.co.uk
Open days 2019:
see website

The Times and The Sunday Times Rankings
Overall Ranking: 101 (last year: =109)

Teaching quality	78.5%	=89
Student experience	76.1%	96
Research quality	7.0%	=78
Entry standards	165	24
Graduate prospects	73.7%	76
Good honours	72.8%	=69
Expected completion rate	84.9%	=70
Student/staff ratio	19.2	=117
Services and facilities	£1,588	121

university. The Advanced Higher Hub offers students in their final year at schools across Glasgow specialist teaching, access to GCU's facilities and preparation for university life.

The university has a series of measures — focusing on academic, social and financial support — for those at risk of dropping out. Completion rates have improved in the latest table; they remain marginally better than the UK average for GCU's courses and entry qualifications.

Health was one of the university's strengths in the 2014 Research Excellence Framework, which placed half of GCU's submission in the top two categories. It was in the top 20 in the UK for allied health research and did well in social work and social policy, and the built environment.

The health building brings together teaching and research facilities, including a virtual hospital. GCU is one of the largest providers of graduates to the NHS in Scotland. As the only Scottish university delivering optometry degrees, it trains 90% of the country's eye care specialists.

However, the university is best known for its fashion courses. The university's British School of Fashion has partnerships with firms such as Marks & Spencer, which has a design studio on the London campus and funds a scholarship programme. There are also courses in fashion business creation, luxury brand marketing and management, luxury retail management and international fashion marketing.

More than half of the undergraduate programmes are accredited by professional bodies and most include work placements. With just over three quarters of leavers gaining graduate-level jobs or going into further study, GCU performs better in this area than in many other aspects of our league table. The School of Engineering and Built Environment teaches three quarters of Scotland's part-time construction students. Glasgow School for Business and Society pioneered subjects such as entrepreneurial studies and risk management, and offers highly specialist degrees, such as tourism management and consumer protection. There are graduate apprenticeships in business and management, IT, engineering and construction.

Student facilities include the Arc sports centre and 24-hour computer labs. Residential accommodation is limited, but first-years and international students have priority in its allocation. Glasgow is a lively city with a large student population, where the cost of living is reasonable.

Tuition fees

- » Fees for Scottish/EU students 2019–20 £0–£1,820
  RUK fees £9,250 (capped at £27,750 for 4-year courses)
- » Fees for International students 2019–20 £11,845
- » For scholarship and bursary information see www.gcu.ac.uk/study/tuitionfees
- » Graduate salary £21,500

Student numbers

Undergraduates	11,090 (2,418)
Postgraduates	1,772 (1,134)
Applications/places	22,055/3,650
Applications per place	6.0
Overall offer rate	65.3%
International students	12.3%

Accommodation

University provided places: 660 (catered 0%)
Self-catered: £100–£113 per week
First years given priority
www.gcu.ac.uk/study/undergraduate/accommodation/

Where do the students come from?

State schools (non-grammar)	96.4%	Working-class homes	34.7%	Black ethnic minority	2.4%
Grammar schools	0.8%	Deprived areas	8.8%	Disabled	1.3%
Independent schools	2.8%	All ethnic minorities	11.3%	Mature (over 21)	35.5%

University of Gloucestershire

A string of new developments have opened for use by students in the current academic year. There is a business school and sports hub on the Oxstalls campus in Gloucester, a design centre in Cheltenham and the Blackfriars residences, where almost 300 rooms are available in Gloucester city centre.

The business school will see students working with and alongside companies, as the building will also be the expanded home of the growth hub, a collaboration between the university and the Gloucestershire local enterprise partnership. The design centre will complement the well-equipped media centre and computing and technology suite on the Park campus, adding professional-standard production studios and research spaces.

The new facilities will allow for further expansion, as Gloucestershire plans to grow by a third. The increased numbers will be on campus programmes, but also at partner colleges, online and through work-based learning. The university already offers seven degree apprenticeship programmes and expects to have 300 apprentices by September this year after expanding into engineering.

While the numbers starting degrees fell in 2017 after three successive increases, Gloucestershire remains in our top 50 for student satisfaction with teaching quality and the student experience, despite a fall this year on both our measures derived from the National Student Survey. Similar results helped the university to a silver award in the Teaching Excellence Framework, the panel commenting favourably on an integrated approach to careers, volunteering and placements that enhances student employability.

Gloucestershire claims to offer undergraduates more time with academics than almost any other university in the UK. In most subjects, students are said to spend at least a quarter of their time in lectures, seminars or other supervised activities. It is implementing a programme to enhance teaching and learning further, after carrying out a full review. More than half of the academics have formal teaching qualifications, one of the highest proportions at any university. The strategic plan promises an even higher rate, as well as greater use of technology to support the learning experience, with online content available wherever possible to support face-to-face teaching.

Gloucestershire was the first university for more than a century to have formal links with the Church of England when it achieved full university status in 2001. The three campuses are only seven miles apart, so students are not as isolated as they are in some split-site institutions. The main Park campus is a mile from the centre of Cheltenham, and houses the business, education and professional

The Park
Cheltenham GL50 2RH
03330 141 414
enquiries@glos.ac.uk
www.glos.ac.uk
www.yourstudentunion.com
Open days 2019:
see website

The Times and The Sunday Times **Rankings**

Overall Ranking: =81 (last year: 83)

Teaching quality	81.9%	38
Student experience	79.7%	=44
Research quality	3.8%	=109
Entry standards	124	=85
Graduate prospects	72.9%	=85
Good honours	71.8%	=77
Expected completion rate	83.4%	=83
Student/staff ratio	19.0	116
Services and facilities	£2,007	88

studies faculty. Art and design facilities, and the education and public services institute are closer to the town centre at Francis Close Hall.

The purpose-built Oxstalls campus caters for sport and exercise sciences, leisure, tourism, hospitality and event management. The site also houses the Countryside and Community Research Institute, the largest rural research centre in the UK, which produced the best results in the 2014 Research Excellence Framework. Overall, 44% of Gloucestershire's submission was rated as world-leading or internationally excellent, but fewer than 20% of the eligible staff took part.

Originally a teacher training college founded in 1847, the university offers primary and secondary training courses that are rated as "outstanding" by Ofsted. There is a good range of work placements for other students, which are undertaken by a third of all undergraduates.

The university has a long-standing focus on green issues and finished second in the People & Planet league of universities' environmental performance for 2017. There are allotments for students and diplomas in environmentalism, as well as sustainability research and development projects that bring together researchers from around the world, undertaking work for agencies such as Unesco.

In addition to its conventional degrees, the university offers a range of two-year "fast track" degrees in subjects such as biology, events management and law. The institution's intake is diverse, with nearly all the undergraduates coming from state schools and more than a third from working-class homes. The projected dropout rate has improved dramatically over recent years, and the latest figure of 8% is well below the national average for the university's subjects and entry qualifications.

Gloucestershire has a strong sporting tradition and is the only university to have a professional rugby league team. Three students were selected for the Great Britain rugby union sevens teams at the Rio Olympics. Sports facilities include a sports hall, eight grass and two all-weather pitches and a cricket pavilion.

All first-year applicants are guaranteed housing in university halls or managed accommodation if they make Gloucestershire their first choice and apply by the required deadline.

Tuition fees

» Fees for UK/EU students 2019–20 £9,250
» Fees for International students 2018–19 £13,840
» For scholarship and bursary information see www.glos.ac.uk/life/finance/Pages/default.aspx
» Graduate salary £19,200

Student numbers

Undergraduates	6,596	(370)
Postgraduates	525	(1,015)
Applications/places	9,075/2,260	
Applications per place	4.0	
Overall offer rate	87.6%	
International students	5.6%	

Accommodation

University provided places: 2,040 (catered 0%)
Self-catered: £100–£190 per week
First years guaranteed accommodation
www.glos.ac.uk/life/accommodation/pages/accommodation.aspx

Where do the students come from?

State schools (non-grammar)	92.4%	Working-class homes	36.4%	Black ethnic minority	4.0%
Grammar schools	3.8%	Deprived areas	15.7%	Disabled	9.1%
Independent schools	3.8%	All ethnic minorities	10.3%	Mature (over 21)	19.9%

Goldsmiths, University of London

New facilities should help to secure Goldsmiths' place as one of the leading universities for the creative arts. A £2.9m performance and teaching space opened last year for student and public use, containing studios and a 200-seat theatre. It was followed by the opening of the Goldsmiths Centre for Contemporary Art, a gallery of eight diverse spaces in a redeveloped listed building that once housed public baths.

But the portfolio of degrees ranges much more widely than performance arts, and includes management, economics, politics and computing. The addition of popular new programmes has helped to encourage seven successive increases in the number of students starting degrees. More than 1,000 students have been added to the annual intake of undergraduates over that period, and Goldsmiths is about to embark on degree apprenticeships for the first time.

The arts remain Goldsmiths' greatest strength, however. It is in the top 12 universities in the world for art and design and just outside the top 25 for the performing arts in the QS subject rankings. Alumni such as Damien Hirst and Sir Antony Gormley are at the top of their fields. In recent years, the director Steve McQueen scooped the best picture Oscar for *12 Years a Slave*, James Blake took the Mercury prize for his album *Overgrown* and Laure Prouvost was named winner of the Turner prize, becoming the seventh former Goldsmiths student to receive the award.

Nevertheless, Goldsmiths was placed in the bronze category in the government's Teaching Excellence Framework, and did not attempt to have the rating upgraded this year. The judging panel did concede that students had access to high-quality resources and benefited from connecting with, and conducting research of relevance to, local communities. But the college was dragged down by low student satisfaction levels, a common problem in London, and poor graduate employment, also a challenge in arts-dominated institutions.

The same failings prevent Goldsmiths from finishing higher in our table. It is in the bottom three for graduate prospects in our new edition. It did well in the Research Excellence Framework, though, with 70% of its submission judged to be world-leading or internationally excellent. The best results came in communication and media studies, and the college did particularly well in assessments of research impact. The entire submission in music was considered world-leading in this respect.

With only 6,000 undergraduates, Goldsmiths remains small for a multi-faculty

New Cross
London SE14 6NW
020 7078 5300
info@gold.ac.uk
www.gold.ac.uk
www.goldsmithssu.org
Open days 2019:
see website

***The Times and The Sunday Times* Rankings**
Overall Ranking: 71 (last year: =63)

Teaching quality	74.8%	119
Student experience	70.1%	128
Research quality	33.4%	37
Entry standards	132	=63
Graduate prospects	58.3%	130
Good honours	83.9%	22
Expected completion rate	79.2%	=109
Student/staff ratio	14.7	=35
Services and facilities	£2,539	31

university and intends to grow further in the next few years. It is based on a single campus that has a mixture of traditional and modern buildings. The Professor Stuart Hall building contains purpose-built media facilities such as radio and TV studios, the Ben Pimlott building boasts state-of-the-art research facilities and studio space for art students, while the flagship Richard Hoggart building has space for outdoor arts and events.

Located in New Cross, southeast London, Goldsmiths is committed to increasing recruitment from the boroughs of Lewisham, Greenwich and Southwark. A quarter of new undergraduates are 21 or over on entry, and there is a growing cohort of international students. More than nine out of ten UK undergraduates are state-educated, and three in ten come from the four poorest socioeconomic groups. A peer-assisted learning scheme helps new arrivals to settle in with weekly sessions run by second and third-year students.

There are integrated work placements on many degrees and workshops help students to develop entrepreneurial skills. Goldsmiths also places great emphasis on equipping students with creative thinking skills. The university's Gold award encourages students to develop the skills and experience that employers are looking for, while its higher education achievement report recognises students' cocurricular achievements.

The campus is ten minutes by train from central London. It boasts a thriving music scene and a varied events programme includes recitals, exhibitions, public lectures and readings. The students' union has a strong tradition in volunteering and in recent years it has won several awards for its campaigning on ethical and environmental issues.

There are almost 1,500 rooms available in halls of residence, many of which are in New Cross, and all are within a 30-minute commute of the campus. Priority for places is given to international students and new undergraduates from outside the London area. There is a well-equipped and affordable gym on campus, but the sports pitches are half an hour away – and not a priority for many Goldsmiths' students.

Tuition fees

» Fees for UK/EU students 2019–20   £9,250
» Fees for International students 2018–19   £13,910–£20,590
» For scholarship and bursary information see
   www.gold.ac.uk/fees-funding
» Graduate salary   £20,000

Student numbers

Undergraduates	6,056	(138)
Postgraduates	2,083	(1,070)
Applications/places		12,085/2,090
Applications per place		5.8
Overall offer rate		76.9%
International students		24.8%

Accommodation

University provided places: 1,500 (catered 0%)
Self-catered: £118–£318 per week
www.gold.ac.uk/accommodation/

Where do the students come from?

State schools (non-grammar)	87.6%	Working-class homes	30.8%	Black ethnic minority	12.9%
Grammar schools	4.5%	Deprived areas	4.7%	Disabled	7.9%
Independent schools	7.9%	All ethnic minorities	47.2%	Mature (over 21)	24.3%

University of Greenwich

The £25m conversion of the historic Dreadnought building has brought together all Greenwich's main student services at the heart of the world heritage site that the university occupies on the banks of the Thames. It houses the students' union and academic and other support services, as well as flexible teaching and social spaces. An enclosed courtyard provides access to a cafe, gymnasium and basement bar.

The development, which follows the completion of projects on Greenwich's other campuses, may help build on last year's rise in satisfaction levels that has helped lift Greenwich back into our top 100. Applications have dropped by more than 20% in three years, but the numbers enrolling have held up well and average entry grades have risen. The university now has more than 22,000 students in the UK, with a further 15,500 taking its courses in 29 other countries.

Greenwich was placed in the silver category in the Teaching Excellence Framework (TEF), which takes account of the student profile in determining grades. The university is one of the most socially diverse in the country. Only five others take a higher proportion of undergraduates from the four poorest groups, while half come from ethnic minorities and more than 40% are older than 21 when they start degrees. There is a range of scholarships and bursaries, and those who do not qualify for them receive an Aspire@ Greenwich smart card worth £200 to spend on learning resources. The university ranks in the top 20 for social inclusion.

The TEF panel praised course design and assessment practices that stretch students and ensure most make progress with their education. It found that personalised provision secures good engagement and commitment to learning from most students, and that the university had invested in high-quality physical and digital resources to enhance learning. The prize-winning Stockwell Street development in Greenwich is one example. Designed partly by the university's own specialists in architecture, it includes 14 landscaped roof terraces and has a large architecture studio, a model-making workshop, and TV and sound studios, plus the main library and other facilities.

A new international college on the main campus, run jointly with a private company, will add to the 5,000 students from around the world by preparing others for entry to Greenwich degrees. There are two other sites, one of which is at Avery Hill, a Victorian mansion on the outskirts of southeast London, which is the base for education, health and the social sciences. It boasts a £14m sports and teaching centre and laboratories for health courses that replicate NHS wards. The campus

---

Maritime Greenwich Campus
Old Royal Naval College
Park Row
London SE10 9LS
020 8331 9000
courseinfo@gre.ac.uk
www.gre.ac.uk
www.greenwichsu.co.uk
Open days 2019:
June 29

The Times and The Sunday Times **Rankings**

Overall Ranking: 100 (last year: =109)

Teaching quality	78.8%	=82
Student experience	76.9%	=89
Research quality	4.9%	=94
Entry standards	135	60
Graduate prospects	70.3%	101
Good honours	74.1%	=62
Expected completion rate	80.9%	=103
Student/staff ratio	17.9	=102
Services and facilities	£2,203	=64

contains a student village of 1,300 rooms, alongside teaching accommodation.

At Chatham in Kent the Medway campus houses the schools of pharmacy, science and engineering, the Natural Resources Institute, as well as nursing and some business courses. The campus, which is shared with the University of Kent, also has a student hub in a listed building, with study spaces, plus a restaurant, bar and nightclub.

The university has increased its focus on graduate employability in recent years. It has almost trebled the number of undergraduates taking work placements and Greenwich is the only university in the country to have an on-campus strategic relationship with a recruitment firm. The service aims to place final-year undergraduates or recent graduates in full-time, graduate-level jobs that are suited to their skills, as well as finding them high-quality internships and other opportunities along the way.

The number of staff with an accredited teaching qualification has been increasing rapidly. Greenwich has a special programme to encourage innovation in its teaching and learning, designed to produce graduates who not only have good academic knowledge but also the skills sought by employers such as a high level of digital literacy, familiarity with new technology and expertise in social media.

The university has also been investing in research. The £18m annual income from research and consultancy is among the largest proportions at any post-1992 institution. More than 200 academics entered the 2014 Research Excellence Framework — a considerable increase on 2008 — and 42% of their work was placed in the top two categories.

Greenwich was in the top 20 in the 2017 People & Planet University League for environmental performance, partly credited to its progress towards a longstanding commitment to cut carbon emissions. Sports facilities are improving, with two all-weather pitches and medical facilities at the Avery Hill campus. Record numbers are also engaging with sports clubs and societies.

The university has also been expanding its residential stock. All new entrants who apply by August 23 are guaranteed accommodation, although those who apply by the end of June have priority for room selection.

Tuition fees

» Fees for UK/EU students 2019–20	£9,250
Foundation courses	£6,165
» Fees for International students 2019–20	£12,100–£13,950
» For scholarship and bursary information see www.gre.ac.uk/study/finance	
» Graduate salary	£22,500

Student numbers

Undergraduates	12,864 (2,680)
Postgraduates	1,483 (2,887)
Applications/places	27,665/3,455
Applications per place	8.0
Overall offer rate	77.2%
International students	18.5%

Accommodation

University provided places: 2,541 (catered 0%)
Self-catered: £114–£273 per week
First years guaranteed accommodation
www.gre.ac.uk/accommodation

Where do the students come from?

State schools (non-grammar)	92.5%	Working-class homes	54.0%	Black ethnic minority	20.4%
Grammar schools	4.6%	Deprived areas	9.1%	Disabled	4.7%
Independent schools	2.9%	All ethnic minorities	51.4%	Mature (over 21)	40.5%

Harper Adams University

Harper Adams is enjoying its third year as the highest-placed post-1992 university and holds a double gold award in the Teaching Excellence Framework (TEF), having earned one in both 2017 and last year. Institutions that had received their TEF rating in 2017 did not have to enter the process again, but the university felt it would be beneficial. Its vice-chancellor, David Llewellyn, explained: "We were keen to test our performance against the new TEF measures introduced this year, and to have achieved gold award again is therefore a significant achievement."

The specialist agricultural university's successes are yet to have an impact on applications or enrolments, however, both of which fell in 2017, in line with national figures for agriculture.

The university has set about expanding its portfolio of degrees. Three new zoology programmes took their first students this academic year and four degrees in applied biology — three of them in combination with agroecology, biotechnology or business management respectively — are on offer this year. Then, next year, Harper Adams hopes to launch a new veterinary school in partnership with Keele University.

Harper Adams was our Modern University of the Year in 2016 and continues to produce excellent results for student satisfaction, both in relation to teaching quality and the broader student experience, as well as registering one of the highest figures for spending on student services and facilities. There are more than 4,500 students, but little more than half of them are on campus at any one time. The rest are on placement years or accredited part-time programmes in industry.

The university is based on a single campus in the Shropshire countryside and already offers degrees in business, veterinary nursing and physiotherapy, land and property management, engineering and food studies, as well as agriculture. The institution's Delta project will see £700,000 invested in learning and teaching initiatives, including the provision of more elearning and the appointment of teaching fellows in each academic department to focus on the development of teaching practice.

Contrary to the stereotypes associated with its agricultural specialisms, the majority of entrants to degree courses — and an even bigger majority of the applicants — are female. About one undergraduate in six went to an independent school, but still almost half have a working-class background. The projected dropout rate of less than 5% is significantly less than the national average for the university's courses and entry qualifications.

Harper Adams has been upgrading its teaching and research facilities and is one

Edgmond
Newport
Shropshire TF10 8NB
01952 815 000
admissions@harper-adams.ac.uk
www.harper-adams.ac.uk
www.harpersu.com
Open days 2019:
see website

The Times and The Sunday Times Rankings
Overall Ranking: =33 (last year: 33)

Teaching quality	83.1%	=22
Student experience	81.6%	=18
Research quality	5.7%	86
Entry standards	128	=73
Graduate prospects	72.9%	=85
Good honours	66.2%	=110
Expected completion rate	90.3%	38
Student/staff ratio	15.7	=61
Services and facilities	£3,459	3

of a small number of locations where the government is funding centres for innovation as part of its national strategy for agricultural technologies. The university previously secured £5.7m for its hub of the Agricultural Engineering Precision Innovation Centre, which now houses its first industry partners, and the "smart dairy", which took its first cows last year.

Among the other innovative features is the Hands Free Hectare, where the university achieved a world first in growing and harvesting a crop without human hands touching it, as researchers automate agricultural technology. The project won the Future Food Prize at the BBC's Food and Farming Awards last June.

The project was among the research recognised in the award last year of a Queen's Anniversary prize for higher and further education. Harper Adams entered only 17 staff for the 2014 Research Excellence Framework — two fewer than in 2008 — but more than half of their work was considered to be internationally excellent or world-leading. There are links with four agricultural universities in China and, since last year, one in Holland.

The students' union, careers service and cafe are all under one roof at the heart of the campus, where open access computers allow students to work and socialise in the same area. The Bamford library holds one of the

largest specialist land-based collections in the UK, but the university's most prized feature is its 1,500-acre commercial farm, which includes the Ancellor Yard, a redevelopment of the original farm courtyard, the former home of Thomas Harper Adams, after whom the university is named. A further 239 acres neighbouring the existing estate were added to the farm last year.

There are more than 800 residential places on campus, with first-years taking priority in their allocation. A shuttle bus runs at key times of the day for students living in nearby Newport to get to the campus and there is free parking for students. Sports facilities include a gymnasium, shooting ground, heated outdoor swimming pool, rugby, cricket, football and hockey pitches, tennis courts and an all-weather sports pitch. There is a dance/fitness studio and even a 4x4 club – unlike most universities, cars are not discouraged here. A rowing club operates from nearby Shrewsbury. The social scene is strong despite the rural setting.

Tuition fees

» Fees for UK/EU students 2019–20	£9,250
» Fees for International students 2019–20	£10,600
» For scholarship and bursary information see www.harper-adams.ac.uk/apply/finance	
» Graduate salary	£21,000

Student numbers

Undergraduates	2,433	(2,523)
Postgraduates	103	(352)
Applications/places		2,715/595
Applications per place		4.6
Overall offer rate		72.9%
International students		4.1%

Accommodation

University provided places: 830 (catered 52%)
Catered costs: £104–£166 per week
Self-catered: £118–£126 per week
First years given priority for accommodation
www.harper-adams.ac.uk/university-life/accommodation

Where do the students come from?

State schools (non-grammar)	71.8%	Working-class homes	44.4%	Black ethnic minority	0%
Grammar schools	10.2%	Deprived areas	7.0%	Disabled	16.2%
Independent schools	18.0%	All ethnic minorities	0.8%	Mature (over 21)	14.8%

Heriot-Watt University

Heriot-Watt has been renewing the 1970s buildings on its main Riccarton campus on the outskirts of Edinburgh and adding new facilities. The second phase of the Learning Commons study space to complement the revamped library opened in 2017, and the Discovery and Innovation Centre will add collaborative learning spaces, teaching and enterprise areas, and more desk space in time for this year's entry. Further library refurbishment is under way.

Little more than a third of Heriot-Watt's 30,000 students are based at the Riccarton site, however. There are campuses in Dubai and Malaysia, and "collaborative partners" in 150 countries. Even a third of those studying in Scotland come from outside the country, making the university one of the most international in the UK. The Go Global programme invites undergraduates to split their studies between any or all of the university's bases, helping Heriot-Watt to become our first International University of the Year in 2017.

Heriot-Watt's recent success in our table (it is a regular in our top 40) is matched by a growing reputation globally. This year's world ranking of =302 in the annual QS World University Rankings is a new high and represents a rise of 67 places over the past six years.

At home, the university continues to pursue a commitment to practical, applied learning with close links to industry. It won the largest share of places in the Scottish government's graduate apprenticeships programme and expects to expand the range for this year's entry. The existing seven programmes cover engineering, design and management. New degrees include statistical data science, British sign language and Chinese, both with applied language studies.

The university traces its history back to 1821, when it was the world's first mechanics institute, and its name honours George Heriot and James Watt, two giants of industry and commerce. The current strategic plan stresses that the university's ambitions will require all academic staff to perform at internationally competitive levels of creativity in research, scholarship and teaching. The awards panel that placed the university in the silver category in the Teaching Excellence Framework complimented the institution on precisely this connection.

More than 80% of the work submitted for the 2014 Research Excellence Framework was rated as world-leading or internationally excellent, and Heriot-Watt was among the leaders in the UK in mathematics, general engineering and architecture, planning and the built environment, where it made joint submissions with the University of Edinburgh. Heriot-Watt features in the top 30 of our research ranking.

Edinburgh EH14 4AS
0131 451 3376
ugadmissions@hw.ac.uk
www.hw.ac.uk
www.hwunion.com
Open days 2019:
see website

The Times and The Sunday Times **Rankings**

Overall Ranking: =35 (last year: 39)

Teaching quality	75.8%	=111
Student experience	75.6%	=99
Research quality	36.7%	28
Entry standards	167	=20
Graduate prospects	79.3%	51
Good honours	76.8%	49
Expected completion rate	84.6%	=72
Student/staff ratio	16.7	=85
Services and facilities	£3,219	7

The £20m Lyell Centre is a main research facility for geological, petroleum and marine sciences, staffed by the university and the British Geological Survey, which has its Scottish headquarters there. The main campus also hosts Oriam, Scotland's national centre for performance in many sports, where world-class facilities are also available to students. The £33m complex features a Hampden Park replica pitch, outdoor synthetic and grass pitches, a nine-court sports hall, a 3G indoor pitch and a fitness suite, plus medical facilities.

The university also has two smaller campuses in Scotland. One in Orkney caters exclusively for postgraduates and specialises in renewable energy, while the Scottish Borders base in Galashiels, 35 miles south of Edinburgh, specialises in textiles, fashion and design, offering one of the few degrees in the world in menswear and the only course in Scotland in fashion communication. Heriot-Watt and Borders College share the merged campus to deliver higher and further education in a region that has been historically underprovided.

The Dubai campus opened 13 years ago and now has almost 4,000 students taking business, engineering, science and technology, or textiles and design courses. Numbers in the Gulf state are expected to rise further. The university's Arabic for beginners course took its first students there last year.

The purpose-built Malaysian campus, which had its first cohort in 2014, has space for up to 4,000 students to take degrees in science, engineering, business, mathematics and design. The £35m campus has a spectacular lakeside location in the administrative capital of Putrajaya, near Kuala Lumpur.

Nine out of ten undergraduates are from state schools and colleges, while more than a quarter come from working-class homes. The projected dropout rate has risen close to 9% in the latest survey, however, marginally higher than the UK average for the university's courses and entry qualifications.

There are separate scholarship and bursary schemes for Scottish students, those from the rest of the UK, and international students. The university also offers sports scholarships, and representative teams do well.

The Edinburgh halls of residence are conveniently placed and house more than 2,000 students. Regular bus services link the campus to the city centre and its wide range of nightlife and cultural events. Music thrives: there are a number of music scholarships and a professional director of music, as well as a varied programme of events.

Tuition fees

» Fees for Scottish/EU students 2019–20   £0–£1,820
   RUK fees   £9,250 (capped at £27,750 for 4-year courses)
» Fees for International students 2019–20   £14,640–£18,480
» For scholarship and bursary information see
   www.hw.ac.uk/study/fees-funding.htm
» Graduate salary   £24,500

Student numbers

Undergraduates	6,988	(427)
Postgraduates	1,984	(1,103)
Applications/places		11,450/1,920
Applications per place		6.0
Overall offer rate		90.6%
International students		29.4%

Accommodation

University provided places: 2,039 (catered 0%)
Self-catered: £112–£210 per week
First years guaranteed accommodation
www.hw.ac.uk/uk/edinburgh/accommodation.htm

Where do the students come from?

State schools (non-grammar)	78.8%	Working-class homes	26.1%	Black ethnic minority	3.1%
Grammar schools	8.4%	Deprived areas	6.3%	Disabled	5.1%
Independent schools	12.8%	All ethnic minorities	14.9%	Mature (over 21)	15.6%

University of Hertfordshire

Hertfordshire was one of six universities upgraded to gold in the Teaching Excellence Framework last year. The panel was impressed by a strong emphasis on work-based learning, entrepreneurship and enterprise, with employability and transferable skills embedded in the curriculum. There had been high levels of investment in physical and digital resources, the panel noted, and courses benefited from "vocationally informed pedagogy supported by the university's educational research network".

The original "business-facing university", Hertfordshire has embraced the concept of degree apprenticeships with enthusiasm. Each of the ten schools has been asked to develop new programmes to complement the 13 now being offered. The university hopes to have more than 400 apprentices in September this year, compared with 48 last April. The new offerings will include programmes for chartered town planners, laboratory scientists, art therapists and social workers.

Hertfordshire's portfolio of traditional degrees is also expanding. New choices include digital media design, physical activity and sports development, regulatory science and sports business management. Previous additions have included architecture, pharmacy and a four-year undergraduate optometry

masters programme, while the university's degree in paramedic science was Britain's first.

Another development this year will see the introduction of the Go Herts award, which was praised by the TEF panel for its links with degree programmes. Until now, the scheme has been restricted to final-year undergraduates, but it is to become available to all students to enable them to receive formal recognition for extracurricular activities. Most courses offer work placements and study abroad.

Hertfordshire's three sites include the £120m purpose-built campus close to the original Hatfield headquarters. The de Havilland and College Lane campuses are linked by cycle ways, footpaths and free shuttle buses, with the former named after the aircraft manufacturer which once occupied the site. Based on student feedback, the university has spent £300,000 on new quiet zones in its learning resource centres on both campuses, study rooms and small study pods in the library.

The Hutton Hub on the College Lane site houses the students' union, a counselling centre, a pharmacy, banking facilities and a juice bar. The campus contains a £50m science building, an art gallery in the media centre and the £38m Forum with its three entertainment spaces, a restaurant, cafe and multiple bars. The Automotive Centre on College Lane delivers up-to-date engineering teaching and many Formula One teams are staffed by at least one Hertfordshire graduate.

College Lane
Hatfield AL10 9AB
01707 284 800
ask@herts.ac.uk
www.herts.ac.uk
www.hertfordshire.su
Open days 2019:
March 16; June 15

The Times and The Sunday Times **Rankings**
Overall Ranking: 90 (last year: 89)

Teaching quality	80.1%	64
Student experience	79.0%	=58
Research quality	5.6%	=87
Entry standards	119	=100
Graduate prospects	80.6%	=44
Good honours	65.9%	=113
Expected completion rate	81.7%	96
Student/staff ratio	17.9	=102
Services and facilities	£2,439	40

The university's third campus at Bayfordbury is home to one of the UK's largest teaching observatories, equipped with seven large optical individually-housed telescopes, four radio telescopes and a high-definition planetarium. There is also a field centre for life and medical sciences.

More than half of the academic staff hold a teaching qualification and over 85% of single honours students leave with a degree that has professional accreditation or approval. The focus on individual development reflects in high scores in that section of the National Student Survey.

The university plays an important role in the regional economy. It runs seven subsidiary companies, including the independent Uno regional bus service which has expanded to run urban bus networks in St Albans and Northampton, as well as routes between Milton Keynes, Bedford and Flitwick for Cranfield University.

More than 40% of undergraduates came from lower socioeconomic groups the last time this was surveyed. The projected dropout rate had been improving but is back above 13% — higher than the national average for the university's subjects and entry grades.

In the 2014 Research Excellence Framework, more than half of Hertfordshire's work was placed in one of the top two categories. The best results were in history, where 45% of the submission was judged to be world-leading and all of it was given the top grade for its external impact.

A new virtual learning environment has been introduced in the current academic year with the Canvas app. It includes reading lists, with help and guidance to plan work, as well as personalised notifications and instant updates about activities. More than 400 different software applications are available for student use, including a Microsoft Office 365 account for the duration of their time at Hertfordshire.

The £15m Hertfordshire Sports Village includes a 110-station health and fitness centre, 25-metre pool, physiotherapy and sports injury clinic and a large, multipurpose sports hall. The university has more than 4,700 study bedrooms on its books, having added 2,500 residential places since 2015 and refurbished 500 more. It is part of Hertfordshire's ten-year plan to provide a "distinctive campus experience for students, staff and visitors, in which the dynamism of the university is embodied in its physical estate."

Tuition fees

» Fees for UK/EU students 2019–20	£9,250
Foundation courses	£6,165
» Fees for International students 2019–20	£11,950
» For scholarship and bursary information see www.herts.ac.uk/apply/fees-and-funding	
» Graduate salary	£22,000

Student numbers

Undergraduates	16,042 (2,873)
Postgraduates	1,625 (4,038)
Applications/places	26,060/4,125
Applications per place	6.3
Overall offer rate	79.0%
International students	14.8%

Accommodation

University provided places: 4,711 (catered 0%)
Self-catered: £110–£187 per week
www.herts.ac.uk/life/student-accommodation

Where do the students come from?

State schools (non-grammar)	94.9%	Working-class homes	42.5%	Black ethnic minority	22.1%
Grammar schools	2.7%	Deprived areas	7.9%	Disabled	5.3%
Independent schools	2.4%	All ethnic minorities	56.4%	Mature (over 21)	23.2%

University of the Highlands and Islands

The University of the Highlands and Islands (UHI) does not appear in our league table because its dispersed campuses, high proportion of further education students and large numbers of part-time staff make it difficult to compare with more traditional institutions. The university is a federation of 13 colleges and research institutions spread across hundreds of miles in the Scottish Highlands and islands, with more than 70 local learning centres.

The demand for places at degree level continues to grow by leaps and bounds. Applications have risen for nine years in a row, including last year, when demand dropped at most universities, and have doubled in the past four years. The intake of new undergraduates has grown by more than a third in the current decade. More than half of them are over 21 at the start of their course.

The addition of nursing to the portfolio of degrees has helped to fuel the university's expansion, as has its growth in teacher training. UHI has taken over the pre-registration programmes in mental health nursing and adult nursing previously delivered by the University of Stirling, adding 40 staff and 300 students. It has also announced plans to develop a degree in optometry, backed by funding from the Federation of (Ophthalmic and Dispensing) Opticians Educational Trust.

A £19m health, social care and life sciences school was established last year with the aim of further extending UHI's work in these areas. This will include collaboration with the University of Dundee and University of St Andrews on the development of Scotland's first graduate entry medical programme (ScotGem) to enhance remote and rural training and the supply of primary care clinicians (general practitioners).

UHI's colleges spread from Dunoon in western Scotland to the village of Scalloway, the ancient capital of the Shetland Islands, in the north. The university's network of campuses is much wider, however. Argyll College, for example, has 13 sites on the mainland and on islands such as Arran, Islay and Mull. Courses are also taught at more than 50 learning centres. Some colleges are relatively large and located in urban centres such as Perth, Elgin and Inverness, while others are smaller institutions, including some whose primary focus is research. The university insists, however, that all have a student-centred culture.

Several of the institutions are in spectacular locations. Lews Castle College UHI in Stornoway in the Outer Hebrides, for example, is set in 600 acres of parkland and claims "possibly the UK's most attractive location to study art" for its harbourside

Executive Office
12b Ness Walk
Inverness IV3 5SQ
0845 272 3600
info@uhi.ac.uk
www.uhi.ac.uk
www.hisa.uhi.ac.uk
Open days 2019:
see website

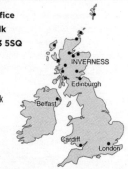

The Times and The Sunday Times Rankings
Overall Ranking: n/a
No data available

Lochmaddy campus in North Uist. Sabhal Mor Ostaig UHI is the only Gaelic-medium college in the world, set in breathtaking scenery on the Isle of Skye, and the Highland Theological College UHI is in Dingwall.

West Highland College UHI does not even have a central campus, although its degree in adventure tourism management is taught in Fort William, close to Ben Nevis. North Highland College UHI has an equestrian centre in Caithness, six miles from the main campus in Thurso, with international-sized outdoor and indoor arenas.

Three quarters of the students are drawn from the Highlands and islands. But the university has begun to attract greater numbers from the rest of Scotland, other parts of the UK and overseas. It has been adding residential places accordingly, and now has more than 600 rooms in nine colleges. Teaching is increasingly through "blended" learning, combining online and face-to-face tuition with small class sizes and extensive use of video conferencing.

The university has one accelerated degree in geography, taught over three years rather than the usual four, but has not so far extended the option to other subjects. New degrees have been launched in archaeological science and food, nutrition and textiles education, with more planned for this year in aircraft maintenance and management, and theatre and festival studies.

There are now nearly 9,000 higher education students and 30,000 taking further education courses. Some undergraduate courses are taught completely online and many offer the opportunity to study entirely in Gaelic. The university was the first in Scotland to produce a Gaelic Language Plan in 2010. A third edition, published last year, included proposals to enhance the Gaelic curriculum, produce more bilingual resources for students, provide training opportunities for employees and increase the amount of Gaelic in marketing and communication materials.

There are a dozen specialist research facilities and an enterprise and research centre on the Inverness campus. They helped to produce some extremely good results in the 2014 Research Excellence Framework. Almost 70% of the research submitted for review was classified as world-leading or internationally excellent.

Tuition fees

- » Fees for Scottish/EU students 2019–20   £0–£1,820
  RUK fees   £9,000 (capped at £27,000 for 4-year courses)
- » Fees for International students 2018–19   £11,100–£12,200
- » For scholarship and bursary information see
  www.uhi.ac.uk/en/studying-at-uhi/first-steps/
  how-much-will-it-cost/funding-your-studies/
  bursaries-and-scholarships
- » Graduate salary   £19,000

Student numbers

Undergraduates	5,253	(2,801)
Postgraduates	217	(448)
Applications/places	4,280/990	
Applications per place	4.3	
Overall offer rate	73.9%	
International students	3.4%	

Accommodation

University provided places: 628 (catered 0%)
Self-catered: £85–£131 per week
www.uhi.ac.uk/en/studying-at-uhi/first-steps/accommodation/

Where do the students come from?

State schools (non-grammar)	96.1%	Working-class homes	46.2%	Black ethnic minority	0.7%
Grammar schools	0%	Deprived areas	6.8%	Disabled	4.4%
Independent schools	3.9%	All ethnic minorities	3.3%	Mature (over 21)	45.4%

University of Huddersfield

Huddersfield has a gold award in the Teaching Excellence Framework (TEF) and continues its rise up our league table. It also had the distinction of topping the first Global Teaching Excellence awards in 2017 after leading educationists chose Huddersfield ahead of 26 other finalists from around the world.

The TEF panel complimented the university on the way that the effective use of learning analytics allowed targeted and timely interventions to boost students' results. It also commended an institution-wide strategy for assessment and feedback, which ensures that all students are challenged to achieve their full potential.

Huddersfield is reaping dividends for its unwavering focus on teaching standards, which includes a commitment to ensuring that its lecturers are the best-qualified in the UK. Two thirds of its academics hold doctorates and the proportion with a postgraduate teaching qualification is the highest at any university. Seminars, as well as lectures, are filmed so that students can revisit the content later online, while a new virtual learning environment will help to tailor students' learning experience by monitoring their performance.

The university's successes are just beginning to be reflected in admissions. The numbers starting degrees rose for the first time in three years in 2017 and applications have stabilised, while most universities saw a decline. A raft of new degrees will give applicants greater choice. New offerings this year will include computer games development, medical engineering technologies, public health, and English language with either sociology, politics or criminology.

Huddersfield has also been acting to improve graduate employment rates. Every undergraduate does some work experience as part of their degree course and a third take extended placements in business or industry, putting the university in the top ten on this measure. Many students now develop their own businesses for the work placement component of their course, taking advantage of the advice and facilities available at the university's Duke of York Young Entrepreneur Centre. Seven out of ten students leave with a professional qualification.

The university is investing heavily in teaching and research facilities and is redeveloping a former industrial site and neighbouring land into a new western campus. A £30m home for the study of art, design and architecture is due to open this year. It is to be named after Barbara Hepworth, the West Yorkshire-born sculptor, and its main frontage overlooks Huddersfield Narrow Canal, which runs through the heart of the Queensgate campus.

Another £30m is being spent on science facilities, which will also be ready in time

Queensgate
Huddersfield HD1 3DH
01484 473 969
study@hud.ac.uk
www.hud.ac.uk
www.huddersfield.su
Open days 2019:
see website

The Times and The Sunday Times Rankings		
Overall Ranking: 62 (last year: 65)		
Teaching quality	81.4%	=44
Student experience	78.6%	64
Research quality	9.4%	62
Entry standards	129	=70
Graduate prospects	80.0%	48
Good honours	74.4%	61
Expected completion rate	82.5%	92
Student/staff ratio	17.0	=92
Services and facilities	£2,234	61

for new arrivals this year. They will include a laboratory for sixth-formers and college students to carry out practical work in areas such as DNA analysis, microbiology, chemical synthesis and forensics.

Huddersfield has always been one of the most successful universities at widening participation in higher education. Approaching half of the full-time undergraduates are from working-class homes and many come from areas without a tradition of higher education. It ranks just outside our top 30 for social diversity.

The dropout rate has been improving, and the latest projection of less than 11% is better than the national benchmark.

The prize-winning Flying Start scheme helps all new undergraduates find their feet. It consists of a two-week timetable of special sessions designed to stimulate academic interest, develop good study habits and provide opportunities for students to work and engage socially. Students take part in quizzes and debates, subject-based film clubs, lab skills workshops, campus orienteering and trips, as well as meeting successful alumni and discussing their career goals.

Some of the most successful areas in the 2014 Research Excellence Framework were in the arts and social sciences. Huddersfield did well overall, entering almost a third of its academics for assessment and seeing nearly 60% of its work rated world-leading or internationally excellent. There were particularly good results in music, drama and performing arts, as well as in English, social work and social policy.

The university does not own its own accommodation, but its preferred provider has enough places — more than 1,600 — to guarantee a room to new entrants. Most are in the Storthes Hall Park student village, with additional residences available at Ashenhurst Houses, about a mile from the campus. The Student Central building has a good range of sports facilities, including an 80-plus-station gym, and the town's leisure centre is within ten minutes' walk of the campus. Town-gown relations are good, although students tend to base their social life around the union's amenities. Leeds and Manchester are easily reached by public transport.

Tuition fees

» Fees for UK/EU students 2019–20 £9,250
» Fees for International students 2019–20 £14,000–£17,400
» For scholarship and bursary information see www.hud.ac.uk/undergraduate/fees-and-finance
» Graduate salary £20,000

Student numbers

Undergraduates	12,878 (1,304)
Postgraduates	1,801 (2,298)
Applications/places	17,765/3,245
Applications per place	5.5
Overall offer rate	84.5%
International students	16.3%

Accommodation

University provided places: 1,666 (catered 0%)
Self-catered: £85–£110 per week
First years guaranteed accommodation
www.hud.ac.uk/uni-life/accommodation

Where do the students come from?

State schools (non-grammar)	96.0%	Working-class homes	46.2%	Black ethnic minority	5.2%
Grammar schools	3.0%	Deprived areas	17.2%	Disabled	8.7%
Independent schools	1.0%	All ethnic minorities	36.2%	Mature (over 21)	21.4%

University of Hull

Hull has been slipping down our league table and has now fallen out of our top 100 for the first time, making it the lowest ranked of the pre-1992 universities. It was one of two universities that applied without success last year to have a silver award in the Teaching Excellence Framework (TEF) upgraded.

The university argued that initiatives such as its Curriculum 2016+ strategy for teaching and learning were improving the student experience but were too recent to be reflected in the data considered in the TEF. The panel praised Hull's course design and assessment practices for stretching and challenging students, and was impressed by its investment in physical and digital infrastructure — but it still did not award the institution a gold rating.

Applications fell by more than 10% in 2017, but the university will hope that a £300m transformation of the campus and the positive impact of Hull's year as the UK city of culture will boost demand in future. The latest addition is the £25m Allam medical building, where medical students work alongside nursing, midwifery and allied health undergraduates, as well as PhD students, advanced nurse practitioners and physician associates. A simulated learning environment enables students to train in a realistic setting in order to make the transition effectively into clinical practice.

Other elements of the campus development plan have seen industry-standard recording and performance facilities installed in the redeveloped Middleton Hall, while a £28m upgrading of the Brynmor Jones library has added an art gallery and provided the centrepiece for the university. A £16m investment in sports facilities will include a 12-court sports hall, 120-station fitness suite and floodlit 3G pitches, as well as a fitness and conditioning suite. To provide more accommodation, a £130m project will see the University Partnerships Programme provide another 1,450 residential places.

More than a third of the undergraduates are local, while one in five comes from an area of low participation in higher education — many more than average for Hull's courses and entry qualifications. The university expects 45% of undergraduates to qualify for a bursary or scholarship. These include merit scholarships of £2,000 in the first year for students, regardless of income, who manage at least 120 points on the UCAS tariff, while those with 152 points receive £1,000 in subsequent years as well.

The Curriculum 2016+ programme has sought to develop a distinctive "vision for teaching and learning", integrating teaching skills with subject knowledge and technology to produce highly employable graduates. An audit three years ago by the Quality Assurance Agency made Hull one of the few

Cottingham Road
Hull HU6 7RX
01482 466 100
admission@hull.ac.uk
www.hull.ac.uk
www.hullstudent.com
Open days 2019:
see website

The Times and The Sunday Times **Rankings**
Overall Ranking: =103 (last year: =75)

Teaching quality	78.5%	=89
Student experience	75.8%	98
Research quality	16.7%	55
Entry standards	123	=88
Graduate prospects	76.0%	=66
Good honours	67.3%	=104
Expected completion rate	82.2%	=93
Student/staff ratio	18.3	108
Services and facilities	£2,153	76

universities in the latest round of reviews to receive a commendation for enhancing learning opportunities.

There is also a focus on employability, which includes the option of a 20-credit module on career management skills. The careers service approaches undergraduates early in their time at Hull and sets up meetings with potential employers. The Enterprise Centre has a successful record with those who would rather start their own businesses.

Hull is trebling the number of degree apprenticeship programmes it offers, focusing on the skills needs of the Humber region. Places are planned to grow from 80 to 300 by September this year, with the addition of new programmes in digital skills, health and engineering.

A longstanding focus on Europe shows in the wide range of languages available at degree level, with the purpose-built language institute heavily used by students regardless of subject. Hull's strength in politics is reflected in a steady flow of graduates into the House of Commons. The Westminster-Hull internship programme offers a year-long placement for British politics and legislative studies students.

More than 60% of the work entered for the 2014 Research Excellence Framework was rated as world-leading or internationally excellent, although Hull made a relatively small submission for a pre-1992 university. The best results were in the allied health category, where 87% of the research was awarded three or four stars, while geography and computer science also did well. Hull won a Queen's Anniversary prize for its research into slavery and played a key role in shaping the UK's Modern Slavery Act.

Another new project will focus on low-carbon energy and clean growth. The Aura Innovation Centre is under construction at Bridgehead Business Park, in Hessle, and is expected to be completed by the end of 2019, providing large businesses and SMEs with the space to collaborate with university researchers on energy projects.

The modest cost of living and ready availability of accommodation adds to Hull's attractions. The city now has plenty of student-orientated nightlife and is less than an hour from Leeds by train. About a quarter of the students stay in Hull or the surrounding area after they graduate.

Tuition fees

- » Fees for UK/EU students 2019–20 £9,250
  Foundation courses £7,195
- » Fees for International students 2019–20 £14,000–£16,600
  Medicine £33,000
- » For scholarship and bursary information see www.hull.ac.uk/money
- » Graduate salary £21,500

Student numbers

Undergraduates	12,196 (1,404)
Postgraduates	1,629 (1,303)
Applications/places	14,520/2,930
Applications per place	5.0
Overall offer rate	89.8%
International students	13.9%

Accommodation

University provided places: 2,853 (catered 11%)
Catered costs: £119–£147 per week
Self-catered: £64–£186 per week
First years guaranteed accommodation
www.hull.ac.uk/choose-hull/student-life/accommodation/accommodation.aspx

Where do the students come from?

State schools (non-grammar)	89.5%	Working-class homes	33.2%	Black ethnic minority	4.9%
Grammar schools	4.8%	Deprived areas	26.5%	Disabled	6.0%
Independent schools	5.7%	All ethnic minorities	14.3%	Mature (over 21)	25.7%

Imperial College London

Imperial's new 23-acre campus is taking shape in White City, west London, where a community of research-focused businesses is in place at the Translation & Innovation Hub (I-HUB). Researchers from the department of chemistry have also moved into the Molecular Sciences Research Hub. The full development will cost a total of £3bn.

The project demonstrates the scale of Imperial's ambitions to produce, in the words of the president, Professor Alice Gast, "a new paradigm of the global university". Imperial has never been out of the top five in our league table and features in the top ten of both the QS and Times Higher Education world rankings. It was named by Reuters as the second most innovative university in Europe.

Applications went up for the sixth year in a row, at a time when they have been falling elsewhere. Over the whole period, only 500 more undergraduate places have been added for an additional 7,000 applicants. Only Cambridge has higher entry standards and fewer than four applicants out of ten receive an offer. Gaining a place here through clearing is not an option either because Imperial has not followed the trend at other Russell Group universities of filling some places after A-level results are published.

Imperial won a gold award in the government's Teaching Excellence Framework (TEF), with the panel praising an "exceptionally stimulating and stretching academic, vocational and professional education that successfully challenges students to achieve their full potential".

This success followed even greater plaudits in the 2014 Research Excellence Framework, when Imperial's research was found to have greater impact on the economy and society than that of any other university. Ninety per cent of Imperial's research was rated as world-leading or internationally excellent overall, a performance bettered only by Cambridge.

Imperial now has nine sites in London, due mainly to the expansion of its activities in medicine in the 1990s. The faculty of medicine is one of Europe's largest in terms of its staff and student numbers, as well as its research income. There are teaching bases attached to a number of hospitals in central and west London, while the UK's first Academic Health Science Centre (AHSC), run in partnership with Imperial College Healthcare NHS Trust, aims to translate research advances into patient care. The centre is one of just six accredited in England, and the largest in Europe. In its first overseas venture, Imperial became a partner last year in a new medical school in Singapore, run jointly with Nanyang Technological University.

The growing business school is Imperial's main venture beyond the world of science and

South Kensington Campus
Exhibition Road
London SW7 2AZ
020 7589 5111
www.imperial.ac.uk/study/ug/apply/contact
www.imperial.ac.uk
www.imperialcollegeunion.org
Open days 2019:
see website

Edinburgh
Belfast
Cardiff
LONDON

The Times and The Sunday Times Rankings
Overall Ranking: 4 (last year: 4)

Teaching quality	75.1%	116
Student experience	78.8%	=61
Research quality	56.2%	2
Entry standards	219	2
Graduate prospects	90.4%	2
Good honours	90.2%	5
Expected completion rate	96.6%	3
Student/staff ratio	11.4	5
Services and facilities	£3,656	2

technology. It is highly rated and is accredited by the three largest and most influential business school accreditation associations worldwide.

Undergraduates in most subjects are based at the original South Kensington campus, which includes the Dyson School of Design Engineering, funded through a £12m donation from the James Dyson Foundation. Imperial is unique in the UK for providing teaching and research in the full range of engineering disciplines. Indeed, it describes itself as the only university in the UK to focus exclusively on science, medicine, engineering and business.

More than a third of the undergraduates are from independent schools — one of the highest proportions at any university and considerably more than the benchmark calculated by the Higher Education Statistics Agency. With another 23.6% drawn from grammar schools, only four out of ten UK undergraduates went to comprehensives.

The Imperial Bursary scheme provides support on a sliding scale for UK undergraduates with annual household incomes of up to £60,000, starting at £2,000 a year for incomes above £55,000 and rising to £5,000 where income is below £16,000 a year. Four out of ten undergraduates qualified for some support. More than a third of the entrants are female – a proportion that has risen steadily over recent years.

The students' union claims to have one of the largest selections of clubs and societies

in the country. Imperial is London's top sporting university, on the basis of results in the British Universities and Colleges Sports leagues. Outdoor sports facilities are remote, but a well-equipped campus sports centre that attracts professional teams offers free gym and swimming facilities, on payment of an initial joining fee.

Recent developments on the main campus near the South Kensington museums have included a second residential complex and refurbishments to the central library, as well as improvements to the students' union bar and nightclub. New entrants are guaranteed one of the 2,500 residential places, as long as they apply by the deadline. The university's Central Library has recently been refurbished.

Tuition fees

» Fees for UK/EU students 2019–20	£9,250
» Fees for International students 2019–20	£28,000–£31,000
Medicine	£41,000
» For scholarship and bursary information see	
www.imperial.ac.uk/study/ug/fees-and-funding	
» Graduate salary	£30,000

Student numbers

Undergraduates	9,522	(0)
Postgraduates	6,828	(1,339)
Applications/places	20,395/2,705	
Applications per place	7.5	
Overall offer rate	43.6%	
International students	50.3%	

Accommodation

University provided places: 2,500 (catered 0%)
Self-catered: £100–£274 per week
First years guaranteed accommodation
www.imperial.ac.uk/study/campus-life/accommodation/halls/

Where do the students come from?

State schools (non-grammar)	39.9%	Working-class homes	16.2%	Black ethnic minority	5.1%
Grammar schools	23.6%	Deprived areas	3.5%	Disabled	4.1%
Independent schools	36.5%	All ethnic minorities	47.8%	Mature (over 21)	11.5%

Keele University

The New Keele Deal, launched in 2017, will see the university, with public and private sector partners, invest £70m in business support programmes to boost the local economy and provide opportunities for students and graduates. A new facility to house the Keele Management School and incubated companies in a sector-leading smart innovation hub has been announced as part of the plan.

The new projects are research-led and welcomed by ministers, but Keele has won even greater plaudits for its teaching. Placing the university in the coveted gold category in the Teaching Excellence Framework (TEF), the awarding panel said there was an institutional culture that "demonstrably values teaching as highly as research", with outstanding levels of student engagement and excellent teaching and assessment practices resulting in a commitment to learning.

Keele is now spending £45m on new and upgraded science facilities, in the biggest single investment in learning and teaching in the university's history. The scheme, which includes a new Central Science Laboratories building on the campus, will be completed by summer this year, underpinning ambitious plans for growth in science and research.

In all, the university is aiming to grow by a third over five years, with postgraduates accounting for many of the new places. The numbers starting first degrees rose by 25% in two years, despite falling applications, but have since slipped back. More than a dozen new degrees took their first students last year, paving the way for growth to restart as the 18-year-old population begins to increase again. The latest offerings include more degrees in business and management, as well as others in physics, pharmacy and forensic science.

The Distinctive Keele Curriculum, introduced as the university celebrated its 50th anniversary in 2012, attracted particular praise in the TEF assessment. It covers voluntary and sporting activities, as well as the academic core, and is the only one in the UK that can lead to accreditation by the Institute of Leadership and Management.

The university's student charter identifies ten "graduate attributes" that include independent thinking, synthesising information, creative problem solving, communicating clearly, and appreciating the social, environmental and global implications of all studies and activities.

The university has also been at the forefront of moves to record in more detail what graduates have achieved through a Higher Education Achievement Report. It has generally been among the leaders on student satisfaction, this year ranking in the top 20 in the UK for satisfaction with teaching quality

Keele ST5 5BG
01782 734 010
sadmissions@keele.ac.uk
www.keele.ac.uk
www.keelesu.com
Open days 2019:
see website

The Times and The Sunday Times Rankings
Overall Ranking: =48 (last year: 50)

Teaching quality	83.3%	=19
Student experience	83.4%	6
Research quality	22.1%	54
Entry standards	128	=73
Graduate prospects	82.1%	=27
Good honours	71.4%	79
Expected completion rate	89.6%	40
Student/staff ratio	14.2	28
Services and facilities	£1,962	90

and sixth for the wider student experience enjoyed by undergraduates.

Nearly all undergraduates have the option of spending a semester abroad at one of the university's partner institutions. Nine out of ten undergraduates are state educated, but the university has been trying to broaden its intake further by offering special projects and masterclasses in local schools and bursaries for students from low-income families.

There is also an Excellence Scholarship, worth £1,000 in cash, paid to students who achieve the highest grades at A-level (or the equivalent), regardless of household income. The projected dropout rate of 6.4% is well below the national average for the university's subjects and entry qualifications.

Keele has the largest campus in the country, 600 acres of parkland in the heart of England, near Stoke. More than £115m has been spent on it since the turn of the century. A new hall of residence opened last year, the first of a series planned across the campus. A third of all undergraduates, as well as many postgraduates and even some staff, live on a campus that includes an arboretum and has won a clutch of environmental awards. Students can grow their own fruit and vegetables on campus, and all undergraduates can take a module in sustainability or environmental studies.

The university's results in the 2014 Research Excellence Framework showed considerable improvement on the 2008 assessments. More than 70% of the work submitted was placed in the top two categories, with researchers in primary care and health sciences, pharmacy, chemistry, science and technology, the life sciences, and history scoring particularly well.

The students' union, which recently underwent a £2.7m upgrade, organises entertainment on campus every night of the week during term time. It won the Best Bar None Gold Award, for responsible drinking and a safe environment, for six years in a row. Sports facilities include a full-size 3G football pitch suitable for all-weather play in a variety of sports to supplement the indoor facilities.

The university is within an hour's drive of Manchester and Birmingham. For those who live off campus, the cost of living in the Potteries and the surrounding area is relatively low.

Tuition fees

» Fees for Scottish/EU students 2019–20   £9,250
» Fees for International students 2019–20   £14,320–£24,000
   Medicine   £32,000
» For scholarship and bursary information see
   www.keele.ac.uk/studentfunding/tuitionfees
» Graduate salary   £21,500

Student numbers

Undergraduates	7,669	(730)
Postgraduates	697	(1,503)
Applications/places	14,510/1,880	
Applications per place	7.7	
Overall offer rate	81.6%	
International students	11.7%	

Accommodation

University provided places: 2,800 (catered 0%)
Self-catered: £89–£159 per week
www.keele.ac.uk/discover/accommodation/

Where do the students come from?

State schools (non-grammar)	83.0%	Working-class homes	32.1%	Black ethnic minority	8.0%
Grammar schools	9.2%	Deprived areas	17.5%	Disabled	7.4%
Independent schools	7.8%	All ethnic minorities	32.4%	Mature (over 21)	13.0%

University of Kent

Kent's impressive progress up our league table has come to an abrupt halt in the past two years with the university falling 32 places in that time, from a high point of 23rd in 2016, when it was shortlisted for University of the Year. A collapse in student satisfaction is the most obvious reason for the subsequent fall with the university now lying outside the top 100 for student satisfaction with teaching quality.

The sudden decline is at odds with other evidence and features of this 1960s-generation university. Kent is one of a handful of universities in the UK to operate a college system, and this was one of the features contributing to a gold rating in the Teaching Excellence Framework (TEF). The panel saw the system as a vital element underpinning a "flexible and personalised" approach to academic support. There was also praise for Kent's "outstanding" Student Success Project, which identifies trends in results and completion rates, and acts to help those likely to fall behind, as well as for the systematic approach to embedding employability in the curriculum and providing employment placements for large numbers of students.

Every student is attached to a college, although they do not select it themselves. Colleges act as the focus of social life — especially in the first year — and include academic as well as residential facilities. Since the addition of the 800-bed Turing College in 2015, there have been six colleges in Canterbury and one on the university's Medway campus.

Almost 20 new courses took their first students last year, most of them including a placement year or a year abroad. They include astronomy, space science and astrophysics, positive behaviour support, autism studies and global philosophies. Another eight are planned to start in September, including business psychology, human geography and three new pharmacology degrees.

Kent's original low-rise campus, in 300 acres of parkland overlooking Canterbury, is seeing considerable development. A new building for the School of Mathematics and the Kent Business School opened in 2017. It was followed by a £3m hub in the Park Wood student village, which includes a shop, cafe/bar and dance studios, in response to requests from students for more social, study and activity space there.

The popular School of Economics, which is so oversubscribed that it raised its entry requirements last year, will be housed in a new building in time for the next intake of students. Canterbury will also be the base for the new Kent and Medway Medical School, a collaboration with Canterbury Christ Church University, which will take its first students in 2020. This is one of five new English medical schools announced last year.

Canterbury CT2 7NZ
01227 827 272
information@kent.ac.uk
www.kent.ac.uk
www.kentunion.co.uk
Open days 2019:
see website

The Times and The Sunday Times **Rankings**

Overall Ranking: 55 (last year: 31)

Teaching quality	77.2%	=103
Student experience	77.0%	=86
Research quality	35.2%	33
Entry standards	138	=55
Graduate prospects	78.3%	55
Good honours	78.5%	44
Expected completion rate	88.3%	46
Student/staff ratio	18.4	=109
Services and facilities	£1,762	111

Kent shares the Medway campus, at the old Chatham naval base, with the universities of Greenwich and Canterbury Christ Church. The site houses the university's business school and the £50m School of Pharmacy, which now has more than 2,000 Kent students. A purpose-built Centre for Music and Audio Technology has also opened there and will accommodate three of the new degrees.

Medway has more than 1,000 residential places and its grade II listed former swimming baths was converted into a student hub that incorporates the students' union, bar and other social spaces. The university also has a base in Tonbridge, mainly for short courses which can be a preparation for degree-level study.

Making the most of its location, Kent is perhaps the UK's most active university in Europe, both in terms of its participation in EU programmes and in its continental ventures. Styling itself "the UK's European university", Kent has postgraduate sites in Brussels, Paris, Athens and Rome, as well as giving many undergraduates the option of a year abroad. Almost 40% of the academic staff are EU nationals and there are partnerships with over 100 European universities.

Almost three quarters of the work submitted for the Research Excellence Framework was judged world-leading or internationally excellent. The successes, led by social work and social policy, music and drama, and modern languages, helped Kent to its highest-ever ranking on this measure.

The university exceeds its benchmarks for widening access to higher education. About 750 students benefit from the Kent Financial Support Package, which is worth £1,500 a year to state-educated students whose household income is below £42,875, if they meet other criteria, such as living in social housing.

Kent is one of the best-provided universities for accommodation, with almost 5,400 places in Canterbury alone. The student centre has a nightclub large enough to attract big-name bands, as well as a theatre, cinema and bars. Some students find both Canterbury and Medway limited in social terms, but campus security is good and the sports facilities include a £4.8m fitness suite, multipurpose fitness and dance studio, and an indoor tennis centre alongside the sports centre in Canterbury. The university is also a partner in the Medway Park sports centre, which has gym and swimming facilities.

Tuition fees

- » Fees for UK/EU students 2019–20 £9,250
- » Fees for International students 2019–20 £15,700–£19,000
- » For scholarship and bursary information see www.kent.ac.uk/finance-student/fees/index.htm
- » Graduate salary £21,000

Student numbers

Undergraduates	15,154	(578)
Postgraduates	2,911	(1,577)
Applications/places	28,655/4,445	
Applications per place	6.4	
Overall offer rate	89.0%	
International students	23.8%	

Accommodation

University provided places: 6,490 (catered 12%)
Catered costs: £119–£183 per week
Self-catered: £115–£186 per week
First years guaranteed accommodation
www.kent.ac.uk/accommodation/

Where do the students come from?

State schools (non-grammar)	91.0%	Working-class homes	32.5%	Black ethnic minority	15.8%
Grammar schools	2.4%	Deprived areas	10.5%	Disabled	8.1%
Independent schools	6.6%	All ethnic minorities	35.1%	Mature (over 21)	9.5%

King's College London

A decade ago, King's was on the verge of the top ten in our league table, but in the latest edition it has dropped out of the top 30 for the first time. It is placed higher in the QS World University Rankings, which are driven mainly by research and academic reputation.

The main reason for the decline of seven places overall in our table is a drop in the completion rate. But the root cause of its problems in national rankings is a consistently low level of student satisfaction. King's is in the bottom seven in both of the measures (teaching quality and student experience) derived from the National Student Survey, in common with other institutions in London.

Professor Edward Byrne, the president and principal, has said that education and the student experience will be the top priority in KCL's strategy for the years running up to its 200th anniversary in 2029. The strategy acknowledges growing demands for increased flexibility - from student time management to academics delivering world-class education alongside world-class research.

Opportunities for students to engage with employers contributed to a silver award in the government's Teaching Excellence Framework. The awards panel commented approvingly on the "excellent" extent to which students were stretched academically and on a "strong research-led culture" that requires all research staff to teach.

King's claims to have the most diverse student population in the Russell Group, with almost 10,000 students from about 150 countries beyond the UK. Half of its undergraduates are from ethnic minorities, but little more than 60% came from state schools, once grammars are stripped out. This performance is bettered on both counts in our new table measuring social diversity by Queen Mary, London, which is the highest ranked Russell Group university in our new analysis of widening participation.

The demand for places has been rising: the numbers starting degrees are up by almost 40% since the first year of £9,000 fees. More than half of all applicants now receive an offer, compared with less than 40% then.

One of the oldest and largest colleges in the University of London, King's has four of its five campuses within a single square mile around the banks of the Thames. Its latest development has been the addition of Bush House, the former headquarters of the BBC World Service, opposite the original Strand campus, where the new King's Business School is based, along with some student services and the faculty of social science.

The Strand site and the Waterloo campus house most of the non-medical departments. The addition of Bush House and its four neighbouring buildings is enabling King's to

---

Strand
London WC2R 2LS
020 7848 7000
www.kcl.ac.uk/study/
undergraduate/apply/
enquiry-form.aspx
www.kcl.ac.uk
www.kclsu.org
Open days 2019:
see website

The Times and The Sunday Times **Rankings**
Overall Ranking: =35 (last year: =28)

Teaching quality	73.1%	124
Student experience	71.2%	125
Research quality	44.0%	9
Entry standards	170	17
Graduate prospects	84.5%	18
Good honours	86.4%	12
Expected completion rate	87.4%	51
Student/staff ratio	12.5	=10
Services and facilities	£2,570	28

upgrade its teaching facilities. It had already expanded into the East Wing of Somerset House, providing impressive new premises for The Dickson Poon School of Law.

Nursing and midwifery and some biomedical subjects are also based at Waterloo, while medicine and dentistry are mainly at Guy's Hospital, near London Bridge, and in the St Thomas' Hospital campus, across the river from the Houses of Parliament. The Denmark Hill campus, in south London, is home to the Institute of Psychiatry, Psychology and Neuroscience, as well as some facilities for dentistry. The Access to Medicine course, which attracts talented students from generally low-performing schools into medical degrees, has now been replicated for dentistry.

King's may become the first UK university to open a campus in continental Europe to protect itself against the possible effects of Brexit. It has collaborated with the Technische Universitat Dresden since 2015 under the Transcampus programme and is now considering establishing a physical base there. King's has already set up one overseas degree: nursing, taught at the Ngee Ann Academy, in Singapore.

King's is in our top ten for research after 85% of the work submitted to the 2014 Research Excellence Framework was judged to be world-leading or internationally excellent. Law, education, clinical medicine and philosophy all ranked in the top three in the country and there were good results in general engineering, history, psychology, and communication and media studies. The successes produced the biggest increase in research funding at any university.

Today's researchers follow in a tradition that has seen King's play a part in many of the advances that shape modern life, including the discovery of DNA and the development of radar. Twelve alumni or academics have won Nobel prizes.

There are more than 4,000 places in university-owned accommodation, as well as access to nearly 400 intercollegiate places run by the University of London.

Some of the outdoor sports grounds are a long train ride from the campuses, but there are facilities for all the main sports, as well as rifle ranges, two gyms and a swimming pool. Recent elite athletes include Dina Asher-Smith, who won three sprint gold medals in the 2018 European championships. She graduated in history in 2017.

Tuition fees

- » Fees for UK/EU students 2019–20 £9,250
- » Fees for International students 2019–20 £18,900–£25,500
  Medicine £37,000
- » For scholarship and bursary information see
  www.kcl.ac.uk/study/index.aspx
- » Graduate salary £26,000

Student numbers

Undergraduates	**16,515**	**(1,737)**
Postgraduates	**7,578**	**(4,734)**
Applications/places		**43,820/5,505**
Applications per place		**8.0**
Overall offer rate		**69.7%**
International students		**32.6%%**

Accommodation

University provided places: 3,917 (catered 0%)
Self-catered: £140–£282 per week
First years guaranteed accommodation
www.kcl.ac.uk/study/accommodation/index.aspx

Where do the students come from?

State schools (non-grammar)	61.4%	Working-class homes	26.2%	Black ethnic minority	10.6%
Grammar schools	14.2%	Deprived areas	4.5%	Disabled	5.4%
Independent schools	24.4%	All ethnic minorities	50.7%	Mature (over 21)	22.4%

Kingston University

Kingston is in the middle of a radical reshaping of its undergraduate portfolio. Students started 24 new programmes last year and 40 more are planned for September. They range from foundation years for the humanities, social sciences and business, to degrees in civil infrastructure engineering, publishing, data science, and media and global politics. At the same time, the university is planning a big expansion in its degree apprenticeships in engineering, business, healthcare and education.

A number of programmes have closed in recent years and national issues such as the withdrawal of NHS bursaries and the decline in the number of 18-year-olds have affected recruitment. Applications to Kingston have halved since the early years of the decade, falling last year for the seventh year in a row. The university has resisted the temptation to raise its offer rate significantly and expects to see some reduction in the current student population of almost 19,000.

Kingston has moved up 12 places in the past two years in our institutional table, but only after falling into our bottom ten for the first time. With 13 other institutions in this guide, Kingston has a bronze rating in the Teaching Excellence Framework (TEF). The TEF panel complimented the university on its award-winning focus on black and ethnic minority students, and a completion rate which is in line with the national average for Kingston's courses and student profile.

Campus developments are gathering pace. The Town House, a £41m teaching building, will open this year, with a learning resources centre, cafes, a covered courtyard, performance space and new landscaping across the front of the campus. The landmark development will bring together the university and the local community, as well as improving student facilities.

At the same time, the highly-rated School of Art is being refurbished, with new academic space and an improved exterior. The school achieved among the best results at Kingston in the 2014 Research Excellence Framework (REF), together with history and English. The university entered relatively few academics for the REF — just 16% of the eligible staff — but 60% of the submission reached the top two categories and there was some world-leading research in each of the nine areas in which it was assessed.

Kingston has been among the top three universities for graduate start-up companies for nine years in a row. The well-established enterprise department gives advice to would-be entrepreneurs in any subject and offers the possibility of financial support to start-ups. A career focus runs through all Kingston's courses and the careers service

River House
53–57 High Street
Kingston upon Thames
KT1 1LQ
0844 855 2177
admissionsops@kingston.ac.uk
www.kingston.ac.uk
www.kingstonstudents.net
Open days 2019:
see website

KINGSTON
UPON THAMES

The Times and The Sunday Times Rankings		
Overall Ranking: =110 (last year: 117)		
Teaching quality	78.3%	95
Student experience	77.2%	=83
Research quality	5.1%	=92
Entry standards	127	=80
Graduate prospects	64.5%	122
Good honours	70.1%	89
Expected completion rate	81.2%	=100
Student/staff ratio	16.0	=71
Services and facilities	£2,362	46

won a national award in 2017 for the best strategy for preparing students for work.

The university markets itself as in "lively, leafy London", making a virtue of its suburban, riverside location southwest of central London as well as its proximity to the bright lights. Two of its four campuses are close to Kingston town centre; another, two miles away and close to Richmond Park, is at Kingston Hill; the fourth is in Roehampton Vale, where a site once used as an aerospace factory now contains a technology block.

Kingston has the third-largest engineering faculty in London, with its own Learjet and a flight simulator to support its highly-regarded aeronautical engineering courses.

The health, social care and education faculty is run jointly with St George's, University of London. There is a link with the Royal Marsden School of Cancer Nursing and Rehabilitation, enabling some students to spend up to half of their course on clinical placements working in hospital, primary care and community settings.

Kingston has one of the most ethnically mixed student populations of any UK university. More than a quarter of the places go to mature students and approaching half to those from working-class families. The university offers unique incentives to its graduates' family members to take courses. The children of alumni qualify for a 10% reduction in fees, as do the spouses of current students or alumni and the siblings of international students or graduates. It ranks 18th in our new table for social inclusion.

As part of the university's outreach activities, laboratories are open to the public to show how science and technology can make an impact on daily life. Kingston also runs Head Start events each summer to prepare applicants for the transition to higher education, including a residential option for those who want to experience hall life.

All new entrants are guaranteed a hall place and Kingston has spent more than £20m on its student accommodation over the years. Most students like the university's location, although — in common with all London-based universities — they complain about the high cost of living.

Tuition fees

» Fees for UK/EU students 2019–20	£9,250
Foundation courses	£7,800
» Fees for International students 2019–20	£12,700–£15,300
» For scholarship and bursary information see www.kingston.ac.uk/undergraduate/fees-and-funding	
» Graduate salary	£22,000

Student numbers

Undergraduates	13,932	(998)
Postgraduates	2,573	(1,967)
Applications/places	25,050/3,045	
Applications per place	8.2	
Overall offer rate	76.5%	
International students	17.1%	

Accommodation

University provided places: 2,720 (catered 0%)
Self-catered: £124–£330 per week
First years guaranteed accommodation
www.kingston.ac.uk/accommodation/

Where do the students come from?

State schools (non-grammar)	93.5%	Working-class homes	47.3%	Black ethnic minority	23.8%
Grammar schools	2.6%	Deprived areas	6.9%	Disabled	7.2%
Independent schools	3.9%	All ethnic minorities	59.6%	Mature (over 21)	31.8%

Lancaster University

Lancaster was our University of the Year in the last edition of the guide, having climbed to sixth in the league table, a position it has retained. It also struck gold in the Teaching Excellence Framework, with the awards panel complimenting the university on the way in which it makes students feel valued, supported and challenged academically. The panel found a "culture of research-stimulated learning" that provided the knowledge, skills and understanding that is most highly valued by employers.

The university believes that these accolades helped it to a 2% increase in applications for courses beginning last year, at a time when many other institutions were suffering a decline. It had already increased the size of its intake of new undergraduates for three years in a row, making a record number of offers in the process.

There will be more options for applicants this year, including new degrees in criminology and psychology, sport and exercise science, and management with modern languages. At the same time, placement years will be added options for almost 30 existing programmes. Hundreds of Lancaster students already spend part of their courses in America, Asia, Australia or Europe. The university has always championed a flexible degree structure in which the majority of undergraduates make their final choice of degree only at the end of the first year.

Further growth will come at the medical school, which has been awarded another 60 places a year, almost doubling the number that will be available from September. The expansion will coincide with the opening of the £41m first phase of a Health Innovation campus, developed in collaboration with businesses and the NHS, alongside the university's main Bailrigg site.

Against national trends, the university re-established a department of chemistry several years ago, and an award-winning building for engineering has helped undergraduate numbers to double. Now the physics building has had a £14m refurbishment, modernising the four large teaching labs. There is even a 365mm Schmidt-Cassegrain reflecting telescope in the department's own observatory on the roof, to which students have access. There are also plans for further development of the highly-rated school of management.

Undergraduates join one of eight residential colleges on the 560-acre parkland campus, which becomes the centre of most students' social lives. The majority of these house between 800 and 900 students in self-catering accommodation. The historic town of Lancaster is a ten-minute bus ride away, and both the campus and town have been rated among the safest in the UK.

Bailrigg
Lancaster LA1 4YW
01524 65201
ugadmissions@lancaster.ac.uk
www.lancaster.ac.uk
www.lancastersu.co.uk
Open days 2019:
June 29, July 13,
September 7 & 14

The Times and The Sunday Times **Rankings**
Overall Ranking: 6 (last year: 6)

Teaching quality	81.4%	=44
Student experience	81.8%	16
Research quality	39.1%	15
Entry standards	158	34
Graduate prospects	89.1%	3
Good honours	76.5%	50
Expected completion rate	92.6%	=20
Student/staff ratio	12.7	13
Services and facilities	£3,244	6

Campus developments have included eco-friendly student residences and an impressive library. Lancaster has won the award for the best halls in the National Student Housing Survey six times.

Lancaster has been the top university in our table from the northwest of England for more than a decade. It has also set itself the target of becoming a "global player" in both teaching and research. Lancaster is the only UK university with a presence in sub-Saharan Africa, having opened a campus in Ghana, and there is a joint institute in China, with Beijing Jiaotong University offering undergraduate programmes in computing, design, engineering and environmental science. There are other partnerships in India, Pakistan, Malaysia and China, and as many students are taking a Lancaster degree overseas as in the UK.

The university's research grades improved substantially in the 2014 assessments, when 83% of its work was considered world-leading or internationally excellent. There were particularly good results in business and management, sociology, English and maths and statistics, and a strong performance across the board.

Lancaster is more successful than most research universities in widening participation among under-represented groups. Nine out of ten undergraduates are state-educated and almost a quarter came from the four lowest socioeconomic classes when this was last surveyed. Outreach activity includes summer schools, masterclasses and mentoring for teenagers, as well as an adaptation of the Minecraft computer game to teach students more about science.

The university hosts a thriving live arts scene for the campus, town and region. It has brought together art, design and theatre studies with a public art gallery, concerts and theatre, and invested heavily in design. Lancaster has also been among the most successful universities at reducing carbon emissions, winning a string of environmental awards for its residences and other facilities.

Some of the nation's most unspoilt countryside, including the Lake District and the Forest of Bowland, is on the university's doorstep. Fitness facilities are good and conveniently placed, with a £20m sport centre on campus. Road and rail communications are good, too, but Lancaster is inevitably limited for off-campus nightlife.

Tuition fees

- » Fees for UK/EU students 2019–20 £9,250
- » Fees for International students 2018–19 £15,680–£18,890
  Medicine £30,330
- » For scholarship and bursary information see
  www.lancaster.ac.uk/study/undergraduate/fees-and-funding
- » Graduate salary £24,000

Student numbers

Undergraduates	**9,683**	**(9)**
Postgraduates	**2,446**	**(1,478)**
Applications/places	**18,720/3,060**	
Applications per place	**6.1**	
Overall offer rate	**91.3%**	
International students	**33.7%**	

Accommodation

University provided places: 6,700 (catered 3%)
Catered costs: £137–£184 per week
Self-catered: £89–£180 per week
First years guaranteed accommodation
www.lancaster.ac.uk/facilities/accommodation/umdergraduates/

Where do the students come from?

State schools (non-grammar)	79.9%	Working-class homes	23.9%	Black ethnic minority	3.0%
Grammar schools	10.7%	Deprived areas	10.7%	Disabled	5.4%
Independent schools	9.4%	All ethnic minorities	15.5%	Mature (over 21)	4.7%

University of Leeds

Always one of the most popular universities in the country, Leeds was back in the top three for the volume of applications attracted in 2017, when it far exceeded its previous highest totals both for applications and enrolments. Another 5% increase in the demand for places last year, against the national trend, saw more records broken.

It is not hard to see why. Leeds moved into our top ten for the first time last year and also secured a gold rating in the Teaching Excellence Framework (TEF). It finished in the top three in Times Higher Education magazine's student experience survey, its own students awarding it high marks for the campus environment, facilities and extracurricular activities, and was among employers' favourite recruiting grounds in the 2018 High Fliers graduate market survey.

The TEF panel was impressed by the strong emphasis on education that is inspired by "discovery, global and cultural insight, ethics and responsibility, and employability". It found that students take charge of their experiences with academic and cocurricular opportunities that can enhance their learning while preparing them for the world beyond university.

More than 80% of the research assessed in the 2014 Research Excellence Framework was considered world-leading or internationally excellent, placing Leeds in the top ten in the UK in 30% of its subject areas. Leeds was back in the top 100 in this year's QS World University Rankings.

The university is investing £520m over five years to try to ensure that it continues to enjoy this level of success. This will include the refurbishment of libraries and lecture theatres, and the creation of new sports facilities. It has already spent £26m on the Laidlaw Library, which was specifically designed for undergraduate students, refurbished the Edward Boyle Library and upgraded and extended the student union building. In the next phase of the plan, the North East Quarter development will bring together physics, computing and imaging science.

The university occupies a 98-acre site within walking distance of the city centre, although much of the accommodation is further out. The student population is highly cosmopolitan, with 6,000 international students from 141 countries among a total of more than 34,000. Leeds also has one of the largest Study Abroad programmes in the country, with nearly 200 options ranging from Spain to Singapore.

There are more than 500 undergraduate programmes, with students encouraged to take courses outside their main subject. The Leeds Curriculum scheme requires undergraduates to undertake a research

Woodhouse Lane
Leeds LS2 9JT
0113 343 2336
study@leeds.ac.uk
www.leeds.ac.uk
www.luu.org.uk
Open days 2019:
see website

The Times and The Sunday Times **Rankings**
Overall Ranking: 11 (last year: 10)

Teaching quality	81.3%	=47
Student experience	81.6%	=18
Research quality	36.8%	27
Entry standards	168	=18
Graduate prospects	81.2%	36
Good honours	86.6%	10
Expected completion rate	92.5%	=22
Student/staff ratio	13.2	=17
Services and facilities	£3,110	9

project in their final year, which is intended to be seen as the "pinnacle of their academic achievement" and is weighted accordingly. The Student Education Service provides support from the point of application to beyond graduation. The university has been awarded 26 National Teaching Fellowships — more than any other university in England.

Leeds has one of the largest new lecture capture and multimedia management systems in Europe, with more than £2m invested in it in 2014. It has since attracted more than 2m views per year and this necessitated an upgrade to improve user experience. The university's virtual learning environment system, instituted in 2008 to allow students to access lectures and other teaching facilities, and to study at their own pace, was similarly relaunched to the latest technology in 2017.

The university devotes one of the largest amounts of any institution to financial support for students, with more than a third of UK and EU undergraduates expected to benefit. The LeedsforLife service — another of the features praised by the TEF panel — provides students with academic and careers advice, as well as help to identify work placements and volunteering opportunities. It is available for five years after graduation. Leeds has created more than 100 spin-out companies, with a market capitalisation of £500m, and seven of these are listed on the AIM (Alternative Investment Market), more than any other UK university.

Sports and social facilities are first-rate, and Leeds teams regularly excel in competition. The university hosts one of six centres of cricketing excellence. It has more playing field space than any other higher education institution, while The Edge sports centre includes a 25-metre swimming pool and a huge fitness suite.

The Brownlee Centre, a £5m facility opened last year, is named after the triathlete brothers Jonny and Alistair who are the university's most successful sporting alumni and train regularly there. It is the UK's first purpose-built triathlon training centre, located alongside a mile-long, closed-loop cycling circuit for cyclists of all abilities, as well as grass pitches used regularly by students for football, rugby and other sports.

The rise of Leeds as a shopping and clubbing centre has added to the attractions of the university. Some 3,500 students volunteer in the local community and 400 are trained as mentors and tutors supporting schools in the region. There are 8,500 residential places, so new entrants are guaranteed accommodation.

Tuition fees

» Fees for UK/EU students 2019–20	£9,250
» Fees for International students 2019–20	£18,500–£22,750
Medicine	£33,000
» For scholarship and bursary information see www.leeds.ac.uk/undergraduatefees	
» Graduate salary	£22,000

Student numbers

Undergraduates	23,888	(455)
Postgraduates	6,873	(2,082)
Applications/places	58,560/7,450	
Applications per place	7.9	
Overall offer rate	73.5%	
International students	22.7%	

Accommodation

University provided places: 8,500 (catered 14%)
Catered costs: £53–£204 per week
Self-catered: £93–£196
First years guaranteed accommodation
www.accommodation.leeds.ac.uk/

Where do the students come from?

State schools (non-grammar)	68.4%	Working-class homes	22.5%	Black ethnic minority	2.9%
Grammar schools	12.0%	Deprived areas	8.5%	Disabled	5.5%
Independent schools	19.6%	All ethnic minorities	18.7%	Mature (over 21)	7.9%

Leeds Arts University

The former Leeds College of Art became the city's fourth university in 2017 and is already reaping the benefits. The 36% increase in applications for courses that began last year is the biggest at any institution in our table. The addition of six new degrees, including comic and concept art, filmmaking and popular music performance has also helped.

It debuts in our table in 54th position, comfortably within the top ten modern universities. It wins our University of the Year for Student Retention with the dropout rate running at only 3.8% against an expected level of 9.6%.

There is plenty of scope for growth: in its previous guise, there were only 1,425 students in 2016–17, with fewer than 100 from outside the UK. Even so, the number of offers had more than doubled in five years, with the chances of receiving one rising from 27% to 42%.

A new £22m building has provided more teaching space and improved facilities at a time when the Blenheim Walk site — which faces the Parkinson tower at the University of Leeds — has reached capacity. The aim is to offer a more diverse mix of courses and provide opportunities for students to collaborate across the university's arts, design and performance-based programmes.

The development's specialist facilities include a 230-seat auditorium, music, film and photography studios. An open-plan atrium-style entrance leads to a public exhibition gallery and coffee shop, together with an enterprise centre that will allow the university to engage more fully with regional businesses and the local community. The building has an urban roof garden and is expected to achieve a high Breeam international rating for its environmental features. Two specialist arts libraries at Blenheim Walk together offer students access to more than 60,000 books, hundreds of magazine subscriptions and over 2,000 DVDs.

The university was founded in 1846 as the Leeds Government School of Art and Design but has been awarding its own degrees only since 2016. Professor Simone Wonnacott, the vice-chancellor, said the institution was proud to have become the only specialist arts university in the north of England and would continue to strive to put itself at the forefront of arts education not just in the UK, but worldwide. Former students include Henry Moore, Barbara Hepworth, Damien Hirst, film director Danny Sangra and London-based designer Omar Kashoura.

As Leeds College of Art, the institution was placed in the silver category in the Teaching Excellence Framework (TEF). The awards panel was impressed that a significant number of teaching staff were practising

Blenheim Walk
Leeds LS2 9AQ
0113 202 8039
admissions@leeds-art.ac.uk
www.leeds-art.ac.uk
www.leedsartunion.org.uk
Open days 2019:
June 12

The Times and The Sunday Times **Rankings**

Overall Ranking: 54 (last year: n/a)

Teaching quality	85.4%	=5
Student experience	82.7%	9
Research quality	n/a	
Entry standards	167	=20
Graduate prospects	57.1%	132
Good honours	73.8%	64
Expected completion rate	90.5%	=36
Student/staff ratio	12.5	=10
Services and facilities	£1,238	131

artists or designers, enhancing the students' exposure to the creative industries. The panel also praised the "highly valued" student support services, which include dedicated advice for mature students and those with disabilities.

The new university has a tradition of high scores in the National Student Survey. Group tutorials are conducted in sessions of between four and eight, while individual personal progress tutorials are timetabled at key points in the year, providing an opportunity to discuss general progress across all modules. The student engagement strategy, which was developed largely by the students' union, commits to involving students in strategic decision-making and operational processes.

The group and individual tutorials make for high National Student Survey scores with top-ten rankings in our table for teaching quality and student experience.

Widening Participation is encouraged through a range of activities with partner schools throughout the year, including Easter and summer schools, an after-school taster course, workshops for all stages from primary, secondary, further education to mature learners, as well as providing mentoring, campus tours and presentations. Some 97% of students are state educated — significantly more than average for the courses and entry qualifications.

Bursaries of £250 in the first year, £350 in the second and £500 in the third are available for undergraduates whose family income is below £25,000 a year. There is also a £500 scholarship, for the first year only, for those who progress from one of the university's further education courses to a degree.

Leeds College of Art did not enter the 2014 Research Excellence Framework but will join the next exercise. There are strong links with industry, which provide placements and allow students to attend trade fairs featuring their work, as well as studios and galleries in the UK and abroad. The university has a Creatives in Residence scheme, providing selected graduates with access to campus facilities and a support network. Internationally renowned guest practitioners visit to critique work and run workshops, and recent speakers include Jake Chapman, Andrew Graham Dixon and Giles Deacon. Other graduates can apply for studio or creative office space in Leeds.

Leeds Art does not have its own accommodation, but most new entrants are offered places in university-endorsed private halls. Only international students who apply by the end of June are guaranteed a place. The city offers famously lively culture and nightlife.

Tuition fees

- » Fees for UK/EU students 2019–20 £9,250
- » Fees for International students 2018–19 £15,000–£16,000
- » For scholarship and bursary information see www.leeds-art.ac.uk/apply/finance
- » Graduate salary £17,000

Student numbers

Undergraduates	1,389	(0)
Postgraduates	8	(29)
Applications/places		3,576/615
Applications per place		5.8
Overall offer rate		38.3%
International students		6.3%

Accommodation

University provided places: 555 (catered 0%)
Self-catered: £118–£140 per week
First years given priority
www.leeds-art.ac.uk/life-in-leeds/accommodation

Where do the students come from?

State schools (non-grammar)	95.0%	Working-class homes	38.2%	Black ethnic minority	1.7%
Grammar schools	2.1%	Deprived areas	10.3%	Disabled	11.3%
Independent schools	3.0%	All ethnic minorities	9.4%	Mature (over 21)	7.2%

Leeds Beckett University

Leeds Beckett continues to rank in our bottom ten despite improvements in student satisfaction. But the university achieved a silver rating in the new Teaching Excellence Framework, when the awards panel commented favourably on the opportunities for students to increase their employability by engaging with professional practice through live project briefs, case studies, practice-related assessments, and placements. Students were stretched, the panel said, and developed transferable and personal skills.

The university has set itself some challenging targets for improvement, such as halving the dropout rate and ensuring that almost nine out of ten students are satisfied with the standard of teaching. It launched more than 20 new degrees last year, as well as extending the range of foundation year courses it offers. The degrees include robotics and automation, real estate and property management, and a number of joint honours programmes with biomedical sciences, politics or international relations. There are also plans to add to the eight degree apprenticeship programmes currently on offer.

At the same time, Leeds Beckett is investing £200m over seven years to create "academic homes" for the 13 academic schools. An £80m creative arts building in the city centre will be one such development. Opening in 2020, it will host the Northern Film School as well as catering for music, performing arts and fashion students. Specialist facilities will include a theatre, 220-seat Dolby Atmos cinema and studios for fashion, music, film and television courses.

A new building on the Headingley campus is due to open this year, with spaces for teaching and research in sport, as well as training facilities for elite athletes. It will include a third-floor sprint track, rooftop walking track, hypoxic lab, and strength and conditioning studio. The Sheila Silver and Headingley libraries have been refurbished this summer. The City campus has already seen a £100m transformation, centred on the futuristic Rose Bowl lecture theatre complex next to Leeds Civic Hall, which houses the business school.

The university has a longstanding reputation for widening participation in higher education and runs a wide range of summer schools. Some 30,000 young people attended outreach events in 2017. But still the number of students starting degrees was down by more than 20% since 2011 and applications have dropped by 40% in that time.

It is intended that all Leeds Beckett students should leave the university with three graduate attributes: to be enterprising, digitally literate and have a global outlook. All undergraduate courses were redesigned with these qualities in mind and all include

City Campus
Leeds LS1 3HE
0113 812 3113
admissionenquiries@
leedsbeckett.ac.uk
www.leedsbeckett.ac.uk
www.leedsbeckettsu.co.uk
Open day 2019: March 6
(City and Headingley)

The Times and The Sunday Times **Rankings**
Overall Ranking: 124 (last year: 123)

Teaching quality	80.8%	=51
Student experience	80.5%	34
Research quality	4.1%	=102
Entry standards	114	=113
Graduate prospects	63.2%	128
Good honours	65.9%	=113
Expected completion rate	76.0%	122
Student/staff ratio	19.4	=119
Services and facilities/student	£1,633	118

at least two weeks of work-related learning a year. A growing emphasis on educational technology is enhanced by 24-hour libraries, which have achieved the Customer Service Excellence standard for 11 years in a row.

There are two bases in Leeds: the City campus, in the centre, and the Headingley campus, three miles away in 100 acres of park and woodland. The latter boasts outstanding sports facilities, including a sports arena and multiuse sports pitches, as well as the Carnegie Regional Tennis Centre and teaching accommodation for education, informatics, law and business.

More than 7,000 students take part in some form of sporting activity, and there is a range of sports scholarships. The Athletic Union hosts 40 clubs and 80 university teams are among the most successful in national competition. Several recent alumni and others who use the university as their training base took part in the Rio Olympics. An annual pass for both the Headingley and City campus facilities currently costs £90. In the first developments of their kind, a new stand was built at the Headingley rugby ground, with classrooms, coaching facilities and social space for use by the university and the two professional clubs, and a pavilion at the adjacent Test and county cricket ground has similar multiuse facilities.

The university almost doubled the number of academics it entered for the 2014 Research Excellence Framework compared with the 2008 assessments. Just over a third of their work was rated as world-leading or internationally excellent, with architecture and sports studies producing much the best results. Leeds Beckett's reputation is mainly for applied research: three interdisciplinary research institutes focus on health, sport and sustainability, and there are ten centres in more specialist fields.

Leeds Beckett is benefiting from the city's growing reputation for nightlife, but it is making its own contribution with a famously lively entertainment scene. With more than 4,000 bed spaces, those who make the university their firm choice are guaranteed accommodation.

Tuition fees

» Fees for UK/EU students 2019–20	£9,250
» Fees for international students 2019–20	£12,000
Foundation courses £9,250	
» For scholarship and bursary information see www.leedsbeckett.ac.uk/undergraduate/financing-your-studies	
» Graduate salary	£19,000

Student numbers

Undergraduates	16,918 (3,197)
Postgraduates	1,597 (3,174)
Applications/places	27,905/4,675
Applications per place	6.0
Overall offer rate	81.3%
International students	6.3%

Accommodation

University provided places: 4,158 (catered 0%)
Self-catered: £94–£187 per week
First years guaranteed accommodation
www.leeds-beckett.ac.uk/accommodation/

Where do the students come from?

State schools (non-grammar)	92.8%	Working-class homes	35.4%	Black ethnic minority	4.3%
Grammar schools	2.7%	Deprived areas	18.3%	Disabled	4.9%
Independent schools	4.5%	All ethnic minorities	20.6%	Mature (over 21)	12.1%

Leeds Trinity University

Leeds Trinity's small size, with fewer than 3,000 undergraduates, can make for big swings in some of the main measures in our league table. It shot up more than 75 places and into the top ten on each of our student satisfaction indicators in the previous edition of our guide, gains it has largely held on to. However, its 29-place rise in overall ranking then has been balanced by a 20-place fall this time.

The university claims to be the only one in the UK to include at least two professional work placements, totalling 11 weeks of relevant experience, as part of every student's degree. Relationships with more than 2,500 employers give undergraduates a wide range of options. More than 60% of students continue to work or volunteer with their placement provider during the remainder of their degree, and 11% find jobs there as graduates. Students have their own placement advisor and undergo an intensive two-week preparation programme. Overseas placements are encouraged, and all form part of an assessed module counting towards final degree classification.

The scheme contributed to a silver rating for the university in the Teaching Excellence Framework. The panel also liked Leeds Trinity's supportive educational culture, innovative assessment and feedback, excellent use of technology, and professional input into its degrees.

Three senior teaching fellows have been appointed to work with staff to pilot and evaluate new approaches to teaching and learning. The university's strategy for teaching and learning stresses student-led enquiry, placing more onus on students to develop and lead their own learning in order to be more employable when they graduate. To guide them from induction to beyond graduation, there is a programme of personalised support from the Learning Hub, which is dedicated to skills development and mentoring.

Both applications and enrolments have dropped by almost a quarter in two years, however. More than a dozen new degrees have been launched to broaden the options available to applicants, with the same again planned for this year. The new offerings include business and enterprise, health psychology, digital media and sociology with police studies. The university also offers accelerated two-year degrees in education and sport, and tourism and leisure management.

Leeds Trinity is one of two institutions given university status in 2012 that are Catholic foundations. It "promotes dialogue and teaching of the Catholic Church" but is not controlled by the church and welcomes students of all faiths and none. The university grew out of two Catholic teacher training colleges established in the 1960s. Education

Brownberrie Lane
Horsforth
Leeds LS18 5HD
0113 283 7150
admissions@leedstrinity.ac.uk
www.leedstrinity.ac.uk
www.ltsu.co.uk
Open days 2019:
see website

The Times and The Sunday Times **Rankings**
Overall Ranking: =87 (last year: =67)

Teaching quality	83.9%	12
Student experience	82.3%	13
Research quality	2.0%	122
Entry standards	101	131
Graduate prospects	68.1%	110
Good honours	78.6%	43
Expected completion rate	83.4%	=83
Student/staff ratio	19.5	121
Services and facilities/student	£1,895	97

is still the biggest subject, but there are also schools of arts and communication, and health and social sciences.

The university is located 20 minutes northwest of Leeds city centre, in Horsforth. Some £15m has been invested in campus improvements, and developments costing another £25m are planned. An extension to the Learning Centre opened in 2017, providing students with new teaching rooms, group study and social learning spaces, and a bigger 24-hour lab and cafe. Students also have access to the Trinity Enterprise Centre if they are considering launching their own business. Its advice and facilities are available to local businesses as well as students.

Only 20 academics were entered for the 2014 Research Excellence Framework, but there were good results in communication, cultural and media studies, and library and information management. The flagship research group, the Leeds Centre for Victorian Studies, has a national and international reputation.

Nearly two thirds of the students are female and Leeds Trinity exceeds all its national benchmarks for widening participation in higher education: more than 22% of undergraduates come from areas with little tradition of sending students to university — one of the highest proportions in the country. The projected dropout rate has improved considerably and is now lower than the national average for Leeds Trinity's courses and entry qualifications. Among the outreach activities is a Children's University, based on the campus, which offers high quality, innovative learning activities outside normal school hours to children aged seven to 14.

The university has nearly 800 residential places — enough to guarantee accommodation to first-years, as long as they apply by the end of June. Sports facilities are good and include a 3G pitch and recently upgraded changing facilities. The university's sports centre has refurbished its fitness suite with £200,000 of new equipment, which caters for elite athletes as well as casual users, with specialist strength and conditioning equipment, and a new functional training rig.

The city of Leeds is one of the most popular with students.

Tuition fees

» Fees for UK/EU students 2019–20 £9,250
» Fees for international students 2018–19 £11,250–£12,250
» For scholarship and bursary information see www.leedstrinity.ac.uk/student-life/student-finance
» Graduate salary £17,680

Student numbers

Undergraduates	2,825	(30)
Postgraduates	392	(377)
Applications/places		5,595/700
Applications per place		8.0
Overall offer rate		87.7%
International students		1.3%

Accommodation

University provided places: 791 (catered 25%)
Catered costs: £121–£139 per week
Self-catered: £94–£125 per week
First years guaranteed accommodation
www.leedstrinity.ac.uk/student-life/accommodation

Where do the students come from?

State schools (non-grammar)	95.0%	Working-class homes	42.3%	Black ethnic minority	3.0%
Grammar schools	2.8%	Deprived areas	20.7%	Disabled	6.2%
Independent schools	2.1%	All ethnic minorities	20.1%	Mature (over 21)	17.2%

University of Leicester

Leicester is to host the new National Space Park, due to open this year, a reward for the university's longstanding commitment to space research. The venture, which will host companies in space-related industries as well as postgraduate teaching and research, is expected eventually to bring in revenues of £40bn and to cement Leicester's reputation in the field. Space is far from Leicester's only area of excellence, however. There are also plans for a life sciences park at the Charnwood site near Loughborough, while the genetics department, where DNA fingerprinting was discovered, is another star feature.

Other current developments are geared more to the student experience. The students' union building is being redeveloped, doubling the amount of social learning space, improving accessibility and creating a spacious food court. Further ahead, new student accommodation and teaching and learning centres are planned, with landscaped areas and pedestrian and cycling routes, as part of a £500m investment programme.

The university has increased its undergraduate enrolments more than any other university since £9,000 fees were introduced, adding 1,000 places to grow by almost a third. The Student Lifecycle Change programme was launched to improve the services underpinning the quality of the student experience and the efficiency of academic administration throughout students' time at Leicester. To stress a commitment to teaching quality, academics can only be promoted to professor or assistant professor if they have a qualification from the Higher Education Academy.

Other innovations, including a new student app, peer mentoring, and the filming of lectures for students to review online, helped Leicester to a silver award in the Teaching Excellence Framework (TEF). The lecture capture system was a response to student feedback — something mentioned approvingly by the TEF panel, who also congratulated the university on engaging students with current research on all its courses.

The discovery of the remains of Richard III by its archaeologists placed the university in the global spotlight. Three quarters of the work submitted to the 2014 Research Excellence Framework was rated as world-leading or internationally excellent, with the School of Museum Studies producing the best results, as it did in 2008. The results, which were also good in clinical medicine, biology, earth science and general engineering, brought a substantial increase in research funding.

The main campus and much of the residential accommodation is concentrated

University Road
Leicester LE1 7RH
0116 252 5281
study@le.ac.uk
www.le.ac.uk
www.leicesterunion.com
Open days 2019:
see website

The Times and The Sunday Times **Rankings**
Overall Ranking: =38 (last year: 34)

Teaching quality	76.7%	=107
Student experience	76.9%	=89
Research quality	31.8%	=38
Entry standards	136	59
Graduate prospects	75.4%	=68
Good honours	79.0%	38
Expected completion rate	92.7%	19
Student/staff ratio	13.7	24
Services and facilities/student	£2,664	24

in a leafy suburb a mile from the centre of Leicester, where a new home for the business school is on the way. The university's first overseas venture opened in 2017 in China, as the Leicester International Institute/Dalian University of Technology. Based in Panjin, it is offering degrees in English in chemistry, mechanical engineering and mathematics.

Leicester aims to provide the most flexible curriculum in the UK, in response to strong demand among students and prospective applicants for more choice in degree options. Undergraduates can choose single, joint or major/minor programmes. Those taking the major/minor route are able to combine a wide range of subjects, spending three quarters of their time studying their principal subject and a quarter on the minor element. The university has also introduced a number of employability initiatives, including an undergraduate internship programme with up to 500 places available each year.

The undergraduate population is among the most socially diverse of any university in our top 40. More than nine out of ten undergraduates come from state schools and 27% came from low-income families when the last survey was conducted. Leicester has 4,200 bed spaces, so first-years are guaranteed a residential place as long as they apply by the end of August. Facilities at Oadby Student Village include study areas, social spaces, cinema room and bar. Many second-year and third-year students also live in halls, although the majority choose to live in private accommodation nearby.

The university has two modern sports centres, one on campus and the other at the student village. Both have a gym, swimming pool, spa, sauna and steam room, and studios. There are also flood-lit tennis courts, all-weather and rugby pitches at Oadby. Students currently pay a basic membership fee of £140 a year to use the facilities.

Its ethnic diversity means that the city of Leicester offers a rich cultural experience, and in term-time 12% of the population are students. It is a more affordable city than most in the UK and big enough to provide all the normal sports and entertainment opportunities, while also offering events such as the biggest Diwali celebrations outside India. The award-winning students' union is the only one in the country to contain an O2 Academy.

Tuition fees

» Fees for UK/EU students 2019–20 £9,250
» Fees for international students 2019–20 £16,700–£20,590
  Medicine £41,945 (clinical years)
» For scholarship and bursary information see
  www.le.ac.uk/fees
» Graduate salary £20,800

Student numbers

Undergraduates	**11,628**	**(445)**
Postgraduates	**3,006**	**(1,721)**
Applications/places	**22,630/3,040**	
Applications per place	**7.4**	
Overall offer rate	**88.0%**	
International students	**24.3%**	

Accommodation

University provided places: 4,237 (catered 14%)
Catered costs: £120–£173 per week
Self-catered: £85–£177 per week
First years guaranteed accommodation
www.le.ac.uk/study/undergraduates/accommodation

Where do the students come from?

State schools (non-grammar)	80.3%	Working-class homes	26.9%	Black ethnic minority	17.7%
Grammar schools	10.6%	Deprived areas	9.8%	Disabled	5.2%
Independent schools	9.1%	All ethnic minorities	49.2%	Mature (over 21)	7.6%

University of Lincoln

Lincoln will open a new medical school this year, the first in the county and a crowning achievement for a university that only moved to its current location a little more than 20 years ago. The school is being established in partnership with the University of Nottingham, which will award the degrees, and will have an initial intake of 80 students. At full capacity, it will train 400 undergraduates a year and offer a foundation year for students without the necessary qualifications for immediate entry to the BMBS degree course in order to attract a wider range of applicants.

The university has a gold rating in the Teaching Excellence Framework (TEF). The awarding panel complimented the university on a strong approach to personalised learning through highly-engaged personal tutors with access to analytics to monitor students' progress proactively. It found that students were involved in the design of courses and enabled to develop their independence, understanding and skills to reflect their full potential.

Lincoln's popularity has been growing, particularly among school-leavers. A 12-place rise in our rankings represents Lincoln's highest-ever finish, while its undergraduate intake has grown by almost a third since higher fees arrived in 2012 and more than

30 foundation year courses in science and technology were launched in 2017. The university is also expanding its range of degree apprenticeships, which were pioneered by its National Centre for Food Manufacturing with the addition of programmes in nursing and social work.

The School of Geography took its first students in 2017. Described by the Royal Geographical Society as "one of the most significant investments in UK university geography for a generation" its teaching is informed by a research centre focused on climate change, flooding and water-borne diseases.

The university is spending more than £100m on upgrading facilities to cope with additional students. Having opened the prize-winning Engineering Hub in 2011 — the first purpose-built engineering school for more than 20 years — it added the School of Mathematics and Physics three years later. A collaboration with Siemens was formally cemented in 2016.

Together with Cambridge, Manchester and Newcastle, Lincoln is one of just 16 universities worldwide to hold Siemens global "principal partner" status. The hub was further extended and redeveloped in 2017 to become the Isaac Newton building. It houses the schools of engineering, mathematics and physics, and computer science, and reflects the vast growth of these three schools in the interim.

Brayford Pool
Lincoln LN6 7TS
01522 886 644
enquiries@lincoln.ac.uk
www.lincoln.ac.uk
www.lincolnsu.com
Open days 2019:
see website

The Times and The Sunday Times **Rankings**
Overall Ranking: 42 (last year: 54)

Teaching quality	83.1%	=22
Student experience	82.4%	12
Research quality	10.3%	59
Entry standards	129	=70
Graduate prospects	81.4%	34
Good honours	73.5%	=65
Expected completion rate	88.7%	43
Student/staff ratio	14.9	=41
Services and facilities/student	£2,054	82

The university's Professional Development Centre provides training courses for medical professionals across the region and is an inter-disciplinary core for academics from the Lincoln Institute for Health.

The TEF panel was impressed by "outstanding physical and digital resources which pervade all aspects of student experience, including state-of-the-art teaching spaces and extensive library usage with investment into the use of e-resources". Lincoln was in the top ten in the health category for the quality of its outputs in the 2014 Research Excellence Framework. Research in the fields of agriculture, veterinary and food science was even more successful. Across all subjects, more than half of a large submission was considered internationally excellent or world-leading.

The university occupies an attractive, purpose-built campus next to a marina in the centre of Lincoln, having initially moved to the site from Hull in 1996. Its headquarters followed in 2001. There are more than 14,000 students, almost one in five of whom comes from an area of low participation in higher education — significantly more than its courses and student profile would suggest. A one-stop-shop provides careers advice, helps to enhance CVs, helps students to gain work experience and find jobs, and supports recent graduates.

Lincoln has won national recognition for its collaboration with business and industry. It runs an expanded graduate internship scheme and a popular summer placement programme. Several degrees can be taken as work-based programmes, with credit awarded for relevant aspects of the job and the university was the first to win a Charter Mark for exceptional service. As well as the courses offered with Siemens, pharmacy undergraduates study in industry-standard laboratories at the £22m Science and Innovation Park in Lincoln, with proposed further expansion of £20m. The National Centre for Food Manufacturing is based in Holbeach.

The city, buoyed by its successful football team, has adapted to its student population with new bars and clubs, while the students' union is effective both socially and politically. A £6m performing arts centre on campus contains a 450-seat theatre and three large studio spaces, and there is a popular venue in a former railway engine shed. The university either owns, manages or endorses almost 5,700 residential places, and guarantees accommodation to new entrants who apply by the end of June with Lincoln as their first choice.

Tuition fees

» Fees for UK/EU students 2019–20 £9,250
» Fees for international students 2019–20 £13,800–£15,600
» For scholarship and bursary information see www.lincoln.ac.uk/home/studywithus/undergraduatestudy/feesandfunding
» Graduate salary £20,000

Student numbers

Undergraduates	10,450	(1,331)
Postgraduates	1,129	(1,194)
Applications/places		16,840/3,810
Applications per place		4.4
Overall offer rate		91.7%
International students		9.3%

Accommodation

University provided places: 5,686 (catered 0%)
Self-catered: £69–£140 per week
First years guaranteed accommodation
www.lincoln.ac.uk/home/accommodation

Where do the students come from?

State schools (non-grammar)	93.2%	Working-class homes	37.1%	Black ethnic minority	2.1%
Grammar schools	4.2%	Deprived areas	19.1%	Disabled	8.2%
Independent schools	2.6%	All ethnic minorities	9.3%	Mature (over 21)	10.8%

University of Liverpool

Liverpool was dismayed to find itself the lowest ranked of the five higher education institutions in its home city — and among the 22 lowest in the country — when the government's first ratings for teaching quality were published in 2017. But it has now succeeded in moving up to the silver category in the Teaching Excellence Framework (TEF).

In a somewhat lukewarm endorsement, the TEF panel said that effective systems of student representation informed policy and strategic developments. It found strategic investment in facilities to support learning, and a comprehensive range of initiatives to enhance performance in highly-skilled employment or further study.

The initial grade appears not to have damaged recruitment unduly. Applications did drop last year, but by half the national average, and after topping 40,000 in the three previous years. The intake of new undergraduates had grown by 1,000 students during that period.

Liverpool is investing £600m in its city-centre campus to make room for the extra undergraduates and improve the student experience. A ten-year development plan has already provided new and improved teaching and research accommodation, as well as additional leisure facilities and more student accommodation. A new teaching hub will be ready this year, providing social study space, more formal teaching areas and new PC suites. The first phase of a new School of Law and Social Justice will be ready this year.

Law is one of the areas of expansion, following an agreement with the University of Law (ULaw) to offer its legal practice course in Liverpool. The development will enable law graduates to remain at the university for their professional training, while graduates in other subjects will be able to take ULaw's graduate diploma in law.

The management school has been extended and the Guild of Students building refurbished, while a £68m Materials Innovation Factory is intended to make Liverpool a world leader in computer-aided material science by 2020. The university previously spent £70m on interdisciplinary research facilities for the health and life sciences to focus on the major health challenges of the 21st century.

Liverpool entered a relatively low proportion of its eligible academics for a Russell Group university in the 2014 Research Excellence Framework, which holds it back in our research ranking even though 70% of the work was judged to be world-leading or internationally excellent. Chemistry produced spectacular results, with more than half of its research considered world-leading and only 1% placed outside the

Foundation Building
Brownlow Hill
Liverpool
L69 3BX
0151 794 5927
ugrecruitment@liverpool.ac.uk
www.liverpool.ac.uk
www.liverpoolguild.org
Open days 2019:
June 21, 22;
September 21; October 19

The Times and The Sunday Times **Rankings**
Overall Ranking: 31 (last year: 42)

Teaching quality	79.5%	70
Student experience	80.0%	=40
Research quality	31.5%	41
Entry standards	146	44
Graduate prospects	85.4%	=14
Good honours	79.3%	36
Expected completion rate	90.5%	=36
Student/staff ratio	13.5	=21
Services and facilities/student	£2,302	55

top two categories. Computer science and general engineering also scored particularly well.

Liverpool has a campus in the historic Chinese city of Suzhou, run in partnership with Xi'an Jiaotong University, and students can study there while Chinese students also get the opportunity to transfer to England. There is also a collaboration with the Singapore Institute of Technology, as well as a postgraduate site in the City of London for professional courses.

Other partnerships involve universities in Chile, Mexico and Spain that will allow students to complete part of their degree at one or more of these institutions. The university is also expanding online, where it is already the largest provider of online postgraduate courses in Europe.

Liverpool also has a site for postgraduates in London which will now be the base for third-year undergraduates in architecture, industrial design or urban planning who want to connect with industry and build contacts in the capital. The London design studio takes a transdisciplinary approach, with collaboration across a variety of areas.

The proportions of undergraduates from state schools and working-class homes are among the highest in the Russell Group. Up to 11,000 young people in disadvantaged areas from primary age to sixth-form take part in a programme of long-term engagement with the university. Almost a third of students qualify for the Liverpool Bursary of between £750 and £2,000 a year. The university is among the best performing of the Russell Group universities in our new table on social inclusion.

Liverpool has one of the largest university careers resources centres in the UK and more than £2m has been invested in student and graduate internships. A programme of "boot camps" gives new graduates opportunities for networking with employers while developing world-of-work skills.

Some £250m has been spent on new student accommodation. More than 2,000 study bedrooms were added on campus in two years and another 489 rooms opened in 2017 at the Greenbank Student Village, which has its own gym. The Guild of Students is the centre of social activity on campus, but the city is famously lively. The indoor and outdoor sports facilities are good and include a 25-metre swimming pool that is also open to the public.

Tuition fees

» Fees for UK/EU students 2019–20 £9,250
  Foundation courses £5,140–£7,500
» Fees for international students 2019–20 £16,550–£20,700
  Dentistry £35,300; Medicine £34,550;
  Veterinary Science £34,550
» For scholarship and bursary information see
  www.liverpool.ac.uk/study/undergraduate/finance/fees
» Graduate salary £22,000

Student numbers

Undergraduates	20,324	(614)
Postgraduates	3,547	(2,586)
Applications/places	40,895/5,290	
Applications per place	7.7	
Overall offer rate	87.6%	
International students	27.7%	

Accommodation

University provided places: 4,660 (catered 30%)
Self-catered: £134–£206 per week
Catered: £149–£207
First years guaranteed accommodation
www.liverpool.ac.uk/accommodation

Where do the students come from?

State schools (non-grammar)	76.7%	Working-class homes	25.9%	Black ethnic minority	2.4%
Grammar schools	11.7%	Deprived areas	10.8%	Disabled	5.3%
Independent schools	11.6%	All ethnic minorities	15.2%	Mature (over 21)	9.7%

Liverpool Hope University

The only higher education institution in Liverpool to achieve a gold rating in the Teaching Excellence Framework (TEF) transformed its Creative Campus last year. The purchase of several buildings adjoining the original campus has enabled Liverpool Hope to add an arts centre, food court, new study spaces and additional library facilities.

The development includes new studios for fine and applied art students, a large refurbished warehouse space, group study rooms and a hub for the student support, wellbeing and students' union teams.

The upgraded campus, the smaller of Liverpool Hope's two main sites near the city centre, hosts two of the new degrees that took their first students in September: popular music and graphic design. There are also two new degrees in robotics, one a four-year master's programme, as well as the same format for maths and a three-year marketing degree. Unusually among modern universities, there are no plans at present to move into degree apprenticeships.

Liverpool Hope has regained its place in our top 50 this year and remains among the leading post-1992 universities after prodigious rises in our table earlier in the decade. It stays in the top ten for both students' perceptions of teaching quality and their wider university experience.

The university boycotted league tables for several years but admitted that its success in them since may have been one of the factors behind a rise in applications in 2017, when most universities suffered a decline.

The TEF panel complimented the university on "outstanding levels of stretch provided through judicious partnerships, good curriculum design and extracurricular activities". It also acknowledged a strategic approach to ensuring outstanding outcomes for all students, and recognition of the value of an inclusive community of diverse learners.

Undergraduates are guaranteed small group tutorials with a named tutor each week, and that all the teaching they receive should be informed by research. They are encouraged to register for the Service and Leadership Award, which runs alongside their degree work. Students can volunteer locally, within the region or internationally as part of Global Hope, the university's award-winning overseas charity.

The university has adopted an integrated curriculum with a "disciplinary core" for each course to ensure that all students have a similar experience and get a more rounded view of their subject. Most opt for combined-subject degrees, choosing after the first year whether to give them equal weight or to go for a major/minor arrangement.

Taggart Avenue
Hope Park
Liverpool L16 9JD
0151 291 3111
enquiry@hope.ac.uk
www.hope.ac.uk
www.hopesu.com
Open days 2019:
see website

The Times and The Sunday Times Rankings

Overall Ranking: 50 (last year: 52)

Teaching quality	85.1%	7
Student experience	83.3%	7
Research quality	9.2%	=63
Entry standards	116	=109
Graduate prospects	83.8%	=20
Good honours	65.9%	=113
Expected completion rate	81.0%	102
Student/staff ratio	14.5	=30
Services and facilities	£2,094	79

Hope was formed in 1980 from the merger of two Catholic and one Church of England teacher training colleges. It sponsors an academy with the same dual-faith character. A university since 2005, its top priorities are student satisfaction and employability, although it includes "taking faith seriously" among its key values.

More than half of the eligible staff were entered for the 2014 Research Excellence Framework – far more than at most post-1992 universities – and there were good results in theology and education. There are research-led seminars in the final year of degree courses to introduce undergraduates to a research culture, and all students produce a dissertation or advanced research project.

The university has increased its national recruitment profile, with nearly 60% of students now coming from beyond Merseyside. There is still, however, a strong commitment to the region. A new university centre was launched in Blackburn, mainly offering degrees in business and education in partnership on the site of St. Mary's College. The Network of Hope takes university courses to sixth-form colleges in parts of the region where there is limited higher education.

Hope comfortably exceeds all the official benchmarks for widening participation in higher education. Almost all the undergraduates are state-educated and almost 20% are from an area with little tradition of higher education – one of the highest proportions in England. It ranks in the top 20 in our new league table for social inclusion thanks to these successes.

The main campus, Hope Park, is four miles from the city centre in the suburb of Childwall. More than £60m has been spent on campus improvements, which include an £8.5m Health Sciences building, housing laboratories for nutrition, genomics, cell biology and psychology, along with facilities for sport and exercise science, including a 25-metre biomechanics sprint track.

A new 3G pitch, tennis courts and a mile-long running track were added last year, complementing the impressive indoor sports facilities. The university also has a residential outdoor education centre in Snowdonia.

The 1,126 residential places are enough to guarantee accommodation for new entrants who apply before clearing. Liverpool is a popular student city and the university has partnerships with the Royal Liverpool Philharmonic Orchestra, Liverpool Tate, the National Museums Liverpool and Liverpool Sound City to develop cultural programmes.

Tuition fees

- » Fees for UK/EU students 2019–20 — £9,250
- » Fees for international students 2018–19 — £11,400
- » For scholarship and bursary information see www.hope.ac.uk/undergraduate/feesandfunding
- » Graduate salary — £19,000

Student numbers

Undergraduates	**3,808**	**(155)**
Postgraduates	**772**	**(506)**
Applications/places	**8,980/1,295**	
Applications per place	**6.9**	
Overall offer rate	**90.7%**	
International students	**3.2%**	

Accommodation

University provided places: 1,126 (catered 0%)
Self-catered: £70–£123 per week
First years guaranteed accommodation
www.hope.ac.uk/halls

Where do the students come from?

State schools (non-grammar)	90.2%	Working-class homes	43.2%	Black ethnic minority	2.4%
Grammar schools	8.6%	Deprived areas	21.1%	Disabled	8.8%
Independent schools	1.2%	All ethnic minorities	9.3%	Mature (over 21)	17.0%

Liverpool John Moores University

A solid performance by Liverpool John Moores University (LJMU) in the official measures of performance, with a silver award in the Teaching Excellence Framework (TEF) and some of the most improved results in the research equivalent, is reflected in its ranking in our table (down just four places after a 16-place rise the previous year). The university claims to be "undergoing a renaissance as the strength of our teaching and research continues to exceed even our own high expectations".

The university has started work on a £100m development that will eventually see all of its students taught in the city centre. Copperas Hill, near Lime Street station, will play a key role in regenerating a rundown part of the city and include an atrium, rooftop terrace and sports facilities as well as teaching and learning spaces. The IM Marsh campus, four miles from the city centre, will close when Copperas Hill is ready for occupation, concentrating the university's activities on a single area.

The first phase of the scheme could see the Student Life Building and Sports Building open next year, with new public spaces close to the Sensor City hub for industrial research, development and commercialisation — a joint venture with the University of Liverpool —

continuing the establishment of a Knowledge Quarter.

LJMU has spent £180m on improved facilities in little more than ten years. Developments include the award-winning John Lennon Art and Design Building and the £25.5m life sciences building, where the facilities include an indoor 70-metre running track and labs for testing cardiovascular ability, motor skills and biomechanics functions. The £37.6m Redmonds Building houses Liverpool Screen School, with its industry-standard TV and radio studios, the Liverpool Business School and the School of Law.

Recent projects have been designed to improve the student experience. Responding to feedback from the students' union, LJMU invested £1.5m to create social spaces in which students can relax, socialise and engage in "casual study". Located in six buildings, they include features such as indoor lawns and trees, IT facilities and phone-charging docks.

The TEF panel complimented the university on a "highly effective institutional strategic drive to improve satisfaction with assessment and feedback", strong recognition of teaching excellence and a consistent commitment to student engagement.

There was also praise for its World of Work (WoW) programme, which is perhaps the university's best-known feature. LJMU was a pioneer of the employment-focused

Exchange Station
Tithebarn Street
Liverpool L2 2QP
0151 231 5090
courses@ljmu.ac.uk
www.ljmu.ac.uk
www.liverpoolsu.com
Open days 2019:
see website

The Times and The Sunday Times Rankings		
Overall Ranking: 74 (last year: =70)		
Teaching quality	80.4%	=58
Student experience	79.2%	=50
Research quality	8.9%	=68
Entry standards	141	53
Graduate prospects	74.9%	71
Good honours	76.0%	51
Expected completion rate	86.0%	=60
Student/staff ratio	17.3	98
Services and facilities	£1,730	115

curriculum that has since become common in higher education. The WoW initiative involves leading companies and business organisations and encourages undergraduates to become expert in eight transferable skills, applicable to a wide range of careers. All students are offered extensive work-related learning opportunities, both paid and voluntary, some of which are based overseas.

LJMU was among the pioneers of degree apprenticeships and offers them in 11 areas, including civil engineering, construction management, quantity surveying and digital and technology solutions. More programmes may be added this year. The Centre for Entrepreneurship supports students and graduates who want to start up in business, become self-employed or work freelance. The Teaching and Learning Academy, launched in 2015, offers assistance from the transition from school, through university and into the workplace.

Named after a football pools millionaire, LJMU draws more than 40% of its students from the Merseyside area. Almost all the undergraduates are state-educated and 40% come from the four poorest socioeconomic groups, helping the university to a strong showing in our new table on social inclusion. A wide range of scholarships and bursaries include the John Lennon Imagine Awards, match-funded through a gift of £260,000 from Yoko Ono, helping students who have been in care or are estranged from their parents.

A growing research reputation is a source of pride at the university. More than 60% of the work submitted for the Research Excellence Framework was rated world-leading or internationally excellent, with the proportion topping 80% in physics. The physics results covered astronomy, where researchers and students use the university's robotic telescope in the Canary Islands. LJMU was ranked second in the UK for sports science and fourth among post-1992 universities for law and education.

Liverpool has been ranked in the ten best cities in the world to visit and is also one of the UK's most affordable for students. Leisure facilities have been improving and there are discounts on theatre tickets and free access to art exhibitions and orchestral performances.

Sports facilities include an Olympic-sized swimming pool, two golf courses, fitness suites and weights rooms, and all-weather football pitches. Students have free off-peak access to Lifestyles fitness centres across the city.

Tuition fees

- » Fees for UK/EU students 2019–20 — £9,250
- » Fees for international students 2019–20 — £13,950–£14,450
  Foundation years — £10,600
- » For scholarship and bursary information see www.ljmu.ac.uk/discover/fees-and-finance
- » Graduate salary — £20,000

Student numbers

Undergraduates	17,238 (1,090)
Postgraduates	2,112 (2,006)
Applications/places	31,795/5,500
Applications per place	5.8
Overall offer rate	82.1%
International students	7.0%

Accommodation

University provided places: 3,800 (catered 0%)
Self-catered: £94–£161 per week
First years guaranteed accommodation
www.ljmu.ac.uk/accommodation

Where do the students come from?

State schools (non-grammar)	90.7%	Working-class homes	39.6%	Black ethnic minority	2.9%
Grammar schools	7.6%	Deprived areas	20.6%	Disabled	4.2%
Independent schools	1.7%	All ethnic minorities	11.2%	Mature (over 21)	16.8%

London Metropolitan University

London Met is the second most inclusive university in the country, according to our new table, with the highest proportion of black students and second-highest presence of mature students, more than half of them from working-class families. But it is just one place off the bottom of our main league table, finishing inside the top 90 on only two measures, students' perception of teaching quality and the amount it spends on student facilities.

Applications have halved since the beginning of the decade, partly because of the closure of large numbers of courses with low recruitment. The numbers starting courses dropped by another 20% in 2017, making a decline of 1,600 places since 2013.

London Met has now embarked on a £125m plan to create a single campus in Islington, in response to student feedback. New facilities for the Sir John Cass School of Art, Architecture and Design represented the start of the One Campus, One Community project. A new social learning hub followed last year, after the conversion of a building previously used for administration, with 11 high-spec classrooms and a cafe.

A new Programme for Improved Student Outcomes guarantees accredited, work-related learning opportunity for all students to provide real-world experience in preparation for the graduate jobs market. Another aim is to create a better sense of community in a university with a particularly diverse student body.

Professor John Raftery, the vice-chancellor, says the changes will "effectively create a new higher education offering in London, with a structure fit to meet the needs of its time".

Having introduced a range of new degrees, the university is planning a big expansion of degree apprenticeships over five years. It aims to have more than 400 apprentices in 2019–20, at least half of them taking degree apprenticeships. New programmes will cover social work, early years education, accounting, finance and law, policing and data analysis.

For the moment, however, London Met is in the bronze category in the government's Teaching Excellence Framework. An unusually negative assessment by the panel said students' achievement is "notably below benchmark across a range of indicators". It acknowledged a range of positive and appropriate strategies to address student satisfaction but was concerned that comparatively few students continue their studies after graduating.

The Science Centre's "superlab" — one of the largest teaching laboratories in Europe — has new audiovisual systems

166–220 Holloway Road
London N7 8DB
020 7133 4200
admissions@londonmet.ac.uk
www.londonmet.ac.uk
www.londonmetsu.org.uk
Open days 2019:
see website

Edinburgh
Belfast
Cardiff
LONDON

The Times and The Sunday Times Rankings
Overall Ranking: 131 (last year: 128)

Teaching quality	78.5%	=89
Student experience	74.6%	=107
Research quality	3.5%	112
Entry standards	102	=129
Graduate prospects	70.7%	=96
Good honours	52.3%	132
Expected completion rate	68.8%	131
Student/staff ratio	21.6	=127
Services and facilities	£1,970	89

that enable the lab to transmit 12 practical lectures simultaneously for different groups of students. The refurbished library on the Holloway Road has more computers, informal learning spaces and a cafe.

The improvements are taking place with an eye to the environment — the university has been shortlisted for a Green Gown sustainability award four times, having cut carbon emissions by half.

London Met entered far fewer academics for the 2014 Research Excellence Framework than it did in the 2008 assessments — only 15% of those eligible. As a result, it slipped down our research ranking, even though half of its submission was rated as world-leading or internationally excellent. English and health subjects scored particularly well.

London Met was the product of the merger of London Guildhall University and the University of North London in 2002, although its origins date back to the mid-19th century. The university has strong business links, especially in East London's "Tech City", where it has a business accelerator which has been ranked in the top five in Europe. It provides regular workshops, boot camps and an incubator programme for students thinking of setting up their own businesses.

The university has always catered particularly for groups who are under-represented in higher education. Student support services have been remodelled and a peer-assisted student support (Pass) scheme introduced, in which successful second- and third-year students coach first-years on their course.

Undergraduates take year-long modules consisting of 30 weeks of timetabled teaching. Over a year, students will typically study four modules and receive a minimum of 60 teaching hours per module. The university is in the top ten for the amount of supervised teaching time and expects first-year students to have 12 hours of teaching a week. Languages are a strength: London Met is one of only 22 universities globally to be members of the UN Language Careers Network.

The university does not own any residential accommodation but works with private hall providers to ensure that new entrants have suitable housing. Many of London Met's students live at home. There are fitness centres on the main campuses, and outdoor sports facilities a short Tube ride away. The competitive teams are successful and the social scene lively.

Tuition fees

» Fees for UK/EU students 2019–20	£9,250
» Fees for international students 2019–20	£12,150
» For scholarship and bursary information see www.londonmet.ac.uk/applying/funding-your-studies/undergraduate-tuition-fees	
» Graduate salary	£21,600

Student numbers

Undergraduates	8,055 (1,349)
Postgraduates	1,194 (1,548)
Applications/places	13,365/1,165
Applications per place	11.5
Overall offer rate	86.09%
International students	10.1%

Accommodation

University provided places: 0
Self-catered: £133–£325 per week (private providers)
www.londonmet.ac.uk/services-and-facilities/accommodation

Where do the students come from?

State schools (non-grammar)	96.5%	Working-class homes	51.4%	Black ethnic minority	37.6%
Grammar schools	0.6%	Deprived areas	7.6%	Disabled	6.1%
Independent schools	2.8%	All ethnic minorities	67.1%	Mature (over 21)	68.0%

London School of Economics and Political Science

When the LSE received a bronze rating in the 2017 Teaching Excellence Framework (TEF), the award caused a huge furore in the media, but this world-class institution says any publicity is good publicity and the poor result was clearly taken with a pinch of salt. Applications for admission last year were up 9%, one of the biggest increases at any UK university.

The LSE did not indulge in the public criticism of the TEF displayed by some other lowly-graded universities, but neither did it make a new submission in search of a better outcome. With more than ten applications per place — the most at any university — it calculated correctly that its global reputation would be more powerful than the new exercise.

Low levels of student satisfaction were the primary reason for the poor rating, although completion rates and graduate employment were also included in the TEF process, areas where LSE is among the top-performing institutions.

Professor Julia Black, then the interim director, said the LSE recognised that it had work to do on teaching quality, although she regretted that its graduates' "exceptional" record in highly-skilled job markets had not been taken into account. Another official report showed LSE graduates to be the highest-paid in the country after five years, a quarter of economics graduates earning more than £120,000.

The TEF panel acknowledged that the proportion of graduates in highly-skilled jobs six months after graduation was much higher than expected, but the LSE still lost marks for the proportion in other types of employment. In our new table, the LSE remains in the top ten for graduate prospects, but also has the lowest score at any university for student satisfaction with the quality of teaching.

Responding to student concerns, the school has reviewed all undergraduate programmes, in collaboration with student representatives, to enhance the learning experience. It has implemented recommendations for greater diversity of assessment and introduced resits for first-year students for the first time. The school is devoting an additional £11m to teaching and learning over a three-year period, including the creation of LSE Life (praised by the TEF panel), which offers students a single source of support for their academic, personal and professional development.

A new app, designed by students, enables undergraduates to keep abreast of activities and connect with others.

Dame Nemat "Minouche" Shafik, former permanent secretary at the Department for International Development, who became the LSE's first female director in 2017,

Houghton street
London WC2A 2AE
020 7955 6613
stu.rec@lse.ac.uk
www.lse.ac.uk
www.lsesu.com
Open days 2019:
April 3; July 4

The Times and The Sunday Times Rankings
Overall Ranking: 9 (last year: 11)

Teaching quality	66.1%	130
Student experience	64.5%	130
Research quality	52.8%	4
Entry standards	204	5
Graduate prospects	86.2%	8
Good honours	88.8%	8
Expected completion rate	96.0%	=6
Student/staff ratio	11.9	7
Services and facilities	£3,023	11

is overseeing the completion of a £120m development of the central buildings to address a chronic need for more space around Aldwych in London.

The new LSE Centre buildings are due to open this year, providing more flexible teaching space in a pedestrianised precinct. Other recent developments have created more areas for students to study, relax and eat, and revamped the library with new facilities and workspaces.

The school is ranked among the top 40 universities in the world by QS and second for the social sciences. More than 30 past or present heads of state have either been LSE students or academics, as have 16 winners of the Nobel prize in economics, literature and peace.

Degrees in international relations and Mandarin, language, culture and society, psychology and criminology are new to the portfolio of courses, which is already much wider than the school's name suggests.

The LSE had more world-leading research than any university in the 2014 Research Excellence Framework. It was the clear leader in the social sciences, with particularly good results in social work and social policy, and communication and media studies. A £10m donation from alumnus Firoz Lalji also created an academic centre focused on Africa.

The school has a long history of political involvement, from its foundation by Beatrice and Sidney Webb, pioneers of the Fabian movement. Its international character not only gives the LSE global prestige, but also an unusual degree of financial independence: only a small proportion of its funding comes from government sources.

More than 30% of the British undergraduates are from independent schools, one of the highest proportions in England. Substantial efforts are being made to attract a broader intake: the school is spending 60% of its additional fee income on student support and other activities to widen participation — the biggest proportion at any university — which might in the medium term address LSE's lowly ranking in our new table on social inclusion.

London's top nightspots are on the doorstep for those who can afford them, and discounted student nights are plentiful. More than 2,800 residential places for only 4,700 full-time undergraduates offer a good chance of avoiding central London's notoriously high private sector rents; there are spaces in hall for all first-years who want them.

Tuition fees

»	Fees for UK/EU students 2019–20	£9,250
»	Fees for international students 2019–20	£19,920
»	For scholarship and bursary information see www.lse.ac.uk/study-at-lse/undergraduate/fees-and-funding	
»	Graduate salary	£29,000

Student numbers

Undergraduates	4,723	(88)
Postgraduates	6,005	(392)
Applications/places		18,225/1,695
Applications per place		10.8
Overall offer rate		38.4%
International students		67.3%

Accommodation

University provided places: 4,599 (catered 35%)
Catered costs: £104–£278 per week
Self-catered: £146–£393 per week
First years guaranteed accommodation
www.lse.ac.uk/accommodation

Where do the students come from?

State schools (non-grammar)	44.7%	Working-class homes	21.1%	Black ethnic minority	4.7%
Grammar schools	23.8%	Deprived areas	7.1%	Disabled	4.3%
Independent schools	31.6%	All ethnic minorities	48.8%	Mature (over 21)	1.5%

London South Bank University

Our University of the Year for Graduate Employment for the second year running, London South Bank University (LSBU) jumped into the top four for graduate prospects, as well as challenging the most prestigious institutions on the salaries secured by its graduates. No wonder the feat is emblazoned across the front of the undergraduate prospectus.

The university is still outside the top 100 in our table, although it moved up 14 places the previous year. But its graduates are earning thousands of pounds more than the national average. LSBU has 1,000 employer partners and operates its own employment agency to help students find part-time work while they study. Almost 7,000 students — more than one in three of them undergraduates — are sponsored by employers.

LSBU received a silver rating in the government's Teaching Excellence Framework. The expert panel was impressed by the "appropriate" contact hours and consistently high levels of personalised learning for a diverse student population, provided by specialist staff and interactive education. This produces high levels of engagement and commitment to learning and study, the panel said.

New degrees such as human nutrition, psychological counselling, and fashion promotion with marketing, are tailored to the jobs market, but there are also fresh offerings in history and in human geography. There are new integrated master's degrees in sport rehabilitation, physiotherapy, and chiropractic.

The university is also planning a rapid expansion of its portfolio of degree apprenticeships, and expects to go from more than 200 to 700-plus apprentices by September this year, with new programmes in areas such as architecture, nursing and chartered town planning.

LSBU has adopted three core principles: student success, real-world impact and access to opportunity. Many of the 13,000 undergraduates take sandwich courses, but the vice-chancellor, Professor David Phoenix, would like even more to spend part of their course in industry. Three quarters of the students are from the capital and just under two thirds are drawn from ethnic minorities, placing the university third in our new table on social diversity.

The main campus is in Southwark, not far from the Southbank arts complex. It includes the Centre for Efficient and Renewable Energy in Buildings, a unique teaching, research and demonstration resource for low-carbon technologies, and the UK's first innercity green technology research centre.

90 London Road
London SE1 6LN
0800 923 8888
course.enquiry@lsbu.ac.uk
www.lsbu.ac.uk
www.lsbsu.org
Open days 2019:
see website

The Times and The Sunday Times **Rankings**
Overall Ranking: 107 (last year: =106)

Teaching quality	77.1%	=105
Student experience	75.2%	103
Research quality	9.0%	=65
Entry standards	107	126
Graduate prospects	87.7%	4
Good honours	68.9%	=95
Expected completion rate	77.0%	118
Student/staff ratio	16.5	=81
Services and facilities	£2,084	80

LSBU has invested more than £50m in modern teaching facilities, and developments costing another £38m are in the pipeline. Its degrees are also taught at a network of overseas colleges that stretches from China to the Caribbean.

Some health students are based on the other side of London, in hospitals in Romford and Leytonstone, while there is a smaller satellite campus in Havering to supplement that in Southwark. The health and social care school works with more than 50 NHS partner organisations and is one of only ten institutions with the highest rating from the Nursing & Midwifery Council.

LSBU is one of the top universities for knowledge transfer partnerships and has dedicated facilities to help students and graduates with start-up companies. The university entered more academics for the 2014 Research Excellence Framework than for previous assessments and scored well on the external impact of its research, with almost three quarters of the submission placed in the top two categories on this measure.

The university has always given a high priority to widening participation in higher education and takes more than half of its students from the lowest socioeconomic groups, far more than other academic institutions with similar courses and entry qualifications. Initiatives such as after-school and Saturday clubs and a summer festival for local people to upgrade their qualifications help to diversify the intake further.

However, the projected dropout rate for undergraduates remains among the highest in the country and the university continues to struggle in the National Student Survey. LSBU is targeting much of its fee income on providing support to help more students complete their education in the expected time.

The student centre has brought the students' union and many support services together to make them more convenient and accessible. LSBU was the first university to receive four accreditations from the Institute of Customer Service for excellent service across its accommodation service, library and learning resources, centre for student life and sports academy. The halls are close by: 1,400 rooms less than ten minutes away.

The sports centre benefited from a £1m makeover, with a multipurpose hall, therapy services and facilities that include a 40-station fitness suite and injury clinic. Southwark council contributed £300,000 to improve the facilities and guarantee public access. The university provides a comprehensive sports scholarship scheme.

Tuition fees

» Fees for UK/EU students 2019–20 £9,250
» Fees for international students 2018–19 £13,125–£15,100
» For scholarship and bursary information see
www.lsbu.ac.uk/courses/undergraduate/fees-and-funding
» Graduate salary £26,000

Student numbers

Undergraduates	8,544 (4,220)
Postgraduates	1,971 (3,250)
Applications/places	20,195/2,130
Applications per place	9.5
Overall offer rate	78.5%
International students	10.0%

Accommodation

University provided places: 1,396 (catered 0%)
Self-catered: £119–£144 per week
First years given priority
www.lsbu.ac.uk/student-life/accommodation

Where do the students come from?

State schools (non-grammar)	97.2%	Working-class homes	50.7%	Black ethnic minority	34.0%
Grammar schools	0.5%	Deprived areas	7.3%	Disabled	11.9%
Independent schools	2.3%	All ethnic minorities	64.6%	Mature (over 21)	51.1%

Loughborough University

THE TIMES
THE SUNDAY TIMES
GOOD
UNIVERSITY
GUIDE
2019
UNIVERSITY
OF THE
YEAR

Loughborough is our University of the Year after moving to its highest ever ranking in our table, put there by successes that include offering the sixth-best graduate prospects for its students. Only five years ago the university was outside the top 20 overall, but now it is in the leading group — and has among the most satisfied students in the UK.

It also has a gold rating in the Teaching Excellence Framework (TEF) to add to its achievements. The TEF panel found that students from all backgrounds achieve consistently outstanding outcomes, thanks to a culture of personalised learning and a comprehensive pastoral and academic tutorial programme. Loughborough also tops the Times Higher Education magazine student experience survey, with particularly good scores for extracurricular activities, social life and campus environment.

That environment should improve further this year with the opening of a £40m student accommodation development with 600 rooms, taking the total to more than 6,500. In addition, an elite athlete centre and hotel is opening this autumn — the first of its kind in Europe — where the facilities include 20 special rooms to mirror the effects of high-altitude training.

Loughborough is best known for its illustrious sporting pedigree: the medal haul of its students, graduates and campus-based athletes would have placed it 10th in the table at the 2018 Commonwealth Games.

But its academic stock has been rising, too. The university, for example, is to house the National Centre for Combustion and Aerothermal Technology, also due to open this year, training aerospace engineers in a critical area for the UK.

Loughborough is a main centre of engineering, with more than 2,800 students in a £20m integrated complex. The Science and Enterprise Park, which is home to at least 70 companies, has the £59m BAE-sponsored Systems Engineering Innovation Centre as its centrepiece.

Only eight universities entered such a high proportion of their eligible staff — 88% — for the 2014 Research Excellence Framework. Almost three quarters of their research was judged to be world-leading or internationally excellent, with sport and exercise sciences producing the best results in the UK and six other subject areas featuring in the top ten.

However, despite a generous package of bursaries, the university misses all its access benchmarks: fewer than a quarter of the undergraduates were from working-class homes when this was last surveyed and

---

Epinal Way
Loughborough LE11 3TU
01509 223 522
admissions@lboro.ac.uk
www.lboro.ac.uk
www.lsu.co.uk
Open days 2019:
see website

The Times and The Sunday Times **Rankings**

Overall Ranking: 5 (last year: =7)

Teaching quality	82.5%	=27
Student experience	84.5%	2
Research quality	36.3%	=30
Entry standards	162	27
Graduate prospects	86.9%	6
Good honours	84.3%	20
Expected completion rate	92.3%	26
Student/staff ratio	13.8	=25
Services and facilities	£3,047	10

only one in 15 comes from an area of low participation in higher education.

Nevertheless, Loughborough's successes have brought growing popularity, particularly among school-leavers, whose applications are up by 50% since 2013. Overall, applications dipped last year, in line with the national trend, but only after five successive increases, which enabled it to be more selective in its intake. Loughborough will not be following the vogue for unconditional offers: Professor Robert Allison, the vice-chancellor, has been highly critical of the practice, saying it can be "tantamount to bribery".

Ten new degrees are being introduced, ranging from the traditional strengths, with sport, coaching and physical education, and robotics, mechatronics and control engineering, to psychology with communication and English literature. Most subjects are available either as three-year full-time or longer sandwich degrees, which include a year in industry. The university is also a leader in the use of computer-assisted assessment, offering students the chance to gauge their own progress online.

Loughborough's sports facilities are among the best in the country, and have seen more than £60m investment over the past 15 years, benefiting elite athletes and social users. The campus boasts a 50-metre swimming pool, national academies for cricket and tennis, a gymnastics centre and a high-performance training centre for athletics. There are two world-class gyms and a fitness centre with cardiovascular equipment, fixed and free-weight stations and fitness studios.

The institution also hosts one of three national sport and exercise medicine centres of excellence, as well as the UK's only centre for disability sport. The programme of sports scholarships is the largest at any university.

Loughborough's 216-acre campus is the centre of most students' social life and the prize-winning students' union is among the most popular in the country with its members. Its community activities also received the Queen's award for voluntary service last year.

The relatively small town of Loughborough, a mile from campus, is never going to be a clubber's paradise, but both Leicester and Nottingham are within easy reach. Loughborough also has a campus for postgraduates in the Queen Elizabeth Olympic Park in east London that focuses on research and innovation.

Tuition fees

» Fees for UK/EU students 2019–20   £9,250
» Fees for International students 2019–20 £17,500–£22,350
» For scholarship and bursary information see
  www.lboro.ac.uk/study/undergraduate/fees-funding/
» Graduate salary   £25,000

Student numbers

Undergraduates	12,790	(142)
Postgraduates	2,815	(1,382)
Applications/places		31,215/3,780
Applications per place		8.3
Overall offer rate		77.9%
International students		20.9%

Accommodation

University provided places: 5,937 (catered 39%)
Catered costs: £159–£198 per week
Self-catered: £93–£164 per week
First years guaranteed accommodation
www.lboro.ac.uk/services/accommodation/

Where do the students come from?

State schools (non-grammar)	69.7%	Working-class homes	21.9%	Black ethnic minority	6.9%
Grammar schools	14.4%	Deprived areas	7.3%	Disabled	8.4%
Independent schools	15.9%	All ethnic minorities	23.3%	Mature (over 21)	3.5%

University of Manchester

All undergraduates at Manchester now explore three "ethical grand challenges", one for each year of their degree. Sustainability is addressed from the start of Welcome Week, with units on the crisis of nature, global citizenship, innovation and leadership. It is followed by social justice in the second year and workplace ethics in the third.

The programme is part of Manchester's Stellify package of extracurricular activities that is designed to make the university's graduates socially responsible and highly employable. The institution was the favourite recruiting ground of employers in this year's High Fliers survey of The Times top 100 companies, although it has lost some ground on graduate prospects in our new league table.

Manchester is comfortably the biggest university in our table — the only one with more than 40,000 students — and applications have been running at record levels, although the numbers starting courses have dropped by 1,000 in the past two years.

The university is in the throes of its biggest campus development programme, having spent £750m already on improvements, with £1bn more to come by 2022. Current projects include the flagship Manchester Engineering Campus Development (MECD), which will be one of the single largest construction projects undertaken by a UK university, and Brunswick Park, a stretch of green space on campus to be enjoyed by staff, students and the local community.

Several key developments have already been completed, such as the Manchester Cancer Research Centre, the National Graphene Institute and the renovation of the Whitworth art gallery, which have all received or been shortlisted for big awards. The eventual aim is to create a single "world-class" campus that the institution hopes will help to secure a place among the top 25 research universities in the world. It has only four places to go in the QS World University Rankings, although a little more in other international exercises.

In our table, with its focus on undergraduate study, Manchester has regained a top-20 ranking, although student satisfaction remains its Achilles heel, as it was when it was awarded silver in the Teaching Excellence Framework (TEF).

The TEF panel acknowledged the investment that was taking place and was impressed by the way that students were stretched, enabling them to progress and develop transferable and professional skills.

More than 80% of the work submitted to the 2014 Research Excellence Framework was considered world-leading or internationally excellent, although the university entered a lower proportion of its academics than many

Oxford Road
Manchester M13 9PL
0161 275 2077
study@manchester.ac.uk
www.manchester.ac.uk
www.manchesterstudentsunion.com
Open days 2019:
June 21, 22

The Times and The Sunday Times **Rankings**
Overall Ranking: =19 (last year: 25)

Teaching quality	77.1%	=105
Student experience	76.6%	=91
Research quality	39.8%	13
Entry standards	168	=18
Graduate prospects	80.7%	=42
Good honours	81.7%	25
Expected completion rate	93.0%	=16
Student/staff ratio	13.4	=19
Services and facilities	£2,898	14

of its peers in the Russell Group. Manchester has had 25 Nobel laureates, the most recent being Professors Andre Geim and Kostya Novoselov, who won the Nobel prize in physics in 2010 and whose work was the inspiration behind the National Graphene Institute. The next phase will be the Graphene Engineering Innovation Centre, which will stimulate the commercial redevelopment of the university's North campus, creating the cornerstone for a "graphene city".

The remodelling and refurbishment of the business school was completed last year, adding a new library and spaces for teaching, research and group work. There is also a 19-storey hotel development and an executive education centre. The MECD, which will bring the university together along the Oxford Road, is due to open in 2020. It will house Manchester's four engineering schools and two research institutes.

Other developments in the masterplan include more teaching facilities and the £235m Sir Henry Royce Institute for Advanced Materials Research. Outstanding teaching is one of the three goals in the university's strategy. The £24m Alan Gilbert Learning Commons provides more than 1,000 flexible learning spaces, high-quality IT facilities and a hub for student-centred activities and learning support services. The Learning Through Research initiative funds undergraduates to work with researchers.

New degrees to be launched this year focus mainly on the environmental and earth sciences, but also include educational psychology and cognitive neuroscience. The university is investing in its digital services to improve the experience of all students, from first contact right through to graduation, via a modern digital platform.

Manchester has been trying to broaden its intake, with a particular focus on increasing recruitment from the city and its surrounding area. The university admits more low-income students than most others in the Russell Group and is now close to the national benchmarks for widening participation.

Manchester's famed youth culture, plentiful accommodation and the university's position at the heart of a huge student population remain great attractions for applicants. There are first-rate sports facilities and the university's teams frequently rank near the top of the British Universities & Colleges Sport league.

Tuition fees

» Fees for UK/EU students 2019–20 £9,250
» Fees for international students 2019–20 £18,500–£23,000
  Medicine £40,000
» For scholarship and bursary information see www.manchester.ac.uk/study/undergraduate/student-finance/2019/tuition-fees
» Graduate salary £22,000

Student numbers

Undergraduates	27,592	(306)
Postgraduates	9,318	(3,275)
Applications/places	63,950/7,325	
Applications per place	8.7	
Overall offer rate	70.1%	
International students	33.3%	

Accommodation

University provided places: 8,082 (catered 27%)
Catered costs: £131–£181 per week
Self-catered: £72–£145 per week
First years guaranteed accommodation
www.manchester.ac.uk/study/experiencee/accommodation

Where do the students come from?

State schools (non-grammar)	70.0%	Working-class homes	21.5%	Black ethnic minority	4.3%
Grammar schools	12.7%	Deprived areas	9.3%	Disabled	7.5%
Independent schools	17.2%	All ethnic minorities	29.7%	Mature (over 21)	9%

Manchester Metropolitan University

A £400m programme of campus improvements is underway at Manchester Metropolitan University (MMU) to cater for a different mix of students. Currently the recruiter of the largest number of UK undergraduates at any institution in our table, it expects their numbers to drop over the next few years and to be replaced by at least 1,000 more international students, many of them post-graduates.

A new eight-storey building for the arts and humanities in the centre of Manchester is the next big project, housing a poetry library, the writing school and language centre, as well as a 180-seat auditorium for the Manchester School of Theatre.

Subsequent plans include a £4m technology hub for companies in the city working on carbon-neutral hydrogen fuel cells, and the new International Screen School Manchester, facilitating the establishment of an interdisciplinary undergraduate curriculum connecting computer science with film production and animation with human-centred design.

There will also be a new institute of sport with leading-edge facilities for academic, performance and participation sport. At the same time, the university is planning to increase the stock of residential accommodation and upgrade its library facilities.

The exception to the gradual decline expected at undergraduate level comes in the growing number of degree apprentices. Always among the pioneers of the qualification, MMU provides one in seven of all England's degree apprenticeships and is working with 13 different groups to expand into areas such as healthcare scientist practitioner and advanced clinical practitioner. The university expects the number of apprentices to rise from the current 700 to more than 1,000 by September. Professor Malcolm Press, MMU's vice-chancellor and a member of the board of the Institute for Apprenticeships, has forecast "exponential growth".

Any expansion will be undertaken with sustainability in mind. MMU heads the current People & Planet league, comparing universities' all-round environmental performance. It has been in the top three for five years in a row, and scored maximum points for environmental policy, auditing and environmental management systems, sustainability staff and education for sustainable development.

The university was given a silver rating in the Teaching Excellence Framework. An unusually brief commentary by the panel praised the inclusive curriculum for providing support for the diverse student population, the use of learning analytics and high levels of engagement with employers.

All Saints Building
All Saints
Manchester M15 6BH
0161 247 6969
manmetuni@mmu.ac.uk
www2.mmu.ac.uk
www.theunionmmu.org
Open days 2019:
June 19

The Times and The Sunday Times Rankings
Overall Ranking: 69 (last year: 80)

Teaching quality	79.2%	=71
Student experience	77.2%	=83
Research quality	7.5%	76
Entry standards	133	62
Graduate prospects	70.7%	=96
Good honours	70.4%	=85
Expected completion rate	82.9%	=86
Student/staff ratio	15.3	=53
Services and facilities	£2,599	=26

MMU is concentrating its activities on Manchester after announcing that the Cheshire campus in Crewe, where there are 800 trainee teachers and 3,000 other students taking contemporary arts and sports science, will close this year. The two Manchester campuses are close to each other, bordering Hulme and Moss Side. A £75m business school and science and engineering buildings have been added at All Saints, while the Brooks building, at Birley Fields, which hosts the education and health faculties, won a prize for regeneration. The Manchester School of Art and the £10m students' union building featured in the Royal Institute of British Architects' national awards.

At least 1,000 courses are offered in 70-plus subjects, more of them professionally accredited than at any other university and many involving work placements. Academics are encouraged to take a teaching qualification, but less than a quarter were entered for the 2014 Research Excellence Framework. Almost two thirds of the work submitted was rated world-leading or internationally excellent, with health, art and design, and English producing the best results.

The poet laureate, Professor Carol Ann Duffy, is creative director of the English department's writing school.

Fashion is one area of expansion. The Manchester Fashion Institute is a multidisciplinary partnership that is intended to be an international hub connecting education, research and enterprise. MMU is also planning a new independent, international medical school in partnership with Manchester and Salford universities, while the Manchester School of Architecture is rated in the top seven in the world by QS.

There is a long-standing commitment to extending access to higher education and MMU lies just outside the top 50 in our new social inclusion table. The First Generation scheme targets young people who would be the first in their family to go to university, providing financial, professional and personal support throughout their studies and into their careers. About 250 students with a household income of less than £25,000 have their fees waived during work placements.

Almost two thirds of MMU graduates stay and work in the northwest. The Talent Match service, in partnership with the Greater Manchester Chamber of Commerce, helps to link skilled graduates to local employers.

The university's sports facilities are good and the city's attractions do no harm to recruitment levels.

Tuition fees

» Fees for UK/EU students 2019–20 £9,250
» Fees for international students 2019–20 £14,500–£16,000
» For scholarship and bursary information see www2.mmu.ac.uk/study/undergraduate/money-matters
» Graduate salary £19,000

Student numbers

Undergraduates	25,019	(1,757)
Postgraduates	3,008	(3,226)
Applications/places		53,335/7,680
Applications per place		6.9
Overall offer rate		79.8%
International students		7.3%

Accommodation

University provided places: 5,050 (catered 0%)
Self-catered: £109–£211 per week
First years guaranteed accommodation
www2.mmu.ac.uk/accommodation/

Where do the students come from?

State schools (non-grammar)	93.8%	Working-class homes	41.5%	Black ethnic minority	5.6%
Grammar schools	3.1%	Deprived areas	16.9%	Disabled	5.7%
Independent schools	3.1%	All ethnic minorities	30.0%	Mature (over 21)	15.0%

Middlesex University

Middlesex is making a serious commitment to degree apprenticeships. It launched 20 new programmes last year and has established the Centre for Apprenticeships and Skills to bring academics and employers together and ensure that the university's programmes meet the needs of industry and apprentices.

The new offerings range from nursing to policing, teaching and digital technology, and another six starts are planned for September, including social work, construction site management and a commercial airline pilot apprenticeship.

Employability is the theme of the moment at Middlesex, which is offering a range of enhanced services to students. MDXcel brokers work experience opportunities; MDXcelerator provides staged intervention from start-up support specialists to help with business plans; MDX: MyMentor connects students with alumni working across the globe; and Unitemps MDX is an on-campus recruitment service that provides part-time work at the London Borough of Barnet and elsewhere.

The university's tailored employability support system for its diverse student body and the embedding of employability within and alongside programmes of study drew praise from the awarding panel in the Teaching Excellence Framework. Middlesex was placed in the silver category, with the panel commenting favourably on students' progress to highly-skilled employment.

Middlesex brands itself as a "university for skills", promising distinctive practice-based learning and embracing the value and power of diversity. Its strategy focuses on a combination of academic rigour and meeting practical needs. One example is the UK's first Cyber Factory training facility, which teaches students to design, develop and maintain the smart factories and cities of the future.

Applications and enrolments both fell in 2017, however, the latter by almost 20%. New degree programmes planned for September are mainly in fashion or environmental sciences, with most including the option of a foundation year for those without the necessary qualifications for degree-level study.

Students on the university's north London campus only just outnumber those taking Middlesex courses outside the UK. There are branch campuses in Mauritius, Dubai and Malta, and partner colleges on five continents. Middlesex was the first overseas university in Malta and opened a new base in Mauritius in 2017, while the longer-established Dubai site has 2,500 students. Altogether, 37,000 students are taking Middlesex courses or engaging in research, including almost 1,400 undergraduates in London from other EU countries, the product of a longstanding focus on Europe.

The Burroughs
Hendon
London NW4 4BT
020 8411 5555
enquiries@mdx.ac.uk
www.mdx.ac.uk
www.mdxsu.com
Open days 2019:
February 27; April 3;
June 29

The Times and The Sunday Times Rankings
Overall Ranking: =110 (last year: 91)

Teaching quality	75.0%	=117
Student experience	73.9%	=113
Research quality	9.7%	61
Entry standards	118	=105
Graduate prospects	73.5%	=81
Good honours	67.4%	=102
Expected completion rate	72.8%	=125
Student/staff ratio	16.6	=83
Services and facilities	£3,170	8

The university has invested more than £200m concentrating its activities on an impressive campus in Hendon. Developments include specialist teaching facilities such as additional wet labs for biology and biomedical sciences. There is a library, well-equipped technology labs and an £80m centre for art, design and media that has won a string of accolades. It includes Sony-designed, equipped and built television studios and newsroom, and flexible performance and exhibition spaces centred on an atrium. The campus even boasts one of the country's few courts for real tennis.

The highly flexible course system allows students to start some courses in January if they prefer not to wait until autumn and offers the option of an extra five-week session in the summer to try out new subjects or add to their credits. There is a range of work-based courses, including the degree apprenticeships, that allow participants to gain recognition and academic credit for learning in the workplace. Many of the conventional degrees include work placements or the option of a sandwich year.

More than a third of the eligible staff were entered for the 2014 Research Excellence Framework, and 58% of their work was placed in one of the top two categories. Art and design produced the best results, with three quarters of the research assessed as world-leading or internationally excellent.

Almost all the British students are state-educated, with more than half of them coming from the four poorest socioeconomic groups. Middlesex does not offer bursaries for undergraduates from low-income homes, believing that outreach and retention activities are more effective means of broadening the intake and improving completion rates, but there are hardship funds.

There are 1,400 residential places on or near the campus, including 630 in a privately run development near Wembley stadium, with more to come in the next few years. New entrants are guaranteed accommodation if they apply by the end of June, or mid-August for international students.

Sports facilities have been improving and now include a well-equipped fitness pod at Hendon with a gym and multipurpose outdoor courts. The West End and London's other attractions are easily reached via the Underground.

Tuition fees

» Fees for UK/EU students 2019–20   £9,250
» Fees for international students 2019–20 £12,500–£13,000
» For scholarship and bursary information see
   www.mdx.ac.uk/courses/undergraduate-funding
» Graduate salary   £23,000

Student numbers

Undergraduates	13,416	(1,391)
Postgraduates	2,005	(2,693)
Applications/places		25,175/3,250
Applications per place		7.7
Overall offer rate		79.0%
International students		23.3%

Accommodation

University provided places: 1,399 (catered 0%)
Self-catered: £143–£178 per week
First years guaranteed accommodation
www.mdx.ac.uk/life-at-middlesex/accommodation

Where do the students come from?

State schools (non-grammar)	96.7%	Working-class homes	56.3%	Black ethnic minority	27.1%
Grammar schools	1.5%	Deprived areas	5.3%	Disabled	4.5%
Independent schools	1.7%	All ethnic minorities	69.6%	Mature (over 21)	27.6%

Newcastle University

Newcastle has embarked on a new round of construction as part of its £350m urban regeneration project with the city council and Legal & General Capital. The flagship development on the Newcastle Helix site (previously known as Science Central) opened in 2017, when the highly-rated school of computing moved into the Urban Sciences building there.

Now, a £34m learning and teaching centre, with a 750-seat auditorium, is on the way. The £50m national innovation centre will follow in 2020, focusing on ageing, data and research innovation. Newcastle Helix is within walking distance of the university's main campus, in the heart of a city that is frequently rated the UK's best for student life.

In recent years, buildings have been added for physics, music and medicine, while science and engineering laboratories have been upgraded and disabled access improved. The prize-winning library is open 24 hours a day during term-time.

Unusually for a Russell Group university, Newcastle has a long-standing reputation for agriculture, with two farms in Northumberland.

A third campus, on the site of the former Newcastle General Hospital, focuses on research into ageing and is another element of the university's lead role in turning Newcastle into one of the six officially-designated science cities. The university also has a campus in London, in partnership with INTO, the company which runs a teaching and accommodation complex in Newcastle to prepare international students for undergraduate and graduate courses. Newcastle University London offers courses from the triple-accredited business school for the international market.

Newcastle was the first UK university to open an overseas medical school, in Johor, Malaysia. It also has an association with the Singapore Institute of Technology, offering engineering and nutrition degrees.

A gold rating in the government's Teaching Excellence Framework added to the university's attractions. The panel was impressed by "exceptional" support for students, including tailored help for disabled students, and consistent engagement of undergraduates with developments from the forefront of research and scholarship.

Nearly all of its degrees include the opportunity to spend up to a year in the workplace. The award-winning ncl+ initiative encourages students to develop employability skills through extracurricular activities. Students commit to at least 70 hours of activity and the award will appear on their Higher Education Achievement Report.

New programmes introduced last year include four-year undergraduate master's courses in mapping and geospatial data

Newcastle upon Tyne
NE1 7RU
0191 208 3333
http://www.ncl.ac.uk/enquiries
www.ncl.ac.uk
www.nusu.co.uk
Open days 2019:
see website

The Times and The Sunday Times Rankings
Overall Ranking: 21 (last year: 26)

Teaching quality	78.8%	=82
Student experience	79.1%	=54
Research quality	37.7%	=21
Entry standards	161	=28
Graduate prospects	85.8%	=10
Good honours	81.3%	=26
Expected completion rate	94.7%	12
Student/staff ratio	13.8	=25
Services and facilities	£2,200	66

science, and speech and language sciences, as well as three-year degrees in speech and language therapy, and psychology and sport and exercise science. The university also offered its first degree apprenticeships in power engineering, and is working with local businesses to add more.

The first students entered the new school of pharmacy in 2017, making Newcastle one of the few universities to offer courses and research in medicine, dentistry, biomedical sciences, psychology and pharmacy. The transfer of Durham's courses in medicine and pharmacy boosted Newcastle's numbers by 2,000 students and staff. The two universities previously had a joint programme, in which Durham's medics spent their first two years at their home university before moving to Newcastle for the rest of their course.

Almost 80% of the research entered for the 2014 Research Excellence Framework was judged to be world-leading or internationally excellent. Neuroscience, English and computing science were rated as leading departments in the UK. Among the university's subsequent research initiatives have been the opening of the Tyne Subsea centre of excellence for hyberbaric testing, and the Emerson Cavitation Tunnel research centre, which tests propellers and turbine blades for the marine industries.

Newcastle is popular with students from independent schools, who took a quarter of the places in 2016, but the university has long-established programmes to attract more students from non-traditional backgrounds and leads a national access programme. It has the Russell Group's highest proportion of students from areas of low participation in higher education but still ranks in our bottom 15 overall for social diversity.

The students' union has been refurbished and a student forum created alongside it as an outdoor social space. The campus hosts an independent theatre, museum and art gallery.

The £75m Park View Student Village opened last year, adding 1,300 rooms and lifting the total to more than 5,000, ensuring that all first-years continue to be guaranteed accommodation.

A new sports centre is due to open on campus later this year as part of a £30m investment in sports facilities. It will include teaching space, sports halls, squash courts and multipurpose areas, supplementing the artificial pitches and new rowing training centre at Cochrane Park.

Tuition fees

» Fees for UK/EU students 2019–20   £9,250
» Fees for international students 2019–20   £17,175–£22,110
   Dentistry £34,000; Medicine £33,600
» For scholarship and bursary information see
   www.ncl.ac.uk/undergraduate/finance
» Graduate salary   £22,500

Student numbers

Undergraduates	18.570	(51)
Postgraduates	4,923	(1,435)
Applications/places		36,505/5,315
Applications per place		6.9
Overall offer rate		87.9%
International students		25.6%

Accommodation

University provided places: 5,150 (catered 16%)
Catered costs: £145–£173 per week
Self-catered: £84–£175 per week
First years guaranteed accommodation
www.ncl.ac.uk/accommodation/university/undergraduate

Where do the students come from?

State schools (non-grammar)	65.0%	Working-class homes	20.3%	Black ethnic minority	2.3%
Grammar schools	10.0%	Deprived areas	9.3%	Disabled	4.9%
Independent schools	25.1%	All ethnic minorities	13.2%	Mature (over 21)	5.8%

Newman University

Newman has been gradually expanding, increasing its intake of undergraduates for five years in a row. The university widened its pool of potential applicants last year by adding the option of a foundation year in more than 20 degrees in the arts and humanities, business and social science for students without the necessary qualifications for immediate admission.

It has also launched three-year degrees in the liberal arts, education, forensic psychology, and sport and exercise psychology.

The university received a silver rating in the Teaching Excellence Framework, whose panel noted that students were "acquiring knowledge, skills and attributes that are valued by employers through work placements, volunteering support and enterprise opportunities, and which proactively embed career skills into the curriculum".

Newman was named among the top three universities in a 2017 calculation by the Economist of salaries five years after graduation compared with their expected levels, given students' backgrounds, qualifications and subjects. The authors acknowledged that part of the explanation lay in the high proportion of Newman students going into teaching and other public service jobs, where employment levels are high and early-career salaries competitive. Nevertheless, they estimated that an average salary of £24,300 five years after graduation was £2,800 more than might be expected.

The university is close to the bottom ten in our latest comparison of immediate graduate prospects, however, and only just outside the bottom ten overall. It achieves a top-ten ranking for social diversity in our new table, however.

About £22m is being invested in the campus at Bartley Green, eight miles southwest of Birmingham city centre. New halls of residence opened last year, adding almost 100 ensuite bedrooms and openplan living spaces. New teaching facilities have been developed, with suites of classrooms and dedicated spaces for interactive learning. One of the main teaching buildings was completely refurbished for use in the current academic year.

Newman was one of three Catholic foundations among the crop of institutions that were awarded university status in 2012. It takes its name from John Henry Newman, the author of The Idea of the University and a Catholic cardinal in the 19th century. His vision of a community of scholars still guides the university, which was established in 1968 as a teacher training college but now has a wider portfolio of degrees, mainly in the social sciences and humanities.

Genners Lane
Bartley Green
Birmingham B32 3NT
0121 476 1181
admissions@newman.ac.uk
www.newman.ac.uk
www.newmansu.org
Open days 2019:
June 15; July 6;
October 12;
November 8

The Times and The Sunday Times Rankings
Overall Ranking: 119 (last year: 121)

Teaching quality	81.2%	49
Student experience	78.5%	=65
Research quality	2.8%	116
Entry standards	120	=94
Graduate prospects	64.7%	=119
Good honours	65.3%	122
Expected completion rate	77.8%	117
Student/staff ratio	16.0	=71
Services and facilities	£1,623	119

The cardinal's influence is apparent in the small class sizes and interactive teaching style adopted by the university, which stresses its Catholic affiliation but also a commitment to be inclusive in its recruitment and subsequent activities.

The campus is in a quiet residential area with views over the Bartley reservoir and the Worcestershire countryside. Its modern buildings are arranged around a series of quadrangles of lawns and trees.

All full-time degrees include work placements, some of which are abroad, and undergraduates can opt to study at a partner university in Europe or further afield. There is a range of part-time courses and foundation degrees, most of which are taught at Newman rather than partner colleges.

The university received one of eight national awards to improve the use of technology in learning and teaching. The successful bid drew on a project designed to boost the digital literacy of the university's students, part of a larger initiative, Newman in the Digital Age.

Although only 23 academics were entered for the Research Excellence Framework, that was twice as many as in the previous assessments. Education and history produced the best results, but less than a third of the research submitted was placed in the top two categories. Newman does not employ staff for research alone, in order to ensure that students have regular contact with active researchers.

Three quarters of the undergraduates are female, almost all of them state-educated, and more than half came from working-class homes when this was last surveyed. There will be no bursaries or scholarships this year, but student support payments of up to £2,450 may be awarded and the university issues supermarket and travel vouchers to those who can demonstrate hardship.

The halls of residence are close to the teaching areas and library, with first-year students guaranteed one of the 292 places. The refurbished fitness suite and performance room have improved sports facilities that include an artificial sports pitch, sports hall, gymnasium and squash courts.

Birmingham city centre offers an abundance of cultural venues and student-oriented nightlife.

Tuition fees

» Fees for UK/EU students 2019–20	£9,250
» Fees for international students 2018–19	£11,250
» For scholarship and bursary information see www.newman.ac.uk/fees	
» Graduate salary	£21,000

Student numbers

Undergraduates	1,835	(462)
Postgraduates	255	(277)
Applications/places		3,440/625
Applications per place		5.5
Overall offer rate		91.5%
International students		1.2%

Accommodation

University provided places: 292 (catered 0%)
Self-catered: £105–£180 per week
First years guaranteed accommodation
www.newman.ac.uk/accommodation

Where do the students come from?

State schools (non-grammar)	98.5%	Working-class homes	56.2%	Black ethnic minority	11.7%
Grammar schools	0.8%	Deprived areas	20.5%	Disabled	10.1%
Independent schools	0.6%	All ethnic minorities	49.1%	Mature (over 21)	30.3%

University of Northampton

Northampton's £330m Waterside campus opened last year, offering high-quality facilities for 15,000 students, residential accommodation for 1,000 and leisure facilities that will be shared with the local community.

Professor Nick Petford, the vice-chancellor, says the new campus will provide teaching and learning space for the 21st century, without lecture theatres for 200–300, where students are "spouted at". Instead, classrooms for up to 40 people and smaller lecture theatres will accommodate "flipped learning", in which students prepare digital material in advance and interact with other students and staff.

The campus development has been funded mainly through a £231.5m bond guaranteed by the Treasury – the first time the government made such a guarantee. Its centrepiece is the four-storey Learning Hub, where most teaching takes place and the new library is open around the clock.

The Creative Hub brings together creative and science disciplines, with laboratories and specialist teaching spaces, while the Senate building includes flexible learning spaces and flexible accommodation for guest lectures and exhibitions.

A grade II listed engine shed was restored to house the students' union, while a sports dome can be used for teaching as well as recreation, supplemented by a pavilion, outdoor games areas and an artificial pitch.

The university's student village contains a mix of flats and four-storey town houses, as well as a hotel and community facilities, including a multifaith chaplaincy, bank, convenience store and health centre. Some residential accommodation on the old Park and Avenue campuses has remained open temporarily to maximise the options available to students.

The university was given a gold rating in the government's Teaching Excellence Framework despite dropping below its benchmark for highly-skilled graduate employment. The TEF panel welcomed "an embedded approach to the involvement of students in research, scholarship and professional practice, with strengths in community-based research and scholarship and sector-leading work on social enterprise".

Northampton was the first UK university to be named a Changemaker Campus by the Ashoka global network of social entrepreneurs and has since been ranked top in the country for social enterprise. Every student has the opportunity to work in a social enterprise as part of their course, developing entrepreneurial skills to make them more employable. This can involve a work placement, volunteering or participating in one of the university's social or economic partnerships.

The university hopes that its impressive

Waterside Campus
University Drive
Northampton NN1 5PH
0300 303 2772
study@northampton.ac.uk
www.northampton.ac.uk
www.northamptonunion.com
Open days 2019:
see website

58-acre campus, a few minutes' walk from the town centre, will help to restore Northampton's popularity with applicants, having seen the demand for places fall by more than 10% in 2017. Petford believes that by bringing back to life a disused brownfield site, the university is also providing a huge attraction to both UK and overseas companies, as well as encouraging graduates to remain in the area through internships, spin-out companies and start-ups.

The Northamptonshire Growth Hub works closely with the university to highlight opportunities for student placements, as well as part-time jobs.

Almost all of the undergraduates are state-educated and four out of ten come from working-class homes – more than the national average for the university's courses and entry qualifications. The Changemaker student award recognises engagement with primary and secondary schools.

The university co-sponsors a University Technical College in the town and another at the nearby Silverstone motor racing circuit. Northampton ranks in the top 20 of our new table measuring the social inclusiveness of universities across a range of measures covering the educational background of students, ethnicity, disability, social class and opportunities given to mature students.

Although it was awarded university status in 2005, Northampton traces its history back to the 13th century. Henry III dissolved the original institution, allegedly because his bishops thought it posed a threat to Oxford. The modern university originated in an amalgamation of the town's colleges of education, nursing, technology and art. It has a focus on training for the region's public services and is the region's largest provider of teachers and healthcare professionals.

The university entered a quarter of its eligible staff for the 2014 Research Excellence Framework. Only 30% of its research was placed in the top two categories, but there was an outstanding result in history, where two thirds of the work was considered world-leading or internationally excellent. There are five research centres, focusing on everything from contemporary fiction to anomalous psychological processes and transitional economics in China.

The town has a number of bars popular with students and the new campus has added to the leisure facilities. The Platform, a students' union venue in the town centre, houses a nightclub, a bar and cafe.

For other leisure avenues, both London and Birmingham are about an hour away by train.

Tuition fees

» Fees for UK/EU students 2019–20   £9,250
» Fees for international students 2018–19   £12,000–£15,000
» For scholarship and bursary information see www.northampton.ac.uk/study/fees-and-funding
» Graduate salary   £21,000

Student numbers

Undergraduates	9,101	(1,383)
Postgraduates	754	(1,611)
Applications/places	14,920/2,285	
Applications per place	6.5	
Overall offer rate	82.3%	
International students	12.4%	

Accommodation

University provided places: 2,500 (catered 0%)
Self-catered: £80–£158 per week
First years are given priority
www.northampton.ac.uk/study/student-life/accommodation

Where do the students come from?

State schools (non-grammar)	96.2%	Working-class homes	40.2%	Black ethnic minority	33.6%
Grammar schools	1.4%	Deprived areas	15.2%	Disabled	6.5%
Independent schools	2.4%	All ethnic minorities	46.6%	Mature (over 21)	32.3%

Northumbria University

Northumbria is the biggest university in northeast England and it is beginning to make its presence felt internationally. A partnership with the Maltese government will see it run a nursing degree on the island to help address the shortage of nurses there, while there is a new agreement with Amsterdam University of Applied Sciences, where a one-year programme in international business will enable undergraduates from all disciplines to enrich their degree.

Master's courses in business and management are also available in Amsterdam, with other subjects to follow this year. There are more than 3,000 students from outside the UK on the Newcastle campus and another 3,600 taking Northumbria courses overseas. This includes a design school in Jakarta, Indonesia, established with Binus International University.

The university was given a silver rating in the government's Teaching Excellence Framework. The panel praised Northumbria for helping students to enjoy their studies and achieve high attainment through a range of academic and personal support services, plus graduate start-up and careers assistance. High-quality physical and digital resources are used effectively both in teaching and by students, it said. The university is up five places in our new league table, partly due to increased spending on student facilities.

Northumbria is investing £52m in its City campus to improve the student experience. The opening of the Student Central zone around the students' union and the extension to the university library bring together services such as careers, welfare and international support.

A new building for computing and information sciences courses is now open and is due to be followed by a new School of Architecture. In addition, the Woon Gallery opened on campus last year, housing rare and contemporary Oriental art on loan from the Woon Foundation as a new resource for teaching and research.

The university had already spent £200m on its city centre headquarters and the Coach Lane campus, three miles away, where the sports centre is located and there is a clinical skills centre, where students learn in simulated hospital environments. There is also a base in the City of London, which is mainly for postgraduates.

Around half of the students are from the northeast, but numbers drawn from other parts of the UK have been rising. More than a third of the UK undergraduates were from the four lowest socioeconomic classes when this was last surveyed. Free one-day taster courses run throughout the year to give prospective students an idea of what

Sutherland Building
Newcastle upon Tyne
NE1 8ST
0191 349 4646
ask4help@nurthumbria.ac.uk
www.northumbria.ac.uk
www.mynsu.co.uk
Open days 2019:
see website

The Times and The Sunday Times Rankings
Overall Ranking: 61 (last year: 66)

Teaching quality	79.9%	66
Student experience	79.4%	48
Research quality	9.0%	=65
Entry standards	145	45
Graduate prospects	75.4%	=68
Good honours	77.0%	48
Expected completion rate	86.2%	=58
Student/staff ratio	16.7	=85
Services and facilities	£2,257	60

university life would be like and there are bursaries of £800 a year for applicants from the poorest homes.

The university was one of the pioneers of degree apprenticeships. It currently offers programmes in chartered surveying, chartered managership and digital and technology solutions, and is planning a significant expansion this year.

More than 560 employers sponsor undergraduate programmes – one of the highest rates in the UK – and accreditation comes from 60 professional bodies.

Northumbria is also among the leading universities for graduate start-ups, its companies boasting the highest turnover in the UK in the last two years for which national figures are available. At more than £80m, a £10m increase on the previous year, their combined turnover was £30m more than the second-placed institution.

All Northumbria's teacher training programmes have been rated as outstanding by Ofsted for 16 years in a row. The university more than doubled the numbers entered for the 2014 Research Excellence Framework compared with the 2008 assessments while improving the results. Sixty per cent of the work was judged to be world-leading or internationally excellent, attracting one of the biggest increases in funding at any university.

The sports facilities are good, and Northumbria has been in the top ten of the British Universities & Colleges Sport (Bucs) league table since 2013–14. There is a £30m sports centre which includes a swimming pool, multiple laboratories, a climbing wall and a 3,000-seat indoor arena.

However, a change in focus to concentrate on participation rather than elite sport has seen the university withdraw all seven of its teams previously participating in national sports leagues. Football, volleyball, netball, basketball and water polo are among the elite sports affected, although the university will remain a serious player in the inter-university sports leagues run by Bucs, with most teams there surviving the cuts.

There is also a generous sport scholarship scheme and these scholarships will be honoured, the university says, despite the cuts to top-end sport.

Most first years are offered places in university accommodation. There are now more than 4,500 rooms available, including almost 1,000 ensuite bedrooms in nearby Gateshead, where there are fitness facilities and a multi-use games area.

Tuition fees
» Fees for UK/EU students 2019–20 £9,250
» Fees for international students 2019–20 £13,000–£15,000
» For scholarship and bursary information see www.northumbria.ac.uk/study-at-northumbria/fees-and-scholarships
» Graduate salary £21,900

Student numbers
Undergraduates	18,571 (2,870)
Postgraduates	2,816 (2,416)
Applications/places	26,365/5,400
Applications per place	4.9
Overall offer rate	85.4%
International students	12.7%

Accommodation
University provided places: 3,653 (catered 8%)
Catered costs: £112 per week
Self-catered: £70–£166 per week
First years guaranteed accommodation
www.northumbria.ac.uk/study-at-northumbria/accommodation

Where do the students come from?
State schools (non-grammar)	90.7%	Working-class homes	37.2%	Black ethnic minority	2.0%
Grammar schools	4.2%	Deprived areas	20.2%	Disabled	5.8%
Independent schools	5.2%	All ethnic minorities	10.4%	Mature (over 21)	20.5%

Norwich University of the Arts

Norwich University of the Arts (NUA) enjoyed one of the biggest rises up our table in 2017, thanks mainly to big increases in student satisfaction, which placed it in the top ten in the sections of the National Student Survey relating to teaching quality. However, a drop in satisfaction with teaching, allied to a sharp decline in ratings for the student experience, has led to the university falling back a little this year.

The university attained a gold rating in the Teaching Excellence Framework (TEF). The panel found that course design and assessment practices encouraged experimentation, creative risk-taking and team-working, providing "outstanding levels of stretch for students".

Investment in physical and digital resources produced a learning environment that is enriched by collaborative working, it added, as professional staff operate alongside visiting lecturers and industry professionals.

Applications to NUA have dipped slightly but the numbers are still twice what they were a decade ago. The university has ambitions to double in size and has opened new buildings in each of the past three years as part of a £10m development plan to allow for growth. The latest of them contains students' union offices, a cafe and a lounge, as well as two labs for new media and facilities for a range of courses.

The Sir John Hurt film studio, named after the university's late chancellor, is in a renovated building in the city centre that also houses the school of architecture. The renovation won an award from the Royal Institute of British Architects.

NUA is widening its portfolio of courses, adding "year 0" courses in photography and illustration this year to bring students up to the standard required for degree-level study. Other areas such as film and moving-image production, graphic design and fine art already had this option. But there are only 15 BA degrees and 2,200 students, 60% of whom are female.

NUA makes a virtue of focusing entirely on the arts, design and media, rather than venturing into business or the humanities and social sciences. The university traces its history to 1845, when the Norwich School of Design was established by the artists and followers of the Norwich school, known for its landscape painting. Former tutors at the university include the artists Lucian Freud, Lesley Davenport and Michael Andrews.

The campus is concentrated on the pedestrianised centre of Norwich. The university's public art gallery enables students to showcase their work and gain experience curating and organising exhibitions, while the

Francis House
3-7 Redwell Street
Norwich NR2 4SN
01603 610 561
admissions@nua.ac.uk
www.nua.ac.uk
www.nuasu.co.uk
Open days 2019:
January 4; June 28

Edinburgh
Belfast
NORWICH
London
Cardiff

The Times and The Sunday Times Rankings
Overall Ranking: 66 (last year: 60)

Teaching quality	82.0%	=36
Student experience	77.0%	=86
Research quality	5.6%	=87
Entry standards	144	=46
Graduate prospects	60.6%	129
Good honours	72.8%	=69
Expected completion rate	87.2%	52
Student/staff ratio	15.8	=66
Services and facilities	£2,176	71

library houses a large specialist art, design and media collection.

The Ideas Factory, which was praised by the TEF panel, provides supported facilities to help graduates with the development of new digital businesses. It also hosts the university's Digital User Research Lab and its creative agency, which provides opportunities for students to work on commercial projects with local, national and international organisations. These initiatives should help address the issue presented by the latest graduate prospects data, which sees NUA in the bottom five in the UK, alongside two other arts-dominated universities, Leeds Arts and Goldsmiths.

Approaching 40% of the undergraduates come from working-class homes and the projected dropout rate is much lower than the national average for NUA's courses and entry qualifications. Most courses include units of self-managed learning and exploration that allow students to concentrate on areas of particular interest to them.

More than half of the work submitted to the 2014 Research Excellence Framework was judged to be world-leading or internationally excellent, with 90% placed in the top two categories for its impact on the broader cultural and economic landscape.

NUA has its own art materials shop, which sells basic and specialist art supplies at discounted prices. Individual studio space is provided for all full-time students in the faculties of art and design, while students in the media faculty have access to digital media workstations.

Workshops for everything from digital video editing to laser cutting provide specialised resources and are staffed by experienced professionals, including graduates and practising artists.

The university has a little over 300 residential places, located in the city centre – enough for four out of five new entrants wanting accommodation. Others have access to a register of more than 1,000 "student-friendly" private residential places

NUA does not have its own sports site but its students have access to the University of East Anglia's Sportspark, which has some of the best facilities in the higher education system, including an Olympic-sized swimming pool.

The city, consistently rated one of the safest and "greenest" places in the UK is attractive and popular with students.

Tuition fees
»	Fees for UK/EU students 2019–20	£9,250
	Foundation courses	£8,750
»	Fees for international students 2019–20	£14,500
»	For scholarship and bursary information see www.nua.ac.uk/study-at-nua/fees-funding	
»	Graduate salary	£17,000

Student numbers
Undergraduates	2,068	(0)
Postgraduates	64	(49)
Applications/places		2,925/750
Applications per place		3.9
Overall offer rate		66.1%
International students		6.9%

Accommodation
University provided places: 305 (catered 0%)
Self-catered: £99–£176 per week
www.nua.ac.uk/university-life/accommodation

Where do the students come from?
State schools (non-grammar)	93.9%	Working-class homes	37.6%	Black ethnic minority	2.0%
Grammar schools	2.6%	Deprived areas	17.6%	Disabled	12.3%
Independent schools	3.5%	All ethnic minorities	10.8%	Mature (over 21)	9.7%

University of Nottingham

International and sporting excellence carry Nottingham to two University of the Year awards and a second successive shortlisting for the overall University of the Year title.

The David Ross Sports Village, a £40m complex with an indoor sprint track, hydrotherapy pool and 200-station fitness suite, is at the centre of sporting activity in Nottingham. Other provision includes a water-based hockey pitch and a 25-metre pool. Nottingham has been in the top four in the Bucs inter-university leagues for the past three years. Allied to an improved ranking in our sports science subject table, it was the overwhelming choice for our Sports University of the Year title.

A central teaching and learning hub, with a 300-seat lecture theatre and performing arts space, and a new health centre for the UK's biggest register of patients are new additions to one of the most attractive campuses in the country. The hub, at the heart of Nottingham's University Park campus, will be the centrepiece of a £40m programme of new and refurbished teaching spaces, while the health centre, which caters for local people as well as students and staff, comes via a £9m gift from the Cripps Foundation, the biggest in the university's history.

Applications were up by 11% last year, more than compensating for a dip in 2017, at a time when most universities have seen demand fall. A gold rating in the Teaching Excellence Framework (TEF) and further progress in the top 20 of our league table help Nottingham to another shortlisting for University of the Year. Medicine, maths, computer science, sociology and economics have seen substantial growth in applications.

Campus developments are not confined to the 330-acre University Park. The Peter Buttery Teaching Laboratory, named after a renowned Nottingham academic, has upgraded the facilities for the biosciences and veterinary medicine, which are taught on the Sutton Bonington site, 12 miles south of the city. The laboratory, which accommodates up to 200 students, can be divided into three zones for different subjects.

There has been considerable investment on the Jubilee campus, which houses the schools of management and finance, computer science and education, as well as 750 residential places. The Centre for Sustainable Chemistry, part-funded by GlaxoSmithKline, is housed in a carbon-neutral building described as the first of its kind in the UK.

The medical school, like the Jubilee campus, is close to University Park, while there is a £4.5m facility for nursing located at Derby Hospital.

Nottingham, which is also our International University of the Year, has been promoting its

---

University Park
Nottingham NG7 2RD
0115 951 5559
undergraduate-enquiries
@nottingham.ac.uk
www.nottingham.ac.uk
www.su.nottingham.ac.uk
Open days 2019:
June 28, 29;
September 13, 14

The Times and The Sunday Times Rankings
Overall Ranking: 16 (last year: 18)

Teaching quality	78.9%	81
Student experience	77.9%	=76
Research quality	37.8%	20
Entry standards	164	=25
Graduate prospects	86.0%	9
Good honours	84.9%	18
Expected completion rate	93.3%	15
Student/staff ratio	13.9	27
Services and facilities	£2,508	35

campuses in China and Malaysia, which are both centres of research as well as teaching. There are more than 6,600 students at Ningbo, in China, and almost 5,000 an hour's drive from Kuala Lumpur, taking Nottingham's total student population to more than 45,000.

With undergraduates encouraged to transfer between campuses and more than 7,000 international students in Nottingham, the university markets itself as a global institution. It is well inside the top 100 universities in the world in the QS rankings, with 20 subjects in the top 100.

The university's efforts to prepare students for the employment market contributed to its TEF rating. Undergraduates across the full range of disciplines are able to undertake a placement year as part of their studies. Nottingham has moved into the top ten on this measure in our new edition, and is among the most favoured recruiting grounds of employers in The Times top 100 companies.

The TEF panel also found high levels of contact time, which are prescribed and monitored; a culture of personalised learning that ensures all students are challenged to achieve their full potential; and exceptionally high student engagement with advanced technology-enhanced learning.

New degrees planned for this year offer the choice of three-year programmes or an extended master's in liberal arts or cancer sciences, in which students examine the entire life cycle of cancer and can include an intensive research project on one type of the disease. There will also be a new BA in international relations and Asian studies.

Nottingham launched a £200m research fund in 2017. The investment will be spread over five years and is expected to leverage more funding from industry, government and philanthropists. It will focus on six diverse areas: modern slavery, future food, green chemicals, precision engineering, propulsion and smart industrial systems.

More than 80% of the work entered for the 2014 Research Excellence Framework was rated as world-leading or internationally excellent. The university was in the UK's top ten in half of the 32 subject areas in which it made submissions, with pharmacy, chemistry and physics producing particularly good results.

The two main campuses in Nottingham are within three miles of the city centre, which has a good selection of student-oriented clubs. Halls of residence and the students' union tend to be the centre of social life for most students, especially in the first year.

Tuition fees

- » Fees for UK/EU students 2019–20 £9,250
- » Fees for international students 2019–20 £17,550–£22,620
  Medicine £40,500 (clinical years); Veterinary science £33,540
- » For scholarship and bursary information see
  www.nottingham.ac.uk/fees/index.aspx
- » Graduate salary £22,500

Student numbers		
Undergraduates	23,470	(595)
Postgraduates	5,760	(2,688)
Applications/places		47,485/6,390
Applications per place		7.4
Overall offer rate		82.2%
International students		22.4%

Accommodation

University provided places: 9,352 (catered 48%)

Catered costs: £150–£176 per week

Self-catered: £101–£173 per week

First years guaranteed accommodation

www.nottingham.ac.uk/accommodation/accommodation.aspx

Where do the students come from?

State schools (non-grammar)	64.0%	Working-class homes	20.3%	Black ethnic minority	7.6%
Grammar schools	16.1%	Deprived areas	8.6%	Disabled	5.5%
Independent schools	20.0%	All ethnic minorities	27.8%	Mature (over 21)	9.3%

Nottingham Trent University

Nottingham Trent University (NTU) is enjoying a period of unprecedented success. Named our Modern University of the Year for 2017–18, it also scooped the Times Higher Education magazine's University of the Year title.

Now it has recorded a second successive ten-place rise in our league table. NTU has reached our top 40 for the first time and only two post-1992 universities are ahead of it in the latest table, both of them specialist institutions.

Although student satisfaction scores have dipped slightly this year, NTU is just outside the top ten on both measures derived from the National Student Survey. Its record in this field helped NTU to a gold rating in the government's Teaching Excellence Framework. The independent panel acknowledged the "considerable" investment in the university's employability team and the provision of high-quality work placements for all students. There was exemplary engagement with employers, "who contribute to the curriculum in a way that demonstrably enhances students' employability", the panel added.

The university's accolades have not gone unnoticed by applicants. Unusually among its peer group, NTU saw a 9.5% increase in applications last year, giving it the opportunity to build on growth of more than 10% in the number of students starting courses over the past two years.

Eight degrees were added in subjects as diverse as filmmaking, policing and ecology, with another eight to come in September, all in education and childhood studies. There has also been a significant expansion in degree apprenticeships, with 17 programmes now running.

NTU has spent £450m on its campuses in the past ten years, including a substantial expansion of its city-centre base, and another £175m has been budgeted for new student facilities in the next five years. They will include a digital media hub and extensive facilities for science and engineering, as well as a new reception area, teaching facilities and exhibition space at the Brackenhurst campus for animal, rural and environmental sciences, 14 miles from the city. The campus includes one of the region's best-equipped equestrian centres, with a purpose-built indoor riding area, as well as 340 residential places.

The Clifton campus, just outside Nottingham, is being redeveloped, with two new teaching buildings and landscaped outdoor spaces, as well as a growing sports village. The Lee Westwood Sports Centre includes a gym, sports halls, studios, and a nutrition training centre, while the outdoor facilities include an Olympic-standard hockey pitch.

The recently-established Nottingham

50 Shakespeare Street
Nottingham NG1 4FQ
0115 941 8418
applications@ntu.ac.uk
www.ntu.ac.uk
www.trentstudents.org
Open days 2019:
February 2, 23

The Times and The Sunday Times Rankings
Overall Ranking: 37 (last year: =47)

Teaching quality	83.8%	=13
Student experience	82.5%	11
Research quality	6.5%	81
Entry standards	144	=46
Graduate prospects	81.7%	=30
Good honours	71.9%	=74
Expected completion rate	85.8%	=62
Student/staff ratio	14.8	=39
Services and facilities	£2,320	51

Institute of Education, which attempts to align teaching and research expertise more effectively, is also based on the Clifton campus.

NTU has 29,000 students, including almost 4,000 from outside the UK. It is best known for fashion and other creative arts, but also has one of the UK's biggest law schools, offering legal practice courses for solicitors and barristers, as well as degrees.

Many courses are sponsored by employers, and NTU is in the top ten for the number of students on year-long work placements, a format that it is keen to promote since establishing that it transforms the job prospects of students from poor backgrounds in particular. A third of the undergraduates come from working-class homes and more than nine out of ten were state-educated.

Most courses include placements of at least four weeks. NTU is also aiming to offer all its students an "international learning experience", which may involve a study or work placement abroad, learning a foreign language or studying another culture or country.

NTU has a more developed research function than most modern universities. It attracted an £8m donation in 2013 from the John and Lucille van Geest Foundation – thought to be the largest to a post-1992 university – to advance the university's work

in cancer diagnosis and therapy. This added to the £8m donated from the same source to establish the John van Geest Cancer Research Centre in 2008.

More than half of the research submitted to the 2014 Research Excellence Framework was considered world-leading or internationally excellent. The best results were in health subjects and general engineering, where more than 80% of the work was placed in the top two categories. The university has since won a Queen's Anniversary prize for new technologies for food safety and aviation security.

There is residential accommodation on every campus. The total of 4,750 bed spaces enables NTU to guarantee accommodation to all new entrants who apply by the end of July.

The university has a strong sporting reputation, frequently reaching the top 20 in the Bucs leagues. Social life varies between campuses, but all have access to the city's lively cultural and clubbing scene. A bus service links the main campuses and the city's tram system serves the university.

Tuition fees

» Fees for UK/EU students 2019–20	£9,250
» Fees for international students 2019–20	£13,900
» For scholarship and bursary information see www.ntu.ac.uk/fees	
» Graduate salary	£20,000

Student numbers

Undergraduates	22,510 (1,088)
Postgraduates	2,902 (2,871)
Applications/places	37,075/7,190
Applications per place	5.2
Overall offer rate	88.0%
International students	13.4%

Accommodation

University provided places: 4,754 (catered 0%)
Self-catered: £97–£173 per week
First years guaranteed accommodation
www.ntu.ac.uk/accommodation

Where do the students come from?

State schools (non-grammar)	90.4%	Working-class homes	33.1%	Black ethnic minority	8.1%
Grammar schools	3.6%	Deprived areas	14.9%	Disabled	6.0%
Independent schools	6.0%	All ethnic minorities	22.9%	Mature (over 21)	12.5%

The Open University

Peter Horrocks, the vice-chancellor of the Open University (OU), resigned last year after failing to win the backing of its governing council for his stewardship of a programme designed to reduce the £420m annual budget by almost a quarter. Professor Mary Kellett, the executive dean of the university's wellbeing and education faculty, took over as acting vice-chancellor, seeking a period of calm in which to review the proposals, but there is yet to be agreement on how to balance the books in the face of dramatically reduced student numbers.

Although still much the biggest university in the UK, with 121,000 students in 2016–17, the OU has been hit by the national collapse in part-time study. Embodying the concept of widening participation even before the term had been invented, the OU remains the model for distance-learning universities around the world, more than 50 years on from Harold Wilson's early 1960s vision of a "university of the air".

However, it is unlikely to retain the whole of its current portfolio of teaching and research. Horrocks's plan would have seen the closure of 41 of the 71 degree programmes, as the OU evolved to become more a "university of the cloud".

The university is already the host institution for FutureLearn, a consortium of leading universities and cultural organisations such as the British Museum and the British Council, offering Moocs (massive open online courses). They are now available in a wide range of subjects, some providing credits towards OU degrees.

The OU is not abandoning developments, however. Seven new degrees have been launched including computing and IT, criminology, and music. The university is also expanding its range of degree apprenticeships, developing programmes in digital technology and cyber-security in the devolved nations, with the expectation of educating more than 1,500 apprentices by September. The OU has the largest Cisco Networking Academy in the UK and is a lead member of the new Institute of Coding.

Our tables have never included the OU because the absence of campus-based undergraduates would place it at a disadvantage in comparisons with traditional universities. There are no entrance requirements, for example, and no need for physical student facilities.

On those measures where a comparison is possible, the OU generally performs well. It is in the top 20 for overall satisfaction in the National Student Survey, for example, and 72% of the OU's submission for the 2014 Research Excellence Framework was considered world-leading or internationally excellent. There was an outstanding result in

Walton Hall
Milton Keynes
MK7 6AA
0300 303 5303
http://www.open.ac.uk/contact/new
www.open.ac.uk
www.open.ac.uk/ousu

***The Times and The Sunday Times* Rankings**
Not applicable

music, where 94% reached these levels, and good performances in art and design and electronic engineering.

Based in Milton Keynes, Buckinghamshire, the university has more than 5,000 part-time associate lecturers (tutors) spread around the country to guide students through degrees.

The OU's "supported open learning" system allows students to work where they choose: at home, in the workplace or at a library or study centre. They have contact with fellow students at tutorials, day schools or through online conferencing and electronic forums, social networks and informal study groups.

In an attempt to revitalise part-time higher education, the university has launched the website Pearl (Part Time Education for Adults Returning to Learn), providing information on the opportunities for adults to increase their skills and progress in their chosen careers. The OU also has a joint apprenticeship service with the consultant KPMG, giving information to employers about the available programmes.

As well as degrees in a named subject, the OU awards "Open" bachelor degrees, where the syllabus is designed by the students combining a number of modules. Assessment is by both continual assessment and examination or, for some modules, a main assignment. Except in fast-moving areas such as computing, there is no limit on the time taken to complete a degree.

Undergraduate fees currently £5,856 in England for the equivalent of full-time study, are the cheapest at any university and eligible for a tuition fee loan. They are cheaper still in the rest of the UK. The OU provides fee waivers for students from poor backgrounds through its Widening Access and Success programme.

Three in ten students are less than 25 years old and three quarters work either full or part-time while studying. More than 60% of undergraduates are female and most live in the UK, but there are now 15,000 students in other countries. The OU offers special support for disabled students and currently has more than 20,000 students with disabilities.

Tuition fees

- » Fees for English/EU students (until July 31, 2019) £5,856
  Scotland, Wales and Northern Ireland £1,968
- » Fees for international students (until July 31, 2019) £5,728
  For scholarship and bursary information see
  www.open.ac.uk/courses/fees-and-funding
- » Graduate salary n/a

Students

Undergraduates	0	(113,477)
Postgraduates	291	(7,853)

Accommodation
Not applicable

Where do the students come from?
Not available

University of Oxford

Oxford has fallen marginally further behind Cambridge in our new ranking, and now heads just one of the nine components in our table, for the proportion of top-class degrees it awards. The gap between Oxbridge and the rest cannot be precise while the two universities' undergraduates choose to boycott the National Student Survey — satisfaction levels in our table this year are based on 2016 responses — but they remain well clear of the rest overall.

Indeed, Oxford is presently rated as the top university in the world in Times Higher Education's research-dominated ranking, although it sits sixth (one place behind Cambridge) in the QS rankings favoured by this guide as an indicator of global standing.

The university has a gold rating in the Teaching Excellence Framework. The independent panel praised its collegiate system and the small group tutorials, as well as the opportunities for students to engage as active researchers with the possibility, in some cases, of co-publishing with world-leading academics. The only negative comments concerned satisfaction levels among disadvantaged students and the immediate prospects for black and ethnic minority graduates holding A-levels.

Controversy has raged over the treatment of black students in the admissions process in recent months after it was revealed that a third of Oxford colleges had admitted no more than three black students in the past three years. The new independent Office for Students has urged the university to be more ambitious in its efforts to admit more ethnic minorities and disadvantaged students.

Oxford finishes well adrift at the bottom in our new table for social diversity that examines recruitment of children not educated in grammar or independent schools, ethnic minorities, the disabled, the working class, those living in deprived neighbourhoods or mature students aged over 21.

Although the university conducted 2,600 outreach activities last year involving 3,100 schools, it still has the smallest proportion of students from comprehensive and other non-selective schools at any English university in our table, at below 40%. Oxford offers the most generous financial support in UK higher education for students from poor backgrounds. Nearly a quarter of all students receive some support, with those from the lowest-income families receiving at least £3,700 a year, and this can rise to £6,700.

Applications have risen for the past four years and are running at record levels, but there have been barely any more places available. Less than a quarter of 18-year-olds applying to Oxford in 2017 received an offer, the lowest proportion in the UK and significantly less than at Cambridge. But

University Offices
Wellington Square
Oxford OX1 2JD
01865 288 000
study@ox.ac.uk
www.ox.ac.uk
www.oxfordsu.org
Open days 2019:
July 3, 4; September 20

The Times and The Sunday Times Rankings
Overall Ranking: 2 (last year: 2)

Teaching quality	n/a	
Student experience	n/a	
Research quality	53.1%	3
Entry standards	217	3
Graduate prospects	83.5%	23
Good honours	93.7%	1
Expected completion rate	98.5%	2
Student/staff ratio	10.5	2
Services and facilities	£3,455	4

Oxford made offers to its highest recorded number of state-school applicants in 2017, nudging 60%.

There are written admissions tests for certain subjects and you may be asked to submit samples of work. Some courses now demand two A* grades and another A at A-level and 99% of successful candidates achieve at least three As at A-level or their equivalent.

The prize is a place at the oldest and arguably most famous university in the world, one that has produced 50 Nobel prize-winners and 27 British prime ministers.

In the 2014 Research Excellence Framework Oxford achieved the best results in the UK in nine subject areas and 87% of its submission was rated as world-leading or internationally excellent, but it entered 87% of eligible staff, compared with 95% at Cambridge, leading to a slightly lower overall score in our research ratings. Since then Oxford has won a Queen's Anniversary prize for collaborations between engineering and medical technology.

Selection is in the hands of the 30 undergraduate colleges, which vary considerably in their approach. Sound advice on colleges' academic strengths and social factors is essential for applicants to give themselves the best chance of winning a place and finding a setting in which they can thrive. Most colleges can accommodate undergraduates for two of their three years at Oxford, if not more.

A minority of candidates opt to go straight into the admissions pool without expressing a preference for a particular college. The choice is particularly important for arts and social science students, whose tuition is based in-college. Science and technology are taught mainly in central facilities.

Oxford has raised a £750m bond to be repaid over 100 years to support a £1.5bn programme of physical and virtual improvements. The new Beecroft building houses laboratory and teaching facilities for physics, while new teaching laboratories for chemistry will provide leading-edge facilities for undergraduate teaching and outreach.

The career prospects for graduates are stellar, although the university has dropped 17 places on our measure of their immediate prospects in the new table.

Sports facilities are first-class. The Iffley Road sports complex — scene of the first sub-four-minute mile by the late Sir Roger Bannister in 1954 — has been upgraded with a new gym and sports hall.

Tuition fees

» Fees for UK/EU students 2019–20   £9,250
» Fees for International students 2019–20 £24,750–£27,240
   Medicine   £37,445 (clinical years)
» For scholarship and bursary information see www.ox.ac.uk/
   admissions/undergraduate/fees-and-funding?wssl=1
» Graduate salary   £27,040

Student numbers

Undergraduates	11,417 (2,848)
Postgraduates	8,099 (2,286)
Applications/places	20,495/3,265
Applications per place	6.3
Overall offer rate	23.0%
International students	33.4%

Accommodation

See: www.ox.ac.uk/students/life/accommodation
College websites provide accommodation details
See chapter 14 for individual colleges

Where do the students come from?

State schools (non-grammar)	39.4%	Working-class homes	10.0%	Black ethnic minority	2.0%
Grammar schools	18.3%	Deprived areas	4.1%	Disabled	5.6%
Independent schools	42.3%	All ethnic minorities	17.6%	Mature (over 21)	2.8%

Oxford Brookes University

Oxford Brookes has recorded one of the biggest rises in our latest table — 21 places — compensating in large part for a decline of almost 30 places in the previous two years. Student satisfaction has improved and there has been a big increase in spending on facilities, although Brookes remains a long way off regaining the sort of positions it occupied when it seemed unassailable as the leading modern university. Applications dropped by more than 10% in 2017, but the numbers starting courses remained close to record levels.

There should be 800 more bedrooms to accommodate them by September, part of the university's £220m development programme. It is also opening a series of teaching and research laboratories, including a specialist bioimaging facility with a 100-seat teaching lab. This follows the opening of a building for the business school, with social learning spaces and flexible teaching rooms that have proved popular with students.

The university was given a silver rating in the Teaching Excellence Framework. The independent panel noted that there had been high levels of investment in physical and digital resources, which are valued by students. It also saw a "developing" focus on graduate prospects for employment or further study, which have indeed improved in our new table.

Brookes recently retained its status as the UK's only representative in QS's world ranking of the top 50 universities that are less than 50 years old. There has been a growing emphasis on its international profile, notably through a global partnership with the Association of Chartered Certified Accountants, which gives Brookes far more students than any other UK university — more than 200,000 — taking its qualifications in other countries.

Closer to home, a campus for nursing on a business park in Swindon was opened in summer 2016. In Oxford, the Harcourt Hill site, which houses the education school, has been refurbished and the sports facilities upgraded. The Wheatley base, the location of the engineering and technology schools, is also being refurbished. The library and student centre has been redesigned too after feedback from students and staff, adding recreational space and a gym.

Another innovative collaboration combines education, clinical practice and research across the nursing, midwifery and allied health professions. The Oxford School of Nursing and Midwifery is a partnership between the university, Oxford University Hospitals NHS Foundation Trust and Oxford Health NHS Foundation Trust, under the umbrella of the Oxford Academic Health

Headington Campus
OX3 0BP
01865 483 040
admissions@brookes.ac.uk
www.brookes.ac.uk
www.brookesunion.org.uk
Open days 2019:
see website

***The Times* and *The Sunday Times* Rankings**
Overall Ranking: =63 (last year: 84)

Teaching quality	79.7%	68
Student experience	78.4%	=68
Research quality	11.4%	58
Entry standards	130	=66
Graduate prospects	77.4%	=58
Good honours	74.6%	=59
Expected completion rate	87.8%	49
Student/staff ratio	16.1	=74
Services and facilities	£2,069	81

Science Centre. Brookes offers perhaps the most valuable bursary at any UK university, in the shape of the Tessa Jane Evans bursary for nursing, worth £30,000 over three years to three candidates from low-income households.

The institution celebrated its 150th anniversary in 2015 of its founding as the Oxford School of Art. There is a tradition of innovation that dates back to its time as a polytechnic, when it pioneered the modular degree system that has swept British higher education. The latest example is the grade point average (GPA) system that gives students a more accurate assessment of their work. Students still receive the traditional degree classification as well, but all their marks from the first year onwards now count towards their GPA.

The 2014 Research Excellence Framework saw Brookes excel, entering more academics than most of its peer group and still having almost 60% of its work rated as world-leading or internationally excellent. There were particularly good results in architecture, English and history. The overall performance produced a 41% rise in research funding, among the top ten increases in England.

The university is popular with independent schools, which provide more than a quarter of the undergraduates — much the highest proportion among the post-1992 non-specialist universities and three times the national average for the institution's subjects and entry grades. Brookes has been trying to attract more students from state schools and has targeted areas in Oxfordshire and the wider region. The university is also expanding its range of degree apprenticeships, with new programmes in health and life sciences, leadership and management, technology design and environment expected this year.

Impressive sports facilities include a 25-metre swimming pool and nine-hole golf course. Brookes is especially strong in rowing, and Dame Katherine Grainger, a silver medallist at the Rio Olympics after her gold four years earlier in London, is chancellor of the university. The cricketers combine with the University of Oxford to take on county teams. The students' union runs one of the biggest entertainment venues in Oxford, a city that offers enough to satisfy most students, although it can be expensive.

Tuition fees

» Fees for UK/EU students 2019–20 £9,250
   Foundation courses £7,200 (at partner colleges)
» Fees for International students 2019–20 £13,410–£14,280
» For scholarship and bursary information see
   www.brookes.ac.uk/studying-at-brookes/finance/
» Graduate salary £22,000

Student numbers

Undergraduates	**12,235**	**(1,454)**
Postgraduates	**1,888**	**(2,226)**
Applications/places		**24,680/3,855**
Applications per place		**6.4**
Overall offer rate		**82.4%**
International students		**18.0%**

Accommodation

University provided places: 5,454 (catered 4%)
Catered costs: £158 per week
Self-catered: £111–£184 per week
First years guaranteed accommodation
www.brookes.ac.uk/studying-at-brookes/accommodation/
prospective-students

Where do the students come from?

State schools (non-grammar)	66.9%	Working-class homes	27.9%	Black ethnic minority	4.5%
Grammar schools	6.8%	Deprived areas	8.7%	Disabled	8.9%
Independent schools	26.3%	All ethnic minorities	16.4%	Mature (over 21)	22.7%

Plymouth University

Plymouth is branching out under its new leadership, it has opened a new school of nursing in Exeter and launched its first dedicated school of engineering. Professor Judith Petts, the vice-chancellor, promises students a university that is "just a little bit different" and they appear to be responding.

The university has moved up 25 places on student satisfaction with teaching and into our top 30 on this measure. It is a transformation that has helped to drive a rise of 14 places in the overall table.

Improved student satisfaction has also helped the university to shed the bronze rating it received in the first year of the Teaching Excellence Framework. The awards panel judged Plymouth's new submission worthy of silver, finding that students were sufficiently challenged and benefiting from sustained investment in learning resources. Although progression to highly-skilled employment was still below the university's benchmark, this was being addressed.

The university is concentrating its investment on academic developments, having spent more than £200m on its main campus. One notable innovation has been the launch of the Plymouth Conservatoire, a joint project with the Theatre Royal Plymouth to teach acting, dance and theatre and performance at undergraduate level. Students will divide their time between the university's performing arts building, the House, and the Theatre Royal.

A new degree in directing will take its first students this year, one of eight new programmes planned by the university in subjects as diverse as international events management, diagnostic radiography and immersive digital experiences. There will also be an additional 250 places on degree apprenticeships, with new programmes planned in engineering and construction.

Plymouth was the only post-1992 university with its own medical school until the approval of five more this year. Having ended its partnership with the University of Exeter in the management of the former Peninsula College of Medicine and Dentistry, the Plymouth school had an initial entry of 75 students taking medicine and kept all 50 of Peninsula's places in dentistry. It now has more than 300 students after an increase in core numbers and the addition of degrees in biomedical and healthcare sciences.

A £17m medical, dental and biomedical research laboratory opened last year, attached to the city's Derriford Hospital. The university is the largest provider of nursing, midwifery and health professional education and training in the region, with nursing provision in Plymouth and Truro, as well as the new venture in Exeter.

Only two post-1992 universities produced

Drake Circus
Plymouth PL4 8AA
01752 585 858
prospectus@plymouth.ac.uk
www.plymouth.ac.uk
www.upsu.com
Open days 2019:
April 27, June 26

The Times and The Sunday Times Rankings
Overall Ranking: 72 (last year: =86)

Teaching quality	82.5%	=27
Student experience	80.1%	=38
Research quality	15.9%	57
Entry standards	128	=73
Graduate prospects	73.6%	=77
Good honours	73.0%	68
Expected completion rate	85.1%	=68
Student/staff ratio	15.9	70
Services and facilities	£1,763	110

better results in the 2014 Research Excellence Framework (REF). Plymouth entered a far larger proportion of its academics for the REF than most of its peer group and still saw nearly two thirds of its research judged world-leading or internationally excellent. Much of the research is focused on business and industry in the region. The Plymouth Materials Characterisation Project, launched this year, for example, will see more than 40 companies working with the university's flagship research facility, its electron microscopy centre.

Plymouth was the first university to be awarded Regional Growth Fund money to promote economic development and now has one of the country's top ten business incubation facilities — part of its managed portfolio of £100m worth of incubation and innovation assets. Focusing particularly on small and medium-sized enterprises, the latest programme provided £8.7m in grants to 100 businesses in the southwest.

Some 12,000 students undertake work-based learning or placements with employability skills embedded throughout the curriculum, while the Plymouth Award recognises extracurricular achievements. There are 13 partner colleges across the Southwest and the Channel Islands delivering the university's degrees, as well as others in Greece, Switzerland, Hong Kong, Sri Lanka and Singapore.

The undergraduate intake reflects Plymouth's position as the working-class hub of the region, with almost 94% of students state-educated and more than a third from the poorest social classes when this was last surveyed. About four out of ten students receive some form of financial support. A range of funds includes one named after a previous vice-chancellor, which provides awards of up to £1,500 to help meet the cost of extracurricular activities.

Student facilities include the £3m health and wellbeing centre and almost 3,000 residential places, many privately operated. Indeed, such is the scale of student-oriented provision in the private sector that the local authority worries many flats will never be occupied.

Upgraded facilities for water sports and an £850,000 fitness centre have added to the sports facilities, while a range of sports scholarships and bursaries support high-flyers. The university was one of the investors in the £46m Plymouth Life Centre and there are sessions exclusively for students at the city's international-standard swimming and diving centre. The city centre is not short of student-oriented nightlife.

Tuition fees

- » Fees for UK/EU students 2019–20   £9,250
- » Fees for international students 2019–20   £13,000
  Dentistry, Medicine   £36,225 (clinical years)
- » For scholarship and bursary information see www.plymouth.ac.uk/fees
- » Graduate salary   £22,000

Student numbers

Undergraduates	16,216	(2,213)
Postgraduates	1,395	(1,821)
Applications/places		19,990/4,545
Applications per place		4.4
Overall offer rate		87.7%
International students		9.6%

Accommodation

University provided places: 2,870 (catered 0%)
Self-catered: £97–£170 per week
First years guaranteed accommodation
www.plymouth.ac.uk/student-life/services/accommodation

Where do the students come from?

State schools (non-grammar)	87.3%	Working-class homes	31.9%	Black ethnic minority	2.2%
Grammar schools	6.6%	Deprived areas	16.7%	Disabled	8.6%
Independent schools	6.1%	All ethnic minorities	10.0%	Mature (over 21)	28.6%

Plymouth Marjon University

Only one university (Aberystwyth) has students who are more satisfied with the quality of teaching than Marjon, an outstanding result taking into account that previously the Plymouth-based university was outside the top 40 on this key measure. Small intakes can make for exaggerated swings — Marjon admitted only 760 students in 2017 — but the improvement of almost five percentage points is one of the largest of recent years.

Satisfaction with the broader student experience, also measured by the annual National Student Survey, is up significantly too, placing the university in the top ten on this measure. A number of initiatives to improve the student experience may have played their part in the transformation. Every student now has a personal development tutor to help with academic skills, careers advice, one-to-one mentoring, confidence-building and resilience. There is also a new student bar and a student hub, with social working space and an information centre.

The positive message certainly appears to be getting through to prospective students. Applications went up by 35%, among the biggest increases at any university, partly due to the introduction of popular new degree programmes. These include business,

commercial music, sport, coaching and physical education, music journalism, and community development and education.

In addition, the university's marketing campaign has been more effective and now targets a wider geographical area. Marjon is still outside the top 100 in our league table, but the surge in satisfaction levels has driven a rise of ten places overall.

Marjon was given a silver rating in the Teaching Excellence Framework (TEF). The awards panel found "appropriate levels of contact time on courses, and a personalised approach to delivery that promotes good engagement". Course design and assessment practices ensured that students were stretched, the panel said.

Nearly all the undergraduates are state educated and approaching 40% come from the four lowest socioeconomic groups. Marjon has two sponsored schools and progression arrangements with another five, where there are targeted interventions at GCSE level and advice and guidance sessions to raise awareness of higher education.

Bursary programmes include one that awards up to £600 to help 15 students to afford an international experience.

Established in 1840 as a Church of England teacher training college in London, with the son of poet Samuel Taylor Coleridge as its first principal, the university describes itself as "arguably the third oldest Higher

---

Derriford Road
Plymouth PL6 8BH
01752 636 890
admissions@marjon.ac.uk
www.marjon.ac.uk
www.marjonsu.com
Open days 2019:
see website

The Times and The Sunday Times **Rankings**
Overall Ranking: 109 (last year: =119)

Teaching quality	86.3%	2
Student experience	82.6%	10
Research quality	0%	128
Entry standards	129	=70
Graduate prospects	63.7%	=123
Good honours	65.5%	121
Expected completion rate	84.1%	=75
Student/staff ratio	22.7	131
Services and facilities	£1,884	98

Education Institution in England". The College of St Mark and St John only moved to Plymouth in 1973. Still officially a Church of England voluntary institution, its Chaplaincy Centre is at the heart of the campus, but there is limited emphasis on religion in the university's promotional material.

Teacher training remains strong, with Ofsted giving an outstanding rating for the leadership and management of courses that run in six counties, as well as in Cyprus and Germany. But Marjon lists sport as its top specialism, with teaching facilities that include sports science labs that boast a climate chamber, bod pod and an anti-gravity treadmill.

Recent academic developments include a new health and wellbeing department, focusing on health professions such as psychotherapy and osteopathy.

Plymouth Marjon suffers in our table for a decision not to take part in the 2014 Research Excellence Framework, which leaves it last in our table for research quality. It was the only publicly-funded university for more than 20 years to submit no work for the official assessments of research. A subsequent research strategy has reversed the policy.

Marjon's campus is located on the expanding north side of Plymouth, close to the Dartmoor National Park and within easy reach of the sea. The green agenda extends to an on-campus duck pond and nature trail.

A new student-centred hub provides a one-stop shop for student support services such as learning support, employability and career development, counselling, placement support and finance advice. It also contains a bar that doubles as a cafe and social space during the day.

Sports facilities are extremely good: there is a floodlit 3G pitch for rugby, lacrosse and football, two further floodlit all-weather lacrosse and hockey pitches, a climbing wall, 25-metre indoor swimming pool and well-equipped gym, as well as a rehabilitation clinic and sports science lab.

There are residential places on campus for 456 students in seven halls of residence and 38 village houses. First-year students are guaranteed places, and those with unconditional offers have first choice of accommodation. Those living on campus may only bring a car in exceptional circumstances, but the lively city centre is a short bus ride away.

Tuition fees

» Fees for UK/EU students 2019–20 £9,250
  Foundation courses £6,000

» Fees for International students 2018–19 £11,000–£11,750

» For scholarship and bursary information see
  www.marjon.ac.uk/courses/fees-and-funding/

» Graduate salary £18,000

Student numbers

Undergraduates	1,839	(155)
Postgraduates	188	(231)
Applications/places		2,340/715
Applications per place		3.3
Overall offer rate		89.0%
International students		3.6%

Accommodation

University provided places: 456 (catered 0%)
Self-catered: £90–£110 per week
First years guaranteed accommodation
www.marjon.ac.uk/student-life/accommodation

Where do the students come from?

State schools (non-grammar)	94.7%	Working-class homes	37.0%	Black ethnic minority	0.7%
Grammar schools	3.0%	Deprived areas	23.8%	Disabled	16.8%
Independent schools	2.3%	All ethnic minorities	4.8%	Mature (over 21)	38.7%

University of Portsmouth

Portsmouth is focusing on providing "real-life" scenarios — both actual and simulated — to boost its students' career prospects when they graduate. Pharmacists dispense medicines for a high-street pharmacy, for example, while forensic scientists work alongside police officers, and dental nurses and hygienists treat patients in the university's dental clinic.

The approach seems to be paying dividends, with upwardly-mobile Portsmouth moving into our top 15 for graduate prospects and helping it to the verge of the top 50 overall.

A 2017 exercise by *The Economist* made Portsmouth the top university in the country for boosting the salaries of graduates, if their backgrounds, qualifications and subjects studied are taken into account. Although the average salaries of Portsmouth graduates were only £26,168 five years into their careers, compared with nearly £46,000 at the London School of Economics, the magazine calculated that this was £3,000 more than might have been expected, whereas the advantages enjoyed by LSE's graduates might have produced £600 more.

The calculations have not been repeated, but the median starting salary of a Portsmouth graduate rose by more than £1,300 to £21,840 in 2017.

The government's Teaching Excellence Framework awarded Portsmouth gold, after the independent panel found "optimum" levels of student engagement and commitment to learning. These were secured through excellent and integrated teaching and assessment practices, and also industry-leading physical and digital resources. The university's provision was actively and consistently used by students to develop their independence and confidence, enhancing learning and progression.

These successes are yet to produce increased demand for places, however. Applications are down by almost 20% after three successive years of decline. New degrees in criminology and cybercrime, physics, modern languages, dental hygiene and data science have provided more options for applicants.

Degree apprenticeships in nursing and applied biomedical science will be added this year in the latest phase of expansion of programmes which already include risk management, civil engineering and architecture.

Well over 90% of school leavers who apply to Portsmouth receive offers, many of them unconditional. Professor Graham Galbraith, the vice-chancellor, has said the increasingly controversial unconditional offers were part of a carefully designed programme allowing for earlier engagement with students. They did not demotivate candidates, he said, because students who took up their offers and achieved their

---

Academic registry
University House
Winston Churchill
Avenue
Portsmouth PO1 2UP
023 9284 5566
admissions@port.ac.uk
www.port.ac.uk
www.upsu.net
Open days 2019:
July 3, 6

The Times and The Sunday Times **Rankings**
Overall Ranking: =51 (last year: 53)

Teaching quality	81.6%	=42
Student experience	81.0%	=25
Research quality	8.6%	71
Entry standards	119	=100
Graduate prospects	85.4%	=14
Good honours	75.2%	56
Expected completion rate	85.1%	=68
Student/staff ratio	15.4	=55
Services and facilities	£2,169	72

predicted grades were awarded a vice-chancellor's scholarship worth up to £1,000.

Almost two thirds of Portsmouth's research was rated as world-leading or internationally excellent in the 2014 Research Excellence Framework, with health subjects leading the way. The best results were in dentistry, nursing and pharmacy, and in physics, with about 90% of the submission reaching the top two categories. The university also has one of the largest language departments in the country, teaching six languages to degree level and offering free language courses to all students. About 1,000 students go abroad for part of their course, and at least as many come from the continent.

A new Future Technology Centre gives engineering students hands-on experience of specialist technology. The facilities are used in the teaching of new innovation engineering degrees, combined with projects that address real-world problems in health, humanitarianism and the environment.

The university has also stepped up its support for students and their wellbeing. Academic staff, including personal tutors, have been trained in awareness of mental health issues and how best to support their students. Portsmouth was the first university to use WhatsUp? an app that promotes communication between students and pastoral services.

The university's Guildhall campus is in the centre of Portsmouth with most residential accommodation nearby. It has undergone extensive redevelopment, including remodelling the library to provide more access to study spaces and IT equipment. Students have access to almost 900 PCs and laptops in the library, with 1,000 more dotted around campus.

A £6.5m student centre includes alcohol-free areas. Planning permission has been received for a £50m sports facility that will be the next part of the university's £400m estate masterplan. The indoor sports facility will feature an eight-lane 25m swimming pool, an eight-court sports hall, a 175-station fitness suite and a ski simulator.

The university's seaside location provides an excellent base for water sports and outdoor sports facilities include an all-weather 3G pitch, suitable for football, rugby, lacrosse and American football.

Many students live in Southsea, which has a vibrant social scene and quirky shops. The university has almost 4,000 residential places — enough to guarantee accommodation to all new students who apply by the deadline and make Portsmouth their firm choice.

Tuition fees

» Fees for UK/EU students 2019–20 £9,250
» Fees for International students 2019–20 £13,900–£15,900
» For scholarship and bursary information see www.port.ac.uk/study/undergraduate/undergraduate-fees-and-student-finance
» Graduate salary £21,840

Student numbers

Undergraduates	17,591 (1,949)
Postgraduates	2,076 (1,887)
Applications/places	26,825/4,805
Applications per place	5.6
Overall offer rate	93.9%
International students	16.3%

Accommodation

University provided places: 3,933 (catered 7%)
Catered costs: £163 per week
Self-catered: £93–£154 per week
First years guaranteed accommodation
www.port.ac.uk/accommodation

Where do the students come from?

State schools (non-grammar)	91.8%	Working-class homes	32.9%	Black ethnic minority	9.6%
Grammar schools	4.7%	Deprived areas	14.6%	Disabled	8.6%
Independent schools	3.5%	All ethnic minorities	29.2%	Mature (over 21)	14.7%

Queen Margaret University

Queen Margaret University (QMU) has broken back into the top 100 in our table, after student satisfaction levels began to recover from a disastrous year in 2017, when it was in the bottom three in both of the measures derived from the National Student Survey. Both applications and enrolments have dipped, but the university expects better figures this year as the first cohort of 120 students begin the new degree in primary education. QMU has already added a graduate apprenticeship and three degrees in business management.

The university has committed to a "student-centred approach", with a culture of personalised support, in its strategy for the years leading up to its 150th anniversary in 2025. As one element of this, it is creating a network of mental-health first aiders to enhance the staff's pastoral role. Nearly a quarter of the university's workforce has undergone Scotland's Mental Health First Aid training. QMU says it has more staff trained to identify and help with problems than any other university in Scotland.

The university's Centre for Academic Practice also provides support for those who teach and study there. It seeks to "optimise learning" through the convergence and successful implementation of pedagogical research and technological advancements.

Three "flagship areas" have been identified for teaching and research: health and rehabilitation, sustainable business, and creativity and culture. QMU expects to add others, such as food and drink, in the next few years. It launched the Scottish Centre for Food Development and Innovation and has a partnership with the Edinburgh New Town Cookery School, run by a QMU graduate, to support students on the international hospitality management degree.

Scottish government funding of £30m will contribute towards the development of Edinburgh Innovation Park on land next to the university campus, a joint development by East Lothian council and QMU. An innovation hub will facilitate an expansion of the food development centre and provide space for small and medium-sized businesses in the food and drink sector. The hub is expected to act as a catalyst for the further development, based around the theme of food and drink.

The university is providing more work placements in partnership with organisations such as Ryder Cup Europe and has a highly successful employer mentoring scheme. The programme matches third- and fourth-year students with experienced professionals who have relevant industry experience.

Named after Saint Margaret, the 11th-century Queen of Scotland, the institution

---

University Drive
Edinburgh EH21 6UU
0131 474 0000
admissions@qmu.ac.uk
www.qmu.ac.uk
www.qmusu.org.uk
Open days 2019:
see website

***The Times and The Sunday Times* Rankings**
Overall Ranking: 97 (last year: =102)

Teaching quality	78.4%	=93
Student experience	74.7%	106
Research quality	6.6%	80
Entry standards	149	41
Graduate prospects	72.9%	=85
Good honours	78.7%	42
Expected completion rate	80.1%	105
Student/staff ratio	18.5	=112
Services and facilities	£1,728	116

dates back to 1875 and was originally a school of cookery for women. It moved into a modern campus, which was designed in consultation with the students, in the seaside town of Musselburgh, to the southeast of Edinburgh, when it was awarded university status 11 years ago. The campus, which won a string of awards, is one of the most environmentally sustainable in the UK, exceeding current standards.

There are 4,300 undergraduates, three quarters of them female, divided between two schools: arts, social sciences and management, and health sciences. The university promises "inter-professional" teaching and research to encourage the professions to work better together. Health is an area of particular strength: QMU has the broadest range of allied health courses in Scotland, from dietetics, podiatry and audiology to art therapy, music therapy and health psychology.

Research ratings improved considerably in the 2014 Research Excellence Framework. Although only 22% of the eligible staff were entered, almost 60% of their work was considered world-leading or internationally excellent. Renowned for its research in speech and language sciences, QMU saw 92%of its work in this area rated in the top two categories, placing the university second in the UK and first in Scotland.

QMU has since launched new centres for research and knowledge exchange, which place academics in direct contact with business, industry and the health profession. In addition, the Business Gateway promotes entrepreneurship and offers free support and advice to student and graduate start-ups.

The campus is located next to Musselburgh train station, from where Edinburgh city centre is a six-minute journey.

There are 800 residential places on campus, which also hosts the sports facilities. The university does not guarantee accommodation for new entrants, although all who wanted one were offered a place in 2017. As part of its accommodation service, QMU runs the ResLife programme in partnership with the sports centre and students' union. This includes a range of social, educational, recreational and cultural activities to help students settle in and feel welcomed and supported.

Tuition fees

» Fees for Scottish and EU students 2019–20   £0–£1,820
RUK fees £9,250 (capped at £27,750 for 4-year courses)
» Fees for International students 2019–20   £12,500–£13,500
» For scholarship and bursary information see
www.qmu.ac.uk/current-students/current-students-
general-information/fees-and-charges/201920-
undergraduate-fees/
» Graduate salary   £20,280

Student numbers

Undergraduates	2,973	(486)
Postgraduates	625	(1,125)
Applications/places		5,875/735
Applications per place		8.0
Overall offer rate		52.9%
International students		21.3%

Accommodation

University provided places: 800 (catered 0%)
Self-catered: £108–£124 per week
www.qmu.ac.uk/accommodation

Where do the students come from?

State schools (non-grammar)	93.2%	Working-class homes	34.4%	Black ethnic minority	2.0%
Grammar schools	2.4%	Deprived areas	8.1%	Disabled	7.4%
Independent schools	4.4%	All ethnic minorities	10.7%	Mature (over 21)	26.7%

Queen Mary, University of London

The launch of a raft of new degrees — more than 100 of them existing offerings with the addition of a year abroad — has helped to boost applications to Queen Mary (QMUL). The popularity of programmes such as global law and a range of international politics degrees taught partly in Paris contributed to an increase of almost 8% in the demand for places, against the national trend.

QMUL had already introduced a new degree structure to improve students' networking and communication skills and provide experience outside their subject. The QMUL Model accounts for 10% of a student's degree, covering activities such as work experience, volunteering in the community, overseas travel, project work with local businesses and other organisations, learning a language, or taking modules from other subjects.

The university sees the system as a new approach to degree-level study, enabling students to broaden their skills as part of their course. The new modules, which count towards students' degree classifications, are compulsory in the first year, but students will choose from a range of options, in consultation with their personal tutor, in subsequent years.

The introduction of the new system is unlikely to be the end of QMUL's innovation. Professor Colin Bailey, who joined the university as vice-chancellor in 2017, is leading the development of a new institutional strategy.

QMUL was given a silver rating in the government's Teaching Excellence Framework (TEF). The panel was impressed by the quality of coaching programmes, mentoring schemes and employer engagement that help students gain highly-skilled employment.

Like other London institutions, QMUL is hampered in our table by low student satisfaction scores. It is outside the top 100 for both of our measures derived from the National Student Survey, in contrast to a top-20 position for both research and staffing levels.

However, QMUL does not suffer from the dispersed nature of other London institutions, with most of its 13,600 undergraduates both taught and housed on a self-contained campus in the increasingly fashionable East End of London. Even its large medical school, Barts and the London School of Medicine and Dentistry, is based in nearby Whitechapel.

The undergraduate intake has grown by more than a third since QMUL joined the Russell Group in 2012. The international options include QMUL's medical school in Malta, where there is a five-year degree

Mile End Road
London E1 4NS
020 7882 5511
admissions@qmul.ac.uk
www.qmul.ac.uk
www.qmsu.org
Open days 2019:
June 21, 22; October 5

The Times and The Sunday Times Rankings
Overall Ranking: =46 (last year: 43)

Teaching quality	73.2%	123
Student experience	73.9%	=113
Research quality	37.9%	19
Entry standards	148	=42
Graduate prospects	78.7%	=53
Good honours	79.8%	34
Expected completion rate	91.9%	29
Student/staff ratio	13.1	16
Services and facilities	£2,524	34

taught by staff from Barts and local clinicians trained by the school. The venture will add to the university's 7,000 students from outside the UK.

More than £100m has been spent in five years on campus improvements. These have included a new graduate centre, a new dental school and redevelopment of the engineering and maths buildings. This summer has seen the completion of Neuron Pod, the £1.9m extension to QMUL's award-winning Centre of the Cell science education centre. The historic People's Palace, which brought education to the Victorian masses, is still QMUL's most recognisable feature and has been restored to host cultural events.

The medical school, which is rated in the top 100 in the world by QS, is based in the £45m Blizard building. Its dentistry institute moved into the first new dental school to be built in the UK for 40 years, when it occupied new facilities in the Royal London Hospital. Another outpost opened last year, with a residential development for postgraduates at the Queen Elizabeth Olympic Park in Stratford.

Medicine and the other health subjects did well in the 2014 Research Excellence Framework, but the best results came in the humanities. About 95% of the research in linguistics and in music, drama and the performing arts was rated as world-leading or internationally excellent. More than 85% of

QMUL's entire submission reached the top two categories.

QMUL has by far the highest proportion of undergraduates from working-class homes in the Russell Group — more than a third — with many coming from London's ethnic minority groups. These two factors contribute to the university's standing as the highest-ranked Russell Group member for social inclusion in our new table. About half of all undergraduates receive some financial support from the university.

For Mile End students, social life centres on the campus, which features a refurbished students' union. A subsidised health and fitness centre has improved the sports facilities.

Students welcome the relatively low prices (for the capital) in east London and their proximity to the lively youth culture of Shoreditch, Brick Lane and Spitalfields. QMUL students can use the sports facilities at the Queen Elizabeth Olympic Park, including the Copper Box indoor arena and the Aquatic Centre's swimming pool.

Tuition fees

» Fees for UK/EU students 2019–20 £9,250
» Fees for International students 2019–20 £16,200–£20,850
  Dentistry £36,280; Medicine £35,000
» For scholarship and bursary information see
  www.qmul.ac.uk/undergraduate/feesandfunding/
» Graduate salary £25,000

Student numbers

Undergraduates	13,620	(7)
Postgraduates	3,968	(1,294)
Applications/places	29,885/3,625	
Applications per place	8.2	
Overall offer rate	81.6%	
International students	31.6%	

Accommodation

University provided places: 3,016 (catered 0%)
Self-catered: £128–£200 per week
First years guaranteed accommodation
www.residences.qmul.ac.uk

Where do the students come from?

State schools (non-grammar)	78.4%	Working-class homes	37.0%	Black ethnic minority	10.0%
Grammar schools	11.6%	Deprived areas	4.5%	Disabled	8.1%
Independent schools	9.9%	All ethnic minorities	65.9%	Mature (over 21)	11.0%

Queen's University, Belfast

Queen's opened its first accommodation in Belfast city centre last year — 1,200 new places with their own services, including pastoral care, security and social activities.

With most of the university's 3,500 residential places at the Elms Student Village, close to the university, on the south side of the city, the new development speaks volumes about the growing attractions of the city centre and the university's ambitions to recruit more students from the rest of the UK and further afield. It is aiming for 20% of students to be international, compared with little more than 10% in 2016–17.

The university has invested £350m in campus improvements and is now planning to spend the same again in the next ten years. A £39m School of Biological Sciences, an advanced manufacturing technology facility and a new cyber security lab are already open. The university won a Queen's Anniversary Prize for research and technology transfer in cyber security, and was awarded Northern Ireland's first Reguis Professorship in electronics and computer engineering.

A £10m centre of excellence in precision medicine is a unique new development, it integrates multiple technologies and analytical tools to target drugs more effectively for cancer patients.

Queen's has held its own inside our top 40, despite a significant decline in student satisfaction in recent times. It has fallen more than 25 places in both of the measures derived from the National Student Survey, almost dropping out of the top 100 for perceptions of teaching quality this year. A better year for graduate prospects, where it is just outside the top 25, helped protect the university's overall ranking.

The university is in our top 20 for research after entering 95% of its academics for the 2014 Research Excellence Framework, a proportion matched only by Cambridge. Despite the large submission, 77% of the research was considered world-leading or internationally excellent and 14 subject areas were ranked in the UK's top 20. There are four global research institutes in food security; health sciences; electronics, communications and information technology; and global peace, security and justice.

A member of the Russell Group, Queen's is recognised as Northern Ireland's premier university, with graduates in senior positions in 80 of its top 100 companies. Enrolments are running at close to record levels despite a marginal decline in applications in 2017.

More than 60% of the undergraduates come from grammar schools, which educate a much larger proportion of the population in Northern Ireland than elsewhere in the UK. This helps explain the university's poor showing in our first table measuring the

University Road
Belfast BT7 1NN
028 9097 3838
admissions@qub.ac.uk
www.qub.ac.uk
www.qubsu.org.uk
Open days 2019:
see website

BELFAST
Edinburgh
Cardiff
London

The Times and The Sunday Times Rankings
Overall Ranking: =38 (last year: 38)

Teaching quality	77.9%	96
Student experience	77.5%	=78
Research quality	39.7%	14
Entry standards	152	39
Graduate prospects	82.4%	26
Good honours	80.0%	=32
Expected completion rate	91.2%	32
Student/staff ratio	15.8	=66
Services and facilities	£2,288	57

social inclusiveness of universities, where recruitment from comprehensive schools is one of seven criteria. The university takes inclusiveness in recruitment seriously, and close to a third of undergraduates receive financial support from a £3.8m pool of funds for widening participation.

A charter has guaranteed student representation, equal rights for women and non-denominational teaching since 1908. Queen's was one of four university colleges for the whole of Ireland in the 19th century, and still draws students from all over the island. However, the majority come from Northern Ireland, and Queen's suffers in our main league table from the comparison of entry grades because relatively few sixth-formers in the province take four A-levels.

Undergraduates are encouraged to take language programmes from a "virtual" language laboratory, which provides online tuition from any computer in the university. IT facilities are good: Queen's was the first institution to meet the national target of providing at least one computer workstation for every five undergraduate students.

The university ranks first in the UK for establishment of knowledge transfer partnerships and fifth for the commercialisation of intellectual property, according to government figures. It has been selected, with the University of Warwick, to run a national programme to promote the commercialisation of university

research, helping to determine whether there is a market for products or services.

Queen's has a cinema, an art gallery and theatre, all of which are open to students and the wider community alike. The city centre has plenty of nightlife, but the social scene is mainly concentrated on the students' union and the surrounding area. New entrants from outside Northern Ireland are guaranteed accommodation. Priority for the remaining places goes to those who live furthest from the university.

The sports facilities, which include a university cottage in the Mourne mountains, benefited from a £20m programme of investment. There is an arena pitch which can host football, rugby or Gaelic sport, another 14 pitches, a recreational trail and conference facilities.

The Physical Education Centre provides physiotherapy, sports massage and podiatry, and there is a £1.2m boathouse on the River Lagan. An Elite Athlete programme offers up to £8,000 of support for leading performers.

Tuition fees

» Fees for Northern Ireland/EU students 2019–20   £4,160
  Students from England, Scotland and Wales   £9,250
» Fees for International students 2019–20   £16,400–£20,100
  Medicine   £38,850 (clinical years)
» For scholarship and bursary information see www.qub.ac.uk/Study/Undergraduate/Fees-and-scholarships
» Graduate salary   £21,500

Student numbers

Undergraduates	15,078 (3,718)
Postgraduates	3,055 (2,001)
Applications/places	28,615/4,100
Applications per place	7.0
Overall offer rate	86.0%
International students	12.8%

Accommodation

University provided places: 4,123 (catered 11%)
Catered costs: £113–£156 per week
Self-catered: £75–£165 per week
First years from outside NI guaranteed accommodation
www.qub.ac.uk/accommodation

Where do the students come from?

State schools (non-grammar)	34.3%	Working-class homes	31.9%	Black ethnic minority	0.4%
Grammar schools	63.8%	Deprived areas	7.6%	Disabled	6.4%
Independent schools	1.9%	All ethnic minorities	3.0%	Mature (over 21)	19.6%

Ravensbourne University, London

Ravensbourne was awarded university status in May 2018, less than a year after securing the right to award its own degrees. It occupies a striking, purpose-built, open-plan headquarters, next to the O2 Arena, on the Greenwich Peninsula, where it specialises in digital media and design.

Professor Linda Drew, the new university's director, said the awarding of university status acknowledged Ravensbourne's academic integrity as a higher education institution with rigorous standards and academic governance. As a specialist creative university designed for industry, it would continue to nurture and inspire people who are valuable to and valued by the world beyond higher education.

Ravensbourne was given a silver rating in the Teaching Excellence Framework. The panel was impressed by the high level of practice-based learning linked to excellent digital resources, as well as by the highly-valued employer input to course design and extensive industry collaboration.

However, like many new universities before it, Ravensbourne makes its debut in our league table in last place. Although close to the top 100 for graduate prospects – often a challenging measure for specialist arts institutions — only the London School of Economics has lower scores for student satisfaction and it did not enter the 2014 Research Excellence Framework, so is hampered in our table by the lack of any score there.

Established only in 1962, Ravensbourne was located on Bromley Common and then Chislehurst, Kent, before moving to its current home eight years ago. Its degrees were validated by the University of Arts London until this year.

University status came too late to prevent a 10% drop in applications in 2017, but the numbers starting courses were still close to the previous year's total. There are fewer than 2,400 students, equally divided between men and women. Ravensbourne's strategic plan is to aim for between 2,500 and 2,700 to be able invest appropriately in staffing and infrastructure to ensure that students' experience is improved while the university grows.

There are new degrees in games design, illustration for communication, music and sound design, user-experience and user-interface (UX/UI) design, and digital television technology. There is also a range of pre-degree courses that combine practical studio projects, workshops and traditional academic learning.

More than 40% of students taking foundation programmes progress to degree courses. As in other similar institutions, admission decisions hinge on an applicant's portfolio or showreel as much as on their academic grades.

Widening participation is among Ravensbourne's top priorities. Almost 40% of

6 Penrose Way
Greenwich Peninsula
London SE10 0EW
020 3040 3500
admissions@rave.ac.uk
www.ravensbourne.ac.uk
www.ravesu.co.uk
Open days 2019:
see website

The Times and The Sunday Times Rankings
Overall Ranking: 132 (last year: n/a)

Teaching quality	71.9%	129
Student experience	67.9%	129
Research quality	n/a	
Entry standards	109	=123
Graduate prospects	68.7%	=106
Good honours	65.6%	=119
Expected completion rate	77.9%	116
Student/staff ratio	28.8	132
Services and facilities	£1,731	114

the students come from homes where the income is in the bottom fifth of the population, and 95% are state educated. There is a range of bursaries for low-income students, the main one being the Ravensbourne Bursary of £500 a year for those with a household income of less than £25,000. All new students receive a £300 laptop bursary.

There is also a programme of free meals for the most disadvantaged students, covering those in receipt of, or having parents who are in receipt of, one or more of a number of benefits.

There is a small cohort of international students, which will expand with the launch of a new partnership with Berghs School of Communication, in Stockholm. Berghs students who successfully complete one semester will be accepted into the a first year at Ravensbourne, and stay on to complete their degrees. The first cohort of students from Berghs will start at Ravensbourne this year.

The single-building campus requires the university to manage its student numbers, room use and teaching model carefully, but the strategic plan envisages further growth, increased commercial activity and more research in the longer term.

Among Ravensbourne's targets is to be recognised as a national and international leader in creative industries education and training. It is already in the top 100 in the QS global ranking for art and design, which relies on academic and employer reputation.

Among Ravensbourne's best-known alumni are fashion designers Clare Waight Keller of Givenchy, who designed the dress Meghan Markle wore for her wedding to Prince Harry; Stella McCartney; Bruce Oldfield; Kevin Carrigan, the senior vice-president and creative director at Ralph Lauren; literary scholar Robert Hewison; handbag designer Emma Hill, sculptor Alison Wilding and the co-designer of the Olympic 2012 torch, Jay Osgerby.

Ravensbourne does not own halls of residence, but it works with a number of private providers to offer students accommodation. No guarantees are given, but first-year students who request accommodation are usually found a room. The university encourages students to apply as early as possible since most providers fill rooms on a first-come, first-served basis.

There is discounted membership for students of a gym within 200 yards of the university building and good transport services on the doorstep for excursions into central London.

Tuition fees

» Fees for UK/EU students 2019–20 £9,250
   Foundation courses £0–£5,421
» Fees for International students 2019–20 £10,800–£14,500
   Foundation courses £9,500
» For scholarship and bursary information see www.ravensbourne.ac.uk/study-here/undergraduate/undergraduate-fees-and-funding/undergraduate-tuition-fees/
» Graduate salary £20,000

Student numbers

Undergraduates	2,224	(1)
Postgraduates	52	(4)
Applications/places	3,145/770	
Applications per place	4.1	
Overall offer rate	55.2%	
International students	9.8%	

Accommodation

University provided places: 0
Self-catered: £144–£255 per week (through private providers)
www.ravensbourne.ac.uk/study-here/undergraduate/undergraduate-accommodation/

Where do the students come from?

State schools (non-grammar)	93.1%	Working-class homes	39.5%	Black ethnic minority	13.1%
Grammar schools	2.0%	Deprived areas	6.3%	Disabled	7.0%
Independent schools	3.0%	All ethnic minorities	37.5%	Mature (over 21)	13.0%

University of Reading

Reading launched no fewer than 43 new degrees last year, most of them existing programmes with the addition of a year abroad, a professional placement or a foundation year for students whose qualifications do not meet normal entry requirements.

Six of them are completely new offerings, including English or another modern language with comparative literature, and a four-year integrated Masters in speech and language therapy. Five more will follow this year – in business management, maths with computer science, and chemistry with a year in industry or research.

There are also plans to expand the single degree apprenticeship programme by adding three more at the Henley Business School in management, financial services and digital solutions. The university expects to have up to 600 degree apprentices, with the possibility of more in early years education.

The expansion of Reading's portfolio of courses complements its 2026: Transform programme, which is designed to make the university a "larger, vibrant and more sustainable institution" by its centenary year. The intake of new undergraduates has increased for five years in a row, adding nearly 1,000 places in the last two years, but there are still fewer than 12,000 students at that level.

The 2026: Transform programme will see more than £200m invested in campus improvements, with the projects shaped by student feedback. By the end of this year, a £40m upgrade of the main library will be complete, increasing study space and improving key facilities, and a £55m health and life sciences building is set to open, housing one of the largest teaching labs in the UK and bringing together a school that is currently spread over six buildings.

Lecture theatres across the campus are being refurbished, as is the students' union nightclub. There is also a new £1m capital fund to be spent on projects selected by the students' union. The first six projects include new "relaxation zones" with massage chairs, bean bags, refreshment facilities and even sleeper pods, more storage lockers and further investment in the filming of lectures.

The government's Teaching Excellence Framework awarded the university a silver rating, with the panel finding high-quality physical and digital resources, with particularly consistent use of the virtual learning environment and effective integration of student support services with academic provision. There is consistent engagement of students with developments from the forefront of research, scholarship and practice, it added.

Reading has dropped eight places in our table this year, mainly because of a decline in student satisfaction, particularly in relation to

Whiteknights
PO Box 217
Reading RG6 6AH
0118 378 8372
www.reading.ac.uk/question
www.reading.ac.uk
www.rusu.co.uk
Open days 2019:
June 21, 22;
October 5, 12

The Times and The Sunday Times Rankings
Overall Ranking: 40 (last year: 32)

Teaching quality	76.7%	=107
Student experience	72.2%	121
Research quality	36.5%	29
Entry standards	138	=55
Graduate prospects	76.0%	=66
Good honours	79.1%	37
Expected completion rate	92.1%	27
Student/staff ratio	15.1	=44
Services and facilities	£2,560	30

the organisation and management of courses, learning resources, the learning community and the student voice, for which the university now ranks in the bottom ten in the UK. However, it remains in our top 40 overall and in the top 200 in the QS global rankings.

Reading was one of only two universities established between the two world wars. It was originally the University of Oxford's extension college and its main campus is set in 320 acres of parkland on the outskirts of Reading, with a second campus in town. The site has won four Green Gown environmental awards in a row. The university also owns 2,000 acres of farmland at nearby Sonning and Shinfield, where the Centre for Dairy Research is located.

The university's business school, formerly a management college, occupies an attractive site on the banks of the river, at Henley-on-Thames. It houses postgraduate and executive programmes, while undergraduates are taught on the Whiteknights campus. Reading also has a campus in Malaysia, which is expected to have 2,000 students by 2020.

International students are attracted by Reading's global reputation for courses and research in agriculture and development, with about a fifth of undergraduates now coming from outside the UK. All first-degree students can take work placements as part of their course, as well as career management skills modules that contribute five credits towards their degree classification.

The university entered more academics for assessment in the 2014 Research Excellence Framework than most of its peers and still saw almost 80% of its research rated as world-leading or internationally excellent. Real estate, planning and construction management were among the leading players.

The 5,000 residential places are either on or within easy walking distance of the main campus. There are more than 50 sports clubs and representative teams have a good record in inter-varsity competitions.

Facilities for water sports include boathouses on the Thames and a sailing and canoeing club nearby. Predominantly a commuter town for London, Reading may not be the most fashionable, but it has plenty of nightlife and the university has a new "street support team", which will work advising and assisting students in three residential areas for a trial period between 10pm and 4am during December, to ensure that the aforementioned nightlife does not end up disturbing local residents.

The town boasts an award-winning shopping centre, although the cost of living is high.

Tuition fees

- » Fees for UK/EU students 2019–20 £9,250
- » Fees for International students 2019–20 £16,475–£19,815
- » For scholarship and bursary information see www.reading.ac.uk/ready-to-study/study/fees-and-funding.aspx
- » Graduate salary £22,000

Student numbers

Undergraduates	11,095	(77)
Postgraduates	2,911	(1,756)
Applications/places	21,905/3,775	
Applications per place	5.8	
Overall offer rate	92.1%	
International students	25.9%	

Accommodation

University provided places: 4,982 (catered 18%)
Catered costs: £146–£187 per week
Self-catered: £122–£256 per week
First years guaranteed accommodation
www.reading.ac.uk/ready-to-study/accommodation.aspx

Where do the students come from?

State schools (non-grammar)	73.3%	Working-class homes	27.3%	Black ethnic minority	5.4%
Grammar schools	11.1%	Deprived areas	6.0%	Disabled	6.3%
Independent schools	15.6%	All ethnic minorities	24.1%	Mature (over 21)	6.8%

Robert Gordon University

Robert Gordon (RGU) is building on its gold rating in the Teaching Excellence Framework (TEF) with a new strategic vision to be an "innovative, disruptive force in higher education". This will include new course models to prepare students for continually evolving careers and greater flexibility in the delivery of programmes.

Four integrated master's programmes in health subjects are among 13 new degrees launched last year. Sport coaching, applied bioscience, design engineering and digital marketing are also offered at Bachelors level, while there are five new graduate apprenticeship programmes in business management and engineering.

The task of implementing the new strategy will fall to Professor John Harper, who stepped up from deputy principal last year, following the resignation of Professor Ferdinand von Prondzynski after a row over the appointment of a business associate as a vice-principal. Although von Prondzynski was cleared of wrongdoing, he said the investigation had caused division and damaged the university's reputation.

RGU was one of only five Scottish universities to enter the TEF assessment. The awards panel was impressed by the range of opportunities for students to develop knowledge, skills and understanding that are most highly valued by employers, and to engage "consistently and frequently" with developments at the forefront of professional practice.

High graduate employment levels have been Robert Gordon's greatest strength since the days, at the start of the decade, when it was the leading post-1992 university in our table. It is still in the top 40 for graduate employment, but that compares with a place in the top 20 in the 2016 Guide – and for many years before that — when the North Sea oil and gas industry was at its peak. Overall, the university has dropped 14 places in our new table and is now just within the top 100.

Applications have fallen for the past four years, although by less than the Scottish or UK average in 2018, but the numbers starting degrees have continued to grow. Students are attracted by the work placements that have become the norm for Robert Gordon degrees and can last for up to a year. Other employability and co-curricular initiatives to enhance career prospects include several innovation skills programmes to prepare students for a changing labour market.

A strong focus on new technology includes an award-winning virtual campus and teaching notes via Moodle, used by on-campus students and the many engaged in distance learning. The system provides notes, online forums and electronic submission options.

All teaching takes place on the Garthdee campus, on the south side of Aberdeen,

Garthdee House
Garthdee Road
Aberdeen AB10 7QB
01224 262 728
UGOffice@rgu.ac.uk
www.rgu.ac.uk
www.rguunion.co.uk
Open days 2019:
see website

***The Times and The Sunday Times* Rankings**
Overall Ranking: 96 (last year: 82)

Teaching quality	80.3%	=60
Student experience	77.5%	=78
Research quality	4.0%	=105
Entry standards	159	=32
Graduate prospects	81.1%	37
Good honours	71.0%	83
Expected completion rate	85.8%	=62
Student/staff ratio	20.6	126
Services and facilities	£1,448	129

overlooking the River Dee. RGU, named after an 18th-century philanthropist, has a pedigree in education that goes back 250 years but its forward-thinking approach can be encapsulated in its landmark green glass library tower, with spectacular views over the city and river, after a £135m capital programme brought the university together on one campus for the first time.

The university made a relatively small submission to the 2014 Research Excellence Framework, but more than 40% of the work was placed in the top two categories, with the best results coming in health subjects and communication and media studies. RGU's new strategy promises investment in sustainable transportation, data and analytics, pharmacy, smart cities and biomedical toxins.

The creative industries are a growth area, but Robert Gordon is still best known for its links with the offshore industries, both in the North Sea and abroad. The RGU Oil and Gas Institute offers drilling and advanced rig training, has the world's only decommissioning simulator, and has provided educational and consultancy services for the offshore industries in Algeria, Japan and Mexico. Nearly three quarters of the undergraduates, however, either attend the business school or take courses in health and social care.

Efforts to extend access beyond the normal higher education catchment have produced a diverse student population, with almost a third of undergraduates coming from working-class homes and 94% from state schools or colleges. The university has a particularly high rate of transfer from colleges in the region via its Degree Link option where students take a two-year Higher National Diploma followed by two years at RGU to gain a degree

Aberdeen is a long way to go for students from other parts of the UK, but train and air links are excellent, and the city regularly features in top-ten lists for quality of life.

Robert Gordon has invested more than £11m in its sports facilities, which act as a social hub at Garthdee while also offering improved sports provision for the region. These include a centre of excellence for hockey; facilities for cycling, netball, volleyball, and gym and fitness classes; a 25-metre swimming pool; and a climbing wall and bouldering courses for students and Aberdeen schools during term time. Although renting in the private sector can be expensive, RGU has enough residential places to accommodate first-years from outside the locality.

Tuition fees

» Fees for Scottish/EU students 2019–20   £0–£1,820
   RUK fees   £5,000–£6,750
» Fees for International students 2019–20   £12,730–£16,240
» For scholarship and bursary information see
   www3.rgu.ac.uk/future-students/finance-and-scholarships/
   financial-support/
» Graduate salary   £22,000

Student numbers

Undergraduates	7,718 (1,348)
Postgraduates	1,271 (2,193)
Applications/places	10,700/2,420
Applications per place	4.4
Overall offer rate	77.9%
International students	17.9%

Accommodation

University provided places: 916 (catered 0%)
Self-catered: £98–£200 per week
www.rgu.ac.uk/accommodation

Where do the students come from?

State schools (non-grammar)	93.8%	Working-class homes	32.0%	Black ethnic minority	2.4%
Grammar schools	0.4%	Deprived areas	4.4%	Disabled	8.7%
Independent schools	5.7%	All ethnic minorities	10.1%	Mature (over 21)	26.4%

University of Roehampton

A new library costing £35m and containing 300,000 books and 1,200 study spaces has become the centrepiece of Roehampton's attractive parkland campus in southwest London. The old one is already being converted into a new home for media, culture and languages, with film, television, photographic and sound studios, editing suites, a flexible creative space for students and a 90-seat cinema, all built around a glazed courtyard. It will take its first students this year.

The prize-winning library may have contributed to a rise in student satisfaction that has propelled the university four places further up our league table. Roehampton has not tried to overturn the bronze rating it was awarded in the Teaching Excellence Framework (TEF), however. The TEF panel acknowledged that the involvement of employers ensured that programmes are contemporary, but low completion rates — where the university ranks 100= this year — were its undoing.

There have been a number of innovations. Roehampton is one of several universities offering undergraduates the opportunity to live in "quieter, more study-focused accommodation", for example. Students living in these areas will be expected to adopt a "moderated lifestyle within their accommodation in respect of alcohol, parties and noise".

Roehampton has also launched the UK's first esports scholarships. Open to undergraduates or postgraduates, the awards are worth up to £1,500 a year, like the university's other sports scholarships, and require a continued commitment to esports and successful academic progression.

Applications were down by more than 8% in 2017, although enrolments have been steady for several years. The offer rate has gone up by ten percentage points since £9,000 fees were introduced, so that nine out of ten applicants now receive an offer. The rate is even higher for male applicants, as the university seeks to reduce the domination of female students, who accounted for two thirds of the places in 2016-17. The gender gap reflects the domination of education, the arts and social sciences in the portfolio of degrees.

Students need not follow any denomination to enrol in Roehampton's four colleges, which all had their origins in teacher education. The Anglican Whitelands celebrated its 175th anniversary in 2016 and was the first in the country to open higher education to women. Digby Stuart was established by French Catholic women, Southlands by Methodists, and Froebel follows the humanist teachings of Frederick Froebel. Roehampton also has a Jewish resource centre and Muslim prayer rooms.

Grove House
Roehampton Lane
London SW15 5PJ
020 8392 3232
www.roehampton.ac.uk/
prospective-students/
enquiries/
www.roehampton.ac.uk
www.roehamptonstudent.com
Open days 2019:
see website

The Times and The Sunday Times Rankings
Overall Ranking: 70 (last year: 74)

Teaching quality	77.7%	=99
Student experience	77.4%	80
Research quality	24.5%	51
Entry standards	109	=123
Graduate prospects	72.2%	=91
Good honours	68.9%	=95
Expected completion rate	81.2%	=100
Student/staff ratio	14.7	=35
Services and facilities	£2,216	63

A quarter of Roehampton students are on education courses. The university's degrees are also taught in Birmingham and Manchester by the private firm QA Higher Education, while international partnerships include an agreement with the EU Business School to offer Roehampton-accredited degrees to students across the continent.

Almost all the undergraduates are state educated, 43% coming from working-class homes when this was last surveyed. The university does not offer bursaries to students from poor backgrounds, other than for care leavers, so only those winning scholarships will receive financial support. Roehampton's diverse intake gives it a ranking just outside the top ten in our new table for social inclusion.

A Student Senate serves as a formal forum for students to raise issues of concern with senior administrators and to be consulted on key institutional matters.

Roehampton entered two thirds of its eligible academics for assessment in the 2014 Research Excellence Framework and saw 66% of its work rated as world-leading or internationally excellent. It outperformed all post-1992 universities and had the most highly-rated dance department in the UK, with 94% of research placed in the top two categories. The results in education and English were among the best in London. These successes produced a 40% increase in funding for research.

A residential development at Vauxhall, 20 minutes from the main campus by public transport, has a swimming pool and other facilities, and brought the number of residential places to more than 2,300. The university guarantees accommodation for UK students who make Roehampton their firm choice and apply by the end of May. International applicants have until the end of July.

The sports facilities on campus have been enhanced, with a new gym, football pitches, running track and multi-use games area. The sport performance and rehabilitation centre provides well-equipped laboratory facilities and performance coaching. The university is a high-performance centre for British fencing and sitting volleyball.

While rents are not cheap in the private sector, students like the proximity of central London and the lively and attractive suburbs around Roehampton.

Tuition fees

» Fees for UK/EU students 2019–20	£9,250
» Fees for International students 2019–20	£13,520
» For scholarship and bursary information see www.roehampton.ac.uk/undergraduate-courses/tuition-fees/	
» Graduate salary	£21,000

Student numbers

Undergraduates	8,205	(316)
Postgraduates	964	(722)
Applications/places	8,820/1,925	
Applications per place	4.6	
Overall offer rate	93.7%	
International students	10.3%	

Accommodation

University provided places: 2,271 (catered 0%)
Self-catered: £112–£178 per week
First years guaranteed accommodation
www.roehampton.ac.uk/accommodation

Where do the students come from?

State schools (non-grammar)	94.2%	Working-class homes	43.0%	Black ethnic minority	23.2%
Grammar schools	2.4%	Deprived areas	5.5%	Disabled	5.7%
Independent schools	3.5%	All ethnic minorities	56.9%	Mature (over 21)	45.6%

Royal Agricultural University

The Royal Agricultural University (RAU) has suffered the biggest fall in our current table — almost 30 places to add to its decline of 35 places in the previous two editions. The university entered our rankings in 2015 on the verge of the top 50 but has now dropped into the bottom 20. A sharp decline in student satisfaction with the quality of teaching and the wider student experience is the main cause for this year's decline.

The number of students starting degrees at the RAU has risen by a third in ten years, however, and applications are up again, bucking the national trend. With fewer than 1,300 students, it is the UK's smallest publicly-funded university, but the number of female students has been rising consistently and has almost reached parity with the men.

RAU was placed in the silver category of the government's Teaching Excellence Framework after assessors commented favourably on the high-quality rural estate and specialist facilities. The panel was impressed by the employer-informed course design, work placements and extracurricular opportunities for students to develop skills and attributes valued by employers.

A £4.2m building which opened last year on the campus outside Cirencester will further enhance the links with agritech companies.

One floor will be used by the Farm491 project, named after the number of hectares available for research and testing here, which offers affordable co-working to entrepreneurs in sustainable food production. The building also houses the Cirencester Growth Hub, helping local businesses of all kinds.

As the Royal Agricultural College, the institution was the first of its type in the English-speaking world, established in 1845 on the initiative of the Fairford and Cirencester Farmers' Club, which was concerned at the lack of government support for education, particularly in relation to agriculture. Since then, every monarch since Queen Victoria has visited at least once.

Today's RAU has been described as the "Oxbridge of the countryside" because of its privileged intake and beautiful Cotswolds campus. It recruits the biggest share of entrants from independent schools of any university — almost half — although almost a third also came from the four poorest socioeconomic groups when this was last surveyed.

The four schools focus on equine management and science; agriculture, food and the environment; business and entrepreneurship; and real estate and land management. There are only just over a dozen honours degrees and four top-up courses for students who have completed foundation degrees, as well as a growing portfolio of master's courses.

Stroud Road
Cirencester GL7 6JS
01285 889 912
admissions@rau.ac.uk
www.rau.ac.uk
Open days 2019:
March 9; April 8;
May 8; July 13

The Times and The Sunday Times **Rankings**

Overall Ranking: =115 (last year: =86)

Teaching quality	75.4%	114
Student experience	75.3%	102
Research quality	1.1%	126
Entry standards	123	=88
Graduate prospects	63.5%	=125
Good honours	65.8%	=116
Expected completion rate	95.2%	10
Student/staff ratio	21.6	=127
Services and facilities	£2,529	33

However, the university has been working with industry to establish a new set of programmes that reflect the emerging needs of the land management and agri-business sectors after Brexit. Two new postgraduate programmes will be launched this year, followed by two at undergraduate level in 2020 focusing on leadership, rural policy and strategy, agri-ecology, sustainability and innovative land management.

Many RAU courses include a 20-week work placement. There is an extensive network of student placement sponsors in the UK and overseas, and part-time work is available both in the university and in nearby Cirencester. The university has been rated within the top ten UK universities and colleges for its enterprise activities.

On campus, there is a well-stocked library and computer suites, as well as specialist laboratories. The virtual learning environment ensures that all teaching materials are available online 24 hours a day.

The two university farms, both close to the campus, cover a total of 1,200 acres. Coates Manor Farm focuses on arable farming, while Harnhill Farm is an example of an integrated livestock and cropping system. In addition, there is an equestrian centre providing stabling and livery facilities, and students also have access to a large dairy complex. All are run as commercial enterprises. The RAU also delivers degree courses in Hong Kong and China.

RAU has one of the lowest scores for research, however. Just 12 staff were entered for the 2014 Research Excellence Framework — a quarter of those with research contracts — and only 7% of their work was placed in the top two categories.

The small numbers and countryside setting encourage a collegiate atmosphere. The campus is the centre of social activities, which includes four balls each year. There are eight halls of residence on campus for undergraduates with 360 rooms — enough for most first-years to be offered a place. Private rentals are available in Cirencester and the surrounding area.

Sport plays an important part in student life and, in addition to the normal range, there are clubs for polo, clay pigeon shooting, beagling and team chasing — a cross-country equestrian sport. There are ample opportunities to explore the Cotswolds countryside and London is only 90 minutes away by train.

Tuition fees

»	Fees for UK/EU students 2019–20	£9,250
»	Fees for International students 2019–20	£10,000
»	For scholarship and bursary information see www.rau.ac.uk/study/undergraduate/fees-and-funding	
»	Graduate salary	£21.000

Student numbers

Undergraduates	1,000	(28)
Postgraduates	242	(11)
Applications/places		1,205/345
Applications per place		3.5
Overall offer rate		n/a
International students		11.9%

Accommodation

University provided places: 329 (catered 75%)
Catered costs: £108–£204 per week
Self-catered: £130 per week
www.rau.ac.uk/university-life/accommodation

Where do the students come from?

State schools (non-grammar)	48.4%	Working-class homes	29.9%	Black ethnic minority	n/a
Grammar schools	4.0%	Deprived areas	n/a	Disabled	10.4%
Independent schools	47.5%	All ethnic minorities	n/a	Mature (over 21)	11.7%

Royal Holloway, University of London

Royal Holloway is broadening the options for undergraduates in a number of subjects as part of a plan for further growth. More than 75 programmes are being launched, many of them new combinations and others adding the opportunity of a year in business or industry. A new modern languages degree, for example, will also be available with 19 other subjects, from international film to maths or music. Wholly new areas include the internet of things, which will be the focus of a degree in computer systems engineering.

The university is close to its target of 10,500 students by 2020, but the numbers starting degrees have plateaued. Applications have fallen by 2,000 in the past two years, although they are still well above the norm before £9,000 fees were introduced. A new science building on the spacious campus will facilitate some expansion. It is intended to attract more female students into science and engineering — an appropriate brief for a college that was founded for women only. The Beatrice Shilling building, named after a pioneering engineer, will house the new electronic engineering department.

Royal Holloway markets itself as London's "campus in the country" and claims to have one of the most beautiful university settings in the world, offering students the best of both worlds: a safe environment in leafy Egham, Surrey, but only 40 minutes by train from central London. Satisfaction levels are the best in the University of London and the completion rate is in the top 20 nationally.

The 135-acre woodland campus close to Windsor Castle and Heathrow is dominated by the iconic Founder's building, which was modelled on a French chateau and opened by Queen Victoria. But a £150m development plan is upgrading the facilities. A library and student services centre opened in 2017 at the heart of the campus, with landscaped and pedestrianised spaces around it. The development, which was designed to complement the Founder's building, includes a cafe, shop, bank and a careers and recruitment hub, as well as a library with seating for 1,150 and different zones to accommodate silent, social, creative and collaborative study.

Royal Holloway was given a silver rating in the government's Teaching Excellence Framework. The awards panel was impressed by the level of investment in elearning facilities and said students were engaged with developments from the forefront of research, scholarship and professional practice.

About 15% of the undergraduates come from independent schools, but the proportion coming from working-class homes is close to the national average for its courses and entry

Egham TW20 0EX
01784 414 944
study@royalholloway.ac.uk
www.royalholloway.ac.uk
www.su.rhul.ac.uk
Open days 2019:
see website

The Times and The Sunday Times Rankings		
Overall Ranking: 24 (last year: =28)		
Teaching quality	80.3%	=60
Student experience	78.3%	=70
Research quality	36.3%	=30
Entry standards	142	=49
Graduate prospects	73.5%	=81
Good honours	80.0%	=32
Expected completion rate	93.0%	=16
Student/staff ratio	15.2	=50
Services and facilities	£2,530	32

qualifications. There is a range of bursaries for undergraduates from low-income households and some for postgraduates so that students who graduate with large debts are not deterred from continuing their studies.

More than 80% of the work assessed in the 2014 Research Excellence Framework was judged to be world-leading or internationally excellent, placing Royal Holloway in the top 30 institutions on this measure in our table. It would have been higher still if a larger proportion of the academics had been entered.

Geography achieved the best results in England, while earth sciences, psychology, mathematics, music, media arts and drama and theatre were all in their respective top tens. Royal Holloway was chosen as an academic centre of excellence in cyber-security research by the UK government, one of only eight such awards nationwide.

The Royal Holloway Passport, which is intended to enhance graduates' employability, recognises the additional skills that students gain from many extracurricular activities. An advanced skills programme, covering information technology, communication skills and foreign languages, further encourages breadth of study. The university offers a number of edegrees and promotes numerous opportunities to study abroad, building on the international flavour of the campus and its links with institutions such as New York, Sydney and Yale universities.

An already plentiful stock of on-campus accommodation was expanded with the opening of 56 new townhouses with spaces for more than 600 students. The halls have social space, laundries and outdoor social and study areas. First-year undergraduates are guaranteed a residential place, as long as they apply by early June with the university as their firm choice.

Sports facilities are good and Royal Holloway has had considerable success with its "student talented athlete recognition scheme", or Stars.

A thriving community action programme involves more than 1,000 students volunteering with various local organisations and charities. The students' union is the centre of most students' social life, putting on entertainment and activities seven days a week.

Tuition fees

- » Fees for UK/EU students 2019–20 £9,250
- » Fees for International students 2019–20 £16,500–£19,400
- » For scholarship and bursary information see www.royalholloway.ac.uk/ugfeesandfunding
- » Graduate salary £20,000

Student numbers

Undergraduates	7,328	(309)
Postgraduates	1,985	(705)
Applications/places		15,560/2,270
Applications per place		6.9
Overall offer rate		90.8%
International students		28.2%

Accommodation

University provided places: 3,501 (catered 29%)
Catered costs: £115–£184 per week
Self-catered: £161–£184 per week
First years guaranteed accommodation
www.royalholloway.ac.uk/studyhere/accommodation/home.aspx

Where do the students come from?

State schools (non-grammar)	74.1%	Working-class homes	28.4%	Black ethnic minority	5.6%
Grammar schools	11.4%	Deprived areas	5.1%	Disabled	6.1%
Independent schools	14.6%	All ethnic minorities	36.3%	Mature (over 21)	6.1%

University of St Andrews

THE TIMES
THE SUNDAY TIMES
GOOD
UNIVERSITY
GUIDE
2019
UNIVERSITY
OF THE YEAR
SHORTLISTED

St Andrews remains the nearest challenger to Oxford and Cambridge in our league table. As usual, it is in the top three in both of our measures — third for teaching quality and top for the wider student experience — which are derived from the National Student Survey. It also has the highest level of overall satisfaction at any university.

By making third place in our table its own, St Andrews earns another shortlisting for our UK University of the Year award. It remains by a distance the best university in Scotland but competes for students on a global stage with international students making up about 45% of the intake, with the largest grouping coming from America.

St Andrews was among a handful of Scottish universities to enter the Teaching Excellence Framework in its first year and achieved a gold rating. The independent panel praised the "exemplary" teaching, and a learning and teaching environment of the highest quality. A culture of rigour and stretch within a research-intensive environment stimulates students' enthusiasm, it added.

Applications are running at record levels and are now 50% higher than they were a decade ago. But the number of places available to undergraduates is lower than it was then — St Andrews having eschewed the huge expansion in places going on elsewhere in higher education in the UK. It means there were more than ten applicants for every place in 2017.

Five new degrees were launched last year, all of them joint honours involving sustainable development. The university is making its own contribution to sustainability with a £25m green energy centre at the Eden Campus at Guardbridge, which pumps hot water four miles to St Andrews to heat university buildings. About 450 professional services staff will relocate to the campus in 2019, releasing space for students and academics in the heart of St Andrews.

Additional space will be provided by a unique swap deal with Fife council, enabling the university to use the site of a secondary school for a new college of social sciences. The school will move to North Haugh, the location for most of St Andrews' science and medical facilities, introducing more pupils to the idea of university and hopefully raising attainment.

The university, Scotland's oldest higher education institution and the third oldest in the English-speaking world, boasts Europe's first Centre for Syrian Studies, an Institute of Iranian Studies and a Centre for Peace and Conflict Studies.

It has also invested heavily in the sciences, which produced some of the best results in

St Katharine's West
16 The Scores
St Andrews KY16 9AX
01334 462 150
admissions@st-andrews.ac.uk
www.st-andrews.ac.uk
www.yourunion.net
Open days 2019:
March 6; April 3, 10, 17

The Times and The Sunday Times **Rankings**
Overall Ranking: 3 (last year: 3)

Teaching quality	86.2%	3
Student experience	85.2%	1
Research quality	40.4%	11
Entry standards	206	4
Graduate prospects	79.6%	=49
Good honours	90.1%	6
Expected completion rate	96.0%	=6
Student/staff ratio	11.6	6
Services and facilities	£2,721	21

the 2014 Research Excellence Framework. More than 70% of the St Andrews submission reached the top two categories and over 90% of two joint submissions with the University of Edinburgh in chemistry and physics was rated world-leading or internationally excellent. Classics and history of art scored particularly well, too.

St Andrews runs the town's Byre Theatre, which is used as teaching space by day and offers productions in the evenings and at weekends. Work is under way on a £12m music centre, funded mainly by alumni and other donors, on a site bordering the historic St Mary's Quadrangle. The facility centre will include practice, rehearsal and teaching spaces for student musicians, as well as a library and a music technology and recording suite.

Many students come from south of the border, even though — together with Edinburgh — St Andrews has the highest fees in the UK for undergraduates from England, Wales or Northern Ireland. It currently charges them £9,250 a year for the full four years of a degree, although there are bursaries for students from low-income families. Scots and other EU students continue to pay nothing.

The university accounts for more than half of the 17,000 inhabitants of the town of St Andrews, itself the centre of the golfing world. Student traditions include third or fourth-year students helping new arrivals, known as "bejants" and "bejantines", adjust to university life through academic 'families'.

Nearly half of the students live in university-owned accommodation, with first-year undergraduates guaranteed a hall place provided they apply by the end of June. Two new halls opened last year, part of a £70m investment to add 900 student beds to the 4,000 the university already owns or endorses.

More than a third of the UK undergraduates come from independent schools. The university is in the middle of a £100m fundraising campaign, £13m of which is to support bright candidates who would otherwise be unable to attend St Andrews. Our new table for social inclusion shows St Andrews to have the least socially diverse intake of any university in the UK, bar Oxford.

Most students enjoy a lively social life in a tight-knit community. A £14m redevelopment of the sports centre has been completed, providing a new sports hall, larger and better-equipped fitness suite, and an indoor tennis centre.

Tuition fees

»	Fees for Scottish/EU students 2019–20	£0–£1,820
	RUK fees	£9,250
»	Fees for International students 2019–20	£22,350
	Medicine	£31,580
»	For scholarship and bursary information see	
	www.st-andrews.ac.uk/study/fees-and-funding/undergraduate	
»	Graduate salary	£23,000

Student numbers

Undergraduates	7,443	(808)
Postgraduates	1,772	(309)
Applications/places	16,875/1,535	
Applications per place	11	
Overall offer rate	50.2%	
International students	45.4%	

Accommodation

University provided places: 4,133 (catered 52%)
Catered costs: £138–£274 per week
Self-catered: £101–£220 per week
First years guaranteed accommodation
www.st-andrews.ac.uk/study/accommodation/

Where do the students come from?

State schools (non-grammar)	54.0%	Working-class homes	14.2%	Black ethnic minority	1.3%
Grammar schools	10.3%	Deprived areas	3.5%	Disabled	3.2%
Independent schools	35.6%	All ethnic minorities	10.5%	Mature (over 21)	2.1%

St George's, University of London

For the third year in a row, St George's has the highest employment rating in our table. While that might not be surprising for the only freestanding medical school in the University of London — and the only one in our table — the institution offers training for other health professionals as well as doctors. Courses include biomedical science and healthcare science degrees in respiratory and cardiac physiology and sleep physiology, while paramedic science and radiography degrees are also taught on-site in partnership with Kingston University.

St George's is one of only 14 universities in our table to hold the (lowest) bronze rating in the government's Teaching Excellence Framework. Although the panel gave St George's credit for an "embedded institutional culture that rewards excellent teaching, and promotes inclusivity among staff and students", its performance was held down by low student satisfaction with assessment and feedback. It also suffers by comparison with other largely medically-based institutions with even higher employment rates. These appear in our subject tables but are too specialised for our league table. In that table, students rate teaching quality at St George's in the bottom three and put it in the bottom eight for the broader student experience.

However, applications have risen 5% this year and there are now nearly 5,000 students studying there. Two years ago, St George's made headlines by becoming the first to advertise in advance that it would have places in medicine available through clearing. It used the process again last summer, not because it was short of candidates — less than a third of applicants receive an offer — but because clearing is considered "the fairest way for us to get high quality students". The previous year, over all courses, 30% of undergraduates won places through clearing.

St George's has done more than most to broaden its intake, and the institution sits in the top 60 overall in our new table measuring social inclusion in undergraduate recruitment. The Adjusted Criteria Scheme reduces the entry requirements by two A-level grades for anyone applying from a non-selective state school whose results are in the bottom 20% nationwide. The scheme applies to medicine, biomedical science, physiotherapy and healthcare science.

A shadowing scheme offers sixth-formers from Wandsworth and Merton state schools the opportunity to accompany a doctor or other healthcare professional at St George's or Queen Mary's Hospital. Three out of ten undergraduates come from low-income households — well above average for the school's courses and entry qualifications.

St George's was the first UK institution to launch the MBBS Graduate Entry

Cranmer Terrace
Tooting
London SW17 0RE
020 3897 2032
study@sgul.ac.uk
www.sgul.ac.uk
www.sgsu.org.uk
Open days 2019:
see website

The Times and The Sunday Times Rankings
Overall Ranking: 80 (last year: =75)

Teaching quality	72.7%	128
Student experience	71.7%	123
Research quality	22.2%	53
Entry standards	166	=22
Graduate prospects	93.8%	1
Good honours	75.7%	53
Expected completion rate	92.6%	=20
Student/staff ratio	12.4	9
Services and facilities	£2,505	36

Programme, a four-year fast-track medical degree course open to graduates in any discipline, which has become an increasingly popular route into the profession.

The original St George's medical school opened in 1868 at St George's hospital, which had been established in 1733 at Hyde Park Corner, in central London, when it was open countryside. Edward Jenner trained there before inventing the smallpox vaccination and the hide of Blossom the cow, the subject of his early experiments, can still be seen in the library of St George's in Tooting, south London, where the institution moved in the 1970s. It shares clinical facilities with the hospital, one of London's busiest.

Continuing a strong research record, which has led to historic developments in cardiac pacemakers and IVF, St George's was second only to Imperial College London for the impact of its work in the 2014 Research Excellence Framework. Overall, 70% of its submission reached the top two categories for world-leading and internationally excellent research.

The school's strategic plan for the next four years focuses on building research strength further. St George's has three research institutes advancing prevention and treatment of conditions with both genetic and infectious causes.

At the Tooting campus there is a preparatory centre for international students coming to London. St George's also offers a four-year graduate entry Bachelor of Surgery degree at the University of Nicosia in Cyprus, where the first intake graduated in 2015.

Most — if not all — undergraduates are offered one of almost 500 residential places, with priority going to students from abroad or outside London.

The sports centre is on campus and competitive teams play in regional and national competitions. Students have use of a rowing club on the River Thames and can also take advantage of University of London facilities for sport. Tooting Lido, the biggest open-air pool in the country, is not far away and the West End is less than half an hour by tube for shopping and nightlife excursions.

Tuition fees

»	Fees for UK/EU students 2019–20	£9,250
	Foundation courses	£7,500
»	Fees for International students 2019–20	£15,500–£17,500
	Medicine	£32,500
»	For scholarship and bursary information see	
	www.sgul.ac.uk/study/undergraduate/fees-and-funding	
»	Graduate salary	£26,600

Student numbers

Undergraduates	2,781	(1,128)
Postgraduates	218	(727)
Applications/places		6,215/470
Applications per place		13.2
Overall offer rate		52.9%
International students		8.6%

Accommodation

University provided places: 476 (catered 0%)
Self-catered: £160–£170 per week
Undergraduates and international students get priority
www.sgul.ac.uk/study/accommodation

Where do the students come from?

State schools (non-grammar)	60.3%	Working-class homes	30.4%	Black ethnic minority	17.3%
Grammar schools	23.8%	Deprived areas	5.8%	Disabled	7.2%
Independent schools	15.9%	All ethnic minorities	64.7%	Mature (over 21)	32.6%

St Mary's University, Twickenham

St Mary's has the most satisfied students in London by a considerable distance, according to the two measures in our league table, and is in the top 20 in the country for their perceptions of teaching quality. The feat has helped to propel it another 22 places up the overall table and into the top 80 — the second big rise in a row.

The university was awarded a silver rating in the government's Teaching Excellence Framework. The independent panel noted that high-quality resources were much appreciated by students and enhanced their learning. Good staffing levels also facilitated personalised and small-group working, it added.

These successes came too late to prevent a 14% decline in applications in 2017, however, and enrolments dropped for the second year in a row. Fifteen new degrees, in subjects from theology, religion and ethics, to communications, data analytics and marketing, and politics, policy and public management, have been launched, giving applicants a broader range of options.

There will be no unconditional offers, however, since the university has decided to end the practice after finding that some of those receiving them failed to achieve their predicted grades.

There are also about 500 undergraduate degree combinations across four schools covering sport, health and applied science; education, theology and leadership; management and social sciences; and the arts and humanities.

St Mary's is the largest Catholic university in the UK, and one of three, the others being Newman, in Birmingham and Leeds Trinity. It has a commitment to training teachers for Catholic and other Christian schools, although it admits students of all faiths and none. The university's first stated objective is "to be a distinctive institution within UK higher education, providing a unique experience for our students and staff by virtue of our values and identity as a Catholic university".

The university has appointed a series of high-profile visiting professors including Dr Mary McAleese, the former president of Ireland; Sir Vince Cable, now leader of the Liberal Democrats; Cherie Blair; and Sir Clive Woodward, who coached England to the 2003 Rugby World Cup. Ruth Kelly, education secretary under Tony Blair, has become Pro Vice-Chancellor of Research and Enterprise.

Founded in Hammersmith in 1850 by the Catholic Poor Schools Committee to meet the need for teachers for the growing numbers of poor Catholic children, St Mary's has historically focused on educating teachers, with a third of all students still training to teach.

It is the university's sporting prowess that regularly captures headlines, however.

Waldegrave Road
Strawberry Hill
Twickenham TW1 4SX
020 8240 2314
admit@stmarys.ac.uk
www.stmarys.ac.uk
www.stmaryssu.co.uk
Open days 2019:
June 12

The Times and The Sunday Times Rankings
Overall Ranking: 77 (last year: 99)

Teaching quality	83.4%	=17
Student experience	81.0%	=25
Research quality	4.0%	=105
Entry standards	120	=94
Graduate prospects	72.6%	90
Good honours	72.2%	73
Expected completion rate	80.0%	106
Student/staff ratio	15.7	=61
Services and facilities	£1,749	112

Twenty-two St Mary's students and alumni at the Rio Olympics won six medals, three of them gold, and would have finished 25th in the medal table, ahead of countries such as South Africa and Poland. They were led by Sir Mo Farah, a graduate of St Mary's, after whom its athletics track is named and who has a scholarship programme for promising young athletes at the university. The £8.5m sports centre is good enough to have attracted teams from Japan and China during last year's World Athletics Championships. There are further sports facilities in neighbouring Teddington.

The campus occupies 35 acres of gardens and parkland close to the Thames with the restored Strawberry Hill House as its centrepiece. The Gothic fantasy was designed by Horace Walpole, the son of Britain's first prime minister, and is open to the public.

The university has opened a new community building in the centre of Twickenham, with theatre space, six multifunction studio rooms and a large conservatory area with a cafe. The Exchange offers training courses for local residents and firms, as well as providing more teaching space for students. Other recent developments have included a £6m library.

St Mary's has a small cohort of international students and is launching an international college on campus, in partnership with an Australian higher education firm, to attract more. The first foundation courses start this year and successful completion will guarantee progression to one of 30 degree programmes.

Almost 40% of the UK undergraduates are from working-class homes and the university has a number of outreach schemes designed to broaden the intake further. Students help selected groups of school pupils throughout the academic year on an e-mentoring scheme that has received excellent feedback. Other initiatives provide academic support and monitor the progress of under-represented groups once they begin courses.

The 710 residential places are enough to guarantee accommodation for new entrants if they apply by the end of May. Most students like the combination of an attractive setting in southwest London that is only half an hour from Waterloo by train.

Tuition fees

»	Fees for UK/EU students 2019–20	£9,250
	Foundation courses	£6,000–£8,000
»	Fees for International students 2019–20	£11,750
»	For scholarship and bursary information see www.stmarys.ac.uk/student-finance/	
»	Graduate salary	£21,000

Student numbers

Undergraduates	3,796	(351)
Postgraduates	548	(838)
Applications/places	5,235/975	
Applications per place	5.4	
Overall offer rate	90.7%	
International students	6.3%	

Accommodation

University provided places: 710 (catered 100%)
Catered costs: £138–£230 per week
First years guaranteed accommodation
www.stmarys.ac.uk/accommodation

Where do the students come from?

State schools (non-grammar)	91.5%	Working-class homes	38.8%	Black ethnic minority	11.4%
Grammar schools	3.1%	Deprived areas	6.4%	Disabled	7.9%
Independent schools	5.4%	All ethnic minorities	28.8%	Mature (over 21)	22.8%

University of Salford

A transformation of Salford's campus is part of a new £800m plan agreed between the university and the local authority to create a new city area linking Manchester's Central Business District and MediaCity UK. The university's share will be £300m of investment split into three zones within and around the existing campus.

The first regeneration projects are already under way. New student residences adjacent to the campus and the upgrading and expansion of laboratories for the life sciences will be ready for the start of the next academic year. A new engineering building is due to open in 2020-21 and the library will be completely refurbished.

Salford had already reshaped its portfolio of courses, narrowing the range of subjects it offers to focus on its strengths and concentrating on four Industry Collaboration Zones, in engineering and environments, health and wellbeing, digital and creative, and sport.

The university described the change as a "bold departure from traditional structures and models of learning". Students will work closely with academics and industrial partners on work-based projects, applying their learning and skills in real-world environments.

New degrees are being introduced to fit the structure. Subjects as wide-ranging as costume design, journalism with public relations, acoustical and audio engineering, and automotive and autonomous vehicle technology took their first students last year. Criminology with security, and psychology with English language will be added this year, when Salford also expects to have more than 200 degree apprentices.

Salford is up seven places in our new table, following a ten-place rise last year, and is no longer the lowest-ranked pre-1992 institution. An attempt to upgrade a bronze rating in the Teaching Excellence Framework was not successful, however. Despite good links with employers and a commitment to learning by students, the panel found that progression to employment or further study remained "exceptionally low". Our table suggests that progression to graduate-level work is broadly in line with the university's overall ranking.

Applications dropped by a little more than the national average in 2017, but only after three successive rises. The numbers starting degrees rose again and have grown by more than 40% since 2012.

Salford is planning a private medical school for international students in partnership with Manchester and Manchester Metropolitan universities and its new British University of Bahrain, opened earlier this year, is the first such UK institution in the emirate.

At home, developments include the £55m New Adelphi teaching centre for art,

The Crescent
Salford
Greater Manchester
M5 4WT
0161 295 4545
enquiries@salford.ac.uk
www.salford.ac.uk
www.salfordstudents.com
Open days 2019:
see website

The Times and The Sunday Times Rankings
Overall Ranking: =81 (last year: 88)

Teaching quality	81.8%	39
Student experience	79.1%	=54
Research quality	8.3%	72
Entry standards	128	=73
Graduate prospects	73.6%	=77
Good honours	69.6%	90
Expected completion rate	81.5%	=98
Student/staff ratio	15.0	=44
Services and facilities	£2,014	87

performance, and design and technology students. It also serves as a social hub. There are opportunities to work with BBC staff and other media professionals at the £30m MediaCityUK building in Salford Quays and the university invested more than £80m in the Peel Park Quarter, with impressive student facilities and 1,367 residential places on campus.

Salford entered only a third of its eligible academics for the 2014 Research Excellence Framework, but more than half of their work was found to be world-leading or internationally excellent.

The university's School of Nursing, Midwifery, Social Work and Social Sciences received outstanding ratings from its regulatory body and the School of Health Sciences has an international reputation for the treatment of sports injuries. Salford's school of health and society has also received outstanding ratings from its regulatory bodies.

Engineering is a traditional strength, attracting many of the 2,300 international students, but it is the business school that has been Salford's main point of growth. Two thirds of the university's courses — and all of them in the business school — offer work placements, some of which are abroad and almost all counting towards degree classifications.

Salford does well on the government's access measures: more than 40% of the undergraduates come from working-class homes and about one in five are from an area that sends few students to higher education. The university ranks just outside the top 30 in our new table measuring social inclusion, with virtually all its students drawn from comprehensive schools and a third from ethnic minorities. From this year, all new UK and EU undergraduates will receive a £150 credit bursary to be spent on study materials, with the amount rising for those from poor families.

Sports provision includes a swimming pool, two squash courts refurbished recently, five fitness suites, and the upgraded multi-function sports hall. There are three grass football pitches and one rugby pitch on the adjacent David Lewis playing fields and students can use the separate Albert Park facility of a 3G full-sized 11-a-side football pitch.

The university's location is one of its chief selling points, with Manchester a prime draw for students. Both main campuses are within walking distance of the city centre and border the River Irwell and Salford's residential accommodation is all within ten minutes' walk of the main campus.

Tuition fees

»	Fees for UK/EU students 2019–20	£9,250
	Foundation courses	£8,250
»	Fees for International students 2019–20	£12,660–£15,960
»	For scholarship and bursary information see www.salford.ac.uk/study/undergraduate/ why-salford#section5	
»	Graduate salary	£21,600

Student numbers

Undergraduates	14,531	(946)
Postgraduates	2,384	(2,136)
Applications/places	24,940/4,380	
Applications per place	5.7	
Overall offer rate	79.5%	
International students	11.4%	

Accommodation

University provided places: 2,100 (catered 0%)
Self-catered: £90–£149 per week
www.salford.ac.uk/study/life-at-salford/accommodation

Where do the students come from?

State schools (non-grammar)	96.5%	Working-class homes	42.2%	Black ethnic minority	7.4%
Grammar schools	2.0%	Deprived areas	21.0%	Disabled	5.0%
Independent schools	1.5%	All ethnic minorities	30.8%	Mature (over 21)	28.3%

University of Sheffield

Sheffield has recruited York's vice-chancellor, Professor Koen Lamberts, to take over the leadership of the university in a rare transfer at this level between two neighbours and competitors within the Russell Group. He will assume the reins at a university where the numbers starting courses dipped in 2017 after four record years. But applications rose again last year against the national trend.

The university was given a silver rating in the Teaching Excellence Framework. The awards panel said students learn in a research-led environment that engages them by combining academic rigour and disciplinary knowledge with real-world connections. It was impressed too by targeted programmes including volunteering, internships for graduates in the locality and the support given to disadvantaged students in gaining work experience with local businesses.

Sheffield has dropped four places in our new league table, however, after seeming close to returning to the top 20. A low score for student satisfaction with the quality of teaching — only just in the top 100 — is partly responsible. Times Higher Education's survey of the broader student experience places Sheffield in the top five (our result, which is based on outcomes in the 2018 National Student Survey, puts it in the top 40), while its students' union has been voted the best in the country for ten years in a row.

Ten new degrees are planned for this year, nine of them combining modern languages and cultures with subjects such as philosophy, economics or music. The other new offering will be a four-year integrated master's programme in chemistry, including overseas study.

The university is also planning to expand its range of degree apprenticeships in management, healthcare and engineering. Uniquely for a Russell Group university, the first priority in its strategy for education and the student experience is to offer the best degree apprenticeships in the UK. Hundreds of apprentices work at the university's Advanced Manufacturing Research Centre with partners such as Boeing and Rolls-Royce, and have the option of taking undergraduate and master's degrees.

Sheffield already has a more diverse undergraduate population than most of its peers, with the proportions from state schools and areas of low participation in higher education higher than average for its courses and entry qualifications. It ranks fifth among the 24 Russell Group universities for social inclusion in our new table, although that still leaves it outside the top 100 overall.

A £81m Diamond engineering building — the university's biggest single development — caters for the growing number of students in one of Sheffield's key

Western Bank
Sheffield S10 2TN
0114 222 2000
shefapply@sheffield.ac.uk
www.sheffield.ac.uk
http://su.sheffield.ac.uk
Open days 2019:
June 22; July 6;
September 7; October 19

The Times and The Sunday Times Rankings
Overall Ranking: 25 (last year: 21)

Teaching quality	78.4%	=93
Student experience	80.3%	=35
Research quality	37.6%	23
Entry standards	156	36
Graduate prospects	84.4%	19
Good honours	80.6%	=29
Expected completion rate	93.0%	=16
Student/staff ratio	14.7	=35
Services and facilities	£2,334	49

strengths. The aluminium-clad hub has 19 specialist laboratories and 1,000 study spaces for students across the university. The highly rated engineering faculty, which has 4,000 students, is adding more laboratories, offices and social space.

The main university precinct stretches into an almost unbroken mile-long "campus" that ends not far from the city centre. The £23m Information Commons operates 24 hours a day throughout the year and was refurbished in 2017.

Of the university's submission to the Research Excellence Framework, 85% was considered world-leading or internationally excellent, with biomedical sciences, control and systems engineering, history and politics all in the top three in the UK. But Sheffield entered a smaller proportion of its academics than most of its peers in the Russell Group. This year it was named as the lead institution in a £4.9m project investigating the development of the internet of things.

The university is among the top 75 in the world, according to the QS rankings, and attracts more than 8,000 students from outside the UK. It also remains one of the top 15 favourite recruiting grounds for *The Times*'s 100 leading employers, according to the 2018 graduate market survey by High Fliers.

The majority of university flats and halls of residence are within walking distance, in the suburbs on the affluent west side of Sheffield. There are more than 6,000 residential places, mainly in two student villages, enough to guarantee accommodation for new entrants. The university caused a stir last year by reserving 12 rooms for lesbian, gay, bisexual and transgender students as a "safe space for students to be themselves".

The excellent sports facilities close to the main precinct include five floodlit synthetic pitches, a large fitness centre with more than 150 pieces of equipment, a swimming pool with sauna and steam rooms, sports hall, fitness studio, multipurpose activity room, four squash courts and a bouldering wall. The 45 acres of grass pitches for rugby, football and cricket are a bus ride away. Sheffield has one of the biggest programmes of internal leagues at any university and elite sport is thriving. At the Rio Olympics three alumnae brought home either a gold or silver medal.

The famously lively social scene is based on the extended students' union. The city has plenty of student-orientated bars and clubs, and town-gown relations are much better than in the majority of main university centres.

Tuition fees

» Fees for UK/EU students 2019–20   £9,250
» Fees for International students 2019–20   £17,600–£22,600
     Dentistry £35,880; Medicine £33,500
» For scholarship and bursary information see
     www.sheffield.ac.uk/undergraduate/finance/
» Graduate salary   £22,800

Student numbers

Undergraduates	19,375	(630)
Postgraduates	6,412	(2,296)
Applications/places	34,605/4,580	
Applications per place	7.6	
Overall offer rate	84.0%	
International students	28.6%	

Accommodation

University provided places: 6,200 (catered 6%)
Catered costs: £79–£156 per week
Self-catered: £135–£168 per week
First years guaranteed accommodation
www.sheffield.ac.uk/accommodation

Where do the students come from?

State schools (non-grammar)	74.0%	Working-class homes	21.2%	Black ethnic minority	3.4%
Grammar schools	13.7%	Deprived areas	11.0%	Disabled	6.9%
Independent schools	12.2%	All ethnic minorities	18.4%	Mature (over 21)	7.4%

Sheffield Hallam University

Sheffield Hallam has launched the first phase of a 15-year development plan costing £220m that is designed to make the campus a gateway to the city and to help achieve the ambition of being the world's leading "applied university". Over the next five years the plan includes new buildings for the business school and social sciences, refurbishing the students' union and creating a university green as a focal point for the institution.

The university — one of the largest in the UK, with about 31,000 students — already physically connects the city centre with the bus and railway stations. Now a former home of the students' union is to become a mixed-use building containing a hotel, restaurants, conference facilities and flats. Other elements of the plan will produce new teaching and learning facilities in the city centre and at the Collegiate campus in the western suburbs.

A separate strategy for the university had already promised to look radically at the way the institution works, to be innovative and respond quickly to new opportunities. More than 200 "specialist flexible courses" mix part-time study, distance learning and work-based education. Business and industry are closely involved in the development of courses and more than half of the undergraduates take work placements.

Hallam's employability activities helped it to a silver rating in the government's Teaching Excellence Framework (TEF), which was chaired by Professor Sir Chris Husbands, the university's vice-chancellor. Husbands was not involved in the decision, but the TEF panel complimented the institution on an exemplary commitment to the region and support for students to be retained locally.

The university is up three places in our new table after a more substantial rise the previous year. Student satisfaction is its strongest suit after a second successive improvement in the two measures derived from the National Student Survey.

Applications have fallen for the past three years, but a higher offer rate has helped to keep the numbers starting degrees stable. Two thirds of the students come from within 40 miles of Sheffield and almost one in five from an area of low participation in higher education. Hallam exceeds all of its access benchmarks and the projected dropout rate is significantly lower than the national average for its courses and entry qualifications.

Hallam is one of the largest providers of degree apprenticeships and collaborates with the University of Sheffield to offer the qualification in engineering. The two universities are the "anchor institutions" for regeneration in the city and the wider region, developing a 25-year prospectus for a post-industrial economy.

City Campus
Howard Street
Sheffield S1 1WB
0114 225 5555
admissions@shu.ac.uk
www.shu.ac.uk
www.hallamstudentsunion.com
Open days 2019:
see website

The Times and The Sunday Times Rankings
Overall Ranking: 67 (last year: =70)

Teaching quality	82.4%	=30
Student experience	80.8%	=29
Research quality	5.4%	=90
Entry standards	124	=85
Graduate prospects	73.8%	=74
Good honours	75.3%	=54
Expected completion rate	86.3%	57
Student/staff ratio	16.9	91
Services and facilities	£2,128	78

The university's Advanced Wellbeing Research Centre (AWRC) will be the centrepiece of Sheffield's Olympic Legacy Park, a joint venture between the university, the city council and Sheffield Teaching Hospitals NHS Foundation Trust, set in the city's advanced manufacturing innovation district. Hallam claims that the AWRC will be the most up-to-date research and development centre for physical activity in the world and is developing a longer-term plan for a health innovation campus on the site.

Planning permission is also being sought for a new centre of excellence for food engineering, alongside the Olympic Legacy Park. Only 16% of eligible academics entered the 2014 Research Excellence Framework, but 65% of their work was considered world-leading or internationally excellent.

Other recent developments have seen the opening of a £30m building for the Sheffield Institute of Education, which has more than 150 academic staff and 5,000 students, making it one of the country's largest providers of teacher training. In addition, the conversion of the city's former post office provided a new base for the Sheffield Institute of Arts, bringing all art and design courses under the same roof.

The university also has a growing international dimension, with large cohorts taught in partner institutions in Malaysia and other Asian countries, to add to the 2,700 who come to Sheffield from outside the UK.

International students and new entrants are guaranteed accommodation, although the large local intake means that many students live at home. The university does not own its own accommodation but has more than 5,200 rooms at its disposal through private providers.

Transport in the city is excellent, with well-run bus and tram services. Sports facilities are supplemented by those provided by the city for the World Student Games in 1991. The impressive swimming complex, for example, is on the university's doorstep. The university has taken over the management of Sheffield's only athletics stadium, which will again be among the facilities used for the British Universities & Colleges Sport annual national games this year. The redeveloped facility is available to community groups, schools and local clubs as well as students.

Tuition fees

» Fees for UK/EU students 2019–20	£9,250
» Fees for International students 2019–20	£13,250
» For scholarship and bursary information see www.shu.ac.uk/study-here/fees-and-funding	
» Graduate salary	£21,909

Student numbers

Undergraduates	22,210 (2,244)
Postgraduates	3,086 (3,277)
Applications/places	35,015/6,430
Applications per place	5.4
Overall offer rate	79.9%
International students	8.8%

Accommodation

University provided places: 5,236 (catered 0%)
Self-catered: £86–£221 per week
First years guaranteed accommodation
www.shu.ac.uk/accommodation

Where do the students come from?

State schools (non-grammar)	93.1%	Working-class homes	40.8%	Black ethnic minority	4.3%
Grammar schools	3.7%	Deprived areas	21.5%	Disabled	7.6%
Independent schools	3.2%	All ethnic minorities	17.9%	Mature (over 21)	16.9%

SOAS University of London

SOAS successfully appealed a second successive bronze rating in the Teaching Excellence Framework last year and was upgraded to silver. Its appeal fell on receptive ears and the panel upgraded the award, praising a strong institutional emphasis on personalised learning and small group teaching, and the presence of specialist resources, including one of the five National Research Libraries.

The panel also recognised a comprehensive student engagement system and outreach initiatives to widen participation. However, the university ranks in the bottom 15 nationally this year in our two league table indicators derived from the annual National Student Survey. In common with several London-based institutions, SOAS has poor levels of student satisfaction with both teaching quality and the wider student experience.

The TEF upgrade coincided with a 3% increase in applications for courses last year, while most universities have seen a decline of similar proportions. Only one new degree — in accounting and finance — has been added in an otherwise unchanged portfolio of courses.

The only specialist institution in the UK for the study of Asia, Africa and the Middle East, SOAS enjoys global prestige. More than 40% of the 6,300 students are from outside the UK and the school is ranked by QS among the top 40 universities in the world for the arts and humanities. Music, drama and the performing arts produced the best results in the Research Excellence Framework, when two thirds of the work was rated as world-leading or internationally excellent.

SOAS covers a much wider variety of subjects than its name would suggest, however. Degrees are available in areas such as law, history and the social sciences, but with a specialist emphasis. SOAS features in the top 25 for music, for example. There is also a more limited portfolio of foundation programmes and language courses.

Approximately 45% of undergraduates take a language as part of their degree and the school has introduced a language entitlement programme that offers one term of a non-accredited SOAS language centre course free of charge. The £6.5m project to transform the library added more language laboratories, music studios, discussion and research rooms, and gallery space.

The school celebrated its centenary in 2016 by moving into the north block of Senate House, the Bloomsbury headquarters of the University of London, which adjoins the SOAS precinct. The five-floor development has brought the school together on a single site for the first time in many years. It includes a student hub, hosting services such as accommodation, counselling, student finance and careers, and a

Thornhaugh Street
Russell Square
London WC1H 0XG
020 7898 4700
study@soas.ac.uk
www.soas.ac.uk
http://soasunion.org
Open days 2019:
June 8

The Times and The Sunday Times **Rankings**

Overall Ranking: 53 (last year: =36)

Teaching quality	75.0%	=117
Student experience	71.8%	122
Research quality	27.9%	47
Entry standards	148	=42
Graduate prospects	70.9%	=94
Good honours	80.5%	31
Expected completion rate	82.6%	=90
Student/staff ratio	12.3	8
Services and facilities	£2,376	42

plaza under a double curvature glass canopy.

The centrepiece of the precinct is an airy building with gallery space as well as teaching accommodation, a gift from the Sultan of Brunei. The gallery lecture theatre has been renovated over the summer and now has room for 270 guests. The library holds 1.5m volumes, periodicals and audio-visual materials in 400 languages, attracting scholars from around the world.

More than nine out of ten applicants receive at least a conditional offer from SOAS. More than 40% of degree programmes offer the opportunity to spend a year at one of the school's many partner universities in Africa or Asia.

A £20m gift from a graduate with a passion for southeast Asian art is funding new posts, building developments and scholarships for Asian students to come to London.

Almost a fifth of the British undergraduates come from independent schools, but more than one in three is from the four poorest socioeconomic groups. The school devotes much of its fee income to outreach activities and bursaries. Among the current schemes is the SOAS Excellence Bursary, which consists of about 300 awards of £750 a year, targeted at those with household incomes below £25,000.

There is no separate students' union building, although the students do have their own bar, social space and catering facilities.

The former University of London Union — now a student centre — is close at hand, with swimming pool, gym and bars.

More than 1,100 residential places are available within 20 minutes' walk of the school. However, SOAS has few of its own sports facilities and the outdoor pitches are remote, with no time set aside from lectures. Students tend to be highly committed and often politically active — not surprising since many will return to positions of influence in their own country — and the variety of cultures makes for lively debate.

SOAS students have been at the centre of some of the recent controversies over free speech in universities and over demands to make the curriculum in some subjects less "white".

Tuition fees

» Fees for UK/EU students 2019–20	£9,250
» Fees for International students 2019–20	£17,750
» For scholarship and bursary information see www.soas.ac.uk/registry/funding	
» Graduate salary	£22,700

Student numbers

Undergraduates	3,246	(28)
Postgraduates	1,958	(1,129)
Applications/places		6,145/715
Applications per place		8.6
Overall offer rate		86.9%
International students		41.9%

Accommodation

University provided places: 1,108 (catered 10%)
Catered costs: £148–£299 per week
Self-catered: £147–£281 per week
www.soas.ac.uk/accommodation

Where do the students come from?

State schools (non-grammar)	74.0%	Working-class homes	35.7%	Black ethnic minority	12.0%
Grammar schools	9.8%	Deprived areas	4.6%	Disabled	8.6%
Independent schools	16.1%	All ethnic minorities	60.2%	Mature (over 21)	16.5%

University of South Wales

The biggest increase in student satisfaction at any Welsh university has helped the University of South Wales (USW) to move nine places up our league table. It makes the top 40 for satisfaction with the quality of teaching and has registered the biggest improvement in staffing levels at any university in the table.

Difficult times may lie ahead, though, especially at the Newport City campus which has lost its large teacher-training intake for 2019 after Wales's Education Workforce Council declined to grant accreditation for its BEd course. There were already concerns locally that the prize-winning base was undersubscribed. USW has resisted media requests for information about the numbers there, but it has admitted that there was already a decline when it took over the site in 2013.

Having closed the nearby Carleon campus outside Newport as an efficiency measure, USW has introduced courses in business, and opened a centre for counselling and therapies in Newport, plus the National Cyber Security Academy. It says that applications to study in the city have been rising and the money from the sale of the Carleon site is being reinvested in a planned Knowledge Quarter.

USW was the product of a merger between the University of Glamorgan and the University of Wales, Newport. The largest campus is in Pontypridd, ten miles outside Cardiff, where two sites cater mainly for science, engineering and health subjects. Recent developments there have included a law school and upgraded laboratories, as well as a £6m learning resource centre.

The greatest investment has been at the Cardiff campus for the creative industries, where the Atrium building replicates workplace facilities for advertising, TV and film set design and fashion, as well as including dance studios, rehearsal spaces and photographic studios. USW's other simulated learning facilities include a trading room, hospital wards and a crime-scene house.

The university was part of a successful bid for funding from the Government's Creative Clusters Programme to promote screen industries in and around Cardiff through research focusing on changing technologies, shifting patterns of consumption and the benefits of creative fusion and collaboration.

The £35m base in Newport opened in 2011 and is USW's home for professional and executive courses. Part of its remit is to attract inward investment and strengthen the local economy.

USW is one of the two largest universities in Wales, and the University of South Wales Group extends its reach further. The group

Pontypridd
CF37 1DL
03455 760101
enquiries@southwales.ac.uk
www.southwales.ac.uk
www.uswsu.com
Open days 2019:
see website

The Times and The Sunday Times Rankings
Overall Ranking: =110 (last year: =119)

Teaching quality	81.7%	=40
Student experience	78.1%	=74
Research quality	4.0%	=105
Entry standards	130	=66
Graduate prospects	63.4%	127
Good honours	67.4%	=102
Expected completion rate	79.2%	=109
Student/staff ratio	15.1	=47
Services and facilities	£1,721	117

includes the Royal Welsh College of Music and Drama and Merthyr Tydfil College, while a strategic alliance brings in further education colleges throughout southeast Wales.

The university also opened a base in Dubai last year, initially offering three courses in aircraft maintenance engineering, one of its strengths in Wales. USW is the only UK university to have a partnership with British Airways that enables students to graduate with a European Aviation Safety Agency licence as well as a degree.

More than a quarter of USW's students are at least 21 years old on entry. Three quarters are from Wales and almost one in five comes from an area of low participation in higher education. The university offers a range of bursaries and has recently introduced three scholarships of £1,000 for undergraduates who study through the medium of Welsh.

Like most universities in Wales, USW did not enter the government's Teaching Excellence Framework. There was a relatively small submission for the 2014 Research Excellence Framework, too, but half of the work was considered world-leading or internationally excellent. The best results came in a joint submission with Cardiff Metropolitan and Trinity St David universities in art and design, and in sport and exercise science, as well as social work and social policy.

Leisure facilities have been improving, with a modern recreation centre and students' union, plus more halls of residence. USW now has 1,230 rooms of its own and another 400 that are privately owned, enough to guarantee accommodation for new entrants who want it.

The USW Sport Park at the Treforest campus — ten miles from Cardiff and 20 from Newport — provides an impressive setting for elite athletes and regular users. It includes a specialist centre for strength and conditioning with 12 lifting platforms and a full-size 3G indoor football pitch, the only one in Wales and one of five in the UK.

The university hosts one of six centres of excellence in cricket. USW has a good record in sports competitions, especially in rugby, football and golf. A new foundation degree in rugby coaching and development has been launched this year, in partnership with the Welsh Rugby Union, Cardiff Blues and the Dragons.

Tuition fees

»	Fees for UK/EU students 2019–20	£9,250
	Foundation courses	£8,000
»	Fees for International students 2019–20	£12,600–£20,500
»	For scholarship and bursary information see www.southwales.ac.uk/study/fees-and-funding/undergraduate/	
»	Graduate salary	£20,046

Student numbers

Undergraduates	14,655 (4,622)
Postgraduates	1,683 (2,504)
Applications/places	14,100/3,100
Applications per place	4.5
Overall offer rate	84.0%
International students	13.4%

Accommodation

University provided places: 1,630 (catered 0%)
Self-catered: £107–£131 per week
First years guaranteed accommodation
www.southwales.ac.uk/accommodation

Where do the students come from?

State schools (non-grammar)	95.9%	Working-class homes	42.0%	Black ethnic minority	2.9%
Grammar schools	1.1%	Deprived areas	22.7%	Disabled	8.0%
Independent schools	3.0%	All ethnic minorities	10.6%	Mature (over 21)	28.0%

University of Southampton

Southampton has re-entered the top 20 in our listing, its 12-place rise among the biggest at the business end of the league table. Its rankings have improved on almost every measure, including entry standards, where only one university has seen a bigger increase. Southampton has also reduced its intake of undergraduates by more than 20% in two years, despite record applications.

The university has succeeded in upgrading a bronze rating in the Teaching Excellence Framework (TEF), one of six to have done so. Southampton led the criticism of the first round of TEF scores. Sir Christopher Snowden, the vice-chancellor, insisted that there was "no logic" in the university's low rating and argued that the process was "fundamentally flawed". An initial appeal was rejected, but a new submission secured a silver rating.

The awards panel noted that satisfaction with academic support was still below the university's benchmark, but it complimented the institution on a strategic commitment to enhancing the quality of teaching and a learning environment in which students participate actively in research. Our analysis of the latest National Student Survey shows that while rankings for satisfaction with teaching quality and the wider student experience have improved this year, they still put the university much closer to the bottom of the table than the top on these two measures.

The university has implemented a strategy that includes reaching the top ten in the national rankings. One element of the strategy has seen a reduction in the number of faculties from eight to five, focusing on arts and humanities; environmental and life sciences; medicine and social sciences; and engineering and physical sciences.

Southampton has launched 15 new degrees in subjects such as aeronautics and astronautics, ship science and acoustical engineering, all of them including a placement year and several also providing the option of a foundation year for those without the normal entry qualifications. The flexible undergraduate curriculum sees some subjects offering a "major-minor" structure that allows students to spend a quarter of their time on a subject other than their original degree choice. There are also interdisciplinary modules that are designed to give students a broader perspective.

The university performed well in the 2014 Research Excellence Framework. It is in the top seven for research quality after entering nine out of ten eligible academics for assessment and seeing more than 80% of their work rated as world-leading or internationally excellent. The best results came in health subjects, environmental science, psychology, physics, chemistry, electronic engineering and music, drama and performing arts. There are

---

University Road
Highfield
Southampton SO17 1BJ
023 8059 9699
enquiry@southampton.ac.uk
www.southampton.ac.uk
www.susu.org
Open days 2019:
see website

Edinburgh
Belfast
Cardiff *London*
SOUTHAMPTON

The Times and The Sunday Times **Rankings**
Overall Ranking: 18 (last year: 30)

Teaching quality	78.7%	85
Student experience	78.1%	=74
Research quality	44.9%	7
Entry standards	159	=32
Graduate prospects	82.1%	=27
Good honours	82.4%	23
Expected completion rate	92.4%	=24
Student/staff ratio	12.9	15
Services and facilities	£2,220	62

also particular strengths in computer science: Sir Tim Berners-Lee, inventor of the web, is a professor and Dame Wendy Hall is a Regius professor in the subject.

A £300m public bond will allow the university to invest further in facilities and infrastructure. Developments have included the £140m Boldrewood Innovation campus, developed jointly with Lloyd's Register — reported to be the largest business-university relationship of its kind in the UK — and five residential blocks with 350 en-suite bedrooms.

Current developments include a new teaching and learning centre, which is due to open this year, as is the £36.5m National Linear Infrastructure Laboratory. The £25m cancer immunology centre — the first of its kind in the UK and funded entirely through donations — is already open.

The university has campuses in Southampton and Winchester, as well as one in Malaysia dedicated to engineering. The main Highfield campus is in an attractive green location two miles from the city centre. The nearby Avenue campus is home to most of the humanities departments, while clinical medicine is based at Southampton General Hospital.

Winchester School of Art has been part of the university since 1996, while other sites include the National Oceanography Centre Southampton, based in the revitalised dock area.

Southampton is in the top 100 in the QS global rankings and the proportion of income derived from research is among the highest in Britain. A recent study showed the university contributed £1.3bn to the economy of Hampshire each year, with almost £1bn going to the city of Southampton alone. The university has 8,000 international students and a growing number of those from the UK spend time at one of the partner institutions in 54 countries.

Almost 86% of the students are state-educated, one of the higher proportions in the Russell Group. Just five of the 24 Russell Group universities recruit more students educated in comprehensive schools. Students act as ambassadors, associates and mentors in local schools and colleges as part of the university's efforts to broaden its intake further.

The university has more than 7,000 residential places, enough for all new entrants who apply by the deadline (and most others). Sports facilities are first class, with an indoor sports complex next to the students' union and a 25-metre pool. Sport and Wellbeing membership provides access to numerous gyms on campus and across the city, while the outdoor sports complex has multiple grass and synthetic pitches.

Tuition fees

- » Fees for UK/EU students 2019–20 £9,250
- » Fees for International students 2019–20 £17,065–£20,970
  Medicine £41,517 (clinical years)
- » For scholarship and bursary information see www.southampton.ac.uk/uni-life/fees-funding.page
- » Graduate salary £23,000

Student numbers

Undergraduates	17,360	(172)
Postgraduates	5,978	(1,670)
Applications/places	39,734/4,270	
Applications per place	9.3	
Overall offer rate	78.5%	
International students	28.3%	

Accommodation

University provided places: 7,000 (catered 9%)
Catered costs: £140–£188 per week
Self-catered: £109–£310 per week
First years guaranteed accommodation
www.southampton.ac.uk/uni-life/accommodation.page

Where do the students come from?

State schools (non-grammar)	71.7%	Working-class homes	23.1%	Black ethnic minority	4.6%
Grammar schools	14.9%	Deprived areas	8.7%	Disabled	4.6%
Independent schools	13.4%	All ethnic minorities	21.6%	Mature (over 21)	10.3%

Solent University

Solent has dropped the Southampton component from its name but has two important things in common with the other university in the south coast city. Like its neighbouring institution, Solent has moved up to the silver category in the Teaching Excellence Framework (TEF) and registered a big increase in our league table. A large rise in student satisfaction, particularly in relation to teaching quality, was the main factor behind Solent moving up 15 places, which has left the university well inside the top 100.

The TEF panel was impressed by students' high levels of engagement and commitment to learning, and by the substantial investment in learning resources and successful integration of research and professional practice into the curriculum. It accepted that the low graduate employment rate that had been the main factor in the university's bronze award the previous year was being addressed, although it remained below Solent's benchmark.

Applications fell for the second year in a row in 2017, when the numbers starting courses were 1,000 lower than in the final year before £9,000 fees were introduced, a drop of more than a quarter. In a period of exceptional activity for the university, Solent is launching 20 new degrees and has overhauled 17 others, at the same time as expanding its portfolio of degree apprenticeships.

The new degrees include a range of sport-based programmes, marketing, architectural design and visualisation and vehicle engineering. Solent currently offers 19 higher and degree apprenticeship programmes in areas including leadership and management, health and social care, engineering, accounting, nursing and digital technology. The university anticipates that the number of apprentices will at least double by September.

The main campus is close to the city centre, with the £33m Spark building at its heart, containing 40 hi-tech teaching spaces accommodating 1,500 students at any one time. A new £28m sports building is scheduled to open this year, providing two sports halls, gymnasiums, fitness suites and teaching facilities for use by students in subjects such as media, journalism and photography, as well as sport.

Other recent developments include new laboratories for applied human nutrition and biomedical sciences, a building for the art design school and facilities for courses in computer games, computer networking and audio production.

Away from the city centre, the university runs the Warsash School of Maritime Science and Engineering. There is strong demand for its courses and the world-renowned maritime academy and superyacht academy serve the

East Park Terrace
Southampton SO14 0YN
023 8201 5066
admissions@solent.ac.uk
www.solent.ac.uk
www.solentsu.co.uk
Open days 2019:
March 9; April 6

The Times and The Sunday Times **Rankings**
Overall Ranking: =85 (last year: =100)

Teaching quality	82.0%	=36
Student experience	78.8%	=61
Research quality	0.5%	127
Entry standards	117	=107
Graduate prospects	70.4%	=99
Good honours	71.3%	=80
Expected completion rate	78.7%	113
Student/staff ratio	15.7	=61
Services and facilities	£2,166	=73

training and research needs of the superyacht, shipping and offshore oil industries. The first phase of a strategy to reshape the university's maritime activities saw cadet training move to a new facility at St Mary's campus in 2017.

Solent is UK higher education's premier yachting institution, with a world champion student team that won the national championships four times in six years and alumni who have gone on to win Olympic and Paralympic gold medals.

The university is frequently among the UK's top ten for graduate start-ups. Students wishing to set up their own businesses or become freelancers are offered rent-free offices and are supported by the Solent Entrepreneur Programme. They have access to the university's creative agency, Solent Creatives, and the Re:So store, the first fully student-operated retail outlet in a UK shopping centre.

The university's support for students, which includes a Graduate Associate Scheme providing employment for 50 recent graduates, was identified as an example of best practice by the Quality Assurance Agency.

Solent recruits mainly in London and the south of England, with a quarter of the higher-education students coming from Hampshire, but about 1,800 are from outside the UK. The university's outreach work to widen participation focuses particularly on progression rates for white males from disadvantaged backgrounds and there is collaboration with other universities designed to combat the attainment gap among black and ethnic minorities. About 15% of first-year undergraduates in 2018 qualify for bursaries.

The university finished bottom of those that entered the 2014 Research Excellence Framework. It entered the lowest proportion of eligible academics at only 7%, and none of its research was placed in the top two categories for its external impact.

Football facilities accredited by the Football Association are used by the city's Premier League team, while other sports facilities include a sports hall and fitness suite on campus and outdoor pitches, tennis and netball courts four miles away.

There are 2,300 places in six halls of residence, including one that has recently undergone a £6.8m refurbishment, which is enough to guarantee accommodation to first-years.

Tuition fees

» Fees for UK/EU students 2019–20   £9,250
» Fees for International students 2018–19   £11,000–£12,500
» For scholarship and bursary information see www.solent.ac.uk/finance/tuition-fees
» Graduate salary   £18,000

Student numbers

Undergraduates	9,428	(1,119)
Postgraduates	226	(289)
Applications/places		12,260/2,610
Applications per place		4.7
Overall offer rate		91.2%
International students		16.4%

Accommodation

University provided places: 2,300 (catered 0%)
Self-catered: £90–£154 per week
First years guaranteed accommodation
www.solent.ac.uk/studying-at-solent/accommodation

Where do the students come from?

State schools (non-grammar)	96.4%	Working-class homes	43.8%	Black ethnic minority	6.6%
Grammar schools	0.9%	Deprived areas	16.7%	Disabled	6.6%
Independent schools	2.7%	All ethnic minorities	17.3%	Mature (over 21)	19.7%

Staffordshire University

Staffordshire is investing £17m in a new apprenticeships and skills hub to deliver more than 6,500 apprenticeships over the next decade to help boost the region's economy. The university was among the pioneers of degree and higher apprenticeships, working with employers such as Vodafone and the NHS and claiming the largest numbers at any university in England taking the qualifications.

It expects to have more than 900 higher and degree apprentices by September, almost trebling the previous total, after moving into areas such as digital marketing, social work and express delivery management.

New three-year degrees are being launched at the same time, including, last year, the first one in esports. Staffordshire is investing in new facilities in this fast-growing area and worked with employers on the curriculum. Other degrees to be launched include artificial intelligence and robotics, and digital life sciences, as well as accelerated degrees in sport and exercise psychology via distance learning and, back on campus, marketing management.

The broadening of its portfolio of courses is part of Staffordshire's "connected university" strategy, which commits it to widening participation in higher education, promoting social mobility and connecting with its communities. Academic enrichment through subject clubs and progression schemes is among the chosen methods of hitting its targets.

The new strategy may have helped to arrest a decline in applications that had persisted for six years in succession. This period included a reorganisation that saw the closure of the Stafford campus, with the withdrawal of some courses, but applications still dropped by almost 40%. A significant increase in the proportion of applicants receiving offers has helped to avoid a similar decline in the numbers starting courses.

Having shot up 29 places in our previous league table, Staffordshire is up another seven in the new edition, taking it to its highest position yet. The university is now in the top ten for student satisfaction with the quality of teaching and it registered the year's biggest rise for spending on student facilities.

The university was given a silver rating in the Teaching Excellence Framework, with the panel commenting favourably on the introduction of a number of initiatives to develop graduate employability skills, close the regional skills gap and provide opportunities for employment and further study. The panel was also impressed by Staffordshire's campus transformation project, which transferred most of its activities to Stoke-on-Trent.

Only the highly-rated nursing and midwifery programmes and other health-related courses remain in Stafford. As well as saving money, the aim was to improve the student experience and create an award-winning, teaching-led university

---

College Road
University Quarter
Stoke-on-Trent ST4 2DE
01782 294 400
enquiries@staffs.ac.uk
www.staffs.ac.uk
www.staffsunion.com.uk
Open days 2019: June 22
(Stoke-on-Trent); April 6,
June 8 (Stafford);
April 10, June 15 (Shrewsbury)

The Times and The Sunday Times **Rankings**

Overall Ranking: 57 (last year: =63)

Teaching quality	84.6%	9
Student experience	80.6%	33
Research quality	16.5%	56
Entry standards	116	=109
Graduate prospects	80.8%	41
Good honours	68.4%	100
Expected completion rate	76.4%	120
Student/staff ratio	14.5	=30
Services and facilities	£2,180	70

with a focus on employability, enterprise and entrepreneurship.

The main campus is at the heart of Stoke's University Quarter project, which forms a gateway to the city for anyone arriving at the main train station. An £80m investment scheme is upgrading a number of buildings, expanding the university library, extending student accommodation and enhancing the public spaces.

Two satellite campuses have survived the reorganisation. Primary teacher training programmes are based at Lichfield, where there is an integrated further and higher education centre, developed in partnership with South Staffordshire College. The other site is in Shrewsbury in Shropshire where nursing and midwifery students are based at the Royal Shrewsbury Hospital.

There are also 15,000 students taking Staffordshire courses outside the UK, about half of them located around the Pacific Rim.

With almost half of the UK undergraduates coming from working-class homes and practically a quarter from areas of low participation in higher education, Staffordshire exceeds all the benchmarks for the breadth of its intake. The dropout rate has been high in the past but is now close to the average for the university's courses and entry qualifications.

Staffordshire increased the size and scope of its submission to the 2014 Research Excellence Framework, compared with previous research assessments, but still entered only 91 academics. The best results were in sport and exercise sciences, although all of the university's research in psychology was placed in the top two categories for its external impact.

Stoke is not the liveliest city of its size, but the University Quarter is attracting more social and leisure facilities, and there is a busy and active students' union.

Sports facilities are good and will see more investment as numbers on the Stoke campus rise. The university has launched Team Staffs Sports Elite scholarships and spent £1.25m refurbishing the sports centre, adding new studio spaces and tripling the capacity of the gym. An accelerated (two-year) degree in football coaching and performance, delivered in partnership with Staffordshire Football Association, has been launched to meet the demand for professionally-trained football coaches at home and abroad.

Until now, the 1,250 residential places have been enough to satisfy almost all first-year students requiring accommodation, but no guarantees are offered.

Tuition fees

» Fees for UK/EU students 2019–20	£9,250
» Fees for International students 2019–20	£12,500
» For scholarship and bursary information see www.staffs.ac.uk/undergraduate/fees	
» Graduate salary	£20,600

Student numbers

Undergraduates	8,317	(4,513)
Postgraduates	637	(1,444)
Applications/places	12,420/2,825	
Applications per place	4.4	
Overall offer rate	87.3%	
International students	4.9%	

Accommodation

University provided places: 1,251 (catered 0%)
Self-catered: £95–£130 per week
www.staffs.ac.uk/support_depts/index.jsp

Where do the students come from?

State schools (non-grammar)	98.5%	Working-class homes	47.6%	Black ethnic minority	7.0%
Grammar schools	0.5%	Deprived areas	27.3%	Disabled	7.1%
Independent schools	1.0%	All ethnic minorities	18.6%	Mature (over 21)	35.8%

University of Stirling

Stirling has set itself the target of becoming one of the top 25 universities in the UK by 2021 and has begun transforming the centre of its famously attractive campus to improve the student experience and further that aim. A £20m sports centre and a new Campus Central development should both be open by 2020, with retail, catering, events space and student support services facilities, as well as more social learning and study areas.

For the moment, Stirling is almost 20 places short of its target in our table, gaining just one place in this edition. Applications have been running at record levels, and even a small decline last year was less than the averages in Scotland and the rest of the UK.

Like most Scottish universities, Stirling did not enter the Teaching Excellence Framework. Its recent scores for teaching quality, measured by the annual National Student Survey, have been modest, with rankings consistently in the 70s among the 130 institutions featured in this guide.

However, Stirling featured among Times Higher Education's top 50 "young universities" until it ceased to qualify after its 50th anniversary last year. It was also awarded the maximum five stars in the QS global rating system, which covers teaching, graduate employability, facilities, internationalisation and inclusiveness.

The 12,000 students at Stirling share one of the most beautiful campuses in the UK, occupying 330 acres of parkland around a loch at the foot of the Ochil Hills. Modern and period buildings nestle in a breathtaking landscape, including the stunning listed Pathfoot building, one of the finest pieces of 1960s architecture in the UK. There are two other sites: one for nurses and midwives in Inverness, and a Western Isles base located in Stornoway.

Facilities on the main campus include a modernised library and dedicated study zone. The university also has a chaplaincy that is open to students and staff of all faiths.

The semester system that has now become popular throughout higher education was pioneered in Britain by Stirling. The academic year is divided into two blocks of 15 weeks with short mid-semester breaks. Students have the option of starting courses in January, rather than September, and can choose subjects from across the institution's five faculties.

The university is famed for its flexible degree structure, and undergraduates can switch the whole direction of their studies, in consultation with their academic adviser, as their interests develop. They can also speed up their progress on a summer education programme, which squeezes a full semester's teaching into July and August. Part-time students can use the scheme to reduce the length of their course, but full-time ones cannot.

A new virtual learning environment has improved students' access to course and

Stirling
FK9 4LA
01786 467 044
admissions@stir.ac.uk
www.stir.ac.uk
www.stirlingstudentsunion.com
Open days 2019:
April 6, June 15

The Times and The Sunday Times Rankings
Overall Ranking: =44 (last year: 45)

Teaching quality	79.1%	=75
Student experience	76.3%	=94
Research quality	30.5%	43
Entry standards	161	=28
Graduate prospects	78.7%	=53
Good honours	79.5%	35
Expected completion rate	85.5%	=64
Student/staff ratio	15.5	58
Services and facilities	£1,823	105

campus information. All lectures are being filmed to make them accessible online for use with lecture notes.

Another target in the university strategy is to raise its revenue by £50m. An increase in the number of international students will contribute to this. The INTO Academic Centre, an international study hub, opened on the main campus in 2017, offering preparatory courses for students hoping to take degrees at Stirling.

Two thirds of the students are from Scotland, but the remainder come from more than 100 different countries. International exchanges are common, with many of Stirling's students going to American, Asian and European universities.

Of the work submitted to the 2014 Research Excellence Framework, almost three quarters was judged to be world-leading or internationally excellent. The best results were in agriculture, veterinary and food science, where Stirling was ranked fourth in the UK. It was also top in Scotland for health sciences and third for psychology.

Stirling is already extremely well provided with sports facilities, having been designated Scotland's university for sporting excellence. The campus is home to national swimming and tennis centres, as well as a nine-hole golf course and a football academy. The refurbished sports centre will include new purpose-built fitness studios, a central gym, a three-court sports hall, indoor cycling studio and strength and conditioning areas, in addition to a new high-performance suite.

The university runs an international sports scholarship programme and manages Winning Students, the national sport scholarship programme for students across Scotland.

There are 2,800 residential places for students after a £38m expansion of accommodation. A centralised student hub team assists with all enquiries and provides support services. There is a lively social scene based around the award-winning union. A multipurpose space has been developed there that can be used generally as a social study area, but is also transformable into a nightclub venue, or space for society meetings or study groups.

The Macrobert Arts Centre offers a full programme of cultural activities for the university and the wider city, while the surrounding countryside offers its own attractions for walkers and climbers.

A counselling and wellbeing service provides support for mental and emotional health, while the disability service assists with a full range of student needs.

Tuition fees

» Fees for Scottish/EU students 2019–20 £0–£1,820
  RUK fees £9,250 (capped at £27,750 for 4-year courses)
» Fees for International students 2019–20 £12,450–£14,820
» For scholarship and bursary information see
  www.stir.ac.uk/study/fees-funding/
» Graduate salary £22,000

Student numbers

Undergraduates	8,016	(571)
Postgraduates	2,114	(1,366)
Applications/places	18,065/2,340	
Applications per place	7.7	
Overall offer rate	59.7%	
International students	20.4%	

Accommodation

University provided places: 2,804 (catered 0%)
Self-catered: £85–£167 per week
First years guaranteed accommodation
www.stir.ac.uk/student-life/accommodation

Where do the students come from?

State schools (non-grammar)	87.9%	Working-class homes	32.1%	Black ethnic minority	1.8%
Grammar schools	5.6%	Deprived areas	8.3%	Disabled	6.4%
Independent schools	6.4%	All ethnic minorities	6.5%	Mature (over 21)	29.3%

University of Strathclyde

Strathclyde is in the middle of a £650m programme of campus developments, the latest of which is a new sport building. A £60m Learning and Teaching Building at the heart of the campus will follow next year, with a new base for the students' union and a number of student services, as well as study spaces.

Other current projects include upgraded facilities for biomedical engineering and a combined heat and power network that will improve the sustainability of the campus.

The university had been climbing our league table, but a big drop in student satisfaction has caused a decline of three places in this edition. Only five universities, including Oxford and Cambridge, have higher entry standards, but Strathclyde is just outside the bottom 20 for perceptions of teaching quality. Like other universities north of the border, it benefited from the uprating of Scottish qualifications when UCAS changed its tariff points system in 2017, but Strathclyde's entrants have higher average grades than those at Glasgow or Edinburgh.

The high grades certainly have not put off applicants. The demand for places has risen by more than a third in four years, with both applications and enrolments up 30% from 2013. Strathclyde's mission to be a "place of useful learning" is as powerful a draw as it was when the phrase was coined with the establishment of the university in 1796.

Nor has Strathclyde's commitment to widening participation in higher education suffered unduly. More than nine out of ten undergraduates are state educated — almost all of them in comprehensive schools and far above the UK average for its courses and entry grades — and more than a quarter were from working-class homes, when this was last surveyed. However, low recruitment from ethnic minorities and areas of deprivation hold Strathclyde back in our new table measuring social inclusion, where it ranks just outside the top 100.

The Learning in Later Life programme has established itself as one of Scotland's most successful routes to education for older people, and Strathclyde has been at the forefront of developing graduate apprenticeships, which only require students to spend one day a month at the university. Two new programmes, in software development and business management, have been launched.

Strathclyde is the third-largest university in Scotland, and with 23,000 students is aiming to be one of the world's leading technological universities. The £89m Technology and Innovation Centre, the largest in the UK at 25,000 square metres — the equivalent of 100 tennis courts — was one of the first projects in the decade-long campus improvement programme and has been selected to run the Scottish government's £8.9m Lightweight

McCance Building
16 Richmond Street
Glasgow G1 1XQ
0141 548 4400
study-here@strath.ac.uk
www.strath.ac.uk
www.strathstudents.com
Open days 2019:
see website

The Times and The Sunday Times Rankings
Overall Ranking: =44 (last year: 41)

Teaching quality	76.3%	=109
Student experience	76.3%	=94
Research quality	37.7%	=21
Entry standards	202	6
Graduate prospects	79.6%	=49
Good honours	82.0%	24
Expected completion rate	86.5%	56
Student/staff ratio	19.8	122
Services and facilities	£1,819	106

Manufacturing Centre. Strathclyde is also the anchor university for the new £65m National Manufacturing Institute for Scotland.

The city-centre John Anderson campus, with the humanities and social sciences faculty at its heart, is where all courses are delivered, enabling staff to liaise on research and teaching. The Advanced Forming Research Centre, a partnership with international engineering firms, operates off-campus near Glasgow airport.

The business school, which the *Financial Times* ranks among the top 30 in Europe, is normally considered Strathclyde's greatest strength. It is among the largest in Europe and one of only 77 in the world to be "triple accredited" by the main international bodies. The school has seven international centres in Europe, the Gulf and Southeast Asia. The engineering faculty is the largest in Scotland, and home to Europe's biggest university electrical power engineering and energy research grouping. Strathclyde is the European partner for South Korea's global research and commercialisation programme.

Strathclyde, like most Scottish universities, did not enter the Teaching Excellence Framework. However, research by the university's eligible academics ranks close to the top 20 in our table after almost 80% of an exceptionally large submission to the Research Excellence Framework rated world-leading or internationally excellent. The university was top in the UK for physics and first in Scotland for business.

Students develop, enhance and test their transferable skills on the Strathclyde Enterprise Pathway while alumni and businesses are supported in the Strathclyde 100 programme for emerging entrepreneurs. The university has helped to launch more than 150 spin-out companies since 2005, one of the largest totals at any UK university, and it aims to grow income from such entrepreneurship by £10m to £30m in 2020.

There are 1,700 residential places in a student village on the main campus and nearby in the Merchant City — enough to guarantee new entrants accommodation, and students are served by the ten-storey students' union building. Proximity to Glasgow's vibrant music scene is a plus and the city has numerous cultural attractions.

Strathclyde Sport, a £31m new building has a 25-metre swimming pool, two sports halls, squash courts, fitness suites and group cycling area. Six students on the elite athlete programme and nine alumni were selected for the 2018 Commonwealth Games, two students winning medals.

Tuition fees

» Fees for Scottish/EU students 2019–20   £0–£1,820
   RUK fees   £9,250 (capped at £27,750 for 4-year courses)
» Fees for International students 2019–20   £14,650–£20,600
» For scholarship and bursary information see
   www.strath.ac.uk/studywithus/feesfunding/
» Graduate salary   £22,216

Student numbers

Undergraduates	13,052 (2,542)
Postgraduates	4,554 (2,809)
Applications/places	28,925/3,985
Applications per place	7.3
Overall offer rate	59.9%
International students	18.2%

Accommodation

University provided places: 1,700 (catered 0%)
Self-catered: £105 - £137 per week
www.strath.ac.uk/studywithus/accommodation/

Where do the students come from?

State schools (non-grammar)	89.5%	Working-class homes	25.9%	Black ethnic minority	1.2%
Grammar schools	0.5%	Deprived areas	5.6%	Disabled	3.0%
Independent schools	10.0%	All ethnic minorities	8.7%	Mature (over 21)	14.1%

University of Suffolk

Almost 20 new degrees, in key subjects such as law, economics and architecture, helped boost Suffolk's applications by 20% last year, while most other "low tariff" institutions were struggling. Two years after achieving university status, Suffolk is still developing its portfolio of courses, with an expansion of its degree apprenticeships also adding to the demand for places. The university expects to have 350 apprentices starting courses this year.

Suffolk has secured a grant to design and deliver innovative technology-enhanced "blended" learning for degree apprenticeships for nurses, police officers and social workers. The model is expected to be suitable for other occupations with contracted hours outside the normal working day. The university is also offering the UK's first two-year, practice-based dance degree, in partnership with DanceEast.

The Ipswich-based university has climbed three places off the foot of the table in this edition. But in two measures it is still being judged partly on its performance as a satellite of the University of East Anglia (UEA) and University of Essex. Suffolk is competitive in some areas, but no score could be compiled for the 2014 Research Excellence Framework.

Founded in 2007 as University Campus Suffolk, it was expected to take 20 years to become an independent university but was granted the power to award degrees in 2015 and the Privy Council agreed to confer the full university title shortly afterwards. UEA and Essex will continue to work with the new university, which has developed an academic strategy and set up a foundation board with a philanthropic role.

Suffolk received a bronze rating in the 2017 Teaching Excellence Framework (TEF) because it was "substantially" below its benchmarks for student satisfaction and graduate employment. About one third of leavers do not land graduate-level jobs, according to our analysis. However, the TEF panel did acknowledge the contribution of employers to course design and found a "developing approach to the creation of research and practice-based communities of staff enabling students to benefit by exposure to scholarship, research and professional practice".

Student satisfaction was high in the early years of the National Student Survey, but has dropped sharply more recently, with Suffolk now in the bottom five for the broad student experience and the bottom 20 for the perceptions by students of teaching quality.

There are 5,000 students on the Waterfront campus and at smaller bases in Bury St Edmunds, Lowestoft, Great Yarmouth and Otley. Nearly 60% of them are over 20 when they start their courses, most of them coming from the region. The university's target is between 6,500 and 7,000 students by 2020.

The proportion of students from working-

Waterfront Building
Neptune Quay
Ipswich IP4 1QJ
01473 338 348
admissions@uos.ac.uk
www.uos.ac.uk
www.uosunion.org
Open days 2019:
April 27, July 6

The Times and The Sunday Times Rankings
Overall Ranking: 130 (last year: 129)

Teaching quality	75.8%	=111
Student experience	70.9%	=126
Research quality	n/a	
Entry standards	123	=88
Graduate prospects	65.0%	118
Good honours	66.2%	=110
Expected completion rate	69.5%	129
Student/staff ratio	17.6	=100
Services and facilities	£2,290	56

class homes, at almost 45%, is higher than average for the university's courses and entry grades, while the percentage from areas of low participation in higher education is among the highest in the country at 30%. This helps Suffolk to a ranking in our top 20 for social diversity in our new table. Suffolk has been devoting a larger-than-average share of its fee income to student support, more than half of its spending going on cash bursaries for students from under-represented backgrounds.

Suffolk recently upgraded its library at the cost of £2.5m and refurbished a teaching building to add specialist facilities for psychology, computer games design, network and software engineering. The Atrium building houses the Ipswich Waterfront Innovation Centre for business and innovation activities and the 3D Productivity Suite. Ipswich council awarded the university £300,000 in 2017 to invest in the 3D printers there.

The university aims to be a "community impact" institution with a focus on science, technology, engineering and mathematics, while its research centres and institutes concentrate on areas such as sustainability, health and wellbeing, heart research, and the study of children and childhood. A £10.3m lottery grant will enable the university to host The Hold, a heritage centre for the county, which will also contain teaching areas. Building work has already started and the opening is scheduled for this autumn.

Suffolk has a partnership with Ipswich Town football club and the university's suite of football sports science and coaching courses cover coaching, performance analysis, sports performance physiology, sports psychology, and strength and conditioning. Placements at Ipswich Town are built into its four-year masters courses.

Suffolk also offers an executive MBA in collaboration with the Maastricht School of Management which ranks second among business schools in Holland.

Many students live at home but there is a privately-operated hall of residence for 736 students close to the campus in Ipswich. The university offers no guarantees of accommodation and is not involved in the allocation of places, but it accredits other accommodation in the town and in its other locations.

Students have access to the sports facilities of neighbouring Suffolk New College and there are student discounts at private and council-run gyms.

Tuition fees

» Fees for UK/EU students 2019–20	£9,250
Foundation courses	£8,220
» Fees for International students 2019–20	£11,790–£14,865
» For scholarship and bursary information see www.uos.ac.uk/content/student-finance	
» Graduate salary	£21,909

Student numbers

Undergraduates	3,662	(961)
Postgraduates	69	(388)
Applications/places		3,915/1,050
Applications per place		3.7
Overall offer rate		73.5%
International students		2.6%

Accommodation

University provided places: 736 (catered 0%)
Self-catered: £85–£165 per week
www.uos.ac.uk/accommodation

Where do the students come from?

State schools (non-grammar)	98.5%	Working-class homes	44.8%	Black ethnic minority	6.9%
Grammar schools	0.6%	Deprived areas	30.6%	Disabled	7.2%
Independent schools	0.9%	All ethnic minorities	13.2%	Mature (over 21)	59.1%

University of Sunderland

Sunderland has been awarded one of the five new medical schools, joining a handful of former polytechnics to have received this accolade. The school will take its first 50 students this year and have an intake of 100 in subsequent years. Its specialisms will address the well-publicised need for more GPs and psychiatric specialists, providing exposure to real-life clinical settings and making full use of the university's own simulation suites in its Living Lab.

The award recognises the university's successes in other health subjects, such as pharmacy and nursing, as well as its leading record in widening participation in higher education, which sees it achieve a top-20 ranking for social diversity in its student population in our new table.

Almost 90% of students on the existing courses are in one or more of the government's target groups for widening participation. About a third come from areas with little tradition of higher education, the biggest proportion in the country, and more than half come from households that are in the poorest fifth in the UK. About 85% of the British undergraduates are from the northeast of England, although there is a surprisingly large cohort — one in five — from outside the UK.

If winning one of the new medical schools was a coup for the university, so, too, was the recruitment of Sir David Bell as its new vice-chancellor. Currently vice-chancellor of the high-ranking University of Reading, Bell is a former permanent secretary at the Department for Education and former chief inspector of schools. He will be looking to build on Sunderland's recent gains in our league table.

Sunderland is up three places in our new league table, its third successive rise. There has been a big improvement in student satisfaction with the quality of teaching, which has placed the university in the top 40 on this measure. Entry standards are also up, in a year when most universities with a similar profile have seen declines.

Applications have fallen for seven years in a row, however, including an above-average decline last year. Their numbers have halved over that period, although there has been a more manageable decline in the numbers actually starting courses.

Seven newly-launched degrees, provide fresh options for applicants in subjects such as biochemistry, medicinal chemistry and teaching English as a foreign language. Another ten will follow in September, including screen performance, forensic psychology and paramedic science. The university is also planning seven new degree apprenticeship programmes in engineering, cyber-security, policing and teaching.

The new Teaching Excellence Framework awarded Sunderland a silver rating, with the panel saying students' academic experiences

Edinburgh Building
City Campus
Chester Road
Sunderland SR1 3SD
0191 515 3000
student.helpline@sunderland.ac.uk
www.sunderland.ac.uk
www.sunderlandsu.co.uk
Open days 2019:
June 8, August 17

The Times and The Sunday Times Rankings
Overall Ranking: 93 (last year: 96)

Teaching quality	82.1%	=34
Student experience	79.0%	=58
Research quality	5.8%	=84
Entry standards	120	=94
Graduate prospects	67.1%	113
Good honours	66.7%	106
Expected completion rate	78.1%	115
Student/staff ratio	15.6	=59
Services and facilities	£2,303	54

were tailored to the individual, with personalised support available. It also praised the exposure of students to professional practice through engagement with industrial and community partners, and the engagement with employers in course development.

There are two campuses in Sunderland, one in the city centre and the other on the banks of the River Wear, built around a 7th-century abbey described as one of Britain's first universities and incorporating the National Glass Centre, a heritage centre for the glass industry.

There is also a London campus, near Canary Wharf, which focuses on business, tourism and nursing degrees, and is scheduled for expansion. In addition, the university now has a satellite campus in Hong Kong.

Generous financial support for eligible UK and EU students from poor backgrounds includes free public transport across Tyne and Wear for a year, or a discount on university-managed accommodation. The Sunderland Scholarship provides selected applicants from households earning less than £42,875 financial support of £1,000 in their first and second years. International undergraduates may apply to a separate programme to get a fee reduction of £1,500 a year.

Support for disabled students is excellent. The main campus houses the North East Regional Assessment Centre, which assesses the requirements of students with disabilities and specific learning difficulties, and there is special provision in the five halls of residence. Tailored modules are available to dyslexics, who are assisted by trained support staff in the libraries and in every academic school.

The university entered almost 40% of the eligible academics into the 2014 Research Excellence Framework, a much higher proportion than most of its peers. However, less than a third of the work submitted reached the top two categories.

Many students take work placements with multinational companies. These include Nissan, which has been displaying a unique first-generation Nissan "half"-Leaf car at the university's Institute for Automotive and Manufacturing Advanced Practice to help students get their own careers on the road.

The city of Sunderland has the advantage of a riverside and coastal location. It has the northeast's only 50-metre swimming pool and dry ski slope, as well as Europe's biggest climbing wall and a theatre showing West End productions.

More residential places are now available in the £12m Forge U-Student Village, bringing the total stock to 1,135 rooms.

Tuition fees

» Fees for UK/EU students 2019–20	£9,250
Foundation courses	£8,200
» Fees for International students 2019–20	£11,500
» For scholarship and bursary information see www.sunderland.ac.uk/help/finance-scholarships/	
» Graduate salary	£18,200

Student numbers

Undergraduates	9,156 (1,568)
Postgraduates	1,453 (844)
Applications/places	8,765/1,735
Applications per place	5.1
Overall offer rate	87.9%
International students	20.7%

Accommodation

University provided places: 1,135 (catered 0%)
Self-catered: £78–£154 per week
www.sunderland.ac.uk/about/accommodation

Where do the students come from?

State schools (non-grammar)	97.9%	Working-class homes	44.9%	Black ethnic minority	3.9%
Grammar schools	0.3%	Deprived areas	34.8%	Disabled	4.4%
Independent schools	1.8%	All ethnic minorities	13.9%	Mature (over 21)	53.0%

University of Surrey

Applications to study at Surrey are more than twice as high as they were when £9,000 fees were introduced in 2012, rising again against the national trend. Record numbers started degrees in 2017 and in the current academic year.

The university received a gold rating in the Teaching Excellence Framework (TEF). A glowing reference from the TEF panel complimented it on "innovative and personalised provision that secures the highest levels of engagement and encourages a high degree of commitment to learning and study". It also found high levels of teaching excellence and an effective approach to the development of professional skills and employability.

Since then, however, student satisfaction levels have dropped sharply, causing Surrey to fall four places and out of the top 20 in our league table, having been eighth only three years ago when it was our University of the Year. The university has fallen nearly 50 places on the key measure of satisfaction with teaching quality, after a decline of three percentage points in the National Student Survey. Satisfaction with the wider student experience has also seen a fall of 25 places.

The university has been investing heavily in health and medical sciences, bringing together teaching and research in human and animal health, launching new degrees and opening the £12.5m Innovation for Health Learning Laboratory.

With a new School of Health Sciences, Surrey was planning to add degrees in medicine but was not among the five universities chosen last year to host new medical schools.

Surrey has been among the UK's most proactive universities in recent years. A second campus, Manor Park, has been added in Guildford, effectively extending the original Stag Hill site, and another opened in Dalian, China, in partnership with the Dongbei University of Finance and Economics. The £45m veterinary school, which opened in 2015, was only the second to be established in the UK in half a century.

The 5G Innovation Centre, which brings Surrey's researchers together with global players in mobile telecommunications, received £58m support from an international consortium. The university has taken the lead in a new £16m hub partnership, demonstrated Europe's first autonomous car and launched the world's first 5G digital gaming initiative.

Professor Max Lu, the vice-chancellor, is keen to develop Surrey's international reputation. It has a high proportion of students from outside the UK — more than a quarter — and more than half of its research publications have an international partner. Students are encouraged to take a free course in a European language alongside their degree.

More than 90% of the UK students are

Senate House
Guildford GU2 7XH
01483 682 222
admissions@surrey.ac.uk
www.surrey.ac.uk
www.ussu.co.uk
Open days 2019:
July 5,6

The Times and The Sunday Times **Rankings**
Overall Ranking: 23 (last year: 19)

Teaching quality	78.6%	=86
Student experience	79.2%	=50
Research quality	29.7%	45
Entry standards	164	=25
Graduate prospects	81.0%	38
Good honours	85.3%	17
Expected completion rate	90.6%	=34
Student/staff ratio	15.7	=61
Services and facilities	£2,714	22

state-educated, just under 79% coming from comprehensive schools. The university targets particular schools rather than areas, where progression to higher education is low. Ranking 95th in our table measuring the social diversity of the student population, Surrey performs rather better than many of its academic peers.

Almost four-fifths of the work submitted to the 2014 Research Excellence Framework was rated as world-leading or internationally excellent. The best results were in nursing and other health subjects. Surrey's research is organised around "grand challenges": global wellbeing, and sustainable cities and communities, and connecting societies and cultures.

Surrey's campuses are ten minutes' walk from the centre of Guildford. Developments since 2000 have cost £400m. The Surrey Research Park, with its focus on science, is one of the largest in the UK to be owned, funded and managed by its host university.

Undergraduates in most subjects undertake work placements of one year, or several shorter periods, often abroad. As a result, most degrees last four years.

Large numbers take engineering and science subjects, but the university has other strengths, notably in business and the sector-leading School of Hospitality and Tourism Management. SurreyLearn, the virtual learning environment, allows students to work with others on their courses online and to take part in discussions, as well as allowing lecturers to set coursework and interact with students.

The business school launched a pilot degree apprenticeship programme last year, with 25 students taking the Chartered Manager Degree Apprenticeship. The university is considering other programmes, in nursing and hospitality and tourism management.

Construction has started on a £75m accommodation project on the Manor Park campus to create 1,200 new rooms. They will be available for the 2019-20 academic year, bringing the total number of residential places to almost 3,000 — enough to guarantee places for new entrants.

The main Stag Hill campus is the centre of social life, although Guildford has plenty of retail, cultural and recreational facilities. The £36m Surrey Sports Park has extensive indoor and outdoor facilities.

The proximity of London (35 minutes by train) is an attraction to many students, although it helps account for the high cost of renting in the private sector.

Tuition fees

» Fees for UK/EU students 2019–20	£9,250
» Fees for International students 2019–20	£15,800–£21,100
Veterinary Medicine	£31,500
» For scholarship and bursary information see www.surrey.ac.uk/fees-and-funding	
» Graduate salary	£24,000

Student numbers

Undergraduates	11,276 (1,052)
Postgraduates	2,552 (1,183)
Applications/places	32,105/3,835
Applications per place	8.4
Overall offer rate	71.5%
International students	27.8%

Accommodation

University provided places: 5,650 (catered 0%)
Self-catered: £72–£170 per week
First years guaranteed accommodation
www.surrey.ac.uk/accommodation

Where do the students come from?

State schools (non-grammar)	78.6%	Working-class homes	28.6%	Black ethnic minority	6.7%
Grammar schools	12.8%	Deprived areas	7.6%	Disabled	4.7%
Independent schools	8.6%	All ethnic minorities	33.9%	Mature (over 21)	14.4%

University of Sussex

One of the biggest falls in student satisfaction has propelled Sussex to a second successive drop in our league table. From a position inside the top 20 two years ago, it is now outside the top 40 overall and in the bottom 25 in both of our measures of student satisfaction.

Yet applications were up by more than a quarter in 2017, the most recent year for which figures are available, after a similar increase the previous year. The intake of new undergraduates was 1,000 higher than in the years before 2015, but the university has not placed further strain on its facilities by taking advantage of the latest increases to add to this number.

One attraction is the growing range of four-year undergraduate master's degrees, which carry an entitlement to student loans beyond the normal three years. New programmes in geography and international development have been added to the list that spans the arts, sciences, engineering, maths, computing and physics. New three-year degrees in primary and early years education, and global media and communications, which includes a year's study in Hong Kong, have also been launched.

Sussex was placed in the silver category in the Teaching Excellence Framework, whose independent panel praised an "outstanding" employment strategy, underpinned by curricula designed to develop transferable employment skills. Students were frequently exposed to, and engaged in, cutting-edge research, the panel added, and significant investment in the university estate boosted the quality of learning.

Since 2007, the university has invested about £150m regenerating the campus in the Brighton suburb of Falmer and expects the total to reach £500m eventually. The Attenborough Centre has become an interdisciplinary arts hub for the university and the wider community, with a 350-seat auditorium, studios and exhibition space and a cafe bar. The £11m Future Technologies Labs, opened in 2017, will enable Sussex to launch new degrees in intelligent systems, smart technologies and 5G.

The university set itself a target of 18,000 students by 2018, to provide opportunities for a more diverse range of students and achieve the "critical mass" that Sussex considers necessary to strengthen the interdisciplinary approach that has been its hallmark since the 1960s, engage with partners and be internationally competitive in research. It is now close to that mark, with more than 15,000 students, almost 80% of whom came from comprehensive schools.

Sussex has extensive bursary and scholarship schemes to broaden its intake, focusing particularly on candidates with no family experience of higher education. A

Sussex House
Falmer
Brighton BN1 9RH
01273 876 787
ug.enquiries@sussex.ac.uk
www.sussex.ac.uk
www.sussexstudent.com
Open days 2019:
see website

The Times and The Sunday Times Rankings		
Overall Ranking: 41 (last year: 27)		
Teaching quality	75.2%	115
Student experience	74.3%	110
Research quality	31.8%	=38
Entry standards	144	=46
Graduate prospects	80.4%	47
Good honours	75.9%	52
Expected completion rate	91.6%	30
Student/staff ratio	16.4	=78
Services and facilities	£2,709	23

prize-winning scheme supports them with rent reductions and scholarships.

Three quarters of the work submitted for the Research Excellence Framework was judged to be world-leading or internationally excellent and Sussex was among the leaders in history, English, psychology and geography. Researchers are building a quantum computer that could be among the most powerful on earth, using the principles of quantum physics to outperform modern supercomputers.

Sussex is ranked top in the world for development studies and has a sustainability research programme headed by the former chief scientist at the UN Environment Programme. There are research centres on adoption, corruption, Middle East studies and consciousness science.

The university keeps Brexit under scrutiny through the UK Trade Policy Observatory, which draws on a large concentration of scholars in economics, law and international relations with experience of trade policy.

A successful joint medical school is shared with the neighbouring University of Brighton, and split between the Royal Sussex County Hospital and the universities' Falmer campuses.

Unless on professionally accredited courses, undergraduates are encouraged to study outside their core area. They can take a language or an elective in another subject, leading to a major/minor degree and opening up opportunities to study abroad. There are two 12-week teaching periods, punctuated by mid-year assessment. The university believes this pattern improves the way students learn and are assessed.

Student support includes a work-study programme to help students earn money, funded work placements and three years' aftercare for graduates to help them find a career. The Sussex Plus programme documents and credits students' extracurricular skills, while Startup Sussex supports creative business ideas and social projects.

A new student village has opened on the campus, which is located within the South Downs National Park, with excellent transport links into the city. New entrants and international students are guaranteed one of the 5,673 places in university-managed accommodation.

There is no shortage of social events on campus and Brighton has plenty to offer. The campus has a well-equipped sports centre and a separate sports complex with indoor and outdoor facilities.

Tuition fees

- » Fees for UK/EU students 2019–20 £9,250
- » Fees for International students 2019–20 £16,750–£20,750
  Medicine £30,450 (clinical years)
- » For scholarship and bursary information see www.sussex.ac.uk/study/fees-funding
- » Graduate salary £20,400

Student numbers

Undergraduates	12,031	(0)
Postgraduates	3,917	(738)
Applications/places	25,960/3,925	
Applications per place	6.6	
Overall offer rate	92.6%	
International students	32.8%	

Accommodation

University provided places: 5,673 (catered 0%)
Self-catered: £90–£156 per week
First years guaranteed accommodation
www.sussex.ac.uk/study/accommodation

Where do the students come from?

State schools (non-grammar)	79.0%	Working-class homes	22.5%	Black ethnic minority	4.0%
Grammar schools	8.9%	Deprived areas	8.2%	Disabled	6.8%
Independent schools	12.1%	All ethnic minorities	19.7%	Mature (over 21)	9.1%

Swansea University

Swansea is our Welsh University of the Year for the second time in three years, having again become the highest-ranked university in the country, a rise of six places in our league table enabling it to overtake Cardiff. It is also runner-up for our UK University of the Year award, after a remarkable transformation in the past few years. The 65-acre new Bay Campus has been the catalyst for expansion, adding new facilities for engineering, management and computer science.

The increased spending on facilities has further improved scores in the National Student Survey for the student experience here. This, plus improvements in completion rates and graduate prospects, have taken Swansea into the UK top 30 for the first time since the first edition of the guide in 1993. The numbers starting degrees are at record levels after five increases in a row, passing 5,000 for the first time in 2017.

The Bay Campus has given the university the capacity for growth on this scale. Its second phase opened last year, adding a £31m "computational foundry" to the teaching and residential accommodation already in use on the site, which has direct access to a beach.

The campus is home to the College of Engineering and School of Management and houses about 1,500 students in halls of residence, relieving pressure on the original campus five miles along the coast.

The latest development is part of a £522m capital plan that includes the redevelopment of the original Singleton Park campus. About £72m has been invested in new facilities, and the programme includes improvements to the library and upgraded laboratories and flexible learning spaces.

Another initiative at the Bay Campus is The College, a joint enterprise by the university and the global education company Navitas, to run preparatory courses for international students hoping to take Swansea degrees. These courses are boosting Swansea's already substantial cohort of international students.

Six new degrees, including medieval studies, medical pharmacology, and modern languages, translation and interpreting, have taken their first students. The university is also developing degree apprenticeships in manufacturing, engineering and digital technology, with the expectation of expanding in the Welsh government's priority areas.

Swansea's strongest suit in our table is in graduate prospects, where it is now on the cusp of the top ten in the UK. The Employability Academy provides paid internships and coordinates career support activities.

Singleton Park
Swansea SA2 8PP
01792 205 678
admissions@swansea.ac.uk
www.swansea.ac.uk
www.swansea-union.co.uk
Open days 2019:
March 9; April 6;
June 15

The Times and The Sunday Times **Rankings**

Overall Ranking: 30 (last year: =36)

Teaching quality	80.7%	=54
Student experience	81.5%	=21
Research quality	33.7%	36
Entry standards	138	=55
Graduate prospects	85.6%	12
Good honours	77.8%	45
Expected completion rate	90.2%	39
Student/staff ratio	15.4	=55
Services and facilities	£2,375	43

The university was given a gold rating in the Teaching Excellence Framework. The independent panel said that personalised learning was embedded across the institution, with a tutorial system and attendance monitoring providing high levels of engagement and commitment to learning and study from students.

Undergraduates are encouraged to venture outside their specialist area in the first year. Many degrees include opportunities to work abroad or study at one of more than 100 partner institutions worldwide. Only 28% of undergraduates came from working-class homes when this was last surveyed — significantly less than the UK average for the university's subjects and entry grades — but the projected dropout rate of 6.2% is much better than Swansea's benchmark figure of 9.5%.

Swansea works with the South West Wales Reaching Wider Partnership to target areas of deprivation and the university has good provision for disabled students, whose needs are addressed through an assessment and training centre.

Four-fifths of the work submitted for the 2014 Research Excellence Framework was assessed as world-leading or internationally excellent, with health subjects, English and general engineering doing particularly well. The university's focus is on applied research with industry — the Engineering Quarter houses two research institutes and there are collaborations with Rolls-Royce, Ericsson, Sony and British Aerospace.

The £20m Sports Village was used as a training facility by the New Zealand and Canada squads during the 2015 Rugby World Cup. It has an athletics track, grass and all-weather pitches, squash and tennis courts, plus an indoor athletics training centre and an 80-station gym. The adjacent Wales National Pool has 50-metre and 25-metre pools and is the Welsh national performance centre.

The 360° Beach and Water Sports Centre is the only university-operated facility of its kind, while at Fairwood, five miles away, the university has grass and 3G pitches built in partnership with Swansea City Football Club.

The university occupies a prime position at the gateway to the Gower peninsula, the UK's first area of outstanding natural beauty. It has almost 5,000 residential places, enough to guarantee places to new entrants who apply by the end of June with Swansea as their firm choice. The city has a good range of leisure facilities and Cardiff is less than an hour away by train for those looking for a change of scene.

Tuition fees

» Fees for UK/EU students 2019–20 £9,000
» Fees for International students 2019–20 £14,500–£18,500
  Medicine £36,750 (clinical years)
» For scholarship and bursary information see
  www.swansea.ac.uk/undergraduate/fees-and-funding
» Graduate salary £22,000

Student numbers

Undergraduates	14,357 (1,564)
Postgraduates	2,226 (1,014)
Applications/places	19,915/3,825
Applications per place	5.2
Overall offer rate	91.7%
International students	18.4%

Accommodation

University provided places: 4,990 (catered 5%)
Catered costs: £134–£139 per week
Self-catered: £91–£149 per week
First years guaranteed accommodation
www.swansea.ac.uk/accommodation

Where do the students come from?

State schools (non-grammar)	85.5%	Working-class homes	27.9%	Black ethnic minority	2.4%
Grammar schools	6.0%	Deprived areas	10.4%	Disabled	4.5%
Independent schools	8.5%	All ethnic minorities	13.9%	Mature (over 21)	13.3%

University of Teeside

The reshaping of Teesside's portfolio of courses continues apace. Having launched about 40 new programmes in 2017, the university added 50 more last year, most of them foundation years leading on to existing degrees for those without the necessary qualifications for immediate admission. Entirely new degrees include clinical optometry, team entrepreneurship, business with change management, and fashion buying and merchandising.

Teesside is also expanding its already substantial commitment to degree apprenticeships. It expects to double the number of apprentices to 400, with new provision for civil engineers, food industry professionals, laboratory scientists, health practitioners and trainee teachers.

The developments follow the adoption of a new learning and teaching strategy that promises to employ Teesside's strength in digital technology to enrich the student experience. DigitalCity, its centre for digital excellence and entrepreneurship, has helped in the creation of hundreds of companies and contributed to a Queen's Anniversary prize for the university's services to business and enterprise.

Teesside was given a silver rating in the Teaching Excellence Framework, with the awards panel impressed by a "comprehensive and well-received investment in high-quality physical and digital resources" and the innovative and well-resourced support for the development of employability. It also praised the investment in internships, which encourage progression to highly-skilled employment.

The university is up seven places in our new league table, a third successive rise, moving Teesside up 17 places over the past three years. It is now in the top 30 for student satisfaction with the quality of teaching and the top 40 for graduate prospects – a considerable achievement when so many of the graduates remain in an area of relatively high unemployment.

Teesside supports the career development of its graduates for a minimum of two years after graduation and is expanding paid work placements as part of a student's course. The Get Ahead scheme provides three-month paid internships and training for graduates, as well as helping with summer placements for second-year students.

The university is known for its commitment to widening access to higher education. Three undergraduates in ten come from areas of low participation in higher education, which is twice the national average for its courses and entry qualifications.

More than 7,000 of the 18,500 students are part-time — a much larger proportion than at most universities since the decline of part-time higher education nationally – and

Middlesbrough
TS1 3BX
01642 738 181
enquiries@tees.ac.uk
www.tees.ac.uk
www.tees-su.org.uk
Open days 2019:
February 23; March 23;
June 15; August 17

Belfast
Edinburgh
MIDDLESBROUGH
London
Cardiff

The Times and The Sunday Times **Rankings**

Overall Ranking: =85 (last year: 92)

Teaching quality	82.5%	=27
Student experience	78.9%	60
Research quality	3.6%	111
Entry standards	120	=94
Graduate prospects	81.3%	35
Good honours	66.0%	112
Expected completion rate	81.6%	97
Student/staff ratio	17.2	97
Services and facilities	£2,399	41

5,600 are taking courses below degree level. Two thirds are from the northeast and around four in ten are 21 or over on entry. It all helps the university to a top-15 ranking in our new table measuring the social diversity of the student intake.

Applications fell by 13% in 2017 after four successive increases, but the numbers starting courses still rose slightly. The Teesside Advance Scheme provides all first-year, full-time undergraduates with an iPad with selected apps and a £300 voucher to buy learning resources and textbooks.

Only 14% of Teesside's eligible academics were entered for the 2014 Research Excellence Framework, but almost 60% of their work was considered world-leading or internationally excellent. Social work and social policy, history and health subjects produced the best results.

Teesside is spending £300m over ten years to transform its campuses, building on the £270m it has already invested, mainly at its base in Middlesbrough town centre. The first phase of an expanded business school has opened, and the £22m National Horizons Centre, for biomedical teaching and research, is being developed at the university's second campus in Darlington.

Further investment will include £83m on additional student accommodation over the years to 2025. Other projects involve a digital production centre, the refurbishment of the university library and a £25m central laboratory facility.

The main campus has shops, bars, cafes and restaurants on the doorstep, and the students' union has been rated among the top ten in the country. Mima (Middlesbrough Institute of Modern Art), the internationally-renowned contemporary art gallery and member of the Plus Tate network, is part of the university.

The cost of living is another attraction for students: rents in the private sector are among the cheapest in the UK and there are 1,000 residential places on campus.

The Olympia sports complex has a large sports hall for tournaments, with room for 500 spectators. There is a £2.75m health and fitness centre, and a water sports centre on the River Tees.

This year the university has added a £1m all-weather pitch to its sports facilities near the Middlesbrough campus.

Tuition fees

» Fees for UK/EU students 2019–20		£9,250
Foundation courses		£6,150
» Fees for International students 2019–20		£11,825
Foundation courses £9,750		
» For scholarship and bursary information see www.tees.ac.uk/sections/fulltime/fees.cfm		
» Graduate salary		£21,909

Student numbers

Undergraduates	10,097	(5,887)
Postgraduates	1,055	(1,515)
Applications/places	12,450/3,210	
Applications per place	3.9	
Overall offer rate	78.2%	
International students	5.1%	

Accommodation
University provided places: 1,012 (catered 0%)
Self-catered: £58–£115 per week
www.tees.ac.uk/accommodation

Where do the students come from?

State schools (non-grammar)	98.4%	Working-class homes	45.7%	Black ethnic minority	3.1%
Grammar schools	0.5%	Deprived areas	33.2%	Disabled	9.7%
Independent schools	1.0%	All ethnic minorities	12.2%	Mature (over 21)	39.3%

University of Wales, Trinity St David

The University of Wales Trinity Saint David (UWTSD) is in our top five for student satisfaction with the quality of teaching, after a rise of 11 places on this league table measure. The spectacular performance has helped it jump 15 places overall, putting it in the top 90 in its second year back in the table after a five-year boycott of all rankings.

Even its score for graduate prospects — which was the lowest in the previous edition of the guide — has seen substantial improvement, with two thirds of leavers now gaining graduate-level jobs or going into further study, compared with the 53% recorded previously.

UWTSD was one of six Welsh universities to enter the Teaching Excellence Framework (TEF) in 2017 and the only one to emerge with a bronze rating. A new submission last year failed to persuade the panel to raise the grade, mainly because of "exceptionally low" levels of progression to highly-skilled employment or further study. The panel was satisfied with the levels of contact time, including personalised provision and additional study support that secured good engagement from most students, and it found that physical and digital resources are well used by students.

Applications are up 4% this year, indicating that the addition of 20 new degrees in 2017 paid off. Another 14 have followed, including vocal studies, adventure filmmaking, health and care of children and young people, and events and festivals management.

UWTSD is also offering its first degree apprenticeship, in ordnance, munitions and explosives, and is bidding for more programmes from the Welsh government's allocation.

The first phase of the £300m Swansea Waterfront Innovation Quarter in the city's SA1 area is now ready. The initial development houses the faculties of architecture, computing and engineering, education and communities, as well as a new library and student centre. The project will see UWTSD collaborating with professional partners to enable its students to engage with employers as part of their studies and to provide opportunities for its graduates. A second phase is due for completion in 2021.

Another important development for the university was the opening of Canolfan S4C Yr Elgin, including the headquarters of the Welsh broadcaster S4C, on the Carmarthen campus. The centre will house a number of companies in the creative and digital industries, giving media students the opportunity to gain valuable experience.

Two mergers in three years created UWTSD: the first saw the former Trinity University College, Carmarthen, come together with the University of Wales Lampeter, 23 miles away. Only Oxford and

---

Carmarthen Campus, College Road
Carmarthen SA31 3EP
0300 500 5054
admissions@uwtsd.ac.uk
www.uwtsd.ac.uk
www.tsdsu.co.uk
Open days 2019: February 9, June 22 (Swansea); February 2, June 29 (Carmarthen); January 26, June 29 (Lampeter)

Edinburgh
Belfast
CARMARTHEN LAMPETER
SWANSEA Cardiff London

The Times and The Sunday Times Rankings
Overall Ranking: 89 (last year: 104)

Teaching quality	85.4%	=5
Student experience	80.8%	=29
Research quality	2.6%	117
Entry standards	106	=127
Graduate prospects	66.0%	115
Good honours	69.0%	94
Expected completion rate	78.2%	114
Student/staff ratio	15.1	=44
Services and facilities	£1,961	91

Cambridge were awarding degrees before St David's College, Lampeter, which became the smallest publicly funded university in Europe. The former Swansea Metropolitan University became part of the university in 2013.

UWTSD ranks in the top 20 of our new table for social inclusion, based on the proportions of students recruited from comprehensive schools, ethnic minorities, the working class, deprived neighbourhoods, those with disabilities or aged over 21 on admission. Only one Welsh university (Wrexham Glyndŵr) has a more socially diverse student population.

It offers students the choice of a rural or urban experience — from the green campuses of Lampeter and Carmarthen to the city lifestyle of Swansea. There are also satellite campuses in London, where international students take business, management and IT degrees, and Cardiff, where the Wales International Academy of Voice is based. In addition, a group structure connects UWTSD with two large further education colleges, Coleg Ceredigion and Coleg Sir Gar.

UWTSD has fewer than 10,000 students and the Lampeter campus makes a virtue of its small size by stressing its friendly atmosphere and intimate teaching style. Based on an ancient castle and modelled on an Oxbridge college, it offers subjects including anthropology, archaeology, Chinese, classics and philosophy. Its Academy of Sinology was established in partnership with the Chin Kung Multicultural Educational Foundation, based in Hong Kong.

The Carmarthen campus, established in 1848 to train teachers, offers programmes in the creative and performing arts, as well as a growing portfolio within the school of sport, health and outdoor education. A centre for outdoor education opened in 2017 a mile from the campus on the All Wales coastal walking path.

The Swansea campus began life as a college of art in 1853, but its automotive engineering courses – especially those focused on motor sport – are now its best-known feature. It is hosting one half of Yr Athrofa, the new Institute of Education, which will also operate on the Carmarthen campus. UWTSD was one of four universities in Wales to bid successfully to run teacher-training courses. The aim is to produce a new and innovative approach to teacher education, with the university and partner schools jointly responsible for the construction and delivery of all training programmes.

First-year undergraduates are guaranteed accommodation on all the campuses.

Tuition fees

» Fees for UK/EU students 2019–20	£9,000
Foundation courses	£4,500
» Fees for International students 2019–20	£11,500
» For scholarship and bursary information see www.uwtsd.ac.uk/finance/tuition-fees/	
» Graduate salary	£18,000

Student numbers

Undergraduates	6,264	(1,918)
Postgraduates	659	(915)
Applications/places		3,625/1,010
Applications per place		3.6
Overall offer rate		84.8%
International students		6.2%

Accommodation

University provided places: 807 (catered 21%)
Catered costs: £109 per week
Self-catered: £70–£140 per week
First years guaranteed accommodation
www.uwtsd.ac.uk/accommodation

Where do the students come from?

State schools (non-grammar)	98.5%	Working-class homes	42.4%	Black ethnic minority	1.9%
Grammar schools	0.4%	Deprived areas	14.9%	Disabled	18.2%
Independent schools	1.1%	All ethnic minorities	7.8%	Mature (over 21)	42.5%

Ulster University

Ulster has recovered nearly all the ground it lost in our league table over the previous two years, moving up 13 places in the latest edition. There have been big improvements in student satisfaction levels — putting Ulster in the top 30 for perceptions of both teaching quality and the wider student experience — after a splash of spending on student facilities.

Applications and enrolments fell in 2017 as the university closed its modern languages department and withdrew other courses to cope with cuts in its government grant. But new degrees have been launched in areas such as football coaching and business management and the university is developing its programme of Higher Level Apprenticeships (HLAs). It expects to more than double the number of apprentices this year, moving into accounting and customer contact management.

Ulster is still hoping to open a medical school on its Magee campus, in Londonderry. It had proposed taking the first 60 trainee doctors this September, but at the time of going to press the university was yet to convince the Department of Health of the need for a second medical school in the province.

An £11m central teaching block has opened on the campus, attached to the library and containing open-plan student hubs and a cafe, as well as teaching spaces. The number of students at Magee is planned to rise from 3,500 to 6,000 in the long term.

The university has upgraded its teaching facilities and opened a £5m sports centre on its Coleraine campus, where new premises for the school of psychology are planned.

The main capital development at Ulster is in Belfast's Cathedral Quarter, where a £250m campus is taking shape. Students at Jordanstown, currently the university's biggest site, will move seven miles to the new development later this year. Only the High Performance Sports Centre, which houses the Sports Institute, will remain in Jordanstown, using the outdoor and indoor sprint tracks, sports science and sports medicine facilities, which will remain available to students.

At present, Belfast concentrates on art and design, architecture, hospitality event management, photography and digital animation. For the moment, Jordanstown remains the location for courses in business and management, the built environment, computing and engineering, health and sport sciences, and social sciences.

The university's campus at Coleraine, on Northern Ireland's north coast, offers environmental and life sciences, humanities, media, film and journalism, and tourism management. A £6.5m media centre there was rated one of the "most impressive in the UK" by the National Council for the Training of Journalists. The BBC has a studio in the

Cromore Road
Coleraine BT52 1SA
028 9036 8821
study@ulster.ac.uk
www.ulster.ac.uk
http://uusu.org
Open days 2019:
see website

The Times and The Sunday Times Rankings
Overall Ranking: 60 (last year: 73)

Teaching quality	82.4%	=30
Student experience	81.5%	=21
Research quality	31.8%	=38
Entry standards	126	=82
Graduate prospects	71.9%	93
Good honours	73.5%	=65
Expected completion rate	82.9%	=86
Student/staff ratio	17.1	96
Services and facilities	£1,910	94

centre, which includes a high-definition television studio, a multimedia newsroom, editing suites and satellite feeds.

The Coleraine site is also home to the Centre for Molecular Biosciences, which produced the university's most highly-rated work in the 2014 Research Excellence Framework. More than 70% of Ulster's submission was considered world-leading or internationally excellent, with law and nursing and health science also producing outstanding results.

The university has since been awarded almost £20m in research funding from an EU cross-border scheme for projects in health and life sciences and renewable energy. The largest share will go to a personalised medicine programme.

Magee has a focus on the creative and performing arts, nursing and social work, computing, business and management, and social sciences. Its expansion will focus on computer science, engineering and creative technologies. The Centre for Stratified Medicine is situated near the campus at Altnagelvin Hospital.

Ulster also has branch campuses in London and Birmingham, offering courses in business, computing and engineering in partnership with QA Higher Education, a private organisation that also delivers apprenticeships and training programmes. Most courses include the option of a year-long work placement.

Although neither of the universities in Northern Ireland entered the Teaching Excellence Framework, Ulster features in Times Higher Education magazine's top 150 universities in the world that are under 50 years old. Business links are strong, and the university is ranked in the UK's top seven for the volume of knowledge transfer it undertakes.

Nearly all the undergraduates are from state schools and more than 45% come from working-class backgrounds. However, the university is held back in our new table measuring social diversity on campus due to the high proportion of grammar schools in Northern Ireland, from which Ulster recruits about 37% of its intake. The 63% who come from non-academically selective schools is among the smaller proportions holding Ulster to a ranking just outside the top 100 overall across a range of social measures, although it is still well ahead of Queen's Belfast.

Accommodation is guaranteed for all first-year students and private sector rents are low by UK standards. There are students' union facilities at every location, including refurbished premises on the Magee campus.

Tuition fees

» Fees for Northern Irish/EU students 2019–20	£4,160
Students from England, Scotland and Wales	£9,250
» Fees for International students 2018–19	£13,680
» For scholarship and bursary information see www.ulster.ac.uk/finance/student	
» Graduate salary	£20,000

Student numbers

Undergraduates	15,958 (3,204)
Postgraduates	1,848 (3,632)
Applications/places	30,315/4,605
Applications per place	6.6
Overall offer rate	84.2%
International students	8.9%

Accommodation

University provided places: 2,275 (catered 0%)
Self-catered: £75–£150 per week
First years guaranteed accommodation
www.ulster.ac.uk/accommodation

Where do the students come from?

State schools (non-grammar)	62.8%	Working-class homes	44.6%	Black ethnic minority	0.3%
Grammar schools	37.2%	Deprived areas	9.0%	Disabled	4.7%
Independent schools	0.0%	All ethnic minorities	2.2%	Mature (over 21)	24.9%

University College London

The boycott of the National Student Survey by those at University College London (UCL) has withered away but the institution has not benefited. Satisfaction levels have fallen since 2016, the last time that UCL undergraduates' responses reached the threshold for scores to be published.

At least £1.4m has been invested in better-quality library spaces, at the behest of students, and the law faculty has been redeveloped with improved teaching and research facilities. A new student centre offers 1,000 extra study seats, group collaboration areas and space for other forms of social learning. Teaching accommodation on the Bloomsbury campus has already been expanded with flexible spaces that will support emerging pedagogies.

The university's strategy is focusing first on assessment and feedback, which has been the greatest source of dissatisfaction for undergraduates. Students have been recruited as UCL ChangeMakers in departments with low satisfaction scores to establish what undergraduates would like and to advise on new types of assessment. At the same time, UCL is adopting a "connected curriculum" to ensure that every student gets the opportunity to engage in research.

Poor perceptions of teaching quality ensured that UCL was restricted to the silver category in the government's Teaching Excellence Framework. The panel found a "wide array of exceptional learning resources, both physical and digital" and complimented UCL on a highly successful approach to supporting students into employment or further study.

UCL remains one of the academic powerhouses of UK higher education, with 29 Nobel prize-winners to its name. It is also in the top ten universities in the world in the QS rankings, which place more emphasis on research. Such was the quality and quantity of UCL's submission to the 2014 Research Excellence Framework that only Oxford subsequently received a higher research grant.

More than 90% of the eligible academics were entered for assessment and at least 80% of their work was rated as world-leading or internationally excellent. UCL had the most world-leading research in medicine and the biological sciences, the largest volume of research in science, technology, engineering and maths, and the biggest share of top grades in the social sciences.

Applications rose by almost 15% last year, against the national trend. UCL has taken full advantage of the ending of recruitment restrictions, adding 2,500-plus places to its intake of new undergraduates since £9,000 fees were introduced. More than 60% of

Gower Street
London WC1E 6BT
020 3370 1214 (020 3108 8520 International)
study@ucl.ac.uk;
international@ucl.ac.uk
www.ucl.ac.uk
http://studentsunionucl.org
Open days 2019:
June 28, 29; September 7

The Times and The Sunday Times **Rankings**
Overall Ranking: 8 (last year: =7)

Teaching quality	72.8%	=125
Student experience	73.2%	=117
Research quality	51.0%	5
Entry standards	191	9
Graduate prospects	83.8%	=20
Good honours	90.8%	=3
Expected completion rate	94.1%	14
Student/staff ratio	10.3	1
Services and facilities	£2,733	20

school-leavers who apply to UCL now receive offers, compared with less than 40% at the start of the decade.

A total of £1.2bn is being invested over ten years to implement the Transforming UCL programme, which could lead to better NSS outcomes. This includes a new campus in Stratford on the Queen Elizabeth Olympic Park in east London. UCL East will bring together expertise in areas such as creativity and material culture, future global cities and experimental engineering. It is the largest capital investment programme UCL has undertaken since building its original Bloomsbury campus, and one of the biggest in UK higher education.

Developments have included a management school in Canary Wharf, and there is also an archaeology and conservation campus in Qatar. The medical school, with several associated teaching hospitals, is among the UK's largest. UCL is a founding partner in the Francis Crick Institute that undertakes leading-edge research in health and disease.

Already comfortably the biggest of the University of London's colleges, UCL now has almost 38,000 students. Concerted attempts are being made to broaden the undergraduate intake with summer schools, outreach activities and campus-based programmes. But the share of places going to independent school students remains one of the highest in Britain, at almost a third.

Students are required to have a foreign language GCSE at grade C or above, although they are allowed to reach this standard during their degree if they have not taken a language at school. In future, British sign language will be accepted as meeting this requirement.

Close to the West End and with its own theatre and recreational facilities, UCL offers plenty of leisure options. Students also have access to the facilities of the student centre in the former University of London Union building in Bloomsbury. Residential accommodation is plentiful and has expanded with the refurbishment and extension of Astor College. Indoor sports and fitness facilities are close at hand, but the main outdoor pitches are a (free) coach ride away in Hertfordshire.

Tuition fees

- » Fees for UK/EU students 2019–20 £9,250
- » Fees for International students 2019–20 £19,380–£29,220
  Medicine £42,230 (clinical years)
- » For scholarship and bursary information see www.ucl.ac.uk/prospective-students/undergraduate/fees-funding
- .» Graduate salary £26,000

Student numbers

Undergraduates	**17,407** (1,202)
Postgraduates	**13,235** (6,059)
Applications/places	**43,930/6,000**
Applications per place	**7.3**
Overall offer rate	**62.9%**
International students	**41.5%**

Accommodation

University provided places: 5,848 (catered 9%)
Catered costs: £149–£181 per week
Self-catered: £98–£291 per week
First years guaranteed accommodation
www.ucl.ac.uk/prospective-students/accommodation

Where do the students come from?

State schools (non-grammar)	50.4%	Working-class homes	19.0%	Black ethnic minority	5.1%
Grammar schools	17.2%	Deprived areas	3.9%	Disabled	2.7%
Independent schools	32.4%	All ethnic minorities	49.6%	Mature (over 21)	10.1%

University of Warwick

Warwick was a surprise absentee from the list of universities given a gold award in the 2017 Teaching Excellence Framework, and a resubmission last year failed to change the panel's mind. The university, which has never been out of our top ten, argued that consistent high achievement by its students and staff, excellent completion and employment rates and exceptional employer feedback met the criteria for a gold award.

The panel was impressed by the culture of research-stimulated learning that challenged students, but did not raise Warwick from the silver category because it missed its benchmarks for student satisfaction and continuation among some groups of students. This finding is borne out by our new league table in which Warwick only just scrapes into the top 100 for student satisfaction with teaching quality, by some distance its worst performing measure among the nine on which the university's overall ranking is based.

Prospective undergraduates seem not to be overly concerned. Applications for courses last year were up by 5%, against the national trend — the fifth successive rise. Warwick has expanded its undergraduate intake by more than 30% since 2012, the first year of £9,000 fees, but there are still more than eight applicants to every place.

Overall, Warwick is down one place in our league table but is on the verge of the top 50 in the world in the research-driven QS rankings. It is also among the three leading universities for recruiters in the Times Top 100 employers seeking the best graduates: only those from Manchester and Birmingham are more sought after.

Only one new degree was added last year, in cyber-security. But the university is expanding its range of degree apprenticeships, which currently attract 500 students in engineering. Another four programmes are planned for September, in civil engineering, social work, health and wellbeing and digital and technology solutions, filling at least 650 places.

A £250m investment programme is under way on the university's campus, three miles south of Coventry. A new mathematical sciences building is under construction and the Arts Centre is being extended and refurbished in time for Coventry's year as City of Culture in 2021. The university is a key partner in the year of events to boost the reputation of a city said to have "constantly reinvented itself to survive".

The university has a host of other projects in prospect, including a new Materials Engineering Centre and the £150m National Automotive Innovation Centre, where research engineers from car manufacturers will work closely with the Warwick Manufacturing Group. The centre is part-

Student Recruitment, Outreach and Admissions Service
Coventry CV4 8UW
024 7652 3723
ugadmissions@warwick.ac.uk
www.warwick.ac.uk
www.warwicksu.com
Open days 2019:
see website

The Times and *The Sunday Times* Rankings
Overall Ranking: 10 (last year: 9)

Teaching quality	77.8%	=97
Student experience	78.4%	=68
Research quality	44.6%	8
Entry standards	182	=12
Graduate prospects	83.2%	24
Good honours	84.4%	19
Expected completion rate	96.1%	=4
Student/staff ratio	12.8	14
Services and facilities	£2,563	29

funded by government as well as by Jaguar Land Rover and Tata Motors.

Almost 90% of the work submitted for the 2014 Research Excellence Framework was rated as world-leading or internationally excellent, confirming Warwick's place among the top eight universities for research. English and computer science produced the best results, but Warwick ranked in the UK's top ten in 14 different subject areas.

The university has reconfigured its research around its Global Research Priorities programme, which focuses on key areas of international significance. Current themes include energy, connecting cultures, food security, global governance, individual behaviour and innovative manufacturing. A new Cancer Research Unit brings together experts in maths, physics and engineering to explore new treatments using digital technologies.

Warwick has a centre for history students in Venice and a close partnership with Monash University in Melbourne. The large business school has a London base in the Shard and last year, Warwick added teaching and research partnerships with L'Université Paris Seine and Vrije Universiteit Brussel, safeguarding its European activities beyond Brexit. However, a planned campus in California for 6,000 students was shelved.

There is a smaller proportion of independent school students than at most Russell Group universities – 22% – although a large contingent from grammar schools means that only 58% come from comprehensives.

The university has introduced a "student lifecycle" approach to widening participation, helping non-traditional students from primary school age to the application stage through to employment or postgraduate study. In 2017, 182 students won places after receiving offers below the norm because of a disadvantaged background. The scheme includes bursaries of up to £3,000 a year for those from families with a combined income of less than £35,000.

The 750-acre campus has 5,662 residential places, with 1,000 more expected to be ready for this year's intake. Another 2,300 rooms off campus are bookable through the university, which also has a study facility for the many students living in nearby Leamington Spa.

A new sports and wellness hub will add to already extensive facilities. They include a running track, indoor climbing centre and an indoor tennis centre, while the new centre will contain a 240-station gym and a 12-lane, 25-metre swimming pool.

Tuition fees

» Fees for UK/EU students 2019–20   £9,250
   Foundation courses   £6,750
» Fees for International students 2019–20 £19,240–£24,540
   Medicine   £39,150 (clinical years)
» For scholarship and bursary information see
   www.warwick.ac.uk/study/undergraduate/studentfunding/
» Graduate salary   £26,500

Student numbers

Undergraduates	14,483	(1,630)
Postgraduates	5,478	(3,456)
Applications/places		37,200/4,615
Applications per place		8.1
Overall offer rate		82.1%
International students		33.8%

Accommodation

University provided places: 6,684 (catered 0%)
Self-catered: £76–£181 per week
First years guaranteed accommodation
www.warwick.ac.uk/services/accommodation/
studentaccommodation/undergraduate/

Where do the students come from?

State schools (non-grammar)	58.4%	Working-class homes	19.3%	Black ethnic minority	7.0%
Grammar schools	19.6%	Deprived areas	6.6%	Disabled	5.1%
Independent schools	22.0%	All ethnic minorities	33.1%	Mature (over 21)	9.8%

University of West London

The exceptional increases in student satisfaction that propelled West London 65 places up our league table in two years have gone into reverse in the latest edition. The university is down by more than five percentage points on both of the measures derived from the National Student Survey and has dropped 27 places in the overall table as a result. It had been targeting a place in the top 50 by 2020 but has now dropped out of the top 80.

UWL's success in the rankings, combined with a silver rating in the government's Teaching Excellence Framework (TEF), encouraged an 11% rise in applications last year, when nearly all of its peers saw the demand for places drop significantly. A dozen new degrees, ranging from interior design and computer games technology to leisure management and aviation with a commercial pilot's licence, have helped the process.

The university is also expanding an already substantial range of degree apprenticeships, moving into new areas such as civil engineering, logistics, education and policing. It expects to have 450 apprentices by September, compared with 110 at the end of the 2017/18 academic year.

The TEF panel complimented the university on its investment in high-quality physical and digital resources, with students fully involved in the design of the new facilities. It also commented favourably on peer mentoring and targeted financial support programmes to improve the engagement of those most at risk of dropping out.

Based in Ealing, UWL has been building a reputation as a career-focused university with fine facilities. The £50m Future Campus, with the HeartSpace at its centre, is popular with students. The Paul Hamlyn Library stretches across all four floors of the campus and has a 24-hour social learning area. The project also added music practice rooms, a new performance space, an architecture studio and a concrete testing lab.

UWL is in the top 15 for spending on student facilities. All students have a personal tutor, as well as access to a team of mentors to advise on non-academic issues. Undergraduates are guaranteed work placements on every course, many of which also boast high-quality simulation facilities. Students on the new aviation management degree, for example, will use a Boeing 737 flight simulator.

The university now concentrates most of its activities on two sites in west London, having closed its campus in Slough. The landmark Paragon Building in Brentford, not far from the Ealing campus, remains the headquarters of one of the largest healthcare faculties in Britain, with top ratings for nursing and

St Mary's Road
Ealing
London W5 5RF
0208 231 2220
undergraduate.admissions@uwl.ac.uk
www.uwl.ac.uk
www.uwlsu.com
Open days 2019:
March 30, June 19, July 6,
October 12, November 9

The Times and The Sunday Times Rankings
Overall Ranking: 83 (last year: 56)

Teaching quality	79.2%	=71
Student experience	77.3%	=81
Research quality	1.6%	123
Entry standards	120	=94
Graduate prospects	74.0%	73
Good honours	72.4%	72
Expected completion rate	76.5%	119
Student/staff ratio	15.6	=59
Services and facilities	£2,893	15

midwifery. There is an outpost in Reading, which houses the Berkshire Institute of Health, and also focuses on nursing and midwifery.

UWL's first overseas venture opened in 2017, with a centre at Hong Kong Nang Yan College, where university staff will teach a range of undergraduate and postgraduate courses.

Many degrees include the option of a foundation year for those without conventional entry qualifications. All students taking these courses receive a bursary of £500 a year for the full four years as an undergraduate. An extensive range of bursaries and scholarships also includes the Aspire programme, which gives all UK and EU full-time undergraduates free books worth £100 in their first year and £100 of credit in subsequent years to spend on books, other learning resources or catering. Part-time students qualify for half these amounts.

UWL is in the top ten of our new widening participation table, with about half of the undergraduates receiving some form of financial support. Half are from working-class homes and an even larger proportion aged 21 or more on entry, while more than six out of ten are from ethnic minorities.

The modern students' union was voted the best in the UK in 2017 for representing its members in academic areas. However, the university is in the bottom ten of our research ranking after entering only 13% of eligible academics for the 2014 Research Excellence Framework. A quarter of its submission was judged to be world-leading or internationally excellent, the best results found in communication and media studies.

The sites in Ealing and Brentford are linked by a free bus service and are within easy reach of central London. The Paragon has more than 800 residential places, but students relying on private housing find the cost of living predictably high. There is a campus gym and students have access to the Ealing Trailfinders sports club. New facilities are being added in nearby Gunnersbury this year.

Tuition fees

- » Fees for UK/EU students 2019–20   £9,250
- » Fees for International students 2018–19   £12,000
- » For scholarship and bursary information see
  www.uwl.ac.uk/students/undergraduate/fees-and-funding
- » Graduate salary   £21,999

Student numbers

Undergraduates	7,491	(1,329)
Postgraduates	704	(868)
Applications/places		12,550/1,695
Applications per place		7.4
Overall offer rate		74.2%
International students		13.2%

Accommodation

University provided places: 839 (catered 0%)
Self-catered: £158–£216 per week
www.uwl.ac.uk/students/support-services-for-students/accommodation

Where do the students come from?

State schools (non-grammar)	95.5%	Working-class homes	49.9%	Black ethnic minority	33.3%
Grammar schools	1.8%	Deprived areas	6.3%	Disabled	6.0%
Independent schools	2.7%	All ethnic minorities	63.0%	Mature (over 21)	56.5%

University of the West of England

A new building for UWE's business school is the centrepiece of a £300m programme of campus developments. It is to be followed by a £9m engineering facility for 1,600 students and 100 staff, already under construction alongside it on the main Frenchay campus. Other elements of the programme include a building for arts and media subjects on the Bower Ashton campus and the transformation of a former NHS laundry site at Glenside to create clinical skills and other practical learning spaces.

The university believes that its new facilities have helped to make it more attractive to prospective students. While most of its peers have seen applications decline, UWE enjoyed a 10% increase in 2017 and demand was up by another 4.5% last year. The numbers starting degrees have grown by 800 in the past two years, although the total is still lower than in the years before £9,000 fees were introduced.

The launch of more than a dozen new degrees has helped to broaden UWE's appeal. Courses in business computing, optometry and construction project management are the latest to be introduced. A further three are planned for September: a four-year integrated masters programme in civil engineering, a BSc in education and technology, and the addition of a foundation year in construction project management for those without the normal entry qualifications.

UWE has almost held its own in our table, remaining comfortably in the top half and featuring on the verge of the top ten post-1992 universities. Awarding it silver in the government's Teaching Excellence Framework, the independent panel praised extensive links with employers and the development of enterprise skills, and said it was meeting the diverse needs of different student groups.

Already the biggest higher education institution in the region, the university's campus masterplan is intended to ensure that it is competitive in teaching, research and student facilities, but has the option of taking more students in future. The three sites in Bristol are mainly in the north of the city, with regional centres near hospitals in Gloucester and Bath that concentrate on nursing and allied health professions. The main campus, four miles from the city centre, has doubled in size in recent years and seen a number of improvements, including the opening of the UK's largest robotic laboratory and the biggest exhibition and conference centre in the region.

UWE's own international college, run in partnership with the Kaplan group, provides preparatory courses for students from outside

Frenchay Campus
Coldharbour Lane
Bristol BS16 1QY
0117 328 3333
admissions@uwe.ac.uk
www.uwe.ac.uk
www.thestudentsunion.co.uk
Open days 2019:
see website

The Times and The Sunday Times Rankings
Overall Ranking: 58 (last year: 57)

Teaching quality	84.2%	11
Student experience	84.0%	4
Research quality	8.8%	70
Entry standards	128	=73
Graduate prospects	76.3%	64
Good honours	75.3%	=54
Expected completion rate	84.3%	74
Student/staff ratio	18.4	=109
Services and facilities	£2,440	39

the UK coming to Bristol. The university's degrees are also taught in a growing number of institutions overseas. Closer to home, Hartpury College, near Gloucester, is an associate faculty of the university, specialising in agriculture, equine studies and other land-based courses.

More than half of the students come from the West Country and the university has broadened its intake considerably in recent years. The proportion of independent school entrants has dropped to under 7%, and the share of places going to students from working-class homes has increased. More than a third of UK undergraduates receive some financial support from the university. The university achieves the same ranking (58th) in our table measuring the social diversity of its student body, as it does in our main academic ranking.

More than 60% of the work submitted for assessment in the 2014 Research Excellence Framework was rated as world-leading or internationally excellent. Health subjects and communication and media studies produced the best results.

As a member of the new Institute of Coding, established to tackle the UK's digital skills gap, UWE Bristol has created an industry-facing student enterprise zone known as The Foundry. The zone also includes a £5m Health Tech Hub, providing businesses with access to laboratories for product development and testing.

The careers and employment service runs an innovative web-based jobs and placement service with the local chamber of commerce. UWE Bristol Futures Award acknowledges extracurricular activities and encourages students to acquire skills that will help in the employment market.

UWE Bristol also has one of the largest internship programmes at any university and graduates can apply to access the Centre for Graduate Enterprise to launch businesses in a new incubator hub at the Frenchay campus.

Bristol is a hugely popular student centre: an attractive and lively city, although not cheap. The university owns or endorses more than 4,700 residential places, enough for virtually all new entrants who want accommodation. A £5.5m sports complex has a 70-station fitness suite, as well as outdoor facilities and further multi-sport facilities are being added next to the Frenchay campus.

Tuition fees
- » Fees for UK/EU students 2019–20   £9,250
- » Fees for International students 2019–20   £13,000–£13,500
- » For scholarship and bursary information see www1.uwe.ac.uk/students/feesandfunding.aspx
- » Graduate salary   £22,000

Student numbers

Undergraduates	**18,915**	**(2,210)**
Postgraduates	**2,285**	**(4,472)**
Applications/places		**30,425/5,855**
Applications per place		**5.2**
Overall offer rate		**79.8%**
International students		**13.1%**

Accommodation

University provided places: 4,739 (catered 0%)
Self-catered: £86–£179 per week
First years guaranteed accommodation
www.uwe.ac.uk/students/accommodation

Where do the students come from?

State schools (non-grammar)	90.3%	Working-class homes	30.2%	Black ethnic minority	4.5%
Grammar schools	3.1%	Deprived areas	16.6%	Disabled	9.8%
Independent schools	6.7%	All ethnic minorities	16.3%	Mature (over 21)	26.5%

University of the West of Scotland

The University of the West of Scotland's (UWS) newly-opened Lanarkshire Campus, costing £110m, has already helped achieve a 7% increase in applications, while most of its peer group has suffered a decline. Based on the Hamilton International Technology Park, the eco campus features a three-storey street atrium linking its main buildings, which contain ultra-modern teaching and learning spaces and a students' union.

Built for 4,000 students and 250 staff, the campus is designed to host courses in health, computing and some business and social science subjects. The gleaming new premises house simulated hospital wards, community and primary care settings to immerse learners in authentic healthcare environments. There are cardiovascular, environmental, exercise science and biomechanics labs, and students use virtual reality and mobile technology for tele-health scenarios.

New student residences are also planned for the site, which aims to be one of the UK's greenest educational environments, with carbon-neutral buildings set in 37 acres of woodland. But for the moment, students will continue to live in the centre of Hamilton, two miles away.

The university's headquarters will remain in Paisley, where more than £30m has been spent improving student facilities and expanding the residential accommodation. This site also has an atrium as its centrepiece, a flexible learning area with interactive technology, meeting spaces and a cafe that is open to staff, students and members of the public. The Hub, which brought together the various student services, was added in 2016.

Another £81m went into developing a modern campus for 2,300 students in Ayr and a further site in Dumfries is operated in partnership with the University of Glasgow and Dumfries and Galloway College. UWS has also spent £12m upgrading its information technology provision.

UWS entered the top 100 universities for the first time in our previous edition, and is up another eight places as it continues to move away from the basement positions it has traditionally occupied. It has recorded big increases in graduate prospects, spending on student facilities and satisfaction with the broad student experience. Like most universities in Scotland, UWS did not enter the Teaching Excellence Framework, but its scores in the sections of the National Student Survey relating to the quality of teaching are now in our top 30.

The university was founded in 2007, the product of a merger between Paisley University and Bell College in Hamilton – institutions serving two less than prosperous towns in areas of low participation in higher

---

Paisley Campus
Paisley PA1 2BE
0800 027 1000;
+44 141 849 4101 (international)
ask@uws.ac.uk
www.uws.ac.uk
www.sauws.org.uk
Open days 2019:
March 23 (Paisley);
March 28 (Dumfries);
April 27 (Lanarkshire); May 11 (Ayr)

PAISLEY
Edinburgh
Belfast
London
Cardiff

The Times and The Sunday Times Rankings
Overall Ranking: 92 (last year: =100)

Teaching quality	82.6%	26
Student experience	79.2%	=50
Research quality	4.3%	=99
Entry standards	142	=49
Graduate prospects	80.7%	=42
Good honours	70.3%	88
Expected completion rate	80.9%	=103
Student/staff ratio	22.1	130
Services and facilities	£2,166	=73

education. Half of the undergraduates are over 20 on entry and four out of ten are from working-class homes. UWS also had places for 100 graduate apprentices in computing, engineering and business last year and hopes to expand into new areas.

UWS is among the largest modern universities in Scotland, with almost 16,000 students. It describes itself as "the local university for a third of Scotland's population", although there are also 1,600 students from outside the UK, many of them from other EU countries. A London campus opened in 2015 and more than 1,000 students are registered there. The site, in Southwark, offers courses in business, health, music, quality management, project management, and education.

The attractive Dumfries campus has 550 UWS students while the Ayr campus is shared with SRUC (Scotland's Rural College) and has a prize-winning library with flexible space.

Many students take sandwich degrees or have work placements built into their courses and all are offered hands-on computer training. UWS was the first UK university to be approved by Microsoft, Macromedia and Cisco. Sony supported a games development laboratory, part of a £300,000 investment in multimedia and games facilities.

The university's School of Health, Nursing and Midwifery is the largest north of the border, and its entries produced much the best results in the 2014 Research Excellence Framework, when 44% of UWS's submission reached one of the top two categories. In a unique collaboration with the International Space School Educational Trust, UWS researchers are applying their knowledge in areas such as gas-sensing technologies to grow healthy plants and study the effects of growth hormone on muscle mass and cognitive function in space.

The top priority at UWS, however, is to become Scotland's most "student-focused" university. It has a formal Student Partnership Agreement with the students' association, which in 2016 won the NUS Scotland's Higher Education Students' Association of the Year award.

The university currently has just 850 residential places, so only international students are guaranteed accommodation. However, the high proportion of home-based students means that, until now, it has been possible to satisfy all new entrants requiring a study bedroom.

Tuition fees
» Fees for Scottish/EU students 2019–20 £0–£1,820
  RUK fees £9,250 (capped at £27,750 for 4-year courses)
» Fees for International students 2019–20 £12,000–£14,000
» For scholarship and bursary information see www.uws.ac.uk/money-fees-funding/
» Graduate salary £22,000

Student numbers

Undergraduates	10,973	(2,421)
Postgraduates	1,576	(986)
Applications/places	18,590/3,745	
Applications per place	5.0	
Overall offer rate	72.9%	
International students	10.2%	

Accommodation
University provided places: 852 (catered 0%)
Self-catered: £85–£149 per week
www.uws.ac.uk/university-life/accommodation

Where do the students come from?

State schools (non-grammar)	98.2%	Working-class homes	40.6%	Black ethnic minority	2.6%
Grammar schools	0.1%	Deprived areas	8.9%	Disabled	2.2%
Independent schools	1.7%	All ethnic minorities	9.2%	Mature (over 21)	49.6%

University of Westminster

Westminster would be well inside the top 100 in our league table were it not for the low student satisfaction levels that plague most of London's universities. It is in the bottom ten in the sections of the National Student Survey that focus on the quality of teaching, and has lost much of the ground it made up in the overall table in 2017.

The university's performance in other areas is much better. It is in the top 60 for research, for example, and the top 75 for the proportion of high-class degrees awarded. Westminster is also inside the top 40 in our new widening participation table, with six out of ten undergraduates coming from ethnic minorities and almost half from working-class families.

Nevertheless, Westminster was given a bronze rating in the government's new Teaching Excellence Framework, which takes account of the backgrounds of students. An unusually brief commentary by the awarding panel praised the consistent support for students at risk of dropping out and acknowledged a strategic approach and commitment to improving employment and entrepreneurship.

The university reviewed all its courses as part of its Learning Futures programme, which came into operation in 2016. The structure of undergraduate programmes changed to promote deeper learning through year-long modules, weaving work-related skills into degrees. It has resulted in new support for employability and international mobility, and awards for students' extracurricular activities recognise outstanding contributions of benefit to the public.

Applications have dropped for four years in a row, although by less than the national average last year. The numbers starting courses recovered in 2017 but are still lower than in the years before £9,000 fees were introduced.

New degrees have been launched in psychology and counselling, and in the production, performance and enterprise of music. There is also an expanded range of courses offering a foundation year in art and design, business management, social sciences, humanities, law and psychology. Degree apprenticeships are available only in building surveying, quantity surveying and real estate, but other areas are likely to be added this year.

The 20,000 students include 6,000 from outside the UK, of whom 2,000 come from other EU countries. Westminster's courses are also taught in nine overseas countries, from Sri Lanka to Uzbekistan, and this won the university a Queen's Award for Enterprise. Expanding the opportunities for students to study or work abroad is one of the main planks of the institution's Global Engagement Strategy.

---

101 New Cavendish Street
London W1W 6XH
020 7911 5511
course-enquiries@westminster.ac.uk
www.westminster.ac.uk
www.uwsu.com
Open days 2019:
March 9, June 22

Edinburgh
Belfast
Cardiff
LONDON

The Times and The Sunday Times Rankings
Overall Ranking: 114 (last year: =106)

Teaching quality	73.4%	122
Student experience	74.0%	112
Research quality	9.8%	60
Entry standards	124	=85
Graduate prospects	70.4%	=99
Good honours	71.9%	=74
Expected completion rate	82.9%	=86
Student/staff ratio	17.0	=92
Services and facilities	£2,022	84

Westminster's ultimate aim is to be the leading "practice-informed" university and it promises a "dynamic synergy" between the creative arts and design, architecture and the built environment, science and technology, business, law, and the social sciences and humanities. It collaborates with a network of more than 3,000 companies and all students are encouraged to undertake a work placement which can form part of their degree.

The university was again among the leading institutions for communication and media studies in the 2014 Research Excellence Framework, when almost two thirds of the work submitted was judged to be world-leading or excellent. There were even better results in art and design, as well as a good performance in English. However, less than 30% of the eligible staff entered the exercise. The Westminster Institute for Advanced Studies has been established since to foster interdisciplinary and independent critical thinking.

Westminster originally became the UK's first polytechnic in 1838. Its Marylebone headquarters, near the BBC's Broadcasting House, houses social sciences, humanities and languages. The university offers one of the widest ranges of language teaching of any UK institution and, together with SOAS, leads the Routes into Languages programme. King's College London, University College London, the University of Roehampton and the Open University are further partners in the scheme to encourage more people to learn a language.

More than £60m has gone into refurbishing Westminster's campuses in central London. Its Harrow site, in the northwest of the capital, is the home of the media, arts and design faculty, the university's best-known feature. A library and resource centre has been added there, as well as a multimedia newsroom, flexible performance areas and a cafe.

Only those who apply early are guaranteed student accommodation. There is a student village for first-years close to Wembley Stadium, as well as a £6m development in Harrow and refurbished halls in Marylebone, but there is no way round the inflated private market at some stage.

Westminster students tend to be spread around the capital but there is a lively social scene on the Harrow campus. Sports facilities are also dispersed, with playing fields and a boathouse in Chiswick and a well-equipped gym at the central Regent Street site.

Tuition fees

» Fees for UK/EU students 2019–20	£9,250
» Fees for International students 2019–20	£13,400
» For scholarship and bursary information see www.westminster.ac.uk/study/fees-and-funding/	
» Graduate salary	£21,000

Student numbers

Undergraduates	12,777 (2,434)
Postgraduates	2,337 (2,104)
Applications/places	24,810/3,495
Applications per place	7.1
Overall offer rate	84.7%
International students	31.4%

Accommodation

University provided places: 1,514 (catered 0%)
Self-catered: £145–£270 per week
www.westminster.ac.uk/study/accommodation

Where do the students come from?

State schools (non-grammar)	94.2%	Working-class homes	49.3%	Black ethnic minority	13.8%
Grammar schools	2.2%	Deprived areas	5.6%	Disabled	4.3%
Independent schools	3.6%	All ethnic minorities	62.8%	Mature (over 21)	20.1%

University of Winchester

Winchester has embarked on a dramatic expansion of its portfolio of degrees, adding 50 new programmes in two years — an increase of more than a third. Among the new offers this year will be anthropology and archaeology, banking and finance, forensic investigative psychology, and development, religion and peacebuilding. There will also be seven new law degrees, pairing the subject with others such as cyber-security and even sport studies.

The range of degree apprenticeships is also being expanded, with new programmes planned in childcare and education, social care and policing. The number of students is expected to rise from 80 to 120.

The new courses, which include a degree in physiotherapy, four in liberal arts and five combinations with computer-aided design, helped Winchester to a 4% increase in applications last year — a rarity among its peer group of institutions. There was a drop in 2017, but enrolments continued at record levels. There are now more than 7,500 students — twice as many as when university status was awarded in 2005.

Winchester has arrested its decline in our league table, making up six of the 20 places it had lost in the previous two editions. Student satisfaction has recovered and the university is now in the top 50 in both measures derived from the National Student Survey.

The university was given a silver rating, however, in the Teaching Excellence Framework. The panel was impressed by the "appropriate" contact hours, tutorials and buddy schemes that produce personalised learning and high levels of commitment from students. Most students are stretched sufficiently to make progress, and acquire knowledge, skills and understanding that are valued by employers, it added.

There are undergraduate exchange schemes with a number of American universities, as well as others in Japan and across Europe. The number of international students coming to Winchester has trebled in the current decade but still amounts to little more than 500.

An award-winning extension to the library added 450 study spaces and extra computers, while a modern Learning and Teaching Building significantly improved the facilities for lectures and independent study. The Victorian chapel has been restored and extended to include a small side chapel and a social and meeting space.

Winchester has split its campus into four "quarters". The compact main King Alfred site is on a wooded hillside overlooking the cathedral city, a ten-minute walk away. Work is under way at the West Downs quarter, another short walk away, on a £50m development for the business school. The

---

Sparkford Road
Winchester SO22 4NR
01962 827 234
course.enquiries@winchester.ac.uk
www.winchester.ac.uk
www.winchesterstudents.co.uk
Open days 2019:
January 12

The Times and The Sunday Times Rankings
Overall Ranking: 79 (last year: 85)

Teaching quality	81.7%	=40
Student experience	80.2%	37
Research quality	5.8%	=84
Entry standards	113	=116
Graduate prospects	63.7%	=123
Good honours	77.6%	46
Expected completion rate	87.7%	50
Student/staff ratio	16.3	=76
Services and facilities	£1,605	120

site will also house Digital Futures, the university's computer science and digital-related degrees. The building is will include a 250-seat auditorium, a cafe and food hall, as well as "contemplation space".

Winchester was one the first universities to appoint its own ombudsman to handle complaints. The university is still best known for its education courses, which Ofsted rates as outstanding, although they no longer dominate in terms of student numbers. A new partnership with the Hampshire Hospitals NHS Foundation Trust covers both teaching and research and is expected to lead to further expansion.

The university held its own in the 2014 Research Excellence Framework. Almost 45% of its work was considered world-leading or internationally excellent, with communications and history producing the best results. John Denham, the former Labour universities secretary, heads the university's Centre for English Identity and Politics, and a Centre for Animal Welfare was established two years ago.

The Sport and Exercise Research Centre was added to mark the 175th anniversary in 2015 of the original institution's establishment as a Church of England foundation for teacher training. It was known as King Alfred College until 2004.

Sports facilities are good, with a gym, fitness suite and sports hall supplemented by the £3.5m Winchester Sports Stadium. Open to local people as well as students, the stadium has a 400-metre, eight-lane athletics track with supporting facilities for field events and a floodlit all-weather pitch. The gym is at the heart of a £12m student village of more than 700 rooms.

Two other complexes adjacent to the King Alfred Campus bring the number of residential places to more than 2,300. UK entrants are guaranteed accommodation as long as they apply by the end of May, with Winchester as their firm choice.

Students value the close-knit atmosphere and find the city is livelier than its staid image might suggest, with a number of bars catering to their tastes. Southampton is not far for those who hanker after the attractions of a bigger city, and London is only an hour away by train.

Tuition fees

» Fees for UK/EU students 2019–20	£9,250
» Fees for International students 2019–20	£13,300
» For scholarship and bursary information see www.winchester.ac.uk/accommodation-and-winchester-life/students-and-money/	
» Graduate salary	£20,000

Student numbers

Undergraduates	5,939	(283)
Postgraduates	510	(808)
Applications/places		8,815/2,260
Applications per place		3.9
Overall offer rate		92.4%
International students		6.4%

Accommodation

University provided places: 2,335 (catered 4%)
Catered costs: £162 per week
Self-catered: £84–£147 per week
First years guaranteed accommodation
www.winchester.ac.uk/accommodation

Where do the students come from?

State schools (non-grammar)	92.1%	Working-class homes	30.4%	Black ethnic minority	2.6%
Grammar schools	3.5%	Deprived areas	15.2%	Disabled	12.9%
Independent schools	4.4%	All ethnic minorities	10.4%	Mature (over 21)	14.1%

University of Wolverhampton

Wolverhampton is back in our league table for the first time since 2009, when it began a boycott of all rankings by refusing to release data about its performance. Its intake of undergraduates has dropped by more than 1,000 since then, despite raising the offer rate from less than 60% to 93% in 2017.

The university has returned to our table in the bottom six, despite ranking close to mid-table for student satisfaction with the quality of teaching and not much lower in relation to the broader student experience. Its entry standards, drop-out rate and staffing levels have dragged it down, this time at least.

However, Wolverhampton is in the top four in our new table ranking universities on the social diversity of their student body. Only one university, Bradford, had a higher proportion of undergraduates coming from working-class homes when this was last surveyed. Nearly all the students are from non-selective state schools and almost a quarter come from deprived areas. The university draws two thirds of its 19,500 students from the West Midlands. It is leading a regional scheme to encourage young people to consider higher education.

Wolverhampton was placed in the bronze category in the first round of Teaching Excellence Framework grades, but has been upgraded to silver this year. The university still missed its benchmarks for student satisfaction and progression to highly-skilled employment, but the awards panel praised the commitment to enhancing students' learning experience, as well as the involvement of employers in the development and review of courses. It was also impressed by Wolverhampton's mental health provision and support systems.

The university is carrying out a £250m investment programme, the biggest in its history, to drive economic growth for the benefit of students and the wider region. The five-year project includes new buildings and facilities, as well as investment in teaching, research and skills training.

It began with an £18m building for the business school, and new engineering facilities are being provided in Telford and Wolverhampton to support the university's courses in automotive and motorsport engineering, electronic and telecommunications engineering, chemical engineering and, most recently, aerospace engineering.

There is a new science centre, the Rosalind Franklin Building, but the most ambitious project will see the £100m redevelopment of the derelict Springfield Brewery site in the city, to create a new campus for construction and the built environment.

The new West Midlands Construction University Technical College (UTC) is already open, as is the School of Architecture and the Built Environment. An Elite Centre

Wulfruna Street
Wolverhampton WV1 1LY
01902 321 000
enquiries@wlv.ac.uk
www.wlv.ac.uk
www.wolvesunion.org/
Open days 2019:
February 2, June 15,
August 17

The Times and The Sunday Times Rankings
Overall Ranking: 127 (last year: n/a)

Teaching quality	79.8%	67
Student experience	78.3%	=70
Research quality	5.9%	83
Entry standards	110	122
Graduate prospects	68.9%	104
Good honours	64.0%	125
Expected completion rate	70.3%	128
Student/staff ratio	20.0	124
Services and facilities	£1,859	100

for Manufacturing Skills is under construction and will complete a range of provision stretching from the age of 14 through to undergraduate and postgraduate courses, to executive education.

The university has also begun to deliver higher education courses in education, leadership and management, travel and tourism, hospitality and computing on a 50-acre campus in Stafford bought by the Chinese-based New Beacon Group from Staffordshire University. Students will be recruited directly from China and locally in Staffordshire.

There are already three bases in the West Midlands: the original site in the centre of Wolverhampton, a campus in Walsall dedicated to sport and performance, as well as education and part of the School of Health and Wellbeing, and a purpose-built campus at Telford, in Shropshire, which focuses on business and engineering.

Among newly-introduced degrees is a BSc in dance science and performance, which offers students research-led scientific study as well as modules in dance training, performance and choreography. It looks at how to enhance the performance of dancers and focuses on their health and wellbeing through the fields of physiology, biomechanics and performance psychology.

In addition, more than 150 students are taking higher or degree apprenticeships at the university in programmes ranging from construction management, chartered surveying and product design and development, to those for chartered legal executives, healthcare science practitioners and paramedics. Future apprenticeships will include digital technologies, policing, social work and nursing.

Research mainly serves the needs of business and industry, as well as underpinning teaching. By far the best results in the Research Excellence Framework were in information science, where almost 90% of the work submitted was considered world-leading or internationally excellent.

Student facilities improved with the redevelopment of the students' union on the City campus and the opening of a new union bar on the Walsall campus. There is a 350-bed student village and sports facilities, including a well-equipped Research Centre for Sport, Exercise and Performance.

The Performance Hub, in Walsall, the university's centre for performing arts, has exceptional facilities for music, dance and drama.

Tuition fees

- » Fees for UK/EU students 2019–20   £9,250
-     Foundation courses   £6,165
- » Fees for International students 2019–20   £12,000
- » For scholarship and bursary information see www.wlv.ac.uk/study-here/money-matters/fees-and-costs
- » Graduate salary   £18,000

Student numbers

Undergraduates	13,022 (3,453)
Postgraduates	1,351 (1,736)
Applications/places	18,080/3,370
Applications per place	5.4
Overall offer rate	93.1%
International students	6.3%

Accommodation

University provided places: 1,000+ (catered 0%)
Self-catered: £88–£106 per week
www.wlv.ac.uk/study-here/accommodation

Where do the students come from?

State schools (non-grammar)	97.1%	Working-class homes	56.9%	Black ethnic minority	22.6%
Grammar schools	1.3%	Deprived areas	23.8%	Disabled	7.4%
Independent schools	1.7%	All ethnic minorities	50.9%	Mature (over 21)	45.2%

University of Worcester

Worcester is leading a yo-yo existence in our league table, moving by at least ten places in each of the past three years. The university is up 11 places in this edition, having dropped 12 last time, after substantial improvement in student satisfaction levels. It is now in the top 15 for satisfaction with the quality of teaching and only three places lower for the broader student experience.

The university achieved a silver rating in the government's Teaching Excellence Framework. The awards panel said that the teaching encourages high levels of student engagement and commitment, with "excellent" levels of contact time, and schemes which involve students in the enhancement of their learning experience.

The numbers of students starting degrees dropped slightly in 2017, but only the two previous years had seen larger intakes. Students applying last year had a dozen additional degrees to choose from, half of them combining business studies with another subject. Another three will be added in September: four-year integrated Masters programmes in occupational therapy or physiotherapy, and a foundation degree for nursing associates.

A new Art House, in the city centre, has opened, providing high-quality facilities for art and illustration courses. The grade II listed building was built in 1939 as a car showroom and many of its art deco features, including a distinctive clock tower, are being retained.

The Art House is located opposite the City campus, which houses the business school and occupies the historic buildings of the former Worcester Royal Infirmary. Almost next door is the university's spectacular library and history centre, the Hive, which was the first joint public and university library to open in Britain and has won several awards.

Worcester has three teaching campuses, less than a mile from each other and all close to the city centre. The main St John's campus occupies a parkland site 15 minutes' walk from the centre. It includes science facilities, the National Pollen and Aerobiology Research Unit, the digital arts centre and drama studio, and an all-weather pitch.

The Riverside campus houses the university's 2,000-seat indoor sporting arena. One of only two specialist sports venues in the UK, it was designed specifically for wheelchair athletes as well as the able-bodied. A proposed International Centre for Inclusive Sport and Health, also to be set at Riverside, will include a similarly inclusive cricket centre to capitalise on the existing partnership the university has with Worcestershire County Cricket Club.

Lakeside campus, a ten-minute drive from St John's, is the third site. It has sports pitches

Henwick Grove
Worcester WR2 6AJ
01905 855 111
admissions@worc.ac.uk
www.worcester.ac.uk
www.worcsu.com
Open days 2019:
March 30, June 30

The Times and The Sunday Times **Rankings**
Overall Ranking: 91 (last year: =102)

Teaching quality	83.6%	15
Student experience	81.6%	=18
Research quality	4.3%	=99
Entry standards	119	=100
Graduate prospects	75.0%	70
Good honours	65.6%	=119
Expected completion rate	84.9%	=70
Student/staff ratio	16.7	=85
Services and facilities	£1,519	126

and a ten-acre lake which has been adapted for a range of inclusive water sports and other outdoor activities. Worcester's commitment to disability sports saw it launch the UK's first disability sport degree.

Originally a post-war emergency teacher training college, Worcester now has approaching 11,000 students, two thirds of them female. A law school opened in 2016 with a mock courtroom, jury room, and a number of seminar spaces.

In the longer term, the university hopes to have a medical school to serve the three counties of Gloucestershire, Herefordshire and Worcestershire. All six NHS trusts in the region have backed the proposal for a new school, which would build on the university's strength in nursing and other health disciplines. The university is the partner institution for the National Childbirth Trust, for example, delivering the trust's antenatal training.

One of the most improved universities in the 2014 Research Excellence Framework compared with previous assessments, Worcester went up 20 places in our research ranking, partly because it entered five times as many academics as in 2008. A third of the work was considered world-leading or internationally excellent, with history and art and design achieving the best scores.

More than a third of the undergraduates come from working-class homes and one in 11 students is in receipt of Disability Support Allowance, helping the university to a creditable ranking just outside the top 40 in our new table measuring widening participation. A team of graduate ambassadors works with more than 200 primary schools to try to broaden the intake further.

The university's Reach scheme gives most students access to ebooks, stationery, art supplies, digital equipment, or other course-specific equipment at discounted prices. New undergraduates paying full fees will receive £100 bursaries to spend through the scheme, and another £50 in the second year. Students also have access to an extensive "earn-as-you-learn" programme.

The university has 1,350 residential places on the St John's and City campuses — enough to guarantee accommodation to new entrants. The cathedral city is not large, but it is safer than many university locations and has its share of pubs and clubs catering for a growing student clientele. An active students' union acts as a social hub.

Tuition fees

» Fees for UK/EU students 2019–20	£9,250
» Fees for International students 2019–20	£12,400
» For scholarship and bursary information see www.worcester.ac.uk/your-home/course-fees.html	
» Graduate salary	£21,000

Student numbers

Undergraduates	7,927 (1,048)
Postgraduates	692 (1,080)
Applications/places	12,850/2,530
Applications per place	5.1
Overall offer rate	87.4%
International students	5.3%

Accommodation

University provided places: 1,350 (catered 0%)
Self-catered: £98–£159 per week
First years guaranteed accommodation
www.worcester.ac.uk/your-home/student-accommodation.html

Where do the students come from?

State schools (non-grammar)	94.6%	Working-class homes	36.9%	Black ethnic minority	5.2%
Grammar schools	2.5%	Deprived areas	17.3%	Disabled	9.1%
Independent schools	3.0%	All ethnic minorities	13.2%	Mature (over 21)	34.3%

Wrexham Glyndŵr University

Glyndŵr is the most socially inclusive university in the UK. Our new table which measures how effective universities are at widening participation sees the Wrexham-based institution come out on top on a range of measures that include the proportion of students recruited from comprehensive schools, ethnic minorities, the disabled, working-class, deprived areas and mature students aged over 21.

Glyndŵr offers among the best chances of securing admission to a university in the UK with just two applications per place and a significant proportion of the intake recruited through clearing. Almost all recruits are educated in non-selective schools, nearly two thirds are mature and around a quarter of recruits qualify for disability support allowance, much the highest proportion of any university.

Although Glyndŵr is in the bottom four in our league table overall, there are a dozen universities with lower average entry grades. And, while its student satisfaction levels have declined in the new table, the university remains in the top half for perceptions of teaching quality.

That was one of the features identified by the independent panel which gave Glyndŵr a silver rating in the government's Teaching Excellence Framework. The university achieved particularly good scores for its part-time courses, and the panel was impressed by the high levels of interaction with industry, business and the public sector. It commented favourably on the quality of work-based learning and on matching the curriculum to the region's priorities.

However, Glyndŵr also has one of the highest projected dropout rates with more than one in five students not expected to complete their courses. This is broadly in line with projections given the student and subject mix.

Professor Maria Hinfelaar, the vice-chancellor, has pledged to improve the student experience, however, and has launched the Campus 2025 programme to this end. Catering facilities were overhauled and expanded, and an innovative science garden opened. Other projects will include new student accommodation, car parking, upgraded academic and research rooms and the reconfiguration of buildings, including the main entrance.

Glyndŵr is celebrating its tenth anniversary as a university. It took the name of the 15th-century Welsh prince Owain Glyndŵr, who championed the establishment of universities throughout Wales, after a long campaign of its own for university status. There are now 6,400 students, more than half of them part-timers and including 1,000 from outside the UK. The university waives 40% of the tuition fee for part-time students living in Wales.

Mold Road
Wrexham LL11 2AW
01978 293 439
enquiries@glyndwr.ac.uk
www.glyndwr.ac.uk
www.wrexhamglyndwrsu.org.uk
Open days 2019:
March 2, June 8,
August 17

The Times and The Sunday Times Rankings
Overall Ranking: 129 (last year: 127)

Teaching quality	80.3%	=60
Student experience	73.2%	=117
Research quality	2.3%	120
Entry standards	112	=118
Graduate prospects	63.5%	=125
Good honours	66.6%	107
Expected completion rate	71.1%	127
Student/staff ratio	19.2	=117
Services and facilities	£1,570	122

The university has been expanding the range of its academic offer, launching 20 new degrees in 2017 and another five last year. There are plans for 14 more this year, ranging from media and communication, comics and surface design to computer games design and cyber security, both with an industrial placement. Many degrees now include the option of a foundation year for those lacking the requisite entry qualifications.

Glyndŵr also offers two-year fast-track degrees and four-year master's degrees in art and design, and computing. The Centre for the Creative Industries hosts the regional home of BBC Cymru Wales as well as providing high-quality studios for the university's television degree. Other facilities include a recording studio, a Chinese medicine clinic, crime scene labs, computer game development labs, flight simulator and supersonic wind tunnel.

The main campus is on the outskirts of Wrexham, with a second base for the art school in the town centre. There are also sites at Northop, in Flintshire, and St Asaph, in Denbighshire. Glyndŵr bought the Racecourse Ground — the oldest football stadium in the world — in 2011 to safeguard the future of the local game. The university leases the ground to Wrexham FC, and its land hosts the 200-bed Wrexham Village next to the Plas Coch campus.

Northop hosts the university's rural campus, specialising in courses on animal studies and biodiversity, where students have access to a small animal unit and an equine centre.

The St Asaph campus houses Glyndŵr Innovations, a research centre that brings together academia and industry, focusing on high-level opto-electronics technology.

There is also an Advanced Composite Training and Development Centre at Broughton, in partnership with Airbus, which has a large plant nearby. Research carried out there will help to improve the efficiency of aircraft and feed into the university's engineering courses.

Glyndŵr entered only 34 academics for the 2014 Research Excellence Framework, but a third of their work was judged to be internationally excellent or world-leading.

A high proportion of the students are local, many living at home, which eases the pressure on residential accommodation. Wrexham is not without nightlife, and the upgraded students' union runs the popular Centenary Bar, in the Racecourse Stadium. The campus also contains a modern sports centre that includes two floodlit artificial pitches, a human performance laboratory and a variety of indoor facilities.

Tuition fees

» Fees for UK/EU students 2019–20	£9,000
» Fees for International students 2019–20	£11,750
» For scholarship and bursary information see www.glyndwr.ac.uk/en/feesandstudentfinance/	
» Graduate salary	£20,000

Student numbers

Undergraduates	2,911	(2,913)
Postgraduates	111	(481)
Applications/places	1,925/425	
Applications per place	4.5	
Overall offer rate	81.5%	
International students	15.5%	

Accommodation

University provided places: 713 (catered 0%)
Self-catered: £79–£160 per week
www.glyndwr.ac.uk/en/Accommodation

Where do the students come from?

State schools (non-grammar)	99.3%	Working-class homes	46.2%	Black ethnic minority	1.3%
Grammar schools	0.7%	Deprived areas	30.8%	Disabled	26.7%
Independent schools	0.0%	All ethnic minorities	2.5%	Mature (over 21)	63.8%

York St John University

After enrolling almost 50% more new undergraduates in two years, York St John (YSJ) has climbed 16 places in our league table. It is not an easy combination to pull off, as rising numbers can stretch resources and make satisfaction levels plummet. Instead, scores in the National Student Survey have risen and there has been a spectacular improvement in graduate prospects.

Low rates of graduate employment in highly-skilled jobs contributed to a bronze rating in the Teaching Excellence Framework, but the proportion of leavers going straight into graduate-level work or further study has risen by 18 percentage points in the latest survey, taking YSJ 50 places up the table on this measure.

The TEF panel commended a scheme that involves undergraduates in research and the innovative measures to support vulnerable students, including those with mental health problems.

The university attributed its increased popularity with applicants to the dramatic diversification of its course portfolio. A raft of new degrees launched in 2017 covered areas including management, police studies, sport and exercise science. They were followed by seven more programmes in events management, marketing and tourism.

Professor Karen Stanton, the vice-chancellor, said the increases reflected the university's investment in new facilities and excellent teaching, and were in line with its ambitious growth strategy. The aim is to be "the best of England's small universities" and to have 7,300 students by 2020, compared with 6,000 in 2016-17.

League tables will be one of the university's measures of success. YSJ had been falling in ours, but is now almost back in the top 100, with hopes of further improvement to come.

Professor Stanton noted that the university was the fastest-rising in the region in the latest edition and said the result showed that YSJ was making an impact both in terms of student satisfaction and in creating strong employment prospects.

The university is a Church of England foundation that dates back to 1841, when the Diocesan Training School opened with just one pupil on the register. Full university status arrived in 2006. YSJ continues to charge the lowest fees in England — only £4,000 in the current academic year — for its foundation degrees in education and theology. But the courses are for a limited range of mature students without traditional qualifications; the fees for all honours degrees are £9,250.

Divided between York and Ripon for most of its existence, the university now concentrates all its activities on York. The 11-acre campus faces York Minster across the city walls and is

Lord Mayor's Walk
York YO31 7EX
01904 876 598
admissions@yorksj.ac.uk
www.yorksj.ac.uk
http://ysjsu.com
Open days 2019:
July 1, August 17

The Times and The Sunday Times Rankings
Overall Ranking: 102 (last year: 118)

Teaching quality	81.1%	50
Student experience	79.2%	=50
Research quality	4.1%	=102
Entry standards	115	=111
Graduate prospects	73.6%	=77
Good honours	64.7%	124
Expected completion rate	84.6%	=72
Student/staff ratio	17.4	99
Services and facilities	£1,831	104

a five-minute walk from the city centre, transformed by £100m of redevelopment already finished or in the works.

The Fountains Learning Centre provides a striking entrance to the university, with 530 computer workstations, multimedia group-work facilities, 24-hour access and an internet cafe and lecture theatre. Nearby, the prize-winning De Grey Court, which serves the health and life sciences, links the university quarter with the city centre.

The York Business School is the biggest school, and offers a number of degree apprenticeships as well as conventional degrees. The university is adding degree apprenticeships for laboratory scientists and police constables. Two thirds of the students are female and there is a growing cohort from abroad.

One in six of the UK students comes from an area of low participation in higher education— well above average for YSJ's courses and entry qualifications. The Aspire scheme gives all UK undergraduates £100 a year towards course materials, with those whose household income is below £25,000 receiving an extra £400. YSJ has been made a University of Sanctuary for its work to assist and welcome asylum seekers.

Psychology produced the best results in the 2014 Research Excellence Framework, when 30% of the research submitted overall was regarded as world-leading or internationally excellent — a big improvement on the 2008

assessments. A new strategy promotes interdisciplinary research, building on current areas of expertise and targeting further improvement in the 2021 exercise.

New entrants are guaranteed one of almost 2,000 residential places if they apply by mid-July with York St John as their firm choice. On campus, there is a sports hall, climbing wall, basketball, netball, indoor football and cricket nets. A sports park, 15 minutes' walk from the campus, has a 3G pitch, outdoor tennis and netball courts and a sprint track. The indoor centre has a sports hall, strength and conditioning suite and six changing rooms.

An active students' union is the social centre for many students, especially in their first year. But York is popular as a student city with a growing range of clubs — as well as a pub for every day of the year, according to local legend.

Tuition fees

- » Fees for UK/EU students 2019–20 £9,250
  Foundation courses from £4,000
- » Fees for International students 2019–20 £12,750–£14,000
- » For scholarship and bursary information see www.yorksj.ac.uk/study/undergraduate/fees-funding/
- » Graduate salary £20,000

Student numbers

Undergraduates	4,843	(272)
Postgraduates	512	(314)
Applications/places	10,125/2,070	
Applications per place	4.9	
Overall offer rate	86.4%	
International students	7.2%	

Accommodation

University provided places: 1,944 (catered 0%)
Self-catered: £100–£178 per week
First years guaranteed accommodation
www.yorksj.ac.uk/study/accommodation

Where do the students come from?

State schools (non-grammar)	93.5%	Working-class homes	34.9%	Black ethnic minority	0.9%
Grammar schools	3.0%	Deprived areas	17.3%	Disabled	8.0%
Independent schools	3.5%	All ethnic minorities	5.6%	Mature (over 21)	10.0%

Specialist and Private Institutions

1 Specialist colleges of the University of London

This listing gives contact details for specialist degree-awarding colleges within the University of London not listed elsewhere within the book. Those marked * are members of GuildHE (**www.guildhe.ac.uk**). Fees are given for UK/EU undergraduates for a single year of study.

Courtauld Institute of Art
Somerset House Strand
London WC2R 0RN
020 7848 2645
www.courtauld.ac.uk
Fees 2018–19: £9,250

London Business School
Regent's Park London NW1 4SA
020 7000 7000
www.london.edu
Postgraduate only

London School of Hygiene and Tropical Medicine
Keppel Street
London WC1E 7HT
020 7299 4646
www.lshtm.ac.uk
Postgraduate medical courses

Royal Academy of Music
Marylebone Road London NW1 5HT
020 7873 7373
www.ram.ac.uk
Fees 2018–19: £9,250

Royal Central School of Speech and Drama*
Eton Avenue
London NW3 3HY
020 7722 8183
www.cssd.ac.uk
Fees 2018–19: £9,250

Royal Veterinary College
Royal College Street London NW1 0TU
020 7468 5147
www. rvc.ac.uk
Fees 2018–19: £9,250

University of London Institute in Paris
9–11 rue de Constantine
75340 Paris Cedex 07, France
(+33) 1 44 11 73 83
https://ulip.london.ac.uk
Degrees offered in conjunction with Queen Mary and Royal Holloway colleges
Fees 2018–19: £9,250

2 Specialist colleges and private institutions

This listing gives contact details for other degree-awarding higher education institutions not mentioned elsewhere within the book. All the institutions listed below offer degree courses, some providing a wide range of courses while others are specialist colleges with a small intake. Those marked * are members of GuildHE (www.guildhe.ac.uk). Fees are given for UK/EU undergraduates for a single year of study.

BPP University
6th floor, Boulton House
Chorlton Street, Manchester M1 3HY
   Campuses in Abingdon, Birmingham,
   Bristol, Cambridge, Leeds, Liverpool,
   London, Manchester.
03331 224 359
www.bpp.com/bpp-university
Fees 2018–19: £13,500 (two-year course);
£9,000 (three-year course)

Conservatoire for Dance and Drama
Comprised of:
   Bristol Old Vic Theatre School Central
   School of Ballet
   London Academy of Music and Dramatic
   Art (LAMDA)
   London Contemporary Dance School,
   National Centre for Circus Arts,
   Northern School of Contemporary
   Dance, Rambert School of Ballet and
   Contemporary Dance, Royal Academy of
   Dramatic Art (RADA)
   Tavistock House, Tavistock Square
   London WC1H 9JJ
020 7387 5101
www.cdd.ac.uk
Fees 2019–20: £9,250

Dyson Institute of Engineering and Technology
Tetbury Hill Malmesbury
Wiltshire SN16 0RP
dysoninstitute@dyson.com
www.dysoninstitute.com
Paid degree courses – no fees

Glasgow School of Art
167 Renfrew Street, Glasgow G3 6RQ
0141 353 4500
www.gsa.ac.uk
Fees 2018–19: Scotland / EU, no fee,
RUK £9,250

Guildhall School of Music and Drama
Silk Street, Barbican,
London EC2Y 8DT
020 7628 2571
www.gsmd.ac.uk
Fees 2019–20: £9,250

The University of Law
Birmingham, Bristol, Chester, Exeter,
Guildford, Leeds, London (Bloomsbury and
Moorgate), Manchester
0800 289997
www.law.ac.uk
Fees 2019–20: £11,100 (two-year course)
£9,250 (three-year course)

Liverpool Institute for Performing Arts*
Mount Street,
Liverpool L1 9HF
0151 330 3000
www.lipa.ac.uk
Fees 2019–20: £9,250

The London Institute of Banking and Finance
4–9 Burgate Lane
Canterbury, Kent CT1 2XJ
01227 818609
Student campus:
    25 Lovat Lane, London EC3R 8EB
020 7337 6293
www.libf.ac.uk
Fees 2018–19: £6,000

New College of the Humanities
19 Bedford Square,
London WC1B 3HH
020 7637 4550
www.nchlondon.ac.uk
Fees 2019–20: £9,250

Pearson College
80 Strand,
London WC2R 0RL
0203 7334 456
www.pearsoncollegelondon.ac.uk
Fees 2018–19: £9,000

Plymouth College of Art*
Tavistock Place,
Plymouth PL4 8AT
01752 203434
www.plymouthart.ac.uk
Fees 2019–20: £9,250

Regent's University London*
Inner Circle,
Regent's Park, London NW1 4NS
020 7487 7505
www.regents.ac.uk
Fees 2018–19: £16,400

Rose Bruford College of Theatre and Performance*
Lamorbey Park,
Burnt Oak Lane,
Sidcup, Kent DA15 9DF
020 8308 2600
www.bruford.ac.uk
Fees 2018–19: £9,250

Royal College of Music
Prince Consort Road,
London SW7 2BS
020 7591 4300
www.rcm.ac.uk
Fees 2019–20: £9,250

Royal Conservatoire of Scotland
100 Renfrew Street,
Glasgow G2 3DB
0141 332 4101
www.rcs.ac.uk
Fees 2018–19: Scotland/EU, no fee;
RUK £9,250

Royal Northern College of Music
124 Oxford Road,
Manchester M13 9RD
0161 907 5200
www.rncm.ac.uk
Fees 2018–19: £9,250

Royal Welsh College of Music and Drama
Castle Grounds, Cathays Park,
Cardiff CF10 3ER
029 2034 2854
www.rwcmd.ac.uk
Fees 2019–20: £9,000

St Mary's University College*
191 Falls Road, Belfast BT12 6FE
028 9032 7678
www.stmarys-belfast.ac.uk
Fees 2018–19: £4,030; RUK £9,250

Scotland's Rural College
Campuses at Aberdeen, Ayr, Cupar,
Dumfries, Ecclesmachan, near Broxburn,
Edinburgh
0800 269453
www.sruc.ac.uk
Fees 2018–19: Scotland/EU, no fee;
RUK £6,950

Stranmillis University College
Stranmillis Road, Belfast BT9 5DY
028 9038 1271
www.stran.ac.uk
Fees 2019–20: £4,160; RUK £9,250

Trinity Laban Conservatoire of Music and Dance
Music Faculty: King Charles Court
Old Royal Naval College,
Greenwich, London SE10 9JF 020 8305 4444
Dance Faculty: Laban Building, Creekside
London SE8 3DZ
020 8305 9400
www.trinitylaban.ac.uk
Fees 2019–20: £9,250

UCFB (University College of Football Business)
Burnley FC Turf Moor
Harry Potts Way Burnley
Lancashire BB10 4BX
Wembley Stadium
London HA9 0WS
(also has a Manchester campus)
033322 06860
www.ucfb.com
Fees 2019–20: £9,250

Writtle University College*
Lordship Lane,
Writtle, Chelmsford, Essex CM1 3RR
01245 424200
www.writtle.ac.uk
Fees 2019–20: £9,250

Index